A Notable Woman

Also by Simon Garfield

Expensive Habits
The End of Innocence
The Wrestling
The Nation's Favourite
Mauve
The Last Journey of William Huskisson
Our Hidden Lives (ed)
We Are at War (ed)
Private Battles (ed)
The Error World
Mini
Exposure
Just My Type
On the Map
To the Letter
My Dear Bessie (ed)

A Notable Woman

The romantic journals of Jean Lucey Pratt

Edited by SIMON GARFIELD

CANONGATE

Edinburgh · London

Published in Great Britain in 2015 by Canongate Books Ltd,
14 High Street, Edinburgh EH1 1TE

www.canongate.tv

1

British Library Cataloguing-in-Publication Data
A catalogue record for this book is available on
request from the British Library

ISBN 978 1 78211 570 0

Typeset in Minion Pro by Palimpsest Book Production Limited,
Falkirk, Stirlingshire

Printed and bound in Great Britain by Clays Ltd, St Ives plc.

MIX
Paper from
responsible sources
FSC
www.fsc.org   FSC® C018072

Contents

Introduction

23 January 1941

I want, I need a husband. Thousands of other lonely frustrated females must be feeling the same way – why should I think that I am to be luckier? Because I intend to try to find one. One must tackle the problem positively, gather together one's assets, accept one's debits and go forth booted and spurred.

Assets: A fair share of good looks, physical attraction, generous nature and more poise than I once had. Subjects about which I know something and can use in work and conversation: architecture, literature, drama, people and certain places.

Debits: an agonising, thwarting knowledge of my deficiencies and general unworthiness; a confused, badly trained, porous mind, a tendency to bolt into silence at the first advance of difficulty.

I must take them, my debits and assets, out into the world, into the battlefield . . . and there must I learn to fight. I may lose, but at least I shall know I have tried while there is still a chance of winning.

In April 1925, at the age of fifteen, Jean Lucey Pratt began writing a journal, and she didn't put down her pen for sixty years. She produced well over a million words, and no one in her family or large circle of friends had an inkling until the end. She wrote – legibly, in fountain pen, usually in Woolworth's exercise books – about anything that amused, inspired or troubled her, and the journal became her only lasting companion. She wrote with aching honesty, laying bare a single woman's strident life as she battled with men, work and self-doubt. She increasingly hoped for posthumous publication, and her wish is hereby granted; the pleasure, inevitably, is all ours.

I first fell under Jean Pratt's spell in the autumn of 2002, but she had another name then. I was visiting the University of Sussex, immersed in Mass Observation, the organisation founded in London in the late 1930s to gain a deeper understanding of the thoughts and daily activities of 'ordinary people'. As the project evolved and the war began, hundreds of people agreed to submit their personal diaries, and Jean Pratt was among them. Most of the diaries (and diarists) were, of course, anything but ordinary: they were diverse, proud, intriguing, trivial, insightful, objectionable and candid. Most entries were handwritten, some were illegible. Some were composed on office paper, some on tissue. Mass Observation soon became a unique rendition of history without hindsight.

I had called at the archive with the intention of collating the material into an accessible book. Many of the diarists wrote from 1939 to the end of the war, but I was more interested in what came afterwards. For the book to work, I knew I would need to tell the story of recovery not only from a political and social perspective, but also from a personal one: the quirks and preferences of the diarists would have to be compelling in themselves, each voice overlapping in the timeline.

Over the next few visits I selected five writers who were different from each other in age, geographical location, employment and temperament. There was a socialist housewife from Sheffield, forever at odds with her husband and hairdresser; there was a pensioner from London, endlessly creosoting his garden fence and writing abominable poetry; there was a gay antiques dealer in Edinburgh; there was a curmudgeonly accountant, also from Sheffield, who got cross when fireworks woke him on VE Day.

And then there was Jean Lucey Pratt, whom I renamed Maggie

Joy Blunt. (I changed all the names: this was in keeping with the broad understanding of Mass Observation's founders and contributors – their words would be used as MO saw fit, but their identities would be protected, a liberating agreement, enabling frank contributions and freedom from prying eyes.)

Jean lived in a small cottage in the middle of Burnham Beeches in Buckinghamshire. During the war she had taken a job in the publicity department of a metals company, where the tedium almost swallowed her. She had been a trainee architect, but what she really wanted to do was write and garden and care for her cats. She took in paying guests; she read copiously; she hunted down food and cigarettes; and entertained her city friends. She researched a biography of an obscure Irish actress at the British Museum. And she kept track of her life in the most lyrical of ways.

My book was called *Our Hidden Lives*. It received generous reviews, and the success of the hardback helped the paperback become an unlikely bestseller. BBC Four made it into a film starring Richard Briers, Ian McDiarmid and Lesley Sharp, with Sarah Parish perfectly cast as Jean. Two further books followed – *We Are At War* and *Private Battles*, both prequels covering the war years – and Jean/Maggie was the only writer to appear in all three. Many readers claimed her as their favourite, and wrote asking whether there was any more. Fortunately there was more. Although Jean Pratt had died in 1986, she had a niece who was still alive. And the niece had treasures in the attic.

I had tea with Babs Everett and her husband at their house near Taunton in the spring of 2005. Babs, in her early seventies, was a familiar name to me: as a young girl she had appeared sporadically in her aunt's diaries, once or twice living with her during the war; her aunt had once complained how untidily she had kept her bedroom; she once referred to her affectionately as the Pratt's Brat. But now she was serving Earl Grey and lemon cake in her living room and wondering whether I'd like to see the rest of Jean's writing. There were several boxes' worth; she had kept diaries not just for Mass Observation, but during her entire life. Two fat folders contained about 400 loose pages, and then there were the exercise books, forty-five in all.

I sat with the journals at Babs Everett's house for a few hours, and made notes. The sentences I recorded included this terse summation of her life to date, composed in 1926 when she was almost sixteen:

> Bare legs and the wonderful silver fountain of the hose. Daddy in a white sweater. School. Very small, very shy. The afternoon in May – taken by mother to Penrhyn. Learning how to write the letters of the alphabet. A beautiful clean exercise book and a new pencil. Miss Wade at the head of the dining room table and me at her right. Choking tears because of youth's cruelty . . .

Very small, very shy. I thought the journals were wonderful – not only their contents, but their physicality; not only the observations but the persistence. I thought immediately about the possibility of a book, but there were snags. Babs was keen on publication, but not quite yet; perhaps the British Library should have the diaries first. Three or four years went by while Babs attempted to find the best home for them. After several further conversations we reached an impasse, and I moved on to other work. I spoke to Babs again a few years later. She still had the journals, but again the timing wasn't right.

In 2013, nine years after our initial meeting, I contacted Babs again. We had another good tea, this time at a friend's house in another part of Somerset. We again talked of how best to bring Jean's writing to a wider readership, but again there was hesitancy. I sensed that the journals were becoming a burden. And then a solution was found. Babs would bequeath the journals to an institution of which Jean would have approved – Cats Protection – and I would be allowed to edit them for publication.

In December 2013 three heavy boxes arrived at my home in

London. The journals smelled faintly of tobacco; they were redolent of pressed flowers and meat paste. I felt privileged, daunted, and responsible. Most of the journals had remained unopened and unread since the day their writer had laid them aside.

How do they hold up, as much as ninety years on? Occasionally they are rambling, anti-climactic, inconsistent, repetitive and opaque, but for the most part they are a revelation and a joy. Not only fascinating to read and startling in their candour, but also funny, unpredictable and so engagingly and gracefully written that I couldn't wait to turn the next page for further adventures. The questing displays of loving and longing (for romance, for life's meaning) are brave and meltingly disarming; her devotion to her cats is heartbreaking; her comic timing owes something to the music hall. At times I felt like an intruder; at others a confidant; I wanted both to scold her and hug her. I found myself rooting for her on every page, willing her to win that tennis game or persuade a man to stay. The life that I had first encountered in her wartime Mass Observation entries now stretched back to her childhood in Wembley and forward to her old age, a snapshot transformed by a greater depth of field. I knew of no other account that so effectively captured a single woman's journey through two-thirds of the twentieth century, nor one written with such self-effacing toughness. When friends asked me for a summary, I could think of nothing better than 'Virginia Woolf meets Caitlin Moran.'

For the modern reader the journals provide many satisfactions. The writer's emotions are universal and enduring: we empathise with her ambitions, disappointments and yearnings. Cumulatively, the journals envelop like a novel: the more one reads, the more one cares what happens next. I frequently thought of Jean's latest challenge or calamity upon waking, and stayed up late to read the latest instalment. I recalled the crowd at the New York docks eager for the latest dispatch from Dickens: would Little Nell survive?

Jean Pratt was not Dickens, of course. She knew how to tell a tale – witness the way she ratchets up the tension over her schoolgirl crushes and her father's new love. And she could draw the sharpest of portraits with a few deprecating lines ('His good qualities seem to indicate a rather "might have been" goodness . . . a plant in decay,' she writes of the man to whom she lost her virginity. 'Not a flattering start.') But there is no plot to speak of here (beyond the biographical one we all enact, the plot of existence and survival), and strands and characters sometimes disappear from sight as swiftly as they appear, without satisfying explanation. She writes that she would have it no other way: in January 1931 she quotes a writer she admired named John Connell.

> It can be no tale of carefully rounded edges, of neatly massed effects, a thing of plot or climax. Somehow life is not like that – it is not symmetrical, measured and finished. The weaver of the pattern doesn't seem to care for neatly tasselled ends and pretty bows – it is all very rough and ragged. Yet through it all there seems to run a purpose and an idea, a kind of guiding line.

Besides, life's like that. And her journals are, after all, only writing; for all her searing honesty, she only records what she can bear to, and what she envisaged would be of value to her as she grew older (and perhaps of value to us after that). Value will date, of course. Not everything she wrote can be of interest to us today, but I was delighted to find that so much of it is.

Jean Pratt was made by the war. Like most who lived through it, the tumult transformed her far beyond the surface terrors and deprivations. Her writing matured, becoming not only more observant, but more worldly-wise. The drama of her war days, which assume a disproportionate weight in my edit, demonstrate the pure thrill of reading something so fresh that it appears still blottable. Completely lacking the hindsight of more familiar accounts, the pages brim with almost overwhelming poignancy: we know how the war turned out, she did not, and such is the power of her writing that we are flung back to doubt our own certainty. Will Hitler invade? Will Jean's home be bombed? Will she aid the war effort? Is Churchill really the man for the job? Is this the night she finally gets laid?

There is far less writing after 1960. Her daily work becomes too time-consuming, her health worsens, and her introspection wanes. The more she knows about herself, and the more her world and ambitions shrink, the less she imagines a life beyond them. Between 1926 and 1959 her writing fills thirty-eight journals; between 1959 and 1986 there are only seven. But she kept at it. In the final years I do feel she was writing less for herself and more for her family and us, the unknowable reader.

At school she may have preferred botany to English, but words were unquestionably Jean Pratt's craft and trade. Her drift into journalism and published biography seems at every stage a natural one (she made several aborted attempts at novels too). She read widely and wrote criticism, and then in later years she successfully ran a bookshop. Anyone who shares this passion for books cannot fail to recognise both a kindred spirit and a talented practitioner, nor marvel at the opportunity to witness a writer develop in style and intellect (let alone track a mindset from teenage *naïveté* to twenty-something disillusion to something approaching adult contentment). On a daily basis, the overriding value of her writing lies in the piecemeal narration and the telling details, the minutiae too often submerged in the bigger histories or airbrushed by heirs and estates. It's a poetic list: the schoolgirl crushes, the depth of a grave as it appears to a child, the loss of a tennis match, bad car driving, classmates Yeld and Grissell, the dress-sense of Christians, the 'Three Ginx in harmony', the shock of Jacob Epstein, the disappointments of Jack Honour, the prominence of hunchbacks, the thoughts of war in 1931, the tears at a train station, girls playing cricket, the sodden film crew on a Cornish beach – the unfettered, absurd humanity of it all, and all this before she turned twenty-one.

How to sum up a life's work? Certainly we may regard it as forward-thinking. She was clearly not the first notable woman to engage with the apparently mutually exclusive possibilities of spousal duty and career, but her modernity singled her out from her parents and the herd. She is not always the most humorous of companions, and her mood swings are often extreme (she doesn't write when she is feeling really low). But her self-effacement more than compensates (and she is often funny without signalling the fact; she was aware of the Grossmiths' *The Diary of a Nobody*, and occasionally I wonder if she is not extending the parody). At times her yearning for spiritual guidance leads her up some woody paths, but on other occasions she champions the principles of mindfulness long before it found a name. I admired her willingness to offend, although her wicked intentions never materialise beyond the page. But most of all I admired her candidacy, the raising of her hand. This is an exposing memoir, an open-heart operation. One reads it, I think, with a deep appreciation of her belief in us.

The dual responsibility (to Jean and her new readers) to deliver a volume that was both manageable in length and true to her daily experience – that is, something both piecemeal and cohesive – has resulted in a book incorporating only about one-sixth of her written material. Shaping her writing was a unique pleasure, but losing so much of it was not, not least because even the most inconsequential passages were refined with ardent beauty. In February 1954, for example, she looks from the window of her cottage. 'Our world is frost-bound. Hard, hard, everything tight and solid with frost. I keep fires going in sitting room and kitchen, all doors closed. I fear there will be terrible mortality in the garden.' Unremarkable in content, the words carry a heady poetic potency, the fine-tuned wonder of ephemeral thought. You will find a thousand similarly weighted reflections in the following pages, the work of a soul singing through time.

Looking for love all her life (from friends, from men, from pets, from teachers, from customers), Jean Pratt may have found her fondest devotees only now, among us, her fortunate readers. A quiet life remembered, a life's work rewarded; Jean would have blushed at the attention. And then she would have crept away to write about it.

Dramatis Personae et Dramatis Feles

(in order of significant appearance)

Family:

Jean Lucey Pratt, a reliable narrator, 1909–1986

George Percy Pratt, Jean's father, an architect

Sarah Jane Pratt (née Lucey), Jean's mother, a concert pianist, died in 1922 when Jean was thirteen

Leslie Vernon Pratt, her brother, born 1901, engineer with Cable & Wireless

Ethel Mary Watson, later Pratt, her stepmother

Prince, the family Airedale

The Joliffe family: Aunt N. is Jean's father's sister, Joyce is her cousin

Margaret (Maggie) Royan, one of Ethel's sisters, Jean's step-aunt

Elsie Watson, Jean's other step-aunt

Aunt Jane, on her father's side, an early loss

Ivy, Leslie's wife

Ethel Lucey Pratt (Babs), now Everett, daughter of Leslie and Ivy

Martin Pratt, a cousin, a touring companion, RAF

Friends and acquaintances from youth, university and early travels:

Arthur Ainsworth, ex-Boys' Brigade, kissed Jean's hair

Jean Rotherham, an early crush

Lavender Norris, another early crush, an early tragedy

Miss Wilmott (A.W.), a significant teacher, another early crush

Joyce Coates, a lasting friend from architecture school

Harold Dagley, a disappointing young man

Lugi/Luigi, real name Dorothy Cargill, another friend from architecture class

Valerie Honour, née Buck, friend from Wembley, (much) better than Jean at tennis, wife to Jack

Gus, also known as Peter, real name Geoffrey Harris, significant long-term friend, actor/writer/interior decorator, pen name Heron Carvic, flamboyant

Phyllis Terry, his actress companion, part of the Terry thespian dynasty

Roy Gornold, delicate and opinionated family friend, artistic tendencies

Joan Bulbulion, a confidant since architecture days

Vahan Bulbulion, her architect husband, Armenian, increasingly annoying

Constance Oliver, artist friend, free spirit, casualty of war

Olive Briggs, tragedian

Eva May Glanville (Mary Kate), university friend

David Aberdeen, architecture student, another fleeting fancy, later famous in his field

Chris Naude, horny South African diplomat on trip to Russia

Mr Wildman, the stand-in vicar

Hugh Patrick (Bill), possible Jamaican hook-up, wife in Truro

Neville, cabin dweller, advantage taker

Marjorie 'Nockie/Nicola' Nockolds, latterly just 'N', enduring friend from journalism course, complicated friendship

Colin Wintle (sometimes Winkle), marriage material in Bath

Dick Sheppard, successful architect, favoured rebel, disabled

Gwen Silvester, ballroom dancing teacher, sister of dancer/bandleader Victor

Charles Scrimshaw, possible beau, good at glancing

Alan Devereaux, appalling marriage material, 'conventionally unconventional', lusts for cream cakes

Monica Haddow, friend, possibly addicted to masturbation, fellow visitor to . . .

Gordon Howe, influential Harley Street psychotherapist

Friends and acquaintances from Wee Cottage, the war and beyond:

Josephine Norris, friend, hypochondriac, ghost-like lover of the actor Leslie Howard

Lady Spicer, generous next-door neighbour

Kathleen Moneypenny, owner of Wee Cottage

D.F., or Francis, good sense of humour, bad nails, goes all the way

Tommy Hughes, a fellow aluminium worker, a lover, a doctor

Jean Macfarlane, an old school chum, legal father

Mac (also M., or Mellas or Alan), Jean's obsession, married and unpredictable, bit of a shit

Hugh Laming, soldier, journalist, friend from Malta, lover of Lillian Gish, lover of Jean, great letter writer

Maritza, his Greek wife

Lydia, a work colleague, a decorator, fellow Mac user

Michael Sadleir, a novelist

Thomas Sadleir, a genealogist, a mentor

Peggy Denny (P.D.), formerly Penny Harding, wife of architect Valentine Harding, fellow Liberal campaigner, dresses like autumn

Clinton G.F., a despised post-war suitor

D.B., another post-war suitor, met on return journey from Portugal

R.W., a girlfriend at the alloys company, reliable source of gossip

Lady B.P., a large, opinionated local friend, often annoying

Miss Drumm, a property owner, a benefactor

Ralph L., an attractive art teacher

Angela, a lanky young shop assistant

N.G., a picture framer, Angela's pash

Lizzie, adventurous painter friend

Mrs V.N., worried about Liz's mental health

Alison Uttley, obliging children's author

Rolf Harris, unnaturally popular at Jean's book stall

The cars, in order of rusting:

A Fiat, circa 1925, father's, once made it to Cornwall

1947 Ford Prefect, cost £40, known as Freddie, rust bucket, got her to Slough and back (ten miles total)

1954 Ford Anglia, bought in 1965. 'Astounding bargain.'

1964 Morris 1000 Traveller, known as Jolly Morris when it worked, purchased late 1969

1964 Singer Vogue, £150 in 1972, tricky switches

Mini Morris Traveller G. reg., purchased 1976; rusted

Suzie Min, Mini Traveller, purchased 1979, radiator collapses soon after

Standard Mini, purchased 1981, got her to Wexham hospital

The cats, in memoriam:

Cheeta, Dinah, Ginger Tom (visitor), Suzie, Little Titch, The Kittyhawk, Ping, Pong, Twinkle, Joey, Squib, Pepper, Walrus, Pharaoh (formerly Tom-Tit), Starlet, The Damned Spot, Pinkie, Pewter Puss, The Senator, Walter, Nicky, Pye, Bumphrey (Bum), Pinnie, Priss, MaryAnne, Buster, George, Tweezle, Mitzie, Jubie.

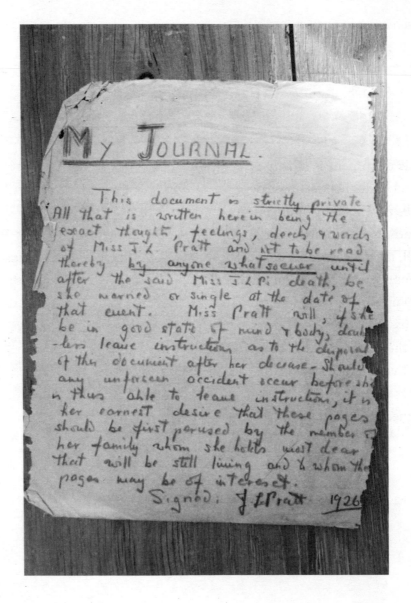

My Journal.

This document is strictly private
All that is written herein being the
exact thoughts, feelings, deeds & words
of Miss J L Pratt and not to be read
thereby by anyone whatsoever until
after the said Miss J L P's death, be
she married or single at the date of
that event. Miss Pratt will, if she
be in good state of mind & body, doubt
-less leave instructions as to the disposal
of this document after her decease. Should
any unforeseen accident occur before she
is thus able to leave instructions, it is
her earnest desire that these pages
should be first perused by the member of
her family whom she holds most dear
that will be still living and & whom the
pages may be of interest.

Signed: J L Pratt 1926

Frontispiece

This document is *strictly private*. All that is written herein being the exact thoughts, feelings, deeds and words of Miss J.L. Pratt and *not to be read* thereby *by anyone whatsoever* until after the said Miss J.L.P.'s death, be she married or single at the date of that event. Miss Pratt will, if she be in good state of mind and body, doubtless leave instructions as to the disposal of this document after her decease. Should any unforeseen accident occur before she is thus able to leave instructions, it is her earnest desire that these pages should be first perused by the member of her family whom she holds most dear that will still be living and to whom the pages may be of interest.

Signed: J.L. Pratt 1926[1]

---

1 Added to beginning of diaries some months after commencement.

O, Why does that Tennis Club
depress me so? I went down
evening: the first time for we
I had two good sets — one
Mr Stuart against Mr Suste
& a ladies four + There were u
two people down there —
a lot of 'civilians' playing
roquet ——— and Leslie told
why do I want to be frien
with him so? It could have
been so easy if 3 years ago
had known what I know no
Yet I wonder? My courage
as soon as I get there +
cannot make myself appea
I should like to appear + I a
a coward: afraid of making a
fool of myself. Afraid of what
people might say ——— I b

PART ONE:
Architecture

1.

Into a Cow

Saturday, 18 April 1925 (aged fifteen)

I have decided to write a journal. I mean to go on writing this for years and years, and it'll be awfully amusing to read over later.

We're going to Torquay next week. I feel so thrilled! We start on Tuesday and drive all the way down in our own car. We only got it at Xmas, and Daddy has only just learnt to drive. It'll be rather fun I think. It's a Fiat by make. I've always longed for a car. I'm going to learn to drive it when I'm 16.

Do you remember Arthur Ainsworth, Jean? Funny bloke – he used to be in the Church Lads Brigade when Leslie was Lieutenant.[2] He used to be my 'beau' then. He used to come and have Morse lessons with Leslie. He used to put his arm round me when he was learning – I could only have been 8 then! And we used to play grandmother's footsteps in the garden and he tried to kiss me – he did kiss my hair. I was quite thrilled – but not overmuch. He used to be sort of Churchwarden at the Children's Service on Sunday afternoon and I used to giggle all the time – even though Mummy was there. I think she knew! She didn't say anything though, the darling – oh how I miss her. I wish she were here now. I'd have been all I could to her.

Anyway, who was my next beau? I can't remember. I think it was

---

2 Leslie her brother is eight years her senior.

Gilbert Dodds. I've got them all down in secret code in my last year's diary. Let's go and fetch it.

Yes, here it is – I've got it down like this:

PR (past romances)
1. A.A.
2. G.D.
3. T.M.
4. K.L.
5. C.B.
6. R.

Gilbert Dodds was the 2nd. He was awfully good looking. He lived at Ealing. The 3rd was Tony Morgan. I hated him, but in my extreme youth I used to go to school with him and I used to go to tea etc. Daddy once suggested he should be my dance partner – was furiously flattered in a way – but I always blushed when he was mentioned. I have an awful habit of blushing, it's most annoying. They've left Wembley now thank goodness. Mr Morgan ran away or something. I couldn't bear Mr Morgan either. He sniffed and always insisted on kissing me. He had a toothbrush moustache and it tickled and oh I hated it. I hid behind the dining room door once till he'd gone.

The next one was a waiter. It was at the Burlington at Worthing and he used to gaze at me so sentimentally. He used to get so nervous when he waited at our table. I never spoke to him – it's much nicer not to speak. The next one was a choir boy at St Peter's. I used to make eyes at him each Sunday and we used to giggle like mad. He was quite good looking with fair hair and pale, rather deceitful blue eyes. At the beginning of the September term I suddenly realised how idiotic it was so I left off looking at him. He was rather hurt at first I think, but he soon recovered and he makes eyes at Barbara Tox and Gwen Smith now.

But in the summer holidays last year I met Ronald. We were all on the Broads for a fortnight. It was at Oulton, and we were moored alongside a funny little houseboat where an old bachelor spent most of his time. Ronald was his sort of manservant. He was quite a common sort of youth, but rather good-looking. I'm sorry to say I went quite dippy over him and gave Daddy some chocolate to give to him. I wonder if he liked me? He noticed me I know – he used to watch me! Another romance where I never said a word. Perhaps it's just as well – he was only a fisher lad – but my heart just ached and ached when he went away. I wish I had a brother about Ronald's age. Leslie's a dear but he's 24 now, and what is the use of a brother the other end of the world? All that day I felt pretty miserable and when we moored just outside Reedham I went for a long, long walk all by myself along the riverbank, and thought things out and finally conquered. I came back because it began to rain. I'd been out an awful long time and they were getting anxious and had come to find me. They were awfully cross and rather annoyed they hadn't found me drowned in a dyke or something – no Jean, that was horrid of you. I think I cried in bed that night and I know I prayed for Ronald.

I determined not to have any more weak flirtations like that. I'm awfully weak and silly, I've been told that numbers of times. That was the 6th. I wonder who'll be the 7th? No, I won't even write what I think this time – but he goes to Cambridge and Margaret says he's growing a moustache – and oh Jean be quiet, you did fight that down once, don't bring it up again. Oh, I do hope nobody reads this – I should die if they did.

What shall I write about now? I know – my past cracks. It was when I was a queer little day-girl in Upper III when I first noticed Lavender Norris. Oh she was sweet! I went absolutely mad about her. She was awfully pretty with long wavy dark hair with little gold bits in it, and dark eyes. Peggy Saunders was gone on her too. I found a hanky of hers once underneath my desk. I gave it back to her and was coldly thanked – she was talking to Miss Prain at the time. One Xmas I sent Lavender some scent of her own name and she wrote back such a sweet letter. We were getting on famously when the next term she got 'flu and a whole crowd of us wrote to her and someone said I was pining away for her. I did write to her again in the Spring hols but she never answered.

She left in the Summer term 1923. Peggy used to write to her and once she told her about Mummy's death and Lavender wrote back and said how sorry she was and sent me her love. Angel! I see her sometimes when she comes back as an Old Girl but that is all. If she was to come back again I should still be mad about her I'm sure – but at present Miss Wilmott (A.W.) claims my affections. Everybody knows I'm gone on her and grins knowingly at me and I hate it. I've walked with her too – I and Veronica – but on one awful walk I shall never forget Veronica did all the talking and I couldn't think of a single thing to say. I came home feeling so utterly depressed that I could have howled. I remember some agonising meal times too that term, sitting next to A.W. They are too agonising ever to write here.

She smiled at me once, quite of her own accord. It was the 2nd of June and we had to go for walks. We were waiting by the gate when I looked up quickly and she was looking at me rather funnily and then she just smiled! I nearly died. She's never done it since – except once, again that term, when I held the door open for her. I went into ecstasies in the dorm. That term was glorious all through.

Sunday, 19 April
Yesterday afternoon Daddy and I went and fetched the car from Harris's. It had been there to get mended. Daddy and I were going to Marlow and Daddy backed into the tree and bent the front axle and crumpled the mudguard to nothing. Harris came down to fetch it on Tuesday and promised it us on Saturday, but when we got there the mudguard hadn't come back from the makers, so we took it without. It does look funny but the car goes all right. I do love going out in it so – being able to go and see one's relations and friends.

Thursday, 23 April

We're down at Torquay at last! Glorious place! We started on Tuesday morning about 9 a.m. and after fetching Miss Watson we carried on till Andover, where we stayed for lunch. Andover is in Hampshire. Daddy drives awfully well!

After we left Andover we went on to Yeovil in Somerset. We meant to stay the night there but everywhere was full up so we went on to Crewkerne. The hills were something awful for the car, but oh the view from the tops was so lovely. Just after we left Newton Abbot something went wrong with the car.

Monday, 27 April

Home again. Such a lot has happened. I shall never forget this trip as long as I live – never.

Daddy has always addressed Miss Watson with more than usual politeness and kindness. I have wondered often if he meant anything. And when we started on this trip my heart grew very heavy. He seemed so, so, I don't know how to call it – so very nice to E.W., and I began to think thoughts, thoughts I could not get out of my mind, unbearable thoughts. Oh Mother dearest! My heart grew heavy for you, darling one – it seemed too grotesquely untrue that Daddy could be forgetting you so soon. Jesus alone knows my heartache when Daddy lingered over saying goodnight to her at Crewkerne in the semi-dusk, and tears would come when I got into bed. I was jealous too – I thought, oh Daddy might not love me so much now. And then it rankled a bit to think of her coming into our home and taking your place.

The next day we arrived at Torquay and we went to see *M. Beaucaire* (the film) in the evening, and it was glorious and Daddy was so nice and dear to me after and I was so much happier.[3]

And then the next day little things cropped up all day – things

3 *Monsieur Beaucaire*, starring Rudolph Valentino.

he said to her, looks they exchanged. I grew sad again until Ethel –
yes, I shall call her that – changed quite early for dinner. Just before
6.30 Daddy came in and sat down. In my heart of hearts I knew what
was coming. (I had pictured a sort of scene to myself, something like
this: Dad comes to me and says, 'Jean darling, we shall have someone
to look after us at last. Ethel has promised to marry me,' or words to
that effect. I knew tears would come and he might say, 'Why Jean,
aren't you pleased?' Perhaps then I'd say, bravely gulping down the
tears and smiling, 'Oh yes Daddy, I'm very pleased, but Daddy, have
you forgotten mother so soon?')

But he just sat in the chair and watched me undress for a while
and then he said, 'And what do you think of Miss Watson?' So I
naturally said, 'I think she's very nice,' but I had to bite my lip hard.
'Jean,' he said, 'I want to ask you a question.' I knew what was coming
but I feigned an interested surprise. 'How would you like someone
to come to live with us?' I just slipped into his arms and cried, and
I tried to get out about Mother but it just wouldn't come. But oh he
was so nice. I never knew I loved him so much until that moment.
He explained that he'd thought of it now for some weeks, and that
Mother had told him before she died that he was free to marry again
(dearheart, that is your sweet unselfishness all over again!). He thought
Ethel the nicest girl he knew and it would be a companion for me.
His friends had often said to him, 'Pratt, why don't you get married
again? You're killing yourself with hard work.' And then he said, 'But
Jean darling, if you think there is anything in this plan that might
come between us I will throw up the cards at once, for after all you
are all that I have got now and nothing must come between you and
me.'

I couldn't have him sacrifice so much – such love must entail a
sacrifice from me. My heart sank and sank, but I said bravely that I
was quite quite sure it would be all right and he need not worry. And
he kissed my hand and said, 'Thank you.' And he also said that he
had not asked her yet, but he must risk that. But when he had gone

– Oh Mother, to think of seeing anyone else in your place. I never
knew I loved you or your memory so much. So I came down at 7
cool, calm and collected, faintly perfumed with lavender. That evening
we went to see Norma Talmadge in *Smilin' Through.*[4]

We came back along the coast – much worse hills but such pretty
country. And I felt tired and sad and a little exhausted, but the level,
smooth stretch of sea peeping between the graceful lines of the cliffs
seemed to comfort the innermost recesses of my soul. And when we
lost sight of it behind high hedgerows I ached for one more sight of
it.

I became drowsy and rather cross, and across Salisbury Plain it
began to rain and I tried to sleep, until Daddy bumped into a cow.
The cow's mild expression of pained surprise tickled me, so that I sat
up once more and recovered my spirits.

Wednesday, 29 April

I have thought the matter over a good deal recently and I have come
to the conclusion that it is a very good sensible thing. The only fear
I have now is what our relations and friends might say. She is very
nice and kind, she can listen to Daddy's business affairs much better
than I can and understand. She will be such a companion for Daddy
while I'm at school. But Mother your memory will always linger: there
are your clothes that I cannot wear, your jewellery, the little things
you gave me, the letters you wrote, the books you read, the piano and
your music. And most of all that large photo of you in the dining
room with your sweet, sad eyes, always smiling at me wherever I am
in the room.

I went to see *M. Beaucaire* at the Crown Cinema. That was the
2nd time I'd seen it but I loved it more and more. I have ordered the
book at Smith's and I'm longing for it to come. After seeing good
films like that I have a strange feeling that I want to film act and to

---

4 A silent melodrama with themes of unrequited love and forbidden marriage.

act well. I'd love to just make people wonder, envy, admire, to be
famous, to be too good for any petty criticism and have certain people
I know say, 'Fancy – Jean Pratt! And when I knew her one would
never have thought her capable of it!' I just want to act, to live, to
feel like someone else, to live in a real world of Romance. I know it
would mean hard, hard work and many disappointments and heart-
breaks, but I should love to feel that I sway men's hearts to a danger
mark, and women's too for that matter.

Last night Daddy, Ethel and I went out to a big Conservative
meeting dinner, and I'm sure I looked so nice. It is the sweetest frock
– very pale blue georgette, cut quite full over a pale blue silk lining.
Right down the middle is a piece of silver lace about two inches wide.
I wore very pale grey silk stockings and silver shoes. I also wore a
blue and mauve hairband and displayed a mauve crepe-de-chine
hankie in my wristwatch strap. I saturated myself in lavender water.
For the reception I wore white silk gloves – I shook hands with the
Duke of Northumberland. I do not like him very much – he has
ginger hair and a moustache, a prominent nose and weak chin and
white eyelashes – ugh! The dinner was great and some of the speeches
were quite nice.

Coming home from Oxford Circus I had to be most tactful. I
pretended to be frightfully sleepy and closed my eyes half the time
and didn't listen much to their conversation. When we arrived at
Wembley Daddy said, 'I hope you don't mind Jean, but we'll see you
indoors and then I'm going to take Miss Watson home.' I yawned and
said, 'Oh I don't mind a bit, all I can picture in front of me is bed.'
Oh Jean, Jean, Jean – may your sins be forgiven you. When they had
left I flaunted about upstairs in my nice clothes and did up my hair
and admired myself in the glass and did a little film acting on my
own. Then I thought I'd better hurry into bed – I heard it strike one
and Daddy hadn't come back. Then I fell asleep. He's been in an
awfully good mood all day today so I suppose his midnight vigil was
satisfactory. Somewhere deep down in my heart it hurts.

Thursday, 7 May

It's over a week now since I last wrote my journal, but there are several good reasons. First, I got *M. Beaucaire* the novel, and, not liking it as much as the film version, decided to write my own account. Second, Miss Floyd the housekeeper has been away for a holiday, so yours truly has had to light the fires and peel the potatoes. Thirdly, IT'S HAPPENED!!!!! Yes, last Wednesday evening about 11.45 I was still reading and Daddy came in saying he'd gone to Ethel's and 'It's all settled!' And he looked so happy.

Ethel is so sweet and nice to me. Daddy was busy buying new shirts and suits etc. It's going to be awfully nice, and everybody's very pleased and excited.

Jean Prat

'I want to do great things, to be great.' Jean at school in the mid-1920s.

2.

Jean Rotherham

Friday, 30 April 1926 (aged sixteen)

Just over a year ago now since I began my journal but I have not forgotten. I am twelve months older now and things are different. I must keep this journal all my life – I just must.

Ethel makes a topping little mother she really does, and to see the good she has done my Daddy makes me feel indebted to her for ever.

So as to give the connecting link between now and then:

My diphtheria two days before their wedding, the hospital on their Day, the weary long drawn weeks there, the first one of aching homesickness, the fighting off of despair. And I came nearer to God than I had ever done in my life. They tell me that I nearly died, but He chose to give me my life.

Then that glorious holiday in Cornwall, Xmas, we got Prince (Airedale), mumps, home again for three weeks, Jean Rotherham. I wonder why I write this? It is not so much the big events I want to record – it's my feelings, my exact thoughts at a certain time. Perhaps in some future generation, when I am dead, they may read these words I am now writing. I wonder who those 'they' will be? Perhaps they will think of this as 'grandmother's writings' or perhaps as 'old Miss Pratt's'. And why have I that feeling at the back of my mind that no one will ever read this? But if anyone ever does read this – if you ever do – Reader please be kind to me! I am only 16 at present, and just realising life and beginning to think for myself. It's all very thrilling in its strange newness.

This time next week I shall be back in that strangely bittersweet prison Princess Helena College. There is not another school like it in the world. To think I've got to go back – that I have to go back to orders and discipline, to Miss White and Botany, to the weary monotony of daily routine, to that conspicuous game of cricket! On the other hand there's Jean Rotherham, whom I shouldn't really mention at all here or anywhere.

Then there's Miss Wilmott, the fun and laughter and companions of my own age, the Military Tournament, the sports and Junior party, the long summer holidays and THEN the event of events – Leslie's homecoming!

To go back to Jean R. The less said the better because I am going back to fight my self-control. She is younger than I am but I think her very sweet, though no one else knows it. I have only told Margaret because I must tell someone.

I wish I wasn't so fat! I've gone up 10lbs again this holiday. It's too sickening for words. Next holiday I must keep myself more in hand. I am now 10 stone and it simply mustn't be – at school last term I was 9st 4lbs.

Monday, 2 August
I'm sorry there's no other ink to write with but I must write. I could never sleep after reading what I've read.

Lavender is dead. Dead. It happened last Saturday evening so the paper said, at Brooklands. I shall keep that cutting and the last photo I shall ever have of her.[5] Lavender – I must have really cared an awful lot because I'm feeling mighty sick. But I bet Mr Cyril Bone's feeling worse, if he can feel at all. I can't send you anything for your grave because I don't know where to send it, but I shall never forget you. And somehow I'm glad you didn't live to get old and ugly, but died

---

5 Helen Lavender Norris was the passenger in the racing car being driven by Cyril Bone at Brooklands circuit near Weybridge in Surrey when it crashed at 100 mph. She was twenty.

still lovely: 'Whom the gods love die young'. Yet it's awful to think you had no time to say goodbye. No one will know how much I really cared.

Sunday, 8 August
Next school year I've got to work like blazes for the General Schools examination in June. Everyone is so discouraging at school. That old beast Miss Pilcher informed me quite cheerfully the last day at lunch that I had no earthly for Schools next year. But Miss P. we shall see. Of course it's absolutely idiotic of her to say that, as I feel inclined to say, 'Well seeing as I'm not going to pass, and you seem so sure of it, why should I bother to work this year at all?' I wish I'd thought of it at the time.

As to J.R. – she was six weeks in the sicker, poor kid, with a poisoned foot, and life was extraordinarily dull while she was there. We were socially poles apart – not even in the same cloakroom. But I think she knows I rather like her, and anyway I've caught her looking at me more than once. She is seen at her best in a tennis match. She's younger than I am, but when I see her playing and forgetful of everything else there is no sweeter sight on earth.

The day after I came back from school we went up the High Street and I got the simply rippingest things.

I.   Fawn tailor-made coat – stunning affair that matches hat, stockings and several things I already possess.
II. Cotton voile frock. White with patterns of yellow roses round the navy neck and sleeves (am going to wear it this afternoon).
III. Stumpy umbrella, black and white, carved handle, birthday present from Ethel in advance. Topping one.
IV. Fawn gloves.
V.   Cream pair silk stockings – unfortunately wore them for tennis yesterday and made irrevocable ladders.

Oh dear, I do love clothes and making myself look nice. It really makes life worth living, but Ethel laughs at me. I'm getting frightfully conceited, and I really wish I was slimmer. But sometimes I think my legs and ankles aren't really such a bad shape in silk stockings, and I'm beginning to wonder if it's purely imagination or are my eyes really quite a nice blue on occasions and sometimes quite big? I know I've got quite a nice mouth – I was told so once at school in 'Truths'. They thought it was my best feature. I overheard Mrs White say that she thought I'd got lovely skin, but I really do not like my complexion. My nails are something appalling and my hips really are too big. In fact I am big – horribly large – and 'well covered' as Ethel puts it, or 'stout' as Mrs White said. It's been a foregone conclusion from the days of my earliest childhood that I've got pretty hair, but I really am beginning to just loathe frizziness and it's getting a really most uninteresting colour, and much thinner since I had dip. And then I wear glasses – that always puts people off a bit!

I was staying with Margaret, and she's got hold of two awfully nice boys who half-promised they'd come to the cinema with us. When she told them I wore glasses they began to kick horribly. But she told them I smoked and liked funny stories (the kind you're not supposed to hear), so they thought I'd be all right after all. But there was some difficulty about another girl and they couldn't come after all. I loathe being thought a prig.

Wednesday, 1 September
Mullion again and the clear sea air!

On Monday we started at a quarter to nine from our house. Ethel and I were so tightly packed into the car, and so surrounded by 'impedimenta' we didn't quite know where we began or ended. We met Uncle Charlie and Auntie Ruth on Ealing Common at 9 a.m., and after that we couldn't get the car started, but at last with Harold's help we were off. On the Bath Road Daddy decided the oil gauge wasn't behaving properly so he hailed an AA man and they spent half an hour fooling with that. We went to Andover for lunch, and Ethel, Daddy and Uncle all slept afterwards in the lounge upstairs – the three beauties – until the maid floated in loudly and woke them with a start.

Sunday, 5 September

Leslie is coming on Tuesday! Not next month or next week, but Tuesday. I'm getting just a little nervous. Will he have altered too much? Does he want to see me as much as I want to see him? How will he get on with Ethel?

Monday, 6 September

Tomorrow morning at 6.30 Daddy and I go to Helston. Leslie. I mustn't forget to brush my hair well. What shall I wear tomorrow? Oh Leslie, just one wild beautiful fortnight and then school and hard work. I mustn't make a sound tomorrow morning . . .

Thursday, 9 September

It's 10.45 p.m. and everyone but me is getting into bed. Writing by candlelight. Tonight let us deal with the biggest subject I have in my life at the moment: my brother. A tall brown man who is at once so very familiar and yet such an utter stranger. I think he feels just as shy at having to deal with a growing-up younger sister as I am at having this manly yet very brotherly brother. He is not used to England yet after three years in the wilds of Brazil. He has the most extraordinary eyes – grey-green, a little piercing, honest eyes.

All the same, it doesn't seem so wonderful – the anticipation was far sweeter than the realisation. It usually is, but it wasn't his or anybody else's fault. I had anticipated too much. After all the excitement was over on Tuesday I was worn out and dead tired and disappointed. I somehow felt he found I wasn't quite what he expected. I cried after I'd blown the candle out. Sometimes you have to. I would never cry in front of anyone if I could help it. But in the dark, just sometimes.

Saturday, 11 September

Yesterday morning a film company came down to the Cove with all their paraphernalia. Most thrilling. They were having a sort of picnic when we left for our lunch, and Geoff and I bolted our food to come down again to the Cove as early as we could. They had collected on the rocks just below the Mullion Hotel, and we clambered up the cliffs and got a topping perch. There were at least a dozen of them.

The heroine, one of those pretty fluffy little creatures with a child's figure, a springy walk and an American accent – she was wearing an orange cap with a long silk tassel over one shoulder, a blue Eton sweater and a green skirt with white shoes and stockings. And her hair was very, very fair and fluffy – suspiciously fair.

The hero – I should think he was an Italian – anyway, something foreign – very tall and slim, black hair just going grey, quite good-looking with clean-cut features and very even teeth. He was dressed as a sailor in long dark blue trousers and a queerly worked belt in gold and black. We discovered today that he is Carlyle Blackwell and the girl Flora le Breton.[6]

Well they didn't do much yesterday afternoon. It was a dull, heavy day and they couldn't get on without the sun. They made up their faces, and fooled around quite a lot, but nothing happened so just about tea-time they packed up and went. We left a lot of them eating mussels at the Gull Rock Hut.

This morning directly after breakfast Geoff and I flew down to the Cove to see what was happening. They had started – at least the hero and heroine were practising a most touching love scene and a sad farewell. So we got some sob stuff gratis. But just as they were getting the cameras ready the sun went in and presently it began to rain, so they all packed up again!

Directly after lunch the sun came out. They went through the

---

6 The film was *The Rolling Road*. Released in 1928, it was co-produced by Michael Balcon some years before his Hitchcock and Ealing classics.

caves onto the beach and started rigging up palm trees. They didn't do much on the beach – only just rigged up the palm trees and took them down again. The producer and his wife bathed, and presently they started packing up.

Saturday, 8 January 1927

Last night I didn't get to bed till past midnight. Leslie and I sat up talking, and he mentioned the fact that perhaps after his next leave (I shall be 21 then) it is possible I might go back with him and 'keep house', provided of course he didn't get married in the meantime. He said, 'I don't think I shall ever get married – of course you never know your luck.'

The idea thrills me to the core: to get away from here, from Wembley, just for a little while, to see different places and people. I know that I shall be in love a hundred times before I find the right man. I don't want to get married – not at least to the struggling domesticated life which seems to belong to every man I know. I want someone just overpowering, who can dance divinely with me, who likes much the same things as I do, who isn't too punctilious or particular, yet dresses well and looks well and is well, who doesn't mind spending money. I don't think I want him to be too rich, but just well enough off so that we can live comfortably, enjoy life and help others, those who really need it. He'll have to be taller than me of course, quite good-looking, not too much so though, he must be extremely witty and popular, a hard worker without showing it, reasonable and sympathetic, dark, and he must be endowed with much the same gifts and ideas as Leslie. He must be English too. In fact he'll be a man very difficult to find, and when I do find him I'll think myself unworthy.

I am so lonely, yet who am I to complain? You are tired Jean. But stand up to these pinpricks, grit your teeth, grin and go on, so that when the blows come with God's help you won't go under. Poor little lonely soul. If I could give you back your mother I would. But hold up your head and never let the world know. It doesn't want to know. You are of no consequence to it, so why should it bother?

Monday, 17 January

On Thursday I go back to the work and the weariness and the routine, the fun and the laughter and the dread of failure. Exams! That will prove if my last term's victory was worthwhile, was sincere. It will seem just impossible to think that someday there will be no returning, that I shall have to say farewell to the place which has played the biggest part in my life so far. And after that? The office with Daddy to see what architecture tastes like, and then perhaps more work and exams and a career . . . when my soul cries out for dancing and film work. I think that after a while you would grow very tired of dancing, and as to films it means very hard work and a lot of pushing.

Yet again if I did take up architecture for a career – and I should never dare to do so unless I was sure I could make a success of it, for Daddy's sake – there'll come a time when I'll have to toss up between that and a home and babies. It'll be mighty difficult, but time and these pages will see.

The smell of eucalyptus, the fluttering of the fire, the ticking of the clock, the occasional rustle of the paper as Ethel turns to read it, her spasmodic conversation, sometimes the dog asleep beneath the table – home and nothing to do. Life would be awful like that.

Monday, 7 February

I have come to the conclusion that I am rapidly 'growing out' of school. This routine, these petty little rules, this kind captivity. But as H.P. pointed out yesterday it is like climbing a hill. You are dying to get to the top but there's still a long way to go. The only thing is to climb – so one climbs.

Sunday, 27 March

Sometimes I hate everyone, everything. Last night I loathed the thought of the life I've got to live: inconspicuous, complacent. I want to do great things, to be great. I can't bear to think of that office, to pass my years insignificantly as an unsuccessful architect. Why won't Daddy see these things? I want to do everything people think me incapable of.

Saturday, 9 April

I am home again. This term's report is a simply amazing one. Miss Harris said to me when I was going, 'Hope you have very jolly holidays Jean – you deserve them.' My English has developed amazingly – that essay on 'Night' was rather a hit. I wonder if I could get Matric?[7] It would be such a splendid triumph.

Last night at half past ten Leslie took me for an hour's run in Pipsqueak.[8] Somewhere out Edgware way. As we sped along some straight wide road Leslie murmured, 'The road is a river of moonlight/ Over the dusky moor.'

It was rather like that – all the flat uninteresting country on either side hidden by a misty darkness, only the moon and the white stars in a clear hard sky. The thrill of the hour, of speeding through places made totally unfamiliar by the night, passing alone with my brother at midnight. Such things are stored in gold in my memory.

Tuesday, 24 May

I said goodbye to Leslie over a week ago. We all got up very early, and Daddy and I went to see him off at Euston. I put on my holiday clothes to see him off. I wonder if he saw the tears in my eyes when I kissed him goodbye. He was standing at the back of the carriage in the shadow – silent – and the train slowly, heartlessly, took him away. All those golden weeks were over. Three whole years, and the most terrible time in front of me.

---

7 Matriculation: the standard necessary to qualify for university entrance.
8 The Pratts' Fiat. Jean has been taking driving lessons with her family for several months.

Saturday, 28 May
We played Luckley this afternoon – cricket 2nd XI. Theirs was more or less an A team. Anyway they won 80–74. I made 9 runs, caught one person out, and took one wicket.

Saturday, 11 June
Today I went home. There were cherries, strawberries, tall blue lupins, white foxgloves, geraniums, early roses. There was the newly painted kitchen, but Leslie's room was empty and silent and a white dust sheet covered the bed. Things he had left behind – magazines, ashtrays, the fencing foils, an old coat – were scattered about my room waiting to be cleared away.

Then I came back to school again, and the Junior party was simply wonderful. They acted *Peter Rabbit and Benjamin Bunny*, then we made handkerchief animals, each form competing. Then we had light refreshments! There were scenes from *Wind in the Willows*, then hide and seek.

There is only one more week before the exams. French oral is on Weds.

Sunday, 12 June
I am in a most amusing and entertaining position at the moment. I think I may safely say that I have no attachments to particular people to consider. I stand a little apart, alone yet never really lonely. There are always plenty of people who are quite pleased to have me if I want to come: Laura, Phyllis Yeld, Rosemary G., Doreen Grove, Phyllis Stephenson and Betty Andrews. The latter I like most of all, yet I don't feel pledged to her in any way.

Then there is Gwyneth and Dorothy. There is only one way to deal with Gwyneth. That is to elude her for a time. I am not strong enough to dominate her or to keep her as my friend. You have to make her run after you. It is a deadly mistake to run after Gwyneth. Gwyneth is an incorrigible gossip – you never know what she might be saying about you behind your back. Today we were in the garden and we could see Laura P. and Phyllis taking each other's photos, and Gwyneth made some unwholesome remarks about them. They couldn't possibly have heard from where they were, but after supper I was sitting with Yeld, Prideaux and Grissell, and during a discussion about people generally Gwyneth and Dorothy were mentioned. 'I always feel,' said Yeld to me, 'that those two are watching us. When Laura and I were taking photos of each other in the garden I was sure they were talking of us.' I chuckled inwardly.

Thursday, 23 June
The worst of them are over – finished. Arithmetic, History, Geometry, French, Algebra and English. I have washed them away in my bath tonight and now I am between clean sheets and in clean pyjamas.

I do not think I have got Matric. I wrote a fairly decent essay on Modern Communication. The Grammar I think I did fairly well on too, perhaps I have got Credit. The Set Books I am not so sure about. Algebra of course that was unspeakable. I have obviously failed in that. The French was better than I expected. The Geom was better in comparison to the Algebra. History of course – well, I cannot say. Miss Stapley said I was her 'hope' just before I went in. One question we have all done wrong: the Civil War of 1649 we all took to be the First Civil War, 1642–46. The Arithmetic was amazingly easy – too easy I think. I have yet to pass in Drawing and Botany, which I think I shall do.

Although it has been a very long week, this week has been by far the nicest. The free half-hour in the garden before the exams, swinging high up level with the gym windows and the wind in your hair, the scent and colour of the herbaceous border, the thrill of being a candidate – the privileges and prestige! It is all over now and the days will never be the same.

Tuesday, 28 June
I had thought there was no heart left in me and I had killed that

wayward passion for Miss Wilmott long ago. But tonight as I came in late from the garden at 8.45 she came in through the doors into the Back Hall. There was no one there but she and I and I was in a hurry, but as I dashed around the corner of the stairs I said 'goodnight' as she passed. The light was dim and the shadows long, but she turned her head and I think she may have smiled as she said 'Goodnight Jean' in the way she used to do two years ago. I knew in that moment I could have died for her and that I shall never be able to forget. 'Those who dream by day are cognizant of many things which escape those who dream only by night.'[9] I believe that she may grow to care more than I have ever cared to hope. What can I do? She lives in a world of games and speed and swift thought – hard practical ideas – and straight, slim eager girls who love to do difficult and complicated things on ropes and bars and things and who scorn such lazy ones as I. She said, 'So long as you try I will help you – I will help you for ever if only you'll try.'

Monday, 25 July

It has come, that dreamed-of long-dreaded hour when I sit alone for the last time in my room at PHC.[10] Miss Parker has made me an Old Girl. I shall be able to come back next term and see those who are not leaving. I cannot believe that it is all over. I have not been able to see or speak to A.W. But at least I can write.

Wednesday, 27 July

And now I am home again. It is half-past six in the morning and I am going to get up soon and make the tea. It is raining.

---

9 From 'Eleonora', a short story by Edgar Allan Poe.
10 Princess Helena College.

3.

Such a Long Way Down

Saturday, 13 August 1927

I just loathe Ethel when she begins making subtle remarks about my future prospects. I hate it. I don't want to get married. She thinks she'll get all the sugar when I've chosen a husband. She shan't. I shall run away – anywhere. She shall have nothing to do with my babies if I ever have any. Mother had all the hard work, and Ethel will get all the 'juicy bits' of being a grandmother. There'll be a bust-up one of these days, such a bust-up. They are both on the landing and Daddy tried the door just now. I am doing 'very private work'.

Sunday, 14 August

I think I must tell you about my farewell to A.W. For the very last few days of term Miss Hawkes had been taking roll-call, but on Tuesday morning (the last day) she went with the Irish mail. I made a rapid calculation that it was 10–1 A.W. might be taking her place. When the 7.40 bell went I prayed it might be so I went to investigate. And she was there, standing just outside the Big Hall watching us drift downstairs. It was my one and only chance and I grabbed it.

'You'll be going directly after breakfast, won't you Miss Wilmott,' I said. 'Well I don't expect I shall see you so I'll say goodbye now.' She shook hands with me. There was a wonderful light in her eyes and she smiled and said goodbye and then waited . . . I believe she knew I might say something else. Then it was like plunging into a cold bath or stepping into the sea. 'Miss W.,' I went on, turning puce, 'I'm awfully sorry I haven't been able to get to know you better here.' We moved a little aside out of the way of people coming downstairs. 'Well Jean,' she said softly, 'there hasn't been much time has there?' 'And,' I hesitated, pulling at the banister with nervous fingers. 'Yes?' she said kindly. 'I may go on writing to you, mayn't I?' 'Oh yes, rather!' she laughed. We moved towards the door, 'Yes Jean, do write. I shall be pleased to hear . . .' Then somehow it was all over. It was wonderful. I am so glad I did it. My school career ended gloriously.

I did just about what I expected in the exams. I failed in Maths, passed in History, Arithmetic, French. I only got a credit for Botany and passed in Drawing. And I got credit in English.

Sunday, 21 August
Ethel and I have talked together about the bigger things. But I cannot say what I feel, what I know. I was surprised to find out how very simple was her nature, how little she seemed to know of life. God has given me a far-seeing vision and a certain amount of understanding – I have an imagination. It is my most precious possession. And it is what Ethel lacks. Her hard practical character is redeemed by a very deep and broad sense of humour which enables her to see things from a wide point of view, but she hasn't yet learnt to dream by day. I don't think she ever will. She is inclined to laugh at all that I hold dear.

Tuesday, 23 August
This morning I took Daddy in Pipsqueak over to Acton and we went to Eastman's [garage]. I came back by myself and all was going swimmingly until I tried to get into the garage. For the second time I nearly knocked down the gatepost, only it was the other one this time and the gate is unhinged. What will Daddy say? These sort of things just

crush the spirit out of you. I wanted to creep away somewhere like an ashamed dog and howl. Why can't I steer straight?[11]

There's no getting away from it – it is my eyes. I must see Mr Roberts this week. I called in on Harris's on the way back about the valves and the reverse gear, the latter being mighty difficult to engage. Of course when he did it it went beautifully and he only laughed.

Sunday, 11 September

I went to Mr Roberts and I have over-strained my eyes. It was part of the price of the Schools Cert. In consequence I am not able to do any of the things I like best, i.e. reading, writing and driving. Also sewing. I shall probably be going to a specialist in the future. I don't think I had better write any more now.

Sunday, 18 September

Do you know a month from today I shall be 18 and I shall be allowed to smoke! O glorious day.

Tuesday, 20 September

Retrospect:

Tipping up in a perambulator left in the conservatory while the others were having dinner. Green peas. Golden curls and blue ribbons. Making houses with the bedclothes before breakfast. Running about naked and thrilling with the feel of it. A white silk frock and a big blue sash and dancing slippers. Dancing lessons. The polka with Noreen. Buddy's cousin. Swinging at the bottom of the garden. Summer days and the smell of citronella to keep away the gnats. Bare legs and the wonderful silver fountain of the hose. Daddy in a white sweater. School. Very small, very shy. The afternoon in May – taken by mother to Penrhyn. Learning how to write

---

11 A mandatory driving test was not introduced until 1935.

the letters of the alphabet. A beautiful clean exercise book and a
new pencil. Miss Wade at the head of the dining room table and
me at her right. Choking tears because of youth's cruelty. Leslie as
a cadet in khakis. Wartime. Air raids. Mother white-faced and
fearful. Mummy and Daddy who were 'lovers still'. Youth's sudden
fierce resentment. Lavender, Peggy, Veronica and I. The Xmas when
Mummy wasn't there. Mummy white-faced and old eyes grown tired
with suffering yet dimly alight with that courage which never quite
died. The sudden night-fears. The long lonely nights that ended and
she was home again. Hot days when she sat in the garden. Nurse
Petersson. Darkness in her bedroom. The electric fan and ice to
keep it cool. Leslie suddenly brought home to see his mother for
the last time. An afternoon in late July when we all came into her
room and she prayed for us. Realisation that my fears were true.
Tears. Tears. A dull sudden despair. Tennis and laughter. Boarding
school next term at PHC! Thrills of the new life before me. Clothes.
Mummy's last kiss on my lips and my eyes dim with tears. Two
shillings in my hand. Gwyneth as a new girl next to me. Bells, bells.
Nights spent praying. The Tuesday morning French lesson. Boredom
itself. Miss Rodger's face round the door. 'May Jean Pratt go to Miss
Parker.' The absurd consciousness of having on my lavender jumper.
The swing doors and Miss Parker beyond. 'Your father is in the
drawing room my dear, he has something to say to you.' The sudden
knowledge of the end of all things. Daddy red-eyed and tired with
open arms and only a sob to tell me everything. Tears. Tears and
unbearable heartache. Home for the day. Aunt Edith outside in their
car waiting for me. Workmen that stopped to stare. A silence that
greeted me as I stepped inside the house. Mother was dead. A sudden
fierce desire to turn round and run away. Anywhere. 'She will be
very still.' The peace that smoothed away the suffering from her
face. And her forehead so cold when I kissed it. The gold of the
sunshine outside. Back to school. Feeling paralysed. Pleased with
sudden elevation of position the simple tragedy had placed me in.

The weekend and the flowers. White lilies that I threw after the coffin. It seemed such a long way down. We left her under the yew tree covered with flowers.

The term went by and the holidays came as all holidays will. Daddy alone. So he worked to save himself from dying of a broken heart. And so the years went by. And Ethel came. And life became what it is now.

Sunday, 9 October

I am beginning to live again – at last! But there is still something lacking – just a boy. To take me to the pictures, to be teased about, to write me letters, to dance with me, to sort of fill Leslie's place. But I must be patient. I know it's my glasses, always has been. Leslie said once, 'I suppose you've got to wear glasses? You know, without pulling your leg, you're a pretty girl.'

And I, fool that I was, answered 'I know!' I didn't mean to leave it at that. I had meant to add that 'my glasses don't improve my looks,' but somehow I couldn't get it out, and he's gone away thinking perhaps I'm conceited. Perhaps he's right.

I have asked Miss Wilmott to tea! Daddy suggested it. I've asked her!

I love the work at the office. I am learning shorthand and type-writing at the moment.

Thursday, 20 October

The dreamed-of has happened. SHE has sat in the drawing room and drunk our tea. I have talked with her and walked with her, as I sighed for long ago. But the things we spoke about were very ordinary, everyday things. I was nervous at first and felt frightfully sick, but by tea-time I gradually calmed down. She was very sweet. Nothing embarrassing happened. Ethel is in bed with a frightful cold and Daddy couldn't get home, so it was just she and I, a whim-sical trick of fate. How extraordinary life is. And yet I'm not as thrilled as I dreamed of being. Sentimental relationships are always embarrassing.

And I'm eighteen! The time one longs for comes around at last. This evening when Daddy came in I was smoking a State Express and neither of us remarked on it.

Saturday, 22 October
It is a miserable day and Leslie has forgotten my birthday.

Thursday, 1 December
I was half awake this morning when the clock struck 8. Then Daddy came in with two letters. One he gave to me – it was only my dividend and he waited till I read it. There was something strained in his attitude. I knew before he told me that he had some sort of bad news. But I knew it couldn't be Ethel. It was Leslie. I had to hold my hand over my heart very tightly to stop it beating before I could open the Company's letter. He has diphtheria. A mild attack they say. He is lying ill now, now as I write this, and we cannot do anything because of the miles that separate us, the miles of this 'small' world. But he is in Montevideo. The Company will let us know how he gets on. But I cannot help thinking of the things that might happen.

And that brings me to the mundane fact of a dancing partner. I must have one for the 21st (Old Girls), but who in the world do I know who can dance? Only one, and he's lying ill in Uruguay.

Sunday, 4 December
So I suppose I must ask Jack Phipps.

Tuesday, 6 December
I wrote to Jack Phipps last night and I have prayed. He will get it today, and I do hope he'll understand and be able to come. I live in suspense waiting for his answer.

Tuesday, 27 December

I had Eric Yewlett for the Old Girls dance. He's learning to be a parson and makes feeble jokes. I can't bear him.

Wednesday, 14 March 1928

Tonight I am going over to Harrow with the Jolliffes to a Conservative dance.

Yesterday morning Joyce phoned through: 'What I rang up to say was,' she said after the usual banalities, 'that I have got you a partner for tomorrow night.' (For a moment my heart sank – I immediately thought of Dennis Rollin.) 'And he,' she went on, 'is so thrilled with the idea that he is ready to put himself and car at your disposal. He has evidently been wanting to make your acquaintance for a long while.'

'But how topping of him,' I said. 'Who is he incidentally?'

'Mr Harold Dagley,' said Joyce.

'I seem to know the name.' And so I do, but for the life of me I can't remember anything more about him. 'What a howl. But I say, Joyce, I'm sure he's thinking of Margaret, not me.'

Anyway he is coming to fetch me from Wembley between six and half-past. I'm nervous, excited, it all seems so absurd. I'm sure it will be like so many of those dreams of mine – will crumble away to nothing. And tomorrow I shall still be in the same place, a looker on. He is sure to be disappointed – they all are. I have got to the stage when depression falls upon me like a blanket. I am going all to pieces so I must think no more about it.

Later:

Didn't I say it would all come to nothing? I have just had another phone message from Joyce to say that H.D. is down with 'flu. So what does it matter what I wear or what the weather is? Damn damn damn. I am fated. Oh God mayn't I ever get to know anybody? Mayn't I have any fun at all? Mayn't I ever meet a few of the people I imagine are in love with me? Or is it to save me from more bitterness, more heartache? But to quote someone else, 'To give up possible joys for the fear of possible pain is to give up everything.' I would willingly suffer a little if I could have lovers – lots of them and a good time.

Tuesday, 27 March

1.40 a.m. Another little Hell – paved with good intentions and roofed with lost opportunities. Oh God, what a fool I was. And the only way to ease the ache is to write and write, even at half-past-one in the morning.

We have just come back from another Ladies' Night – the Borough of Acton – and Geoffrey Roberts was there. I caught his eye in the entrance hall before we went up for the reception. He came over and was introduced as 'Mr Roberts'. He stared hard and said, 'Am very pleased to meet you.' I just smiled faintly and turned away, thinking, 'Oh, Geoffrey Roberts . . . he can wait.' And it was there I made the first mistake, I know now.

Then I let slip another opportunity. After dinner, while we were waiting for the dancing to begin, Ethel and I and one or two others went up the stairs to look at the awful flash-light photos of ourselves. Having thoroughly studied and reviled same, they stood back against the wall and I leant over the bannisters looking down onto the hall below, wondering idly why I had been so cold to G.R. He was standing with the crowd. He is tall and dark, and again his eye caught mine, and almost at once he came upstairs to look at the photos beside me. Should I have spoken or given some sort of encouragement? All the torment begins again when I think of it.

I try to comfort myself with the thought that Ethel and Mrs Halter were just behind so it would have been impossible, but it wouldn't have been. We had been introduced, and it was my place to speak. I had hoped he would have asked for a dance, but having behaved so abominably beforehand I hardly blame him for not risking getting snubbed again.

There is no sleep for me until 2, and even now I shall lie awake a long, long time. Am I really in love, or is it another one of those dreams which are always dreams?

Later: All day long my nerves have been keyed to a pitch I can hardly describe. All the time my mind has throbbed with a single thought – a suffocating desire to meet and speak with him who has haunted my thoughts since we last looked into one another's eyes.

Sunday, 1 April

I have slipped back into the old ways of looking at life, merely as a bystander. No man turns from the stream to wait upon me, they do not come in numbers as they seem to come for Margaret. I am just amused, cynical, hating myself – dreading the thought of tomorrow and the disillusionment it may bring. 'At 18 we are so innocently vain' – I am quoting from Isobel. As she says, we want everyone to love us. And why not? I shall never be 18 again. And I have never been kissed. Oh damn it, and I know I ought to have been. Other people think I have.

Sunday, 15 April

The days slip by so quickly. It is nearly a year since I left PHC, and of what value has that year been to me? I know now I should have stayed on. I could have helped PHC, could have made myself useful in the library, could have got Matric and learnt more of things I was just beginning to enjoy. I have gained nothing by stealing this year from my school life.

Wednesday, 25 April

No further news of Harold Dagley.

Thursday, 3 May

I had a long, long letter from Leslie this morning. It seems so wonderful after all this time. And he writes all the news to me, treating me no longer as a baby sister, and sends all the snaps to me.

Sunday, 6 May

I mustn't fall in love with someone at the Tennis Club. It will be so awkward, yet I can't help thinking of him. On no account will I be made to look a fool. Oh, he wears such wonderfully creased flannels. I am going to the club tomorrow evening. I went yesterday too.

Temple Silvester has just passed, and I can't imagine who it was with him. One of the girls in an awful red frock with the Alsatian.

Sunday, 20 May

Ethel has not meant to, but she has stolen away all possible intimacy between me and Daddy. I only see him now as a man growing old – a little eccentric, a little vulgar, irritating – the difference between our ages forming an almost unsurpassable gulf. Yet I know that I love him.

Daddy I want to win you back some day. There is work I must do for you, for myself, for our name. And perhaps I am lazy and weak-minded. Perhaps I do find the position of junior typist a very comfortable and easy one, and perhaps I am not doing as much and learning as much as I should.

I hate myself for being a coward and a cad. I eat with them, I smile and talk with them, I take all my father has to offer, and then write these sort of beastly things about them without them knowing.

Wednesday, 6 June

'I don't think I could take a boy of my own age seriously enough to marry him,' I told Miss Walker some 15 minutes back as she stood by the window watching the traffic at work. At present I am not worrying myself particularly about it at all. I would like to go to the pictures with Geoffrey Roberts. Or have coffee with Barrett at Lyons. Or meet Harold Dagley. Or go for a walk with Jack Honour. Any of these to amuse me, laugh with me, tease and be teased. Except Jack: I would want him to make love to me.

'Very small, very shy.' Jean prepares for the battles ahead.

4.

Two Girls Who Whispered Once

Tuesday, 25 September 1928 (aged eighteen)

This 'year' is nearly over. I have come through fairly all right. I took Miss Walker's place and stood the test. It was work I rather enjoyed in spite of the few long letters that got me down. It was hard work, doing the work of two at a busy time. But it gave me a sense of well-being and I gained in self-confidence.[12]

Tomorrow I start lessons in architecture at the Ealing Institute. Wednesday and Friday mornings at 10 to 12.30. Shall I be the only girl? And if so, shall I be an awful mug? Shall I be able to do anything?

Wednesday, 26 September

She came in some 10 or 15 minutes after the class had started. Tall, thin, dark-eyed, smiling impudently.

'Come, come,' said Mr Patrick, pulling out his watch. 'First day of the term – this is dreadful.' But there was a corresponding twinkle in his eye that I noticed afterwards always came when he spoke to her. Lazy, amusing, vibrant in every fibre of her . . . one of those people who go through life in a don't-care-a-damn-for-anyone-life-is-fun mood. Aggravating to live with but lovable in spite of her faults.

---

12 Jean's work at her father's architecture practice consisted of secretarial and administrative duties. Many of her diary entries contain passages where she is staring out of the window.

Character and personality – or what Elinor Glyn has termed 'It' – counts more than brains or beauty.[13]

A piquant face not altogether unattractive, teeth a trifle prominent, skin almost sallow, lanky shingle, but lovely eyes. A button off the cuff of the short tweed coat she wore, darned woolly stockings, large flat-heeled old brown strap shoes, a wispy skirt of a thin dark blue artificial silk. And yet the most impelling personality in the room – at least I thought so.

She came and inspected my instruments. 'Aren't they nice?' she said. And, 'Where do you get your set-squares from? I've tried all over the place in Ealing and can't get them with the rounded edges like that.' Making herself charmingly agreeable in case she might want to borrow something. After she had gone I scratched my name on the set-squares.

After all, it was quite simple. There are 7 of us starting Architecture – 3 boys and 4 girls. The rest are doing their 2nd and 3rd years. One helped oneself to a drawing board, bought a sheet of paper in the next room, took a T-square and chose a place in the front row. And it was all fairly easy to begin with.

I wonder why these personalities dominate me so. Immediately I come into contact with anyone I take a fancy to I want to be like them.

Sunday, 11 November

For two minutes today we paused and dreamed. There was heartache and pain and awe in the silence, and the cry of a frightened child, and a man who coughed, and two girls who whispered once. And there was promise and peace and a vast universal stillness.

I am so very proud and glad I was there in Whitehall with all

---

13 Glyn was a popular and sometimes scandalous British writer. Her novel *It*, published in 1927, popularised the concept of a person – male or female – possessing a certain talent of mind or character which makes them instantly attractive to a member of the opposite sex.

those thousands. Within a few yards of the King and his family. And to see the people who came: coarse, loud-voiced women. Slim supple girls. Old men and young. A cockney and his vacant-eyed wife – one of the bloody Tommies perhaps who came through. All of them bound together for one indefinable space of time by a relationship stronger than blood or spoken word. And the service at Albert Hall tonight, when songs and hymns were sung so familiar and so clear, grander than the men who first thought of them.[14]

Saturday, 15 December
Against the dictates of all reason, and minimising the chances of my eyesight ever becoming better, I must write. Today I watched a bride and bridegroom sent away by their relations and friends smothered in confetti. Confetti was thrust down their necks, bags of it emptied over them, their car lurid with it. Horrible, gaudy stuff that brings no happiness. And so my resolve is strengthened more fiercely than before: If I ever get married, mine shall be the quietest of weddings. I don't want a lot of people for whom I care nothing get tight on Daddy's champagne and ogle me at church and whisper to one another.

I have dreamed it all so often. One morning, Sunday perhaps, very early I and He, Leslie, Ethel and Daddy and his most intimate and necessary relations in a little church, and then to shy away. No fuss, no ribaldry, no hateful insincerity.

Sunday, 12 January 1929
Last night I met Harold Dagley. Margaret and I went together to join in the celebrations of P.'s 21st (next year I shall be 21!). And he came late. They had partnered me off with him, but as it happened, Martin was partnerless so I went round with him. H.D. was distinctly disappointing even at first sight – slight, thin, dark and weak-

---

14 The first Armistice Day commemoration was held within the gates of Buckingham Palace on 11 November 1919.

chinned. He is one of those boys who cannot be friends with a girl without wanting to flirt with her. And it is no use getting away from the fact that I am not a flirt in the same way Margaret is. I don't think there's anything frightfully admirable in that. Perhaps I said that because I am a bit jealous. I know that if anybody wanted to kiss me I wouldn't refuse him – and yet damn it all I've just remembered that Percy did on Boxing Day under the mistletoe and I smacked his face.

Oh I don't know – it's all wrong. How often have I wondered: to give up everything for an ideal, or lose sight of it in the murk of an everyday existence? Is it made up of little things – washing up, typewriters and shoulder straps – or must one climb the hills to reach the stars alone?

Wednesday, 17 April

Daddy has hurt me so. I came in from the tennis club meeting full of the fun I had gleaned from it, and I told Daddy that Valerie had been elected to the Ladies Committee. 'Oh, you are hopeless – if Valerie can, why can't you?' And it hurt, hurt, hurt. Why can't parents help you by thinking a bit for themselves, instead of bringing up the same old platitudes? I am too damn proud ever to talk of these things with other people.

Monday, 23 December

'The War has ruined us for everything.' He is right. 'We are not youth any longer. We don't want to take the world by storm. We are fleeing. We fly from ourselves. From our life. We were eighteen and had begun to love life and the world; and we had to shoot it to pieces.' (From *All Quiet on the Western Front* by Erich Maria Remarque, translated by A.W. Wheen.)

I have not the time to say all I would about this book, nor to copy all the paragraphs I should like to. I think all my generation and all later generations should read it. We never knew the true ghastliness of war, its utter futility, its horror, the pitiless suffering of men. We should pray every night and every morning for no more war.

This book brings it home to you more than anything I have ever known. The details are harrowing – it spares you nothing, it makes you feel physically sick. Yet how much better for us to learn like this rather than ever enact it all again.

Monday, 6 January 1930

And so I pray. My one big belief is prayer. I pray that if all other faiths fail, this one may not. But the question that weighs heaviest on my mind at the moment is this one: Shall I leave the Tennis Club or not?

The idea came to me just before Xmas. At first it seemed the one thing left for me to do to establish my happiness. I want to write it all down so that I can get the pros and cons in a cold systematic review.

Pros: I shall be free every day to do exactly as I like. No one at the club cares whether I go or not. It is too large for me – I fit in nowhere. I cannot somehow play tennis well enough to arrest the attentions or kindly regard of the upper sects. The bright young people boss me. I am not able to drift with them: self-consciousness overcomes me. My eyesight, nerves and weakness generally are against me. I love tennis. If only there were someone who wouldn't mind practising with me. No more mental agony, that lounging about in the summer hoping someone will ask you to make up a decent four, but no one does because there is always someone else. Then eventually to hide one's shame and get one's money's worth, make up a four myself with a lot of old women.

The cons: Perhaps I didn't try very hard last summer. I missed the tournaments quite by mistake – that always gives a bad impression. Many people are kind: no one is ever rude to me or obviously shuns me like they do Mrs Warner. There is always a chance that I may sometime convince them I can help, organise, could be of value to the club, can be light and amusing and attractive.

But I think the biggest and most important Con is Valerie. It is so hard not to be jealous. She is young and has won a gallant place among them. I don't want to lose her, she is one of the best friends I have. If it wasn't for her I shouldn't think twice about leaving. Oh God, I don't know what to do.

Sunday, 12 January

There is a dream: an exquisite little house set down on the borders of Cornwall and Devon near the sea. That may never come true – those counties are already overcrowded during the summer, what will they be like in some years' time? Maybe a husband, maybe a husband at sea, maybe a husband who is difficult, divorce, perhaps death. I should like 2 children, a boy and a girl with 2 years' difference in their ages. Most of the time they are at boarding school.

Monday, 17 March

As far as I can gather, I come into an annual income of about £300 in October. I could devote one-sixth of the amount to the improvements in the office I so much desire. It has also occurred to me whether I couldn't invest that amount in something solid and remunerative, such as flats or gilt-edged securities. The flats appeal to me, buying up old property, altering and redecorating and then renting them.

The alterations in the office will cost money. There will be one very, very unalterable condition if I do this though, and that is that G.P.P.[15] must get rid of W.S.B. and engage some more reliable draughtsmen. If I had my way I would turn out W.S.B., E.H.S. and I am afraid J.G.P. I do not think I shall really speak of this until I am 21. I am then within my legal rights and should be capable of voicing an opinion. I am very serious about all this. In the meantime, a little patience and much thought.

---

15 Her father, George Percy Pratt.

Wednesday, 9 April

A success such as I have never known! How I have worked and prayed and dreamed, and now it is all over, their congratulations still ringing in my ears. And Mr Worrall, Mr Worrall himself came to me – asked for me – and told me he considered I was the best in the whole show. I'm just overwhelmed.[16]

And what a weapon I have in my short-sightedness. Without it I feel convinced I should not have done nearly so well. I could see nothing beyond the footlights, a faint blur that conveyed nothing to me, only sounds that came from that darkness. I didn't feel nervous because I couldn't see their faces or note their expressions.

Monday, 2 June

I have the inferiority complex, the hump and indigestion and a few other things. Yesterday Joan Hughes beat me 6–0 6–0 in the Open Singles. I know she's good, but damn it all – not a single game! And after my prayers and that gay, calm confidence I instilled into myself. If I think of it too much I find myself asking absurd and desperate questions. Is there a God? Does he care or hear us?

I quite see that the best players don't wish to play with weaker ones. Naturally it spoils their game. They will see that score, and all the committee, and they are the people that matter most, and they will say, 'Good Lord, Jean's even worse than we thought she was.'

Yet why should I let a tennis tournament so dampen my spirits? Only that I had hoped that by this year I might have proved to other people that there was some strength in me. The whole world is a dark and murky place and I am afraid I shall never rise to the heights I dream of, afraid that I shall settle down to an irritating existence of

---

16 She was taking part in an unnamed play for her local amateur dramatic association. The journals contain no further details, and no mention of rehearsals.

domesticity and the narrow little life of the average woman. But I shall always have the chance to write.

I have two more tournaments to play yet. And I must beat Elsie Warden.

Thursday, 5 June

Tonight Leslie Northam and I played Kit Rayner and Ken Matthews. They won the first set 6–0, and I thought, 'Hell! This is going to be a repetition of Sunday's fiasco.' Then something in me stirred and I cannot quite explain it, but I started a sort of auto-suggestion in my mind. I brought my willpower into full force. We won the first two games – they only just beat us 7–5.

I have been thinking a lot today. The idea took a final shape in my mind as I walked to Sudbury Town. I am getting soft. My position at the office as daughter of the boss is too comfortable, and I am able to do too much what I like. It will never do: I cannot be a subordinate to Pop in that way, but as his partner I can do immense things.

They need doing badly too. He has worked the business to a certain point and here we have stopped. To be any use at all I must get my Associate RIBA certificate, and I shall never do that on my own at the office. I haven't the ability and there is no one to coach me for the exams. I have decided – I want to go into another office, a large, modern and well-organised affair where they will help me achieve my work for the Intermediates. I shall see how a well-run office ought to be managed. Daddy is getting old and I feel it is essential that I get on with things.

Sunday, 21 June

Have just been glancing through my last entry and since then I have been brought to realise that it must be a school, a day school. I have written for prospectuses to the London University, Central School of Arts and Crafts, the Northern Polytechnic, the Regent Street Poly – it is the latter which I think I shall really prefer.

Tuesday, 17 July

And so another period of my life ends. Two years at the Ealing Art School. Today for the last time I bent over a drawing board in Room 15, and for the last time walked those bare stone corridors and clattered down the stairs. I said goodbye to Mr Patrick, waved farewell to Mary Moyes and Elise Folkes. I am not sorry it is over, the time I spent was but a stepping stone to something better.

Wednesday, 30 July

We eventually decided on the London University and I went up for an interview. It was most satisfactory, and I start on 6 October.

Now if I can only convince Daddy of my seriousness. I can encourage him to hang on for another five years. Then I will return to him and do all the things that need doing so badly. With all his long years of experience to help back me up I should be able to make a splendid thing of this. What a fool I have been! If I can only make him realise that he has someone here on whom to rely he will feel encouraged to carry on for a little longer. And Oh God I must not fail at the University.

And all my friends – they have not the first idea of the direction or depth of my ambition.

Monday, 4 August

The early passion of the garden is blown, and heavy rains have beaten the colour from the roses. Delphinium, larkspur and foxglove have died, Aaron's rod is beginning to throw golden spikes up the border by the fence, phlox, gladioli, geranium and dark red antirrhinum bloom among a profusion of foliage washed deep green. Peaches are being gathered and lavender is nearly ripe for picking, and there is a whisper of autumn in the wind.

Thursday, 7 August

Supposing Daddy had been a singer or a cook, or anything but an architect, and I still had my income when I was 21, I dream of how I would plan my life:

Freelance journalism.
Music.
Cooking.
Dressmaking.
Gardening.
Golf.

I would get up at 7.30 for 8.30 breakfast every morning except Sundays. From 9 to 10.30 I would practise – singing, piano lessons, elocution too perhaps. Then the rest of the morning to English study and writing, and in the afternoon dressmaking, gardening or cooking. I would drive a car and play golf for recreation, and there would be social obligations to fit in in the afternoon and evenings. Yet I don't know. I think I would rather go the way I have chosen. Something more reliable and strengthening about it.

Sunday, 5 October

A national disaster has occurred – the R101 has crashed.[17] 40-odd people burned to death (all men). Terrible, ghastly, tragedy stark and dramatic. The papers will be full of it, much sympathy will be expressed for the remaining relatives, the men will be made heroes and their widows provided for for life, there will be whip-rounds and memorials and long, stirring speeches, and all the world will be horribly thrilled.

But I know of worse tragedies that go on every day unnoticed: patient, plodding workers scraping all they can together so that their children may have a better start than they had. I cannot forget that timorous little creature who came into the office for an education

---

17 Before the Hindenburg, the British-made R101 was the world's largest airship. It crashed on its maiden overseas voyage over France, killing 48 of 54 passengers and crew.

grant for her daughter. She was so shrunken and nervous and terribly anxious to get the best for her girl. She confessed to having had to borrow £4 for clothes. The patience of these people. What do they ever get from life?

Friday, 10 October

Thoughts accumulated during the past week: that in no other place apart from university can one be so completely and unintentionally ignored. I may hate the newness of it all, and the hardness of it, yet I must fight on. If I am to be the only girl in a class of boys, then let me get to know those boys. Already two have shown signs of friendliness.

Saturday, 6 December

Joyce Coates: A charming little person, rich, with a good taste in clothes and attractive manners. More in her perhaps than at first might be imagined.

Joan Hey: She is in the act of growing up. In fact she is only just beginning. Nonetheless she is easy to get on with and likeable, and has plenty of willpower.

Elsie Few: A most interesting personality. There is something of the texture of satin or cream about her, and above all she is an artist.

Thursday, 1 January 1931

So seldom have I succeeded in keeping any New Year Resolutions that now mine are rarely made in January, but at odd sudden moments in unconventional places.

But I have recently reached a conclusion on a point I have been considering for several weeks. I inherited from my mother the desire to write. This desire has haunted me from the time when I first scrawled the alphabet in coloured letters across a clean white page. I must write, even now, with my career chosen and my training begun. It is in my blood and will not be subdued. To satisfy this desire I am going to keep this Journal which I shall make as entertaining as possible. I am learning truths too, as I grow older, that I am unable to discuss at present, and I fear that with the coming years ideas will be forgotten unless I make an effort to keep them. So let this be my New Year Resolution – that I leave behind me something worth reading, which even if it doesn't attract strangers, may at least surprise my friends and relations.

Saturday, 17 January

Pooh went back to work today.[18] Our lives are made up of meetings and farewells. Think of the meals now! Once more 'they two' and me.

Ethel and I will never be more than superficially good friends. We are mentally opposed. I always feel that anything she does for me is rather a nuisance. When I was in bed the other day with a cold I felt the most brutal burden. She won't read: how much she has missed. And if a discussion is started on anything more advanced than the latest family scandal she shuts up like an oyster at first signs of opposition.

But it isn't her fault any more than it is mine. I admire all she has done for us tremendously, and she runs this house as if it were a ship. And she has looked after and cared for Daddy. But oh this banging about in the mornings when she makes herself do the housework she's not feeing equal to. This agitation when a guest is late for a meal, this pride in her home. There is no sort of adventure about it, and she is too practical, too afraid of sentiment. I wish sometimes she might suddenly leave dusting the drawing room one morning and take a bus to Kew because Spring seemed suddenly to have arrived and she wanted to see young, green growing things.

Since I have so many more advantages than she has ever had and I have learned so much more from books than she has, I must be the one to regulate the friendship so that we do nothing to hurt each

---

18 Her brother Leslie.

other. If she'd had the education, good school, made to work, college, a degree, travel. All desires outside her circle have been repressed by the atmosphere in which she was brought up – Wembley all her life.

I feel brutal writing these things, but . . . Mummy used to read Shelley and Keats and Tennyson. She'd have loved Rupert Brooke and Alfred Moyes and Walter de la Mare. Poetry is never something that has taken a very big place in Ethel's life.

Saturday, 24 January

Tonight we played 'cutthroat' and Daddy won (1s. 5d.),[19] and we half-jokingly urged him to put it to Dr Barnardo's. But this he firmly refused to do. 'It is wrong,' Ethel said as he went to do the greenhouse. 'He plays for what he can get.' And later, when we were discussing the possibility of visiting Wisley Garden, a good Sunday outing in the car, she said, 'But we never go out in the car. I never had a run all last summer. Daddy just will not use the car except to get him somewhere definite. We never use it and we never shall.' So she too finds Daddy a little disappointing. There are times when I am ashamed of him – yet I love him. He came from his Saturday night bath very pink and clean, with his white hair fluffed in a halo round his head. I think I love him like that best of all. If in 5 years I manage to become an Associate of RIBA he will be 70. 70. Oh why wasn't I born sooner?

I was smitten earlier this evening with a tremendous idea. I would write a book within the next 5 years and see if I could get it published. And here I am going to quote from Mr John Connell, for I must confess his book was partly responsible for the inspiration:

'It can be no tale of carefully rounded edges, of neatly massed effects, a thing of plot or climax. Somehow life is not like that – it is not symmetrical, measured and finished. The weaver of the pattern doesn't seem to care for neatly tasselled ends and pretty bows – it is

---

19 A three-handed variation of the card game Euchre.

all very rough and ragged. Yet through it all there seems to run a purpose and an idea, a kind of guiding line.'

And so I conceived the idea of writing a book on similar lines.

Friday, 30 January

This morning I felt foolish talking to Mr Ashworth. I kept imagining that he was wondering why on earth I had chosen Architecture and not Decoration, or in fact either.

On our way back from tea today Joan Hey and I passed the little 2nd-year decorator Philips. She was alone and her eyes were red and swollen and I heard her sob as she passed us by. 'I am so sorry for her,' said Joan. 'She's so dull and inanimate, but I expect inside she wishes she were dashing and attractive. Everything is against her. She has the ugliest figure.'

It is true. And I am sorry too. I know that feeling only too well.

Saturday, 31 January

This book I am going to write. I shall start with my schooldays and fill the first chapter or phase of the book with as eloquent and entertaining a description of PHC as possible. Then those bitter years, a very light and rather cynical sketch but quietly indicating growth of thought and so on, and I shall write I think in diary form. I must suppress all egoism. It's going to be difficult. And then student days.

Lacrosse this afternoon, played in a bitter wind. I'm not very good but I love it – the tang in the air, the movement, the superb cleanness of it all. I wear my gym tunic under my coat now and don't bother to change. It amuses me to see the sly, curious glances of the gentlemen in the direction of my knees as they become exposed with the flapping of my coat.

Tuesday, 3 February

Copy of letter to my father

Darling –

While I've got this still in my mind –

I've been thinking such a lot – I am really worried about you. You are the absolute centre of my future: without you I should be like a rudderless ship; all my inspiration would die. So it is absolutely essential that you keep well. And as I said the other night, you won't keep well if you have to worry about the business.

Now the business is far more important than me – it even matters perhaps more than any of us. I can be of no practical use to it for at least five years, and even then I shall be very young and inexperienced to take up any sort of responsible position.

The only way out that I can see is for you to ensure the future of the business firm by taking a partner as soon as you can. You must have someone reliable, trustworthy and hardworking in the office. I am praying day and night that we may find the right man. I know it's damn difficult – but don't let W.S.B. do you down any more! If only you could find the right person to buy a share of your practice, and for you to leave your share to me in your will, then I shall not feel I am undertaking an impossible task as I do sometimes in moments of depression. And your health will benefit by easing your mind.

Sunday, 8 February

In bed with one of these blasted colds again – what a miracle and a blessing is the wireless. I think that with a good portable set, a library subscription, fountain pen and paper and ink, I should enjoy being bedridden. Through these mediums I could explore the world. I lay in the semi-darkness listening to some vaudeville in which The Three Ginx in harmony gave a delightful performance and Ann Penn contributed some very clever impersonations, particularly one of Gertrude Lawrence in the song she sang with Noël Coward in *Private Lives*.

Friday, 20 February

To and fro swings the pendulum: to have my hair cut or leave it long? On Tuesday Elsie Few put it to a vote in the studio, and most people seem to think it would improve my appearance rather than otherwise. 'It would make you look so much more charming Jean,' said Few. 'Really we want the world to be as beautiful as possible – you owe it that. And think – you'll have all the young men simply flat my dear.' But Cargill objected. I respect Cargill's opinion. 'Don't you have it done Pratt – it looks jolly nice as it is.' And today Joyce Coates rather surprised me by saying, 'Don't you have your hair off Jean – I shan't have any more to do with you if you do.'

And of course at home from Ethel: 'Oh, you would be very foolish if you did it.' 'You'll be no daughter of mine,' says father magnificently.

Cheap – that is of what I am afraid, looking cheap. But if I were cheap I should be so now with it as it is. Outwardly it cannot make anything but a superficial difference: it is what I am that matters. So I shall have it done![20]

Saturday, 28 February

God – what dream is this? We study the architecture of Rome, and the vaguest fantasy rises before me: a dream of the City Beautiful.

To build a perfect city: buy an area of lovely untouched English country somewhere in the South. Plan first two straight wide roads, one running from N to S, the other from E to W, and where they intersect is the centre of our city. On the corners should be erected the most important buildings, i.e. the police station, GPO, council offices, fire station, possibly a bank etc. Shops should range on either side of the two main roads, the front portions being built out with flat roofs that could be used by restaurants in fine weather. The

---

20 This formed the last entry in a crimson exercise book. The back of the book contained an exclamatory list of 'Danger Dont's': 'Don't play at being "last across" on any road or street! Don't hang onto a vehicle nor climb on it! Don't forget to walk on the footpath, if there is one!'

residential area should be built at the back of these streets, and all designs would have to be essentially twentieth century. No faked Tudor houses or ugly Georgian facades.

Fireplaces for coal fires would only be allowed as a luxury. For all domestic and industrial purposes gas or electricity should be used, and each house could only have one chimney stack.

Everywhere there should be as much light and air and clean lines as possible. And all designs would have to be passed by a Committee of men selected for their knowledge in good construction, hygiene and, most important, their appreciation of real beauty and proportion such as the Greeks knew.

Garages and hotels should be built at the four entrances to the town. Large recreation grounds provided for the inhabitants, sports grounds for tennis, golf, cricket, rugger and all athletics. Public baths built to Roman ideals: open-air baths for the summer, covered in for the winter. A gymnasium, dance halls, skating rink. Everything should be provided for public amusement: one or two good theatres, cinemas – everything for a residential people, no industries or factories of any kind would be permitted. This should be a city where the more successful workers of London might live, driving in their cars or going by the specially prepared railways to London each day and back at night. So that London may eventually be left to its fogs and dirt and manufacture, salesmanship and business. A rather preposterous ideal, because I doubt whether London's entertainments might ever be excelled. But might it not be possible, if the world's finest financiers were gathered together and formed a syndicate or something. And then the world's best engineers and greatest architects and artists to plan and design the Perfect City?

There is no reason why it should not be international: let its inhabitants be as cosmopolitan as is reasonable. Possibly England has the best climate in the world, for all our complaining. To promote world peace we may not stand aloof and exclude any other country, and this applies to every race.

No building should be commenced until the general layout of the city was arranged. And the building would be lovely – their proportions please the eye, their design satisfy the artistic judgment. No tramways either. Perhaps even the main roads built with subways for heavy traffic and special paths for pedestrians. And another thing from Rome: the main streets colonnaded so that shoppers were not inconvenienced by a shower of rain.

Tuesday, 3 March

The only thing of importance I have done today is to visit the Leicester Galleries and seen Epstein's *Genesis* for myself.[21] Admittedly at first sight I was shocked but not repulsed. The more I looked the more I marvelled. I am hardly in a position to pass any criticism on the technique of his work, but all the busts in that room possess the same characteristic – i.e. strength, a vitalising staggering power that overwhelms one, as if one had been plunged in cold water. And the work strikes me as being sincere – the manifestation of a magnificent mind. And it is not crude or gross, but rather a beautifying of a crude and gross subject. I could feel the pain of that expectant negress myself. Because his art is not conventional he is condemned. Epstein is setting a totally different standard. That is where we fail: unconsciously we compare his work with standard works (i.e. the Greeks). It is what we have been brought up to do. We learn in our youth what is supposed to be beautiful and what is ugly, so that by the time we have reached the age of discerning these things for ourselves we are already a little biased. Most of us find it so difficult when we meet with something totally different. Epstein sees further.

To watch those who came to see for themselves was distinctly amusing. Nearly all betrayed a look of shocked propriety, hastily

---

21 Jacob Epstein's majestic *Genesis*, a sculpture in white marble, showed a naked woman in the later stages of pregnancy. Controversy raged: the *Daily Express* called it 'You white foulness!' A cloud of thinly disguised anti-Semitism presided over other critiques.

suppressed. 'We are broadminded of course, this is the twentieth century,' they tell themselves. One woman murmured, 'I haven't seen anyone looking like that – funny sort of figure.' She was the bulky sort of person who, without her clothes on, would look far funnier than *Genesis*.

Friday, 6 March
Conversation at Aunt Janie's this afternoon, on Epstein's work. Mrs H.: 'Well, there's something about it . . . makes you come back for another look. Lovely bit of white marble to begin with. Of course the anatomy's all wrong. I went with a doctor, that's how I know. Of course Epstein's a bit mental. Never washes.'

Thursday, 12 March
Lecture on Modern Architecture by Austen Hall. Architecture must express an adventure of the mind. Design must have strength and wit and character. In trying to break away from traditions we are taking the wrong path – must find a way of refreshing the old without eliminating all necessary detail, for some of it rightly applied is very beautiful. There seems no point in doing without a cornice (or as one modern architect does, wear a collarless coat).

Thursday, 19 March
Tomorrow is the long talked- and thought-about Foundation Dance at UCL. We are eight: Jo Coates, Dorothy Cargill, Alison Hey, self, Goulden, Tarrant, Gresham and Stoneham. Beginning the evening with the 2nd evening performance of Cochrane's revue, we go on to dance at college until 5 a.m. God grant the evening will be a success! Tom Goulden is the only boy that knows us all. Tarrant we know to exchange an occasional greeting with. Gresham and Stoneham not at all. Stoneham is causing us all a certain amount of curiosity. I wonder if he will prove very disappointing.

5.

A Man Shorter than Myself

Sunday, 22 March 1931

Over now! And how marvellous it was, just what I had prayed for.
Nothing embarrassing happened. Gresham brought me home in his
Morris Minor and I arrived feeling so wide awake and gay that I
slipped off my frock for a skirt and blouse and took Prince up the
Harrowdene Road, a marvellous hour, dawn. It seemed that we shared
a secret, the birds, the dog and me.

The loveliness of Alison in her slim pink frock and exquisitely
dressed fair hair. Cargill in blue, Jo in green, me in yellow, the new
chiffon yellow frock that has cost me £8 8s. and down which I spilt
lemonade that Tarrant gallantly mopped up with his handkerchief
and made little remarks about for the rest of the evening. For
instance, when I had finished an ice, 'Now, have you eaten that
cleanly?'

My beads that Tarrant was hanging round his shirt front . . .

From the Revue: 'I'm a little stiff from tennis . . .' 'I don't care
where you come from . . .'

And Valerie is getting engaged to Jack Honour.

Wednesday, 25 March

The truth weighed suddenly in on my happiness.

The best work I can offer is only 3rd rate. I have spent many extra
hours on that sheet, and I have put what I thought was my uttermost

into its execution. I had dreamed for a moment that it was better than either of my other orders (Doric and Ionic). There was the possibility of my getting an 'M', and all I have received is a 'C'. No good saying that this is better than having to do it again, or that Goulden also has a 'C' or that Decorators must be marked more leniently than Architects. Jo has an 'M' and I a 'C'.

I have terrible visions of the future, of never being able to rise above mediocrity. Of drifting my life away in a dry, dusty office, a dull and stupid spinster who cannot rise out of herself and has not the strength of character to seek adventure.

The trouble is bare before me. What can I do? Fail and fail and fail again.

Sunday, 12 April
Valerie and Jack are having such a tough time. Who could have thought it possible that her mother should be so hidebound, so stupid by convention, that she objects to Jack's position. He isn't good enough – not good enough! 'As a matter of fact,' said Valerie, 'his blood relations are much better than mine if we choose to go into it. But of course she won't, just because his family lost all their money and they have to live in Lonsdale Avenue.'

I cannot understand Mrs Buck's point of view. I suppose she had dreams for her daughter, saw her carried away from Wembley by the conventionally magnificent hero amid a shower of envy while she stands proudly by. The pitiful narrow selfishness of it.

I have just finished reading *Bengal Lancer* by Francis Yeats-Brown. There is so much food for thought in this book, and it brings up the question of Gandhi's fight for India's supremacy. Why shouldn't India be allowed to rule herself? A vast continent of many different races, surely it could be more ably done by natives who understand the condition and circumstances of the people. What right have we to force Christianity on them? Will they necessarily remain hostile to us if we were to evacuate? Surely an exchange of ideas and trade would still be welcomed? We need spiritual training more than anything.[22]

Tuesday, 28 April

There is Pooh, 30 years old, unmarried. A roamer on the surface of the world and likely to remain one until the long hours of night duty and the restlessness kills him. They are pensioned off at 50, rarely last longer than 55.[23] Is that to be all for you, my Pooh? Another 20 years controlling the messages of the world? The pain and pleasures of the peoples of all nations by the lift of your little finger.

Friday, 8 May

I wish Ethel would leave me to spend my money in my own way. Trying to make me pay for supper at the church bazaar to which she dragged Margaret and me! It makes me wild – I didn't want to go. She pretends she dislikes these functions yet really adores them, as happy as anyone there, dashing around in her new blue hat saying how do you do to everyone and feeling immensely important as the wife of the Vicar's warden. God preserve me from marrying a man who will lead me into such a life. Thank goodness I have a career. It makes me keener than ever to work and work and get away from the terrible 'Christian' atmosphere. Anything less Christ-like is hard to imagine.

It always annoys me the attitude E. takes to my clothes. Am always being told to get something 'decent' and 'good', but when I take a little time and trouble thinking out a respectable sort of summer ensemble

---

22 Such questions would only be resolved (and then only partially and with much violence) with the partition and independence of India in 1947.
23 Jean had recently visited her brother stationed at Porthcurno, near Penzance in Cornwall, the hub of England's telegraph and underground cable network that would play a vital role in communications during the Second World War. Leslie Pratt was employed by the Eastern Telegraph Company (later Cable & Wireless), and Jean witnessed her brother read out a message to an occupant in Sloane Square, Chelsea. 'Heartiest congrats. Another of life's customs passed. All my love, David.' She noted other messages coming in from Alexandria, Singapore and Newfoundland.

that will be suitable she accuses me of collecting a trousseau and asks when I am 'introducing him'.

I do not dress to attract men or any man, I dress entirely to please myself. Funny though: I was looking at some rather delightful nighties the other day, but passed them by thinking that if I did get any there was no one to appreciate them.

To travel! But one needs a companion, and the best sort of companion is a man. Even to my socialistic mind I think it would be better to be married – more convenient, double rooms being usually cheaper than singles.

Sunday, 10 May
Thinking of 'Things I Shall Buy My Wife' (article by Bev Nichols) has given me to consider what I should buy my husband. But beyond a particularly interesting kind of dressing gown which we would choose together and cigarette case I should choose myself, my mind will not rise above tobacco and ties. From there it was all too easy to draw an imaginary picture of the 'man I shall marry' so that I feel rather like a schoolgirl again when I decided he must be tall and dark with wavy hair and blue eyes, and I vowed I would die a spinster rather than walk from the altar with a man shorter than myself.

But I hope he will like music and poetry and the same kind of books as I do, besides being able to drive a car, and that we shall have a sufficiently adequate income to go abroad or roam round England just as we desired. And that at least once a year we would separate for a few weeks. A house in the country because I must have a garden, also an income large enough to enable our employing an adequate number of servants, for I know only too well how soul-destroying domestic trivialities can be.

Wednesday, 3 June
A Canadian architect visiting the college spoke to us of the great possibilities that lay before us. There was a germ of greatness in the modern

movement. We are no longer hampered, as he was, by the conventional theories of the Royal Academy and RIBA – the war exploded all that.

Now I am at last clear in my own mind that I do not want the conventional finale to a young girl's career – her marriage. Let the conventionalists laugh; from now on my career becomes of first importance. I will learn all that I am possibly able. I will build a new world!

Friday, 26 June

I feel disloyal when I say things against Daddy and E. Yet I don't know of anyone among my friends and acquaintances who are on terms of complete and happy understanding with their parents. I think mine are the most tolerant and kind in their way, yet I can confide in neither. Nor have any desire to do so. It seems too much trouble even to hope to make them understand.

There is Harris (Gus). He has had so many rows with his father that he has been turned from the house and told never to come back again. He has an allowance and is now utterly happy in his newfound freedom. There is Few, whom Joan and I have envied with her independence, her lack of home ties. Then Cargill – she is older, and her parents seem more tolerant, but she is not happy and I have heard her complain of the parental attitude. And Joan – how she grumbles at her home life. And Alison: 'My mother is very sweet of course, but I like her so much better at a distance.'

We want complete independence, to be turned out of our homes as the birds turn out their young. How many years since Shakespeare wrote Crabbed Age and Youth? And still we have not learned.[24]

---

24 Crabbed Age and Youth
   Cannot live together:
   Youth is full of pleasance,
   Age is full of care;
   Youth like summer morn,
   Age like winter weather;
   Youth like summer brave,
   Age like winter bare . . .
   (Attributed to Shakespeare)

Friday, 3 July

'Next time,' said Aunt Janie to me in the interval this evening as we sat in the two seats I had taken in the upper circle at His Majesty's Theatre almost immediately behind Valerie and Jack who were celebrating V's birthday, 'Next time I come to the theatre with you I hope it will be with your fiancé.'

The last time we argued about this I upset a cup of tea all over the tablecloth in the dining room. I will not be made to believe that this is the ultimate reason for a girl's existence. I will not bind myself to any soul-destroying life when the chance to live so fully lies before me. Yet how much do I want to fall in love!

'There is nothing very remarkable about getting married or having a child,' writes Ethel Mannin. 'But when you get down to rock bottom, love is the greatest of all human happiness because it is the only source of lasting, fundamental satisfaction, and there can't be any lasting delight in beauty, work, travel or anything else unless one's life is right at the core, and it can't be right at the core unless one's love life is right.'[25]

Wednesday, 23 September

4.30 a.m., Have sat talking with brother Pooh since 1.30 a.m. The possibility of my having Phyllis Robinson as a sister in law.

Sunday, 27 September

The lights failed this evening. The glow of candlelight stirred a number of indefinable emotions within me. Is the secret of living that we should consider life as a series of episodes, and joining Walt Whitman on the Open Road, treat the body's death as an accident only, having no cognisance either at the beginning or end of our travels? So that were a World War suddenly to ravage the earth, severing me from

---

25 Mannin was a prolific novelist and memoirist. Among the first, alongside Jean's other favourite Beverley Nichols, to be published by Penguin.

the placid security of my parents' home, scattering my friends, killing those I love, depriving me of my independence and prospect of a career, turning my stable life upside down, even carrying me captive to a strange land – I might look upon it merely as one scene in a play, one stage of a journey on which I am bent solely to garner wisdom in search of beauty and truth.[26]

Phyllis Robinson teaches cookery and needlework and could make an excellent housewife. But she is perhaps too fond of her own way. It's for him to decide. I only hope his loneliness won't drive him into an alliance he'll regret.

Thursday, 29 October
I fear of inking the sheets again as I write in bed. I have got another '1st Mention', the highest mark, for my Studio work. Although no mark I am afraid will ever again fill me with such amazement and rapture as the '1st Mention' I received for my Classical Composition at the end of last term. After three consecutive Cs I began to think I could not improve. I have now every encouragement to work hard at this career I have so strangely chosen, and I must forget that I would rather be able to write a good book.

Friday, 20 November
'I live as speedily as I can,' said Olive Briggs in the cloakroom the other day. 'I was having a conversation with my mother this morning when she asked me whether I had ever considered the value of my life. Had I ever asked myself should I mind if I died tomorrow? I asked myself that long ago, and I'm quite sure I shouldn't.'

I too wouldn't mind were I to die tomorrow, except that I might hurt the two people I care for more than anyone else in the world. If I could build one monument to the beauty of mankind, if I could write one book of real worth, I should feel I had not lived in vain.

---

26 Jean was reading Walt Whitman's *Leaves of Grass*.

[Note added later and pinned to her journal:] Olive Briggs became a fully qualified and competent architect and later married the son of a wealthy collar manufacturer. They were both found dead in his car on a lovely part of the Yorkshire Moors – voluntary suicide, from the car's exhaust. It was widely publicised in the press, with the note they left. He could not face the future, the world seemed to him on the brink of chaos and nothing could save it. She took her life willingly with his. 'Loyalty,' she wrote, 'I believe to be one of the virtues.'

Sunday, 13 December

'What I believe,' writes Bertrand Russell, 'is that when I die I shall rot, and nothing of my ego will survive.' And this conviction is based on an expert knowledge of physical science.

Sometimes the idea of immortality has appalled me – that there shall never be an end and we must go on living through untold and inconceivable eras. But behind it all there must be some purpose. Why must we suffer so here on earth? Why should one be physically attracted to some people more than others? What is it that makes me believe I shall one day meet someone who will mean more to me than the satisfaction of sexual desires? Why torment us with a little knowledge and then stamp us out? Why are we here?

Until someone can answer these questions for me I will not surrender my belief in God or in life after death. There are so many questions that will go unanswered, but I cannot believe we shall never know the truth.

Boxing Day, 1931

We dined yesterday at 'Milton', the home of Ethel's two unmarried sisters. They belong to a class dying out with their generation, the middle-class gentlepeople who lived in the quiet villages around London before the increase in road traffic developed them into the present revolting suburbs.

The girls were brought up with the main idea of finding a husband as soon as possible, and during the interim amused themselves at home with all the other young people of their own social standing in the village. They lived in big, comfortable houses run efficiently by a thoroughly domesticated mother and two or three servants. Entertaining was their chief interest: tennis and river picnics in the summer; musical at-homes and dances in the winter. They did a little sewing and possibly helped with the cooking and arranged the flowers, and could devote themselves to parish church work if they wished. No one found it necessary to question the religion offered them. They accepted what had satisfied their parents without demur, and were not troubled by their personalities or concerned with psychology. No passionate discontent urged them to leave home in search of adventure.

The main road where the trams now go clanking by was a long and lovely lane flanked by tall poplar trees, and I can remember the land ablaze with buttercups on blue May mornings, and two magnificent oak trees whose shade was favoured by lovers at dusk. All have gone. The buttercups were raked up long ago and the ground divided into neat little plots. One is called 'Dreamcot', and in another there is a collection of children who scream all day long and keep their dog chained up so that he is continually lifting his voice in complaint.

But the remnants of the old, gracious families still gather together at Xmas time, pathetic fragments of a society scattered and storm-tossed by the war, and shaken and bewildered by its aftermath. I must go my way. I can never go theirs.

'We are never satisfied with what we have.' Jean in her Chelsea Arts frock, 1932.

6.

The Popular Idea of Love

Monday, 4 January 1932 (aged twenty-two)

'The charm of modern London is that it is not built to last,' says Virginia Woolf in her article on Oxford Street.[27] 'It is built to pass. Its glassiness, its transparency, its surging waves of coloured plaster give a different pleasure and achieve a different end from that which was desired by the old builders and their patrons, the nobility of England. Their pride required the illusion of permanence . . . Today we knock down and rebuild . . . it is an impulse that makes for creation and fertility. Discovery is stimulated and invention on the alert.'

But to me it is all horrible. This cheapness, this tawdry turmoil and haste and sham values – I can only see it as the manifestation of the ghastly little minds of the people who tolerate these conditions. And ugliness of mind is inevitably inherited by the next generation as a physical deformity that they will not thank us for. It will be more difficult for them to knock down the heritage of deceit and insensitiveness than the walls and facades that seem 'made of yellow cardboard and sugar icing'.

Nowhere in the suburbs, nor growing provinces, nor welter of humanity and toil in the thoroughfares of this degenerate London may be found peace or pause. If there is by some mischance a cessation of noise in some backstreet, the silence is empty and vacant.

---

27 Published as 'Oxford Street Tide' in *Good Housekeeping*, 1931.

But how well she has described it, the Babel and glitter of Oxford Street, and with what courage does she try to discover a value for its existence. 'The mere thought of age, of solidity, of lasting for ever is abhorrent to Oxford Street.' It most certainly is: who would want Oxford Street embalmed as a memorial to our present age? God forbid. So let us sweep it away before the harm of its ugliness reaches far into the lives of those who succeed us.

Saturday, 16 January

My discontent can be used as the ruling power of my life. After school it drove me from home into the office, from the office to college, and from suburban life to one of independence in town.[28] I feel suddenly secure, knowing that so long as I am never content with any one state and achievement I shall go on to discover new people and make new things. I shall never grow smug and suburbanised and narrow-minded so long as I can overcome a natural apathy and lazy desire to dream. So long as the little material things of life don't crush me down or hem me in so that I lose all vitality.

I find myself carrying a banner with a strange device: across it in letters of gold and flame is flung the word 'Excelsior'.[29] I discovered it in the train this morning as I was coming home from a night's dissipation in town and I had stayed with D.V. Cargill. We had been with Peter and his brother to *Bow Bells*, and supper at the Troc. I wondered why such a delightful evening lacked something I couldn't define. It was an excellent show, and my companions are charming and amusing. What is this nagging desire that will not be quieted?

Wednesday, 10 February

'Immortality is hard to achieve,' says D.H. Lawrence. I believe it, but

---

28 Jean was now living alone in a rented flat in Charlotte Street, on the edge of Fitzroy Square, surrounded by what she called her 'madly bohemian friends' from college.

29 Elsewhere she translates it from the Latin: 'I must go higher yet.'

I want immortality. If I find I cannot create great architecture I shall give it up.

God, why did I get a 'C' for my Farmhouse? I said I would get a '1st Mention' for it. I know I didn't finish it, but that alone couldn't have given me so low a mark. I am still stamped with the stamp of suburbia. I cannot somehow get any stability into my work. Or am I right that everything I have done that has been well marked was more of other people's brains than my own? Admittedly I had little to do with the Town House elevation, but the dovecote was quite a lot of my own . . .

But this is sick-making – only when I have strong influences to guide me do I turn out good work. If I am to face this truth, then dare I go back to the office at the end of this course? I shall be dragged under, mutilated.

'I wish I had your profile,' Joan said to me one day, but I wish I had her colouring. We are never satisfied with what we have. How can I tell her how lovely she is when flushed with excitement when watching Crockett come in at the studio door – her hair is a light, ripe gold, and her eyes are wide and blue and very bright, and she sits tensely upright on her stool, swinging her legs or waving her T-square in the air, and there is a vividness about her I envy. She may be childish now, but she will grow out of it and grow into a far more interesting person than I shall ever be.

She will outgrow her passion for Crockett. She has tried to persuade me to go with her to Cannon Street where she thinks he lives. 'But what *good* will it do you?' I argued. 'Oh, but it's *interesting*,' she said. 'One can imagine him so much better at home if one knows his surroundings, but you don't understand.' She added patronisingly, 'One day you will . . .'

Johnny Hodgson despises me and I hate him for it. He described me more aptly than anyone else could have done. When he said, 'Miss Pratt would never do anything unusual unless someone else was doing it too,' I hated him for it but I knew he was right.

Saturday, 5 March

Peter (Gus) – I cannot bring myself to admit I am in love with him, for I don't know how much is sheer animal sex and how much true affection.[30] That at times I am terribly fond of the little blighter I mustn't deny. I have messed around with him so much and taken him so much for granted that it is a little alarming to believe that I am growing to care.

He is weak and selfish and terribly affected, and at times irritates me beyond endurance, but I am thinking far too much about him to ignore facts. He is clever definitely, and interests me: who couldn't be thrilled with the designer of my Chelsea Arts Frock? It is a dream, a miracle, something that completely transfigures me and which is of course so eminently pleasing to one's vanity. But then he is so ridiculously young for his age, and I am afraid of what he may become now that he is going on the stage – he is so easily influenced.

At times I am consumed with a terrible lust for power. Power over men, power to make that light come into their eyes like I have sometimes seen with Peter's when they look at me. That is the beast in me. I doubt whether anyone suspects it. 'The Wee Bear' says Peter. 'Something soft and fluffy.' Me. Me! Soft and inoffensive and wholly ineffectual – Christ! Is it any wonder I lust for power?

Monday, 14 March

Amazing what a difference my meeting Roy has made to my feelings for Peter. I had a wonderful weekend at the Gornolds', but it was chiefly on account of Roy.[31] He is quite the sweetest thing I have met for a long time, and I am desperately anxious our acquaintance won't end there. At first I wondered if he was just a spoilt and pampered

---

30 Jean's college friends are seldom short of nicknames, but Peter/Gus outdoes them all. Neither Peter nor Gus are his real name: he is known to his parents as Geoffrey Harris. In later years, as a writer, he adopts the *nom de plume* Heron Carvic. His sexuality also seems to be in raging flux.
31 The Gornolds were family friends in Brighton.

boy amusing himself with a studio and a few paints. He is intensely selfish and lazy, but evidently frightfully delicate, and has consequently been waited on and surrounded by female adoration since birth.

I wondered at first whether his interest in art was not just a pose. We had a tremendous argument about Epstein on Saturday evening, and he was horrified when I spoke in favour of Epstein's work. 'But it is the produce of a distorted mind!' he said.

It was on Sunday morning that he impressed me most. We walked along the front before lunch discussing the future of Britain. 'Britain is the coming race,' he said. 'There never has been such a nation, and I still think the Britisher is superior to all foreigners.' I had mentioned Russia and my interest in its future. 'Rot!' Roy had said. 'Utter bunk! For one thing the people are physically so degenerate it will take about 900 years for them to produce a clean, perfect strain, even after a few generations of what appears to be more or less normal healthy stock. You will get throwbacks and lunatics being born. It takes years to get rid of all that in a country. Besides, with the equalising of women, Russia will cut its own throat. As soon as the women of a nation become equal with men that nation falls – it happened in Rome, in Persia, in Egypt.'

I asked how. 'Why, men lost their respect for women and women became cheap. The Britisher has always idealised women, but if she once cheapens herself Britain will be in danger.[32] It's a woman's job to look attractive and appear to do nothing. There comes a time when man needs and relies on women's intuition. He doesn't really care to live with an intellectual woman: he would rather be persuaded to a point of view with subtle flattery than argued into it, however clever and convincing the argument.'

It was all decidedly stimulating and exciting. I want to know more of him, to continue our discussions. Possibly he finds me a little boring, for I gave him little in return except a certain amount of

---

32 Voting had been extended to women in the UK in 1928.

spirited opposition. But I cannot forget those ghastly moments when he was seeing me off on the 10.15 to Victoria last night. In his eyes was the expression of the man who is deliberately avoiding the words the woman wants him to say. 'When dealing with women you are dealing with danger,' he had admitted in the morning, so perhaps he would not mention anything about a further meeting lest I construed too much from the situation. But heaven forbid I should ever marry him! He would wear me out in a week.

Friday, 1 April
Letter to Joan in a vain endeavour to disencumber her of this Crockett business:
'I am beginning to give up the popular idea of love. It is so grossly exaggerated in our cinema and cheap novels and magazines. I am putting it aside as a myth, a fantasy, a poet's dream.

'To me, friendship seems the most important thing in life: to know well as many interesting people as possible. And if it remains purely intellectual it doesn't matter whether one's friend is a man or woman. I cannot see that "love" is anything apart from a combination of these two elements – sex and friendship. It's this damn silly sex business that makes friendships difficult and induces one to expect too much of marriage. One is either first physically attracted and then attain[s] mental agreement or vice-versa, and "love" is built out of these two together. Its perfection lies in the balance obtained between them. Tragedies occur when there are wrong proportions on either side, such as one's attraction being purely physical and the other purely intellectual. Love must be built on a very deep and wise understanding of the other person's heart and mind – only then may one indulge and enjoy sensual pleasure. Love is a thing to be learned, a very long and arduous process of continual building.'

Friday, 8 April
Strange to hear the history of one's family. Of my mother, dominated

and oppressed by the fear her own puritanical and severely minded mother inspired all through the years of her childhood until she was 20. Her own father could not pick her up and caress her in the presence of his wife. And the wild, troubled spirit of Uncle Fred, mother's youngest and favourite brother, the one adventurer in that terribly sober and phlegmatic family. And the kindly old man who was my grandfather, and the good position his father held as Lighterman of the City of London on the Thames.[33] And the change in the family's fortunes with the invention of steel and steam.

After that comes an emptiness and sense of futility. Grandfather sleeping with his housekeeper. Uncle Fred leaving his selfish wife in England, sailing to New York, making love to a woman, building up a splendid business, instigating the jealousy of his colleagues, going for a voyage on a private yacht and being buried at sea.[34] And I am left wandering – is it all a pageant to please immortal eyes?

Sunday, 10 April

I am being cowardly again: postponing the hour of study will not help me in June. But I could scream at the *flaccidness* of this household. Why can they not take an intelligent interest in any of the arts? What does Daddy know about modern architecture? Precious little of any real value. Blount does all the designing in the office – that is probably why it is so rotten.

What I need at home is either intelligent opposition in my pursuance of the arts, or definite encouragement. I meet with neither, and flounder hopelessly when I come into contact with it outside. I wish with all my heart Mother were still alive. She played

---

33 A skilled operator of a trading barge.
34 Her maternal uncle Fred Lucey was treasurer of Philip Morris & Co Ltd in New York. In 1916, *Tobacco World* magazine wrote: 'F.S. Lucey, of Philip Morris & Company, is one of the keenest students in the trade of conditions which affect their business, and has always on tap a few most original deductions which epitomise the true state of affairs.'

Chopin exquisitely and was the artist here, not Daddy. Ethel is just a very conventional materialist. I am grateful for all she does, and if she had been at all intellectual she might not have been content to stay here and look after the house. Damn money. I want pots of it – enough anyway to provide me with an adequate number of servants, trained people who will look to the care of my wardrobe and meals and all these petty irksome little details that take up so much of one's time. And here am I, wasting what little I have to spare when I should be starting a thesis on the architecture of the French Renaissance.

I had left Peter on Thursday evening in rather magnificent form. 'You will become hard and efficient and live in the suburbs,' he said. 'I couldn't bear it! Why don't you take up dress design? You respond so quickly to clothes in the right colours . . .' And then the other night I took off my glasses and combed back my hair, and surprised him more than he had ever been in his life. 'But you are almost beautiful!' he said. 'We could make something really astounding of you – will you let me try please?'

I know he is not flattering me in the least – he is no more in love with me at the moment than he is with anyone else. For his art is the art of creating beautiful women, and I know he has extreme genius in this direction. Together we might be able to establish an amazingly good business. If he provided the ideas and I could see to their execution, I would make a damn good manageress. We would dress all the elite of the world! I see myself superbly accoutred in black velvet, moving suavely up and down softly carpeted luxuriously lit rooms, advising gracious and lovely women to wear what had been specially designed to enhance their personality. We would have a special beauty parlour and medical adviser, hairdresser, manicurist and chiropodist. Even perhaps a psychologist also, for what is the point of clothing the body if the mind is not also well appointed?

I don't want to become one of those whom Ruskin describes as having 'fat hearts, heavy eyes and closed ears'. The only way to do this is to live beautifully, fully, by striving to attain an ideal that is perhaps beyond my reach, to reach for the stars.

This was Jean's last entry in an exercise book until October 1933. She continued to write for the next 18 months, but in a more random way; she wrote on scraps of loose-leaf paper, and her handwriting appeared more rushed. The file in which she kept these notes also contained several letters, although many of these were drafts and incomplete.

7.

All His Honeyed Deceit

Thursday, 23 June 1932

Nearly two months have slipped by and the exams are over. The passion that rules my life at the moment is to get to know David A., that tall, nervous intense young man with the slender hands and white sensitive face. Last year he wore spats until Joan teased him out of it. Spats! I want to understand that mixture of wistfulness and superficial conceit and I want to win his confidence. It is going to be difficult, for if I force myself on him in the least he will leap back into that shell out of which he is beginning to creep. I think I am suffering a little from the hell others have suffered – being interested in someone who cannot give you back all your passion and desires. I want him to care – terribly. No one has ever fallen in love with me to any intense and palpitating degree. Mon ami, what a lot I could give you if you would only let me.[35]

Friday, 24 June

Perhaps I shall be able to indulge in some passionate affair while touring Russia during the summer vacc.

---

35 This is David Aberdeen (1913–1987), who went on to become a successful architect. He is best remembered for the Swiss Centre in Leicester Square and Congress House in Bloomsbury, reportedly inspired by Corbusier. The courtyard of Congress House contains a wall relief by Jacob Epstein.

Tuesday, 5 July

What a fool I was to give David A. *The Conquest of Happiness* (Bertrand Russell). I underestimated his intelligence. It was written for the average man who cannot think very acutely for himself, and he is anything but average. I'm definitely losing ground there. He thinks I'm a half-wit.

Monday, 11 July

Ten days before the end of term and up heaves my tutor. 'Now, Miss P., I am in a position to discuss your case. We have got all the results through. You have failed in Construction, Hygiene and Engineering, and I am afraid it will mean you will have to do the 2nd Year again.'

It was so ridiculous. Everyone was very kind and sympathetic, particularly David A., at which I felt gratified. 'I mean, isn't it silly,' said David, 'just for the sake of 6 hours to be put back a whole year . . .' Perhaps after all it would be better to chuck Architecture completely and go in wholeheartedly for Interior Decoration. Gus of course was delighted when I told him this.

So I went and explained it all to Pop, who was kind as he always is but I know terribly disappointed to discover his precious little daughter was not the brilliant young undergrad he had given everyone to imagine. But it is a miracle to me how I got through my History exams, having produced a beautiful plan-section of Rheims Cathedral and firmly called it Notre Dame.

However Pop was not satisfied and came up to see my tutor. The next morning my tutor strongly advised me to continue with the course and could he give me his special course of coaching in Engineering? 'I suppose at the time something was distracting your attention,' he went on. 'I don't know what it was of course, but I might make one or two guesses. I'm no psychologist – the men students are bad enough, but the women completely baffle me. It might have been books or an interest in higher art, or theatre or men. You know it's a very terrible thing when the students fall in love with one another. We can't do anything about it, but it's most distracting, most distracting . . .'

I could have smacked his face. I have chosen to do Decoration.

Mid-July
[Draft of letter]
Pooh darling,

Ethel has been frightening me into fits by the wildest suggestions for the reason of your rather strange silence. She firmly believes something has gone wrong and conjures up pictures of you sitting haggard-eyed before the good old gin bottle contemplating suicide because the girl has let you down. I don't believe it.

No Pooh, if things have gone wrong for you I know that however difficult a time you are having now you will pull through. Naturally I think Pop is a bit anxious, but nevertheless he has faith in you also: your life has not been saved for you to tear to pieces within two years of its salvation.

Although we have not written we are thinking about you. We keep hoping for a letter from you first. In all your troubles Piglet prays for you.

Thursday, 28 July
I lay awake the other night in a sudden state of panic wondering why I had even contemplated joining the Student Tour to Russia on my own. I was visualising those five days at sea travelling tourist class on a Soviet ship with people I have never met nor know in the least. Accommodation may be cramped and uncomfortable, the North Sea may be very rough and I shall be ill. Conditions I am told in Russia are appalling.

We shall travel everywhere 'hard' class and sleep two or three to a room at the hotels of the cities we visit. Why was I then so rash to pay down my £25 I can so ill afford for three weeks that may be torture?

'You are brave!' people have said in awed tones. And, 'Russia? Are you sure it's quite safe?' 'Of course you will only be shown what they choose to show you.' 'I think you're making a great mistake. Some women I know who were on a party that went to Moscow broke down at the sight of the squalor in which they were expected to exist while there.'

But Soviet Russia is a force that may not be ignored.

Mid-August

[Fragments of a copy of a letter to 'Chris'[36]]

We accomplished the journey from Kiev without mishap and were only one-and-a-half hours late. Something contrived to bite me 13 times on the left arm and I am very glad to be at sea again. The ship is at least comparatively clean, and so far the Baltic is behaving itself admirably. I sought in vain among the letters at Leningrad and was more depressed (than ever) with that decayed city when I failed to find one from you. But perhaps it will be waiting for me at home.

I've missed you terribly. Were you beginning to be a bit disappointed with me, to think I was a flirt and merely after all the admiration and attention I could get? I'm sorry if I seemed cheap, but please, please believe me when I tell you I am *not* in the habit of allowing my male acquaintances to make love to me as you did. And you do do that divinely![37] Whether from experience or instinct I wouldn't like to say, but I don't think it matters much. The fact remains. Dear Passing Ship, please linger a little longer within my sight that I may grow to know and understand you better. You were marvellously kind to me, and that I shall never forget.

---

36 Jean met Chris Naude not long before her trip to Russia, but there are no details of the event. We learn elsewhere that his parents are probably friends of her family, and that he has a diplomatic role at the South African High Commission in Trafalgar Square. Jean visited the building in 1932, a few months before it opened, and she had previously attended a lecture by its architect, Sir Herbert Baker.

37 Up to a point: it becomes clear later that she did not lose her virginity on the trip.

And now I will try to pull my scattered thoughts together and endeavour to tell you something about Russia. We were not there long enough to receive more than the briefest of impressions. Everyone told me before I went, we 'were shown only what they wanted to show us,' which nearly drives me epileptic with rage, as if they covered up their decaying buildings with dust sheets, screened off the food queues and chained off all undesirable parts of the city and prepared special places for tourists. Heavens, as if every city in the world has not backstreets and ugly buildings and bad factories they don't wish foreigners to see.

But certainly to anyone used to the average luxuries of modern Western Europe, living in Russia is not exactly exciting at the moment. Many of the people are physically splendid to look upon, the younger generation particularly, but they are all clothed in garments that are shoddy and badly made. That no amount of propaganda even attempts to deny it is a sign of the poverty of the race. Imagine if you can, London completely overrun with the working classes, the shops and clubs and restaurants of Piccadilly and St James's and Knightsbridge closed or converted into factories or worker's guilds, no subtlety or graciousness or dignity left anywhere, a bland, naive young people, enormously enthusiastic, mind you. And they know where they're going and what they're trying to do, whereas we muddle along.[38] Their government is centralised, and so long as every member of the ruling party remains uncorrupt and lives up to their ideals I think they have every chance of success.

I think I see wisdom in their suppression of individualism. It tends to do away with all selfishness, individual gain, ambition and greed. I envy them their singleness of purpose, each one of them as part of their new state has a reason for living. Russia is undoubtedly one country with a future in a world where all other systems of civilisa-

---

38 Later in her journal she regrets that a strictly observed career path may leave no room for dreaming or a more imaginative temperament.

tion and administration are rocky and cracking and decaying. I am not convinced that for us there are no means of discovering new ideals and new methods without going through the same ghastliness of war and revolution and suffering that Russia suffered. Revolution perhaps, but God let us hope it will be bloodless. The test of their experiment is not now, but in 10 or 20 years' time.

I will phone you on September 1st.

Monday, 12 September
There is a strange streak of hardness in me somewhere – cruelty, and a desire to mar the perfection of things, such as trampling in new-fallen snow.

Now supposing Chris were suddenly to go away without saying goodbye or seeing me again: what should I feel? My vanity would be hurt. I am terrifically proud of possessing so popular a male as a friend. He is a divine lover. But I am yet to know him as a companion. We have extraordinarily little in common. I never know what to talk to him about when we are alone, so he fills in the silences by making love to me.[39]

I feel I am making myself cheap, I feel as though we have both somehow reached a dead end. I should be terribly hurt if he were thinking the same thing. I should like to make more of it than this, invest it with some *permanence*. Kisses alone are not enough to cement a friendship.

Friday, 14 October
> When Mausie goes down to the Strand for tea
> She's no thought for David and none for me
> She's lost in joyous, abstracted bliss
> With her charming and lovable diplomat Chris[40]

---

39 A while later, Jean added: 'These were petting parties. I was never his mistress.'
40 As hand-written on Jean's lecture notepaper by Joan Hey, UCL. Several of Jean's college friends call her Mausie in this period, although the origin is unclear.

Strange how life goes on. I decided I must do the Decoration Course and refused to consider the idea of 2nd Year Architecture again. But here I am, doing it and rather enjoying myself. I think I am happier than I have ever been. My days are filled with many people and interesting work, I am independent of home influences, my room is delightful.

Friday, 25 November
As I walked down Tottenham Court Road tonight I again realised what a marvellous time I had had at college, how dear and familiar London had grown, and what memories each part brought back. Teas at the Criterion, Swan & Edgar, the Arts Club where I lunched with Gus and his mother for the first time, the delicious sensation of being well-groomed just after a visit to that hairdressers in Dover Street, Harrods where I once lunched alone off Welsh rarebit, all the theatres in Shaftesbury Ave, the nights we have queued for pit or gallery, the strange snack bar somewhere off it where Gus and I once had the most marvellous waffles, the Coventry Street Corner House at 3 o'clock in the morning, teas at Boots, Regent St by bus and on foot and in a Daimler, the gramophone shops where Gus and I have listened to many records, Charing X Rd, its books and News Theatre and Doctor's Pills.

Mid-December
[Fragment of a copy of a letter to Chris]
At last this term is over. Quite triumphantly too, for I've got a 1st Mention for my Classical Ballroom. It's been such a long time since I managed to get one of these. It's not the mark I care about, it's the knowledge of my power to turn out good work.

But you know if you never lift your nose from the drawing board what marvellous things one would miss. I want so to *live*!

. . . God bless you and may another letter arrive from you soon! (So far I've had one from Toronto which I answered).

Jean.

Monday, 2 January 1933

I have been trying to restrain myself from writing about this thing, but . . . how immeasurably it helps. It seems to release this terrible unending torment, and I find for a little while a great relief and a little rest.

That Chris should have *lied* to me I think hurts most. And yet for all my tears and pain I cannot believe it of him even yet. There seem to be two parts of me: one sits serenely and patiently on high, still full of faith and hope, while the other rages at its feet despairingly. There was something in him that was good and beautiful and strong that appealed to all that was good and beautiful and strong in me. Something lovely began to blossom between us, and in our selfishness we would not heed it but trampled it to death at our feet. Oh that I understood – that he would write to explain. I know I must wait a long time yet before that letter comes, as I think it will do, and in the meantime endure this sickness and heaviness of heart. But I shall not be cowed by this event.

All his honeyed deceit – I still believe he would not have hurt me so deliberately had he realised how much I really cared. He would never believe me when I said I loved him. And all he wanted was to make love to me. 'It would be so *marvellous*,' he whispered. 'But you won't let me . . .' I wish I had given in to him, accepted the affair as he wanted me to, as the passion of a moment, and then let me be. If only we could have understood one another I could have kept the incident as a sacred and lovely memory. What is my virginity to me? I don't want to keep it. It would have been so sweet to satisfy that desire. And yet of course for a woman it is different – just because he kissed me a little. Those natural desires for a home and children were roused in me until they possessed all my waking moments and he was woven into the centre of my dreams.

Thank God I have written this. It is the first time since that dreadful letter came for Mr and Mrs Pratt announcing Chris's marriage to some poor lucky fool of a woman that I have been able to get at the core of the matter and see things as they are. I have been waiting to hurl the bitterest of accusations at him. I understood why women are driven to the streets or suicide or murder, yet I knew were he to come back to me with or without any explanation I should love him still.

When he told me marriage could never come into his life he meant perhaps marriage with me, but was afraid to say so because he knew it would bewilder me. So he lied. I want to get all those letters he wrote and trace this idea through them. Oh it is a tangled and twisted misery that must be endured – he can never be mine. I know he is capable of ineffable depths of tenderness and affection for the woman he chose to marry. I am so jealous of him and Josephine, but I hope they'll be happy.

It is no good, the pain goes in. I love him, love him, love him and he doesn't want me. Enough of this self-torture. Life must go on.

[Undated letter – possibly never sent]
My dear dear Chris,

What agony I'm going through this weekend! Do you know what happened? I'm at home you see for this last fortnight of the vacc, and though I left my address at Belsize Park for them to forward all letters to me, they didn't, damn them! So you see we suddenly got the announcement of your marriage addressed to Daddy and E. without a word of explanation to me.

God it was *Hell* Chris! It was so unlike you, to betray our friendship like that. But oh how typical of you, you dear thing. Was there anything you ever did that wasn't a frightful rush? Of course you may count on me to help you . . . to the end of the world Chris. I will not fail you.

Wednesday, 4 January

I am climbing out of the dark well of my despair. Chris did write to me, even as the honourable man I believed him to be. Brief, sincere, concealing. I think I admire him more for the complete lack of an attempt at an explanation than I could have done for any number of bitter excuses. I must accept the truth of all he told me, and if it is so then his difficulty must be even greater than mine.

It must have been true when he told me marriage couldn't come into his life, and that if he married anyone not a S. African his father had told him he need not go home again. It must have been a very desperate situation that forced him into this marriage. And I know from his letter he needs help, and time will prove whether mine will be of any value to him or not. I will give of what I have to give abundantly, whether it be kindliness, farewell, or a deep and intimate relationship. And of these three the last would be easiest for me, for I know that to be once more crushed in the strong comfort of his arms would bring to me a relief so overwhelming that I daren't contemplate it.

Thursday, 12 January

Gus said: 'Before you went away you were beginning to stand on your own feet, beginning to express your ideas, and they were no longer suburban. Then you fell in love and you went back, threw your whole weight on the man. You were *dangling*. I saw that sooner or later you must drop, and only hoped we should all be there to catch you when you fell.'

I was so impregnated with his point of view at the time he said this that I wasn't able to contradict him. I see now he is wrong. I never dangled. Not once. But he was a little blinded I think. For a little while I withdrew myself from him and he was jealous. Perhaps it went to my head a little: oh the thrill for a woman when she realises the strange power she can have over a man!

'You will never be happy,' said Gus. 'You want too much and your sympathy is too deep.' Probably. But what do I want? What does Gus want? What is it we search for and call vaguely an ideal? I owe Gus a tremendous lot, and I think he is right when he says, 'I feel I have taken you as far as I can, taught you as much as I know. Now it is either someone else's turn or you are to go on your own.'

He hopes he may train me into that ideal companion for which he knows he is seeking in vain, and I am resisting it with all my strength. It is impossible because of his tragic difference. He is sexless.[41] And I, if I am to live, must have sexual satisfaction. 'Leave sex alone,' says D.H. Lawrence. 'Sex is a state of grace and you'll have to wait.' I shall surely have to experience this sex fully. I can wait.

It may be I am to write as a woman for women. Perhaps in my writing I shall find the consolation I need. If I must face the truth that no one person will ever be able completely to fill my desires, then let me be brave about it. I have no passion to paint or dance or sing – only to write.

Wednesday, 25 January

From *Since Then* by P. Gibbs:[42]

'Problem of the young woman who wants to fulfil the natural destiny of womanhood but cannot find her mate. It is the outstanding problem of England today . . . These legions of girls are wistful for male companionship. They want to meet nice boys who will give them the chance of marriage. They crave to be loved . . . all the books they read intensify their yearnings to experience the biological purpose of their being, without which they have been robbed of the greatest adventure in life with essential meaning. One thing is certain. These women are not going back again behind the window blinds.'

Tuesday, 11 April 1933

An idea for a novel is germinating. Mainly about me (M.), but the chief characters are all to be based on real people. Briefly the theme is to be this. M. is at college, just realising that what she really thinks she wants is to get married and run a home, instead of a career as

---

41 Jean added later: 'No. Homosexual.'
42 An analysis of the post-war world. As well as providing a social survey of women's role in society, Philip Gibbs's study examined the rise of fascism in Germany and Italy, the civil war in Russia and the role of the League of Nations.

an architect. One love affair having just ended rather badly, leaving her feeling bleak and lonely. Her best companion of some years' standing is G.; he is younger, consumptive and training to dance.

Then she meets the new curate of her home suburb. He is 30-ish, falls in love with her and finally asks her to marry him. She finds she doesn't know how to answer him. Her complexity is acute. She is not romantically in love with the clergyman, although she likes him well enough and finds him marvellously sympathetic.

It is this character about which I am most hazy at the moment. I want to meet Mr Wildman, the locum here while the Vicar is away. Ever since I heard of his coming the thought has been developing. 'Seems a manly man,' Ethel wrote. 'Doesn't mind going to a pub for a drink and won't wear clerical garb but goes about in flannels etc.' Which I thought sounded dangerous, such an easy way of attracting people in these days of general scepticism. A cheap bid for popularity. Yes, I do want to meet him, just to see if he is like that, and if he could be built into this book.

I am prepared to let the affair go as far as an engagement, and then in a sudden panic she breaks it off – crashing through all her theories and deciding to go her way alone.

All the time, of course, G. has a tremendous influence over her. He is in love with her and she not a little with him, but this they don't dare to admit to each other for marriage is quite impossible, even if his health permitted.

Friday, 14 April
In collecting material for the 3rd character of my novel I feel I am in danger of letting myself in for something I shall regret. Supposing what I am now imagining were really to happen! It seems now that I hear of nothing else but the marvels and strangeness of Mr Wildman. Here is an account of his interview with the *Wembley News*:

"'Many of the Church's practices and customs are inconsistent," he said. "There is a vast amount of hypocrisy in our modern church life . . . People are too easily shocked by frank references to the facts of life. Sunday cinemas? I am strongly in favour of them, provided that people who take this recreation go to Church first." Mr W. has led an adventurous life. He has served on a windjammer and travelled all over the world. He has been a journalist and worked in a bank.'

I don't like the photograph of him in the paper, but when studied carefully he has interesting eyes. Nonetheless I am deeply sceptical. I know exactly what I would like to say to him if I ever get the proper opportunity.

Easter Sunday, 16 April
Have just been to the 7 a.m. service. I have been trying to find out why I bother to go at all. I think it is mainly to appease my conscience and appease Daddy. I went too to see Wildman, but he was not taking the service. He handed round the wine and stood by the porch door afterwards: a pleasant voice and a pleasant face with very alert dark eyes. He is going bald on top of his head, but on the whole the impression was favourable, except for the callow youth who stood by his side. Ethel spoke of this youth: she has seen him about with him. Perhaps I'm being unfair. My putrid mind would leap at once to homosexuality.

Later: I am working myself into a positive fever over this man. It is quite absurd. I can't forget his eyes. I know I'm riding for a fall, but I want desperately to meet him. To talk to him and get it over. The difficulty is that it may be weeks or months before it occurs. I would like to get my teeth stuck into his theories and worry them out with him, but I will not go to church to hear him, I will not be numbered with the unmarried spinsters who swell the congregation on his account. Until I have grasped the reality, until I have felt it, knocked against and bruised myself perhaps, I cannot continue the romance in my mind.

Sunday, 14 May
Well we have met Mr Wildman. He came over the other evening and stayed till 1 a.m. drinking Daddy's port and telling the most entertaining

stories. He horrified the parents and amused me vastly. I have no fear of complications ever arising between myself and him.

He is typical of the age: coarse, sincere and dramatic, very sincerely dramatic, plays to the public from the pulpit and is not ashamed to admit it. Nor to take out his front tooth to show how it is attached to the plate, not to tell us of the woman who invited him to sleep with her because of divine inspiration she had received from God.

Cheap – yes he is cheap, and appeals thereby to the poorer classes. He much prefers to turn the mangle while Mrs Jones gets on with the dinner than be entertained in the front parlour. All good in itself, certainly. He talked an awful lot of scandal in a deliciously unmalicious way.

I am going to Jamaica. I shall see Pooh again.[43]

Undated, probably early June
Damn, Hell and Blast. Ethel cannot see that my hair looks any better after it has been done by Mr Ed of Dover Street than when I do it myself! She is so blind stiff she cannot see that the paint is cracking off her own wooden nose. God what a mood I'm in tonight.

Monday, 5 June
I have never known Ethel to look so charming as she did this afternoon serving tea to us in the drawing room, wrapped in a thin, pale blue dressing gown; it gave her a strange air of gracious freedom. I think I am often unfair to her. I know she resents the fact that I don't confide in her as much as I might do.

This morning I was again accused of being inconsiderate; it is always the one weapon she can most easily handle against me. And all the evidence is in her favour. I am selfish and inconsiderate and often strangely rude and unkind to her. Don't I often come down to

---

43 Her brother's work with Cable & Wireless took him to a new country. A local woman named Ivy soon became his wife.

breakfast very late so that she is put to the most immense inconvenience of getting me a fresh one? Don't I often come in very late at
night and disturb her in her first sleep? She always does her best, and
is working now without a maid for the sake of the family's overdraft.
And what do I ever do to show my appreciation? How many times
have I compared her to a little wooden doll whose limbs will only
move in certain set directions? I love my father – there is sun in him.
And I had a great and dreadful thought the other night that she is
one of those people who are sunless.

Thursday, 6 July

The more one dreams of a thing, the more it recedes from one in
reality. I could have given him so much. Marriage with Gus would
be hell I know, but it would have rich compensations. But he doesn't
know I have been in love with him for the past 18 months. Perhaps
he never will know. Why should he?

I think the idea of marriage with any of his most intimate friends
terrifies him. He is sexually so very fastidious. How may I teach him
that the thing that matters is that hard rich jewel of trust, and that is
what we could have. It is as if I have seen a lame man trying to hobble
along without a stick and wanting to lend him my arm, but he would
rather endure his difficulty alone rather than the humiliation of
support.

I am free anyway to consider further advances, and if none come
then at least I shall have had Chris and Gus and Roy and David, each
for a few brief moments. I have considered marrying them all but
have failed to run my dreams into reality. It is the bourgeois taint –
that sickly desire, fostered by cheap novels and films, to hear a man
say, 'I have been waiting for you all my life . . . we were made for
each other . . . it is fate.' Miracles I suppose do happen – but they are
rare, and there is no reason to believe they might happen to me.

I am afraid of loneliness as everyone else. 'Somewhere, somewhere
afar, a white tremendous daybreak' – what is it Rupert Brook says?

That is what we aim at. I will **not** give Gus up. I know he is not the type to grow old. He couldn't live quietly in a cottage. He belongs to the night and the footlights and all the glamour of the city and the circus. And I belong to the soil.

8.

Of Her Own Accord

Saturday, 22 July 1933 (aged twenty-three)
Jamaica.
It is astonishing how easily I am able to disconnect myself from the
affairs and atmosphere that affect me in one place and absorb those
of another. These last few days there has been a devil raging within
me, and it was roused by the devil in Hugh Patrick ('Bill').

He has been such marvellous fun to know even for a little while.
But now I am crazy to know more of him, to search those deeps in
him that I know are there. There was something in him that responded
to the cry in me. Oh, if I could have him for a few hours at ease by
my side, that I may say all I want to say and hear all I know he would
say in return. It was not that he is in the least like Chris either – feature
or figure – but he has the same latent depth and warmth of feeling, the
same light in his eyes when he looked at me sometimes, the same rather
stiff, amused little gestures, the same masculine magnetism, the same
superficial gay recklessness that I find so irresistible. God, what a lover
he might be, and how wild and impossible my ideas sometimes are.

But he sails on Tuesday back to his wife in Truro.

How magnificently he will work in as the character of the tragic
love affair in my novel – he and Chris combined. Why do I always
get my deep feelings roused by married men? It wasn't the sea. I want
to have him teasing me again, pulling my hair and being thoroughly
rude, then growing suddenly quiet. Miss Neil (fortune teller) read my

hand on board: 'You will not get married until you are about 45, then it will suddenly happen.'

And now I must not waste Pooh's electric light any longer, it is past 1.30. The Jamaican night is raucous with the odd strange calls of its creatures. My sheet is scattered with moths and insects, fireflies glitter past the windows, mosquitoes nibble at any bare part of me they can find. It is marvellous being with Pooh again. To think I am the aunt of a most magnificent niece![44]

Monday, 31 July

Heat, damp sticky breathless heat, mosquitoes, flies, many moths, deep banks of green fern round the verandah, black ants scurrying across these atrocious Victorian tiles, Sam watering the roses, whistling as he handles the hose.

I never realised how hideous European clothes were until I saw them worn here. The girls adore pale pink georgette and bright shiny satins and flimsy hats. And why is our civilisation so efficient and so ugly? Everywhere one goes one finds the inevitable mark of the white conqueror's Victorian heel. Beastly little houses, American advertisements, petrol pumps, cinemas. If someone would only put the black woman into loose brightly coloured skirts, beads and the gay head handkerchiefs many of them still wear. But as soon as she has won her freedom she must have her silk stockings and high-heeled shoes. And although they copy us so exactly and slavishly they hate us – all the black people. One can feel it everywhere. Except that everywhere the white man is feared and respected. But their deep envy and hate is there. Possibly the backwash, as Pooh suggests, of the bitterness of the slave.

Monday, 14 August

I am bored to the soles of my feet. Domestic bliss is all very well for

---

44 This is Ethel 'Babs' Everett, the inheritor of these journals (see Introduction). In a later entry, Jean writes of sewing bunnies onto her blue woolly shawl. Elsewhere, Babs is also referred to – affectionately – as 'the Pratts' Brat'.

the two people most closely concerned, but my God how tedious it can seem for the mere onlooker. I never realised how much older Pooh is to me until I met his wife Ivy and her friends. It is odd how the men in my family are attracted to the conventionally minded female. I feel rather mean to be criticising her while still a guest in her house, and she has admirably sterling qualities and will be loyal to her last breath. And she will look after him as he so badly needed looking after.

I don't think a sub-tropical climate is really good for me. On Friday I shall have been here a month, half of my precious holiday will have gone, and I have done hardly anything. And I am not going to try to be Christian-minded about it. I came out here to have a good time, and I could have had it too if there were someone just to take me about a bit. It is a great pity Pooh must be so busy just as I get here.[45] I must have the most amazing powers of self-control and self-restraint that I can screw down my impatience and restlessness so that none of them seems aware of it.

I wonder if Pooh's awkwardness with babies is due to my mother's distaste for them – her fear of having any and her efforts not to have Pooh. It is all rather terrible, but she was marvellous enough to us when we did arrive.

I am tired of these correct, nice people with their stiff and settled ideas on proper ways of living. I want London and Gus again and a little Bohemianism.

Wednesday, 16 August
If I have to sit on that verandah much longer I shall explode. But what with hurricanes and snapped cables and babies I am hemmed in and doomed for 8 weeks. And even if the trams did manage to get going again tomorrow, where on earth can I go? The slopes of Kingston

---

45 He was still working for Cable & Wireless. Kingston had just been hit by a hurricane.

bore me to tears, and I am frightened of exploring those backstreets on my own. Well I can go home and tell the usual lies.

Saturday, 19 August
Please God don't let this go on.

Tuesday, 22 August
Pooh is still repairing cables.

Monday, 28 August
I do so badly want a home of my own, wherein I could experiment with all the exciting recipes I came across in such mags as *Good Housekeeping*. Varieties of sandwiches for tea; stuffed vegetables for supper or light lunches; new kinds of sweets, grated milk chocolate for instance, with mashed banana and cream.

Now supposing I was suddenly left a million pounds, what should I do with it? Clothes of course. Learn French. I would take a room again in town. I would give the old folks a new car and chauffeur and a boiler for constant h.w. And I think I should give up architecture for the two-year Journalism course at UCL.

And now the damned idea's got hold of me I realise there are no practical obstacles to prevent my taking the course. Only fear has held me from considering the idea seriously. Writing is the only thing that has meant anything to me. I've been doing architecture for nearly six years now (three years at the office and three years at college), so I ought to know whether I'm capable of dealing with it or not. And honestly, I'm afraid I'm not.

I am going to write books and plays and articles.

Wednesday, 30 August
I cannot really believe that this may be true. I am about to do the thing I have always dreamed of doing. Rain drips from the verandah, the mad Jamaican ants scurry across the tiles, and I am deciding to

make a bold mad plunge into a river I don't know. Nothing is going to shake me or make me change my mind anymore. But give me words, not bricks, to play with and I will build you palaces for kings.

Difficulties? Millions of them! Failure? Inevitable.

Thursday, 14 September

The last idle hour I shall probably ever have in Jamaica. A stray breeze blows through the room that has sheltered me for so many weeks. Net curtains fixed to the lower half of all the many windows. Cream-washed cracked plaster walls. Grey paint on sills and frames and boarded ceiling. The curtain rings of the wardrobe rattling in rhythm with window sashes. The cupboard door under the table blown open. Outside bananas and bamboo fronds. Coffee berries. Lime and orange trees. Ebony, pear, Spanish oak. Mauve convolvulus creeper, hibiscus flowers. Heavy sweet scent by the waterfalls. Night coming down over the mountains. Lights of Kingston miles below.

Tuesday, 19 September

I am the only unmarried female aboard.

Wednesday, 20 September

I am hating all these lousy old men, old men who want to make love to you. I would like to wring their necks and slap their faces, but I don't. I encourage them by holding their hands, and then offend them by not trotting off into some dark corner after dinner to be slobbered over.

Dear God I'm getting some experience of men. But they are nearly all old, at that stage where any fairly young girl could amuse and flatter them enormously. How I hate being mauled about. Poor Billie B. (my brother's boss in the Kingston office) – what a fool! What an undersized and boring fool! 'You're not *afraid* of me are you?' as he tried to make me go for a drive with him. *Afraid.* If I had only said, 'My dear man, I'm bored to tears with you, take me home at once,' instead of soothing him gently by murmuring 'Oh, I think you're very nice . . .' And how could I explain that foolishness when we danced at the Silver Slipper after eating ham and eggs, and that his touch excited in me memories of other men and other moons, and that as a man I despised him utterly, and that I compared him to some rotten, undeveloped kernel, green and mouldy in a dry and brittle shell.

Friday, 29 September

I don't know whether I am more amused or angry with myself. But I do know there are a damn sight too many men on this ship, and I was very foolish to allow Neville into my cabin to say goodnight.
I loathe myself for that, and I don't know how I'm going to get beyond this. There's not one of them wouldn't make love to me (or hasn't tried) if I encouraged them enough, from the Captain downwards. Whether they have bets on it or not I can't guess, but I know I've gone just a little too far with Nev and I wish to God I hadn't. Reason said, 'Why not?' and instinct said, 'No'. And once he was in my cabin, instinct said 'Let him stay' and reason said, 'Send him away at once'. And there he is now writing letters. His presence naturally disturbs me. He has just asked me if I write poetry and says he is writing a fairy story. Oh Lord, oh Lord, what have I done?

Saturday, 30 September

'But listen Jean,' said Nev. 'Making love on board ship means *nothing*.' Which is just the crux of the whole matter. The whole bitter point of it. I want someone who will mean something to me.

My physical needs as a normal woman are badly wanting fulfilment. I've got to somehow make them understand that I have no anchor; that an ordinary full-sexed woman must centre her interests on one man, otherwise she must inevitably go to pieces.

I've learnt a lot from this voyage, and one thing from Nev which is forceful and important – that platonic friendships *are* impossible. To show my trust in my little boyfriends I left my door unbolted; although they had drunk too much, I knew I could trust them. But I've bolted it again.

Undated

Dearly beloved Pooh and family,

Home again, and I'm wondering if it's three months or three minutes that I've been away. Everything is exactly the same here. The voyage was on the whole gorgeous fun. I was the only young unmarried female on board, and what a time I had. There were twelve passengers altogether, and they were all damn decent to me and danced divinely, added to which I got off (disgusting expression) with the Captain, quite an achievement if you know the Captain, while the ship's doctor tried to get off with me. I used to annoy him by calling him Daddy. His wife was also on board, doing the round trip as a holiday. Then there was the fat and amusing little German commission agent. When I sat curled up on one of the settees at tea-time he used to stroke my ankles and tell me what a faithful husband he was and what a bad girl I was, and once when he had drunk too much beer said that it was fortunate we had not met sooner or there might have been trouble. Piglet managed to keep her head well above water although it was a strain at times.

Now I'm trying to concentrate on the session ahead of me. Pop has taken my decision to transfer to Journalism amazingly well. If he was at all distressed he is quite resigned to the change by now.

Wednesday, 18 October

I sat in the Refec drinking tea by myself feeling acutely lonely and very old.[46]

How is one to get beyond oneself? To get into contact with people – easy and friendly contact. I must get to know the journalists of my year. It is not in the nature of human beings to remain solitary. One wants to feel one is popular and liked. But one wants only a few very intimate friends – people who really matter in one's life.

All a matter of growth – of patience and endurance and courage.

---

46 It was her 24th birthday.

9.

The Young Girl Glider

Wednesday, 25 October 1933 (aged twenty-four)

*The good diarist writes either for himself alone or for a posterity
so distant that it can safely hear every secret and justly weigh every
motive. For such an audience there is need neither for affectation
nor of restraint. Sincerity is what they ask, detail and volume.*

Virginia Woolf[47]

Today begins the Journal I have made so many attempts to commence
since the idea first occurred to me one Saturday in the April of 1925.

The desire to express myself in words is so great. ('From
Architecture to Journalism! It's rather a leap isn't it?' as David said in
the Bartlett School studio this morning.) I have left the promised
security of my father's protection, and have forsaken the quiet, familiar
waters which I have loved so well, to navigate my ship alone upon a
stream whose course may lead me God knows where.

Was I right in changing from one thing to another so abruptly?
At least these pages shall remain as a record of my endeavours and

---

47 Jean begins her fourth hardback journal. Woolf kept a journal between 1915
(when she was 33) until a few days before her death in 1941, leaving behind 26
volumes. She regarded them not only as a record of events and people she had met,
but as a critique of the writing of others and a method of trying out new rhythms
and techniques of her own. Leonard Woolf produced an edited version named *A
Writer's Diary* in 1953, but the complete journals are also in print.

despair; that it may be known I was not without ambition and lamentably ill-defined faith in myself. So if this self-portrait fails to interest posterity, then my life will have been dull indeed, and I shall have grown into the stupid and tedious woman I have, at heart, such a horror of becoming.

Monday, 30 October

I would I could recall the intensity of my feelings as I came home in the tube tonight. I will write like Virginia Woolf or E.H. Young.[48] I will write better than either of them! I am so tired of tubes and trams and washing up, cheap clothes and a bad complexion.

It is now 1.30 a.m. and I am in bed, my hair brushed and my muscles duly stretched, but I cannot sleep. What is one to do when one seems possessed of ideas and ideals too big for one's meagre capabilities? I can go on living this mediocre life, helping to wash up and entertain and play bridge, queue for shows, go to the pictures, dance occasionally, and read hurriedly in what little spare time I have left. Thus may I continue, placidly, manicuring my nails, patching my vests, planning next season's outfits, and never achieving anything. On the other hand I could neglect my nails and my hair, leave my stockings undarned, sleep as long as I like, torment Ethel and make myself thoroughly unpopular – that I might have more time to read and study, more time to write and learn. Oh God, what is one to do? Remain pleasant, agreeable, and careful of trifles, stunted and underdeveloped? Or grow fat and selfish and temperamental, dropping deeply into the store of old learning and wisdom and culture, encouraging the growth of one's intellect?

Friday, 24 November

This evening Lugi gave a farewell party for Gus and Howard who sail

---

48 Young (1880–1949) was an independent-minded novelist and suffragette, and for many years lived infamously as 'Mrs Daniels' in a *ménage à trois* in London with a married man and his wife.

on Wednesday for Marseilles. Five of us were squeezed into that little room, already hazy with smoke when I arrived about 7.30. She had prepared quantities of food: grapefruit served in teacups, cold roast beef, salad and baked beans, lemonade and home-made jam tarts and cream.

I sat curled up on the divan next to Howard who waited on me hand and foot. I think he grows more charming each time I meet him. Gus disapproved strongly of the black crepe-de-chine triangle I had tied around my throat. 'Mausie, take off that *bib*!' he said suddenly. 'It looks awful! We know you have several double chins, but you needn't draw attention to the fact.' But I thought the effect on my green frock rather attractive – I wouldn't concede.

We played Slippery Anne round one of Lugi's drawing boards that she placed over the diminutive table. Lugi asked me what I was doing for Xmas, and whether I would care to go with her for four days into the country. 'But,' I said, 'I've never left the family for Xmas before. It may be difficult.' 'Then it's high time you began,' said Gus. 'Do them good.'[49]

It is so sad to think there will be no more evenings like this for some time to come. With Lugi and Gus I have no fear, no feeling of restraint. I want a room of my own again badly.

Friday, 8 December

Marjorie Walker sat and chatted to me over the dining room fire this evening.[50] While discussing her recent activities she related the account of a visit with The Ramblers to the new South Africa House one Saturday afternoon. I wanted to ask them who had shown them round but hadn't the courage.

'We had tea,' she said, 'in one of the rooms overlooking Trafalgar Square. All the woodwork and panelling is simply beautiful – in

---

49 She did get away, to Alfriston in Sussex.
50 A family friend.

stinkwood. I don't know why they call it that. We asked them but they didn't seem to know. And in the Governor's Room (I think she meant the High Commissioner's) is a really gorgeous Persian carpet. They told us it cost 250 guineas!'

'Oh, the new South Africa House,' said Ethel coming in at that moment. 'A beautiful building isn't it?' I wanted to be dramatic, to say with an exaggerated air of carelessness, 'Yes, I was taken over part of it last year before it was completed. I knew someone who worked for the South African government, and had thought at the time how grossly they were decorating the interior.' But I threw the stub end of my cigarette into the grate instead and answered, 'How nice!' wondering with an odd spasm of pain if he was still helping to control the affairs of his country in London. But his is a name I never bear mention now for fear of the embarrassment it might cause me. *Adieu, mon cher vaisseau passant!*

Saturday, 30 December

I have not yet broken the news of my intended departure to the family. I am strangely fearful of doing so, yet I must start room-hunting on Monday and move in next Thursday or Friday so that I shall be settled there before the term begins. It seems as though I have been trembling over this secret for months.

Friday, 5 January 1934

I informed Daddy as we waited for the Hendon Lane bus on our way to see Uncle Jack and Aunt Claire. He made no comment whatsoever. Ethel I told a little later while we were washing up. She was in a singularly good mood and I congratulate myself that I chose my moment well. Before I left yesterday she heaped me with groceries and carried one of my bags to the station. My fear of her spite is grossly exaggerated.

I trailed round London for two dismal days at the beginning of this week searching for rooms. A more depressing occupation could not be found. In desperation I at last returned to Belsize Park, and they welcomed me back like the lost sheep. It is not the same room I had last year but one exactly like it at the top of the house. It is really too expensive on £3 a week, and until I can find something cheaper I must manage my finances as skilfully as I can.

Today I unpacked my belongings and arranged them to my liking. 'Don't you find it very *lonely* there?' asked Aunt Elsie yesterday afternoon. 'Not a bit!' I lied glibly. 'I've no time to be lonely. I'm either working or entertaining or going out.' Wonder what she would have said if I'd answered, 'Yes, damnably at times.' Loneliness is the price one has to pay for freedom.

Friday, 19 January

Loneliness did I say? I'm beginning to think my answer to Aunt Elsie's question was, after all, true. There are many minor triumphs I would like to record: little parties I have already held in this room; the gin and tonic Barrel stood me at the Duke of Wellington the other day and his apparent eagerness to accept an invitation to coffee here one evening; the invitation I have had from Marjorie Nockolds (whom I have wanted to know of all the new people I am now meeting at College) to visit her flat in Kensington; the Regent Institute's approval of my article on Modern Architecture – I have sent it, as suggested, to the *Morning Post*. Life begins to assume some shape and colour.

Tuesday, 23 January

My triumph, it seems, is to be short-lived. This evening I am threatened with a very bad depression which I shall endeavour to overcome. As Arnold Bennett says somewhere in his journals, 'It's a good thing I don't write here my moods and things . . .'

I feel rather like Elspeth Myers remarked in the cloakroom the other day, 'I feel as though I'm due to fall in love again!' But no one sufficiently presentable and interesting appears on the horizon. It makes one feel humiliatingly undesirable.

Thursday, 25 January
The *Morning Post* has just returned my article. I shall not feel justified until something of mine is in print.

I must get through those damn exams at the end of this year. So I will put on one more record, light a cigarette and perhaps eat a couple of raisins, and dive once more into *Richard II*. 'For God's sake let us sit upon the ground and tell sad stories of the death of Kings!'

Tuesday, 6 February
'Happiness is an unreasonable state,' said A.J. Cronin's Dr Leith in *Grand Canary*. 'Examine it and it disappears.' To which Mary murmuringly replies, 'You don't want to examine it . . .'

One daren't examine it. But I don't want to forget today. College for a psychology lecture and returning to Belsize Park for supper with Nockolds: Lyons cold tongue and pressed veal and ham, olives, loganberries and a junket that had actually condescended to set, and ginger wine. No, I dare not boast, save that I like her enormously and am immensely proud that she has been my guest.

The room is still fragrant with the memory of her presence. Oh this I am sure is a secret of living – to develop one's capacity for making friends with the right kind of people. In this way one may defeat that dread fear of loneliness.

I have had notice today also that it is possible to get vacation work through the college authorities in some newspaper office for at least four weeks. This is magnificent, an excellent reason for not going home.

Sunday, 4 March
I am to work this vacc on the *Bath and Wilts Chronicle and Herald* and am now waiting to hear from the editor.

Wednesday, 28 March
Bath.
The newspaper staff gave me the most bewildering welcome. My first

job was to write up a wedding from certain notes provided. They even printed parts of it quite unaltered. It rather tickled me to write that the bride looked charming when I had not even seen a back view of the lady in her everyday clothes.

Mr Winkle (actually <u>Wintle</u>, one of the reporters) heard me express myself rather forcibly about the restrictions of my hostel, and has introduced me to the most comfortable and inexpensive digs. Mr Winkle is, I think, the type of young man I shall probably marry. I never realised before how exciting journalists were to know. I believe it will prove the kind of work I shall find most satisfying. It teems with interest and perpetual variety. But I must go – it never leaves one with nothing to do!

Later: To what place have I ever been where I have not sooner or later lost my head over somebody?

Good Friday, 30 March
I am sure Mr Winkle is the one who is always detailed to take visitors round. We went to Mells this afternoon, a fascinating place. I sat in the car while he went in to speak to the Rector. I respond too quickly to my environment, too eagerly adapt myself to suit the temperament of the first man who attracts me in a new place. It is ridiculous.

Saturday, 31 March
My Easter prayer: that soon, soon my body's hunger may be satisfied! Not by many lovers, for I have had my chances at that. In the end, as Gus said, I should only hate myself. Mere satiation of physical desire would poison my mind and wound my heart beyond hope of healing. But to have no lover at all would be even worse. For then, being denied a normal woman's experience, my mind would swell with obscene fancies and my heart would die. Those ghastly visions of the virtuous virgins – hard, bright acidular old age!

No, before I can live I must go through the crucifixion of marriage; it seems inevitably the part of Providence to find me the right man.

The only suitable one I have met up to date walked away suddenly and married someone else. All I want is someone reasonably young and healthy and sufficiently in love with me to trust me a little while, and I will make him as happy as is possible. Then will my body be at peace perhaps and leave my mind in a more balanced condition.

If Mr Winkle is not what I am afraid he is, he is really eminently eligible. He is at least the most interesting member of the staff on this paper. But again I am probably jumping to the wildest conclusions. Besides, it is absurd that I should discover the solution so easily on my first expedition. Oh Hell . . .

Easter Monday, 2 April
Once more I stumble from the great heights of hope into the dull valley of disillusion.

Mr Winkle is evidently a young man easily discouraged, or I imagined there was more underlying his attention to me than there actually was. Why did he trouble to find me these digs? Why did he offer to show me the nearest pub? Why did he take me to Mells? I knew things had begun too well.

Unfortunate that I should write an article in which I have said in the first paragraph, 'Were the beauty of Bath advertised, the desecrating, curious public will come in their chattering hordes . . . and we shall be left with nothing but a skeleton, floodlit', when only three weeks ago it was arranged to spend £3,000 boosting the damn place. 'Do you know,' said the Editor, 'that we had 20 Welsh miners down here a little while ago and they all took off their hats when they entered the Pump Room!' However, he's going to print the thing as it is tomorrow, with his own beastly little footnote.[51]

I have today done nothing but write up weddings, weddings and yet more weddings. Dear God! What fools these mortals are! Brides

---

51 This being Bath, our heroine's romantic adventures cannot but henceforth take on a distinctly Austen-ish air.

in satins and suede georgettes and heavy crepe white and cream and pink and blue. Bridesmaids in chinions and silks carrying bunches of tulips and roses and lilies and pearls and ponchettes and crystal necklaces, the tawdry gifts of the groom. It's enough to make one a spinster for life.

Tuesday, 3 April

All the sub-editors this afternoon toasted me in tea, upstanding. I was very touched, dear old things! But Mr Cox has a painful habit of making the most appalling puns. If they don't send me out somewhere tomorrow I shall throw a fit. Mr Walker pointed out to me yesterday that I had referred to a High Street Council School teacher as a High School teacher. 'Just the difference, you see . . .' he said. Christ!

I have just returned from a visit to the Theatre Royal where the English Repertory Players are giving *On the Spot* this week. I can't help admiring Edgar Wallace his gift for sensing dramatic situations.

Thursday, 5 April

It is Spring and there is no one here to make love to me: that is the trouble.

Friday, 13 April

I like the Wintle family very much indeed. Ann and her mother who run the snack bar seem delightful, and they all know how to work hard. Ann came up to me the other night and asked me how I was getting on, and if I had good digs and so on. Her interest surprised and pleased me, and left me wondering why she had taken the trouble, whether it was merely idle curiosity or anything her brother may have said, or pure kindness. Anyway, their coffee and hot dogs are excellent.

An idea for a play has been germinating. Tomorrow I am going to get a notebook from Woolworth's in which to start gathering in the fragments as they form. Roughly, the theme is to be a young girl's experiences on a provincial paper. Characters to be drawn from the *Chronicle*. And the influence she has on each individual delicately portrayed. She comes and goes leaving no tangible trace of her visit, i.e. she doesn't marry the most eligible reporter or shatter the News Editor's domestic tranquillity. But leaves a very distinct impression on the minds of those with whom she has worked, and with several of them unconsciously changes their outlook on life. Scene might be set throughout in the Reporters Room.[52]

Sunday, 15 April

A suicide. Neville came to the office yesterday morning to tell me an old man had jumped into the river at Newton Bridge. I was rushed off there and then with Colin Wintle to view the scene of the crime and gather information generally.

Monday, 16 April

I must get this nonsense out of my head. Because Colin Wintle asks me what my Christian name is and if I'd go out with him on some job this evening doesn't necessarily mean he is going to propose to me.

Tuesday, 17 April

I think I have control over this situation at last. I went with Colin Wintle after lunch to the inquest in the Newton Bridge suicide and felt perfectly at case with him throughout the afternoon. He has started calling me Jean, which is too amusing. I suppose he'll never know the romantic illusions he once evoked, that they are over and finished with.

Wednesday, 18 April

How soon is last night's exaltation withered! This torturing see-saw of emotion.

---

52 She called it *The Suburban Chronicle*. It soon turned from a play into a novel, and would take her three years to complete.

Colin Wintle is a nice boy but I have no business to be thinking of him as much as I have done. I have already suspected him of being incapable of falling in love with any woman – he gets on too well with too many of them. But I found myself consumed with the most absurd form of jealousy when I heard him making a date with Molly Taylor over the phone.

Thursday, 19 April

After trying to interview Miss Meakin, the young girl glider, this morning, Colin storms into the office saying she is an unmannerly little bitch – awkward and difficult, out of which nothing could be got. 'Well, she's terribly young,' I interposed. 'Young!' he snorted, 'She's older than you are. She's 22. You're not 22, and if you are you ought to be ashamed of yourself.' Which I am not sure is quite as complimentary as may have been intended. Lord, I must seem sweet and innocent. I think if I get the opportunity I'll tell him I'll be 21 in July.[53]

Thinking it is over this afternoon, I realise it is not at all funny. I do behave like a schoolgirl when I'm with him.

Saturday, 21 April

And this time tomorrow I suppose I shall be home. It will be fun meeting my lousy crowd of friends again.

Later: It's over, it's over, it's over. The drink and the dinner and the farewells. Only Colin has not said goodbye. He got up suddenly after the speeches were finished, presumably to write them up. And hasn't been seen since. Why the hell should I care? I ought to have learnt something of men by now, but I haven't. They all do it, the ones that have seemed to matter most – Chris and David and Bill Davies – just get up and walk out.

---

53 She'll be 25 in October.

Wednesday, 25 April

Wembley. And the packing was done and the train was caught and I am home again. But only for a few days. The room next to Lugi's in Dorset Square will be vacant this weekend and I am to move in on Sunday.

Now I am trying to forget how much I enjoyed myself in Bath in spite of those dull periods of depression which are inevitable wherever I go or what I do. Trying to forget, too, how much I want to go back and convince Colin that I am not a schoolgirl and behave on occasions like a normal human being. Having discussed the matter fully with Gus (oh my friend, my friend, how shall I get on without you?), I have no doubt in my mind now that Colin is homosexual. 'I have been meaning to warn you for a long time,' said Gus. 'They will always be a great danger to you, because they understand women so well and are so easy to get on with. It is very hard on the woman admittedly, because they are liable to mistake their intentions.'[54]

Wednesday, 2 May

A lovely room this, for summer: wide and high and cool, looking out upon the green trees of the Square. I shall be happy here, with Lugi opposite coming in every morning and evening in her cheery way, the kind of independent companion I need.

Thursday, 3 May

I would like very much to get to the bottom of homosexuality.

I cannot believe it is such a *crimina carnis contra naturam* as Kant makes out. The Greeks accepted it without dispute; the Romans tolerated it; it was unquestioned in England and also Europe I suppose

---

54 According to his biography on the flap of a book he wrote about the history of Hampshire, Colin Wintle went on to work in Fleet Street for the *Daily Mirror* and *News Chronicle*. He became a major in the Special Operations Executive (SOE) during the war, and upon demobilisation established a public relations company, working principally for charitable and voluntary organisations.

until the end of the eighteenth century, when certain moral philosophers became terribly self-conscious about sex generally. They misunderstood it, were shocked and ashamed.

Examined by itself, it is disgusting. But a lot of our physical functions are disgusting, yet they aren't wrong and they aren't necessarily demoralising. Yet if one accepts homosexuality as an inevitable and natural condition in some men, then one should also accept lesbianism similarly in women, and what Kant calls onanism and sodomy. All of which are almost too sickening to contemplate. The root of it lies perhaps in the psychological side of the problem, the effect that all sexual intercourse has on the mind and the general composition of the person's finer and more enduring qualities.

10.

Twentieth-Century Blues

Thursday, 24 May 1934 (aged twenty-four)

Dorset Square.

I have given up smoking until the exams are over. Why I don't quite know; I suddenly decided last Sunday morning when I was at home that it might be quite a good thing to do. I must say it's damned hard at times. I never realised how much it meant to me.

Aunt Elsie nearly died last Sunday. She has been in hospital nearly a fortnight now, and I have been convinced that her operation will prove successful and we shall eventually see her out and about once more.

Friday, 25 May

What mockery is this – Aunt Elsie died last night at 10 o'clock. Ethel has just phoned to tell me. She saw her yesterday afternoon after visiting me here, and the grapes I sent were never undone. She was my step-aunt: a quiet shadow of her sisters. How shall I write to them and what flowers shall I send?

Tuesday, 29 May

They buried her yesterday on Harrow Hill. The flowers, said Ethel, were magnificent, 'and we felt really happy about it all – if only she could have seen them.'

I feel very tempted to pinch one of Lugi's cigarettes. I have not kept to my resolution very well, having had one or two a day since Thursday and about half a dozen on Sunday. This weakness over so small a thing alarms me. Within a week or two I shall probably be smoking as much as I did before I left off. I like smoking and I want to smoke and at the present time I have no proof that it does me much harm.

Thursday, 14 June
I am angry and bitterly ashamed with myself. Gus is absolutely right: I have let myself slip, am getting fat and not paying enough attention to my clothes.

It seems damned unfair that some people – Joan for instance – can look marvellous by just stepping into the right frock and combing her hair, while I must spend increasing energy to achieve an effect which barely lasts longer than half an hour. I could, I know, look a little less suburban. In 50 years' time some damn prig of a critic will be saying, 'she lacked the necessary control of the organisation of her impulses'. Oh, we are bound with a thousand chains! For a hundred years we struggle to free ourselves of one, and while trying to file through the next discover that the other has once more twisted itself round our ankles.

Saturday, 23 June
For another fortnight I shall be in London making whoopee, wildly and without restraint: sherry parties, dinner parties, theatres, dances, art exhibitions, films – then peace, perhaps somewhere alone for a few weeks before I return to Bath.

As Virginia Woolf urges of young writers, I must not forget my patron, Posterity. And Posterity I must ask to be lenient with me, remembering that this is only an experiment. Stella Benson, I read a short while ago, has left an enormous journal to be published in 50 years' time. 50 years![55] If I live I shall be 74 – dramatic thought! If I

---

55 It is yet to appear. Stella Benson, a feminist, novelist and travel writer, was popular in her day (Virginia Woolf mourned her passing), but is now largely forgotten.

succeed in making of life what I think perhaps I may, my Journal shall not be left so long unfriended.

I sent six letters to Bath the other day, five of which I owed to the people there. But the sixth was to Colin Wintle, and I swear I had no intention of writing to him when I began the others. I have not, after all, forgotten Colin. What will come of this affair God knows.

The July issue of *Good Housekeeping* printed the attached letter which I wrote after reading Sewell Stokes's article in the June number:

A Girl Defends Her Own Generation

While I agree with nearly everything Mr Sewell Stokes has said concerning the 'education of our parents' in your June number, I feel that I must protest that his theory is not so simple to put into practice! Mr Stokes must be fortunate in having an exceptionally broad-minded mother. My own is dead, but my father, though he does not want to be educated in the least, is sufficiently good-natured to let me go my own way without trying to interfere. However, I do know only too well of the strife that goes on in the majority of homes today . . .

It is no good telling us to be patient with their obsolete opinions on drama and art; to 'teach them tactfully all we have learnt,' for they are not always 'surprisingly good pupils.' They adhere doggedly to the 'We've lived so much longer than you have, my dear, and therefore must know better' principle, simply refusing to admit the possibility of their being wrong . . .

We cannot introduce them to our Chelsea friends unless we are sure they will receive them without unreasonable censure. But it happens often that anything new or unexpected, anything they cannot easily understand and which does not fit into their own knowledge of the world, the older generation will set aside at once as unacceptable . . .

Miss J.L.P.
University College, London

Tuesday, 24 July

Colin Wintle – the maddening flippancy of his letters throws me back into a torment of doubt and sick dreams. What does he mean, what does he want of me, what does he think of me? Who writes on the back of GWR pamphlets?[56] 'If only you were in Bath now . . . I *am* looking forward to seeing you next month . . . we'll make a date now, for I'd love to take you out.' It is bewildering. He may not be at all what I have thought he might be. Or he might be running away from himself, hiding behind the first woman who seems interested. It is possible, Gus said, to go either way or both.

Thursday, 26 July

Dollfuss killed in Vienna.[57]

'This is a very terrible thing,' said Mary Kate as she seized the Rice Krispies this morning. It seems she knows something about it.[58] 'The League of Nations is no good whatsoever. They've tried to suppress Germany and Austria, which is futile.'

War . . . war . . . the muttering goes on on all sides. War in the air. England's lovely countryside devastated. No escape anywhere.

Yet supposing it happened. Bombs dropping, bombs bursting away the slums of London and Leeds, and the dirt and depression of all our big cities. Life will be lost of course, blood will flood the streets, beauty will be desecrated. But afterwards – for it couldn't last long this war in the air – if any of us have survived, if any of us can still pick up the torn threads of our lives and go on, what a magnificent chance for us to begin again. Given men of foresight and wisdom and sensitiveness, we have every opportunity of creating an age more golden than the Elizabethan.

---

56 Brunel's Great Western Railway.

57 Engelbert Dollfuss, the Austrian Chancellor since 1932. Dollfuss, a Christian Socialist, established an Austrian fascism modelled on that of Mussolini. He was assassinated in the Chancellery in an attempted *coup d'état* by a faction of Austrian Nazis.

58 Mary Kate Glanville, a new friend and holiday companion. Jean writes that she was related to radio pioneer Guglielmo Marconi.

Monday, 13 August

Bath.

'Never trust your memory,' Mr Richard Pearce, one of the clerks of the Acton Police Court, advised me last week. 'Make a note of everything.'

And here I am again. Was welcomed warmly by all in the office today. Colin . . . oh, I don't know about Colin. He is still as baffling, still as distracting. What right have I to think he can mean anything to me or I to him? Actually I know remarkably little about him. His worth has not yet been tested or proved at all. His father was a well-known doctor in Bristol and played an active part in the affairs of the city during the war. Colin himself went to Eton, to my immense satisfaction. There *is* a distinction about a public schoolboy that cannot be denied.

Wednesday, 15 August

I've got to get to know Colin. I've got to cut this nonsense out of me. Since those drinks with him this evening I've been in a flat stupor. Perhaps I shouldn't have had gin on top of poached egg and tea. If I can't make him want to marry me then I'll give in and have an affair with him. Loved I must be or go on the streets. It is electric.

Perhaps the real difficulty is this: that I want to watch the play and act in it at the same time. I want to watch the evolving of my own drama.

Saturday, 25 August

I wish I were middle-aged and married, placidly touring England with a companionable husband, fat, comfortable and content, like the two Americans I saw at lunch.

Was it prelude, or merely an incident, that touch of his lips on my hand three days ago?

Tuesday, 28 August

I went round the works of the *Chronicle* again today. A sordid, confusing, dramatic process, printing. Colin I haven't spoken to for a week. I feel that any day now I shall hear of his engagement to some Bath beauty – impending disaster is in the air.

Such an adorable and consoling letter from Howard this morning. 'There seem to be very few men in London at the moment,' he writes. 'I suppose they've all followed you to Bath. Do come back home soon, we miss you so here.' Nice, nice, nice! Howard and Gus have started rehearsing at the Old Vic for *Anthony & Cleopatra*.

Thursday, 6 September

For heaven's sake, Jean, stand up and be brave! If you cower and slide and shiver anymore behind your silly little curtain of doubt and indecision he will never know or see or understand you. Can you really doubt what you've seen in his eyes?

Saturday, 8 September

I must go back and finish my last year at college, even if Mr Walker offered me a job now. It is my only chance of acquiring an extra amount of knowledge and academic training for which I think I shall be grateful in the future. Therefore it is no good encouraging Colin to fall in love with me. If I were not so clumsy I could do what I liked with him. My life I am still centring round my work; everything else must be embroidery.

Thursday, 20 September

Four more days in Bath. Then will begin the impossible scramble to get all I have to get done done. Move into Blandford Square, the unfurnished flat I'm sharing with Mary Kate; meet people; Liverpool at the weekend to meet Leslie and family who are now on their way from Jamaica.

I'm sure that I could win Colin completely. But it would be slow and delicate work requiring infinite patience. First to establish confidence in myself in order to establish confidence in him; then gradually to unfold myself, securing him cautiously by the thin, frail threads of mutual experience until the whole net is woven. Only then will he lose his fear of me and begin his own pursuit and struggle for conquest, while I, pretending to be blind, watch every movement and help every step.

Saturday, 22 September

White moonlight and hell. The black shadows and pale stars' slate roofs like snow-drifts; wind through the pear tree, and drifting, broken races of cloud across the sky.

Colin makes love exquisitely. It is all I ever dreamt it might be, and he doesn't care. No one's touch has ever thrilled me more. But it exhilarates him only for the moment.

'I may never see you again,' he said without the slightest concern. And 'I'm not a permanent sort of person.' A passionate, casual devil who is going to break my heart. His, I believe, was broken long ago, and all his ideals shattered. 'Yes, I had a stab at that when I was your age, but it's not any good.'

I have absolutely no fear to restrain my desire this time. The cup has been lifted to my mouth and I am already intoxicated. It is real I know now, this wild dream of mine. He is as much in love with me as it is possible for him to be in love with anyone. Yet if I could only make him feel again, only break through the crust of his cynicism, then all this torment will not have been in vain. Fate will you be kind to me?

That terrible moon has moved from my window. What was it Colin said last night? 'There are hundreds and thousands of people, married and with large families, who've never had a romantic moment in their lives. They are just stodgy, they fill up the world but don't matter very much. It's those people with that streak of lighting in them that makes the world go on.'

Thursday, 27 September

Wembley.

On Monday evening I discovered exactly the extent of my power over him. He has no desire to get married, but would be more than willing to have me as his mistress. 'Can't you pigeonhole the episodes of your life?' he asked. 'Tuck Bath away somewhere with Colin. "Oh yes, he had rather a nice mouth . . ."'

I know where I am at last. And I am not unhappy.

Sunday, 7 October

I am going to live as Francis Stuart lives, as Balzac and Goethe and Shakespeare lived – 'prodigals of life, spendthrifts, gamblers. Adventurers, not studying life from a desk but in the midst of it.'[59]

I must read his *Notes for an Autobiography*, reviewed in this week's *Sunday Times*, it sounds interesting, stimulating. A book, he says, 'shouldn't be in your head. It should be in your flesh and blood. There are too many books written from the head.'

We are to move from this flat. Being almost on top of the Great Central Railway, the noise of the trains is too much for Mary Kate. Her heart is weak and the doctor says we must leave.

Wednesday, 10 October

I met Nockie today as I returned from lunching with Leslie at Simpsons (divine roast beef!). She is starting as Science Correspondent for the *Daily Mail*. She was running around London enthusiastically, determined to do her best with it, looking incredibly attractive in grey and scarlet. In love again, she says, with someone new. Shall I, I wondered as I watched her scrambling gaily onto a 536 bus, also have to submit to the conditions of the age, loving only as circumstances allow, my only anchor work and a certain inner fortitude?

Sunday, 14 October

Wembley. I have just finished reading Noël Coward's *Post Mortem* and am greatly bewildered. Coward is representative of London's

---

59 Francis Stuart was a prodigious and popular Irish novelist. His activities in Berlin during the war gained him a reputation as a Nazi sympathiser, an accusation he denied.

moneyed classes, a society which seems altogether rotten and horrible and terrifies me to death. I have always felt Coward's work is always of the same kind, and a little too rich, of the caviar and champagne variety, emphasised always with such vehemence that it leaves one wondering if there really is anything in the world but caviar and champagne. But I know that there is: I discovered it in Bath and can discern it occasionally at home. It flows deeply and quietly . . .

And just as I was beginning to get all smug and sentimental about the happy English house, I went down to tea. Now I am not so sure, not at all so sure. It began to seem rather futile, their conversation, and the absurd fools they make of themselves over that child, although I'm just as idiotic when I start playing with her, for she is rather sweet.[60]

I don't know that it is worth it: rearing children to dullness and complacency or death and disaster. Just because of a smile in a man's eyes and the momentary touch of his hand. A fleeting second of divine intoxication which came and went and may never come again. Domesticity is not what I want, but being at home normally has this effect on me after a little while. Feel suffocated and depressed. The twentieth-century blues get me down badly in Wembley.

Monday, 22 October
Blandford Square.
The blues get me down not only at home. Colin gave me a month in which to forget him. I have done my best. I knew he had meant goodbye when we parted.

At home such an abundance of life has filled the house. Footsteps and scraps of conversation everywhere – a child's voice, and a child's belongings, and a half-dozen grown-ups running up and down stairs and from room to room in untiring attendance. And I, when I am there, feel very much on the surface of things.

---

60 This is Babs, Jean's niece, now aged one.

Never have time to do anything thoroughly, to think or feel or dream. Half an hour at this, an hour at that, and interruptions every 20 minutes. Half a dozen pages of Shaw, two scenes from Shakespeare, an act from Dryden, half a tale of Maugham and a chapter of Virginia Woolf. A paragraph in *The Times*, the headline of the *Herald*, the photos of the *Mail*, the glimpse of an article in the *Spectator*, a rapid survey of the *Bookman*. No time to digest them or form one's own opinions or remember what one's read, too busy planning the hours to be spent on Boswell, Matthew Arnold and Tennyson, on Plato and Kant and John Macmurray, plans that never materialise because of a pair of stockings that have to be darned, nails that must be manicured. Then a telephone bell rings or a letter arrives. Little bits of scattered knowledge cling uselessly to one's memory. So much to do, so much worth doing, but in trying to do it all, one does nothing.

Wish that train would go. It has been hissing beneath our window for the past five minutes until even my nerves begin to feel a trifle shaken.

Saturday, 27 October
Colin is engaged to a Miss Flora Wagstaff of Claverton Down, Bath. God! And what a name.

But putting all personal heartbreak aside, I'd give a lot to know what has made him change his mind so quickly. Little over a month ago I know he had no intention or desire to get married. What is it in me that makes the boyfriends – after an exciting petting party or two – rush off hastily to marry someone else?[61] That I do excite something immoral in men seems unquestionable, and the reaction makes them go all pure and domestically minded. It's rather humiliating. I must manage my affairs very stupidly indeed.

'Oh, what is this crazy thing called love? I'd like to know.'

---

61 When discussing this issue a few days later, Jean states: 'Think what England will owe to me! I shall have saved half its population from going to the dogs, and been responsible for more stalwart sons than I would ever manage on my own.'

I suppose I shall write: books upon books, and they'll be good. Love to be only an incident. Work to be everything.

Sunday, 25 November

Let me try then once more to get this straight. What are for me the most important things in life? First, living: making friends, knowing and understanding as many different types of people as possible without destroying my own integrity; taking a constructive, intelligent interest in all contemporary art and literature; reading and knowing enough of the past to give the present its full value; travelling, not touring, which will involve a more serious study of languages; clothes, health and exercise.

Friendship is perhaps the most important thing. Love will come out of friendship, or is part of friendship, love in its purest and non-physical form. We want a new word for love. Love is so associated with sexual passion it is difficult to think of it without. Sexual passion is necessary and usually inevitable, but is only of relatively minor importance. We have sentimentally confused it with love.

And secondly, writing. If I am reduced to scrubbing steps and drinking gin I shall still keep a journal. Writing is so much a part of me that even if I never get anything published and have to earn my living in other ways, I shall continue in private. Living and writing – I desire to live fully only in order to write fully.

Thursday, 29 November

Bond Street has gone all carnival. All England seems to have come up for the Royal Wedding.[62] And London seems to have withdrawn very discreetly. Elegance has retired with a graceful wave of the hand, leaving his favourite haunts free for the curious, eager mob to explore.

7 p.m. Christmas Day

Wembley. Reading over the confused outpourings of the last twelve

---

62 Of Prince George and Princess Marina.

months I don't think I should like posterity to know quite how foolish I've been this year.

The major difficulty with which a diarist must contend is this: that since he jots down the day's activities as they occur, he cannot work to any preconceived plan. He cannot collect his facts first, as does the novelist, and from them make a unified and symmetrical pattern. But that doesn't mean he need make no pattern at all. Facts are showered upon him indiscriminately day by day, and these he must sort and arrange into a kind of mosaic which only a biographer may round off and frame. And he must have intuitive knowledge of the values of these fragments which pile up around him hourly. He must know what to choose, and having chosen, how to arrange them in an intelligent and interesting manner. To spread one's thoughts and feeling too lavishly over the pages makes too loose a picture, while just to record events impersonally like so much scientific data becomes essentially tedious. Facts, and the feeling and ideas they may arouse must be combined by the chronicler without destroying any of their essential spontaneity or upsetting a certain balance which must be studied and maintained. Really, I believe a good diarist is born, not made. And I'm not a good diarist. I always want to say too much.

The diarist must do what other writers may not. His emotions are not recollected in tranquillity; his ideas are not necessarily formed after long and studious reflection. Nor is his narration of events picked from imagination or memory. His purpose is special and peculiar. He has to capture and crystallise moments on the wing so that 'This,' future generations will say as they turn his glittering pages, 'was the present then. This was true.'

11.

T.S. Eliot Surprised Me

Monday, 28 July 1935

Wembley, 10 p.m. I eat too much at home, that is the trouble. And Daddy sits up obstinately listening in when I want him to go to bed. Someone on the radio is talking about the Abyssinian situation. 'Full of difficulties,' Daddy says. 'It all depends on the League meeting on Wednesday.'[63] Are we to be plunged into war again? Oh God, not yet, not yet.

Monday, 12 August

I believe neither in love nor in happiness, but only in living. If they are real they will come as the natural consequences of living, as by-products. I am not going to waste further time searching for them. That is the conclusion I have come to in my 25 years of experience, and that is the conclusion my little heroine Anne is coming to at the end of my novel.

Sunday, 18 August

Just to amuse myself I am going to make a list of my present friends, relatives and acquaintances.

---

63 Although Jean's interest in global politics was limited, she did tend in her journals to select key events that would shape her own world. This was one: the conflict between Italy and Ethiopia (which resulted in Italy's invasion in October) would have direct consequences on the Second World War. Fascist Italy would soon ally itself with Germany, and the League of Nations would prove itself ineffective as a force for peace.

To begin with, blood relations: My father, George Percy Pratt, ARIBA, JP, who practises in Acton, Middx, and lives here, in Wembley. His wife, my mother, who was Sarah Jane Lucey, and died when I was just 13. His second wife, my stepmother, Ethel, the daughter of Mr Watson, sometime brewer of Sudbury, near Harrow. Leslie Vernon, my brother, an electrician in Cable & Wireless Ltd, now working in London, but usually abroad. His wife, Ivy, from Jamaica. And their two-year-old daughter Ethel Lucey. Then there are various aunts, uncles and cousins whom I cannot be bothered to mention here and now.

Of my oldest Wembley friends I think Valerie is the most import-ant, and her husband Jack Honour, who live now out at Oxley. Now my college friends, who are certainly the most important, are: Lugi, who is Dorothy Cargill, daughter of Mr Cargill, an ophthalmic surgeon in Cavendish Square; Gus (Peter/Geoffrey), the son of Dr Wilfred Harris, a nerve specialist of Wimpole Street; Joan, daughter of Stephen Hey, dental surgeon of Wimpole Street, and her husband Vahan Bulbulian, architect. Marjorie Nockolds ('Nockie'), journalist, whom I have not heard from for months; John Rickman, Tarrant, Colin Gresham – all sometime scholars of the Bartlett School of Architecture (at UCL); John is learning to be a taxi driver and studies London at night on a bicycle. Eva May Glanville, or Mary Kate, of Irish extrac-tion, a librarian at Bedford College; Constance Oliver (or Oggie), artist, of Adelaide Road, who had her first picture hung in the Academy this year. And others I do not care to mention.

Wednesday, 21 August
Molly Taylor has given me the address of Dick Sheppard. I will try to get in touch with him, but am rather frightened of the idea.

Friday, 23 August
I sent brother Pooh 'Denied in Youth' (my study of Ethel), and I have just received a postcard from him. 'Best thing of yours I have read

so far. Have only read it through once very hurriedly but it seems excellent.' This is infinitely encouraging.

Thursday, 29 August

I am to meet Dick Sheppard next Wednesday. 'We shall both be wondering what sort of person we're to meet,' he writes. 'I believe you'll be superb – from your letter you're not dumb.' Molly tells me he is now fully qualified as an architect. He is a cripple and was once in love with Molly. They trained together at Bristol until he came to the A.A.[64] But he met with an accident some time ago, which paralysed him for several months. He will never, I understand, have complete use of his legs again – and a very good athlete at one time. Tragic.

Friday, 30 August

Wembley. I feel on the verge of hysterics. I am in a state where everything at home irritates me to distraction. But I remain outwardly agreeable.

To lighten the hour I must note down the story Aunt Jane told me the other day. A collection of old maids were discussing their wills at a tea party. One, when asked, replied, 'I have left my money to my two daughters.' There was consternation. 'But you've never been married, have you?' 'Oh no – but in my youth I was never neglected.'

A nephew in law once asked Aunt Jane, so she told me, 'Aunt Jane, are you still a virgin?' And out she came with the answer: 'In my youth I was never neglected.' Delicious.

Now I am going to be sordid and vulgar, to drag all my vulgarities firmly before me. With the names of the men I have known I could pen something so obscene and so exciting it would be the biggest bestseller on record. Those futile affairs of my youth . . . Arthur A., Gilbert D., a choir boy, a young waiter, Ronald on the Broads, F.E.S., Leslie J., Geoffrey R., Leonard W., Stanley B., David A., all the names

---

64 The Architectural Association in London.

collected from the Russian tour, Chris, Hugh P., Neville, John M., Neil A., Colin W. – oh it makes me feel quite sick, and I have forgotten half of them. This is what happens from being highly sexed, imaginative and timid. Damn good job I was timid too. But I am not so timid as I was.

Tuesday, 4 September

And now I have met Dick Sheppard. Interesting. We talked about everything and came to conclusions on nothing. I am passionately sorry for him but dare not allow him to see it. Vital, twisted, strong, impressionable, unambitious, morbid. We talked about perversions, sex, pregnancy, homosexualism, the bloodstream, death, Robert Graves, Stephen Spender, Hemingway, Evelyn Waugh, Donne, Webster, Marlowe, Corbusier, Paul Nash. Is interested in Communism, politics, crooked commercial gambling. The astonishing things he told me of the power of these big firms and the wretched use they make of it.

I like him. He is stimulating, amusing, he contradicts everything one says and himself. In the true modern tradition he believes in nothing and bullies convention. There is something fundamentally big and generous about him, yet one feels it is distorted – those terrible twisted legs have twisted his brain.[65]

Wednesday, 5 September

It occurred to me as I woke this morning that Dick was making an extra effort to appear interesting for my benefit. He moved around the room apologising at intervals for his lameness. Aunt Jane asked me this morning, 'Did he make love to you?' Really, she sometimes shocks me to the core.

---

65 Sir Richard Sheppard CBE, 1910–1982. It was not an accident, but polio. His firm Richard Sheppard, Robson & Partners designed many schools and university buildings, including Manchester Polytechnic, Imperial College London and Churchill College Cambridge. His firm, still thriving, was a pioneer in sustainable architecture.

The attitude he reflects is the fashionable one of 'I hate the country, open fires and little children' – a healthy reaction to the sentimental value of these things.

'If you want to get your book published,' said Dick, 'you'll have to be the publisher's mistress. I shouldn't think you'll have much difficulty . . .'

And he tried to perform an operation on his pregnant cat with a knitting needle because he thinks she's too young to have kittens (not while I was there of course).

He works for Louis de Soissons at the moment, and is living in one of the flats designed by him out at Larkhall.[66] Dick condemns them heartily.

Sunday, 16 September
I have driven the Fiat to Wimpole Street and back, alone. Up the Harrow Road, across the Edgware Road and along the Marylebone Road, soon I shall be able to take that car anywhere anytime.

Monday, 23 September
The most extraordinary thing happened to me in the train as we neared Waterloo. I was finishing *A Farewell to Arms* (Dick Sheppard had read me fragments of it – he knows it, he says, almost by heart) and I had reached the description of Catherine's confinement. I like this book immensely. It is written in a very hard, terse style I would do well to study. Catherine – I do not think I have ever disliked a character so thoroughly. She seemed to me completely impossible, until I came to the birth of the baby. Then I suddenly was Catherine; I was suffocating, dying with her. I had to close the book for I could not read further, the agony was too acute. I was nearly fainting, and then was sick, literally, out of the

---

66 Louis de Soissons was best known for his work on the development of Welwyn Garden City and around fifty European war cemeteries.

window. It was terrible; I could do nothing. At Waterloo the man opposite took my case down from the rack and asked if I would be all right.

I got into the Watford train and pains began, but at Kilburn Park it was all over. I didn't tell my family, they would never have believed it was caused through the death of Catherine. But there can be no other reason. I was well: fed, warm, dry, and my period was over 10 days ago.

Thursday, 10 October

Gus positively brutal with Part One of my novel – how bad my style is, how poor my construction. I am in such a state of despair I could almost commit suicide.

Friday, 11 October

I am consoled. Herbert Read in his treatise on *English Prose Style* criticises a passage of Kipling's in exactly the same manner as Gus criticises my work.

Friday, 25 October

Last night I went to a meeting of the Tomorrow Club on the introduction of Constance.[67] Mr Adrian Arlington read a paper on School Stories. Mr Harold Raymond, a director of Chatto & Windus, was in the chair. An entertaining evening. I was interested to see a director of Chatto & Windus. Someone from the same firm came to the Bartlett School once, and in both I recognised the same quality: superlative culturedness. But I shall try Faber & Faber first: they might not be quite so alarmingly refined. I wonder, though, how far that refinement goes? What is Mr Raymond's home like?

---

67 The Tomorrow Club, a precursor to the International Pen club, was established in 1917 by Catherine Amy Dawson Scott as a place where young writers could meet and hear established authors and publishers. Based in Covent Garden, speakers included H.G. Wells, Siegfried Sassoon and T.S. Eliot.

He rose last night and said he had been given the most astonishing piece of information. *Eric, or Little by Little* still sold at the rate of 4,000 (or was it 40,000?) copies a year. Who, he asked, was there reading it today? Who could there be possibly who took it seriously enough?[68] But the effect of last century's ideals die hard. Uncle Herbert and Aunt Mary Lucey send me an improving book every Xmas. I am quite certain they would have sent me *Eric* long ago if they thought I had not read it. It has suggested this to me: to attempt a novel of a girls' public school; to question and criticise women's education as has been done to men's.

I shall go on November 7th to have a look at the editors of the *News Chronicle* and *New Statesman*.

Monday, 4 November

Pop was too sweet this evening. He was about to leave, booted and spurred, for a Masonic meeting at the Connaught Rooms at 4.55 p.m. 'I am supposed to be there at 5,' he said as he filled his cigarette case. 'But I am making a point of being late. I have to be announced: "Worshipful Brother Percy Pratt, Assistant to the Grand Superintendent of Works, demands admission," and everyone has to stand up for me.'

Wednesday, 6 November

How incontestably right Ethel always is. I have left my bedroom door open again. 'Jean, how many times have I asked you to keep that door shut? I have only to ask you to do something for me and you forget it immediately. You are selfishness personified. I am an older woman and feel the cold more than you do. If you're going to live at home you must try to remember it's my home, not yours.'

I try to keep within her narrow tracks, and then, because I am thinking

---

68 The book, by Frederic Farrar, was first published in 1858. A moral fable set in a boys' boarding school, it follows one pupil's descent from privilege to what the author calls 'all folly and wickedness'; the only solace is religion. Parents bought it as a warning; school children were given it as a threat.

of the next chapter of my book, I leave a door open and am a monster of selfishness. If Leslie and Ivy had not been through all this also I shall begin to believe I am. I don't deny I am careless and even selfish, but I could prove she were more so if selfishness is lack of consideration for others. How very deliciously dramatic it would be if I could say, 'Then if I am such a disturbance to you in this house, where I was born and which is mine legally, I must go to live with Gus. He has been asking me to for months. And you will have the pleasure of knowing you have driven me to living in sin.' I wish I were big enough for that.

Friday, 8 November

Last night a very tired editor told the Tomorrow Club something of his problems. He was Mr Vallance of the *News Chronicle*. [He spoke of how] advertisements have tremendous influence on the daily paper. Advertisers of pills and toothpastes are the most powerful group in existence in England. Offend them and half the paper's revenue is forfeit. The paper cannot refuse their advertisements although they know the majority are quack medicines and a danger to public health.

And this was amusing: reader-interest of the popular paper has been categorised as that which appeals between the knees and the neck. Above the neck interests and opinions differ widely, but the appetites of mankind are universally similar. Sex, death, food. Too dismally true.

Thursday, 28 November

I am almost converted to Socialism by a letter of Gerald Gould's in last week's *New Statesman*. I have always had leanings in that direction, but weight of family feeling and insufficient knowledge has kept me vaguely Conservative. I voted obediently for the National Government because Daddy insisted that I should, I had not arguments to support contrary opinions.[69]

---

69 The National Government was a Conservative-dominated coalition led since June 1935 by Stanley Baldwin.

But I believe eventually we shall achieve economic freedom for the masses, which is the Socialistic aim. And I approve of it unreservedly. As Gould says, 'It does not worry me that you have a bigger income than I have, but it worries me to death that so many people are underpaid or on the dole . . . and I believe that ultimately freedom is the one thing that matters.'

I think a great many honest people are struggling hard to achieve this freedom for everyone in the economic sphere, and I believe eventually they'll win. We have such excellent tools – clean streets, tidy houses, orderly shops, comfortable theatres and cinemas, facilities for every kind of amusement and intellectual pursuit, museums, colleges, schools – the haphazard list is endless. And the material is there, good material, silks and cottons, steel, concrete and brick. But we don't know how to use it. We distort it, ruin it, degrade it, and there is ugliness everywhere.

But you cannot aim at health, you cannot aim at beauty. But you can aim at the conditions which produce health and beauty.

Friday, 29 November
Wembley. I come home from a lecture by Stephen Spender on Poetic Drama, loathing the suburbs. And I wake up on a fair morning, glad to be here and disinclined to go again to London this afternoon. But this, I know, can never be the centre of my activities. I am right in loathing the suburbs; only if I fail shall I be forced back to them. I must make my own centre.

T.S. Eliot surprised me. All distinguished people surprise me when I see them. I expect them to appear in halo and cloak, but they never do. I expected Eliot to be taller. He seems such a very tired scholar – one never suspects him of being a poet. Spender is surprisingly young. He went to UCS. I read his account of it in Graham Greene's *The Old School*. Pooh went to UCS, but I don't expect he knew Spender.[70]

---

70 University College School, a liberal public school in Hampstead, north-west London. The editor of these journals went there too.

Wednesday, 4 December

I don't know whether my artistic consciousness is particularly low this afternoon (i.e. I am ready to accept anything without criticism), but I think I have just read the best article about money I have ever come across, by James Hilton in *Good Housekeeping*.[71] Or is this the view of all sane, intelligent humans?

'The real advantage money confers is the power to ignore it in the daily traffic of life. I believe that money and more money for the most of us is a good thing, and that far more lives are ruined by having too little of it than by having an excess. It is the possession of money that enables you to put money in its proper place, which is a secondary place.'

The great point in dealing with money is to get value, and the way to do that is to form your own private scale of values, and to watch that it is kept quite independent of fashion and prices. Do I want a new, patent, self-acting chromium-plated, electrically operated cocktail shaker to save me from one of the few forms of physical exercise that can be performed in the drawing room? I do not. Does it matter to me whether Mr So and So has one, or whether (as I am assured by all the advertisements) all Mayfair has one? It doesn't.

Tuesday, 10 December

Have just hit on a brilliant solution of my difficulties. I will look for a small unfurnished room near Charlotte Street, at a minimum rent, which I can use for work and work only. Shall live with Gus at 109, but shall keep all manuscript and temperaments at the 'office'.[72]

Friday, 13 December

I have been feeling spasmodically very foolishly subjective and sentimental about the departure of the Pooh family. Having the

---

71 James Hilton was the author of *Lost Horizon* and *Goodbye, Mr Chips*, and won an Oscar for the screenplay of *Mrs Miniver*.
72 Gus has rented a flat with an actor friend named Zoe, and for weeks has been asking Jean to join them.

Brat about the place has made me want one of my own desperately. I get very melodramatic to myself over the sensation that I am never to have any. It is expected of me as a natural sequence. The next event in the family, Jean's wedding, how very gratifying. 'In three years' time,' said Ethel to the baby yesterday, 'I expect you'll come back to find Auntie Jean pulling on the pants of her *own* little baby . . .'

Saturday, 14 December

I do hope this awful feeling of loneliness will pass. I hope it is only subjective, due to stifling influences at home. What is there to keep me at home? Except that I love my father. I love him. But then no one could help loving my father. As Nockie says, it is no credit to Ethel that she is devoted to him. And because of that (and partly too of fear) I have kept quiet within his house. I have climbed down, have tried to meet them on their own level, and what is the result. I am ignored. I lose touch with my friends in town, and here no one cares a damn what I do. I climb down, I climb down. I discuss the weather and menus and listen to family scandal without controversial comment. I have no rows with my family. I am not turned out of the house, but when I am here everybody seems to be wondering why I'm here and why I don't go. It hurts. I am like a plant trying to find some suitable corner in which to grow and having to uproot myself perpetually.

Friday, 17 January 1936

I had my hand read the other day by a Europeanised Indian at the Caledonian Market. Usually palmists leave me sceptical or despondent and I try to forget what they have told me immediately. But this man seemed to be reading my mind rather than my hand.

'You might seem to have a bright and happy disposition,' he said, 'but actually you are easily and often depressed because you are of an impulsive and highly sensitive nature. You feel that no one understands you. By the end of this month things will be much better for you. At the moment you are in an indecisive state of mind.

'Early matrimony is indicated. Possibly this year. It will be a good thing for you. You will be happy, so long as you have courage. You are not financially embarrassed, and although money is not your ambition, you will prosper. You will always be surrounded by the elegances and graces. The next three years will be especially prosperous – 1939 will be an excellent year.'

12.

Like a Knife, He Said

Sunday, 19 January 1936 (aged twenty-six)
I have a small room in Howland Street and am moving in on Monday with folding chair and table, books and pen etc. Next week I hope to begin work in earnest.

Ethel took us to see *On Wings of Song* this evening. Daddy touches the heartstrings: 'I once was ambitious to sing,' he said, 'but I found I wasn't good enough.' Shall I be saying that in 50 years' time? 'I once wanted to write . . .'

Monday, 27 January
I have an odd conviction that these journals will have a value, perhaps scientifically. Every time I go through them, they pull at me. I cannot throw them away. They seem to be demanding recognition, acknowledgement in their own right, as they stand, so I will let them have their way.

I am in more danger of being submerged by Gus than I have admitted. It is a difficult fight: every day something happens to draw me deeper into service for him. Day by day my affection grows. I stay up late at night, I linger over meals, I help him entertain his friends.

Marriage with him looms in my mind significantly. But I cannot imagine him in love with me. And I do not honestly want to marry him − socially I doubt if I could rise to the demands of such a position. But vanity urges me to bring about desire in him if it is possible.

Monday, 3 February

Gus blinds with gold-dust. He feeds the vanity of others in order that they may feed his. And I am blinded with the rest. 'Your view of the young man,' said Nockie, 'seems at the bottom to be proprietary. He gives you excitement which you do not get at home.' I want to believe I can give him what no other woman can.

I am thinking of Gus's room. It is essentially theatrical – too theatrical. One piece of furniture out of place, or a cushion crumpled, spoils the effect. There is no place in it for anyone but Gus, a room of mirrors.

Tuesday, 11 February

Gus and Zoe may be going to join a repertory company at Amersham next week. They have tried for so many other jobs at various places that I can't believe this one will materialise.

Friday, 21 February

I am 26, still feel myself neglected, still wanting to be in demand, surrounded by admiration and attention, I want the homage of men and the respect of women – but peace, peace – I don't really want these things. They are but abstract symbols. It is time I stopped chasing these shadows. What I want is quality – quality in everything I do and possess. I want to be elegant, graceful and elegant without being snobbish; I want to be sophisticated and accomplished without being metallic; I want to be smart without being cheap or theatrical, dignified without being cold or stiff, honest without being dull. Kind without being stupid, be generous without being complacent, steady and reliable without being obstinate and narrow. I want wit without rottenness or meanness, excitement without lust. I am sick of mediocrity, the kindness of cows, the beaming kindness of uncultured women.

Gus and Zoe are playing at Amersham. I went to see their first night performance – a cruel journey, a dreadful little theatre, and an odd, under-rehearsed, barely organised company. The man who is running it seems quite inexperienced and has no money. Consequently Gus and Zoe are given huge parts they cannot manage. It is strange that whenever I see Gus on the stage I can get no grip of the character he is playing at all. I still believe he has great ability, but he is years of hard work away from its full development.

Sunday, 23 February

I have been troubled by the effort involved in living. Why, if I like being lazy, staying in bed, reading easy literature, going to a film or play, drifting around from friend to friend and adventure to adventure – why should I not live like that? I have the economic means, I do not have to support anyone but myself. Why should I bother to write a book? Why must I always be making the effort to improve, to progress?

It would be easy to quieten my conscience by finding a job – in the provinces as a journalist, as a freelance architectural correspondent, or teaching English to a French family. I could even go back to Daddy's office. It is the continual nagging inside me somewhere that will not let me rest, will not let me laze or relax. One must grow and develop. One must exercise one's faculties, or without exercise everything atrophies, physical or mental. So I must get my book written. My reading I shall reduce to the *New Statesman*, the *Sunday Times*, a few good fiction books, some poetry, and a book or two on style, construction and criticism. But I will do it. I will do it.

Monday, 24 February

Mrs Harris (mother of Gus) came in just now. She sat down on the arm of Zoe's chair and asked me what I was doing now. 'Writing a book? A novel? But how interesting.' And she has promised to give me some introductions for placing it when it is down. And then Pansy Leigh Smith phoned: 'I know a man in Cassell's and a publisher in New York.' And Vahan knows a reader at Macmillan. Seems as though there'll be a fight among the placers.

Thursday, 12 March

Extraordinary. I don't know quite how to record all that has happened over the past few days. Daddy's appendix was removed in Wembley Hospital on Tuesday night at 11 o'clock. I lived through the worst half-hour of my life when Ethel phoned me on Tuesday evening. She simply said, 'can you come home,' and was crying so much she couldn't go on.

I now feel, as I always do at home, that I have been here for ever and will be here for ever. The phone goes perpetually. Somebody calls every half-hour. We are calling Leslie (rather touching to feel one can be in communication like this with people the other side of the world). Ethel, outside the genuine anxiety she naturally feels, is getting a tremendous kick out of the situation. 'What it is to be the wife of a public man!'

Saturday, 14 March

'I should have known,' said Nockie on Thursday, 'that you'd been at home with your stepmother even if you hadn't told me.' That's the effect it has – it muffles me and it shows. I loathe it, I loathe it. This murderous atmosphere. Am not even allowed the full hour with my father at the hospital.

Sunday, 15 March

What agony it was to sit by Daddy this afternoon while his life flickered like a guttering candle. 'I'm being worn out,' he said. 'I've no strength left, no strength. I don't want any food.' One could barely hear his whisper. Ethel found me crying by his side. He turned to me and said, 'I'm afraid I'm not much entertainment for you.' How could I help crying?

But this evening he was better. He was being fed on Benger's Food, which pleased him.[73] He made the nurses quite hysterical by conducting

---

73 A popular, easily digested formula for babies and invalids.

the evening service over the wireless with a spoon. 'I should like a cigarette,' he said afterwards, 'but I must wait until this irritation on my chest has moved.' The coughing disturbs him dreadfully, 'like a knife,' he said, 'ripping me open.'

Monday, 16 March
Uncle Len is with us (he is Ethel's brother), and I am flirting with him outrageously.

Wednesday, 18 March
Ethel has been charming this last week with Daddy ill. But tonight, for a moment, the claw showed. She suggests the house should be made into flats, so that she should not have as much to look after. The house, she said, was too big for them – what did she and Daddy want with seven rooms? My God, I feel sick again when I think of it. And what does she imagine Daddy's feelings are? But she doesn't. If she thinks Leslie and I will spend our capital on altering the house into mean little flats at the expense of our father's pride, she is mistaken. Daddy wouldn't tolerate the idea for a second. This house is not big, and IT IS NOT HERS.

Friday, 20 March
Pop's stitches were removed today. His progress is very satisfactory, so that on Monday I hope I shall feel free to go back to the flat. It worries me perpetually why I cannot live at home. It seems so strange to me that all my relations are so tediously unambitious – all, that is, except Mummy's youngest brother Fred Lucey, to whom I owe my economic independence.[74] I wish I could discover he didn't die in America before the War (it was only a rumour), and that he is now alive and very wealthy. Because I feel he might have approved of this niece.

---

74 Jean is living off an income of £200 per annum: inheritance from her uncle Fred Lucey, and her father.

Saturday, 21 March

In this week's *Wembley News* (they rang me to enquire earlier in the week):-

Favourable Progress

Mr G.P. Pratt, who, as I mentioned last week, has undergone an operation for appendicitis at Wembley Hospital, is, I hear now, progressing favourably. Mr Pratt lives at 'Homefield', Crawford Avenue, Wembley, and has lived at Wembley for 42 years. His enforced, but fortunately only temporary retirement from public life, is being deeply felt in many circles, particularly among the parishioners of St John's Church, where he is vicar's warden.

Friday, 3 April

Daddy is to be X-rayed again. They don't know the cause of the pain about which he complains. Sister told Ethel that we must realise Daddy will not be the same again although he has come through the oper-ation so far very satisfactorily considering his age.

Wednesday, 15 April

Daddy came home from hospital last Saturday. 'Good,' I thought, 'he will not mind if I don't go to see him now until Wednesday (today).' But the first words with which I was greeted: 'So you *have* managed to leave your friends to come to see me. I was very disappointed you didn't come yesterday to see your poor old father.'

How to convince him that I am not playing in London, that my book is my job which gets badly neglected? He looks so thin and tired and beaten; I can't bear it. He still complains of a pain. Daddy would like me there the whole time, but Ethel leaves no room for me, and I cannot tell him that.

Have just been trying to write a letter to Pooh, but find an ex-planation of the situation to him quite impossible. He would only reply, 'Ethel be damned. If the Governor wants you at home, you jolly well go home.' And so a truth comes to light: I do not want to go home, even to please my father.

Met Mrs Barkham in the High Street after tea. She is the wife of our squire, Titus G., who is a director or something at Express Dairies and caused a scandal some time ago by having an illegit by one of his parlour maids. He is a hunchback. Mrs Barkham said to me, 'Been to see your father? He's had a bad time. Touch and go. Touch and go. You nearly lost him.' I'm damned. I think I'm the one to know that.

Monday, 20 April

I must endure this torment until – yes, let me write it – until my father dies. I admit my deep contempt for Wembley and all things suburban. Perhaps Ethel is right, and I am conceited and selfish. I try to offer my services, but my intense fear of her makes the offer appear ungracious. There is not a spark of generosity in her nature: she bristles. I shall call these disturbances at home Wrestles in the Dark with a Pygmy.

Friday, 1 May

Papa is to have another operation tomorrow morning at 8 o'clock. When will all this agony be over? Ethel would have it that it is very serious, but I shall not believe it. He is in good condition and the doctors are not in a hurry to operate. 'He's wonderful, isn't he?' Ethel said as we left him in hospital this afternoon. 'A little abnormally cheerful perhaps, but not thinking of himself at all, only of us.' Dramatising, dramatising the whole time. 'The garden, so lovely, and he not here to see it . . .'

Saturday, 2 May

My father died this afternoon at half-past two.

I am free. But at what cost. He died in such terrible pain. We had to stand and watch him die.

Sunday, 3 May

Death is lovely. Only life is cruel. I know that now. He lies in the drawing room now, awaiting the final rites, and his face is like an exquisite wax mask of him at his very best asleep. I am so happy. All agony for him is over.

11 p.m.: I have been mean and selfish. If my love for my father had been allowed to grow as I know it was capable of growing, Ethel's threats and tantrums wouldn't have mattered. I let my subjective fear of them stifle my love's development. Love when it is strong enough defeats such miserable obstacles with ease. If I had loved my father as I should, I should have known how much he must have suffered. I was too impatient and cruel.

Tuesday, 5 May

4 a.m.: Death is a great healer. All animosity between myself and Ethel has shrunk to nothing now that the object of our love and jealousy has gone.

I cannot sleep. I would like to marry some well-armed and powerful fighter of disease that I might help to make living and dying easier. My mother suffered dreadfully for years, and Daddy must have suffered much more than anyone ever realised. I had wanted to believe he would live to see my book published, but perhaps it is well he didn't; he might have found my ideas difficult and hurtful.

Birds are beginning to sing. We shall be leaving his home and garden. How that would grieve him, but neither I nor Ethel have any wish to remain here without him. I have the power to create the same loveliness elsewhere; I hope I may even be able to improve upon it, although I shall be told I expect that nothing my father did could be bettered. There is a great deal of sentimentalism one has to fight, but the feelings he inspired are genuine. He was very greatly loved.

The doctors spoke of his operation as a simple affair: just another three weeks in hospital. That was the way in which I was seeing it. It was so cruel that it had to be so unexpectedly terrible. He was like a child with the pain: it must have been awful.

When love is real and big enough, the ability to see things in their right proportion cannot lessen it. There have been things about him at which I was irritated and impatient, but what makes me go on my knees to him now, as it always did, was the natural unconscious sun of his spirit. It is that sun in the heart of men that makes them great. We were all warmed by it, so that only the brightest memories remain.

Thursday, 7 May

There will be no more green springs for us in this garden, no more summer hay or night-blue grapes at autumn. The blossom-starred branches nod in the evening wind, but his step is not on the stairs, he locks his doors no longer and sings no more in the morning, for his long trick is over, his quiet sleep and sweet dream found.

Oh God that he should have died before I could show him how much I love him! But I shall take my love away. I shall take it with me all over the world and plant his roses everywhere.

Friday, 8 May, *Wembley Observer and Gazette*

Death of Mr G.P. Pratt
Vicar Warden at St John's
One of Wembley's Oldest Residents

It is with deep regret that we record the death, which occurred at the Wembley Hospital on Saturday, of Mr George Percy Pratt, of Homefield, Crawford Avenue, Wembley, at the age of 70 years. Mr Pratt, who was taken ill in March, went into hospital to undergo an operation for appendicitis. He had been a resident of Wembley for 42 years. His life was an extraordinarily active and varied one and his interests were numerous. By profession he was a chartered architect and surveyor . . . he was chairman of the Acton Bench of magistrates up till his death . . . a prominent freemason, a member of many lodges. His principal hobby was gardening, and for many years he was a prominent member of the Royal Horticultural Society. He grew roses mainly.

Mr Pratt leaves two children, a son, Leslie, who is in the cable business, at present stationed in British West Indies, and a daughter, Jean, both by his first wife, who died in 1923. In August 1925 Mr Pratt remarried, his bride being Miss Ethel Watson of Sudbury, daughter of the late Mr Dewar Watson, who owned the old Sudbury Brewery.

Saturday, 6 June

I am battling with house agents, expiring and antiquated insurances, solicitors, removals and warehousing plans, bills, relations. If I were the great artist I want to believe I am I would sweep all these things aside and allow nothing to come between me and my creative urge. But I have been left with half a house to look after and all the furniture: responsibilities increase daily, and each new difficulty proves my immaturity. I have never felt so tired and worried and alone, yet everyone tells me how well I look.

Monday, 8 June

The thing that looms largest on the horizon now is our move from Wembley and my move into a new flat in Hampstead. Vahan and Joan are converting a house in South Hill Park: they are to have the ground floor, and I am having (I hope) the attic.

Monday, 27 July

I'm here, at 83, South Hill Park, Hampstead. I have signed an agreement for 3 years. I have been here a fortnight, and my lodger (Vahan's younger brother) arrives on Thursday. 'Homefield' is empty, its garden rich with rain, flowers and maturing fruit, and everywhere are rumours and threats of war. How can one feel settled?

Cecil Lewis has written in *Sagittarius Rising*: 'World state, world currency, world language . . . would demand new allegiances, new deals. Possibly two or three more world wars would be necessary to break down the innate hostility to such changes . . . It is a fight between intellect and appetite, international ideals and armaments. The latter will probably win the first two or three rounds; but if civilisation is to survive, the ideal must win in the end. Meanwhile, if a few million people have to die violent deaths, that cannot be helped. Nature is exceedingly wasteful.'[75]

It will not matter: war and death and the spoliation of one's loved possessions. Whether we live violently and die damnably, or long and die in peace, we die. We die and our loved possessions must become possessed of another's love or crumble away unloved. Only the love we can give out in passing matters; it is the only thing that lingers after a person dies.

I wish brother Pooh was in England. Homefield is a big responsibility for me alone. Ethel went away on July 1st, and I had to undertake the move and warehousing quite by myself. Lonely? No, I haven't felt lonely yet, there has been too much to do. War? Then let there be war, I can do nothing to stop the mass foolishness of barbarians. My room here fills me with delight. But if I could send a message to Heaven, I would ask an angel to tell my father that I love him, that I love him.

Tuesday, 18 August
I have acquired a kitten. Its curiosity is insatiable. Writing is difficult with Cheeta walking over the page.

Friday, 21 August
Next Friday I start with cousin Martin and his girlfriend Dorothy on

75 C.A. Lewis was a fighter pilot in the First World War, and *Sagittarius Rising* documented his exploits. He was a founder of the British Broadcasting Company, the precursor to the BBC.

our motor tour in Europe (he has an Alvis). Belgium, Germany, Switzerland, N. Italy, Nice. And then I may take up ballroom dancing with Joan Silvester at the Empress Rooms in October. I am also getting involved with a Communist movement in Hampstead. I even typed some cards for them yesterday. What will the Conservative relatives say . . .

Tuesday, 25 August

The movement is not specifically Communist, but a movement to establish a Popular Front in England involving all parties, sects, religions and classes. A good thing and an urgent one I feel.

Nockie was full of scorn at first at the ballroom dancing idea, but the more I think of it the more I approve. I need hardening, smartening: if I dance I shall have to care for my hair, nails, clothes, and I think it should give me the confidence among the sophisticated that I lack. Clothes, or rather one's physical appearance, is the symbol of character. A really smart woman must be intelligent. The tragedy is that not all intelligent women are smart.

Thursday, 27 August

I add my name (humbly) to the list that appears at the end of the letter in the *Statesman* this week on Britain and the Spanish War. 'It was almost universally held that the noblest contribution of the British to European civilisation has been our theory and practice of political liberty and parliamentary democracy . . . It has taken over 300 years of our history to establish and consolidate this characteristically British freedom and we have had to defend it against our own kings, aristocracy, army leaders and . . . Spanish, French, German monarchs, dictators, conquerors . . . At present in Spain a constitutional government, elected by the people, is being attacked by a junta of generals who have declared their intention of destroying parliamentary democracy in that country . . . We who sign this letter agree in retaining belief in the British ideals of political freedom and democracy.'

Everyone at present is afraid that Socialism and Communism means an attack on their property; the idea is fostered by a capital-istically controlled Press. But I don't see why the confiscation of individual property must be necessary to bring about the reforms needed. Everyone is so smug: so scared for their own safety. But there is evidence of immense wealth in this country, and I am sure it is only a matter of readjustment and intelligent control of the situation. Not by Fascism or military despotism – that is death, not life to the people. The individual's material needs are limited: after a certain point luxury becomes a vice, and possessions superfluous. The trouble is, I suppose, that the surplus millions are controlled by a small set of powerful persons who have so strangled themselves spiritually that they can only kill and corrupt life.

I am all for the *Vogue* way of living: elegance, grace, culture. I consider it necessary to fine living, and know it to be a difficult achievement. But my sense of justice demands that everyone is given a fair chance to achieve that social height. The finest intelligence and most artistic nature should be at the top, but not bolstered there by immoral economic support. Give every man and woman sufficient means to feed and clothe and house themselves, and let the intelligent and artistic rise as they should by the natural development of their capabilities. Let us be snobbish about ugliness and meanness and lies, and let us encourage kindness and cultivate manners and good taste.

Friday, 28 August
On the eve of this long-planned motor trip in Europe it has occurred to me that I have made no will. I have been told repeatedly I should make one, but it is such a complicated business I have shirked it. But supposing something happened, who on earth would settle my affairs?

In The Event of My Sudden Death during coming fortnight, I appoint (or request) my friends Marjorie Nockolds and Joan Bulbulian executrices.

My share of the property at Wembley and all invested and current monies I leave to my brother Leslie Vernon Pratt (c/o Pacific Cable Board, Barbados, BWI), with the exception of the War Loan Stock, which I should like transferred to my friend Marjorie Nockolds, and £100 to my friend Constance Oliver.

I should like Constance Oliver also to choose whatever furniture she cares to have from the lots stored with John Sanders of Ealing Broadway, with the exception of the grandfather clock, which I leave to my cousin Margaret Royan, and the piano, which I leave to my cousin Joyce Joliffe.

And furniture for which Constance cannot find a use I should like my stepmother Ethel Mary Pratt to have in the hope that she may buy her cottage soon.

<u>All MSS, Notebooks, Diaries etc to be burnt please without being read.</u>

My new fur coat (purchased this week and being stored with John Lewis of Oxford St) I leave to my friend Mrs Valerie Honour. My other clothes to my friend Zoe Randall (109 Charlotte St), and also to her my sewing machine.

My jewellery I leave to my sister in law, Ivy Pratt. My typewriter to John Rickman. My best deep-blue tea service to Gus (Geoffrey Harris). My plants and kitten to Joan Bulbulian, and my good wishes to everyone I haven't mentioned.

Thank you all,

Jean Lucey Pratt

'Only the brightest memories remain.' Jean's parents, George and Sarah.

13.

Israel Epstein

Saturday, 29 August 1936 (aged twenty-six)
Luxembourg.
For a fortnight I hope no one can send me bills, solicitors cannot disturb me, and property need not worry me. We drove to Dover last night, lost our way and Martin his temper, arrived half an hour late but allowed on board. Belgium incredibly boring, drab, beaten, until we go beyond Brussels. Picnic lunch in Soignes Forest, lovely. Scenery from Namur to Bastogne and Luxembourg boundary enchanting. Dorothy and I sleeping in car, Martin in cart at side. Soon must wash in babbling brook.

Wednesday, 2 September
We have come through Luxembourg into Germany via Trier, the Saar, Hamburg, Karlsruhe, Freiburg, Titisee, the Bodensee, Meersburg, into Austria, Bregenz, and are now camped in the valley somewhere between Bludenz and Partenen. Nothing but mountains, fir trees, river blue sky and a sun setting on the further side of the valley. Martin and Dorothy have gone in search of milk.

It took me three days to realise I was abroad again: everything seemed so like England – trains, roads, cars, trams, European clothes. The civilised countries are getting alike. Everything in Germany very clean, efficient, stolid. A nation of mechanics, without imagination, kind, but ugly, bullet-headed, fat, corpulent, cigar smokers, beer drinkers. In Bavaria flowers in the windows everywhere. We went to a Biergarten last night in Lindau, but though the people there were well fed, I thought them dull, heavy, drably dressed.

Atmosphere in Austria a little different. A more dreamy light in the eyes of the people, villages still clean, but not so tidy. As Dorothy remarked, Austria seems the same as Germany but without that solidity.

M. rather mean-minded. Haggles about halfpennies and begrudges us a postcard. Dorothy is pretty, feminine, a little stupid, but easy to know.

Sunday, 6 September

We are now at the Gasthaus in the Falkenstein. Yesterday we spent partly at the Freiburg baths, and today we walked a little way into the Black Forest. They aren't walkers, the others. I am not a walker either, but can walk the others tired without much difficulty. Martin doesn't drink beer or spirits or smoke; his only appetite is for tea, which he drinks at any hour of the day. Lovely country, but a little too lush, too dark. I feel hemmed in, bowed down by mountains, vision barred and escape impossible.

Monday, 7 September

No marks left for a meal. We are feeding off nuts and peaches.

Friday, 11 September

Hampstead. Arrived back soon after seven. Cheeta was sweet but thinner and larger. Plants dusty and badly watered.

Wednesday, 16 September

Do not feel I have had a holiday at all, swept as I am into the turmoil again. Find I have been elected a member of the People's Front Propaganda Committee.

From *The Sunday Times* . . . am gratified that I heard this story weeks ago:

'There is this story, which is enjoying great popularity in Berlin. A lion escaped from a menagerie and arrived at a crowded restaurant in the dinner hour. Everybody fled in terror except one little man, who refused to move until the lion was near to him, when he took up a sharp knife and cut its throat. A news-paper reporter, who saw the affair from a doorway, rushed up and congratulated him "on the bravest deed I have ever seen," and promised a full report in his paper the next morning. "May I have your name, please?" "Certainly," replied the hero. "My name is Israel Epstein." The journalist lifted his eyebrows and walked away. Next morning the following headline appeared: "Cowardly Jew attacks defenceless lion."'

Sunday, 11 October

Our democratic liberties are in danger, so I am told. Everyone seems convinced of this – some say in the form of Fascism, an unreliable government, individual industrial interests, the Jews, Communists. The People's Front may even be a mask from Moscow. Who is one to trust?

We want peace, individual freedom, free speech, equal opportuni-ties. We would not tolerate a dictator. But we have no peace when partisan demonstrations cause disorder in our streets, when free speakers are bespattered with bad eggs, and opportunity is obviously the privilege of the minority.

'The movement for a British Popular Front,' wrote *The Sunday Times* political correspondent last week, 'about which a good deal of noise was made in some quarters during the summer, is fizzling out.' Is it? Although the People's Front movement has brought these perplexities to my notice, and roused my sense of justice, I am still hesitant about its essence. If it is really a democratic movement, why has it not drawn in the more intelligent democrats? From what I have seen of them, the original members of the movement are regrettably peevish individuals, midgets with a grievance, hoping they have found something at last that will make them seem important. There is everywhere so much distrust. I would like to shrug my shoulders and leave it all for someone else to work out, which is an invitation to Fascism. We must learn to think and decide action each for ourselves.

Sunday, 18 October
For the first time in 27 years I celebrate the anniversary of my birth without either parent responsible for it. I have spent the whole day alone. Pooh has sent me a cable.

Saturday, 24 October
The exquisite Charles Scrimshaw is storming my imagination. I shall endow him with the usual extraordinary sensibilities and understanding, convince myself that his glances every Tea Dance in my direction are full of significance, and settle myself with him for the rest of my life – until I (if ever) speak to him. Then I shall discover he is not yet 25, is either married, thinking about it, or 'pansy' as Joan Silvester declares he is, because being inordinately conceited he combs his hair frequently before one of several mirrors.[76]

Saw Charlie Chaplin's *Modern Times* this evening. A moving plea for the underdog.

Wednesday, 4 November
His glances in my direction seem more significant than ever. Nockie read my teacup a short while ago: 'You're going to be swept off your feet. Not a very tall man, and dark I think.' Well, I wish the sweeping'd begin. I won't endure another of these feeble infatuations. It is so easy, so fatal to fall in love with an idea.

The tenant moves with his family into Homefield this week. Cheeta has run away. I am afraid she has gone for good.

---

76 Jean had been taking dancing classes at the Empress Rooms in Kensington for three weeks. Her teacher, Gwen Silvester, was the sister of bandleader and ballroom connoisseur Victor Silvester.

Monday, 9 November

Events have taken an unexpected turn. Mr Watson (of the People's Front Propaganda Committee) descended upon me on Saturday with some letters to type, stayed to tea and wants me to have dinner with him one evening. I am flattered. Now Nockie has phoned to say that what she prophesied for me has happened to her. Did she read the wrong cup?

Saturday, 21 November

Nockie is in the thick of her affair: the situation is an astonishing one. Both are madly in love with one another, but he is married, and still loves his wife to whom he has been married only six months. He says he never believed a person like Nockie could exist outside fiction, and neither knows what to do next.

Friday, 27 November

I still feel in danger of drowning when I see Scrimshaw looking at me the way he does. He is insufferably conceited: he may only think he has found another mirror in me.

Saturday, 5 December

I am now collecting opinions on the King-Simpson bombshell.[77] My hairdresser was the first to tell me it was in the papers on Thursday morning. 'One could forgive him making a fool of himself over something young and dainty, but an old hag like that . . .'

'Thinks nothing of sending her £5 worth of flowers every week,' said Mrs Rogers. That's the sort of boyfriend I'd like. Aunt Emmie was so funny about it when I saw her in the summer: had I heard of

---

77 The abdication crisis had been raging since October. King Edward VIII's devotion to Wallis Simpson, who was still married to her second husband, caused both a social and constitutional scandal. Edward was the titular head of the Church of England, which forbade the marriage; he chose to abdicate rather than give Simpson up, and their marriage the following year lasted until his death thirty-five years later.

someone at Belvedere who warmed his slippers for him?[78] Of course it was a dead secret and she mustn't repeat names, but the lady in question was married, her name began with an S, and there was a firm of the same name in the Strand . . .

I am intensely sorry for him. I think the whole nation is (but no, I heard of someone's uncle on Thursday night who said he needed horsewhipping). I do agree with the *Statesman*'s leader writer: he is being honest, and why won't the government make a special law that the King's wife need not be queen?

'One did hope,' said Aunt Maggie, 'He would have chosen someone fresh.'

Thursday, 10 December

I pray that the King will neither abdicate nor give in to his ministers.

Tuesday, 22 December

King Edward abdicated. I was so sure he wouldn't. Now everyone says War is upon us. I am so sure there won't be a war.

The Scrimshaw infatuation continues to ferment.

Wednesday, 30 December

I have been reading through my Journals again. That affair with Colin in Bath – what a fool I was during the first weeks we met. I had him in the hollow of my hand, but like a strange toy in the hands of a clumsy child he slipped through my fingers. It was too late when I returned in the summer. Sometimes I think I will burn the Journals, rough notes and all. But when I read them through I know I cannot.

Saturday, 6 February 1937

I have not had such a bad attack of inferiority complex for months.

---

78 Fort Belvedere was the country house in Windsor Great Park where their relationship first blossomed.

For the past week I have had grave suspicions that Joan Spall has transferred her affections (for the third time since October) to Charles Scrimshaw. I have tried to ignore them and the pain it gives me. I have only the slenderest evidence and have been making mountains of it. I woke at 7 this morning in tears about it.

This is not an isolated instance: it has happened continually through my life, and weighs upon me heavily. Unless I make a supreme effort it will continue, so that I shall miss the affection and tenderness I crave. Without it, life is empty, however full of other things. The heart is hungry for the stimulating flow of love, and without the gift of it from another, the source in oneself dries up.

Tuesday, 9 February

The Empress Rooms . . . Joan Spall didn't rush off to catch her train at 6.30, but was waiting suspiciously for someone in the lobby. I would so like to believe that C.S., in a discreet effort to get to know me, is trying to win Joan's confidence first.

Wednesday, 14 April

I have finished *The Suburban Chronicle*.[79] It must now be read and criticised by sundry friends, then typed and turned loose among the publishers. I do not expect that it will be accepted anywhere very easily, but if it only brings me into contact with literary circles I shall be satisfied.

Sunday, 9 May

Coronation, coronation, coronation. The crowds nauseate and excite me. They nauseate me because their voices are loud, their clothes ugly, their manners vulgar. They excite me because they are excited and so friendly and good-humoured. I shrink from the vulgarity and

---

79 Her *roman à clef* of her Bath newspaper days. See 13 April 1934.

messy emotionalism fostered by the commercial magnates – this sort of thing [from the *Evening News*, 8 May]: 'If you are amongst those who have still things to buy – clothes, extra delicacies for the table, something new for the home, seats for the shows you want to see – utilise the short time left to your best advantage. Make an extra careful study of the advertisement columns of *The Evening News*, so that you may know without delay where your requirements are to be met to your certain satisfaction.'

I would like to feel one of a great, unified people paying homage to their new King, but I cannot. It is all so false. I wonder how much interest and loyalty they would show if it didn't suit our tradesmen and the Church to excite it through the Press. People are saying it's the last Coronation England is likely to have.

Saturday, 15 May
Saw something of the Coronation crowds and the fireworks on the Heath. Brilliant in spite of the rain. Had a long letter from Nockie, she suggests I go out to share a flat with her in Malta. Had a bad Scrimshaw attack on Thursday. Extraordinary. Thought I'd got over it.

Saturday, 22 May
The Suburban Chronicle came back, so magnificently typed and bound that it took me two days to summon my courage to read it. I felt as an artist must feel when he sees his first picture framed and realises it is not as good as it seemed on his easel. But I have sent it now to Jonathan Cape with a letter.

Sunday, 14 June
Jonathan Cape have returned the *Chronicle*.

Friday, 23 July
The Gods have given a sign. In returning *The Suburban Chronicle*,

Lovat Dickson himself writes to me.[80] 'The manuscript shows ability and cleverness. It reads rather like a first effort at writing by a talented person who does not know what she wants to write about. I think if you were to alter this or attempt something else you might do well with it. I want you to know that we shall always welcome and give careful attention to anything that you may send in to us to see.'

Sunday, 22 August

Today I must get the *News of the World*. On Monday 9th I went to the tennis court but no one was there, and someone had left a *News of the World* in which a buyer's glove-judging contest tempted me. I spent the evening entering for it – a foolish bait of £500. Results published today.

Friday, 27 August

There was peace in Hampstead this afternoon as I walked up Willow Road, Flask Walk and Heath Street. People passing quietly about their business, children playing, old women walking their dogs, cats in the gutters. A cool afternoon, the sky a far, faint tremulous blue, fishes along the edges of the ponds, and I have never seen reflections in the water so clear and still. We shall remember such days with longing.

Thursday, 16 September

[From affixed blue letter paper headed 'British India Line'.]
I have . . . boarded this tub for Malta. The travel agency phoned me on the Tuesday to tell me of this vacancy. I nearly died in the rush to get on board in time, and am now dying again with boredom.

Crowd on board mixed. Am singularly fortunate to be in the same cabin with Mrs Molly Joy, a nurse at the military hospital. Pretty, rather plump, full of energy, very outspoken and sure of herself within

---

80 Dickson was a highly regarded publisher and biographer, initially with his own company, and then at Macmillan.

her orbit (anyone outside it is accordingly an imbecile). I like her. Gorgeously selfish. I doubt she would have noticed me if I hadn't been in her cabin.

There are several young females on board, but most of them going East of Suez and chaperoned. One slender young thing called Kitty – whom everyone seems to despise – an artist of sorts, and I'm not sure I shouldn't get on with her well. She skips and hops a lot – they say she's affected. The half-caste who sits opposite M.J. at meals interests me. He has a very cultured voice, a Scotch name, good manners, but the colour in him is unmistakable – African probably, and it makes him, I think, a little self-conscious. (Later: I've nicknamed him Sharkie.)

What I detest about life onboard ship is its close, gossipy, uncharitable atmosphere.

Monday, 20 September

Malta. Never, never can I regret this evening. Landing at 10.30 p.m., a riotous party onboard, Nockie to meet me, drinks, drinks, drinks, and now here I am at 26, Strada Tigue. This is going to be no ordinary foreign excursion. I can hardly believe I'm here, the depressions of the past week washed away in gin, white wine, Benedictine, shandy and beer. Dear Sharkie, I'm glad I'm not staying on that boat or I might have fallen heavily, coloured though he was.

I have been given a room with a marvellous view: wide, wide windows, air wafting over the rooftops from the sea. We are going to have a good time here, Nockie and I, and I shall write my novel for Lovat Dickson.

Saturday, 25 September

Within a week the sirocco has reduced me to tears, for no particular reason except possibly the foretaste I have had of the difficulties that lie ahead. I know that Nockie is not going to be easy to live with. No person of her intense individuality could be. For the

English here she has a supreme contempt, she dismisses them as a chattering, artificial horde of hysterical women and half-witted men.

My impressions of Malta: sticky, sticky heat, dust, ugly sandstone houses, bright sunlight, tiring on the eyes, the colour everywhere is dead – the colour of bleached bones, ill-treated cats, herds of degraded goats driven about the streets, screaming children, bawling hawkers, few trees, tawdry shops, priests, church bells, a gale-whipped Mediterranean from my window, wind, always wind. But through Nockie the place becomes a treasure island; treasure hidden, waiting for us to discover it.[81]

Thursday, 3 March 1938

I am on Spinola Palace roof, watching the Fleet go out for their spring exercises. An aircraft carrier seems to be leaving, decorated with bunting. Far out at sea were four destroyers and four cruisers. They have turned, and stand as if at attention.

The sky is grey with light, low clouds. Sounds of rifle practice from nearby barracks, traffic along the road, dogs barking, the flip-flop of Carrozzi horses, the wind has carried away my blotting paper,

---

81 She didn't find much hidden treasure. Jean lived in Malta for ten months. Despite her initial optimism, her days were beset with the usual feelings of inadequacy and self-doubt, combined with the now-standard flirtations with unsuitable and exploitative men. Her virginity remained securely intact (while Nockie cheated on the married man with whom she was having an affair). Her journals concentrated on her new friends and her architectural explorations of the island, but most entries were unremarkable. Her greatest success came when she was commissioned by *Architectural Review* to submit an article with photographs about Valletta. She also continued working on her novel *The Suburban Chronicle*, and despite her avowed attempt to develop her character and 'build something solid of my own' (rather than being 'swamped' by the influence of others), she became enamoured with the writing of the spiritualist and psychotherapist Graham Howe, an early practitioner at the burgeoning Tavistock Clinic in London. She frequently wanted to return home, but felt she should remain on the island until Nockie also returned. Only towards the end of her stay did she pay much attention to the gathering storms of war.

below me wanders a fat boy playing with carnival ball, imitation leopard-skin hat on his head. Four aircraft carriers have passed in a long line northwards.

Thursday, 24 March

Nockie is in a deep depression over the possibility of war. If Mussolini bombs Malta we shall be lucky if we have 24 hours' notice. The Spanish may seize Gibraltar and close the Straits. What should I do, I was asked, if I was suddenly awakened by guns?

Yet for all this talk of bombs and dictators and death I believe that I shall survive, and that my journals – if nothing else – shall survive with me. Some of the old faiths must remain. I shall pack my papers and send them home.

Friday, 25 March

We are seeing the death of democracy, says Nockie. Sooner or later we shall have to fight for our Empire, though not perhaps for a few months. There will come a form of Fascism to England. We may win if we fight.

Monday, 28 March

Nockie describes me sometimes as an engaging rabbit who will not leave its burrow, and that I must go out and suffer experiences as she has done: 'I have had more experiences crowded into my 34 years than most people have in a lifetime. A war would not help me, but it might do you a lot of good.'

It's time I went home. God, please let me survive the next three months.

Wednesday, 5 July

The luggage has gone. Just like that. A completely wasted year as far as my work is concerned. Have learnt something more of life, met many people, but in essence am no happier, no clearer, no surer of myself or path. But if it is possible, this ambling is going to stop as soon as I get to Graham Howe.[82]

Friday, 15 July

Hampstead. And now I am back again where I left off. Malta is an awkward dream that seems to have left little impression. Joan and Elsie Few gave me an uproarious welcome. The flat looks spotlessly clean, Joan has arranged flowers charmingly in my room.

It rained heavily as we approached Victoria. England was very grey and very green. I do not think that there are anywhere more beautiful trees than those in England. It is lovely, lovely to be home.

Friday, 22 July

I want a love affair. Something really exciting, stimulating. I know I am not unattractive, but I also know that love affairs don't drop into one's lap. I'm stuck, in danger of losing whatever little charm and ability for living I once possessed. Marriage with some worthy, reliable male seems the only hope. Today I counted up 8 or 9 possible paths to follow: architectural journalism, short story writing, the novel, ballroom dancing again, a job on the *Dancing Times* (through the Silvesters), furnishing and subletting flats as a commercial proposition, working for an architect's diploma, marriage (to someone like Alan Devereux) or cutting adrift completely. I want, as Monica Haddow puts it, 'to be rescued from virginity'. Feel myself growing flabbier and flabbier.

Urging myself to write to Graham Howe.

Monday, 25 July

I have been obsessed with the appalling idea of marrying Alan

---

82 The analyst ran a practice in Harley Street, proposing a spiritual course of enlightenment called the Open Way. R.D. Laing claimed him as a significant influence, although others shunned him for his vanity and lack of scientific methodology. Jean's favourite book of his was *I & Me*, published by Faber.

Devereux. In many ways so suitable – provincial upbringing, passion- ately fond of music, a very bad architect, loves argument, good physique, plays tennis well, owner driver of reasonable DKW,[83] tends to be conventionally unconventional, I like his sister – but oh one wants something more than this. I must be sure of physical reliability and possibility of satisfaction. I compare every man I think of in this way with Colin Wintle. I had no doubts about my desire to sleep with him at all; I still think that if we met again now I shouldn't hesitate to have an affair with him. I wish we could meet and lay this bug.

I have had a cable from Barbados. Pooh and family expect to be in England by August 31st.

Friday, 29 July
I am still obsessed with the A.D. idea. I think it will be a long and difficult task, for he is obviously rather woman-shy. The idea is being most villainously encouraged by my friends. The Devereuxs go to Bavaria on Thursday. I made up my mind to join them so that I might have a chance of considering and settling this foolishness.

Wednesday, 3 August
The idea is with me day and night. All because I come home starved of affection, attention, caresses, a little scared by the approaching 30s, a little more tolerant of the idea of marriage, less willing to live alone.

A dream I had the other night is worth recording. I was stranded in Italy, brought into Mussolini's presence, lavishly entertained and courted by him, was flattered by his attentions, had no doubt as to his intentions, but decided it would be amusing to lose my virginity to a dictator. But when he discovered I was a virgin he slapped me into prison. I tried to console myself with the thought that he is said to have syphilis.

Tomorrow we leave for Bavaria.

---

83 The Dampf-Kraft-Wagen, a once-popular German make.

Friday, 19 August

I blush at my last entry. Nothing to record but another failure. We were bored with and irritated by one another. The object of my meditations was a muddler, fussy, with a tendency to meanness and narrow-mindedness. He bit his nails and gobbled his food and has a humiliating lust for cream cakes.

The Devereuxs, so Elsie tells me, are descended from Robert, Earl of Essex, their mother's family from an illegitimate son of James II. I'm supposed to have an Elizabethan ancestor too, but it doesn't seem to help very much.

Today I shall write to make that appointment with Graham Howe.

Friday, 26 August

I am

going to see

Graham Howe

(oh God!)

14.

Into the Woods

Saturday, 27 August 1938 (aged twenty-eight)

I have chosen to visit Graham Howe on Monday morning rather than be at Plymouth to meet Pooh and his family. I am afraid Pooh may be hurt, but I want to see Dr Howe before – I want to feel not quite so hollow. Pooh may suggest my asking along a Boy Friend to make a foursome for something or other, and I Shan't be Able to Find One.

Monday, 29 August

2 p.m. I went through dull torture from 7 o'clock this morning until I began to answer Dr Howe's questions. I am interested at how still I sat, how quietly I spoke, and I answered everything he asked me as honestly and fully as I could. He suggested that the death of my mother had left a serious blank in my life which I have ever since been trying to fill. I have looked for this maternal understanding in the men I have known and imagined, and have made a refuge of my writing when it should have been an attack. 'If, by talking things over with you, I can give you a new orientation in life . . .' Orientation – I have never properly examined this word.

Dr Howe said that he did not believe in long analysis if he could get to the root of the problem by more direct methods. Most psychologists apparently go in for the long analysis. I am to go to him twice a week throughout September. 24 guineas. Thank God I have the 24 guineas.

Friday, 2 September

Pooh and family very well, very happy, niece adorable. But myself alien, taut, awkward. This evening Graham Howe taxed me with stiff mental exercises. Made me draw diagrams on paper to his dictation. I must have that protective Mother-Dictator. I have been seeking for someone exactly the same as myself so that I may identify myself with them: a oneness with the person I love. But in the centre of the self is the mother, the cup, the receiver, and on the outer circumference the father, the agent, the active member. The mother-dictator I seek is the centre of myself, the inspiration, the creative force which my marriage with the outer circumference of technique and opportunity will produce the work of art.

That I have lived so long with the idea of writing is my guarantee that the spark, the possibility, is there. I have been looking at myself from the outside, rudely, striving after ideas with a clenched fist instead of an open hand. I must make myself permeable. I must cut out these negatives, do more adding and less subtracting.

I walked down Marylebone Road trying not to cry. Astonished that anyone could have diagnosed my troubles so clearly. 'Your only difficulty seems to be the difficulty of letting yourself go, until you reach the bottom, as far down the chambers of the self as it is possible to fall – to fall asleep, to fall in love. And when you have learnt to relax, you will be able to write, to live, to love . . .'

It seemed so simple as he said it, and as clear and sweet as bell notes. But I grew immediately suspicious and distrustful. If he goes on being as sympathetic and stimulating as this I shall start falling in love with him, which is absurd and must not happen. I wonder how many of his lady clients do, and how he copes with such a situation.[84]

---

84 Elsewhere, Jean describes his Harley Street consulting room: 'There are always

Tuesday, 6 September

The astonishing, astonishing things Dr Howe twists out of one's dreams! Last night I was in a train passing through wide, wide fields, almost prairie land, set out with small piled-up hammocks of cut grass. In one field some black-clad men, one of them distinctly in the conventional costume of Hamlet, short black coat, tights, a sword, with a bomb in his hand which he placed carefully, furtively in the centre of the field, and began with the aid of the others to cover it with cut brush wood. Then I was in an attic, in a bathroom having a shower, by the seashore deciding to bathe, but had to go into some shelter to remove underclothes which I had on under my bathing costume, and then with the Silvesters in a ballroom I didn't recognise.

And he said, was I bomb or seed, was I Hamlet, full of doubt and indecision? Bomb and seed both contained immense energy, but one burst in timelessness and was destructive, and the other grew in time and was constructive. To experience life, he said, one must *plunge* into the sea of the emotions; one doesn't experience life through thought and criticism. I've been a sardine in a tin taking my tin with me.

But I am still full of doubt and indecision. Will he really be able to get me out of this mess, and help me to make peace with myself?

Tuesday, 13 September

Something somewhere up or down in the darkness sits and watches me betraying myself to Dr Howe, watches Dr Howe betraying himself, and is vastly entertained. I told him about Gus, and he knew at once what I was trying to say. 'In homosexuals a woman will find a baby

---

several vases of garden flowers about the room. His desk faces an open window. His patient sits in a deep armchair in a corner on the right hand side of the desk. There is a divan along one wall covered in soft green.' There is a mirror above the mantelpiece and a photo of a woman on his desk. 'A strong, open, pleasant face – is it his wife?'

to handle, a man to dominate her, but never a man to love. He does it with such glamour: the salads he makes for you (God, how did he know?) are supreme, and his opinions are supreme but fixed. There must be no opposition, no hostility. And if they are strong enough they will succeed, and you can point to their success, but over a trail of corpses.'

And then the torture began. I said all the things he expected me to say in answer to his questions. There is nothing he has told me about myself that I do not know, there is nothing he can tell me that I could not find for myself in his books, and yet I cannot disentangle my problems alone. I am still looking for a nice comfortable prop, for someone to pat me on the head and say, 'Poor little thing, how you do suffer. But you will win through, you will have everything you want in time.'

Thursday, 15 September

My article on the old fortifications in Malta has been accepted by the *Architectural Review*. 'The best thing that could have happened to you,' said Dr Howe. 'A new day has dawned for you.'

That letter from [editor] Richards this morning was in the nature of a miracle. I still can't believe it's true, that this thing is happening to me. Some dam in me is breaking down. I have started to live.

Monday, 19 September

Living begins to be simply heavenly, but I can't believe it will last. I think Dr Howe is a magician and one day the spell will break. It is beyond explanation – a feeling of deep, spreading warmth inside me, like being in love.

Tuesday, 20 September

Now from that deep bed of warmth I slip into a well of darkness, down and down and down, just as he said I must. He is far, far away on the edge, watching me with indifference, then not watching me at all. 'Treasure your secret places,' he said. 'Learn to love that darkness, that emptiness. Out of the darkness comes the creator. There must be light and darkness.' And so I am letting myself go. Perhaps I shouldn't even try to write about it.

I am only one of many patients. I have so much to learn, so long and lonely a road to go. Grabbing at the next man I'm attracted to will be no solution. 'But learn,' Dr Howe said, 'to make the best of what you have. If you can't have *that*, you have *this*. Learn to love *this*.'

Friday, 23 September
Graham Howe says that there will be no war.

Tuesday, 27 September
War, war and yet more rumours. Why must everything threaten to crash just as I am beginning?

Wednesday, 28 September
Gus says it is agony playing in *Idiot's Delight* this week.[85] Houses are packed and absolutely silent. The world at the mercy of a madman.

Midnight. And now the Four Powers are to meet tomorrow in Munich. Perhaps, says Grig,[86] Hitler in the end will be the means of creating a real world peace and a real League of Nations.

Thursday, 29 September
Hampstead. I return to a London plunged into a kind of fatalistic, smiling gloom. We've been told that everyone who can get out of London should. This panic leaves me cold with fury – why run

---

85 An American comedy by Robert E. Sherwood. The film of the play featured Clark Gable singing 'Puttin' on the Ritz'.
86 Grig was a new friend from Bournemouth.

away? Tomorrow I have to be fitted for a gas mask. The Edgware-Highgate tube is closed for Air Raid Protection measures. And yet underneath I cannot believe there will be a war. Joan just rang the doorbell. They have been listening to news and I am going to join them in Flat 1.

Friday, 30 September

We stayed up until 2 a.m. waiting for news. Panic spreads quickly. I mustn't lose my nerve, I won't succumb to this wave of terror.

I didn't know whether to keep my appointment with Dr Howe or not. I told him that the panic in London was unnerving me. And what, he asked, would I want to do if the crisis occurred? I want to stay in London. I might be able to help, do first aid. Living, I said, was so pointless if one didn't create something.

Our meetings are over. I tried to say I was grateful.

Monday, 10 October

Nockie came yesterday. She is full of gloom for our political future, believes that war is inevitable eventually, or conditions of dictatorship in England that will be worse than war, and urges me to go abroad away from it all as soon as I can. Hitler's curve, she says, is parabolic. Watch it. We went to see Charles Boyer in *Orage* at the Everyman, and also the GPO film *North Sea*. As Nockie said, the struggle to live goes on while Hitler marches into Czechoslovakia. And fishing in the North Sea will go on, for even dictators must eat.

Tuesday, 20 December

We are bound by a hard frost and snow, brought, I am told, by winds from Siberia. The pipes in the flat have frozen and we still have no hot water. I have oil stores on the landing and in the bathroom. I am wearing three thick sweaters and two pairs of socks. On Sunday I walked over the Heath to Highgate. The wind cut so that it hurt to breathe.

Tuesday, 27 December

My Xmas has been one of pleasant plenty – presents, cards, warmth and enormous meals, disturbed a little by the thought of those in want, and the possibility of days of poverty for myself in the future. I am nearly 30 and have no right to all this comfort, security and kindness. I want to earn my right to them.

On Sunday I went with the Poohs to a family party at Milton (Ethel's sister). I went with them yesterday to see *Peter Pan*. Soon they will be on their way to Suez. Pooh means more to me than he has ever done. His marriage is one of the most successful that I know: Ivy is a very fine little person and an excellent mother. I wish we were not so nervous of one another.

Saturday, 31 December

'How Some People Approach 1939' [Cuttings from the *News Chronicle*, with each comment accompanied by a photo of the speaker.]

Miss Marjorie Oakham, of Morden, Surrey, secretary: 'I have made up my mind that in 1939 I will be less impatient and more tolerant.'

Mr Tom Calvert, of Hackney, chef: 'As far as business goes, 1938 was quite good, but with better prospects of peace ahead, I am looking forward to a still better 1939.'

Mrs B. McGrogan, of Belfast: 'My wish for the New Year is a wave of prosperity and content. My motto is, "Keep Smiling".'

Mr Hampden Butler, of Heston, commercial artist: 'I think that this war scare will be overcome, that the pessimism of 1938 will turn to optimism in 1939.'

Mr Harry MacDonald of Highams Park, Essex, hotel proprietor: 'If 1939 is no worse than 1938 I shall be satisfied. I think the prospects seem hopeful.'

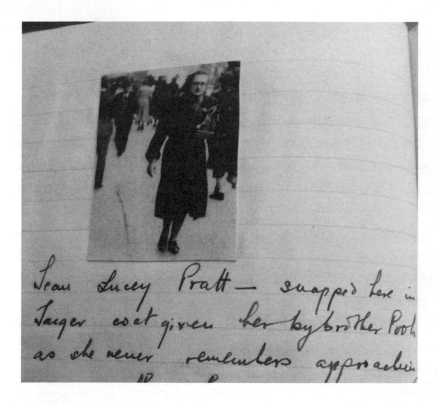

While Jean Lucey Pratt – snapped here in the 12-guinea Jaeger coat given her by brother Pooh – approaches it as she never remembers approaching any other year, all nicely set on her marks, full of plans and hope.

Tuesday, 10 January 1939

Last night I was at the Behrends' 'At Home', at which Sophie Wyes accompanied by Benjamin Britten gave a recital of German, French and English songs. The English section was a selection of poems by W.H. Auden set to music by Benjamin Britten. Auden was present, and St John Ervine, Ashley Dukes and probably other celebrities. It was very Bloomsbury. A party of us went on to the Four Hundred.[87] It is most discreetly, beautifully decorated. The Duke and Duchess of Kent were there for a while, looking exactly like their photographs (they didn't seem to be real people to me at all). I danced most of the time with Julie's boyfriend, the architect John Greenidge, a very good natural dancer whose style would lay Gwen Sylvester prostrate with horror. I came home in the early hours of the morning feeling frightfully pleased with myself.

Friday, 17 February
I had my fortune told again last night in teacups and cards. The thrill one gets from this sort of nonsense is incredible. I was promised a successful career and a successful marriage. She saw great possibilities ahead of me, with hard work. She saw engagement rings around two men, but thought I had not yet met the one she would choose for me. He was charming, fair, my type. I might meet him at a party, or in connection with some business. He would probably have a government post, something to do with aeroplanes. I am going abroad again in about six months, partly on business, partly on pleasure. A hot climate. Water is lucky for me. I shall be in an old building, looking through files. An elderly man will give me much help. I must beware of crossroads. A small debt will be paid by a fair woman, unexpectedly.

It is the first time a clairvoyant has seen 'the possibilities of great things' ahead for me in connection with my work. I want so much to believe it is true, yet dare not. A successful career and marriage – too good, too good.

Monday, 6 March
The disturbing atmosphere of Baker Street. The syncopated rhythm of modern life: the smartly dressed women, the flowers, the furs, the

---

87 'Top people's' London nightclub.

colour. Oh, the money in the N. West of London! The well-fed faces, the good warm clothes, expensive hats, fast cars, scintillating modern life, vulgar, gaudy, fascinating. How can I sit here now and work (at my desk) with that movement still throbbing through my veins? I have no real part in it. Oh, to feel one was working with and for society, part of it, part of the means to the known end – justified, good, progressive, thrilling and alive, not rebuffed by it.

Thursday, 9 March

In December 1920 (I was 10!), Katherine Mansfield wrote: 'There is no limit to human suffering . . . suffering is boundless, it is eternity . . . I do not want to die without leaving a record of my belief that suffering can be overcome. One must submit. Do not resist. Take it. Make it part of life . . . I must turn to work. I must put my agony into something, change it. Sorrow shall be changed into joy.'

I know that I have not known suffering like it; I don't think I have suffered yet at all. Shall I ever have the courage to destroy my 'huge complaining diaries'? [88] But I still think they are interesting, scientifically, and will not destroy them yet.

Tuesday, 21 March

The unabridged translation of Balzac's *Droll Stories* that Ivor has lent me[89] is hugely diverting, but fills me with humiliation that I am still a virgin. It is preposterous. I am not flat-chested as Joyce Joliffe is; I have, I know, an exceptionally attractive body, and that I have to be so fastidious about is exceedingly hard. Oh, the French are artists! The Englishman's approach to vulgarity is so clumsy that it makes it

---

88 As Mansfield referred to her own journals. She did indeed destroy the bulk of those she kept between 1909 and 1912. In an earlier entry, Jean had noted: 'How lovely to be able to write [, as does Katherine Mansfield]: "The idea of fame, of being a success – that's nothing, less than nothing. I love my family and a few others dearly . . . " And, "Life without work – I would commit suicide. Therefore work is more important than life."'

89 Ivor Brown, her new co-lodger in her Hampstead flat.

seem dirtier than it really is, but the Frenchman lifts it with a light, dexterous touch onto a plane of inimitable humour. To go to bed with Balzac is to know what one has missed all one's life.

Sunday, 26 March

I often wonder if I shall look back on these easy-comfort days with longing, when I do not have to save on cigarettes or think too hard about catering, taking extra cream when I feel like it, meals out, buying good fruit and vegetables, not worried overmuch by bills, or having to deny myself the price of a gallery seat or an afternoon picture show.

Friday, 31 March

Ivor's favourite expression: 'The country will be split from top to bottom!'

A man in the clothing trade has told him that the cheap tailoring firms have had a government order for 5 million khaki suits, 1914 pattern.

Elsie and I are taking First Aid classes in April. It is all very comic – now.

Such a heavenly day. I dallied back from the library in Keats Grove (why have I not been using this library instead of trailing down to Antrim Grove?) across the Heath. England did seem in that hour a land of hope and glory. There was a swan on the pond that would chase one of the drakes. The trees along the shore of the farther pond were a shower of delicate, pale green and a glowing burnt ochre kind of red. On the bridge strode a child, the mother in a red-brown coat, the child in dull orange – nothing against that brown and red and green could have been more perfect, the dark shade of the water and the blue shadows, faint it seemed with the hope of summer.

Mrs Boddy (the new char, name alone worth 1 shilling an hour) was telling me today of a well-to-do Jew in Germany who has been sent into a concentration camp. He is a friend of a husband of someone she works for – 'was a gentleman, good and kind, never done anyone any harm. One can't help what nationality one's born into, now can one? But his friend may never see him again. He's broken-hearted about it, everything been taken away from him, and never done anyone any harm, one of the nicest.'

How long will this absurd sort of cruelty persist? Why do the German people allow such things to happen? Could it ever happen – this persecution of the Jews – to the same extent, now, in England?

Wednesday, 5 April

I am contemplating a complete move to the country when my lease here is up in July.

Wednesday, 17 May

I'm too excited to work or read or practise or study first aid. I have found it, the place I must have – not must have, but want. A small cottage and a larger one in a gypsy clearing in Burnham Beeches, being excellently decorated by one of Alan's friends, owned by one of *his* friends, with all modern convenience: electric light, hot water, fires, a charming garden, near the London Green Line bus route and buses into Slough. Gypsy Cottage East and Wee Cottage. I can't, daren't believe it. Something may happen to snatch it all away from me. The cottages belong to a Kathleen Moneypenny but are looked after by her brother. £115 per annum plus rates and insurance.

Tuesday, 6 June

I move to Burnham Beeches on the 24th.[90] Gus and Phyllis drove with me there on Sunday and fell in love with the place. Gus now wants to give up Charlotte Street and live in Gypsy Cottage East whenever he is out of work.

---

90 Jean chose isolation. Wee Cottage and next-door Gypsy Cottage East were situated in a clearing deep within the Beeches (more than 500 acres of ancient woodland), and about half a mile from the nearest main road. Beautiful and bleak, according to mood and season.

A very wide-awake kitten is trying to bite my elbow. Nockie brought her for me from her sister's chicken farm on Whit Monday. A black atom of fierce fluff. I am calling her Dinah.

Thursday, 8 June

An ARP official called on Joan the other day insisting that she accepted one of the government's Air Raid Shelters. She is going to cover it with earth, scatter it with Woolworth's seeds and let Geoffrey play in it. They expect no trouble, they told Joan, but We've Got To Be Prepared.

We hear that there will be no war because vested interests do not wish for one. We hear that there will be a war because vested interests require one. Chamberlain is tied hand and foot by vested interests.

The Duke of Kent is a kleptomaniac and has a man following him continually to replace the objects he takes. On one voyage he was locked into his cabin because of his moral indiscretions – 'too fast' was he for his fellow passengers.

Thursday, 22 June

I should have *worked* for these cottages, not inherited capital which places them at my disposal. It is grossly unfair that the valuable comforts of life can so easily be bought. The feeling I have now is that I shall make a success of architectural journalism and I shan't with short stories.

Tomorrow . . . and then on Midsummer morning into the woods!

Sunday, 2 July 1939

Wee Cottage, Egypt, Burnham Beeches.

I am in heaven. I am in love. All the week I have been wanting to write this down. I am happier than I have ever been.

I wrote to Nockie: 'I must be very selfish, but I adore being on my own.' To which she replied, 'I don't think you're selfish. Sensible. One can't grow properly if one's roots are muddled up with someone else's.'

All the week I have been hard at work in house and garden. The Devereuxs drove me and Mrs Boddy after the removals van last Saturday. Mrs Boddy stayed the weekend helping me. I saw her onto the London bus and walked back through the woods in the still evening wanting to cry, wanting to write here how she had said so quietly, without rancour: 'It makes me a little envious, seeing all this. My grandchildren, they'd go mad here they would.'

This afternoon Gus and Phyllis and Julie came to tea. Charming, yet when they had gone I felt cold and the old unrest. It may have been because they didn't state their approval of my arrangings.

Thursday, 6 July

I want to indulge in a little wail. It is raining and the willow tree outside my study window waves sad glistening leaves at me. Desolation will creep in – a threat of it rather. I fear I may be drowned by it: a deep, dreary soughing sea of melancholy.

Elsie came yesterday with her bicycle which she sold to me for £2.

Monday, 17 July

The willow tree branch has been cut from my window. Yesterday I waited in hope for answers to my Gypsy Cottage advert in the *New Statesman*.[91] Two nasty young men from South Audley Street arrived in a sleek greige car and went over the place uttering scarcely a word. Only the balcony seemed to amuse them slightly. It was the discovery that I should be such a near neighbour that finally startled them into saying No. I can only think that they wanted to practise Black Magic. No answers from the *Lady* advert.

Sunday, 23 July

I have been having tea with my neighbour Lady Spicer. An exquisitely

---

91 It appears that she has taken on responsibility of finding a lodger for the neighbouring cottage, a task that will later pass to the owner, Ms Moneypenny.

British move on her part to invite me informally this morning. She was oh so charming. I see her pass with her Alsatian daily. We can now be formally informal. I suppose I could ask for her aid in time of need, and I suppose she will ask for mine if ever such an occasion arose. Everyone was so class conscious, she said; you never find that atmosphere on the Continent. Abroad the workers are not ashamed of being workers. That seemed to her very satisfactory, that they should know their place. But that surely is an attitude belonging to the old order of things.

Sunday, 20 August
Our foreign policy seems at last firmly defined. We shall fight if Germany tries to interfere with Poland. But perhaps Germany won't interfere with Poland: perhaps she will do something completely unexpected and we shall be as indeterminate as ever.

I am planning a tinned food store. Wondering if I must have thick curtains.

Saturday, 26 August
My near neighbours Jack Payne and Peggy Cochrane are now *On the Air*.[92] Crazy world. I find it rather uncanny to be waiting to know whether my future is to be chaotic and painful, or will continue its meandering fog-bound course undisturbed, on the word of one man. Yet it is all so like last year's crisis it is comic. The same sickening fear, bewilderment, resentment and wonder. Lady Spicer returned from her holiday this afternoon: 'We shall find ourselves allied to Germany next, fighting France and Italy – or at war with America.' Everything is so fantastic I'd be surprised at nothing.

Peggy Cochrane about to sing. They say that she and Jack swear at each other something awful.

---

92 A popular and famously moody bandleader and his pianist/singer wife.

Monday, 28 August

I had been telling myself after reading the *Statesman*'s leader that although a war would smash my life and the lives of thousands like me, it might release those of millions. The last one hastened the emancipation of women, broke down much class prejudice, and swept away much stupid social etiquette. Life is more democratic than it was, although class friction continues. So perhaps a war might benefit mankind more than the terror and idea of it will let us see.

9.15 p.m. And still we wait. Two panic-stricken women [came] to see the cottage this afternoon. They made me furious, sick and ashamed. They wanted to park themselves and families into Gypsy East for one month. They scarcely looked at the place they were so scared. 'Let us be safe. Let us be safe!' Now I know what the local agent means when he speaks of 'the rats'. War at the moment seems absolutely inevitable. I am as scared at bottom as anyone, but may I never show such mean cowardice as these women are doing.

I stand to lose everything – my money, my house, my treasured belongings. Many of my friends may be killed or badly injured. I may be killed, and that would be the easiest solution. What I dread most is physical pain. Spiritual torture I believe I could now endure or learn to endure.

I believe they are drilling on Farnham Common. I can hear a voice above the trees shouting like an army sergeant.

Tuesday, 29 August

A wave of optimism. Hitler did not hand his reply to Sir Neville Henderson until after 7 p.m. We don't know yet what it is, but the hope is that as he hasn't marched into Poland yet he daren't because the odds are too heavy for him.

Lady S.'s houseman, a marine reservist, has been called up. He told me that there are now 4 million regulars ready for the Front Line. Many are already on the Continent, others waiting at Newhaven. There is a heartening feeling of confidence in the air. It looks as though

Hitler is in a nasty corner. Is this the beginning of the end of the Nazi regime?

Wednesday, 30 August

Another long day of uneasy waiting. We still don't know what Hitler's demands are, or what our reply is. Report has it that he insists on the return of Danzig and the Corridor. Russia is fortifying her Polish frontier. Holland and Belgium have offered Poland their services. France is requisitioning all her railways tomorrow and has already handed over her broadcasting stations to military authorities. Switzerland has appointed a commander-in-chief. All over Europe I see doors closed on secret government conferences.

Thursday, 31 August

Tomorrow schoolchildren and other 'priority' classes are being evacuated from dangerous centres. The Prime Minister wishes it to be made clear that this doesn't mean that war is inevitable. I sat and wept through the 9 o'clock news. This part of the nation's confidence and calm is oozing away. I can think of only one prayer that now seems adequate: 'Thy will be done.'

Friday, 1 September

Hostilities have broken out in Poland. Lady S. is expecting four evacuees, she doesn't know when. I have bought black paper for the windows. There is difficulty in getting butter and sugar. Lady S's houseman, so his wife tells me, has had a month's salary in advance and Plymouth is in a complete state of war. He may be in France now.

6.30 p.m. I cannot believe that this is happening to us. Germany has been bombing Polish towns since 5.30 this morning – obliged, so Hitler says, 'to meet force with force.' But no one knows (I mean I don't) who started the bombing. The British government is . . . 'inflexibly determined to stand by her obligations.' Chamberlain – speaking in Parliament now – says that the responsibility for plunging the world into this frightful position rests on the shoulders of one man. I shall stay here as long as I possibly can.

Saturday, 2 September
Nockie arrived about 9 p.m. with the two Haynes girls – very, very charming Scottish Canadians. Parliament meets this afternoon. Butter is difficult to get. Spong can get me no more cigarettes.[93] Parties of evacuated children are playing in the Beeches. The *Chronicle* reports that Hitler has said he is 'ready to wage a 10 year war on Britain.'

Tuesday, 5 September
We are at war with Germany.

---

93 The Spongs ran the local grocery store. Mrs Spong is still remembered in the village for her home-made cakes.

PART TWO:
News as it Happens

15.

The Boys in the Village

Wednesday, 13 September 1939 (aged twenty-nine)
No air raids yet. An atmosphere of resigned curiosity has settled over England. Rumours are current of deserters from the German army, of strikes along the Siegfried line. But our heavily censored press prepares us for a three-year conflict. News of aid from the colonies and dominions and India, opinion largely in America on our side makes me hugely optimistic – I fear too optimistic.

Monday, 30 October
My darling journal. That lost golden month of September. A sodden, gone October. And not a line here written. I have written letters, cooked, gardened. I have written an article on Malta for the *Canadian Geographical Journal*, I have sewed and knitted and read, and one day gone into Slough and one day went to Hampstead to see Joan for a few hours. We read together and talk and ramble through the Beeches, and enjoy our food and sometimes the radio, always the *Band Wagon*.

Gypsy East is let to a nice quiet couple with baby: Campbell.

Wednesday, 1 November
I have found a few notes made since the outbreak of war.

We were bored with the news, and calling the Ministry of Information 'The Ministry of Little or No Information' and 'The Ministry of Misinformation'. Latterly someone has called it 'The Ministry of

Malformation'. There seems to be a strong undercurrent of dissatisfaction with the government – I wonder how strong, how dangerous.

We are under a polite dictatorship. We do not really know what we are fighting for, and our government fears the spread of Bolshevism in Europe as much as Nazism. We were all gloomy conjecture, waiting for air raids. The first time I came up to London after war began I accompanied Nockie to Swiss Cottage, and the number of uniforms and the general atmosphere increased the feeling of rebirth within me. Memories of the last war returned with startling vividness: my earliest memories are connected with uniforms, thin newspapers, ration cards, potato cakes, margarine instead of butter, a shortage of sugar. I dreamt of a lettuce with a rotten heart.

On September 25th we were reading *Sense and Sensibility*, the Beeches were yellowing. Jane Austen carried us away completely. A lovely age, of peace and orderliness, good humour, security and comfort.

On October 18, my birthday, I scribbled: I am 30, unmarried and still a virgin. If I am not bombed or bankrupted by this war I suppose my declining years are to be spent here with Nockie. Friends may come and friends may go, but she goes on forever.

Tuesday, 14 November

On Monday Nockie begins work at the Forest of Dean in the Forestry Dept of the Women's Land Army. I shall be unable to believe that my freedom will last any favourable length of time.

We have had our ration books. I cannot get butter now from the milkman. No difficulty about other food. Blackout regulations still rigid. Windows every evening an agony. Tonight Gracie Fields entertainment to the BEF[94] Somewhere in France was broadcast: the troops did not know the words of her *Shipyard Sally* song 'Wish Me Luck'. Naughty digs by variety artists on the radio at Hitler and his gang

---

94 British Expeditionary Force.

are endless. The German broadcasts in English are entertaining. On one occasion Bournemouth was in flames.

Monday, 20 November

Alone again. Curtains drawn. Little cat out saying hullo to the new moon. Some woman drivelling on the radio.

I have just listened to the six o'clock news. More ships sunk by mines. Air battles over Holland. One plane brought down, two men killed. This idiotic war: hundreds and hundreds of civilians, neutral and belligerent, drowned and drowning and a handful of fighters killed. No air raids, no battles. We, the luckier ones in England, continue to eat and sleep in comfort, our anxiety dulling.

Why I like living alone: I can organise myself to suit myself – i.e. rise and breakfast without fear of disturbing another, potter about my chores without interference, be in garden without a guilty conscience of being unsociable, and work in the evenings instead of having to be agreeable by the fire. No tension from disagreement. No interruption.

My little cat is resting her chin on my right wrist. One cannot be lonely with this little companion, an individual with seductive, provocative and independent ways, one of the dearest animals I have ever known.

Tuesday, 21 November

I am lost in a pleasant dream: to buy the Gypsy Cottage block from the Moneypennys. To do this I shall have to enlist Pooh's aid, sell Homefield, which I can contemplate calmly now with the idea of possessing Gypsy Cottages in its place, and probably release some of my already threatened capital. Perhaps I would not need to touch the War Loan and the Gilt Edged, and I might still be able to rely on £100 per annum from them. This evening began to coat bedroom floor with Liquid Lino to give it a glossy finish. A very tough rabbit for supper.

Thursday, 23 November

I am trying to cut down my cigarettes from 25 to 10 a day by not smoking until after tea. The *New Statesman* reports a rumour that Germany is to begin her attack on the West on May 1st, and will have defeated Britain – so her authorities calculate – by mid-July.

Monday, 27 November

Dinah followed me for 10 minutes into the woods this afternoon. She trots behind with her bushy tail erect and amber eyes wide and staring, a picture of studied determination to keep me in sight. Every now and then she stops and looks about her with back arched, as though she suspected enemies in every bush.

4.30 p.m. I can smoke now. But they are bitter little cigarettes, 4s. 6d. a 100 from Rothmans. I must not get any more for 10 days. From breakfast to tea-time I say to myself, 'Wait, wait – think of the rates. I have been smoking 15 du Maurier a week. In a year that would pay the rates on Gypsy East and Wee Cottage.

Tuesday, 28 November

A man came this morning selling newly shot duck. He said he was from Lord Burnham's estate. I bought a pair for 4s, and a couple of tiny things he said were teal duck. They are swinging now in the shed outside, such beautiful feathers. I saw the man again in the village later. Something rather harassed about him.

Thursday, 30 November

A group of young evacuees was walking home with a girl as I returned from village. She was reading some letters they had been writing. 'I have been evacuated from Shepherds Bush. I like it better in the country because I can go and play in the Beeches and collect conkers. Sometimes I pick up wood for the Lady.' One hears echoes of this happiness of town children everywhere.

9 p.m. Russia has invaded Finland. Russia has said that she bears

no malice towards the Finnish people – only their government. That sounds like a leaf out of our book. It is beginning to be a little ridiculous: each belligerent country declares undying respect and affection for the people of the nation it is fighting. Each states that it has the good of the people at heart.

But oh, what is the matter with the people of this world that they have let such governments lead them into this path of destruction? It is surely the fault of the people – me and you – too lazy, too limited, too self-centred to care who rules so long as the responsibility is not ours. I am afraid that we are to pay a heavy price for our indolence.

Friday, 1 December

From Lionel Hale's 'Life Goes On' column in today's *News Chronicle*.

'Looking back these 13 weeks: the curious feeling of a gas mask on your shoulder; the pitch black buses; the feeling your way from pillar box to lamppost; a crop of jokes about Hitler; his Last Will and Testament sold in the Strand for a penny; the lovely shine of the balloon barrage in the September sun; an ARP post in a Knightsbridge cellar furnished with carpets, chintz, radio, magazines, a bowl of goldfish.'

Ethel has sent a telegram to say she cannot come. I was looking forward to entertaining a pukka visitor – roast wild duck and orange salad all to myself now. I feel gloomy.

10.30 p.m. Alas for the duck! When the poulterer brought them plucked and prepared they were bright green. The ducks – all four – are now buried in the compost heap.

Friday, 8 December

I have asked Josephine Norris here for Xmas. I feel tired at the thought. Why did I do it? I think the statement that I am like Russia and pursue a policy of cold self-interest not unjustified.

Friday, 15 December

Josephine is coming for Xmas. I wish I were going to Ethel's. I have started a separate notebook for my war diary: Nockie, the dear, wrote me a letter of enthusiastic constructive correspondence after reading my first instalment.

Sunday, 17 December

As I sat playing patience half an hour ago, the German cruiser *Admiral Graf Spee* scuttled herself just outside Montevideo harbour. Hooray, hooray – Germans dead and wounded and defeated, a fine piece of engineering gone, gone just like that. All because of man's inhumanity to man. I don't want that sort of victory.

I was waiting up to hear a Mozart pianoforte recital, but I am not listening to it. I can only feel the humiliation and despair of men who have had to scuttle their pride – and the Bulldog's chortle of triumph. Listen, listen now to the beating of Mozart's heart . . .

Thursday, 21 December

I am enjoying myself enormously. Josephine arrived yesterday and she seems so happy here. I like people to feel at home, comfortable, warm, well-fed, pleased with the country and my company. What are the things that please me? Fires, warm rooms, hot water, things I can provide for my guest, food, the sun through winter trees, my cat – and, be honest Jean – the little Scot who works for the Ray Frasers.[95] I have an admirer, only a 'workman', but so intensely gratifying. He has stopped to speak to me on his way to the village, has thrown dead wood over from their ground into mine. It is going to my head. Ah, if I could only let myself go.

Thursday, 28 December

Today I feel dreadful, literally full of dread and pain and desire. Snow has fallen. My visitor is still with me. The trouble is that they like staying with me so much that they don't want to go. I want so much

---

95 The Frasers are neighbours in the Beeches.

to be alone again. I am shocked to the core at this passion for my own unadulterated company.

Saturday, 6 January 1940

Alone again. The relief is heavenly, like the first immersion in a hot bath. I saw her off at Slough this afternoon – if only she hadn't stayed so long. I want to write the third instalment of my war diary.

At the beginning of December, Jean learnt that Nockie had been keeping a diary of the war that she hoped would prove to be a useful social document in years to come. She decided to follow suit, opening a separate notebook to tackle less personal issues than those covered in her journal. Every few weeks she sent copies of her new diary to Mass Observation, the private organisation established in 1937 to record everyday life in Britain (see Introduction). Although many of her entries are unique to this new diary, after a few months her private journal and her account of the war began to merge, and carried similar or identical passages.[96]

Saturday, 20 January

I have stayed with Joan in Hampstead, seen the films *Goodbye Mr Chips* and *Juarez*, and the thriller *Ladies in Retirement*. I have bought things in the West End I couldn't afford, stayed with aunt Maggie and Ethel where I was thoroughly spoiled, saw Diana Churchill in her new show and visited her afterwards, missed the last Bakerloo Watford train and walked home in the blackout without a torch. I played mah-jong with Elsie Devereux, saw Fargeon's *Little Revue*, spent the night in Gus's new Primrose Hill studio flat, called on the Silvesters. And fallen in love again.

He is a boy – or should I say man? – whom Gus met and liked

---

96 To read more of Jean's Mass Observation diaries (1940–1948) please see *We Are at War*, *Private Battles* and *Our Hidden Lives* (all edited by Simon Garfield and published by Ebury Press).

when playing in *Young England* before Xmas. Tall, charming, danger-
ously like Colin Wintle. I know it's hopeless. I know that in a week
the excitement will have died from my mind. He might arrive unexpectedly one day in spring at the cottage gate and I would show him
the garden and we would talk of the country, which he says he adores,
and poetry and ballet and pictures. But I think it will be a long while
before we meet again. It was a spark . . . It will die, although of course
I hope and like to imagine it won't.

Yes, a lovely London visit, but what a welcome home: frozen pipes,
burst main, flooded kitchen, plumbers and chills. It has been an
agonising 24 hours. I have never known such a hard winter.

Sunday, 21 January (Jean's Mass Observation War Diary)
Vahan is employed at the moment by a Borough Council to inspect
air raid shelters in which he says he has little faith. They might save
one from flying shrapnel and falling masonry, but exact safety depends
entirely on where a bomb may fall: the open centre of a street might
be the safest place.

Less than 50 per cent of the population seems to be carrying gas
masks now. Joan and I decided to take ours when we went out, on
principle, but it was an effort and an irritation. The blackout has
slackened considerably. I noticed streaks of light from doors and
windows which would never have been allowed at the beginning of
the war.

Sunday, 28 January (War Diary)
Salisbury Plain manoeuvres have brought the army into much
evidence in this district. Houses in the forest have been commandeered
for the military, and disused saw mills, stables, vicarages, are being
used as billets. There are soldiers in our village too. A large new garage
was commandeered at the beginning of the war, and khaki coloured
lorries and officers' cars being driven in and out of it are a familiar
sight. No doubt spy rumours abound. When I was in London I was

told of enemy transmitting stations discovered in an old church tower and the petrol tank of a woman's car. One might do worse than cash in on spy stories now. I could imagine myself as a suspect.

Sunday, 4 February (War Diary)

A glassy thaw began on Wednesday when I had an appointment with my bank manager in London. He was grave and kind. He advised me to reinvest in the old 3 per cent War Loan, the government stock being not only a patriotic investment, but as safe a one as any, since if the government crashes everything else crashes too. 'But it will not come to that,' he said, 'though we have hard times to face. Government stock may drop still further. Taxes are heavy. We shall all suffer. I am receiving less now than I was two years ago although I am earning more.' He can grant no more private credit: all available credit is being reserved for the Government. Money for bombs at all costs.

Fanny has heard that Hitler is to be in London on April 21st. She said with a twinkle, 'Don't you arrange to go up *that* day, Ma'am!' It is reported that he intends to be King of England. An odd ambition.

Sunday, 11 February

Now for a sentimental interlude. I have been listening to the BBC's 1930s scrapbook. Oh, but I was standing on the edge of things in 1930! All the world was singing the Song of the Dawn: the government was Labour; they subsidised opera for five years but it didn't interest me then; Sydney Bridge was finished; Amy Johnson flew to Australia; we were humming 'I've got such Happy Feet'. I went to college in October, I was 21. I saw and was enchanted by *Private Lives* and later *Grand Hotel* and *All Quiet on the Western Front* (the book appalled and moved me mightily). And one of my first memories of Gus at a Buildings Construction demonstration. And Valerie was engaged to Jack Honour, and Daddy alive and Ethel cruel. Well, it is over. Ten years ago.

Saturday, 24 February

The weather is mild now, no trace of snow or frost remains anywhere, buds are swelling, birds are bursting with song; I go round the garden each morning with greedy eyes, the moist earth eager with life. One wants to make plans – one's blood stirs as the sap is stirring – and then an aeroplane casts a black shadow over the future. How can one think of the summer?

Monday, 26 February (War Diary)

I was working in the kitchen this afternoon, knitting and books and newspapers, letters and cigarettes, face flannels and a table cloth on a clothes-horse, coke crackling in the range, kettle humming, Dinah on my knee – when I saw a sprightly lady in a costume the colour of Parma violets pass this window. She was scented and made-up discreetly, wore a brown felt hat, a fox fur, brogues and dark thick stockings. She was small and bony and I recognised her at once as the owner of a dachshund I have met in the Beeches. I have heard her talking to the dachshund as I talk to Dinah and ordering him about as I would never dare my little cat.

She asked if I had heard of the National Salvage Campaign, looking at me doubtfully as though a young woman in grubby grey slacks with untidy hair and a dirty face might very well be ignorant of it. I had heard of it. I asked the Lady in Violet into the kitchen with due apologies, while Dinah sat on the hearth rug looking very annoyed. The Campaign was explained, and a list of salvage items (waste paper, metals, textiles, bottles, glass, rubber, even electric batteries and bulbs), and the address in the village where they were being received.

Summer Time began again yesterday. The new stock of Woolworth eau-de-cologne is in bottles of very reduced size for the same price. 'I think it's wicked,' said the girl who served me. 'You have a big bottle while they're still some left.'

Dinah's love affairs are reaching a conclusion. Ginger Tom, by a really awe-inspiring determination, is established as the accepted suitor. I had great difficulty in keeping him out of the cottage if Dinah was in it. The moon grew full. Dinah stayed out night after night while my sleep and probably my neighbours' was disturbed by Ginger Tom's piercing love songs and Dinah's replies in tones of terror and excitement.

But I forget. We are at war. Nockie has resigned from the Forestry Department of the WLA. An architect of my acquaintance who has had no other employment since war began save that of waiting in a London Auxiliary Fire station, is planning to join a contingent for Finland. His wife is in the Censor's office, translating Hungarian. Gus has testily given up reading or listening to war news, distrusting all information given to the public. Some friends of his discount 95 per cent of all they read and hear. The boys in the village are leaving one by one. 'Soon,' said the butcher, 'there'll only be us old ones left.'

16.

Your Mother in Englant

Monday, 18 March 1940

Since 1933 I have been using these 6d. Woolworth's notebooks at a pretty regular rate of two a year for my journal. Now, at the same price, they are selling them one quarter or less this thickness.

I'm frightened tonight: the future seems so fearful. Italy is promising to join Germany and Russia against us – fighting lovely Italy! Oh the world is mad. Somehow one has a ghastly vision of Turkey turning traitor, of the Scandinavian countries withdrawing from us, of America suddenly, strangely allying with Germany, of unrest in Britain spreading, dying in our common desire to defend ourselves from our foes and, like Finland, fighting fearful, hopeless odds. England beaten by the Dictators! Hitler as King – really tonight nothing seems too fantastic to be possible. At least half of my friends would commit suicide or be imprisoned.

A year ago I was beginning a new book and reading Katherine Mansfield, as I am now. I had hardly decided to leave Hampstead for good. I did not think there would be a war. At the back of me are still those dreams. I could recall and re-establish them in a moment: a warm, thrilling, satisfying male companion with me on a couch by a sitting room fire, and later in bed. I had no clear picture of the man's features, only his strength and warmth and a dark sparkle of admiration in his eyes, his sense of humour, his passion and tenderness and desire which equalled mine.

Tuesday, 26 March (War Diary)

No spring attack on England has been made yet. Fighting in the air and at sea continues. Tension over the Balkan situation increases. I am anxious for the possible fate of Suez, as my brother is stationed there with his wife and small daughter. We do not seem to be dealing with the unrest in India very successfully. Changes in our Government are mooted.

Though these events determine our future we have no control over them. We live from day to day in a kind of resigned doubtfulness, unable to make plans for more than a month ahead.

One night after 11 p.m. I was experimenting with foreign wavelengths on the radio when I heard a cockney voice speaking from a German station. A German announcer said in English, 'Now give your name and address. Come, speak to your mother in Englant.'

'I am a prisoner in Germany ' said the English voice, 'I am not wounded. I am in the best of health. I send my love and kisses to all at home.'

More prisoners were brought to the microphone. Each gave his name and address. The address of one was near Bath, one near London, one in Berkshire. Said the announcer to one of them, 'You are keen on football, I understand? You took part in a match against the German team, did you not? State in your own words the result of this match.'

'The Germans won,' came the reply without enthusiasm. 'By 3 goals to one.'

To another prisoner the announcer remarked, 'You have not shaved this morning?'

'No,' answered the Englishman, 'I have no kit.'

'Why is that?'

'I left it in the trenches.'

'You did not bring it with you?'

The Englishman began to stammer and was faded out. 'No . . . I . . . it was all too quick . . .'

Monday, 8 April

For nearly twenty-four hours I have been saying No, I must not write in here. But my short story 'Prodigal Daughter' has just been returned from Penguin Parade and I cannot contain my feelings any longer.[97] I am grateful that I have a fire and food and pleasant surroundings, but am depressed utterly that I have so much and have given so little. Perhaps I am just to be a proof that talent and desire and opportunity are not enough to make an artist. Or perhaps I'm struggling along a road I'm not and never have been meant to follow. All that I want to do crumbles and seems nothing. I think I know what a flower might feel that was not pollinated. I think now that I shall never be anything else: fit only to rot in time.

Wednesday, 10 April

A sense of impending disaster has haunted me these last few days. I put it down to my own depression. But now I wonder. Yesterday we heard that the Fleet had sown minefields in Norwegian waters. Today that the Nazis have overrun little Denmark and occupied certain strategic towns in Norway. The Germans certainly have a genius for organisation. This movement of theirs will lead to momentous doings.

Sunday, 14 April (War Diary)

I sit alone, grinding out short stories which no editor wants, and wonder whether I should not be playing a more active, a more obviously useful part in this war. Voluntary ARP work for instance or a full Red Cross training. Yet something (it may be laziness) says, WAIT.

It is difficult to understand why the German people tolerate and even approve, as they seem to do, the actions of their rulers. There are two opinions current in England at the moment. One is that we are fighting the Nazis, not the German people, and that if we destroy

---

97 Penguin Parade was a series of short books previewing new stories and poems by contemporary and largely unknown writers.

the Nazis everything will be all right. The other is that Nazism is the natural expression of the German character and therefore the whole German nation must be punished. I don't see what right we have to punish the nation for Nazism. I think it is more important to find out where its roots lie and to see if its energy can be diverted into saner channels.

Sunday, 28 April

I have been staying with Joan in Hampstead for a fortnight. When I left here the garden and the trees were still hesitant, waiting. But the weather changed last weekend, and I returned to find the grass on the lawn three inches high, tulip buds showing lines of colour and bees chorusing in the flowering currant. Dinah's kittens had arrived too – squeaking triplets. She is so delighted and proud. I wanted to send telegrams to everyone.

I think I shall have to find work of some sort soon, a daily job in High Wycombe, Slough or Windsor. If only I could get some freelance journalism. The depression deepens, it doesn't go.

Saturday, 4 May

Dinah's husband Ginger Tom was collected by his owner at the beginning of the week (after living here since January). But he returns every night in the dead hours to see his wife and family; he jumps through my bedroom window miaowing lustily. Tonight about 11.30 he didn't go to Dinah's saucer at once as he usually did, but waited for me to stroke his head and speak a word of welcome. Dinah jumped up from her box and ran to greet him, touched his nose with hers.

Sunday, 5 May

Last night the King of Hearts fell from the patience cards at my feet. I want to fall in love again. I want to fall in love with someone who will fall in love with me. Oh God, is it too late?

Thursday, 9 May

A debate has raged in Parliament. We have proved that we are still a democracy, that we may still criticise our leaders. Chamberlain seems to me a tragic figure. I have a respect for him, the feeling I might have for a Tory Uncle. A silly old fool but well intentioned, and he has dignity. His policy and views may be narrow and prejudiced but I feel that as a man he has character.

Graham Howe told Monica Haddow that he believes the war will end this year and will be followed by the beginnings of a great, bloodless social revolution all over the world. I find slight indications that this may be so. The feeling in nearly everyone I meet is that changes in a big way are necessary.

Friday, 10 May

Germany has invaded Holland and Belgium. Has it begun at last this war?

I have just heard from Canada: The Geographical Soc has accepted my article on Malta for their journal. They cannot publish it before 1941. But the relief and exultation!

9 p.m. I think Chamberlain is magnificent – magnificent! And I'm going to tell everyone I think so.

(War Diary)

Attacks have been made along the Western Front. The Whitsun holiday has been cancelled for all government workers. The paper this morning was full of Chamberlain's possible resignation. The withdrawal of our troops from Norway was a bitter surprise – it made Hitler's 'strategical blunder' into another masterstroke of strategy and we feel humiliated. What lies before us now? Is it coming at last, the terror we long since ceased to expect? Will Hitler reduce England to a small insular state, take away our colonies, gold, platinum, radium and 80 per cent of our merchant fleet, make Egypt into a German protectorate, 'free' India into an associated state with Germany, and so on and so on.

I have just heard Chamberlain broadcast his resignation. I think that was a magnificent gesture – not the broadcast, but his resignation at this moment. He might, under the present stress, so easily have patched things up and gone on under the same administration for a little longer. I believe he has always acted, in his own view, for the good of his country – beyond any personal advantage. He has proved it now.

Churchill has been appointed new Prime Minister.

My little cat chases butterflies on the lawn.

Wednesday, 15 May

Ethel came for the day. Such a sad, lonely little person now, it wrings my heart. It upsets me to see someone as nice as E. unhappy. Is there nothing I can do for her – short of offering to share my life with her, which somehow I cannot bring myself to do. She is so kind to me now, loves to refer to me in casual conversation to strangers as 'my daughter'.

Thursday, 16 May (War Diary)

Units of men between ages of 17–65 are being formed to protect coast towns and villages from parachute jumpers. They will wear uniform, carry arms, and receive training in their spare time, and be known as Local Defence Volunteers.[98]

Friday, 17 May

I have been racing through Barbellion's journal.[99] He uses words with fine, scientific clarity and an exquisite artistic sensibility. He writes much better than I do, yet he gives me courage that mine may be

---

98 Later to become the Home Guard (and later still Dad's Army).
99 W.N.P. Barbellion was the pseudonym of Bruce Frederick Cummings (1889–1919). *The Journal of a Disappointed Man*, printed initially with a preface by H.G. Wells, details his love of natural history and his battle with multiple sclerosis, and is regarded as a classic memoir. It remains in print.

read one day also. If I could be certain I should relax and be happy. Barbellion told his intimate friends about his journal, he discussed it with them, let his wife read it. Not one solitary person in the world knows of mine.

(War Diary)

In Germany it is reported an institute has recently been established for a two-year course for housewives, ending with an examination and the conferring of title 'Master Housewife'. This helps to give domestic activities the character of a profession which is publicly acknowledged and encouraged. Some sense in this. But as for its effect in Germany, see also 'The Position of Women Under Nazi Rule' talk published in the *Listener*, 16 May.[100]

Sunday, 19 May

Have spent the day at Whipsnade with Gus and Phyllis. We saw baby bears, peacocks, flamingos, black swans, three ugly black baboons in a very playful and entertaining mood, oh, and the tigers and the lions and the polar bears, the elephants, the wolves and the little free wallabies, and all manner of other interesting creatures, high on the North Downs. Then drove back through a countryside so rich in young greens, May blossom, lilac, laburnum and all the pageant of early summer.

Tuesday, 21 May (War Diary)

Went today to see Joan in Hampstead. She thinks London will be safer than the coast and is going to bring her son Geoffrey back from Bournemouth.

---

100 This article was by three women: A.F. Cunningham, a Mrs Hardinge, and 'Lisl'. It argued convincingly that the position of women under Nazi rule was increasingly inferior compared to the Weimar Republic, with little influence over social issues, much less political ones.

Wednesday, 22 May

Germans have reached Amiens. I have housework to do, I have letters to write, books to read, but I can settle to none of them. All I can think of is: the Germans are coming, the Germans are coming. They have got everything so far they have planned to get. Something is rotten in our state and in our armies. Each time we are taken by surprise. God, let me live to help build a new and real democracy, or let me die . . .

Tuesday, 28 May

The Belgian army has capitulated.

I have just returned from taking Ginger Tom to see a vet in Slough. He has strained a ligament in one of his hind legs, and must be made to rest as much as possible. The vet is a big, fair, good-looking man of about 40. He is physically rather attractive, but I affect not to notice it when in his surgery. He handles animals firmly and efficiently and speaks to them kindly. Something a little cynical in his manner: 'These fussy women – how gladly they part with 2s. 6d. for their pets.'

(War Diary)

I don't think I shall be able to keep out of this war much longer. I begin to see what I must do, but God I do not want to do it. I must join the Civil Nursing Reserve. I cycled through the woods this morning trying to think it out. Perhaps I shan't have to go – shall I wait a little longer? But isn't that just what we have all been doing, hoping. And now we and the French are alone against the Nazis in Europe, and they are on our doorstep.

Wednesday, 29 May

On the bus back to Farnham Common from High Wycombe I saw that they hold a course for architects in the evenings, beginning in September. I began to think: would it not be a good thing to ask for more details and see if I could work again for the Intermediate RIBA?

This would give support to my architectural journalism efforts – a qualified person has more authority in writing.

Afterwards, alone in the cottage, I continued this conversation with myself: 'I should like to join the Civil Nursing Reserve, but I cannot leave this place unless I can find someone to look after it for me.' I thought of Ethel. I thought that this is just what she would love to do. I am still weeping. I do not want to do it.

Thursday, 30 May
The British Expeditionary Force cut off in Flanders is fighting its way to Dunkirk on the coast where communications are still open and ships are bringing supplies. Attacks are being made from the Channel by the French Navy and RAF.

'Sensible People' are to be nominated in every district to act as guides, under the authority of the Ministry of Information, to kill false rumours and circulate information in the event of a breakdown of ordinary communications.

Friday, 31 May
With the cooperation of the Allied Air Forces, the navies have carried supplies to the rearguard in the Flanders wedge and evacuated the first contingent of BEF, French and Belgian troops. A defeat has been turned into a great achievement. But how soon the Germans will turn towards Paris or attempt the invasion of England no one can say.

All signposts on the roads of Britain are being taken down. Saw some on a lorry by the Common this afternoon.

Saturday, 1 June (War Diary)
The evacuation of troops from Dunkirk continues. An epic.

Malcolm MacDonald urges the immediate evacuation of children from the East and SE coasts – Government consider raids imminent.

Monday, 3 June (War Diary)

Fanny tells me that a local man, one of the BEF, just returned from Flanders saying that the papers do not exaggerate. Germans bomb the wounded; he saw them. It was hell let loose. They had to run – how they had to run! – and he a man of 50 who had served in the last war. Troops were crossing in all kinds of craft – little fishing boats, motor boats, anything. The Admiralty has issued a statement describing how these were summoned and how they responded. What a magnificent achievement.

We hear the sound of guns on still days. I thought it was practice somewhere near but I am told it is the guns of Flanders. This is no longer considered a 'safe' area. They fear for the trading estate and are taking all precautions. The LDV is on duty in shifts the whole time.

A story is going round the village of a caretaker cleaning in a church one evening. A clergyman came in, said he was tired and wanted to rest. The caretaker went on with her work and left, but for some reason returned and heard a lot of noise in the belfry. She went for assistance and they discovered the 'clergyman' with wireless set transmitting messages to the enemy.

Friday, 7 June

London was calm. There are more sandbags and shelters. The sky was sprinkled with barrage balloons. But the daily life of the city seemed terrifyingly normal. I lay in bed in the morning listening to the footsteps of early workers in South Hill Park, the leisurely progress of a milk cart. The West End was not crowded but was by no means empty. Women shopped as usual. June sunshine had brought out a crop of light frocks, white hats, sunglasses. Strawberries were on sale. The weather is perfect.

Saturday, 8 June (War Diary)

Germans have launched a furious attack on the Somme but we are holding them back. On the outcome of this battle, says the *New Statesman*, the future depends.

These are days of most appalling tension. One lives from hour to hour. Raiders are over the South and East coasts nightly but no serious damage or casualties have been reported. When I was in London I heard of people in Deal who say the town is barricaded and wound with barbed wire like nothing in their knowledge. Their house shakes nightly. All townsmen who can have left. Troops are in possession.

Ethel and Aunt Maggie have Belgian refugees. I met them – a master plumber and his wife, homely, pleasant folk. Ethel said that when they arrived they were in a terrible state. He burst into tears. They left two sons in Belgium, one recently married, a gendarme, but they have no news of them. They think their home and business are gone. They help in the house. They speak very little English but he speaks French. He told someone he was so glad that this house was clean, a point we overlook: while we fear 'dirty' refugees (I remember stories from the last war), we forget there are decent folk among them who may fall into bad billets. The couple were refugees in the last war (think of it – twice in a lifetime!).

Sunday, 9 June

The heat seeps down. It is as hot as it ever was in Malta. I was up before 7 a.m. and gardened for three hours in the coolness of early morning. The *Listener*, the *Sunday Times* and a Pelican edition of George Moore's *Confessions of a Young Man* curl in the sun.

My championship of Chamberlain is short lived. I have not studied politics long enough to realise the extent and enormity of his crimes . . . Scarcely anyone but Fascists have a good word for him now. In fact, one is suspected of Fascist tendencies if one says anything for him.

Monday, 10 June

Italy has declared war on us. Land of colour and enchantment! Now my brother and his family in Suez are cut off from me. Malta is a little besieged island, a lonely fortress in the Italian sea. Slowly the ground crumbles around me at the march of Fascist armies.

Tuesday, 11 June

Two children got off the bus with me this morning and followed me along the narrow footpath towards home. A little boy and a little girl – he possibly 9 and she 7 or 8. Presently they overtook me and we began to talk. They were returning from school, the Dair House School in the village. Did I know where they lived? No. 'Shall I tell you? In that big white new house just round the corner. You wouldn't think from the outside that it was a very big house would you?' said the boy. 'But it is. It has 13 bedrooms.'

It is a modern, reinforced concrete house, whitewashed, with flat roof and flush doors which I have noticed with interest. I had been told that it was the work of a young architect but did not know who.[101] I find that he is the father of these children. 'But he's in the army now,' said the little boy. They chattered on. 'Do you know my mummy?' asked the girl. 'I'll tell you her name and I'll tell you ours. I'm Janet and he's Richard . . .'

Thursday, 13 June (War Diary)

Paris is becoming a deserted city. A great tide of humanity is fleeing towards the West.

All Church and Chapel bells are to be used now only to notify the arrival of parachute troops.

Friday, 14 June

Because of the food shortage all dogs in Germany are to be killed.

Sunday, 16 June

---

101 Their father was the architect Valentine Harding. Jean was to become good friends with his wife Peggy.

A depression of such blackness envelops me. I hardly know how to write about it. The Germans are in Paris.

I have been reading A.A. Milne's Pooh stories. Beloved little animals in the forest – our foolish, childish, blundering selves . . .

The Germans will not gain control of France and leave us untouched.

Monday, 17 June
I have met Janet and Robert again. Their father has been killed in Belgium.

17.

Gas-Filled Cell

Thursday, 20 June 1940 (aged thirty)
We wait. We wait interminably for the word of the Dictators. I hope there will be a place and work for me in the new order. I hope I shall be able to preserve my journals and my books. I only want to keep my journals because of the conceit I hold that they will be of interest and use to posterity.

Friday, 21 June (War Diary)
Still alone waiting for news. French plenipotentiaries have met German and been handed peace terms which have not yet been published. So far there have been no alerts near here or London. Neighbour Mrs C. has just told me that if there is a raid here I may go and sit with them, which is very sweet of her.

Our turn will come. I MUST do something. The *New Statesman* this week points to the millions of men and women who if invasion comes will find themselves useless civilians. We have not been organised or called upon. I suppose it is left for us to volunteer but it should be made more constructively possible for us to do so. There should be some urgency and appeal about it.

Am reading Maugham's *Of Human Bondage*.

Monday, 24 June
The stocks smell heavenly tonight. The terms to France are monstrous

but nothing less than one expected. Germany is to occupy all the Channel and Western coasts, the whole of Northern France and territory from Tours to the Pyrenees. At cessation of hostilities all artillery, tanks and weapons to be surrendered and the armed forces to be demobilised. French fleet to return or be interned. Everything in fact is to be done to aid Germany in the war against us. Italian terms are yet to come. I think that the war is over. We cannot withstand them for very long.

Tuesday, 25 June

Last night we had our first air raid warning since last September. I woke at 4 a.m. to the 'all clear' warden's whistle. Tonight I am keyed up, excited, not at all depressed. Have a new filter fixed to my gas mask, have placed bucket of ashes and shovel by back door, filled the bath with water, have torch, gas mask, patience cards at hand and my clothes all ready to dive into.

Damage and casualties have been reported from east and south coasts and Midlands. One of the towns hit was near Cambridge I heard from the sweetshop man. I lay awake this morning listening to an early cuckoo and the receding All Clear sirens, picturing Wee Cottage on fire and the cats writhing under gas.

Hitler, I am told, is to be in London now by August the 18th.

Wednesday, 26 June

Another warning last night which I slept through until the all-clear sirens went.

Monica has made a summary of a sermon Graham Howe gave in St Martin's Church on the day of National Prayer (Hospital Sunday). He said that there is much more at stake than the matter of which side wins this war. If this war is not to end in utter waste it must be followed by a great spiritual revival. 'Then he swept away all the beloved props to which people cling so fiercely. We must not fix our hopes on a life beyond this – our business is to live *now*. Then he said that each of us should say to himself, "It all depends on me," and each one of us should act as if it did all depend on us."

Friday, 28 June

There has been little (comparatively) damage from air raids in Britain so far. But they will come. 'No one should be allowed to imagine,' writes the *New Statesman*, 'that the air raids that have come our way so far are more than reconnaissance and trial flights.'

I received a cable from Pooh in Suez. Mails home have been stopped temporarily, but the family is all right so far.

Tuesday, 2 July

Still nothing definite happens. Woman in antique shop in village today sounded panicky but prepared. Fanny told me of people she knew who had left coastal towns, their houses deserted and gardens planted with vegetables. The finest summer we have had for years, and instead of seaside resorts thronged with satisfied visitors – barbed wire and troops.

Sunday, 7 July (War Diary)

The war seems as fantastic and far away as ever. Successful air attacks by the RAF on enemy objectives continue. The Italians show up poorly as fighters.

I can still get as much good food as I need. London, except for the balloons and sandbags, ARP notices and black-out, seems as normal as ever. Shops are in full summer sale array. Went to the bank, the dressmaker, and attended a family lunch party. Bought new grey slacks at Peter Bobs. Bank manager said to me, 'They will never get London.'

There has been an improvement recently in BBC *Postscripts*, with another good one tonight by Priestley. This is a war between despair and hope. Nazism is an expression of despair, a death worship. People were watching the other night a brood of ducklings on Whitestone Pond in Hampstead. A symbol of hope.

Sunday, 14 July (War Diary)

A week of showers and cool wind, of chores and letters and ARP lectures, of garden and books and restlessness.

Tea is now rationed to 2ozs. Next week total allowance of butter and marg to be 7ozs. Green Line and country buses are to have women conductors. Bevin is to present a scheme for women, including the middle-classes, to relieve hard-pressed regulars in factories, and if this comes about I might volunteer. I have started the Home Nursing course and begin more First Aid on Monday.

The South Bucks anti-gas instructress is a terrifyingly efficient person. She is slim, trim and precise with a very upper-class manner. Her complexion is shocking – she looks as though she is worked to death. Some of our First Aid unit are going in for their anti-gas exam and were put through their gas drill the other night. When everyone's gas mask had been properly fitted and tested we were shepherded into a gas-filled cell. The masks are certainly good, even the civilian one I have that has been dumped and bumped about enough this past year and not once cleaned. We tested for gas, i.e. took a deep breath, thrust two fingers into the side of our mask and 'pecked' thrice. Eyeballs began to prick at once. Just before we came out we ripped off our masks and took a lungful – and rushed out weeping. It was a harmless experience.

Monday, 16 July

Am grateful for what I have now. I thank God sincerely for my cottage comforts, the garden, the cats, my books and food and clothes and health and the long, quiet nights. But how can I sit in my solitary peace writing 'The Confessions of an Old Maid' when the world is being shaken and shattered around me? I want to be in contact with life when the old order crumbles, I want to be in at death, part of suffering, growing humanity, not a dry isolated speck in security.

Sunday, 21 July

My Little Titch has been taken. A family came last night and took her away within 10 minutes. They were nice people and will look after her I know, but I have never wept at the loss of a pet as I have for her. She had inherited all Dinah's most attractive characteristics without Dinah's timidity. There was such sweetness to be drawn from her, and now she is no longer mine. Really it hurts.

Monday, 22 July (War Diary)
My first duty at the FAP last night.[102] The Point is in the gym of a boys' prep school on the edge of the Common. We sleep on camp beds which we have to erect and make with our stock blankets and of course clear away in the morning. I should have worn uniform but it had never occurred to me and no one had told me. Did not sleep very well but night was without incident. Returned home by 7 a.m.

Wednesday, 24 July (War Diary)
The new Budget: Income tax 8s. 6d.; 1d. per pint on beer; ½d. on ten cigarettes, 1½d. on 1oz tobacco. A tax on entertainments.

Saturday, 27 July
We are beginning to think now, 'Perhaps the threatened invasion will not take place, not perhaps immediately, perhaps never . . .' Hitler is evidently having to change his plans and he will have to hurry to be here by August 18th.

London Philharmonic Orchestra is to tour music halls instead of being disbanded as was feared through lack of financial support. This happened through the publicity given to the matter by Priestley and the *News Chronicle*, which roused Jack Hylton 'whose personal enthusiasms go far beyond dance music,' to act as sponsor. A curious situation, but results may be excellent.

---

102 The FAP stood, variously, for First Aid Post, First Aid Point and First Aid Party.

Military activity in and around the Beeches. Lorries parked. Troops marching.

Sunday, 28 July

This afternoon began to read John Strachey's *Why You Should Become a Socialist*, which I have had since 1938. These figures stick in my mind, and in my throat: approximately 90 per cent of the population earns £250 and under per annum, a large proportion of which are families of four living on £2 a week. 'With individual exceptions, the employing class cares nothing about the conditions which the existing economic system imposes upon the working class.' I'd say rather that the major part of the employing class (if he means the middle classes as a whole) *do not know* the conditions. They never come into contact with the real workers. Only by desultory reading have I become conscious of the magnitude of social inequalities and injustices. At one time I honestly and happily believed that the working classes were a minority of the total population.

The *Canadian Geographical Journal* is publishing my article in the August issue. Think of it – it must be in print and in circulation now!

Wednesday, 31 July

It is exciting to ride off late at night, through the dark woods and along the edge of the mist-hidden Common as mysterious as the sea, with bright beams of light searching for an aeroplane and a pale moon edging its way between low clouds. No signs of life. In nursing frock and apron with gas mask swinging from one's shoulder one feels original and important. But the night spent on a hard strange camp bed in the unfamiliar darkness is more oppressive than too many blankets. The pillow is bumpy and too low. One sleeps lightly, with one ear open. One turns and sighs, conscious of strange and vivid dreams, hearing one's companion stir in the next bed. An owl seems to be crooning all night on the doorstep. One wonders if daylight will ever dawn again.

Days are drawing in. I am not looking forward to the winter. I hope to have some coal sorted. But what will the food supply be like? The other night I had half of a steamed mackerel (3d.) with new potatoes (2d. or 3d. a lb), spinach from the garden, and parsley sauce made from lard, wholemeal flour, water and home-grown parsley, and stewed fruit and bread and butter. Black treacle, important for my health, is difficult to get but I have managed so far.

And then the long black nights, the awful business of blacking-out. For six weeks or more I've had to black out scarcely at all, simply by going to bed when it was dark and getting up early.

J.B. Priestley's broadcasts are excellent. I am astonished that the BBC allow them. He says insistently that this war is not to restore the old order, that we must not return to the old muddle and injustices. Already, he says, he has had letters telling him to get off the air before the government puts him where he belongs.

A film called *Grapes of Wrath* has just been released and has had startlingly good criticisms in every paper. It tells a story of American life that is not often mentioned, of unemployed and down-and-outs trekking across the Continent in search of work. There are no stars in the cast[103] – characters are all played by ordinary men and women. It is being shown at the Leicester Square Odeon.

Sunday, 18 August
I have been counting up the 'eligible' men I know.

1. Alan D. The innocence at 34 is astounding. Elis is quite sure that if he were married he wouldn't know how to have children. The sexual instinct seems entirely lacking.
2. Clinton G.F. Twice married and looking for a third wife. But has no attraction for me at all, nor have I for him. Just a silly little man.

---

103 Apart from Henry Fonda, who received an Oscar nomination for his portrayal of Tom Joad.

3. Ivor Brown, who lived in the Hampstead flat with me. An enigma. Too timid. Did not appeal.
4. Mr Ratcliff, who was a neighbour last year and now lives in large, gloomy house on the Common with his old mother. A cruel and mean nature, altogether twisted and undesirable.
5. Hugh L. – now in Palestine. A problem I couldn't tackle. I could only have him because N. didn't want him. Hugh would be difficult – I could never trust him.
6. Psychologist Jennings W. Again no appeal.
7. D. Mitchell. Poet and scholar who lives in Hampstead. I might find him attractive but I know by instinct he has got himself into a comfortable middle-aged groove and doesn't want to be disturbed out of it. No desire in him for a wife, and considers himself over and well out of the passionate stage.

Wednesday, 21 August (War Diary)
Ethel and Aunt Maggie have evacuee mother and two children from Southend. Mother is bone-lazy and has no control over small boy aged 2. His hands perpetually sticky. Loves coal, dustbin and drain. Mother does minimum of housework. Baby lies in pram on pillow always wet. Stories of other evacuees in neighbourhood with disgusting habits. Our own people – it is shocking. And to think that the Belgians they housed (with a not too sanitary reputation from last war) were clean, industrious, grateful.

Troops in the Beeches today: they seem to come and picnic every midday and go off again. One day a machine gun in a lorry trained skywards just outside the cottages.

An astonishing growth of feeling towards a new order is manifest everywhere.

Sunday, 25 August 1940 (War Diary)
Yesterday I received a telegram from brother Pooh in the Suez to say that he and family were well but mails were badly delayed and he

wanted news. I cabled a message back and have today sent a letter. I parted with it with a pang of fear. What is to be its route, its adventures, and will it ever arrive at its destination?

It is sometimes difficult to believe in this war. This afternoon it was so quiet in the garden. From the sultry sky came the sound of one far-off plane. Churchill has made another impressive speech this week. He is undoubtedly a figure in our history. Trotsky has been murdered in Mexico. Our belated account of recent air battles has impressed America who had been given the impression by swift German reports of a shattered and demoralised Britain.

Animals must be suffering more than we are from this war. Proper food for them is difficult to get. Ginger Tom has been looking wretched for weeks, and in desperation at the sores around his head and his thinness I took him to the vet yesterday. I was told he was not being fed adequately. He needs quantities of raw, red meat. Raw, red meat. I wheedled some pieces from the butcher but he told me we were liable to two years' imprisonment! I wonder what Lady S. does for her Alsatian.

Monday, 26 August
This weekend London has been raided. The enemy has changed his tactics from mass attacks to small formations and single bombers. We are warned to expect raids nightly now. So far near here we have heard little noise, only the noise of aeroplanes and distant thuds. Bombs fell at Datchett, only a few miles from here, and Chertsey. The Devereuxs propose taking me with them to Stratford this weekend to see some Shakespeare.

My home nursing exam is on the 6th. I am in a twitter this evening, having asked my commandant to tea. I don't know whether this is 'done', whether I'm not being too impulsive. She has been so kind and is now offering to coach me for the exam.

Sunday, 1 September
We saw *Measure for Measure* at the Shakespeare Theatre. We sat by

the river on Saturday morning and I practised home nursing bandages. When they slept here on Friday night, Elsie said that the noise of gunfire and bombs that she heard was worse than it had been in London, although they have been spending every night in basement shelters. I seem to sleep through everything and will only wake I suspect when a bomb falls in the garden.

Monday, 9 September

Raids over London are incessant and of increasing intensity. Damage and death over the docks and East End have been terrible. But Hitler won't win. Rash perhaps to prophesise, but I believe I can feel a spirit awake and moving among our people. We will not be subdued. We will have a better world. Confound German arrogance. Damnation to them who machine-gun our women and children, and they do. Only last week a hundred or more factory girls were killed in this way during their lunch-hour at Weybridge. There are people in the village who once knew the dead. One girl escaped by diving under a hedge.

We have had our adventures too. Bombs at Burnham and Farnham Royal. Cows killed and property damaged. German planes are over every night. The cottage has been shaken by explosions. Shrapnel has fallen over the village.

Life goes on. That is what amazes and thrills me. In spite of this increasing terror and destruction over London and the constant rumours of invasion, we get our food, our papers and letters. Buses and trains run fairly well to time. Work in factories and offices and shops continues. I have a great feeling that this is the death and birth of ages . . . the old order passing . . . and life in fire from the sky descending.

Thursday, 12 September

Raids on London every night. Homes destroyed, death to hundreds. The city in flames. One can not imagine it. Joan writes that the fires seen from Parliament Hill 'have been terrible but oh so beautiful. Bombs have fallen near Haverstock Hill, noise has been shattering, but somehow I don't mind half so much as I thought I would before it all began, and there is something almost exhilarating about people's new comradelyness.'

It makes me wish I could be with them. There is something in the Britisher when his life, his heritage or whatever is threatened which refuses to be beaten. That's my feeling now. Damn those arrogant Germans who think they can destroy our beloved city and cripple our spirit! We are not as effete and inefficient and rotten as Nazi propaganda has made out. I think the Nazis have miscalculated – they do not understand British psychology. I don't think anyone does, least of all ourselves. Are we downhearted? Never! I am thrilled to be here, a Britisher in England. I am willing, ready and waiting to take my place in the fighting line.

9 p.m. News: Bombs have fallen on Mme Tussauds, Regent Street and on some newspaper offices.

10.30 p.m. Local sirens have just wailed their dread warning. Usually when that happens a deep silence follows. But a thought: German resources must be great, perhaps greater than we are being led to believe. Suppose the Nazis do go on and on attacking – really, how long can our little island stand it? My thoughts touch on these things repeatedly, particularly when the sirens wail at night. When all communications with the capital are broken and war civil defence services worked to exhaustion (I in my place with the Red Cross) – then and only then shall I grow a little discouraged and afraid.

Bless me, if that isn't the all-clear!

Monday, 23 September (War Diary)
How endless this war seems. On neither side are resources or courage exhausted or full force of attack released. Destruction in London terrible: churches, hospitals, schools, Buckingham Palace, big stores in Oxford Street, Regent Street and the Strand have been hit. Raiders creep through

singly at night and do this damage. Mass raids in the daytime are a conspicuous failure. 187 enemy planes shot down a week ago.

I have heard of several cases of lynching of fallen Nazi airmen. This seems to me barbaric, horrible in the extreme. Last week a ship carrying evacuee children to Canada was torpedoed and many children and adults drowned in a stormy sea at night.

Wednesday, 2 October

Constance Oliver was killed when a bomb hit a house she was visiting in Adelaide Road in Swiss Cottage a fortnight ago.[104] She was visiting friends two doors from her own house. A direct hit. Her own house was untouched. This news brought the war into sharper perspective.

London, one hears, is a shambles. A friend of Lady Spicer's is driving an ambulance there. At night it is terrible, bomb craters in the road which they cannot see. No time to pick up the dead or give first aid to the wounded – all they can do is to move the living away from dangerous places as quickly as possible.

Tuesday, 8 October (War Diary)

Red Cross activities in abeyance, and I have withdrawn from duty at the Slough centre. There is never anything to do there, we never get any practice and the people bore me. Jean MacFarlane has just called to say the local Point is closed for the time being. There is infantile paralysis [polio] in the neighbourhood and the headmaster of the prep school where we had our Point has put the school in quarantine.

The sirens are going again. Wail upon wail. How agonising not to know can be.

Wednesday, 16 October

How quickly the year passes. October. Rain. Long nights. On Friday I shall be 31.

---

104 See past entries, 18 August 1935 and 27 August 1936.

Each time I go to London I am astonished at its indestructibility. One can walk down Regent Street in full October sunshine, buy a hat at Dickens and Jones, lunch at Lyons Corner House while sirens wail. Crowds throng the pavements, familiar traffic lines the roads. What is this talk of air raids, devastation, death, and crumbling empire? But we have heard of the massacre in the East End, people made homeless in a night, districts without water, gas rationed, and millions sleeping for safety in the stuffy bowels of London's underground. Nor does London alone suffer. East, west, north and south the raiders pass over our country, Bristol, Birmingham, Liverpool and Brighton. Last week a string of bombs fell across the Common, a land mine exploded in the Beeches not very far from the cottage, cracking one window pane. Our first war scar, of which we are very proud.

Monday, 28 October

We shall discover in time that history is made by people. It is not a series of reigns, battles, and party politics, but an unending story of events created by living people: people moved by emotions, ideals, passions . . .

We shall learn not that the Duke of Marlborough won the battle of Blenheim in 1704 and so saved Vienna from the Elector of Bavaria and the line of James II from being restored in England, but *why* this battle was fought. We shall ask questions back and back until we come to the motives that governed the actions of the people. We shall find them – the people, crippled with jealousy and greed and fear; we shall ask why and go seeking further.

I know that every record we now have – the treaties, the letters, the laws, the pictures, verse, books and songs, buildings, clothes, everything – each has its place in the pattern of time, and can be knit into one piece and solve many puzzles. A moving web leading always to tomorrow.

Thursday, 31 October

The winter is here. Yesterday I found the dahlia leaves blackened by frost. And I lifted and stored the tubers and cut the remaining flowers. What shall I be doing and feeling by the time those tubers bloom again? Shall I have a) found a husband, b) had a real love affair, c) written a book of fiction or a good short story for publication, or achieved all three? If I had a husband I could not be more content – only very surprised. I think I should die of astonishment.

Monday, 4 November

Heart of my heart! Six or seven bombs have just fallen it seemed outside my back door. I heard a plane and then zzzoom! . . . zzzoom! . . . zzzoom! . . . one after the other. I felt the ground shaking and dived for the table. We have had a land mine in the Beeches which cracked a sitting room window pane, and five or six bombs at Hedgerly Corner which destroyed two council houses. I heard the soldiers stationed in the woods shouting 'Lights! These people aren't blacked out at all!' It is not easy to keep a slither of light from showing now and then. The times I have pulled and tacked and padded my black-out. God, the silence now . . . and the darkness. In this quiet, withdrawn spot it is the unexpectedness of such an event that is so terrifying. I would rather be in a city and hear the barrage guns.

Saturday, 16 November

Gus and I were hanging out of the window of a top floor flat in Marylebone High Street from 1 to 3 o'clock in the morning. Plane followed plane over our heads and we got to know almost to the second when they would release their bombs. 'He's due to lay!' Jules would say. And down they would screech – to the right, to the left and far ahead of us. The awful noise of rent air: the scream of metal as it hit the waiting city: the explosion blast and shiver of the wounded earth – Heavens, what a night! Rooftops pallid in the light of a full moon, echoes of gunfire rolling along the still streets, shrapnel sweeping past our window like hailstones, and in the distance a carillon of fireballs, the horizon above the chimney pots coloured like the afterglow of sunset. We didn't know whether the next bomb would be ours but it didn't seem to matter.

I am home again after an exhausting journey. It is night and the planes are once more overhead, the guns in action. Last Monday afternoon a plane swooped out of the clouds just over a bus I was in on the outskirts of Slough and machine-gunned the road. The nights are very long.

Tuesday, 26 November

Joan is on the verge of having an affair with a conscientious objector. He objects to fighting in this war though he went to Spain because he believed in the cause of the Spanish people. He thinks we shall have Fascism here whether we win or lose, financial interests have such a hold upon our country and its institutions. He is prepared to go to prison for his convictions.

Monday, 2 December

I have written so much about Ethel in the past – before Daddy died – that it is worth saying here how she has changed. I don't know how deep it goes, but all her prickliness and hardness is much tempered. She is lost and unhappy but how much softer and more tolerant. The war has been making her think, ask questions, and want to discuss fundamentals she would never have considered as valid at one time. There no longer seems to be stiff disapproval in her of anything she doesn't understand or hasn't experienced. I must be more generous, and talk more and give more freely to Ethel.

Monday, 9 December

A pretty, fading widow serves at the Red Cross Canteen on Monday mornings. She came with the news that London had had another very bad night. 'Another Coventry,' the paper says . . . The screams of children under the debris . . . terrible! Hitler is a wicked man. There never has been a wickeder.

'I would like to hang, draw and quarter him . . . Really, if only I could get my hands on some of these Germans that come murdering our women and children! We *must* go on with this war. Did you see that six men in parliament had the nerve to propose making peace terms?'

The village hall is being used as the Canteen. Gas radiators have been installed, a long counter in front of the platform, and a sink and a gas cooker. They have pinned posters on the walls, a bookshelf is nailed along one short wall, there are little tables and chairs round the sides of the room, a ping-pong table, a gramophone, notepaper and periodicals. Soldiers come and go in a fairly steady stream. I like to study them, but if they find you staring they think you are making eyes at them. Most of them are very young.

Saturday, 28 December
Xmas is over. Monica, Nockie and me all crowded into Wee Cottage somehow – a wonderfully elastic cottage. Discussion of Monica's problems has been the principal topic.[105] I find this drama vastly interesting, but I am a little tired of playing spectator to other people's dramas.

Sunday, 12 January 1941
Nockie and I went to London on Friday – she to stay with Monica at Swiss Cottage and me to stay with Gus and Phyllis in their new flat in Gloucester Place. Jules and I worked most of the time on the novel, he as usual tearing my efforts to pieces.[106] But on Saturday afternoon when we went to see Bette Davis and Charles Boyer in *All this and Heaven Too* at the Warner in Leicester Square. The blitz began in the middle of it. A bomb fell somewhere near and the building rocked.[107] Not a soul stirred, there was scarcely even a murmur. When

---

105 She is pregnant; the father is absent.
106 Jean's new novel, inspired by her experiences with Ethel, was called *The Widow*.
107 Sometime later, Jean added: 'I think this was the bomb that wrecked Green Park Tube Station.'

we came out Gus said, 'I am not given to singing the praises of the British nation but when I see the way we can behave when something like that happens I begin to think we are not such a bad race after all. Abroad there would have been pandemonium.' Perhaps Londoners are used to these shocks by now and anyway only the type who can stick it are in town now, the rabbits have long since fled, as we in the country know. The excitable, panicky type of foreigner has left too. A visit to London is a tonic.

Gus and I walked back from Leicester Square to Gloucester Place. Guns were going at intervals but no shrapnel was falling in our direction. Fires lit the dusk to East and West of us. We could see one raging at the end of Bond Street from where we stood in Oxford Street.

Nockie and I were delighted to discover, quite by chance, Graham Howe beginning a series of broadcast talks under the name *Blueprint*. This seems to me very significant – I wonder how they will be received. Priestley's *Postscripts* have been published too. The world is stirring. There is hope for the future.

Monday, 13 January

Nockie and I have had an orgy of reading. John Hampden's *Great English Short Stories*. Maugham's *Altogether* and extracts from his *Gentlemen in the Parlour*. Some Hazlitt essays. John Steinbeck's *Red Pony*. *Richard II*. Around me now I have Clough Williams-Ellis' *Pleasure of Architecture*, J.M. Richards' *Introduction to Modern Architecture*, Ramsay Muir's *Future for Democracy*. Have finished *Idiot's Delight* and Shaw's *Major Barbara* and begun *John Bull's Other Island*. So much and so much. And so much more to read. One gets mental dyspepsia with it all.

Friday, 23 January

I want, I need a husband. That is so obvious it requires no more comment. Not *any* man: not any man that I now know; but a Chris or a Colin whom I've yet to meet. Thousands of other lonely frustrated females must be feeling the same way – why should I think that I am to be luckier? Because I intend to try to find one. One must tackle the problem positively, gather together one's assets, accept one's debits and go forth booted and spurred.

Assets: A fair share of good looks, physical attraction, generous nature and more poise than I once had. Subjects about which I know something and can use in work and conversation: architecture, literature, drama, people and certain places.

Debits: an agonising, thwarting knowledge of my deficiencies and general unworthiness; a confused, badly trained porous mind, a tendency to bolt into silence at the first advance of difficulty.

I must take them, my debits and assets, out into the world, into the battlefield . . . and there must I learn to fight. I may lose, but at least I shall know I have tried while there is still a chance of winning.

Saturday, 31 January (War Diary)

There has been a sinister lull in enemy attacks on this country since Xmas. Except for the fire blitz on London and short concentrated raids on Cardiff, Portsmouth, Plymouth and Southampton, our nights have been so quiet 'you could hear a bomb drop' as David Low told America.[108]

We are not starving, we are not even underfed, but our usually well-stocked food shops have an empty and anxious air. Cheese, eggs, onions, oranges, luxury fruits and vegetables are practically unobtainable. The fruit shops fill their windows with tinned goods and expensive spring flowers. Housewives are having to queue for essential foods. We live on potatoes, carrots, sprouts, swedes, turnips, artichokes and watercress. We are encouraged to use oatmeal to help out the meat ration which was cut at the beginning of the month and now includes all the offal we could once buy without coupons. Cigarettes and sweets are difficult to get though not impossible if one has time

---

108 Low was a political cartoonist on the *Evening Standard*.

and patience to search the shops. We are warned by statesmen repeatedly that Hitler intends to invade us if he can when the weather improves. Our men are still called up in large numbers. Those under 19 and over 36 and women from 18 to 23 are to register soon.

J.B. Priestley is our spokesman. He has become the representative of British Everyman. I am continually astonished at his popularity. He has even impressed some of my most conservative relatives. He voices the opinions and hope of millions – plainly and with understanding, as one thoughtful man to another. It will come, our better world, though through how much more pain it is impossible to say.

18.

The Big Moment Passionate

Tuesday, 11 February 1941

Re-reading Katharine Mansfield's journal. Did all artists and intellectuals ignore the last war as she seems to? According to her journal it means nothing to her. She stands aloof from it, accepting it as she might an earthquake that affects her only indirectly, something in which she has no responsibility and no part although she suffers because of it. This was the dangerous attitude to politics we inherited, and is partly why we are at war again. When feeling came to be regarded as improper, the artist was ostracised from society, being forced to live in such unhappy isolation – although his vision might have saved it had it listened.

Churchill made his most heartening broadcast of the war on Sunday.[109] Even the weather cheered up. He is a magnificent war leader. He spoke of invasion as still a grave possibility for which we must all be prepared. I could endure invasion, parachute troops, more bombardment, even mild gas attacks, so long as I do not get caught and detained in London, or am ordered to leave the cottage. Dreadful

---

109 This was Churchill's first address to the nation for five months. His speech closed with the words he said he would offer President Roosevelt: 'Put your confidence in us. Give us your faith and your blessing, and under Providence all will be well. We shall not fail or falter; we shall not weaken or tire. Neither the sudden shock of battle nor the long-drawn trials of vigilance and exertion will wear us down. Give us the tools and we will finish the job.'

pictures of a sudden evacuation haunt me. The cottage desolate, the cats crying for good and affection, or gasping their poor last under gas with no one by to help. What is one to do for animals in a gas attack? Instructions for ourselves are vague enough.

I will try to write a description of this house I love so much. There is a road that runs from Farnham Common parallel to the main Beaconsfield–Slough route. It runs through an avenue of old spread beech trees, birch and some sapling oak, and is, roughly, the east boundary to a carefully tended stretch of woodland known as Burnham Beeches. Half way along, as it runs from the Common, it curves round a triangular clearing and there stands a group of redbrick farm cottages converted with restraint into clean, comfortable middle-class homes.

When the cottages were the homes of farm labourers, Wee Cottage was a stable. In Wee Cottage a young woman lives alone, except for a couple of cats to whom she may often be heard talking in tones of deepest affection. Her neighbours see and know little of her. She has frequent women visitors to stay with her for long intervals; men have been seen to come and go during the day, but not many and not often. The sound of a typewriter can be heard when alone. She is seen sometimes going off on her bicycle to the village and returning with the basket laden. She doesn't dress particularly well or carefully and nearly always wears rather shabby trousers, except when she goes off with a small suitcase for a few days when she puts on a skirt and high heels and appears to have taken a little more trouble with her toilet.

She never tells her neighbours where she goes on these occasions, yet it is generally known that she visits London. The trades people find her easy to deal with and fairly prompt in paying her bills. One of the village women 'does' for her one morning a week and reports no scandal whatever – only that she is a writer, has many friends, is not too fussy about the house, 'though mind you it's never dirty.' She has some nice pieces of furniture and pretty cushions and lots of books, pays well, is interested in what goes on in the village but is never what you might call malicious.

Monday, 17 February (War Diary)

Although I adore the country and have the greatest difficulty in uprooting myself from the cottage, London casts a spell upon me as soon as I reach its straggling boundaries.

Going round the City I have realised that report and rumour exaggerate bomb damage grossly. If we are ever to have a better capital, I fear that a drastic number of more bombs must fall. There are of course many buildings and street corners in ruins – heaps of rubble and twisted, rusty girders, but life goes on as though these ruins had been there for years. Water supply, lighting, bus and train services, telephones, cafes – all are functioning again. Business continues at the Guildhall which was said to have been destroyed completely. The workers stream out for lunch at midday, passing, as usual, with dull eyes the churches Wren built. It is a lost city. A square mile of tortuous streets which the hand of trade has choked with its monstrous offices.

Not long ago a doctor broadcast on 'suburban neurosis' from which many women who have worked in such offices suffer after they have married and settled down in an instalment-paid villa. After a while, he said, they found life in these cheap housing estates unbearably dreary; they had no interests beyond the meagre limits of their home; through shyness or snobbery they 'kept themselves to themselves'. They would not go to the local pub and there were no clubs; but the war had at least opened up for them new ways of living, given them new interests, a new sense of comradeship with their previously ignored neighbours.

Meanwhile it freezes and thaws and the sun grows warmer. Yellow crocuses are out on the rockery. The Army which had possessed our woods all the winter is now wiring them in. Huge lorries, like futuristic elephants are parked right to the edges. The air is poisoned with the smell of heavy engine oil (I realise now what make me seasick). The soft ground is torn by heavy tires. Lady Spicer who has a permit to walk her dog through the woods daily says there is no joy in it.

We did not know how well off we were before the war.

Monday, 24 February

A letter came from D.F. today asking me to meet him one day this week.[110] 'Dear Miss Jean Pratt.' I am flattered to the marrow by the unconcealed eagerness in the letter to visit the damaged churches with me. This promises to be a situation in which I must summon courage to keep my balance, and get what I hope to from it. So wildly does my imagination run.

Tuesday, 4 March

Yes, dear Reader, I went City 'site'-seeing with D.F. He wore a hideous cap and his nails were filthy. But he has charming manners. His enthusiasm for the old buildings is inspiring, and he seems to be a very conscientious worker. I have no 'feelings' about him at all. Beyond our one mutual interest is a blank. I cannot imagine myself getting any further and don't really want to. We are still Miss Pratt and Mr F. to each other in letters, which is painfully stiff, but in conversation we avoid calling each other by any name. My dread is that he'll start prodding.

Sunday, 9 March

I have just had the most glorious idea. How ever did it originate? Perhaps partly from last week's brooding on my past sex failures, and then from wondering what the brothels were like in foreign parts where our Services are stationed. But here it is. The brothel becomes in future a recognised institution for the instruction of the young in the arts and crafts of lovemaking! Nothing smutty or forbidden about it, but part of our educational system where female adolescents could go to learn how to make the best of themselves – attention to physical

---

110 This is a strange start to the record of a significant relationship. There are no clues as to who 'D.F.' is, at least not at this stage, although he is clearly keen on architecture, and the pair have evidently been writing to each other. Later we will learn that his first name is Francis, and that he is not the most glamorous of men. But he is available, and, after an initial reluctance, Jean plans to take full advantage.

health, use of cosmetics, elements of dressing well, and full instruction on all matter of sex, including a course on the bearing and rearing of children and possibly other domestic matters.

But the whole point being to apply this theory in practice – all its young students to be given every opportunity of meeting the opposite sex and forming alliances as they are inclined. Experimenting as much as they like, marrying if they want to or 'living in sin' if they want to. Competent adults – doctors, psychologists, nurses and experts of all kinds to be in control, to give guidance and advice when needed. What a healthy improvement it would be. And for those who want to lead a completely domestic life, an opportunity to learn methods of birth control and how-to-keep-one's-husband and so forth. I think it's a magnificent idea.

Monday, 10 March

Last night wrote a moving 'last letter' to Ethel, who, poor darling, would have the fearful task of sorting and clearing up my possessions. I was so overcome by the end of it I felt I had already died, and decided I must make a 'last entry' in here too. I was so fascinated by the spectacle of scenes in the cottage after my decease I could not sleep for hours. Today I feel very alive.

Tuesday, March 18

A growing feeling of optimism. Lady Spicer thinks it will all be over by the autumn. She was given an onion yesterday for her birthday. Her cook flavoured bread sauce with it and then used it for something else.

Monday, 21 April

Are we really going to lose this war? The Nazis sweep from triumph to triumph making no mistakes while we make all the mistakes.

'I would rather die than live under Nazi rule,' says Nockie. Nockie said that someone had read in her teacup that she was to be left some money through the death of a friend. Hope that's not me. I don't want to die at all, just as I seem to be getting a grip of living. Besides, these journals are not ready, are not finished. Death, yes, in its appointed time, but not now. God alone knows what the living will be called upon to endure these next few years. Planes overhead again tonight.

Tuesday, 22 April

Mental torture. 1) Will he get the letter before he leaves for work tomorrow morning and phone me in the evening? 2) Will there be a blitz on London on Thursday night and 83 be bombed? 3) Will all this torment bring on a period? 4) Shall I really be able to cope with the situation so that there are no 'consequences'? 5) Perhaps he will be engaged on Thursday? 6) Perhaps it won't be as tremendous as it promises to be? 7) Perhaps I'll suffer the whale of a reaction and never want to go near him again?

I've never felt less romantic about anyone in my life. It is very naughty of me. But it's too strong for me – if it doesn't happen this week, it will the next time we meet, so I must be ready. Leaden, leaden hours.[111]

Wednesday, 23 April

He phoned last night without having had my letter, and the fever suddenly subsided. I am a little horrified now at what I am about to do – but not much. It's too late to retract, and I should be happy to have to, now that I have made up my mind. It's something I cannot resist.

Thursday, 24 April

Again, last night, he phoned, having had my letter. He really is the nicest person. 'Oh, this can't be love, I feel so well!'

---

111 'F', whom we can only assume was recently 'D.F', has taken the room Jean once rented in Hampstead (83 South Hill Park), the location for most of their trysts. We do not know what her letter proposes. In another entry she says she is reading a play he has written, but she is not impressed. We only learn more of his identity after a year.

I'm in a strange, golden haze of anticipation, waiting for a door long-closed to open for me.

Monday, 28 April

Churchill's speech last night – well, everyone at the Canteen this morning pronounced it excellent so I suppose it was. But the division of aims among our own people and our maddening inefficiency threaten, I think, to lose us the war. There are people who want a new social order, but not Hitler's. There are the powerful sets, apparently in control of the war and trying to preserve 'democracy' for their own ends. The confusion is terrible. Germany solves it at the moment by liquidating all opposition to its one ideal, ruthlessly. It is not the right way, but it is, or appears to be, the quickest.

Sunday, 11 May

Time waits. The sun shines in a pale sky. Clear bird notes fall through the quiet woodland. Leaves and branches are moved by a light, cool current of air. The clock is now two hours ahead of the sun and spring is a month behind.

A bad blitz on London again last night, much damage done and casualties feared heavy. One's heart tightens with anxiety for friends one knows who were there. One cannot grieve any longer for all the wounded and bereaved, there are too many, inevitably.

Tuesday, 13 May

Rudolf Hess, Nazi Party leader and Hitler's deputy, has flown in an ME110 from Augsburg and landed by parachute on farmland in Scotland, without arms or ammunition and is now somewhere in GB recovering from a broken ankle. If this is true, if the man is sane, if it is not part of some deep laid Nazi plot, the implications are tremendous . . . and the romance of it! It is the best piece of news we have been given for months.

Shall I or shall I not record something of the incredible adventure I seemed to be facing on Sunday April 20? I have refrained, I think, purely from vanity; I wanted to wait until I could state here that I AM NO LONGER A VIRGIN. But I still am, and the situation seems to have reached a rather dreary dead-end. What is interesting is that I have no qualm of conscience about the matter. Ought I to lose my chastity by this particularly unspectacular and neurotic little man with whom I am not in love (nor is he with me)? The difficulty is that he finds more satisfaction in imagining – with great vividness and in powerful Laurentian detail – his love affairs, than in participating in them actually. For me he was my first real potential lover; I thought I was to be initiated at last. It was largely my own fault that I wasn't, yet I know it wouldn't have been a success that night.

I have at least learnt more of the practical details of love making – much more. Layers of sentimentality about LUVE have peeled off. And I begin to think that so many DUVs (Dried Up Virgins) are so because they have lacked knowledge of these very practical, unromantic details (how and when to insert pessaries for example, what kind to use, whether and how to use a douche and so on), when their virtue and conventions were challenged, and having no friend they could trust for the information, as I have had in Nockie. (She has behaved magnificently, been my guide throughout the whole affair.) If I had known as much six years ago I might even be married by now, and successfully married. Now I feel: I am over 30, what the devil is the good of my chastity to me any longer? I have enough experience and resources in other spheres to pull me through any severe emotional crisis, and I want, most passionately, to have *this* experience. Though it seems now that I shan't with this man. But I don't mind. I am without shame.

Tuesday, 27 May
HMS *Hood* has been destroyed and intense fighting between British and German forces is going on in Crete. The whole Mediterranean

situation seems to depend on the outcome of this battle – the destiny of Suez is being decided.

But I am enveloped in my own affairs. My period is two days late, and although I have no cause at all for alarm, I am alarmed.

Wednesday, 28 May

How big little moments can sometimes seem. Ethel has just left. I saw her off at Beaconsfield and have just returned to a mournfully empty cottage. Am in a suicidal mood today. Everything seems to be going wrong and I don't know what to do. Had better read some Graham Howe. Want to sink into a comfortable coma and emerge to find all the kinks and mountains removed. I hate the feeling of restriction when people are here with me and hate the emptiness when they are gone, as though with them have gone opportunities I didn't use, things I never saw or understood that I should and could have understood. Like having a book in my possession that I didn't bother to read properly.

10 p.m. Period is now over three days late. If conception can take place without that man's organ being inserted into the vagina and without the woman being conscious of the passage of anything between them although the organs are in contact, then nature's ways are incredible. I don't believe it is possible, I won't believe it . . . All the same I shall not rest until I *know*. I have a plan of action.

Sunday, 1 June

False alarm, thank goodness. But I didn't know until I had sent an express letter to Nockie on Thursday. How she will laugh. Incapacitated as I was, I am still a virgin, but unless fate interferes with our third set of arrangements, I shan't be this time next week. Oh God, if I am to burn for this, as St Paul threatens me, then I'll burn. For this is desire without love. I can't help it and I don't care. 'Finlandier!' said Joan at the Odeon on Saturday when Sibelius was being played. She looked at me and F. beside her – 'Philanderess!'

I wish I understood the situation. An irresistible, physical attraction between a hungry, passionate virgin and an oversexed, neurotic, incomprehensible man.

We have lost the battle of Crete with very heavy losses. Clothes are to be rationed.

Tuesday, 3 June

For *five* weeks this ad has been appearing in the *Architects' Journal*: 'Vacancy exists for woman architect or architectural student on the editorial staff of an architectural publication. Candidates must be able to write easily and well. An interest in the presentation of buildings illustrated in architectural journals and general knowledge of our current events in the profession and building industry are also desirable.' The last one appeared on May 22nd and I have to see it *now*. I could kill myself, am weeping wildly. I have written, but it's too late, I know it's too late. What a lesson for me. To think that I have had all those ruddy journals in the house and had not bothered to look at the adverts, which I did do regularly at one time. What came over me? It's as though they were trying and trying to get hold of me. Am frantic. There'll never be another opportunity like that. I, and I alone, am to blame.

Sunday, 8 June

Now I can record it – the death of an Old Maid. But whether I've the energy to write more at present I don't know. The experience has been Pleasant and Unpleasant, and I am now exhausted. I don't regret the experience one atom. But I think there is something wrong with me physically. He, obviously, wore himself out with anticipation – those long, incredibly detailed letters, that emphasis to 'working up' to the crisis, his anxiety that I should be properly thrilled. Have I fallen into that trap again – of wanting too much, too quickly?

There was I, 31 and a virgin and likely to remain so unless I grabbed at the very next opportunity – which turned out most surprisingly to be F. Vanity thy name is Jean Pratt. Let things drift a bit now. He gets hugely worked up at the thought of me and when he kisses me, but fails to get me into a sufficiently responsive state for the big moment. I've been over-anxious too, and immodestly frank to him about my desire – gave him no reason to doubt my intentions, no thrill of pursuit.

I am a little worried as to how much the neighbours have over-heard! He has a peculiarly penetrating voice and talks about love-making with almost as much restraint as he writes of it in his letters. One story he told me I enjoyed immensely. It was written by Alec Waugh. A young girl after the first experience remarked, 'Well, if that's Divine Love it's given me a pain in the stomach.' Which is exactly how I feel.

Monday, 9 June

F. phoned tonight and reminded me of it. When he had played with me in the French manner (too long I think) to work me up to the Crisis, the Big Moment Passionate and so on, I left him to make my preparations and then lay back on the bed and said in a sepulchral voice, 'Now I'm ready for the worst!' Well, it was damned painful, though I didn't know it was going to be.

I have quite recovered from my pain in the stomach and am in a rare good humour, have been all day. It is such a relief to feel one is no longer completely ignorant.

19.

Francis

Friday, 13 June 1941 (aged thirty-one)

Too much lovemaking in one week, and I as cold as a fish last night, so cold I thought I was sprouting fins. Perhaps there is something wrong with me, or is it because we are in love only physically? I feel now that I shall never feel amorous again. I was *faint* with desire not so many weeks ago, and now, unsatisfied, there is not a spasm of desire in me.

Saturday, 14 June

Received this morning a timely reminder from Nockie about using the word fuck. It has sunk, she says, very low in the social scale and reveals F's attitude to sex.

I am now going to analyse F. ruthlessly. He is slight, about the same height as myself, no, taller, but his thinness makes him seem smaller. His face and features are long and sharp, his mouth small, vicious, his eyes and hair dark. His hair is wearing thin at the back of his head and grows thickly above his temples and is apt to stand out wildly when blown or rumpled. He has ugly hands. He has now a wizened, shrivelled appearance, but not without the suggestion of having once possessed lean good looks in a romantic, poetic fashion. He must be 40 years of age or more.

As a companion he is exhausting, irritating. He likes to call himself highly strung but I think he is badly neurotic. (He bolts his food, rarely stops to look at anything, never sits still, never listens to one speaking for long.) He is maddeningly dogmatic about everything and morbidly absorbed with sex once you have passed the barriers of communication with him.

I have drawn him thus darkly, as darkly as I can, deliberately. For on the other hand he has a sense of humour, some tolerance, sympathy, gentleness. His instinct for cultural values seems to be right – his interest in literature and art and music and life in general is always in the right (i.e. my) direction. But he has an unconvincing, unattractive way of expressing himself in conversation. He has failed at everything he has attempted so far and has a brother seven years younger who has been comparatively very successful. His good qualities seem to indicate a rather 'might have been' goodness, a goodness suffocated and dying instead of free and growing and passing out into life – a plant in decay.

That is the man who is my first lover. Not a flattering start.

Thursday, 19 June

High summer came upon us without warning on Sunday. We have been hot, burst out in light and white and airy garments, the soil is dry, there is perfume in the air, dust on the roads, mosquitoes in the garden, greenfly on the roses. And my moods have been past belief – up, down and indifferent. I have been overcome with nausea, crying with D.H. Lawrence 'From all the mental poetry of deliberate love-making, from all the false felicity of deliberately taking the body of another into mine, O God deliver me!'[112]

Seeing F. as one of the rather nastier types of mosquito, sympathising with brides who are not in love with their grooms, with wives who are bored with their husbands, with wives who are 'used' by their husbands, with tarts who have taken to prostitution because there was no other means for them of getting a meal. Then forgetting F. altogether and feeling as though nothing at all had happened between us, then wondering when I should see him again and what I would do when

---

112 From the poem 'Chastity'.

I did. He phoned on Sunday evening but I was vague and indecisive and shocked him a lot I know – I have taken enough initiative in this affair, now it's his turn. What I am really dreading is next week when my next period is due. If it is late again I shall go crazy.

The cigarette problem is acute. Have failed to get any in Slough these last three weeks. The local man yesterday had a few Woodbines. In London last week I managed to get 100, which I am trying to make last, but with the greatest difficulty. It shocks me to find that they have such a hold on me. F. tells me it indicates a craving for sex. I would really (at the moment) rather have the cigarettes.

Saturday, 21 June
A letter from him this morning. I am now a very sweet and desirable person, and he wants to see me again very much but is afraid that I have been struck by qualms of conscience and am worrying and thinking about the matter too much, which I am not to do. We are to take things easily and naturally – let things develop without trying to *understand* the situation.

So unreasonably reasonable of him. But I scent a clue in this sentence: 'I did feel that in you I had found someone who was completely natural about sex.' I may be, but I don't think he is (or what is natural to him is not natural to me).

Really life strikes me as so pleasant at this moment – I must say so here. After a long winter and a frozen spring the weather has swept into a train of royal summer days. Roses and lupins and foxgloves, oriental poppies, purple and yellow iris bloom in the garden. The heat is Mediterranean. At night a sheet on the bed is too much.

Only the constant passing of airplanes reminds me of war. I have more than enough food for my needs. I have clothes enough, money in the bank, interesting work, a lover, books, papers, radio, a few very good friends and many agreeable acquaintances, two cats and kitten, a heavenly garden and cottage – what more could a woman want? (Cigarettes. This woman does. A certain 20 or even 15 a day would suffice.)

Sunday, 22 June

On the hottest day of the year we hear at 9 a.m. that Germany has invaded Russia and at 9 p.m. that the declared policy of the British Government is to aid all nations who are victims of Nazi aggression. We are going to help Russia! Churchill made one of the cleverest speeches of his career. ('Any man or State who fights against Nazism will have our aid. Any man or state who marches with Hitler is our foe.') I smoke my last cigarette to him. I think this is the most important day of the century.

Tuesday, 24 June

The wages of sin is/are anxiety.

Wednesday, 25 June

Thank you God, oh Thank you God! Now I will enjoy this day. The ways of the Lord and science are truly wonderful. The relief of knowing I haven't to worry this month!

Thursday, 3 July

Have just acquired an informative little book on *The Technique of Sex* by Anthony Havil. It treats the subject in a healthy if rather abbreviated scientific matter. It is undoubtedly useful. It is very smug. I intend to visit F. in Hampstead again (oh heaven help me).

Sunday, 6 July

Gus and Phyllis have just left. They belong to a class and age I just missed being born into. That their class and age are dying doesn't make any difference – I am filled with wistful envy. I adore them both. Why they should be so sweet to me I do not know, coming that vile journey from London on a blistering day to see me. I am very touched, very flattered. Phyllis bought me 300 cigarettes, chocolate, a jar of jam, Parmesan cheese. The privileged class. They accept the inevitable and with such good-humoured dignity: that this is a class war and that nothing they can do will stop the advent of social revolution. They belong to an age when aristocracy mattered and had real influence.

During the last blitz on London, about 6 weeks ago, Marylebone 'got it'. Druce's in Baker Street has been obliterated. Gus and Phyllis's flat is in Gloucester Place just behind. Fires raged round them all night. Their house was one of the only 4 in the block which was not burnt. A sudden change of wind favoured them. High explosives fell not far away. At one time Gus could not go into the street: the wind was blowing smoke and sparks with such intensity. They were up until 7.30 a.m. helping to quench fires. Sheets of flame blew over their roof. It was the worst night they had ever known. But they describe them, these bad nights, with great gusto. They face danger magnificently. It is a great, dramatic adventure. IF you are hit, well that is just too bad. So let's just enjoy the drama of it while we can. I wish I could face all kinds of danger like that.

Ginger has come into my room and is now sitting by my bed, and when I am working in the garden he and Dinah will both come and sit somewhere near. I adore being caressed as much as a cat apparently does. To be stroked! Heavenly! But to be stroked by someone who really loves you! Impossible?

Monday, 14 July

F. is the most difficult of persons. He is one of those men Who Won't Be Told. He rolled up like a hedgehog on Saturday, and watched me getting crosser and crosser with delight. It was far too hot to be made love to on Friday night. Besides, I am not at all sure that I want F. to make love to me anymore. The truth is we are two damned selfish people unwilling to alter our lives one iota for the other. If I met someone who attracted me more and was more human, I should drop F. without a qualm. At least I think I would. But perhaps he'll drop me first.

Wednesday, 16 July

I want to smash something but will escape here instead. Am typing out final copy of that blasted short story which I intend to send to 'Penguin Parade'. But it'll come back, I know it will. I want to hammer and hammer at my typewriter until its parts are scattered and destroyed.

Just before I woke this morning I dreamt that F. was making love to me in a way I particularly dislike. I got up and ran away from him. He chased me into dark and fearful corners but I escaped at last up steep stairs and onto a cliff from where I dived into the sea with my clothes on. He stood above me threatening with a gun, but I dived underwater. On shore was the handsome young officer who comes sometimes into the canteen and I hoped he would rescue me, but I woke before that delightful event occurred.

Friday, 25 July
Tomorrow I join Nockie at St Bees for 10 days' holiday in the Lakes and am now suffering a bad bout of disinclination. I want to go but do not want to undertake that frightful journey. Weather is warm again. Cannot get on with packing and arrangements here, do not want to leave the cottage and the cats, it is all too silly. Suppose I shall be up very late finishing and then have to scramble for 9.20 bus in the morning and arrive at destination exhausted. What will I do if I have to leave here to do war work? I heard yesterday that the women born 1910–1916 are to register within the next three months. The 1909s will be next. I am in a state.

Tuesday, 12 August
It was a good holiday. We stayed on a farm at Crossdale, near Lake Ennerdale. We fed on butter and cream and large starchy meals and became liverish. No fruit, few greens or salads. Farm people have no excuse for these sort of shortages but they were the type who do not consider greens or brown bread important. Kind people. Mrs Edmondson, ridden with arthritis, ruled the household from her chair by the kitchen stove. The domestic help Maggie did all the work. There were 5 dogs, 10 cats, cows, a bull, pet lambs, chickens, ducklings

– every farm animal you can think of. The weather might have been worse. We returned to London by the night train.

[The day's entry straddles two exercise books.]

The satisfaction in beginning a new book! What will its pages tell? I know no more than you, dear mythical reader. No, 'hypothetical' reader is more accurate.

Tonight as I write I hear planes in the night outside. Though we have had no enemy activity over this area for many months, that sound still spells a dread. My home-made black-out frames are falling to pieces.

In October we are to be rationed to ½ pint of milk per adult per day. I can manage with this but with 3 cats it will be a watery ½ pint and there will be no milk puddings.

Saw Greta Garbo in *Ninotchka* this afternoon. It seemed in rather bad taste to be laughing at the Bolsheviks now.

Thursday, 14 August

I want particularly to note the food I live on during this war. I still maintain that there is no need to be hungry or undernourished. For breakfast I have tea, a cereal, black treacle, (the best medicine for my innards – it has required ingenuity and forethought to keep myself supplied but have sufficient in store now for some months). Cereals are becoming very scarce. Am considering rice (still plentiful) as a substitute. For lunch nearly always I have a green or raw veg salad with cheese if I have it, or marmite on bread, and then something starchy and sweet such as brown bread and jam. Jam is a real difficulty now. I have only a very small stock of it and the ration of ½lb a month does not go far. For supper usually a hot meal with cooked veg and a pudding. Tonight I shall have egg and bacon, runner beans, cooked lettuce and potatoes and the rhubarb steamed pudding to which I have today added stewed apples I consider this a sufficiently wholesome and satisfying diet, though possibly the quality of the flour in bought products is not as good as it was and there is certainly less sugar in cakes and biscuits.

Paper today is full of the exploits of the RAF during recent raids on Cologne and Berlin.

Friday, 15 August
F. phoned this evening. The war situation fades into the background.

It amounts to this: I would not mind at all if I never see him again. If I had a good excuse I'd use it. And then my conscience flickers: I fear that I have and am treating him rather badly ('You never sent me a postcard even.'). Then another fear: that I am running away from something of value, and that if I had the courage I might find treasure in what I thought was dross. Imagine him here for even a few days. The neighbours would know. Winnie the cleaner would know. The tradespeople would know. I could say openly that I was letting a play-wright friend stay here for his holiday – no one is to know what we do at night. Yet I fear my name in the village would be mud. I haven't the courage – not for F. If it were someone I loved, loved as much even as my cats or my cottage – but I do not love him at all.

Monday, 18 August
Reading *I Came Out of France* by Cecily Mackworth: story of a young woman's escape last year when France capitulated. Written quietly, easily, it gives a vivid picture of the fantastic horrors the refugees went through. One can hardly believe it. People swarming from the north, from the south, over-running country towns and villages; no food, no medical attention, no petrol; wild rumours, contradictory orders; suspicion, mistrust, hunger, illness, death; civilians machine-gunned, press and radio under German control. One feels one had no business to be sleeping comfortably and eating well when the French nation was suffering so much.

Tuesday, 19 August
Went to Wembley today. No cigarettes or sweets anywhere. In Sudbury

I tracked down some Players Weights and chocolate caramels and liquorice all-sorts. And in Beaconsfield on my way home a packet of Woodbines and 2ozs of broken block chocolate.

The young man is very determined. He has nailed me down to next Tuesday, to meet him in town.

Wednesday, 27 August

Gus is doing well at the BBC repertory, enjoys the work, likes the people and Val Gielgud.[113]

Met the boyfriend as arranged yesterday and spent a most successful 24 hours with him. Not *completely* successful, but very much more pleasant than any previous time. It made me dig out an old ring to wear on the third finger of my right hand. So silly. Slight summer madness.[114]

Thursday, 28 August

I would like him to fall in love with me so seriously that he makes me fall in love with him. To love as he has never loved before. I have vain moments when I think I could do it. He is feeling the need of companionship, of a home atmosphere to return to after work, of someone to share his experiences with. But I shall not offer to satisfy it. I must keep a little aloof and appear to be indifferent, but never jealous of his other loves or ideals. Sympathetic without cloying. Friendly, independent, and beyond his power to hurt me until he owns my power to hurt him. Do I say slight summer madness? I should have said Grave Autumnal Lunacy.

Friday, 29 August

I must take my cue from Graham Howe, who said in one of his lectures that one of the first problems he had to tackle with the

---

113 Val Gielgud, a pioneer of radio drama at the BBC, was John Gielgud's brother.
114 The significance of the ring placement is unclear; occasionally it may signify marriage, but generally it signifies unattachment.

majority of his male patients was that of disentangling them from the tentacles of half a dozen women anxious to 'do' things for them.

I see F. as a forlorn and wasted individual, a heart desiring affection; and affection is stored in me, ready to be lavished on the first man who asks me for it. It would give me a gratifying feeling of power to satisfy my much-neglected maternal instinct. That is not love. But I do want him to go on making love to me – I want *him* now, not anyone new, which I certainly have not felt before.

Sunday, 31 August

Nockie has been talking a lot of sense with me. Marriage to him would be spiritual and mental suicide. Do not let him persuade you into consenting until you have had something to do with someone else first (and then, says N., you won't want to have anything more to do with F.!)

I shall not marry F. (always supposing he asks me). I should only consent to do so on condition that we lived together first for at least three months. I should soon get over any sentimentality roused by our physical intimacy. I think one month would be enough. How nice to have one's meals cooked properly, he sighed; you need a house-keeper, I replied, but I am not offering to be one for you.

Physical attraction can trick one into endless fake feelings. But what is one to do about the physical attraction? Satisfy one's lust soullessly and then forget about it? Or wait for 'the real thing' – perhaps too long? How is one to know what the real thing is without some practical experience?

Tuesday, 2 September

The fever subsides. Curious. Three hours in the garden, cutting the grass and weeding, left me exhausted. This morning, for the first time since I dug it out last week, I did not put on the ring. By this evening I was hopeful he wouldn't phone. But he did. I was so cool, have promised to see him Thursday evening. Really I don't care, I wish the affair would end. It doesn't seem worth any effort, and the scheming for and snatching of an hour seems so sordid.

Wednesday, 3 September

Two years ago, we are reminded by the press and the BBC, war was declared. For two years I have been lucky, living so happily here. But the time is coming when I shall have to make my sacrifice. There seems no hope of the war ending. The future appears dreary and incalculable. I cannot expect anyone to understand what it will mean to me to give up my indolent cottage lifestyle. The problem of what to do with the cats seems appalling.

Friday, 5 September

I have no business to feel tired so often and so much. It is wearing me out. Even my passion for gardening is not what it was. This evening I layered the carnations but at the outset it seemed a task demanding more energy than I could summon. Apart from that little job I have done nothing important beyond chores all day. Perhaps my mail this morning is responsible: the publicity department of the Ministry of Works is full. There is no vacancy on the staff of *The Builder*. Yesterday I tried to crash into the press department of the British Council, but Mr Forsdick would not see me. It is incredible how a few refusals can depress one, make one feel unwanted, a meddling amateur or a tiresome pusher. I shall be pushed into uniform . . .

F. is ill. He seems to me to be on the verge of cracking, in a terrible state of nerves, for which I can do nothing, though I offered to have him here for a rest. He was abominably rude and loathsome last night, very repressed and explosive, rigid with a hate of life.

Monday, 8 September

One is living at an intense tension. This dreary war. Endless, vindictive slaughter, drama, heroics, destruction. While a serene moon shines full upon ally and foe. What does the future hold? Will Germany defeat Russia? Canadians, Australians, all the men who have given up their lives overseas to fight with us are asking – *Why* is Britain one of the world's leading powers?

Our genius, says Priestley, is for improvisation not organisation. We need to be inspired, as we were inspired after Dunkirk. But with so many Stupids in authority, who is there to inspire us? He is too glib, is Priestley. He says, 'We must be as fiercely democratic as the Nazis are fiercely Nazi . . . we should believe intensely . . .' Yes, yes, yes Mr Priestley, we must, we must! But how, when the heart of us is being eaten away with disease?

Saturday, 20 September

I

have

got

a

job

on

the

ARCHITECT AND BUILDING NEWS.

I don't believe it, but there it is. I am to begin on October 2nd. Now I have so much to do in preparation and tidying up, don't know where to begin. I do thank you, God. Please let me benefit from all my past experience – use everything I have learned to make the most of this opportunity. Please let nothing happen to spoil this chance.

Germany claims to have taken Kiev but Russian communiqués do not confirm this. The fighting on Russian soil is terrible, *terrible*. We feel that our aid is tardy, we fear the weight of anti-Russian influences in power.

I stayed in Hampstead last night. F. is such an odd and difficult creature. No one likes him. Vulgar, vain, mean. Yet just something about him attracts me to him. I cannot end it or keep away.

20.

The Whole World Involved

Tuesday, 23 September 1941 (aged thirty-one)

I have worried myself into a fever over the prospect of this job. My temperature last night was 100.6 – am sure due to over-anxiety. So terrified that I shall do something foolish and irrevocable when I begin.

Glancing through this week's *Radio Times* I see the names of commodities that are now part of the fabric of the nation, such familiar names but they may not be used in articles, stories, novels, plays and broadcasts – in any of the things that make familiar things more familiar to us. But they have their influence and place. In my life, for instance, Gibbs Dentifrice: a pink block in a silvery tin that I used when very young until something about it enraged me, and I smashed the tin and have never used it since. Odol, toothpaste and gargle which I bought with enthusiasm when they first appeared because of their bright light blue and white packs. Kruschen Health Salts in a dark brown glass jar from which I began to take in my early teens believing with ardour that they would solve all my problems. Malteser chocolates – delectable sweets, introduced to me by June at Hampstead but now seldom to be seen except at the Canteen when I hand them over the counter to the Tommies. Peak Frean biscuits, Sifta salt, Pepsodent toothpaste, which I was warned by a cousin-in-law dentist against using as it scratched the enamel, but did use. Senior's fish and meat pastes. Carter's Little Liver Pills – the name spread on huge hoardings facing railway tracks that run through open country. Caley's chocolates, Grey's cigarettes.

What a pity that there are so many odd men about, their oddities just a bit too much of a barrier to make one want to marry them. There's the psychologist Jennings White, who lives in South Hill Park. He is searching for a housekeeper/secretary he can marry. Joan sees him often and finds his loud, hysterical laughter most embarrassing. And David Mitchell, the poet, plump, middle-aged, nervous, easily offended. And Jill's tall, neurotic bachelor friend Clifford, a typically mother-swathed egotist. Is there no healthy, attractive, unattached male for me now in the world? Even my one neurotic seems to have deserted me.

Thursday, 25 September

Nockie has been warning me not to underestimate my ability, not to allow myself to be exploited by a Tory editor, to stick out for my own work, not to sign away my liberty, to insist on a rise at the end of 6 months. I am starting at £3 10s. a week, but if it had not been for Nockie I would have meekly asked for £3 and accepted £2. 10 without a murmur.

Wednesday, 1 October

Yesterday my last full free day in London. Ordered a coat and skirt at Peter Jones for 13 guineas. An appalling price and has taken most of my coupons, but I look on it as an investment. I can manage now with the clothes I have for at least a year (undies will need renewing). Stockings will be the only problem. At present I have six pairs and shall be able to wear one pair a day through the week, rinsing every worn pair as I take them off at night.

A letter this morning from Cousin Martin. He says that the Russians have obviously been concentrating on armament production for a long time, that they are supremely confident of victory, have not even yet fully mobilised the army and that the British have been well and very efficiently received.

Army manocuvres here all this week, at least in the Slough and

Aldershot areas, against a mock invasion. On Monday fierce air fights were going on overhead.

This time tomorrow! I'm scared.

Thursday, 2 October

An incredibly casual office. It does not matter if I do not get there until 10 a.m. Everyone clears off at 4.30 p.m. We do not work on Saturdays. Tea at 11 a.m. and 3.30 p.m. No one pays any attention to the contract one has to sign. Most of the work seems to be done by Mr Musgrave and his secretary Miss Stuart, aided by typist Peggy. So far I have read papers for 'news' and have been handed a series of articles on roof construction to sub. I am not threatened at the moment with overwork. The strain of going backwards and forwards will not be nearly as great as I feared it would. I catch the 8.20 Green Line bus in the morning which takes me to Hyde Park Corner by about 9.30, and a bus home from there about 5 p.m. so that I am back here about 6.30 p.m.

Fetter Lane – there is hardly anything left of it.

Sunday, 5 October

Still not a word from the incalculable F. Joan, Nockie and Ethel have each phoned to find out how I liked the new job. If he were really interested in me you would think he would have made some effort too.

He thinks he knows all there is to know of the art of making love. He does not know even how to begin. It does not begin in his room with port wine and a verse or two of Keats.

Monday, 6 October

Met Joan for lunch. She brought a casual and most offhand message from F. and was boiling with rage at him. I came home in the bus planning a letter I would write, saying a few straight things cruelly. But was too tired to start it when I came in. And then he phoned! Most incomprehensible of men. And I, most foolish of women, am happy.

The exchange of prisoners between us and Germany seems to me fantastic. In the middle of the bloodiest, the most hot-headed of wars, the two governments pause, bow to each other at a polite distance above the heat of battle, command a truce over an area of the Channel so that the wounded, the women and children of each can return to their own countries. If they can do that why can't they agree to stop the war altogether?

[Note added later:] These ships did not sail. All arrangements were cancelled and the prisoners sent back to their camps on October 8th. That *monster* Hitler.

Thursday, 9 October

I am full of hate tonight: for the deadly, humourless, efficient, destructive Prussian; for the men in power who, I am certain, put every obstacle in the way of our aid to Russia; for the feeble little Britishers who on their homeward journeys from the office tonight are saying, 'I suppose it was to be expected.' The public think we can 'take it' because we withstood last year's raids. Does it imagine that the German High Command has not since been preparing in elaborate detail plans for our total destruction? God, is the age of miracles over? Can you not send a plague or earthquake to demolish the German High Command and all its works?

My position at the office is delicate. There is very little work at the moment. I must make work for myself, make suggestions and be prepared to carry them out. I feel like the new girl at school again.

Friday, 24 October

The position at the office improves.

F. only gets in touch with me when he wants to sleep with me, which makes me feel like a concubine.

Sunday, 26 October

London has had a long lull from bombing, but people still sleeping in the tubes, probably because they save money thereby, but what a way of living. As the war drags on a Tube Dwelling community will develop. A thousand years' hence excavations will be made and the site of some bombed and long-forgotten stations discovered, disclosing skeletons and relics of Tube Dwellers.

Friday, 14 November

A jagged jolt. Soon I shall have lost the job. I am not up to expectations, says Mr Wood. There is no work for me to do, I have failed to create any, and I must therefore look round for something else elsewhere. He hoped I would develop a news-sense, which I show no signs of doing. There has been nothing for me to do but read the newspapers, but there has been no building news; he wanted me to make bricks out of straw. I'm a failure, a bloody failure. Beware a casual office! The notice is three weeks.

Sunday, 23 November

So I have been seeing people. Mrs Clarke of the Fabian Society has offered me a temporary job cataloguing the Blue Books.[115] But I'm off the track again, lost in a fog.

Saturday, 29 November

It is a vile age. An age that has bred generations and generations of frustrated, disillusioned, cynical men and women for whom there is now no future but death or a change of heart (and who can work that latter miracle for us?) We were born sensitive, imaginative and energetic, but the fight in the world was a competitive, brutal one for material advantages which we in our hearts despised. Pressure from this heaving, confused world moulded us into dreamy, idle and shy adolescents. We have become miserable, haunted, dying people. We

---

115 The Fabians are a left-leaning think tank, founded in 1884. The Blue Books were the Society's manifestos and tracts.

have become frigid, dull or aggressive – we shrivel, rot or explode. We are the ghostly train of the Also-Rans.

Sunday, 30 November

Gollancz yesterday, speaking to the Fabians.[116] An emotional, sensitive Jew, with tremendous domed, intellectual head. He does not believe the entire German race are to blame for this war, and explained the growth of Hitlerism very ably. Insists that we must win this war, but that we must also help the German people to break the power of the Prussian militarists, the Junkers and the industrialists. This can only be done by accepting and helping to establish International Socialism, and this implies – though he did not say so – breaking the power of our own militarists, landowners and industrialists. We must regain a passionate faith.

Monday, 1 December

The milk ration has knocked us sideways, reduced to 2 pints per adult a week.

There is to be a debate in parliament on making conscription of women to the Services and industry compulsory.

Tuesday, 9 December

A light fall of snow and Japan's declaration of war surprised us on Sunday night. Now the Pacific is in the news and America is in the war. The whole world involved.

The whole world at war. It is almost too gigantic a thought for human intelligence. The German campaign in Russia has come to a halt. (Those marvellous Russians!) But German power is not broken. During the winter one supposes they will now turn their attention to us and the Atlantic again. We hear that the North East coast was badly raided last night.

---

116 The publisher Victor Gollancz, an earlier champion of George Orwell and Daphne du Maurier.

Thursday, 2 January 1942

New Year. There seems no hope of suitable employment for me anywhere. 'The department is advised that your qualifications and experience do not fall within the range . . .' 'Your application has been receiving our consideration but . . .' 'We regret that there are no vacancies on our staff . . .' A little batch of these sort of letters has greeted me every night this week on my return from the Fabian Society. My date for Registering with the ATS looms nearer and nearer (Jan 24th).[117]

For the sort of jobs I am after I lack, at the age of 33, *experience*. Oh God, those wasted years! If this is ever read by posterity, let posterity ponder on this: You cannot run away from life. If you try, life will only catch you in the end, and the longer you've been running the more it will hurt. Learn to be hurt as early as possible, welcome being hurt; face pain, humiliation and defeat in your teens; accept them, let them go through you, so that you cease to be afraid of them.

Saturday, 4 January

What a tin of plums will do! One in my store had been oozing and I went to consult the Campbells as to the wisdom of eating contents or not. The conversation veered to jobs and Mr C. advised me strongly to explore the possibilities of the Slough Trading Estate. Not that there will be anything in my narrow line, but there are advantages attached to a job in Slough that I can not ignore. Mr Campbell suggested welfare work.

Thursday, 8 January

I wrote to Nockie at New Year, and her reply I must quote – it is such sane and sensible wisdom which I know in my heart to be true. 'Lot of nonsense about your wasted years. No such thing if carefully analysed. We can't all be ready to make a spring off the board on

---

117 The Auxiliary Territorial Service. The female branch of the British army, no longer a voluntary organisation.

leaving college. Think of all the advantages of the spirit you have had in the past years.'

Saturday, 10 January

I want that job. I reach bursting point about it. Nockie has sent me a packet of information about alloys.

F. has just phoned. I wish, I wish he weren't quite so much F. It isn't fair that I should still be disturbed by him physically. (Nockie calls it lechery, bless her – she says it can't be physical attraction because he is such a poor physical specimen.)

We have been, and are, promised to be the best-fed nation in Europe. My relations are saying that they can remember in the last war feeling hungry but have not done so yet in this. They have high praise for Lord Woolton the Food Minister. If I had no stores in I could still feed myself adequately. A regular supply of butter, marg, cooking fat, cheese, bacon, sugar and tea arrives each week. As much bread and flour as I need. Custard powder and starchy things like rice, tapioca and so on can be had at intervals liberally without 'points'. The milk ration is helped out by tinned and powdered varieties. There are still plenty of tinned beans, carrots and soups. Eggs are very scarce. Meat is more difficult than it was, but there is often sausage meat and corned beef as substitutes and makeweights. Fresh and salt fish can be bought at controlled prices in fairly good supply. Cakes and pastries are still obtainable by order or by queuing from most reliable confectioners. Sweets I hardly ever see. The biscuit supply varies. But now, the papers warn us, Japan's attack on American merchant conditions will make a difference and we must expect to 'tighten our belts' and may yet get poorer menus.

Clothes restrictions are more severe than they have ever been. I need a new warm dressing gown badly, should much like a winter swagger coat. The dressing gown I may get by buying furnishing velvet and thin felt and getting one made.

I cannot grumble about clothes. I have heard recently of an old well-known Wembley couple (the Dudley Wrights, who had a very large house and corresponding reputation in the old Wembley days) who were torpedoed on their way home from Canada and are now interned by the Germans somewhere unknown. He lost his teeth and she her glasses. They have so few clothes that she has knitted herself shoes from the string saved from parcels. The terrible tales that will be told after this war are beyond one's imagination.

Have discovered a small zoo shop in Slough that will take kittens, so perhaps can get rid of the next lot more easily, and am relieved at the thought. I had visions of the cottage developing into an enormous cattery – generations and generations of Dinah's family swarming in and out of the windows and disturbing the neighbours, until I was driven to live in the shed.

Thursday, 15 January
I have been accepted as a Technical Journalist in the Publicity Department of High Duty Alloys. I feel oddly confident.

21.

What Being a Woman Means

Tuesday, 20 January 1942 (aged thirty-two)
I want to know everything about the future, all at once.

Yesterday was worn to a shred with the nervous strain of 'being new' again and bearing the abiding horror of being turned out. The situation has similar points to the one at the *Architect and Building News*. 'Nothing very much for you to do at present Miss Pratt – I hope you won't find it too boring.' Agony.

I work with an attractive young Irish publicity engineer called Hughes and a good natured youth called Buckland, our 'commercial artist', rather pink and white, who poses a lot but is probably quite good at his job when he has anything to do. There are two other men, Goldsworthy and Lessel, whom I haven't met yet, and a swarm of typists in a room of their own. The firm's doctor (I had to be medically examined) spluttered and stuttered that he couldn't understand why they kept on so many young people doing nothing. 'Now they are taking *you* on. If you were to replace one of the young men I could understand it.'

We do not have to be punctual in the morning but I don't know how late I dare to be yet. One foot of snow outside my cottage door delayed me half an hour today. We were all allowed home early tonight because of the weather. I am learning an awful lot about metals and alloys.

Saturday, 24 January

Think I am falling heavily for the young Irishman (Hughes). He might be anything between 25 and 28.

Tuesday, 27 January

My imagination was busy with Mr Hughes all over the weekend.

Stevens (my boss) came in to see me today. He wants me to get a picture clear in my mind of what the aluminium industry has done in the past and hopes to do in the future.

Wednesday, 28 January

Hughes and Buckland have disappeared. No one at the office has seen or heard of them for three full days. Poor Mr Stevens, he really has no control over them. I have a sad feeling I shall not see Hughes again. He was a bad young man, but there was about him that fatal Irish charm, and he could talk with sympathy and eloquence on many subjects that move and delight me. There seemed to be a promise there of our being able to build a rare and exciting friendship. It is as though I held a book in my hands that I very much wanted to read, and some twist of fortune has taken it from me before I had even finished the preface.

Thursday, 29 January

Such a simple explanation – flu! The point that made us suspicious was that both Hughes and Buckland were absent together and sent no explanation. Now forget Mr Hughes. There is a girlfriend, anyway, in the laboratory.

On my way to the canteen today, which lies back from the street-front buildings among the sheds and untidy offices that straggle for miles across the estate, I peeped into one of the workshops. Passions of white flames from furnaces lit the whole interior. Enormous parts were being heated and hammered. Brawny men moved about naked to the waist or with shirt sleeves rolled. The sound of hissing flame and hammers on metal, the pale lights in the high roof, the shadows and the steam. Artists should paint it, poets should pen it, musicians translate it. Modern industry, all turned now to making guns. 'Thirty thousand a year!' said Lord Beaverbrook last night. Thirty thousand guns! Forty thousand guns . . . fifty thousand . . .

Monday, 16 February (War Diary)
School magazine arrived last week. Old Girls are ATS and WRENS and WAAFS, VADs and other volunteers in alarming array. Others are in the Land Army, the War Office, the Air Ministry, helping in welfare centres for evacuees – all kinds of Government work. One is Official Indexer, whatever that may be, another a District Inspector for the Ministry of Health, another is interested in the International Women's Organisations and their plans for reconstruction. And one girl whom I knew quite well (although in Selfridges not long ago we decided not to recognise each other) has been working a longboat on the Worcester Cut with another woman, carrying freight, and is now to train women to do the same kind of work for the Grand Union Canal Co. Many are scattered about the Empire.

Electric torch batteries – no No. 8s in the village now. Bought 3 in 3 weeks at Boots recently – they all gave out before I had used them more than twice. Man in village shop says that all batteries are now only half-filled owing to shortage of materials.

Wednesday, 25 February (War Diary)
Allowed morning off last Saturday to attend cousin M.'s wedding. When I asked for this my boss said it was *most* irregular but grinned broadly when he heard Martin was in the RAF and had just returned from Russia.

Sat next to cousin-in-law Peggy in Church. She has just been put in charge of a large scabies-clearing depot and gave me detailed description of the cure while we waited for the bride. 'Our skin man told us that it was caught chiefly from your bedfellow. It just depends who you sleep with.' Glad I've been warned.

Bride in white satin, bridesmaids in dark green velvet carrying daffodils. Guests for the most part were huddled in cheap drab fur coats. Best man was the pilot who shot down the plane over Victoria station. Snowstorm as we came out of Church. Reception at hotel in Acton, where M. had been head of ARP until he joined up. Food, provided at 4 days' notice, remarkably good – chicken and ham sandwiches, trifle, fruit salad and cakes in quantity. Drinks not so good. I had a thimbleful of sweet white wine. On Monday B. asked cheerfully if I had got tight at the wedding. Impossible for anyone to get tight at that wedding.

Tuesday, 3 March (War Diary)

Our department is hectically active just now preparing for propaganda for the Works for Warships week. Slogans and posters everywhere. Buckland's desk looks as though something has hit it. He spent hours last week trying to find out the colours and order of the flags of Nelson's Last Signal. Phoned Selfridges Information Bureau (closed for the duration owing to shortage of staff), the Imperial War Museum, the Admiralty and God knows what else. No help anywhere. Miss de Groote found it eventually on an Xmas card. We are going to have a tall flat staff with the signal fluttering on one side and little sailors climbing the other, each holding a notice giving the Savings achieved every day. Buckland drew out the model sailor yesterday to unending and useless criticism from everyone who saw it.

Saturday, 7 March (War Diary)

A soldier has dug my two cabbage patches for me. He is stationed in this area and seems to get quite a bit of free time in which he comes to aid the gardener-less folk around here.

Chemist had no Vapex or anything of that nature. No talcum powder. This is difficult to get anywhere now. A store in Slough has a window full of cheap and unnamed product and I bought a packet marked 'Sample' for 1s. 9d. at a hairdressers not long ago. Our chemist was selling jars of his own make of cold cream and liquid shampoo.

For supper – mutton stewed with sundry vegetables and one onion; rhubarb and prunes and a mince pie. All very good. (Feel like Pepys.)

Wednesday, 11 March (War Diary)
Made such a noise coughing at the office this afternoon P.A. sent me home.

Stayed Monday night with June. She saw a film recently in which Churchill and Stalin appeared. For Churchill – a few polite claps. For Stalin – a storm of applause.

Menu outside a Piccadilly restaurant quoted pheasant at 25s. or 27s. a helping.

Monday, 16 March
Cough has gone. I can smoke again.

Monday, 23 March
Gus phones. Tells me that Phyllis is now working in a cigarette factory and will be able to send me 100 a week.

Thursday, 23 April
Next week Buckland joins the RAF. I am hoping to have his desk.

Friday, 24 April
We said goodbye to Buckland today. He shakes hands flabbily. He wants to be a pilot, to be at the controls. I have a hunch that he'll get there – he is the type that has surprised and frustrated the German High Command. Undisciplined, effete, but able to withstand dramatic attack. No one, as far as I know, told him to his face that he will be missed.

Sunday, 10 May

Have begun to chronicle an office romance between the Linnett (a little plump, reddish colouring, pale skin, an efficient secretary) and Tom Hughes (the young engineer). In short it all began with a bicycle. With the cut in the petrol ration Barbara Linnett expects to have to abandon her car in June – in its place she decided she must have a bicycle. But good 3-speed cycles are not being made today, and Tommy Hughes set out to get a second-hand one for her. He knows a lot about bicycles, he liked chasing the adverts, and she kept him at it. The hunt began about four weeks ago, and on Friday they found one. Are they riding out together today? I'll not be surprised if she receives a proposal of marriage, but I shall be very surprised if she accepts it, at any rate the first time.

So many women seem to be waiting, as I wait, for something wonderful to happen. For the man-they-want-but-never-find to appear and carry them off to Paradise – some not even that, but just to be married. I'm sure that if B.L. ever accepts T.H. it will be partly because she feels herself getting older and opportunities fewer. The majority of women want marriage – there is no doubt at all of that. Careers are only of secondary importance unless they have genius (and very few women have that), or until they realise their best chances of marriage are past.

At work Lizzie de Groote expressed frustration that she had lived nearly a quarter of a century and what had she done? I should have said to her that it is not what one does, but what one is in the process of becoming that matters. *Being* is so much more important than *doing*, although it is true, too, that what one does so one becomes.

There is no doubt that women are not happy, that men lack a certain quality that we look for. It may be because women are going through a great stage of change, have reached a new point in their development, can not now go back to the old way of living (and do not want to), and haven't yet discovered the right way in a different world. This deep trouble has its effect on the men they bear and love.

We have enormous influence, enormous power, a great part to play, but not as servants or toys of men, but as living, independent individuals, as women in our own right. But we do not know yet what being a woman means.

Wednesday, 27 May

I hope to see Graham Howe again on Friday. My problem, as briefly as possible, is this: how to get what is in out? I absorb so much, I have gobbled experience, but I do not seem able to use it, or rather it seems to lie in me in heavy undigested lumps. In my job there are occasions when one has to talk clearly, coherently and intelligently. I am asked a question or expected to say something about a particular subject of which I claim to know a little, and I get grossly confused and inarticulate. It is childish and inexcusable. Given time I can get quite a lot out in a rather clumsy manner, and if the person I am talking to knows me well (such as Nockie) I feel that the clumsiness doesn't matter. But with a new acquaintance or in company (a strange, critical audience, judging me, as I imagine, by my performance) I stumble, blush perhaps, dry up and make a complete fool of myself, and feel sure they must think me an utter fraud.

I have read and listened to millions of words on politics; I have read hundreds of good books (classics and non-fiction). I have studied architecture, I have known artists, I have seen and loved many ballets, plays and films, and I shall go on doing these things. Out of all that absorbed material I should be able to produce something individual and interesting when the occasion demands – an anecdote, an opinion, a description, some appropriate contribution. But I have sat in company recently and felt miserable because I was unable to contribute nothing, and was afterwards asked 'I hope we haven't bored you . . .' No remark could be more shattering!

A good deal of talk in the Press just now about planning for the world after the war. 'We have done,' says Laski, 'once and for all with the mad competitive economic system which spells poverty for all peoples and war as the outcome of that poverty.[118] I believe that is true. We shall eventually have a more justly planned society.

The kittens dart over the floor like mice. I wish I could keep a cattery. My pleasure in it would be unending. Why should I not do that? Breed cats for a living, starting at Homefield, the portion of orchard left at the bottom of the garden would do very well. I would bother no more about clothes, cosmetics and hair-sets. I would forget all I had learned, I would burn my books, give away my fountain pen, and devote my time to the garden and the cats.

Letter from F. last week. He wants to meet me again. Quite unable to answer as I don't know if I do.

Sunday, 21 June

10 a.m. Red Cross canteen in the village. Local policeman came in for a cold Horlicks. Four ducks were stolen from a house near his last night. People, he says, are helping themselves liberally to small items – his neighbour's chickens, washing etc. One woman had joint taken from oven while helping another to hang out her washing.

Monday, 24 June

Winnie left me – a shattering blow – to work full-time for our local fishmonger's wife who has cancer. Have found a very good woman, Mrs Hawthorn, who comes in twice a week and 'does' most thoroughly. A bit of a dragon though, and much more expensive.

Political situation most depressing. Tobruk fallen. Shipping losses grave. Some German successes in Russia. We are at times an infuriatingly feeble nation. We talk and blah about our superiority in this and that Service, but when put to the test crumple up like cheap tin.

Went one Sunday to Hampstead to see the exhibition of Modern Painting and Sculpture at Goldfinger's house in Willow Road.[119]

---

118 Harold Laski, the influential socialist economist and future chairman of the Labour Party.

119 The work included Duchamp, Max Ernst and Henry Moore. The architect

Modern artists, the sincere ones, are saying new and exciting things, and their work cannot be explained. One accepts them as inexplicable and tries to learn, slowly, or one rejects them arrogantly as 'rubbish'.

Monday, 13 July

Part of me wants to have done with Francis, to draw a line and close the book, but I haven't the courage to convey that to him. I am sorry for him, and still interested, although he bores everyone else. What I must do is to let him come on Sundays (but not for a weekend), and meet the other people who come, and let him find his level among my old and new friends. It would be abominable of me, but if I had to choose between F. (and all that he means to me physically) and my friends, I should choose my friends. I've lived nearly a year now since the last 'flutter' (disgusting way of putting it – 'Experiment' is better) without any other Experiments. It is only vanity and pity that keeps me from breaking up our relationship.

My work for Mr Stevens has met with his approval: material for a brochure on aluminium in the Post-War home.

Sunday, 26 July

I received a bonus on Thursday. Firm is making so much money it does not know what to do with it.

Francis came last Sunday for the day, but I kept him most skilfully at a distance. He takes everything for granted, that I am quite ready to collapse into his arms at the first opportunity. He never takes any interest in my work or new friends. All he wants is to make love to me and to talk about himself. He called me a little bitch because I would not let him touch me. What a man.

Erno Goldfinger lived in this modernist row of houses from 1939, but its design was opposed by local residents, including Ian Fleming (who probably named his villain Goldfinger after him).

Friday, 7 August

Concern over our Government's interventions with regard to a Second Front to help our terribly pressed allies is universal.[120] ('Second Front *Now*' was scrawled in white paint across the road at Henley's Corner a few days ago but has now been removed). Even people who take relatively little interest in the political aspect of this war are getting worried.

Many people say, 'We are not ready.' Why are we not ready? Authorities should have foreseen this Second Front possibility last year, surely, and begun preparations at once. We should have at least some plans made, men trained and material collected for launching an attack on the Continent *now*. One loses heart and faith in the people who are in control. We have the feeling, strongly, that Powers That Be wish to see Russian might crippled before they will move a finger to help. They do not want Russia to have any say in the Peace Terms. Capitalist interests are still vastly strong, and the propertied bourgeois, although a minority, have still an enormous influence on the conduct of our affairs and are terrified of the idea of Socialism.

But the more our reactionaries try to resist the progress of Socialism, the greater will be their downfall. Socialism is inevitable. Any intelligent individual needs but an elementary knowledge of history to see that it is something which has been developing through centuries and can not be stopped. It will reach fruition in its own time, like all growing things, though it may take centuries more yet of blood and toil and tears and sweat.

Saturday, 8 August

I have made 2lbs of cherry jam. I was cutting thyme for drying when a Jerry swooped over the trees just after 6 p.m., sprayed the searchlight

---

120 The concept of the Second Front entailed an allied invasion of Europe to divert German forces from the Russian conflict.

post by the Farnham Common Hotel and peppered the Beeches. He was so low I could have read his number but for the mist which curled about and swallowed him. Guns went tardily into action but he rose and disappeared. A Jerry right over my cottage and I saw it! I began to feel excited again about the war. Action on my doorstep. Later learned that the machine-gunning was directed at a local fete in progress, and that 3–4 bombs were dropped on the trading estate. Two policemen killed.

Am reading *I Had a Row with a German*.[121] It is interesting, but this sort of sentence makes me feel ill: 'My last chance would be gone to send some loathsome murderer to his end.' Precisely what distinguishes the RAF fighters and bombers as heroes and the Luftwaffe as 'loathsome murderers'? If that's our service mentality, Lord help our post-war world.

Monday, 10 August
Gandhi and Congress leaders arrested. The *Star* splashes an account of Gandhi's luxury prison quarters in the Aga Khan's Palace at Poona – Empire and American raisins, a special British type of soap, rooms furnished by the most expensive London firms, the bed in the Royal boudoir large enough to sleep 18 and where a millionaire Mohammadan slept with all his 12 wives at once, sheets of silk, gardens cooled by fountains . . .

Gandhi is a man in advance of his time. India is a vast country with a complicated history. There must be other reasons for our refusal to give India her freedom now, besides those relating to our Imperial interests which the Communists shout about. Time may reveal.

Am having a fight with my laundry. The curtains I took to be cleaned on June 20th have been dyed black in error.

---

121 An account of the Battle of Britain, 1940, by Squadron Commander Tom Gleave, published anonymously as 'RAF Casualty'.

Friday, 14 August

Well! The phone rang – F.! He is Coming For The Night one night soon. There's perseverance for you – God knows I've given him little enough encouragement. But as there is no one else I cannot keep him at a distance any longer. Better an affaire without love than an embittered chastity. I have no motive for resistance. I am really rather ashamed of myself. Wish some St George would deliver me from this Dragon.

Mrs Hawthorn has not been since Bank Holiday now. What an abominable creature.

Tuesday, 18 August

I came to the conclusion after much serious thought during the weekend to finish with F., and wrote him a letter to that effect as firmly and as kindly as I could. If this decision means I must do without a lover then I must endure the situation. I am not the only woman who must do without. There will always be some without lovers, either from natural chastity, misfortune or their own psychological tangles. It is a problem for each of us to solve for ourselves – it is not solved by snatching sex out of its place and time.

I have no desire to meet F. again. I have no regrets, either, at having known him.

Wednesday, 19 August

The news of Churchill's visits to Moscow and Cairo have heartened us but tonight's account of our latest Commando raid brings a familiar depression. We have lost, apparently, many men and planes and much material. If this is the start of a big attack it would not seem to matter so much, but these nibbles at the French coast – what do we gain by them?

Still without domestic help. Have reduced living to its simplest. Except at weekends all meals and ablutions in the kitchen (the bath and sink being in the kitchen and no other taps in the cottage). Someone said today the war would go on for another 6 years.

Monday, 21 September

Lizzie de Groote and her friend Peter became engaged last Tuesday – Lizzie's happiness is a joy to behold. They are two fine, lovable people. But I am envious, terribly envious of Lizzie's happiness. A happiness it seems I am never to know. I go round my cottage saying, 'I have this. I have independence, an interesting job, good friends, many interests. These things are valuable and satisfying.' But living is not quite complete. It is the promise of fulfilment that is the essence of Lizzie's happiness, a knowledge of growth and future growth. Without that, however 'full' one's life, living is at the core hollow and desolate. It is like being a plant that lives in shadow, that never knows the sun.

Thursday, 1 October (War Diary)

Day off on Monday to shop in town. Searching for winter coat: Weatherall's no. 1 (top of Bond Street) – no stock at all. Weatherall's no. 2 (Regent Street) – the coat advertised in *Vogue* was in window. In *Vogue* it looked smashing and just what I wanted. Actually frightful, a sort of gabardine with trashy lining. Tried on a navy, belted, fairly good, fashionable cut, said to be 'pure wool' but badly finished with a ghastly Red Cross red lining (all their coats now seem to be lined with this material). It needed pressing and looked shoddy. Price 15 guineas. Jaeger, Regent Street – stock extremely limited and nothing under 19 guineas. A very indifferent assistant did not want to show me anything. Wanted to use strong language but went instead to Nicholls further down Regent Street. There the assistant was most helpful. A choice of several good coats but I fell for the first one I tried on – a very soft, real camel hair, great, belted, of classic cut and perfect fit. 13 guineas. Shops generally: stocks very low and much absolute rubbish being sold at high prices. Saw *Bambi* after lunch.

American soldiers to be seen everywhere. Vahan reports that there

is much ill feeling in British ranks at Americans' better pay and conditions. Tommies not openly hostile but are resentful. Must be a difficult situation. (Barbara Linnett says Americans in Wycombe are not
very popular. She finds the typical American to be 5ft nothing with
a leathery skin and not her fancy at all). Vahan says that the trouble
with the British private is that he does not know how to complain
(grumbles enough, but when an officer appears is dumb). Is it due to
the pressure of class distinctions, inadequate education, or inherent,
characteristic British shyness?

Gone with the Wind being shown in Slough this fortnight. One
hears it being discussed in every bus and queue.

22.

Asbestos Front

Friday, 2 October 1942

Did a spectacular faint the other evening when I went with Barbara Linnett to see *Gone with the Wind* and had to be taken home by ambulance. Scared B.L. to death. Am tired of these unexpected dramatic pass-outs which occur at such irregular intervals. Some weakness I think in the organs within the pelvis. Pains there fairly frequent but from apparently different causes. Have decided I must seek medical advice although I detest making a fuss. But have made an appointment to see Graham Howe on Monday. Any excuse to visit him again.

Monday, 5 October

Saw Graham Howe. Highly satisfactory. A picture to remember: star-light from the mountain piercing the waiting water lily.

Sunday, 11 October (War Diary)

The defence of Stalingrad magnificent. Clamour for Second Front continues, but many people, while agreeing that it is desirable, say we can not do it – we haven't the men, material or sources of supply necessary for a continued attack.

A Bristol Hercules engine is on show in the canteen. We supply all the aluminium alloys for this engine and the R.R. Merlin, besides making many aircraft parts, e.g. prop blades.

Tomorrow we start at 8.30 a.m. at the office. For this extra effort our Cost of Living Bonus has been changed from the 10 per cent on salary to a universal 10s. for all women and 15s. for all men receiving salaries of £7 and under. Why it should cost women less to live than men I don't know.

The question of women's equality with men cropped up. I maintain that women are not equal, or inferior, but *different*. Joan's little boy is at a school in Cornwall for small boys and girls, ages anything from three to thirteen. All the boys are keenly interested in aeroplanes and engines – Joan's son (7 years) knows every plane by sight. 'That's a Whitley,' he tells his mother who hasn't the least idea herself. On the other hand the little girls show no interest at all in aeroplanes and engines or any of the things that enthral little boys.

It is true that we have been given a vote and are accepted as independent individuals. It is true that we can work for the same exams and do as well and sometimes better in them than men. It is true that we have proved our ability in many spheres once governed only by men. But we find that in achieving this 'equality' we do so at a sacrifice of much of our private happiness and fulfilment. We have come out of the kitchen and away from the cradle to find that we are still women and masses of us are drawn year by year by instincts stronger than reason back again. Yet for many of us it isn't enough. We want to compete with men – and when we find ourselves on a level with men, doing men's work, the difference remains. We are in a state of perplexed growth and experiment. We are aware of our difference but haven't yet discovered how to define it or in the least how to use it outside our familiar domestic enclosure.

Sunday, 18 October
We are an astonishing, incalculable race. 'We do not know our capabilities and our power. A year or two ago our pilots and navigators and airgunners were the people we rubbed shoulders with in the streets. We took no particular notice of them then. They were clerks

and mechanics, they were sheep farmers, they sold second-hand motor cars and life insurance and radio sets.'[122]

Which reminds me that the latest news of Buckland is that he is *flying*. No one at the office thought he would stick out the course.

Sunday, 25 October
Wednesday at the RIBA all day and saw the Technicolor film of the prefabricated Homasote House which has been bought back from America. Intensely interesting. All parts of these houses of timber or wall boarding fabricated and cut to standard measurements in factory, transported to specially prepared site and erected within a few hours. Are being built in California for Emergency Defence Housing.

On Friday to a dance for Allied Nations given at the Slough Social Centre. London's Lord Mayor was there, and various of our directors and other local notabilities. French sailors, Polish airmen, Czech soldiers, British, Canadian, American forces, Land Army, Wrens, Waafs, ATS thronged the hall. Roped off were the Mayor and Officers. A grim affair. Girls and men stood about in self-conscious groups. No attempt beyond one very untidy Paul Jones and some Excuse Me dances was made to mix us up. Various entertainment turns throughout evening. Cabaret, Grand Pageant (our history stopped with the Stuarts). I was picked up by an army captain and swept into a date for next Friday before I knew where I was. He struck me as a rather inhibited creature, the sort that does get attracted to me. I will keep the appointment – the curiosity is too much for me.

Friday, 30 October
Have been late 3 times. Received an infuriating letter from the cleaners who ruined my curtains. Shall have to let solicitors deal with the

---

122 From *The Raft* by Eric Linklater.

matter. This evening's date with the Captain – I kept it, but he didn't. Feeling cold, lonely, inadequate and generally browned off.

Wednesday, 4 November
A supply of Coty rouge available in Slough. All typists in our department invest and are immensely excited.

Thursday, 5 November
Took an Intelligence Test this afternoon, voluntarily, (when asked if I would, I found it difficult to refuse). It was a paper set by the Institute of Industrial Psychology for clerical staff, and all our typists have taken it. Was in a panic about it – have had no clerical experience and thought it rather unfair, but P.A. was very soothing. He told me that several long established executives have taken it and with appalling results.

Sunday, 8 November
Weekend at Wembley. Ethel and I walked up Harrow Hill, the miles and miles of vile little houses wrapped softly in jade, people sitting along the church yard wall in rows looking over the land – the fair, spoilt land of 14 counties.

Her neighbours the Davies have relatives in Guernsey. News reaches them in this form: 'Mother Hubbard very evident' and 'A brasserie would be welcome.' 'Gerald is in your room and likes it very much.'

Saturday, 21 November
Attended a lecture by Sir William Beveridge to the Fabians this afternoon. Conway Hall crowded out. A very interesting lecture followed by a barrage of questions, but came away feeling unutterably lonely and depressed. Wanted to discuss it all with someone, either a friend at the meeting or someone waiting for me at home. Went straight to bed, ate a large bowl of hot onion gruel (a Pratt special).

Wednesday, 2 December

Beveridge Report issued and general reaction favourable.[123] Peter, who reads nothing but the *Telegraph* and steers clear of all 'politics', considers the proposals good. P.A. wanted to borrow my paper to study the account further. Mr Oliver muttered something about 'only the old insurance racket.' Lizzie says that the people she lives with turned Beveridge off the radio the other night – the report, they said, was no concern of theirs. They have no interests outside their home.

My WEA classes are in abeyance.[124] The Replanning Britain ones have been postponed on account of lecturer's illness.

Entertained two American officers from Wycombe about three weeks ago. Barbara Linnett cycled over with them (met them at the Allied Nations Dance). They brought cane sugar, canned beer, boiled sweets, chewing gun, pop-corn, packets of Philip Morris. We walked them through the Beeches to our 'lakes' on the edge of the Common but they were not impressed. We played silly games – Lt Fairman was a great sport and worked very hard to keep us all amused. Then we brought them back to the cottage for tea. They remarked on our English afternoon tea custom, which is unknown in the States. They paid a tribute to the women of England – said that if American women had had to put up with half as much as we have they would have made a terrific fuss. We played silly games and they appeared to enjoy themselves but under it all was a feeling – what? Sort of 'we are strangers and resented.' I don't know how they are received in Wycombe but British provincial people can be abominably hostile to any 'foreign' element. I proposed this tea party weeks ago which made

123 The Beveridge Report laid the foundations for the Welfare State. The economist William Beveridge identified 'Five Giant Evils' in society (Squalor, Ignorance, Want, Idleness, Disease), and the ambitious prospect of their eradication proved highly attractive to a population who believed the end of war was at last in sight. The principles of a modern benefits system and the National Health Service sprang directly from the report.

124 The Workers' Educational Association had been established in 1903 to provide a broad range of adult education courses.

B.L. want to give one herself but her mother said, 'I'm not having any Americans in my house!' She was, however, persuaded in the end, and after the one who came had gone she remarked, 'He is rather fascinating, isn't he?'

Thursday, 3 December

Home early tonight on account of fog.

Mr G. had me into his office today for an 'informal chat'. Was told again that we must cut staff to a minimum in order to appease demands from the Ministry of Labour and that as many of our people as possible will be transferred to the Laboratories or other departments. The Government is checking up hard on all extravagance, and preventing as far as possible private firms making plans that would interfere with progressive post-war reconstruction. High Duty Alloys' plans for development are positively nil, and is obviously hopping with terror at the idea of Government interference. Seems as though if I stay after the changes are made, that my work will be mainly routine and very, very dull. But the job has such potentialities am loath to abandon it now. The cottage is, besides, an overwhelming factor. I'd put up with a lot in order to go on living here in spite of domestic problems. Purely selfish, as P.A. pointed out the other day when I was 'on the carpet' for being late. I was explaining some of my private difficulties and he said, 'Haven't you an aunt or sister or something who would come and live with you?' At which I answered with emphasis that I valued my independence much too much. The outcome of this interview is that I have been granted an hour a week for shopping, allowed only as a rule to married women employees.

Tonight ate cheese sliced thinly and cooked in margarine with tomato and milk, and pudding made from stale scone and some vile ABC jam sponge cake, soaked in prune juice, mixed with plenty of homemade plum jam and steamed. Jam was beginning to go mouldy: Joan says she has heard of many people's jam doing likewise, possibly due to wartime proportion of sugar and to it being beet instead of cane sugar. So cold. Fire won't burn.

Wednesday, 9 December

Hughes, Lizzie and Miss Lucas are to be released from Publicity Dept. I shall have a lot more to do, and it looks as though my job will become a lot more interesting. I shall be working as the Head's chief assistant.

Sunday, 27 December

'You do not *know* what Wee Cottage means to me,' said Nockie. 'I feel certain you saved my life by having me down at your heavenly home.' These and other contributions I am vain enough to treasure. I say, 'Everyone falls for the cottage,' and Lizzie answers, 'But you *are* the cottage!'

I have reached a point now where I am established as an independent, individual woman, with a definite life of her own, something to share with a man. It does not depend on the cottage, but the cottage is its first flowering.

A lovely Xmas. Nockie here. Plenty to eat! I roasted a rabbit and some pork, managed to get some mince pies from the village at the last moment and had made an 'austerity' Xmas pudding from a recipe in *The Listener*. I made jelly and custard and stewed some diced fruit. Iced a cake. Received a good number of Xmas cards and presents such as Book Tokens, handkerchiefs, soap, calendars. Fire in the kitchen all three days.

Sunday, 24 January 1943

Last night Barbara Linnett gave a party at her house in Wycombe. Thanks to the Americans it was a whale of a party. The Americans I have met are strangers to me in a way the Britisher never is. On the surface they are so much more sharply defined than we are: scintillating, unselfconscious, but I'm not sure that it isn't the unselfconsciousness of children. There is a naivety about them. Their confidence doesn't seem to be an adult one, not the confidence of men who have laboured through all the painful process of learning to know themselves. But so far I have only met officers. There is something about the officer class which is trying in all nations.

I enjoyed that party enormously. It ended up with some terrific rough and tumble kissing games. Barbara managed to find a taxi to help the long-distance people home after midnight. It brought me and Thomas Hughes to Egypt [Wee Cottage]. He had left his bicycle at the cottage to take him back to Slough. He came in quite willingly when I suggested tea, looked at the kitchen stove (he has ideas now for keeping the fire in for long periods), and then we sat in the sitting room talking very easily about – oh, all sorts of things in the usual Tommy manner, i.e. he did most of the talking.

He eventually came out with the idea of our starting, after the war, a sort of library reference service for industry. Just as High Duty Alloys has its Bulletin giving abstracts from current technical journals and notes and news of anything of importance to the aluminium industry, so might an outside agency work for several industries. Any manufacturer wanting all the available dope on a certain subject has only to phone, and the references are sent to him in a couple of days. It's an idea with immense possibilities which appeals to me, and I'm flattered beyond measure that he has thought of me. He left at 5 a.m.

One of the games we played last night was 'Truths'. Questions shot at me included, 'Have you ever been in love?' (From T.H.) Answer: 'Several times.' And 'Are you in love with anyone now?' Answer: 'No.'

Sunday, 21 February

And now it is Sunday evening, and Nockie has just left and I await the arrival of Thomas to cut an asbestos front for the kitchen stove. I suppose that for as long as I know him I shall have to endure his *maddening* instability. I wanted him to come before Nockie went and suggested 5 p.m. I am always so damnedly good-humoured to his face about his shortcomings – he's got into the habit of thinking 'Jean won't mind.' Yet bad temper and nagging wouldn't do any good. I begin perhaps to know him, but I do not understand him. What the hell should I worry for anyway? What have I to do with a lunatic Irishman? Perhaps he won't come tonight at all now. Does it please him to be disappointing to his friends continually?

Wednesday, 3 March (War Diary)
In the house I manage much better than I thought I should. The chief thing is not to worry about dust in corners. As an article in a recent *Housewife* explains, many people are discovering that the 'woman' can be done without and that the kitchen floor does not look dirty if it is never scrubbed.

Barbara Linnett bought a Hovis the other day and hugging it to her said 'If only I had half a pound of butter I'd sit down and eat this now!'

A cable and airgraph from my brother in Suez this week. He and family all well. Sold his car nearly a year ago owing to number of passes required to get anywhere. Sister in law says prices high. Niece Babs at school in Cairo and happy.

Monday, 15 March
This dark and firelit north-facing study. The furniture is old, drab and here for a purpose only, not to be decorative. Books on the table, the desk, the chest of drawers, papers, journals, a pot of Gloy and a box of pins, a trunk behind the divan, my old worn drab toys of childhood, Big Teddy, Little Teddy, Piglet, limp with sawdust pouring from their unpatched sides. A scarlet scarf, a powder box, a silver-topped pot of rouge, lipstick and lotions, an ebony elephant who has lost his trunk, chromium earrings, talcum powder, a tiny cup of dying primroses, a nest of small, brightly coloured wooden bowls which I brought from Russia. I love it. The scene is set for the Bloomsbury garret. Here struggles the young writer, here weeps, here rests the growing woman.

23.

Hiduminium Aluminium

Monday, 21 March 1943 (aged thirty-three)

A new book with a red cover (promise of passion), and I have to start it with tears. The dream and the hope live on, although one knows one may be wasting one's time with a ghost. Yet the person is real and one knows him a little better now. The agony is one of frustration and anxiety, and the awful threatening finger of 'Too Late! And it was your own fault.' The opportunity missed, the wrong word, the wrong action . . .

Last night I lay awake coughing until 5.30 a.m. This morning I visited the doctor, he tapped and sounded me very thoroughly, told me there was 'nothing to worry about,' and stuck a piece of adhesive tape marked 'HCB' across the top of my shoulder blade. I am to go again on Wednesday.

Thursday, 25 March

Sky-rocketed by this paragraph in a letter from Nockie, which I just cannot refrain from giving here, although it betrays me irrevocably.

'Things are turning out for you just as I expected. I thought he would be going his own way again. And it will be some time again before he comes round I should think, but not so long as before because his appetite should be a bit more stirred now, even if he is a dilly-dallying, shilly-shallying, unreliable, thoroughly attractive and upsetting Irishman.

'About my giving you advice with regard to the managing of such a highly complex example of God's work: I think Cleopatra would take a chance on things, and if she made a wrong shot, she'd just have to wait again until the time was ripe again to try another kind of shot.'

I have no Cleopatranine technique nor can ever hope to have.

Wednesday, 31 March

Am asked frequently, what do I do with my evenings? This is what I do. As soon as I get in: light study fire, view mail and collect goods left by tradesman, prepare a meal, make bed, empty hot-water bottle and slop pail, do black-out, eat meal, then possibly write letters, make phone calls, an hour or two's work on WEA class or war diary, mend some stockings perhaps, clean a pair of shoes, iron a blouse, boil kettles. No dusting or sweeping gets done until the weekend, washing up I attend to perhaps twice during the week.

Chest X-rayed this afternoon. To know the worst tomorrow.

Tuesday, 13 April

The strength of the Old School Tie – Jean Macfarlane to the rescue again. I twice left light on in bedroom recently when I departed in morning, and as I did not return on each occasion until long after Black Out, the light shone brilliantly into the darkness and was reported by military. Local policeman had to climb in window and turn out offending illumination.[125] I didn't go to court for first summons, and was fined 30 shillings. Last night I received second summons and a charge for wasting fuel. The office sent me dizzy today, telling me that second fine likely to be very heavy, that I must attend court in person this time, that I should certainly obtain legal advice. I phoned Jean when I got home and I am to see her father tomorrow evening. Am deeply touched.

---

125 Later she writes: 'Policeman very nice about it. Said he had to charge a Chief Constable's wife not long ago.'

Thursday, 15 April

An elderly, precise, big-hearted, hard-headed Scotsman – Jean M.'s father. They are such kind people. They live in a large, pleasant neo-Georgian house, and their garden is spacious but rather desolate. There are daffodils in abundance under trees, but the lawn needs cutting and there is no colour in the flower beds. If, said Mr Macf, the case had been at Slough court he might have been able to get it withdrawn for me, but as it is at Burnham where he has no influence he can do nothing. Jean, however, is going to bring her influence to bear on the Inspector who has brought the charges (through a Farnham Common Red Cross commandant). If he can be persuaded to be lenient, the Bench will possibly be kind to me. But I must plead my own case on Monday – I am guilty! No lawyer could say anything in my defence that I could not say myself. What would my darling Papa say? Much banter about me being a hardened criminal.

Wednesday, 21 April

I attended the Court as bidden on this last Monday morning, quaking. I was expecting to have to pay out £5. I pleaded guilty, accepted the policeman's evidence and explained in a small voice that I worked from 8.30–6 every day, was alone in the cottage, had no domestic help and had to get myself up and off in the morning by 8 o'clock, had not been well and was that week losing sleep because of troublesome cough and that therefore in the early morning rush it was easy to forget the light. The Bench went into a huddle and then I heard the Chairman say '£1 for each charge.' £2 in all! Which I paid promptly. What wires Jean and her father have been pulling I don't yet know but I have them to thank for this I am sure. Everyone at the office as astonished as myself and think me very fortunate. But Heaven help me if I do it again.

Tuesday, 5 May

I saw my first X-ray diagnosis last night: everything as it should be except for some 'scattered opacities in the right lung which suggest tubercular infection.' The second X-ray was taken this afternoon and I am in a most mournful mood. I don't want to be ill, to be subjected to some monstrous treatment and be shut away from the world. I wept this evening. What, I asked myself, have I to live for? Why should I fight for a life that seems aimless and vapid? What have I given that the world should want me?

Darker and darker grow the shadows in the garden. From here, in the sitting room with the light on, the sky is a theatrical dull green-blue, the trees and shadows ultramarine and black. An orange glimmer from a neighbour's window.

Thursday, 6 May

I dread to hear the doctor's verdict.

Sunday, 9 May

A little girl demands that I record this confession. She knows him to be a vain, unreliable, deceiving scoundrel. She is often shocked and chilled by his behaviour, his aloofness, his lack of real sympathy. Yet she would give him the earth if she could. She dances with joy when she hears him coming. She thinks of him day and night, and although he has proved his worthlessness again and again, although he is never there when he is wanted, she likes to be with him, likes to know he is around. She will believe anything he tells her. She would stand by him through any misfortune. She weeps at her own foolishness. She knows that the other girl in the laboratory is much more of a friend to him than she can ever be. And yet and yet . . . the dream and the hope go on. Her heart floods with bitter happiness at the thought of him.

The second X-ray has shown that there are no changes in those disturbing 'opacities', and the doctors have come to the conclusion that they are therefore inactive. Nothing to worry about. Do not smoke too much and do not neglect colds. It was like being released from long-term imprisonment.

Monday, 24 May
Thomas Hughes has been moved to the labs.

Sunday, 30 May
Feeling as chill and mouldy as a tomb. Your will to love gets pressed down and blacked out. If that pressure grows heavy and black enough there's no other way out of the problem – you're weighted down, wedged, suffocated. All paths but one seemed blocked to you. I am nowhere near that state but I can see how it can begin. It is a terrible mood: to feel useless, unwanted, unloved.

Tuesday, 15 June (War Diary)
This last Whit weekend I spent at Hove. The Brighton shore is mined and guarded with barbed wire, many of the huge hotels along the front have been taken over for the Services, and The Lanes, where the fashionable strolled on summer evenings after dinner, have gone to sea-dried seed. The appearance of the front is very depressing but holiday crowds (90 per cent of which seem to be Jews) still promenade when the sun shines. The doors of the Norfolk Hotel, The Metropole, The Queens, the Old Ship and a host of others still swing open to visitors. The antique shops in The Lanes appear well stocked and thriving.

The front has not suffered much from bomb damage, only those parts of the town near the station, the viaduct and the gasworks. Many shops thereabouts are boarded up or to let and many houses empty. When raids are bad the population begins to leave.

On the whole I think the war has improved Brighton. The glare and publicity to attract the cheap holiday trade has subsided. Now the Georgian era can be seen – faded but enchanting.

Wednesday, 16 June (War Diary)
Our Wings for Victory Target was £15,000. On Friday it had reached £7,000. Today the total was announced as something over £15,400.

Was told that the management would not allow our total to be less than the target at any cost.

Sally who works in wages and was responsible for the Savings receipts said that one man last year brought in £150 in £1 notes – she told him to bring it the next year in £10 notes, and he did.

Tuesday, 29 June (War Diary)

Our film *Forgings in Hiduminium Aluminium Alloys* is now making its debut. We saw it last week. I didn't have anything to do with it so I can say freely that it is really an excellent technical film. It has had one or two special showings and has been very favourably received.

Blitz First Aid lectures and a Prisoners of War Fete held last Saturday at which I helped at the coconut shies. No real coconuts, only wooden dummies. Anyone who knocked one off received 3d. or another turn. Lemon, grapefruit and orange drinks. An Auction: silk shawl that went for £10, a necklace for £27, lemons and peaches for 20s. or 30s. each, a live rabbit for 10s. Goods included champagne, port, dolls, a patchwork quilt made by an old lady of 82, Maltese lace, a tea cosy and a statuette for which no one would give a bid, not even for Prisoners of War.

Wednesday, 30 June

What I am seeking is *poise*. That has really been the essential motive of all my wanderings. More than writing, more than lovers – I want to feel sure of myself as a full-growing balanced person, meeting defeat, pain, humiliation without losing that balance. A person of wisdom and quality.

Saturday, 10 July

Cats have had 5 kittens between them. The foundation of life is in young creatures. Their curiosity, courage and joyousness seems inexhaustible – I could watch them without tiring for hours.

To be loved – not merely made love to – that's what I want. It is comparatively easy to find someone willing to make love to you. But to be loved – that lies beyond your conscious power to control. All you can do about it consciously is to become worthy of being loved.

Monday, 2 August

Here I am, with Elsie D. as companion, at the Fabian Summer School in Dartington. We have been here since Saturday evening, and by tonight should have got to know at least one or two males sufficiently well to be asked for, say, a couple of dances each. I came away deliberately from the dance hall to write this, leaving Elsie alone there: I think she stands more chance of being asked if she is on her own. I hope she'll stay for a little while and chance her luck.

I'm not here for any spectacular romance or to find a husband, but I had hoped we should fall in with a pleasant group and mix fairly freely. But people seem to have ignored us as if we had the plague or weren't there. I'm not sure whose fault this is: E. is more retiring than I am and really rather a bore. We have isolated ourselves too much and E. doesn't help matters. I think we sit around in corners too much looking superior.

It's not being a success, this holiday. This question of lonely people: there should be here a sympathetic hostess and I would like to be it: just to keep my eye open for the solitary members of the party, find out if they are so by choice or mischance, and tactfully get the lonely people together. It would be so easy for me at this stage to fall into a bitter, sour-grapish criticism of the Fabians. They have a power for good, but they won't succeed unless they explore thoroughly all the potentialities of their members. If you leave it too much to the individual's initiative, the work will be grabbed by the exhibitionists, the people who crave limelight and power.

Midnight: E. has returned. She has danced with a certain Czech.

Tuesday, 3 August

Midnight: All, all is changed! Another familiar situation: to have met someone you're attracted to, who is attracted to you, and wanting the obvious climax to that attraction yet not knowing at all what to do about it. Reason, upbringing and fear all preaching caution, and then impulse and instinct urging you violently to take the plunge. When one is hungry for something and sees food one doesn't stop to consider the principles of eating. Tomorrow evening – oh, let's go to bed now and wait till that time comes.

Sunday, 8 August

I must go right back. About 11.30 p.m. on the evening before my holiday at Dartington the phone rang. To my astonishment it was Tommy. He had asked me at the office about the chances of getting a room at Dartington (his idea, not mine). As usual he had made no plans for his holidays. On the phone he said he had been unable to get accommodation there, but might come to Devon with his bicycle, stay somewhere near and look in. This pleased me enormously. I have in no way for a very long time made any effort to pursue that young man. Since March the fever subsided and all sentimental hopes and desires died. If he approached I welcomed him, easily and frankly, but set no 'nets'.

We returned from Dartington yesterday and I am still in bed. The villagers consider us all lunatics – our reputation for immorality is terrific. Both accusations are to some extent justified. I don't think I want to go again. One lives at a very fast pace, crowding as much as possible into a very short space of time: two lectures a day, endless discussions, walks, dancing, tennis, activities of all kinds to suit every inclination. Everyone is greedy for the maximum amount of enjoyment. People grab at pleasure, and the timid and diffident get left out. We seemed to have an unusually unmeldable collection that week. A top group, formed of brilliant, scintillating young people who mixed easily with Fabian notables. Only their own pleasure was considered. People who could not live at their pace or come up to their standards were ignored. I am thinking of a young woman called Barbara Betts, and a young Jew called John

Lewis – the intolerant type that thrive on competition and make my type shrivel.[126]

Things began to improve for myself and Elsie on Wednesday during a long walk. We got to know people, and the awful rain was a great help. I began to fall quite seriously for a Czech (not the one E. danced with) called Otto. He was large, rather like Charles Laughton, his manner a little conceited and ludicrous, but I think it was due to loneliness and shyness. I spent quite a lot of the day with him.

I think my agitation and misery at the beginning of the week was largely aggravated by the thought of Tommy's possible appearance. I did not want him to come and find me left out of everything in the humiliating position of wallflower. On Wednesday evening Otto made very definite advances, which pleased me, but I was undecided as to what course I should take. Thursday was a disappointing day until the afternoon – E. and I tried to go to Paignton but spent all the afternoon queuing for buses in the rain. When we eventually abandoned the idea and returned, I found a note in my room from Tommy. He came to the lecture that evening.

Well, in this extraordinary, feverish atmosphere of young passion, wit, ideas and so on, the climax for Tommy and me was obvious. There was only one obvious course for me to take that night, although not with the person I had been considering the night before. I spent Thursday and Friday night with Tommy and I am not at all ashamed to admit it. Why be ashamed of sex?

We learnt a lot about each other. I think we may be able to help each other a lot too. He has lived with the girlfriend who works in the laboratory (just as I have always expected) for years – I suppose he still

---

126 Barbara Betts: this was the young Barbara Castle, the future long-standing Labour MP for Blackburn and influential cabinet minister under Harold Wilson. More than thirty years later, on seeing a newspaper report on Castle, Jean recalled in her journal: 'Met at a Fabian summer school in the 40s, I think at height of my T.H. affaire. Barbara sat next to me at a meal and soon sized me up and had dismissed me of no account. Very vital she was then, young, slim, bouncing about on platforms. No doubt at all that she would get somewhere.'

does. I don't feel at all jealous: I am not in the romantic sense at all in love with Tommy. I like him. I feel this morning quite calm, happy, ready for whatever may lie ahead. I leave our next meeting to him or to chance. One just doesn't make plans where Tommy is concerned.

Monday, 16 August

The sort of day when marvellous things should happen but rarely do. Left office early to have my hair done – new hag at the hairdressers had booked me for *next* Monday in error. She looks an awful old witch and I'd like to get fixed up elsewhere, but hairdressers so fully booked these days. Cottage for once tidy, cool and delightful, but Dinah missing. She has been missing since last week and am distraught. No letters, not even a bill. And not a word from that young man. As far as I can discreetly find out, he has not yet returned to the office from his holiday and I have seen nothing of the girlfriend either. This is so typical of him. But I went through too much agony last year over this sort of strange vanishing to worry more now. Am of course eaten up by curiosity and a little anxious lest something may have happened to him.

Sunday, 22 August

Tommy came back to the office on Tuesday. Dinah limped home with a badly damaged paw on Wednesday to my great joy. Ethel is here and the cottage begins to glisten again, thanks to her. But if the period due at the end of this week doesn't come then my future will be hard and complicated. The thought doesn't scare me at the moment but I don't want to have to go through difficulties and complications of that kind – I don't know that I would have the necessary amount of 'guts' – and I mean either way, to have a child or get rid of it. I think I would want T. to share the decision with me, but I'd never ask him or get him to marry me as a way out – I would rather die. And if the decision was to get rid of it, I'd go to my own friends, not his. He just makes me feel that way.

To him I am just an adventure in the Beeches. In fact to all the men I have ever had much to do with I've been just an adventure, an entertaining interlude. I am getting tired of it. What is exasperating, humiliating, is that I am sure if T. really wanted to be different he could be. I enjoy being with him, oh, enormously really! But the Irish – yes, they do scare me. That Irish background of his, the circle of friends I never meet, only hear of. I couldn't cope with them. And besides, in that circle, the girlfriend is accepted more or less as his 'wife'. It is that quicksilver quality of theirs that is so bewildering to the stable English.

Monday, 30 August

I want so badly now a lover interested in me positively, dynamically – but I guess all men are too selfish and much too egotistical. And I too bitter, independent and elusive.

Waiting for the kettle to boil in the kitchen just now I was suddenly overtaken by the humour of the situation. I stood there and laughed and laughed as the cats regarded me with solemn horror. That impossible young man. There the girlfriend and I sit in the canteen, knowing a whole lot about each other and the young man – the shared young man. Oh she can have him, he's much too much a coward for me!

Friday, 3 September

Four years of war. And now we are invading Italy.

Our new boss Mr Botterell has arrived at the office. He knows nothing of Publicity or Advertising.

Thursday, 9 September

I am feeling so awfully pleased with myself. The position at the office has now been clarified and I appear to have come out with flying colours. I am Mr B's assistant definitely – I have been doing a good job of work and didn't know it. I am always so surprised when I receive a pat on the back. When it's a big pat it affects my balance even more than a kick in the tummy does. But think of it: I have established myself in the eyes of management as one intelligent, competent young woman!

I wish I could be half as successful in my affaire with Tommy. I have not even *seen* him for a week. N. thinks, as I do, that the girl-friend is an even greater tie than she would be as his wife. Why doesn't he marry her? All the men I've ever cared about have done that – married someone else.

Friday, 17 September
He came into our office this week and talked to me for half an hour. Otherwise – nothing. One could say he's had all he wanted, his curiosity is satisfied and now you're finished with, dropped, discarded. He is about with the girlfriend a lot these days, and there is no avoiding that they do seem a pair. It's that that I'm jealous of – she is his woman whatever extraneous adventures he may indulge in, and she knows it. I can under-stand the desire of a woman to break up a happy relationship; when one is hungry and alone it is a damnedly provocative situation.

Friday, 1 October
His behaviour is both insulting and humiliating, though I don't think he intends it to be. Not a word, not a sign – perhaps I should write 'Finis' to this episode and let go.

I keep hoping that if I accept this humiliation, endure the emptiness, the desire unfulfilled for a man's steady affection and companionship – that God will be pleased and reward me with what I want. But I have got to accept these facts: that I am a hungry, haunted woman *now*, reward in the future or no. That is much harder to face and bear than T.'s actual neglect. I am one of the Adamless brigade, have always been, may always be. It is, however, much more difficult to live successfully without that means of letting one's love flow. The easiest way to be happy and to give out one's happiness is when one has a successful sex life, isn't it? Some people would say No, its the economic life that counts.

Friday, 8 October
And as I stood in a queue this morning waiting for a bus to take me

into Slough, he came down the road and I waved and he came across to me and said he was just on his way to see me. So we stood and chatted amiably on this mild, bright October morning, and when the bus came he got on it and came with me into Slough, although that had evidently not been his intention. He has promised to come and mend a light switch for me this weekend (I have had to grope around the kitchen with candles).[127]

Tuesday, 19 October

I returned through driving rain from a High Duty Alloys discussion group on 'Equal Pay for Equal Work' (for women). There we were, nine men and four women, and the women put up a very poor show. Maggie Gray and I were the only two who spoke. Maggie became more positive and sure of herself towards the end, but I suddenly felt how pointless was the argument and relapsed feebly. Equal pay for equal work unanimously agreed, but can women contribute equal work? That was the point really – can she and does she want to? Hasn't she other kinds of work to do which men cannot do, and why therefore should she compete with men? If she does, who is to look after the house?

I cannot compete with men in logical argument! How apparent that was tonight. The men did all the abstracting, generalising, summing up. I felt fussy and muddled. But at least I am now saying something in public, which at one time I could never do, not even ask a simple direct question.

Lizzie hurt and surprised me the other day. She suddenly said (and meant it) that my two cats Dinah and the Kittyhawk 'gave her the pip.' I must not, she went on, lose my sense of proportion, I must not forget that they were only animals. I do, I admit, talk of them foolishly, and I am foolishly fond of them – I adore them. But I never prattle about them unless invited to, never impose them on other people as The

---

127 Note added later: 'He didn't come.'

Most Wonderful Cats In The World, never demand that others should see them as I do. I had believed Lizzie understood. She doesn't. That little, hard, rigid streak. She has all she needs as a woman to lavish her affection on (and a baby on the way), and she does not have to find substitutes. I thought she had more sympathy, more tolerance. But I shall not give up loving my cats because of her remarks. No one should be despised or reproved for loving something, however extravagantly, however unworthy the subject. 'I say this for your own good,' she said. God, the cruelty, the damnable cruelty of these narrow, hard women who would destroy love in another for 'their own good'!

T.? No, T. has not been near me. It hurts, it hurts, to see him about so much, so closely with the girlfriend, to hear everyone's remarks and speculation on the matter ('Almost hooked!'). I wanted so much to know him better, to share more of what I have with him.

Saturday, 20 November (War Diary)
We had great difficulty in obtaining permission to make 16mm copies of our *Forgings* film but sanction came eventually from the Ministry of Supply and we have now about half a dozen copies which are going the rounds of various aircraft firms and training centres. A film on Castings is now being made. Incidentally we make the Halifax undercarriage. It is the largest magnesium casting in the world and we are awfully proud of it.[128]

The long evenings have begun. The kitchen blackout I leave up all the week (and the cottage *beams* on a Saturday morning when I take it down before going to work because it knows that the kitchen will have the whole day of whatever sunshine there is and that there will be a fire in the range).

The London Symphony Orchestra was performing on Wednesday for war factory workers only. I should have been one of them but for

---

128 The Halifax was first employed in 1941, and although widely considered less effective in its bombing raids than the Lancaster, it boasted higher crew survival rates and proved highly effective in Italy and North Africa.

somebody's error – ENSA sent 2,000 vouchers which were allotted to the various factories including ours, but the hall holds only 1,000 people and at the last moment all our vouchers were recalled.[129]

Wednesday, 24 November
Am still vastly dissatisfied with my personal progress. I am 34 and shudder at the thought. I still believe in my potentialities, and that I may realise them – that I can achieve something concrete yet, make some worthwhile contribution to life. Am at the point now when I am sure many people like me feel they are failures, and that it's no use trying any more. And they give up, shrivel, go bitter, miserable, silent.

As a woman, before anything else I feel I should be married, happily married, with possibly a young family. I have an appalling sense of failure, inferiority and insignificance about this which cuts deeply. It seems that something must be very wrong somewhere that I have failed to attract myself the right mate. And I should be now settling into a defined career and making headway in it. I wanted to write, I still want to write, but have produced really nothing.

Saturday, 27 November
One fact I often forget: there are 3 million surplus women in Great Britain. But I am resentful that I have to be one of them. There's no good reason for it, except my 'unapproachability'. No lost, dead lover. No physical defects. No domestic inability. No lack of potential warmth! Only that first awkwardness, fear.

I am stripping and whipping myself ruthlessly because I am so sick of this sickly sense of frustration. But however I advance in the future, and for as long as I write here, I swear to be honest – as I always have been. As honest as such a subjective approach can be.

---

129 ENSA, the Entertainments National Service Association. Also known as Every Night Something Awful.

24.

Good Dyed Squirrel

Sunday, 12 December 1943

The cottage was burgled on Friday. I came home about 6.30. It was only just after sunset, the moon was full and the evening light. One or other of the cats was around my feet as I unlocked the back door. I noticed with a start that the black-out screen at the window had been moved and the things on the windowsill pushed onto the table beneath. I couldn't find my torch. I went into the sitting room and turned on the electric main switch. The 'front' door (which is never used as it is right at the back of the cottage) immediately opposite the stairs (the stairs run straight up to the first floor, dividing the cottage; as you face them, the small store room and kitchen are on your right, the sitting room on your left). The front door, as I was saying, was open.

I was shocked and frightened and turned all the lights on. Cupboards were open. Upstairs – chaos. Every drawer in the bedroom had been opened, and the contents of several of them thrown on the floor. Boxes under the bed had been dragged out and emptied. In a recess at the top of the stairs I keep, behind a curtain, an old stand that once held my mother's music, with boxes containing evening shoes, belts, oddments – most of these had been opened, and one evening shoe (how many times had it carried me to the theatre or a dance?) was in the bedroom. The jewel box had been ransacked but its secret drawer left undiscovered.

The study had also been searched. All drawers open, papers scattered. I felt sick. I felt very, very angry. I rushed to my neighbours. I telephoned the police. My fur coat was gone, two clocks, the electric iron, various pieces of jewellery, including all long strings of beads, some of them quite valueless, and an old rosary which was in a box in the sitting room (but none of my earrings).

The police (first our local Sergeant Brewer who climbed in my bedroom window twice last winter to turn out the light, then the inspector and his assistant, three enormous, uniformed men), went slowly round, making notes, discovering footprints in the flower bed outside the kitchen window, the pane cracked, my bicycle pump (which I keep indoors) by one of the sheds

Lady Spicer offered to put me up for the night. But I thought no, I must go on, see this thing through. My cottage has been insulted, raped. I will not desert it in its hour of humiliation – my beloved cottage!

I restored some order to the bedroom. I stayed at home the next morning, and a nice young man came and took casts of the footprints and looked for fingerprints. The police suspect a man in the neighbourhood who has done several jobs similar to this. He has a woman who gets rid of the stuff for him.

Tuesday, 14 December

The BBC is giving an account of Mr Eden's speech on the Tehran Conference.[130] I should be listening but I'm too happy. So rarely do I write that here. Really happy. It is only for a moment, I know. It will pass, it must, but I savour the moment as full as I can. I owe it to these journals to record why, although I know the danger there is of destroying it as I do so.

He came into the office when I was alone at lunchtime, looking

---

130 This first official meeting of Churchill, Roosevelt and Stalin discussed options for a Second Front and early plans for a post-war settlement.

for a camp bed he had left in one of the cupboards. I asked him to
buy a Russia Today Xmas Draw ticket. He said, with his arm around
my shoulders, 'And how's the little girl?'

'Feeling a bit neglected.'

'Who's neglecting you?'

'Who do you think?'

'It wouldn't be me, would it? Would it?'

'It might be . . .'

And the Little Girl (yes, I've just realised it, he *does* call me that!)
stirred and was dancing, dancing . . .

He talked then in his usual way. I don't remember what about.
Ireland I think But it didn't matter. He asked if there was anything
he could bring us back from Ireland (he is going home for Xmas).
Silk stockings?

Warmth. That's what mattered. The whole light on living changed.
How long will it last? But while it does, let me relax in it. Heavenly,
heavenly moment. Oh you crazy, foolish woman.

Friday, 17 December

The moment was very short-lived. At one o'clock I was alone in the
office again and went down to the typists' room and found him by
the telephone. He was busy with the phone so I did not stay. I
hoped he'd come up before he went off, but he didn't. He swooped
out without a sign to me. I've no doubt he had plenty of good
reason for doing this, but it shows what a completely masculine
disregard for my feeling he has. He's a swine and he knows it, and
he'll go on behaving like that for as long as we know him. Girlfriend
was around – I followed them out of the canteen. She's always
around.

And when the Almighty asks me, 'Well, and what besides yourself
did you love on earth?' I shall answer, 'My cats and my cottage . . .'
And if He goes on, 'And did anyone love you?' I shall have no
answer.

Tuesday, 28 December

One more Xmas over. Had a bad cold. Nockie was with me with a bad cold too so we sat and wheezed at each other over the fire most of the time. From all accounts everyone had quantities to eat over Xmas. I heard of one girl who had turkey for middle-day dinner on Xmas Day and goose in the evening, chicken the following middle-day and duck in the evening. I also had a rabbit which I stuffed and roasted and some pork from my butcher. I was able to get some mincemeat and made a large mince pie, the first time I had ever made pastry, and it was an enormous success.

Mass Observation is asking its Observers to keep a Daily Feelings chart throughout January. Maximum cheerfulness is to be marked 10+, deepest depression 10-, and 'normal' i.e. neither cheerful or depressed, 0. I think this is going to be very difficult. How can one assess one's feeling over a day like that? I might start 5-, rise to 7+ and sink to 1-, and, being tired, put myself down for the day as 8-.

Friday, 31 December

New Year's Eve, 11 p.m. In bed. I wasn't going to open this book tonight, but then I thought, well, wish good things at least to your family and friends. So I'll wish nice things to my family and friends and be asleep before the New Year is in. Leslie and Ivy and Babs. Ethel. All the Pratt and Lucey relations to whom I owe good feeling. Nockie, Joan and Vahan and their family Gus and Phyllis. Lizzie and Peter. Lugi. These and other unnamed. Now I am going to sleep, wishing you all a Happy New Year my loved ones. And to my pussies, past, present and yet to come.

New Year's Day, 1944

Oh fertilise me, fertilise me, God, that thy servant may not die fruitless!

Tuesday, 4 January (War Diary)

Of course none of the stolen articles or the thief have been traced. The police suspect a man of 60. He goes about as a jobbing gardener asking for work, then watches the surrounding houses. Several people have said to me, 'But if the police know him why don't they go and arrest him?' which in England you cannot do without evidence. They never seem able to get the evidence.

I must admit that for a week I quaked when I returned each night, but the qualms soon wore off and I come back now as intrepid as ever – though possibly greeting the cats a shade more enthusiastically than formerly.

I am covered by an All-In Policy but not for the wartime increase in values. The iron, for instance, cost me 15s. in 1939. Now, if you can get such a thing, they are about 30s. My coat was a good dyed squirrel, bought in 1936 and had just been cleaned and remodelled (£10. 10 had gone on that). The furrier told me it would sell like that today for £150. It cost me originally £40. The Insurance company are sending someone to see the house this week – but what I am to show him beyond a cracked window pane and a practically empty jewel box I don't quite know.

Saturday, 8 January
In bed. Cough has developed vilely.

Sunday, 9 January
Still in bed. Shall not go to office tomorrow. In some ways it would be a great relief to be told that I had only, say, 6 more months to live. Or perhaps a little longer: just long enough for me to edit my journals and arrange for their publication, tidy up all my affairs, remake my will, and then slip out, quietly, gratefully. I am not being morbid. I am tired of struggling against what is apparently my fate – i.e. to be alone, unloved, unfertilised, unfruitful. Just tired of trying to find out why it should be so, and of trying to alter it. I wanted, *needed*, someone who *understood* me, and that person I never found . . .

Thursday, 13 January
The doctor has been and pronounced me suffering the after-effects

of flu. 'You don't look well,' he said, and prescribed for me all the things I want to do most – rest, rest and rest. An enormous relief, to be able to be lazy with a clear conscience and just enjoy the cottage. Delicious. And people are so kind. Ethel had offered to come earlier in the week if I needed help. Cousin Joyce would have come but I wouldn't have wanted her, however ill I was. Lady S. has been very sympathetic since she heard yesterday – all this kindness makes me want to cry.

I am to have sun-ray treatment and to see the doctor again next week. Extraordinary faith one has in a doctor's word; one feels he must know everything and is as near being God as anyone can be on earth.

Friday, 14 January

Why have I not become a writer – why should I accept the idea that I shall never be one now? At first Gus made me conscious and ashamed that my style was suburban, not aristocratic. Then Nockie made me conscious and ashamed that my experience had been negative not positive. How could I be a writer, a good writer, with a suburban style and negative experience? Yes, I blame both Gus and N., as well as myself. So go on, if you can, from here. Do not prophesy, dream or hope. Just work.

Monday, 17 January

This morning a little old lady who lives nearby with her sister and with whom I have but the barest nodding acquaintance came trotting in and insisted upon doing the sitting room fire for me and getting in the coals. She has brought me some of their Bramley Seedlings and is bringing me a custard and baked apple tomorrow. She had heard from Mrs G. that I was ill and was so concerned. 'We' she said, referring to herself and sister, 'can look after each other when we are ill but when you are all alone . . .'

Air raid warden came round this evening to test gas mask. Have not had mine out for nearly two years. It was very dusty but apparently in good condition. He thinks that perhaps the authorities fear gas attack when our invasion does begin. It does seem now that we are going to invade Europe.

Friday, 21 January (War Diary)

I keep telling everyone I feel better, so I suppose I do, but I said to myself quite solemnly this morning, 'I don't know whether I am ill or not because I have forgotten what it feels like to be well.' There is no bone where my spine should be, just an ache. What I want more than food or sleep is sunshine and fresh air. The air of Slough is bad. I am sure that thousands and thousands of people are suffering from this same lack of sunshine. When I go back to work I shall ask the clinic doctor if I can have sun-ray treatment there – the apparatus is provided and employees may have treatment free.

At 6 p.m. went to keep my appointment for a blood test, but the doctor was not there and his secretary who does this minor operation for him is now ill so I had to trail home again feeling cold and exhausted. Coal crisis has occurred. Have used all my small stock of coal except about two scuttles of slack and a tin bath of small pieces which I sorted this morning. Am doing without kitchen fire and trying to burn anthracite in sitting room grate but it is not a success.

Monday, 7 February

She said: 'This time next year you'll either be, or be preparing to be, married. Yes, you have met him, spoken to him, and the acquaintance will develop. There's been another man – oh, you are very well out of that!

'There's a gold wristwatch coming to you. You'll move from where you now live. You'll have your photo taken. Diamonds are your lucky stones, and then sapphires. Six is your lucky number. And Monday, Wednesday and Friday are your good days.'

And when she had finished with the cards she took up the crystal.

Messages came from George, William, Mary and Joe. All will be well and as you wish, they said. The future is bright, full of good news, entertainment and health.

Thus and thus did she speak to me for nearly three-quarters of an hour. Well it all sounds delightful. I said there was not the remotest possibility of my getting married. 'Nothing is impossible,' she answered. I asked what he was like. 'He is taller and older than you,' she said. 'With hair brushed back and a kink in it, and he smiles with his eyes. He is or has been married, but very unhappily. You will be in clover . . .'

How do we lap up this nonsense. I wish it could all come true, but it won't, it never does. Yet every fortune-teller has seen marriage for me; I don't know why just now I should have such an *ache* for it. To deliver up one's independence – is it worth it, just to satisfy the body's hunger?

Companionship? Yes, that is desirable too. Loneliness is a big thing to bear.

Sunday, 27 February
At the office: Mr Botterell (new boss) pleasant, very pleasant, but uninspiring. I see no interesting prospects for Publicity under our present boss. Mr Oliver has been doing propaganda posters for the works, for which there is a big demand. He wants to break away from our department and set up one of his own under the title 'Technical Illustration and Works Posters', and suggests that I move in too, as a copywriter. The position would give me an easier conscience – should feel that I was really doing something at last of some value towards the War Effort. It would be interesting, creative work, demanding good use of my intelligence, training and experience, and Mr O. is very optimistic. But I have seen too many good schemes at HDA turned down and trampled on. From every department one hears tales of mismanagement and lack of imagination and courage.

Monday, 28 February

God, I know what makes a woman drive a knife into a man! His whole attitude to me is insulting, *insulting* – and I wish I could make him see how much I feel this to be so. But nothing penetrates. And I, I am only feeble when we meet . . . do nothing, say nothing, not a sting, not a slap. Just amiable and silly.

Wednesday, 1 March (War Diary)

Had sun-ray treatment at Clinic up to last week when nurse went sick and am taking three halibut liver oil pills a day.

Gunfire is terrific. My cottage shakes like a jelly and I wonder when the ceilings will collapse. I lay in bed one night watching the flares. Various relatives and friends in districts near London tell of damage and fires. Some complain of 'nerves' from which they have not suffered before, others say they find these short, sharp raids easier to endure than the old Blitz. Nockie, at Swiss Cottage, who is suffering from colds and sinus trouble and much the same debility that I had, says that she feels much more likely to die of illness than under a bomb.

Sunday, 5 March

Tommy sent me a message last week to get Horrabin's book on *Post-War Problems*, now on sale in Slough. Why should he trouble to do that? And why, if he goes that far in thought for me, not go a bit further and buy me a copy (a 9d. Penguin)?

Received full amount from Insurance for burglary, and to my astonishment 18 coupons from Board of Trade for fur coat. The fur coat I have been lucky enough to replace with a kitten musquash which my London tailor and furrier happened to have in stock. He let me have it without coupons: did not enquire too closely why, but assumed it to be secondhand, cleaned and remodelled. It is quite a success and many people say they like it better than my old one although I am not passionately fond of musquash. Cost me £60, which some folk think much too expensive, but most of the amount was covered by Insurance money and tailor has given me a replacement value certificate for £100 for Insurance. The other items I consider lost to me.

Friday, 10 March
Mr Botterell makes my gorge rise. He is flaky. He is a parasite. He treats me as if I were a log of wood, to be turned over and sat on when required and meanwhile left to rot. I despise him utterly. He is a maggot. He never takes me into his confidence, rarely gives me any interesting work.

I must make an effort to talk over the position, amiably, with him. I am sure that if my old boss Stevens had had half as much evidence of my potentialities I shouldn't have been pushed aside like this. All Mr B. does is travel the country with our *Forgings* film – he is away now until next Friday and has left us with nothing to do but supervise mail and cope with queries. This firm doesn't know how to use its staff. I must approach him somehow, because then if I don't get satisfaction I shall go to higher authorities.

Wednesday, 15 March (War Diary)
Last night another big raid on London. Guns here were active and I got all my Red Cross uniform ready. We are not being called but have to use our own discretion about going to the Point. Can hear our bombers going out now. A continual hum, like the dynamo of some fearful machine.

Saturday, 25 March
Shortly after my outburst on 10th March, the general manager, Mr H.G.H., gave me an opportunity to voice something of my discontent. Since then I have been sent to our Redditch works where employees and visitors stay at a super guesthouse known as 'The Cedars' at the firm's expense. There I met with an unexpected adventure, and now

wait in humiliating, sickening suspense, going as usual over and over the episode to find out where I went wrong (if I did) and what I should do if the next move is made. I feel now, fear now, that it is all over as suddenly as it happened.

I knew he was coming to The Cedars on Thursday evening, met him at the top of the stairs and introduced myself (we knew of each other and had conversed over the phone, but had never met). I found him pleasant, easy to talk to and obviously attracted. He asked me to go out for a drink after dinner, and on our way (with the firm's petrol) to the pub the magic began. He said he had wanted to meet me, had heard a lot about me – that I was one of the most intelligent women on the HDA staff, capable of holding down any job, and so on and so on.

In the bar this sweet and terrible flattery continued. He asked leading questions, had all my barriers down. Here was a man (a small man, but attractive) showing a deep, personal interest in me. He could not have used a more subtle or effective weapon to disarm and win me. I couldn't believe it was happening to me – making love to me with his eyes. It was too unexpected, too sudden, too marvellous. I wept in the cloakroom, I wept unashamedly in the car afterwards (and that must have shaken him!). And when he began to make love to me my response was electric. Indeed I had the greatest difficulty in refusing him that night but said 'No' emphatically when he asked if he could come to my room. Nevertheless he did come – and I really didn't expect him. But he went when I asked him to.

I couldn't sleep and felt simply frightful the next morning – just drawn, white, rigid. Could make no contact at all, although he took me into Birmingham where I was catching a train back to London. I was too tired and bewildered and cold to know what to do or say. I wanted some sort of warm and definite lead from him but of course did not get it.

I must now consider what I know and sense about him. Because it seems a familiar story – an entanglement with the old type, the philanderer, the fickle, fascinating breaker of hearts. He has a very good, responsible job at HDA, definitely an important member of the Senior Central Staff. In his late 30s but looks older. Is married and lives about two miles from this cottage. He has, I understand, something of a reputation with women and his wife is *not* envied.

He has no interest in or knowledge of Art and admits it, and I doubt whether he has in any of the other arts. He is out to make money and have a good time – I suspect him of being quite appallingly vulgar and uncultured. So I probe anxiously for the darkest aspects of his character, feeling more and more dead towards him every minute. Oh, he said such unbelievably lovely things on Thursday! Yes, like 'I love you . . . Do you love me? As soon as I saw you I had a feeling we were out of the same barrel . . . You will ask me round to the cottage, won't you? . . . We'll have rows, but we'll have a good time too . . . You're grand, I think you're just grand!' And the thirsty, hungry woman had indigestion all night.

He asked vaguely, diffidently, after some hours that morning, when he should see me again. He hinted at need for discretion in Slough. I eventually told him my phone number. But he hasn't used it yet. I shan't do any chasing. Shall just suffer the old, old agony in solitude. I must have patience. You know nothing about him, Jean. He is just now an indistinguishable figure in a veil of silver light. Find him first.

Sunday, 26 March

All right. I'll pay. What a fool, *fool* you are, Jean. If he had been *really* interested in me he would have phoned by now to have found out at least how I was. I was not at all well on Friday morning, he knew that. Damn these men. Damn them. I did not tell him of my 'past', but did not deny that there had been other men when he tried to find out. Was it that that shocked him?

I forgot that I was dealing with a middle-class mentality which still retains a Victorian view of sex. He thought I was a 'nice' girl and then discovered I wasn't. He probably has had no contact with the modern, intellectual outlook on these matters. Sex something nice but naughty, and not indulged in by unmarried, respectable young women.

Where do I go from here? Am I labelled now, shall I ever have a chance to put forward a different view? These men are comic. They themselves may sow what wild oats they like, may be unfaithful to their wives, may initiate virgins – but women must remain 'unsullied' until fate places them in their path. Yes, now I know that this attitude still really and truly exists.

My poor little heart! Pieces chipped off and scattered through Britain, a bruised and battered heart. But it grows whole again, and I am not sure that it doesn't improve with time, as pruning strengthens a fruit tree. It will be worth a lot to the man who can win it *all* and in good health.

25.

The Robot Plane

Tuesday, 28 March 1944 (aged thirty-four)

Happy, though no reason to be. Passed him today and exchanged smiles – oh very warm smiles! Was convinced he had forgotten all about me up to that moment. A philanderer, definitely. You can see it in his face. Yet the knowledge doesn't depress me unduly.

T. came into the office this afternoon too. I was able to meet him as I don't remember ever meeting him before: listened and talked to him and flirted with him openly and unashamed.

Wednesday, 29 March (War Diary)

People are seething. Nearly everyone I have spoken to about it was disappointed in Churchill's speech. (The one he broadcast last Sunday.)[131] Many want to know why he spoke at all – they resented his cracks at his critics when no one could answer him back, and felt he was trying to win the country's sympathy for a possible coming election. We are restless and anxious about the Second Front – some

---

131 The speech outlined recent progress against Mussolini, confirmed his resolve to succeed in Italy and the Balkans, praised the Russians and Americans, and described plans for house reconstruction to replace the estimated one million homes lost to date. Churchill also promised a swift and fair demobilisation, hit back at critics of the government, and stressed there was much work to be done: 'Britain can take it. She has never flinched or failed, and when the signal is given, the whole circle of avenging nations will hurl themselves upon the foe and batter out the life of the crudest tyranny which has ever sought to bar the progress of mankind.'

people think it will start in the Balkans, some favour Norway and few think we shall try through France. And we stick in Southern Italy, while Russia moves from strength to strength.

Photographs are needed, for advertising purposes, of certain aircraft components. This means 1) getting the Part Numbers from the Sales dept; 2) obtaining permission from the head of Central Planning to have the parts released from their despatch batches; 3) contacting Inspection from where they will have to be collected and delivered to the Photographic Dept; 4) getting the Librarian to look them over and decide which are most suitable for our purpose. By the time all this is done the war will be over.

Sunday, 2 April

Double summer time.[132] Quotation from the Yeats Letters:

'And happiness – what is it? I say it is neither virtue nor pleasure, not this thing or that, but simply *growth*. We are happy when we are growing.

'It is the primal law of all nature and the universe . . .'

Monday, 3 April

Yes Jean, sit tight and wait while the long-awaited spring rain falls. It is a matter of chance as to whether the affair will develop or not. The world seems to be full of these fascinating, dangerous men for me. How it hurts – so easily tricked, so helpless, so forlorn! But just take a look at your own unstable emotions: a Czech in the summer when interest in T. had flagged, then T. again, then a faint curiosity in a Communist at the India classes, and now Mac.[133]

---

132 Largely because of black-out restrictions, British Double Summer Time was a wartime scheme to extend 'natural' evening light (which meant darker mornings). It was achieved by not turning the clocks back at the end of summer in October 1940, and advancing clocks by the normal hour in March 1941. The 'double time' ended in 1945. BDST was reintroduced for one summer period only in 1947 to ease the fuel crisis.

133 Jean refers to her office obsession variously as M or Mac (his surname) and

Tuesday, 4 April (War Diary)

Last week Manny Shinwell MP came down and spoke to our Discussion Group.[134] His subject was Post War Britain, and more than 300 people came to hear him. He said that he thought world economic and political unity an excellent ideal but we must be realists. He could not see how we could achieve this perfection while such differing ideologies as that of Soviet Russia and that of individualist, capitalist USA existed together in the world. We must realise the competition that would face us from these enormous empires after the war – and possibly China and India – and that we must organise our industrial resources to the very fullest extent if we did not want to fade to a 4th or 5th rate power. It could be done if we willed it. We had the resources and the skill. All the more mature industries and the public services he thought should operate under state direction; not Civil Service direction as we know it today, but by personnel drawn from the workers and technicians in industry who thoroughly understand it. It was a stimulating speech, given impromptu without notes, and was received with tremendous enthusiasm.

Thursday, 13 April

I would like to know whether he is 1) smitten by sudden and unsuspected diffidence or 2) very, very busy (most probable), or 3) very, very callous.

Sunday, 16 April

Just back from a weekend in Hampstead with Nockie and am in one of those vile, bitter pre-period moods which all sensitive, imaginative, unbalanced women suffer. Let men note this. Difficulties loom enormous and insurmountable. One sees daylight only from the depths of an unclimbable pit.

---

also as Alan and Mellas.

134 Shinwell, a popular trades unionist, was one of the founding fathers of the Labour Party.

I want Nockie's sympathy, approval, help and encouragement, of course I do, and I get them in large measure, and yet in the next breath she will have got her claws into a dream and will have rent it asunder. She cannot let well alone. As I lay in bed last night and when I woke this morning I felt bruised.

She cannot bear to think that I might at any time find a greater happiness than she has done. Or that I should do any work which she herself could not do too and excel in.

When she comes to analyzing my doings she draws from her own experience – and the yardstick of her own ego is brought out. She wants me to be happy, to have a happy love affair or marriage. But to her own standards. She will never wholly approve of any man I fall for. Because I have fallen now for a business type, she suggests 'a tall American who'd call you "honey"'. Because she is in love with an American, I must fall in love with an American too. Because she is not really happy in her job and despises the people (civil servants) she works with, she thinks that I must not like my job and companions either. If I followed her pattern, if I were like her, she knows she could beat me and be 'top'.

Wednesday, 3 May (War Diary)
The long evenings are here again. Weather brilliant, blossom everywhere profuse, spring in all its perfection. Last night about 11.15 a plane dived with a terrific roar over the trees and houses here. I saw a brilliant burst of flame as it crashed and exploded out of sight. The sky in the west glowed for a long time and one could hear crackling and sharp reports. Was told this evening that it was a Mosquito, landed on a common about three miles away, set fire to hay ricks but did no other damage. The crew of two was killed.

'Salute the Soldier Week' in Slough this week. Our firm aims at £15,000.

Five new kittens.

Thursday, 4 May

This evening as I rushed over to the main office for some information Mr Botterell had failed to send to our advertising agents who were needing it urgently, I turned and saw Mac in the corridor behind me. I waited for him and heard him say, 'Hello stranger! I nearly cycled up to see you one night last week. But I was too scared.'

And myself answering, 'Go on! . . .'

'Yes,' he said, 'I was. Plumb scared! It was Wednesday or Thursday . . . were you alone?'

'I had a visitor all last week (Josephine), but I'd be *very* pleased to see you anytime . . . Next time, don't be scared.' (Vilely inadequate.)

Heart bounced up and hit the roof, so that Mr B. found me singing at the top of my voice, 'I'm singing in the rain . . .' when I thought everyone had gone. I went duty bound, to see the film of Mme Curie, but took little of it in, and certainly did not weep as everyone else seems to have done.

Sunday, 7 May

In the interests of this record, although I am damn tired, I must note that I really do seem to have developed, and am becoming the person I always felt I should be. And now that I have written that, I want to retreat and have gone all bashful.

Barbara Linnett brought two young Americans over this afternoon, and one of them, a lively, sensitive young animal, appeared vastly intrigued by me. Until quite recently – until I went to High Duty Alloys I think – the only men who ever showed any interest in me were poor, inhibited creatures like myself, but now the much more normal and anything-but-inhibited variety are taking notice. It is immensely gratifying. HDA has done me a lot of good.

Thursday, 25 May

He has a daughter. Sally-Ann.

Wednesday, 31 May

The torment does not automatically cease. He said, 'I still intend to come one evening to have coffee or whatever it is you give people.' That was all. He was on his way to collect his daughter and was very late. Imagination still easily panders to flooding desire. And then I heard a dance track on the wireless which took me back to 1936–37 when I was with Gwen Silvester at the Empress Rooms. I was then a victim of passion for Charles Scrimshaw. The dreams, the hope, the palpitations and desire. Don't think I even exchanged two words with him.

Tuesday, 6 June (War Diary)

INVASION DAY. It really is rather thrilling to hear that the long awaited action of our armies is at last taking place.[135] The BBC announcement was being relayed over the work broadcast at noon today. We crept to our places in the canteen in a cathedral-like hush. 'There'll be many worried homes today,' said L.S. Work went on as usual in the afternoon with a sort of subdued excitement prevailing. Several people suggested that we have been waiting, not for any particular day, but for the fall of Rome. Many claim that they had 'feelings' last night of pending events.

Went to see Lizzie and Peter on Sunday and their son and heir, born on Easter Saturday. Lizzie is trying to cope with baby and belongings in two rooms in someone else's house – sharing kitchen and bathroom. Peter when he comes home at night washes the nappies. I have never heard of a father doing this before but Lizzie mentioned several others who do the same now. What a war will do to the middle classes.

Bought a new coat and skirt at Peter Jones. 'The Govt. want us to go about badly dressed – that's what it amounts to,' said the assistant.

---

135 The D-Day landings on the beaches of Normandy brought more than 150,000 Allied troops ashore. After long battles with many casualties, Paris was liberated eleven weeks later.

Tuesday, 13 June

Tomorrow it will be a fortnight since he phoned and promised to come and help water my lettuces. It has rained almost every evening since then and I have not heard a word. Yet hope persists. Any reasonable person would tell me I am a sentimental, vain, silly woman, clinging to a dream because of a few passionate kisses and impulsive words exchanged three months ago. How many women, I wonder, build a dream from less than that and live with it for years, believing that he will come again and life will glow once more?

Wednesday, 14 June

One of the ginger kittens (Ping, or is it Pong?) has the lambs-wool sock from my bedroom slipper in its claws and is licking it furiously.

I think the two Americans have been swept off by the invasion.

Saturday, 17 June

Pong – or was it Ping? – has met with a most tragic, pitiful end. I came home late this afternoon and was greeted as usual by the family from all directions, but missed Pong (or Ping). Did not start looking until I had had my tea, and then I found him in the shed, rigid and cold, his little chest covered with blood, his pale eyes glazed and lifeless. I had to find out the cause and washed the blood away (that stiff, icy little body that only last evening was curled warmly in my hands).

A round, deep hole like a small bullet wound reached down perhaps to his heart. There were a few bird feathers on the floor near him, and I can only suppose it to have been the beak thrust of some poor wretched bird caught and surrounded by the kittens. The bird had its revenge before it died, and the kittens had their revenge for the death of their brother. Death is a most strange thing, happening somewhere every day, every hour.

Germans are causing excitement over here now with their pilotless aircraft.[136]

Saturday, 24 June
Have been told in confidence by Mr O. that Mr B. is getting £650 p.a. + bonus + expenses. It is scandalous.[137]

Sunday, 25 June (War Diary)
The Germans' new weapon, the robot-plane . . . The first day they came over we were sent to the shelters. I took one look at them and fled and a great many other people did the same. We have not been sent since although we have had many alerts. One or two of the bombs have fallen quite near. I never hear the alert but am awakened by the vibration of the bomb as it lands. The blast is terrific, everything shakes. Nockie writes that their effect in London is demoralising, to hear them coming and not knowing where they will fall. There is no defensive gunfire. She says she prefers the ordinary Blitz and has I gather had very little sleep recently. She has even sent me a copy of her will to keep in a safe place. Have been told that there are only enough to last another fortnight when they will be replaced by some other Secret Weapon.

The feeling that the war is nearing its end at last is not viewed by all of us with unalloyed jubilation. In fact I have seen no evidence of jubilation anywhere at the thought. The question that is in everyone's mind is, what will post-war conditions be like? Shall I be able to keep my job or get another of the kind I really want? We feel too that preference will be given to people coming out of the Services – who have of course lost contact as much as any of us. It will be largely a matter of luck and of knowing the right people. It will be a ghastly scramble for work.

---

136 The V-1 guided missile was first used this month as a direct response to the Allied landings, and its buzzing descent lent it the nickname doodlebug.
137 Jean was earning £300 a year.

What our firm will do or intends to do no one seems to know or will say. We have just launched a New Company 'to co-operate with designers and manufacturers in all industries on the use of light alloys for post-war purposes.' We have put out some splashy advertising.

Sunday, 25 June
There is so much in this world to make me happy. Small things such as cats, a good meal, one's garden, trees in spring and autumn, clouds, colours, fabrics, clothes, companionship, books and music and films, a drink in the friendly atmosphere of an English pub, a ride in a bus, a letter from a friend, staying in bed when one is tired, firelight, starlight, waves breaking against rocks, evening sunlight on a flight of bombers.

Saturday, 8 July
Nockie, bless her, has come to stay with me to get away from the doodlebugs. She will travel to Paddington and back every day. She is in a bad state of nerves.

Saturday, 15 July
The bubble is pricked, and the foolish, foolish heart has had evidence to prove its foolishness. What happened was this. Nockie and I decided last night to cycle down to the Crown for a drink. The Crown is near his house, and I know that he frequents that pub. We got buried deep in a settee so that he did not see us for quite a long time and I was able to watch him unobserved. Surrounded by women – one of them Nockie is fairly sure must have been his wife. She looked *nice*. Really a nice, pleasant, attractive type – quietly dressed, not over made-up, no elaborate hairstyle. Oh he is a devil. Yes, it must have been his wife (whom he has never once mentioned to me) because when he did turn round and see me he did not come and speak to me. He did not even dare to speak to me outside when we went out to collect our cycles. I have nothing to reproach myself for, except for indulging

for so long in sentimental fancies. Wonder what I shall do, what he
will do, when we meet again. Or perhaps we shan't meet again.

Saturday, 22 July
He was back yesterday at the office and gave me a lift to the Pump
[pub] and stood me a drink. He may be a rogue but I do like him.
It came out in conversation with acquaintance in the pub that
Sally-Ann is 10, and for the first time I heard him speak of his wife.
They have two evacuee children staying with them – a girl of 15 and
a girl of 2.

Monday, 24 July
While I moan about my insignificant difficulties and frustrations,
dreadful, dreadful tragedies are taking place a few miles away. A bomb
fell near the home of a friend of Nockie's and badly unnerved this
young woman who had seen legs and arms among the rubble and
glass in her road. These doodlebugs are diabolical. We had one over
on Saturday evening here. It sounded as though it were flying right
over the cottage, then it stopped and drifted for 2-and-a-half minutes.
It fell, we are told, at Marlow. Out of a clear sky, with no sound, no
warning, falls a terrible destruction.

     And in spite of our triumphs in France and Italy and the great
Russian push along a 1,000-mile front, and the attempt on Hitler's
life and rumours of revolution in Germany – these raids go on,
unnerving the war-weary, hardworking population in London and
southern England, as they are meant to do. Shall we stand the strain?
Yes.

Saturday, 29 July
On Monday I go to Cornwall with Joan for a week. I took the last
two kittens and The Kittyhawk to the Cats Home this morning and
went through agony. How is it one can suffer so acutely for a cat? I
loved The Kittyhawk and now she is no more. I shall never again see

her black and dull gold little body uncurl from the bushes to greet me, or follow me to the post, or those big, black accusing eyes lifted. All over. In a way a great relief – three cats to feed was no joke, and the problems with recurring families just insurmountable.

Saturday, 5 August (War Diary)
Cornwall. We expected the journey to be grim. The weekend before conditions at Paddington had been simply appalling – I heard nothing but the most depressing tales of crowds and jammed corridors. Settled eventually in corner of non-smoker, two Canadian sailors sat opposite. We gave them some of our sandwiches just before they embarrassed us enormously by showering quite a dozen packets of chocolate from their kit bags onto our laps.

We were met by Jill (Joan's eldest sister) whose husband is stationed with the RAF Transport Command at Newquay. They had just moved into a cottage at St Mawgan and insisted upon my staying with them. My face is shining like a beacon, my hair has dried to the texture of hay, I feel a little middle-aged and aunty-ish, but I am on the whole well and happy. All round here is full of RAF and evacuees. Was told of one little boy who had been in bad raids in London who threw himself flat at the sound of the first plane overhead.

Sunday, 20 August
Allied successes on the Continent. Russians on Prussian soil. The Americans in Paris.

And my heart and intuition rejoicing over a triumph of their own. It *is* all rather unbelievable. I am ridiculously happy and very scared. He gave me a lift again on Friday. We arranged to meet at the One Pin, and we came back to the cottage. Nockie went to bed early. I am not going to describe what followed.

I am not yet his mistress, but I hope and intend to be. I said, 'I am not a husband snatcher and it's time you went home.' He replied slowly, 'I am not a husband that wants to be snatched,' and did not go home. Later he said, 'I am a *hungry* husband – hungry just as you are.'

He loves his wife, there is no doubt about that. But for some reason she can not have any more children and 'for no selfish reasons on her part' dare not have anything to do with him. He is quite obviously an unsatisfied man physically, and as intuition told me right from the beginning, a very genuine, intelligent, trustworthy person. He said that he had cycled round here time and time again wanting to see me, not daring to call. Still find it hard to believe – the things he said, the warmth of him, the warmth in his eyes. It envelops me wholly. I will accept what he says and what he offers and demand no more.

Tuesday, 22 August

He has decided to come on Saturday – his wife and daughter evidently still away.

It's no good letting one's imagination leap ahead with this affair. I must take it step by step, problem by problem. A handful. Heavens yes! Perhaps he has exhausted his poor wife, perhaps that is the answer. As for me I am just *terrified* – of failure, humiliation, disillusionment, and all the possibilities of being hurt and shaken by this new adventure. It is an experiment and must be so regarded. But it is real and true and down to earth at last. No more slipshod, sentimental dreaming and desiring. Have wished for it for so long and now it is here, very hard and sharp and actual.

Saturday, 26 August

11.30 p.m. Black. So black I can hardly write about it. But I want to record my deep, deep gratitude to my unfailing, wonderful friend Nockie – I don't know what I should be doing without her – near suicide I suspect. He never came, or let me know why.

Heart has suffered a bitter reverse and is numb. All the interest I have had for him since Redditch seems dead in a single blow, and there is no desire or feeling left for him at all. Not even hate. But *anger* – that he should treat me like that. I went to quite a lot of trouble in my preparations for the evening's entertainment, and until 6 o'clock I felt happy and sure about his coming. Then doubt crept in, increased and grew intolerable.

He told me he was coming back from Winchester today via Ascot and would come to me from there. *He* chose this evening. My feeling is that he has got in tow with someone else and forgotten all about me, or shelved the problem of letting me know. Some crony or old girlfriend at the races and been drawn into a party with them.

'Don't show that you're angry, don't let him see that it matters,' Nockie says. 'You have probably learnt more about him tonight than you would have done had he come.' She doesn't think I am in love with him. I don't know. Tonight certainly I am not.

Sunday, 27 August
We have exhausted all the possibilities and I will not believe the worst until I have proof of it. He has not phoned or sent any message. I cannot believe he is quite so callous and rude. I pray for him, wherever he is. It is ignoble of me to think such evil of him. God please help me through this.

26.

Arsenic Blue

Thursday, 31 August 1944

He lost so much money at the races on Saturday afternoon that he got roaring drunk and was in no condition to come to see me in the evening. That was what he told me on Tuesday, and only then because he happened to catch sight of me in the bus queue as he passed in his car and gave me a lift. And was not going to explain, I am sure, if I hadn't been bursting with rage and demanded it. I said that he might have at least phoned on Sunday, but this had not occurred to him. It is all terribly, terribly galling. He realised he had behaved badly, but I doubt if the thought much troubled him after I had gone. A very sordid, shabby little man. Phoney, like everything about HDA and its leading personnel.

Yet desire is such that the heart (all beaten and battered again) cannot forget or leave go. I now want to help, perhaps tempted by the role of 'saving angel'.

My motives are selfish: I want to be made love to. I want to help him because of the hope of ultimate reward. Would I offer to help him if I knew I could never have that? Offer friendship without sex and see what happens. Would he, could he, accept and give as much back again?

Friday, 1 September

I yearn for some real hard work that I can do well and that will be appreciated. Our department at HDA has practically nothing to do now. I am sure there is no future for me in Publicity.

Wednesday, 4 October

I have made an appointment to see Dr Howe again on Friday. I have *got* to get out to him the story of my latest emotional entanglement.

I have had only one further meeting of any consequence. About a fortnight ago I was walking down the main office corridor and heard someone behind me call 'Miss Pratt!' When I saw who it was I smiled back and walked straight on. He can catch me up if he wants to, I thought. But he didn't.

One word about Tommy. He has left HDA and takes up his medical course in London next week. He does not intend to lose touch with me nor I with him. All the emotional complexities dispersed, and what remains is a pleasant and strong friendship.

Tomorrow am going to see *Lady in the Dark*.[138]

Saturday, 7 October

I walked the streets of London yesterday after seeing Graham Howe, feeling as though I owned the earth. G.H. was interested and amused, and summed M. up as the type of man with unusually quick and sure intuitive powers, living in the 'Eternal Now', able to assess a person and a situation in a moment, and make a woman feel as though she is the only one that matters in that moment, skimming the cream of the situation for himself with skill, and then forgetting all about it in the next new and different moment. His emotional life has no continuity and his wife justifiably will find him 'impossible'.

'You must be realistic about him,' said G.H. Also I must uproot that morbid little plant sown by the old hag in Hove who promised I should be married 'to a married man' next year. The trouble, G.H. explained, about these fortune-tellers was that only 50 per cent of their shots reached the right target, and they pick up one's fantasies

---

138 Starring Ginger Rogers as a woman being courted by a married man. For answers, she turns to a psychoanalyst.

and desires and tell one what one wants to hear. So go away, Ghost.
You have possessed me too often and too long.

Wednesday, 11 October (War Diary)
Life at work is all shamefully 'cushy' but I don't know what to do
about it. I sit back watching events and personalities, fascinated. Our
production programme has been greatly decreased, shops are closed
and men turned out by the 100 (they say there are over 1,000 unemployed in Slough now; Labour Exchange has no work to offer them).

Attended a meeting with Sir George Schuster on 'Can We Afford
the Peace?' His speech followed the theme of several of his recently
published articles on the same subject. We must concentrate on
increasing our industrial productivity, make plans for industry at home
first so that full use is made of our natural resources and industrialists
should come forward to the Government with their own plans.

I read somewhere the view that the change from war to peace
would be so gradual we should hardly notice it. It will not be something definite and spectacular like Lights Up, Bananas for all, unlim-
ited fully fashioned real silk stockings at 2s. 6d. a pair and everyone
with a job they like and able to afford their own plot and bungalow.

Thursday, 26 October
Have spent a good part of this and last evening sorting through papers,
books, pamphlets and letters accumulated over the past four or five
months. It appals me, the swift passage of time, all there is to notice
and absorb, and how little of this information I take in or use in any
way. Daily papers, the *Listener*, *Radio Times*, *Architects' Journal*, Fabian
literature, miscellaneous monthly periodicals – lent me, given me,
bought myself – and all set on one side to read when I have the time.
But I never have the time, and the mass of printed matter becomes
too much. I abandon it all, store it on bookshelves and forget about
it. (And then the letters I should write . . .)

Ethel brought out (she left here on Monday) the other evening a photograph of the loved one (Father) taken by a street photographer in Acton many years ago. It startled me into remembering how much I had loved him too. It was an excellent, exact likeness. The amused twinkle in his eyes, the dear, lived face, the creased suit. Silken white hair and a grey tobacco-stained moustache. Was I 'in love' with him? Is it my father I am seeking? Is it his image I impose? But I never wanted him physically – that I will deny vehemently to my dying day – consciously or unconsciously. But the warmth and sympathy and happiness he gave me, perhaps I *am* seeking that. That gladness of heart at the sight of him, – the little girl full of deep trust and joy running into outstretched arms, sure of her welcome, sure of sympathetic attention and guidance and comfort.

Saturday, 11 November

God, I am so lonely. It is not the practical fact of being alone that is difficult to bear, it is this personal isolation – this being on a hill – this wanting to share my life, an arm to link mine to, a *warm* companionship. And a female companionship wouldn't help at all, really it wouldn't. Yet for years women have struggled to free themselves of man's domination, and to stand alone, free and independent to make their own lives in their own way. All that these women fought for I have, and I am crying, 'It is not enough!' We are incomplete without our men. We are unlit lamps.

Monday, 13 November

I came home in a vile mood, really deep arsenic blue, thinking of M. as usual, and more than usual having seen him three times and spoken – actually walked down the main corridor with him – once. ('Good morning! And how are you?' 'Oh, very well – and you?' 'Bearing up.' 'So long as you are not bearing down . . .')

I lit a fire in the study, moped for a while wanting and wanting something terribly exciting and unusual to happen, did the few chores, got some supper and gradually soothed down under the influence of warmth and food and kind Kilvert's diary.[139] The phone rang. Thomas! As usual wanting something (did I know of accommodation in London?) but we had a nice long most warming conversation. I then settled down to an evening with Kilvert. The phone rang again. Nockie, from a call box. She had spent the evening with Hugh Laming – in England and before going off on urgent Army matters to the Balkans. He *very* much wants to spend a few quiet days somewhere in the country, and is entranced by the idea of spending them here with me. Will I phone him tonight, late, or early tomorrow morning? He is very tired, has nowhere to go, and would so like – and so on.[140]

She is a witch. She would like me to get into bed with him. I will NOT do it. But unless I can somehow warn Hugh, he'll expect it. His capacity for sexual affairs is fantastic. I would like him to come, though. He will be great entertainment and very interesting. He has been all over the Mediterranean, has a wife in Greece,[141] has been in France. But perhaps he'd be bored with me. However he can read all he wants to while I'm at work and we can pub-crawl in the evenings.

There it is then. The *terribly* exciting something. I feel alternatively furiously angry with Nockie for foisting this situation on me and very delighted. No, I will not phone Hugh tonight. It would look too eager.

Tuesday, 14 November

I have seen him again – my darling, my darling – and I still do want him so, foolish, misguided, untamable woman! I swore in tears as I came home that I loved him. I am in the grip of something I can't control. It is so strong sometimes that I move in a daze. When I knew Barbara Linnett wasn't going home at 6 o'clock tonight I calculated

---

139 Francis Kilvert's diary of rural clerical life between 1870–79 was published posthumously in 1938, and has remained in print ever since, a calming and fortifying read. The original diaries were destroyed by Kilvert's niece after publication, while the original transcription by editor William Plomer was destroyed in the Blitz.
140 Hugh Laming, a journalist friend of Nockie and army officer, has been mentioned by Jean once before, in August 1940, when he was stationed in Palestine.
141 Note added later: 'No. Greek wife in Palestine.'

and engineered my movements so that I might be passing his office just after 6.15 when I knew he might be coming out. It worked. It was like a miracle (I had to walk into the women's cloakroom at the end of the passage and light a cigarette and come back again). He instantaneously stopped me and asked if I would like to be taken down the road 'to save me waiting at the bus stop'. And then there I was in that beloved car again! Jean, you are the world's prize idiot among women.

The moment was a sombre one. He has a sore throat, and is worried like most people are in the firm. The firm is losing money – or the losses are now becoming apparent. At the height of war production the profits were so enormous. It is going to get worse too, I gather. Perhaps he was trying to tell me I was on the staff redundancy list.

We drank Guinness at the fireside of one of the pubs at the Pump. We argued about heating, and the advantages and disadvantages of coal fires. He asked me about Lydia whom he sees me with at lunchtime (it occurred to me today to give her a friendly word of warning about him). No reference to the past at all, yet all accepted and 'forgotten'. When I said I had taken on the cottage for another three years but might, when the war ended, want to go abroad again, he jumped out an offer to take it in my absence. Now thinking it over I am deeply offended – he would possess the cottage immediately if I left it, but never comes near it when I am there!

He guided me with his torch towards the bus stop – no touch, not much warmth in him tonight. God forgive me, but please let him come to me. No one who has come to know me well has ever regretted it.

A message from Hugh. He has had to go to his mother in Sheerness, but would like to come to me on Friday.

Sunday, 26 November

Hugh and I have had a wonderful week. I am still too near to it to say much yet, except that I am not in love with him and don't think I ever could be. Curious that Nockie should plant him onto me. He is exactly the type that I usually fall for with pathetic heaviness.

All my urgent lecherous yearnings are now satisfied. How could I have expected Hugh to stay with me here at such close quarters without getting into bed with me? I didn't want to, should never have chosen him as a lover myself, yet what a marvellous lover he is! He is thoroughly and incurably naughty and I am quite sure could never remain faithful to Cleopatra herself – or satisfy any sensitive woman deeply for long. Restless, restless, restless, even here where most people do seem to find repose.

Physically I am happier and calmer than I have ever been. A starving woman fed. I feel no shame. I have come and gone, not caring what the neighbours and tradespeople might be thinking. How is it such a delightful physical relationship does not touch the emotion at all? I still think of M. and look out for him in the office. If Hugh went abroad tomorrow I should be sharply disappointed – I want to see him again – but the heart would be little moved. A thoroughly selfish male, but so honest, and what enormous fun for a little while!

Hugh Laming and son John in the offices of the *Sydney Morning Herald* after the war.

sensual mouth, small moustache, temperament of a Latin and a continental lover's technique. A butterfly's (his own word) intense interest in nearly everything, witty, sharply intelligent, talking endlessly of himself and his adventures, – sublimely, disarmingly egotistical, sensitive, mercurial, *exciting*. Belongs essentially to the 1930s – Noël Coward, Somerset Maugham – a scintillating cynicism, a little shallow, brittle, the fascinating Fleet Street smart alec (he says he is tired of that role now, the war has been changing his values). An individualist of the pre-war years who won't fit into our Brave New World (he calls me a 1946 woman). He like to think he has no illusions, knows all the rackets, sees through and despises the Left, knows all about women and how to deal with them. Happy? As happy as he can be, snatching, flitting, nibbling at this, flicking through that, taking in two or three things at once: does any of it stay?

I understand a little better now Noël Coward's 'Let's Say Goodbye'. 'Let our affair be a gay thing . . .' The feeling of that glittering, trifling era between the wars. He has given me a lot, my sweet Hugh, a lot that I thought I had missed or hadn't got or was never to know. Somewhere from the Victorian age I have a hangover to be an inspiring, guiding, ministering angel. But all I do is encourage a man's lust and laziness! My self-confidence shares have gone up though. How *dare* M. keep away from me?!

Monday, 27 November

I have had a charming, charming love letter from Hugh. He wrote and posted it on Saturday, while he was still here and I was out. Although I am such a damnable little sceptic I believe he means it: 'I have been happier here than I dared dream. You gave me rest of mind and body when I needed both so desperately. Whatever the future may hold for us one does not forget these hours. Time has stood still for us; we have not spoken of love for fear of hurt, thus am I silent still . . .'

I don't know how to answer this. I can be honest and cruel here. I didn't refrain from speaking of love for fear of hurt. I didn't want to – love, my idea of it anyway, just hasn't come into the picture. But I don't want to hurt him. I have had no chance of growing sentimental over Hugh. We knew him well in Malta. His first wife was ill with TB and he was blatantly unfaithful to her – we heard of his infidelities. He told me himself last week of the two–three day affair he had with Lillian Gish, who wanted him to go out to Hollywood to be her re-write man.[142]

He kept in touch with Nockie, and I have heard of him and his adventures through her. He told me a great, great deal about himself and his family last week. His frankness is engaging; one cannot help liking him for it. But I can't forget that he is on his father's side of a family of philanderers. He would live on my money without a qualm. He couldn't give me the love I want, though I don't know if physical fidelity in this is so important. There's a virgin in me yet that no man has ever touched and won.

Saturday, 9 December

Hugh returned last Sunday evening, stayed until Wednesday morning and may come back again anytime. Why is it that just the sight of M. at the office makes my pulse race in a way it never does for Hugh, even in his most impassioned moments?

Do I really want H. here again? I have invited him for Xmas if he cares to come. I want something good to come of this relationship – sex seems to me less and less important. I could have him here now and do without if he would, and be as happy, perhaps happier. It is nice to have a man around, however tiresome.

Tuesday, 12 December

I am helping Lydia decorate a club room in Slough with murals. Much to my amazement I have been painting mountains and trees on the

---

142 Gish was one of the few stars to make the transition from silent movies to talkies, enjoying a long career that stretched from D.W. Griffith's *Birth of a Nation* (1915) to *The Whales of August* (1987).

walls with a flourish, gusto and effect. Would never have undertaken such a thing on my own initiative, but Lydia got me there on Sunday night, put a brush in my hand, and said 'Do what you like'. I was terrified, but thought: well, mountain outlines are fairly easy, and I always did like doing blodgy trees in charcoal or very thick pencil. Landscape all the way round, mountains, valley and sea, and somewhere there is to be an Inn. Our efforts are really very amateurish, but our heart is in the right place.

This club is run by Curly, a friend of Lydia, and one of Slough's worthy small tradesmen. He is I can see a very kind, good soul and devoted to Lydia in a rather dumb-dog fashion. He owns a radio business and was able to drive me home tonight.

Hugh is prancing about town with a (male) American he picked up recently in the Poland Street King's Arms. (This is Hugh's focal point in London: if one meets Hugh in town it is at the King's Arms.) I discovered that H. had figured to bring him down here for his leave. I should have collapsed. Hugh on his own was strain enough. He grumbled at stew, did not like sweets, wanted everything fried, wouldn't of course eat salads or fruit and grumbled also if I spent too much time in the kitchen. I came home one night to find him cooking the evening meal in the frying pan, ignoring all the prepared food which I had intended to curry. I began to seethe inside. He would never, either, blackout the uncurtained windows, which annoyed me too, and it annoyed him that I insisted on blacking out. And so on. There were a dozen or more such jags daily. Yet he did try to help. Chopped wood, filled the coal scuttles, even made my bed twice and cleaned my shoes once.

Wednesday, 20 December

A week ago Hugh phoned to say he had been posted to Burma and could he come and see me again that night. He came (there was a thick fog as there has been today), stayed until Monday and is coming back for Xmas. I am happy about it all now, immensely happy, but can't write it down (as I have to when unhappy). Strange. This should be called a Blue Moods Journal.

He has said to me, 'Why haven't you married? Academically speaking, would you marry me? You are the only English woman I'd ask. My first wife was a mistake of youth. Academically speaking, I'd marry you.'

Academically speaking, I would not marry Hugh, but I am very touched and flattered. But he doesn't know me well enough yet, he needs someone like his present Greek wife Maritza – scintillating, fascinating – I could never compete with her. She met Hugh in Paris in 1940, and later again by chance in Athens in 1941. She was a café singer. Then the Germans came, and he had to move with the British Army, and she escaped to Beirut, walking barefoot over the mountains of Smyrna. He returned to Beirut with a staff job in Intelligence, but then the invasion of Italy began and he had an urge to volunteer for active service again. Will he go on obeying that urge that keeps him always on the move? I do think he is running away all the time from himself. I am but a harbour at the moment for a somewhat battered ship.

New Year's Day 1945

A letter from Hugh which ended, 'I miss you damnably.' Well I miss him too, but there is nothing much we can do about it.

I have dallied with the idea of being married to Hugh, and I'd make a success of it because I'd tackle it as a full-time job demanding all my wit and intelligence and charm. I'd have to submit myself to rigorous discipline, housekeeping, catering, cooking, grooming, clothes, health all kept at 100 per cent efficiency – but without any jarring or nagging! I'd have to have some help in the house if I wanted to do any work of my own. But I'd better get on with my life as it is.

27.

Plenty of Time for Dick

Sunday, 7 January 1945 (aged thirty-five)

Have been reading Eric Gill's autobiography. Most absorbing.

Hugh has phoned. Wonder if we shall meet again before he goes abroad? The affair is over, dead. But the friendship remains.

And having coped with the British Army it now seems possible I may have to cope with the American. That attractive young Irish New Yorker phoned again last week.[143] He is stationed once more in Wycombe and says he wants to see me, and would I put him up for the night if he came over? Fantastic. Do wish someone would come and rescue me from this situation. I like making new friends and entertaining the Services enormously, but really I do not want to have affairs with every one of them.

Am in a sort of vacuum about this. I must be firm with Dick. But I thought I was going to be firm with Hugh.

The point is, is it essential to get into bed with a man before you can have a friendship (that is worthy of the name) with him? What is to prevent one going on like this, from one man to the next?

'The barren and destructive road.' I came upon this phrase of Eric Gill's describing loose physical relationships almost immediately afterwards. That is just what they lead one into – a barren and destructive road. And that is what I am afraid of, have always feared. Satisfy your

---

143 This is Jack's friend Dick.

curiosity if you must, but don't be tempted further by vanity, and know where the one ends and the other begins. Be strong on this. And then you may, perhaps, as Eric Gill did, 'enter the enchanted garden of Christian marriage . . .'[144]

Friday, 19 January

Hugh has written me nearly every day from Rotherham. It has been wonderful to find his letters waiting for me every evening – warming and supporting. One person at least thinking of me pretty frequently and wanting me. Yes, still wanting me, so he says. He was expecting to receive orders for Burma, but now tells me it is all off and he is to stand by for France.

Monday, 29 January

Have been frantically busy with arrangements for our discussion group meeting at which Sir William Beveridge is to be the speaker next week.

Hugh has orders now to sail for France on Feb 6th. He thinks the war in Europe will be over in six months, Tommy thinks it's a matter of weeks but that surrender will not be total. I think it may be longer than six months. The Germans, as Hugh says, have their 'backs to the wall' and are in the mood to die fighting to the end.

Tuesday, 30 January (War Diary)

Frantic day at office with Beveridge meeting arrangements. Our chairman is away with flu just to make things more difficult. Mr Oliver yesterday on Beveridge: 'This little man, quite determined that his plan for Social Security is possible. Nothing daunts him. He is a big draw. Prepare for an overflow. You know, when his report was first published the BBC and press were told to pipe down on it. But they couldn't.'

---

144 Eric Gill, the sculptor and typographer, was perhaps not the best moral guide in these matters, having (it was subsequently revealed) had sex with at least one of his daughters and at least one of his dogs.

Have no post-war plans or ambitions. Don't know what I shall do and may in that mood let myself be 'directed' if the Government goes on directing us after the war. One's life isn't one's own and won't be as far as I can see for several years yet, if ever.

Saturday, 10 February

I was about to settle down to an evening of Diary (War and this) and domesticities on my own when the phone rang. None other than that attractive young Irish-American Dick. He just invited himself over for the evening and to sleep and that was that. When he arrives at Hedgerly Corner he is to give me a ring and I shall go and collect him. That arrangement was made over two hours ago, since when I have been busy preparing food and tidying up, muttering to myself the while, 'Fantastic, fantastic – the British Army, the American Army, but the one man I want, *never*.' There is of course plenty of time for Dick to change his mind or lose his way, but he evidently intends to come one weekend and I would rather it were this than any other for the simple security reason (oh, what one can confess in a private diary!) that I have a period.

Sunday, 11 February

I dealt with Dick much as I dealt with T.H. in the summer. Just packed him off to bed and hoped he would sleep well!

Monday, 12 February (War Diary)

The question I was instrumental in asking Sir William Beveridge at our big meeting last Wednesday (and his answer) was quoted by *The Times*, the *News Chronicle* and criticised severely by Maurice Webb in the *Sunday Express*.[145]

---

145 The brief report of the meeting in *The Times* on 8 February was headlined 'Sir W. Beveridge Studying State Machinery' and reported: 'Sir William Beveridge, MP, after explaining his plan for full employment to workers at Slough last night, was asked whether it would necessitate a change in the machinery of Government. He

Our first rocket fell on Sunday about 5 a.m. Landing on Stoke Common, roughly a mile from my cottage. It shook me from a deep sleep and I heard the whistling sound of its descent and the explosion quite clearly. Am told one person killed, two old people taken to hospital with shock, many houses in adjoining village damaged, and ceilings in house of one of our directors down.

Tuesday, 13 February
Since there is no one I can turn to as fully as I desire on this matter these journals must be burdened once again. By the end of March High Duty Alloys intends to have rid itself of 250 of its staff, senior and junior (this M. told one subordinate, in confidence, who told it to his wife, who, being a talkative little creature, let it out to Lydia with whom she works). That I am numbered among those 250 I am positive. That Lydia *isn't* I am also positive and madly jealous over. She estimates castings and has impressed M. very much by her ability – so much so that he doesn't want to lose her, I know. They have never had any direct contact but I am sure that when the opportunity comes he'll make the most of it. That thought fills me with sheer agony.

I am prompted by all these feelings to make a move to get out before I am politely dismissed. I hate having to do it. ~~Uprooting myself and starting again. I have written after one advertisement for 'Capable woman required as Assistant to Advertisement Manager'.~~

Thursday, 15 February
Barbara Linnett paid me a visit and told me what she had heard in confidence (and I swore not to repeat). And that was that Mr Botterell was to be offered the post of sales representative in our London offices

---

replied: "Yes, and if I ever write another book, it will be on that subject. I am studying the machinery of State at Westminster now, and I shall make a real study of it. We shall want a Government that can resist lobbying propaganda and Press pressure.'"

when they open. They'll find some other nitwit to take his place I have no doubt. I heard further that our department, being such a small one, is to be left untouched by the redundancy purge, but I should like to get that confirmed.

A letter, at last, from Hugh last night, describing the crossing. 'Foursome in corner playing bridge in whispers. Outside, in corridor, troops more jovially playing pontoon. Wonder why officers prefer bridge. Anyway, cards awful bore. Prefer writing to the Noun . . .'

That's me. One of his special names for me. Grew from a joke we shared. 'Moog' is another – he read the word in one of Saroyan's stories.

'She'll be sleeping cat-like now, forgetting the Hugh interlude. For Hugh a lovely one, unforgettable, nostalgic. She *must* wash her ears. All sorts of thoughts tumble madly – stoated kittens.' (Two of Dinah's last brood were attacked and killed by some wild wood creature. A grisly business.) 'Talc; weariness, gentle soft wearing of contented passion; *Observer* in bed; chopping a forest of trees; stew and beer; endless radio Christmas carols; the Moog moralising immorally; warm welcoming fire; Christmas frost and New Year snow; Kew Theatre and crumpets; hours of solitary reading while Lucie . . .' (his usual name for me) 'earns my keep. Wondering why Lucie hasn't married –p'raps she has – and how lucky for Lucie it wasn't to me.'

He is in Brussels now. Nice Hugh. Dear Hugh, our memories – yes, thank you for them. Now my memories come forward: Hugh, the first Sunday he was here, getting up first to get the tea and coming up and sitting on the edge of my bed. 'Tell me, do you usually have a big bush thing right outside the sitting room door? Well, it's there now.' Gale had blown over the rose arch.

And then sulkily, army overcoat over pyjamas, army boots on feet, coming to deal with squealing stoat-attacked kitten. And saying, 'You know, Lucie, I have *missed* you. I'm not used to missing people.' Slouch hat and my raincoat over civilian clothes, his face outlined against the white night Xmas sky. Stretched in armchair by the fire flipping through books, and catching my arm – 'Don't go . . .' His dark head on my pillow and impudent dark eyes over the edge of the sheet. Stamping snow from his boots all over the clean kitchen floor.

Saturday, 17 February
Have been reading through 1944 entries, and forgot all about pork chops cooking, and they are now leather.

Redundancy 'purges' have been carried out periodically among the staff since the autumn and now the Central Production department, already reduced to about 13, has been told that it will cease to function by the end of March and they can all look for other work. The stamp shops will be closed down entirely by then. Already familiar faces are missing, like candles on a Xmas tree being blown out one by one.

At our Wycombe works there has been a strike because 20 men were sacked and 20 Italians taken in place of them (lower rates).

Sunday, 18 February (War Diary)
In Windsor yesterday afternoon, after a hair appointment, bought some scrubbed carrots. When I remarked on their cleanliness the woman said that it was still a penalty to scrub root vegetables.

Nockie is now on the senior staff of an aircraft firm at Edgware [de Havilland] writing about aero-enquiries.

Monday, 19 February (War Diary)
The Machinery of Government question has caused a crop of letters in *The Times* and *Telegraph*.

A letter from Hugh. 'This office is a military almshouse for the lost and lame – I fear contracting the palsy. The Demon Rum is a great evening temptation and I sit with another Desert Rat beside a wood stove in a café and reminisce garrulously. Verily we have become Desert Mice. Have not reconnoitred the local blonde market yet but preliminary observation not encouraging. Their teeth are bad after four years of Boche occupation. Anyway, only Yank privates and British quartermasters can afford them. I hear there is a war on somewhere near here but can scarce credit it. Slough is more embattled.

'Nearly all here fear the future and look upon the Army in their inner consciousness as an uneasy refuge. I pray for your letters.'

Tuesday, 20 February (War Diary)
Went to see Gas Association's Kitchens Exhibition at Dorland Hall. Crowded with women opening and shutting oven doors, peering into cupboards and refrigerators.

Items of interest: scoop drawers of plastic or glass (plastic were much lighter) for flour, cereals and other such loose foods used in cooking; one or two new patent door fastenings; an Ascot heater covered in transparent plastic presumably to show its innards; plastic table tops that looked rather like cork which would not show marks from hot plates; coloured enamelled steel sinks, possibly easier to keep clean. On the whole, however, was disappointed. Enamel was chipping on some sinks, and much substitute material used which gave appearance of shoddiness. Notices informed me constantly that 'This is a dummy'.

Thursday, 1 March
At office R.W. telling me this afternoon domestic details of the Royal family. She and her parents have lived in Windsor all their lives. Her father owns a pub. They know several of the Castle staff and hear a good deal of gossip.

Of the two princesses, Margaret Rose is the most popular – she chatters to the servants and takes a lively interest in their activities. Elizabeth acknowledges them but remains aloof. One or other of them often accompany their mother when she goes on her tours of inspection. There is an air raid shelter 12 feet below the castle – made as a flat with every convenience – and stock for a six-month sojourn.

Lunch menu in staff canteen today: kidney soup; sausage toad, herrings in tomato sauce; chips, spam, pickles, mash, sprouts; chocolate steamed pudding, rice pudding, dried peaches and custard. The food has not been nearly so good since the canteen management has been taken over by Mrs F. To hear her you would think her rissoles were the most delectable food on earth.

Friday, 2 March
Saw Mr Oliver this afternoon. A few weeks ago he fell off a bus and broke his wrist and has not been able to do much work, but hopes to turn out something for our next big Discussion Group Meeting on the Case for Private Enterprise. We discussed a possible design for this poster. He suggested a photograph of the firm's first two bays – to imply how this particular private enterprise has flourished – but we decided that that would be too personal and finally decided on a silhouette of two bays and of a large factory. This co-operative bringing to birth of an idea made me feel good for ½ an hour or so. It always does – it's something very few people understand about poster work.

Monday, 6 March
Hugh phoned late last night. He is in England again – originally on some special, secret mission until he fell down some stairs and broke his wrist. He says he MUST see me, and threatened to come here today, but phoned again tonight to say he was in hospital once more.

Thursday, 8 March
So happy. I found him sitting in the armchair on Tuesday evening, the fire lit, the curtains drawn. His arm in a sling but looking well – in fact, better than I've seen him. I was surprised at how pleased I was to have him here again. Surprised to find that I wanted to be made love to again. We are planning a weekend in London before he sails.

Saturday, 10 March (War Diary)

On Tuesday the Management gives a Premiere showing of our new film on *Castings to the Aircraft Industry*. A message from W.'s secretary that one of the men invited is dead.

Came in and made bed with clean sheets and then set about de-fleaing Walter. I have had him in the cottage only twice & on each occasion was atrociously attacked – never have I been so bitten in England. 'Keatings' is now unobtainable but the Ministry of Food (why the Ministry of Food?) issues little cartons of Mixed Pyrethrum Powder. I sprinkled this inside an old pillow case and put Walter firmly in it & rubbed him thoroughly.

Tuesday, 13 March

I'd been looking forward to the weekend with Hugh too much. I was *longing* for it, planning all the details and bubbling with happiness yesterday. I ought to have known better.

This evening I receive a message to say that he has been sent overseas on a special mission – returning Monday. If his orders to sail for the Middle East next weekend still stand, then it's all over and it will be very unlikely I'll ever see him again. Oh, does it so much matter? It seems to tonight. We both satisfied a need in each other. My need will go on. He heads for his dream in Greece and his wife in Palestine.

This time last week he was with me.

Wednesday, 28 March (War Diary)

Allied cruisers are swarming across the Rhine. Churchill says the end is in sight, Eisenhower that the Germans are whipped. Two women in the Doctor's surgery this morning said, 'Why don't they give in now? If they would only give in so much more bloodshed would be saved.'

My ears troublesome again. Dr B. treated them just after Xmas – had been having boils in them and much discomfort since time before. He said it was a kind of eczema. Also, developed a septic finger last week, I think from handling some old and dirty forgings. I must rest it as much as possible and he had a splint applied. As it is my right hand it is infuriating. I can't do a thing and shouldn't really be writing this.

Saturday, 31 March

I wait in desolation for my meal to cook. It has been on the kitchen stove for nearly an hour and a half. Stewed mutton and Spanish onions. Broccoli and rhubarb which arrived only half an hour ago. My finger is no better, no worse. The Doctor saw it this morning – said 'It's in the balance now. You *must* keep your hand in a sling or I won't answer for the consequences. That woman who has just gone out, she had the same trouble and now she has lost her nail.'

Everyone I have met recently or heard from is expectant, even exultant. There is much hope in the atmosphere. Young men on leave at the Social Centre, so Jackie told me, were saying 'It'll all be over by Easter Monday.' D.J. more soberly, 'The end in sight very possibly. But it may take another 3 months.' I offered to take Ethel to the theatre for her birthday in February but she did not like the idea of running the gauntlet of V bombs. Now she writes, 'Is not the news thrilling? One wonders just how soon one may expect Victory news. Yes, then you may take me to the theatre. Do! What a treat!'

Tuesday, 3 April

Have tried to obey Doctor's orders – finger looks about the same.

Curly bought a wireless in place of mine. Mine apparently in a rather bad condition. Curly owns a wireless & sports shop in Slough and is having this done for me all out of the kindness of his heart.

He has just had a raw deal, he told me, and feels that by doing someone a good turn that he gets himself readjusted to living. He has been helping to run a Club but has a very poor view of its members – the petit bourgeoisie of Slough. All out for their own interests, he said. 'And you feed them today knowing that if they saw you in the gutter tomorrow they'd tread on you.'

To see a Red Cross film show tomorrow: *Blood Transfusion*; *ABCD of Health*; *Green Food for Health*; *First Aid on the Spot*; *Conquest of a Germ*.

Sunday, 8 April

Nockie has been here and it has been a wonderful and exciting weekend. The fantastic thing was that last night M. phoned. I still don't believe it. I thought it would be Curly to say he was returning my radio. I heard a voice saying, 'So you're not alone this evening?' I gasped, 'What?' 'You're not alone this evening?' 'N-no . . .' 'Well I did say I'd phone and I have. I'll try again . . .' 'Yes, phone again . . .' 'When?' 'When you like . . .'

Not once did we exchange names. I knew his voice. Oh, it was ridiculously fantastic! Nockie could not know or feel the wonder of the miracle of his having phoned at all. It was honeydew that my imagination fed on to saturation point nearly all night.

Tuesday, 10 April

Lydia at lunch said she had had an unexpected visitor last evening. She seemed elated and happy and would not tell me who the visitor was. That look in Lydia's eyes as though she knew something I didn't. I may quite well be imagining it, or misinterpreting. But oh, I am so beaten up by the old hunger, that desperate desire for something which seems adult and important, and to the brink of which I am always being led and then left, deserted, shivering and bewildered.

28.

Oh, the Swine!

Thursday, 12 April 1945

Just after lunch yesterday Lydia let fall a remark which shot me up. Pointing to one of Mr Oliver's posters she said, 'M. doesn't think much of Oliver as an artist. We were looking at a cartoon, and I mentioned Oliver, and M. said . . .' And so on. I *had* to find out when and where she had had this conversation with M. All afternoon my mind was in a turmoil. If he was playing the same game with her as he had with me then it was time she knew my story.

We had arranged to see a Dancing Display (Aid to China show) at the Social Centre in the evening. This was my opportunity. Now I like Lydia enormously, enormously. She is attractive, has courage, brain, imagination and grit. She has a sense of humour and a lively interest in many things. She is a flower opening. Whatever M. was up to with her, it was only fair that she should know of his 'line' with me. Besides, I was burnt up with curiosity and jealously. I have had my suspicions for weeks – ever since he asked about her, and have sensed from stray looks and several remarks and intuitive hunches that something was taking place – though I didn't like to think what – between them.

I found it very difficult to break through, to frame and utter my first question, but I did it. 'Do tell me – I am eaten up with curiosity. Where did you have this conversation about Oliver with M. . . .' Something like that. There wasn't time before the show to go further, but afterwards over a cup of coffee we had it out.

I told her my story first. Hers is a business offer. She could not give me details, and I don't want them, but M. has plans for starting something on his own with one or two other men, and making use of Lydia's artistic talents and engineering experience. It was a good offer and interested Lydia very much when first made five weeks ago. But then he apparently hung fire (how typical of M.: not a word, not a gesture!) and she was very offended. However on Monday he approached her again, and had some drawings to show her, and wanted her to meet him that evening. Of course she said come round to my flat. Which he did, and discussed the matter in a business-like way with much enthusiasm. But, business finished, he then began the patter he put over to me with such success at Redditch.

Heart, could you have more Proof Positive of his villainy? Lydia was surprised and a little uncertain as to what she should do. She had no personal interest in the man (I believe that) and wanted to regard the whole affair on a strictly business footing. However, she humoured him (they danced to the wireless) and eventually turned him out at about 11 p.m. (from what she said he would obviously have stayed given the slightest encouragement).

I failed to board the last buses home, all full to overflowing, so went back with her for the night. We went into my story in great detail. She thinks his business deal is genuine enough, but this new light on his character is making her hesitate. I would not spoil a good chance for her – but oh, the swine! That he should be making passes at her too! Not of course surprising but painful to hear about. I am a fool! Foolish, foolish little man. I could have loved you so much.

Thursday, 19 April
This evening at the office Mr B. called me in to say he was releasing our office girl J.C. as there was so little work for any of us at present. He thought Miss W. and myself could manage. He evidently realised I am quite valuable to the department and that I can stay on if I want for a few more months at least. Which I do, strange as it may seem.

More letters from Hugh. He has sent me his Will and made me his executor.

Wednesday, 25 April (War Diary)

'God is pleased' said N. 'that we are freeing the concentration camps in Germany.' The horrors that have been revealed by the Allies are past belief. All the people I know cannot understand how any human being in a so-called civilised nation could treat other human beings like that. We just cannot understand it. The authorities who ordered such torture, and the men and women who had to supervise and control the camps must be mad, terribly mad. One suspected the Nazis of a certain amount of brutality and sadism, but not on this scale, involving the death by starvation & deliberate degradation of 1,000s and 1,000s of men, women and children – the children the worst of all. As at least one newspaper correspondent has pointed out, if they were trying to wipe out their enemies it was at least logical to gas and cremate them. But these methods are hideous, unvarnished sadism. All civilised, balanced people must be shocked to the soul at the reports that have come out – German people among them – and it is said that some have claimed and do claim that they knew nothing of what was going on.

It is indeed a terrible lesson to the whole world. Did the Nazis think they would never be discovered? They must have done. As to the whole German race bearing the blame – maybe they should and must. But as M. said, when your loved ones are threatened what can you do? Would you be brave if your husband, mother, child might be whisked away from you if you didn't submit to the authorities? I suppose the fault is in being so ignorant and disinterested in 'politics' as to let the State grow to such power. This seems to me the moral – the lesson we have to learn from the story of the German concentration camps, and it should be broadcast and bought home to everyone. But officialdom won't do it.

I thought that I should revel in not having to draw curtains any more at night. But as soon as it gets dark an unprotected window makes me feel guilty and uncomfortable. I draw my curtains.

Thursday, 26 April (War Diary)
Letter dated 6th March from brother Pooh in Suez received before Easter:

'We are under orders for Alexandria and expect to be leaving Suez at the end of this month or beginning of next. We are both quite pleased about it as it will make a change and in some ways may be better for us than coming home.' They have been in Suez since the beginning of 1939 & should normally have had 3 months' leave at the end of 3 years.

'We are all going strong though still broke. Prices are still going up and up. The Egyptians, having made lots of money out of England and the British troops during the past few years, pay the most astounding sums quite cheerfully. Jay was in Cairo the other week & watched a fat old Egyptian woman in a big store buy twelve pairs of Nylon stockings at £9 a pair, a silk nightdress at £25 and various other odds and ends, the total of which came to nearly £200. She calmly opened her handbag and paid down spot cash for this little lot.'

Friday, 27 April (War Diary)
The Russians and Americas have met in Germany. In Italy the German Army is crumbling fast. Mussolini, it is reported, has been captured. Dramatic news. Much speculation as to what is happening now to the Nazi chiefs – evening papers say Goering has left the country with wife, daughter and £5,000,000. I wondered aloud coming home with Mr Ch. in what currency he could have taken it.

I think Hitler will commit suicide, and only Hitler. Mr Ch. doubted it: 'It takes a lot of courage.' But thinking this over, yes it takes courage for the 'normal' person, but suicides are never 'normal', and Hitler is not normal.

Tuesday, 1 May (War Diary)

Important hours, important as those days at the end of August in 1939 preceding the declaration of war. This is tension of a different kind, expectancy, preparations being made for a change in our way of living. But the tempo is slower. We wait, without anxiety, for the official announcement by Mr Churchill that is to herald two full days' holiday and the beginning of another period of peace in Europe. We wait wondering if Hitler is dying or dead or will commit suicide or be captured and tried and shot, and what his henchman are doing and feeling.

We had ice cream in canteen for lunch today – the first for two, or is it three, years?

Wednesday, 2 May (War Diary)

One can hardly keep pace with the news. 'Hitler Dead' the *News Chronicle* informed me this morning in 12-inch type across the front page. Doenitz has either been appointed to succeed him or has seized power over Himmler's head. We discussed the situation all through lunch, wondering how much longer the war would now continue with Doenitz in control. At the office an atmosphere of suspense but little obvious excitement.

Thursday, 3 May (War Diary)

Mr B. gave me the afternoon off. About 8 p.m. the rain turned to snow. I ate my supper watching the enormous snowflakes fall, wondering if any other country in the world could present such a scene – snow on tulips and broken lilac blossom, snow falling through bursting beeches and the sky ash, snow on shivering pansies and wan forget-me-nots. A fantastic spring.

Friday, 4 May (War Diary)

When the first newsflash came through the radio announcing the surrender of the German forces in north-west Germany, I was in bed mopping my ears. We had looked at the headlines in the *Evening News* in the office just before 5 p.m. and decided that the end *must* be near now, as the enemy was collapsing on all fronts.

I asked R.W. what she intended to do on VE day and she said that she didn't know. Her people keep a pub in Windsor and they have not decided whether they will keep open or not. If they do (and the brewers want them to) they will not have more than their normal rationed supply and will be sold out by 9.30 p.m. Her father thinks he will invite in all his pals and keep the pub closed to the public.

No one seems very certain what they will do. There are to be some Victory parades and special services and bonfires. It looks as though I shall spend the day and days following in close, solitary seclusion. My ears are a most revolting sight and even Dr B. is baffled. He talks of sending me to a specialist but I am to treat them myself this weekend with rainwater and special ointment. I am worried and tired and do not want to go out or meet anyone. My friends are sympathetic and anxious but I feel rather a leper and imagine all strangers to be goggling at me.

I came home at 5 p.m., collected ointment from the chemist, and, while waiting for it to be made up, some new stock arrived including a small box of Wright's coal tar soap. I have not seen any of this for a long while and the girls said they would not have any 'for ages' so I bought two tablets.

Girls in cloakroom were chattering excitely this afternoon. 'Oh, I do hope it'll happen while we're at work! – It won't seem the same will it?' The official notice asks us all to assemble in the canteen where news of victory is announced over the works broadcasting system. We are then to have the rest of the day off and the two following days. The girls began twittering about their husbands – what group for demobilisation did each belong to? I left them, feeling rather old and forlorn.

Listening now to the repeat broadcast of General Montgomery from Germany this afternoon. My emotions at this moment are indescribable: enormous pride in the fact that I am British, wonder and excitement. 'Tomorrow morning at 8 a.m. the war in Europe will be over . . .' The war in Europe is over . . . This is a tremendous moment.

The war is over. I cry a little. I think of my dearest friends, my stepmother, my brother in Egypt, of those men in the fighting services I have known – and I wish I had taken a more active part; it is too late now. But it is not too late to take part in the new fight ahead. I am not moved to rush out tomorrow and wave a Union Jack in the village high street. I think it is a good sign that people are saying universally, 'Our troubles are just beginning,' because it would be idiotic to assume they are over with the end of hostilities.

We want a better world and we must fight for it. That is where we must distinguish between pessimism and optimism. I believe with the utmost optimism, faith, hope and joy that we can have our better world (and note that one says 'a *better* world' – not the perfect or even best possible world) – yes, that we can have it if we know clearly what we want and fight for it.

Midnight news now being read. The announcer sounds tired. Pockets of German resistance still remain. I have been down and turned off the radio. For once I waited to hear the whole of the National Anthem, moved suddenly again to tears by this historic, this incredible moment. I stood with my hand on the radio switch listening to the National Anthem and to the voices of a thousand, thousand ghosts. They came over the air into that unlit, silent room, I swear it.

It's time I tried to sleep. One of the cats is outside my window waiting to be let in. Tomorrow and tomorrow and tomorrow stretch before me. Infinitely more full of promise and interest than the war years have been. I feel that new and exciting events await me. But that may be due to the influence of tonight's news. The atmosphere is charged with a release and potentiality.

And the bottom sheet, in an exceedingly frail condition from old age and much hard wear, is now torn beyond hope and redemption. I am sick to death of patching worn linen.

From Italy, Hugh wrote on 1 May:

'Last night German resistance on the northern Italian front ended. I was at my desk with two very young officers and my OC who was a captain with me in Greece in 1941. He said, "It's been a long road." We opened a bottle of Scotch and had a tot – two tots. Yet the old real Desert Rats – my old 7th Armoured Division – are still battling around Hamburg. The youngsters felt more exhilaration than we. My thoughts, strangely, were on the safari track from Bug Bug to Maddelena – two graves long since covered with sand. The end is near now and a great sense of emptiness. A new desert of emotion to be explored and fought over . . .'

Tuesday, 8 May VE Day

I cannot put this down in my War Diary for Mass Observation – that I feel intensely lonely and that it is somehow my fault. That feeling I have had ever since I was a little girl and was conscious of such feelings – of being left out of things and not understanding why I should be.

I want desperately for someone to ring me up and ask me to share in the day's celebrations. If I had someone staying with me now it wouldn't seem to matter so much. If I were in London and Joan were at home I should get drawn in there, and almost certainly have some contact with Nockie. I phone Lydia, but she had already been 'nabbed' by her friend C., and if I had phoned earlier I might have been included – they are going to a dance tonight probably. I should dearly have loved a dance. But my intention is to cycle to see Lizzie and Peter after I have heard the PM at 3 p.m. They are almost certain to be home between 5–6 because of the baby.

So here I sit with so much to give, longing to share what I have, and knowing that I as always will have to make the first move. I would like to see the cottage (the sitting room now so bright after its spring clean) full of happy people this evening.

11.30 p.m.. I cannot, cannot confess this agony to MO. They play on the radio at this moment: 'I'm a Little on the Lonely Side Tonight'. The dance music, the happy voices that come with it, the sound of happy people dancing – their cheers and applause only increase the agony. God, I am lonely, lonely. I want to be in all this somewhere celebrating with happy people. It was good being with Lizzie and Peter. We cycled round looking at the local flags, bunting, lights and bonfires, but they had to go home to the baby, and I came home alone. Left out. Forgotten. Not very much wanted by anyone. All my life this has gone on. I have built up pretences and found ways of escape, but here is a moment where the truth faces me and I cannot avoid it. And with it the constant feeling of guilt: you pay now at times such as this for your cowardice and selfishness, you get out of life what you put into it.

I wish Nockie had phoned. I don't think I can endure listening to the Victory Night ball at Covent Garden much longer. I can hear people saying casually, 'What – all alone? Doing nothing on Victory night?'

PART THREE:
A Starving Europe

29.

A Large Bag of Biscuits – Chocolate and Plain

Monday, 14 May 1945 (aged thirty-five)

I have reached a point, a stage, where I need something to integrate my life. There are two things I feel I should possess as I possess hands and feet – a wedding ring and a publisher.

Monday, 21 May

There is, surprisingly, a lot of good common sense in some of the women's journals. An intellectual snobbishness bars one from it. I am often drawn to them by their attractive layout and colour, and the hope of finding useful household hints. There are dozens of these journals – from the cheap weeklies like *Woman* to the more expensive and better class monthlies such as *Good Housekeeping*, and, seen on a bookstall, the temptation to buy is great because nowadays they are so seldom seen. And often when one has bought and devoured greedily one feels nauseated: it has been, or has seemed to have been, all ersatz cream.

But sometimes one finds something really solid for digestion – in the June *Woman and Beauty* for instance. 'There are many women entirely ready to marry, but unable to win proposals from any man they consider eligible. As a group, they are well bred, well educated, unusually intelligent, attractive at least as the average. But they have all conducted themselves on the general principle that if a man isn't discerning enough to recognise and appreciate their good qualities, it is just too bad – for him!'

The article goes on, 'You should take definite, effective steps to enlarge your social circle. And if you have to move to do that – well, you'd better move.' And then later in the article: 'Don't make the mistake of trying to marry a man less able than yourself. On the contrary, aim high! Recent studies show that men do not tend to marry girls more capable or better educated than themselves. That's one of the reasons, incidentally, why so many professional women are unmarried. There are not enough really knowledgeably superior men available for them!'

When one starts to analyse these sorts of articles one finds them full of holes, but the grit in this one for me is being more positive about marriage. I am not in the professional women class nor anywhere near it, I am not an ardent careerist, but all my experience and training seem to have been preparing me to be a first-class wife. At 35 I am more attractive than I have ever been, I have more poise, I am happier and I have more to give. Now – *cherchez l'homme*! That is the command I recoil from. I want the *l'homme* to fall into my lap, out of nowhere. I don't want to be thought a husband-chaser. I shrink from the effort required, the possible humiliations to be suffered.

The point is to admit frankly, fairly and squarely that one wants to marry, to enlarge one's social circle – at the cost of a cottage if necessary, but I don't think that it need be. I feel that if I am just at this moment uprooted from the cottage I shall bleed to death.

(War Diary)

Collecting milk from next door, Lady Spicer bears down on me with a triumphant, exultant gleam in her eye: 'I have always said that our troubles would begin when the war was over – now everyone is out for himself and there is a clash of interests everywhere. Power goes to heads of these people who have not been brought up to rule.' I agree that the future promises to be chaotic and that there will be trouble with Russia but can't believe it will be as black as she seems to think. Spent the weekend with stepmother Ethel (Aunt Maggie also there). Listening to the report of Ellen Wilkinson's speech on the one o'clock news I was suddenly struck by the thought of how extraordinary it was that the BBC should allow Labour propaganda such prominence.[146] When I am with Conservatives I find myself agreeing with Conservative opinion, when with Liberals with Liberal, Labour with Labour, Communist with Communist. Conscience, and the fact that my politically minded friends will expect me to, will probably make me vote Labour. (The election may be held, we are told now, in July, which seems too soon, too much of a rush. But why should we have to put up with the present Government until the war with Japan is over?) There are people even now who have never used a ration book for themselves. For example, an elderly female cousin of Ethel's and Aunt Maggie's, of fantastic wealth, who has been living with an elderly companion in a remote part of Scotland during the war. They have not, either, heard a gun. They are now in London staying in a hotel near Welbeck Street. Two useless, parasitical old women. And what a lot of apparently useless people there are in the world living on money someone else has earned. Is it entirely their fault? I am not at all sure that unearned income is not more demoralising than dire poverty. When no effort has to be put into living the character grows fat, flabby, feeble.

Wednesday, 23 May

I'm high as a steeple. I am floating on a cloud. I am in heaven. I am tight.

Such a delectable, delicious sensation. Now the world is my oyster and I am capable of all things. Love, and this and that. Dinah sits with her back to me, shocked, disgusted.[147]

Nothing to eat since lunch. A bitter, bitter moment when I thought I saw M.'s car sliding out of the car park this evening just three or four or five minutes ahead of me. If it was – oh Fate why do you do

---

146 The Labour MP Ellen Wilkinson was the post-war minister of education until her death in office in 1947.
147 Her handwriting is distinctly looser and messier.

these things? And if he saw me walking to the gate as he might have done – why could not he have waited . . . just those few minutes?

But at the bus stop I met my very old and trusty friend Dr R.L. and a colleague of his. They took me off to the Pump and we went and drank at the Duke's Head. A Guinness. A bitter. Two gin and lime. I feel soothed and somehow compensated and defiant. Damn M. Has he any idea of what he is missing? The primus stove gives a faint high note when lit that might be the telephone bell (so does the vacuum). I thought it was, I was sure it was. But no.

A letter from Hugh awaited me. 'Your charming VE day descriptive letter came today. I read it to an appreciative ward. Why don't you write a novel?' Why don't I? Oh God, why don't I?

I have a new short 'utility' Jaeger jacket. Blue. Madonna Blue, Lizzie Cecil called it. It is an enormous success. It is an incredible blue – greenish, Prussian, and goes with nearly everything I possess. It makes my eyes bluer, says Lydia.

Friday, 25 May (War Diary)

I am having help in the house again, after three years without. A woman recommended through friends came last Thursday for the first time. Certain things had been put back on their shelves and ledges with the symmetry so beloved of Mrs Mops. The bedroom floor had been polished and looked very nice, the kitchen stove blackened, the parts of the stone floor I could see washed, the stairs swept. But the carpet hadn't been touched and a mat carefully arranged and disguised the fact. A table by the bed, in a rather dark and difficult to get at corner, had not been dusted. And so on. This sort of slackness and cheating enrages me. We have to pay 2s. an hour for it and be thankful. I gave her something for one of her children, told her to make herself tea, showed her where the biscuit tin was and intend to let her have flowers as she likes. My manner to these women is always kind and sympathetic and I always hope not patronising. I feel sympathetic to them and like to hear about their families and troubles. I am probably too kind, too trusting.

Tuesday, 5 June (War Diary)

Prisoners of war returning now thick and fast. Their stories differ tremendously. An acquaintance of Jacky's, for instance, has come home looking well, tanned and happy. Speaks well of the ordinary German soldier – the non-Nazi – who shared parcels of food with the prisoners. On the other hand, R.W. met a friend in the RAF who has been a prisoner for two years. He was so thin she would not have recognised him but for the uniform. He was in an army prison with Russians. All were fed in this camp on cabbage water soup and bread, one loaf between ten men a day. They were so hungry they would steal rotten turnip peelings as they were carted through the camp. The Russians would keep the bodies of dead comrades as long as they could and take them into roll call in order to get the extra rations. Punishment for the slightest offences were severe – R.W.'s friend had frostbite cracks between the toes from having been stood out in the winter cold for two hours at a time. Russian Cossacks liberated them. They had not sufficient food for the prisoners but allowed them to roam the town and loot what they could. Men were shooting cattle and pigs and gorging themselves on these. Some died from it. A month later he was flown to England, medically examined and given six weeks' leave.

An extraordinary cigarette shortage since VE day. For at least the last two weeks, when I have been in London, ordinary Virginian brands have been unobtainable. They have been increasingly scarce here, locally, but so far I have managed to get at least twenty a day from the canteen kiosk (but not my favourite brand). People talking of getting their cars on the road once more.

Sunday, 17 June (War Diary)

Catering difficulties increase rather than decrease. There is a shortage of potatoes, soap, fresh fruit and greens. Our fat, cheese and sugar rations are being cut. We have had nothing but cabbage on the menu in the canteen for weeks and weeks (I mean as a second vegetable to potato). A woman who shops in Slough was told by the managers of two big food stores recently that they expected this winter and next to be the worst we have yet known. There are now no food reserves in the country and supplies are going to Europe. She was told: 'We are having to do it because the Americans won't. Why should we? We've gone without willingly all through the war because we've known it's been going to Our Boys. But why should we feed Europe? I resent the idea of helping the Germans or the French. I have a family of young children to feed and I think the essential foods should at least go to them first.' There are some people who in all seriousness thought that as soon as the war ended the shops would be filled with pre-war goods and we should be free to buy what we liked. Have Huxley's *Eyeless in Gaza* out of the public library.

Yesterday Ethel and I went to see the Aluminium exhibition at Selfridges, lunched at the Bolivar and then went to see *Arsenic and Old Lace*, in its third year, I think. Really delightful entertainment, though it has not pleased everyone.

Tuesday, 19 June (War Diary)
Some evacuated children do not want to return to their own homes, and their foster parents don't want to let them go. Jacky talking this morning of a young cousin: 'My uncle's little girl was taken at five years old, by a wealthy family in Scotland at the beginning of war. They have adopted her as companion to their own daughter and given her the same education, clothing and attention. Now she's a proper little lady. She won't want to go home – her people being rough and ready farmers . . .'

Friday, 22 June
Have been to a skin specialist about my ears (a woman). She asked me if I were worried. I replied, 'Not excessively.'

I have made an appointment to see Dr Howe again.

Monday, 25 June (War Diary)
Some extracts from Hugh's letters from Italy.

30 April. I'm scribbling this on my bed in the tent. I shall probably head north very soon. My batman, now snoring, said tonight, 'The War's nearly over – then the real one begins, xxxx it!' Comment of one officer: 'The next war centre is Tehran – oil interests.'

2 May. 2nd General Hospital. Now in hospital. In an hour's time they take out my blasted appendix. Was taken ill at 3 a.m.

4 May. I am weeping weakly because I can't stop pain in my belly and three days without food, and on top of it the emotional storm of the great victory. Let me weep. Six long years, my dear. And I end them here, in a shabby Italian barracks . . . But my complaints are for the wounded who cannot celebrate. Funny. I have never wanted to weep so much before and I know others are weeping silently. The radio blares victory after victory after victory.

8 May. So it's over. Listened to Churchill's speech. Then came, to us, the most pleasing thing – the thin clear notes of the 'Cease Fire'. And so I snuggled down to sleep. Wonder where Hitler, Goering, Goebbels & Co. swine are. Possibly we shall hear of a Terence O'Goebbels editing the *Cork Courier*.

25 May. So there's to be an election. This snap election may lose Labour much of the military vote, but it has a 2:1 chance of winning. I fear its foreign policy but welcome its internal plan for nationalisation. The pledge to the Jews in regard to Palestine is especially dangerous. May set the Arab world ablaze – and more poor British Tommies will die in a cause they profit not by.

Wednesday, 27 June
This afternoon's meeting with G.H. was one of the most important I have yet had.

Do not try to avoid frustration, he said. Living is difficult, and frustration is part of the difficulty. See how my poor mother struggled against it. I remember one night, as a little girl, being wakened by the sound of her practicing scales joyously. I called down, 'Mummy you woke me up . . . please don't.' The scales stopped, she left the piano and I could hear her setting the table for my father's supper. From the way she handled the cutlery I could feel her anger, resentment and despair. It flooded up to me alone and frightened in the dark. I can imagine her mood now: 'Even my own children! . . . I never wanted them . . . I wanted to go on with my music . . . I shall never play now – never, never. Why did I have to fall in love? Why did we have to be poor? This war, I suppose. No help in the house, meals to get, mending, scrubbing, cooking, incessant demands that I can't ignore because I love my husband. When Jean grows up may she never be tied like this. May she be free of all the insatiable demands of men and family life. She will have a little money, and I will help her all I can to a career . . .'

Saturday, 30 June
I ran into M. this morning. Warned by his car parked in the works yard that he was somewhere about, I was not too embarrassed to come face to face with him outside the Inspection Shop. I hesitated. He mumbled, as well he might. It was difficult to hear above the noise of the works and 'Music While You Work'. He said, 'Are you still Publicity, still at the cottage? Can I ring you sometime?' I said I was still on the telephone.

I want a chance to say all the things I've been longing to say for months. Lydia is 'washing her hands of him'. That is the sane thing, the rational course to take. But I'm not rational about this. He had on a new light fawn tweed suit, looking smarter than I've ever seen him.

Monday, 2 July
Tonight I receive a letter from Hugh dated 28 June. 'Lucille, my sweet. No mail from you. I shall parade outside your cottage with a picketing

banner: "Pratt so unfair to Laming", singing to the tune of "The Red Flag":

> A trollop is Jean Lucey Pratt
> And all Slough is aware of that;
> She also has a trollop cat
> And 50 kittens on the mat.
> Then Comrades I'm assuring you
> That Lucy is unfair to Hugh.
> Reactionary cat is Pratt
> And bites the ear of Desert Rat.

This delights me, delights me. Could any woman fail to appreciate such flattery?

No phone call. Of course no phone call, as I told Lydia in answer to her enquiry today. All I want is a chance to be rude to that wretched little man. But he's not going to give me the chance.

Tuesday, 3 July
M. again in Slough. His car at the filling station at the George when I passed. He was outside paying for the petrol and made a gesture which might have been 'Lift?', but which I soon discovered meant 'No lift tonight'. He did look a scab this evening. Shabby blue suit, tired, flushed, as though he had been drinking heavily all day. A really shoddy little business man. Pah!

Monday, 9 July
Heart is singing again. M. phoned and came round on Friday evening. And stayed. Yes, I am his mistress now, his mistress. I do not care what others say or reason dictates. I am his mistress, and as far as I am capable of loving a man, I love him. The current between us is too strong – it is more that I can resist.

I tried to be angry, to get some explanation out of him. But all he could say was, 'I have at least come back. You know now you are not forgotten.' And later I asked, 'How many girlfriends have you?'

'Five,' he replied promptly and coolly. 'Three are in Sheffield.'

'That is bad luck for you. Do you ever get there?'

'About once a year.'

'Just to tell them they are not forgotten, I suppose . . .' Which made him laugh.

He mended the kitchen light for me. Brought a large bag of biscuits – chocolate and plain – tomatoes, cigarettes and gin. 'What a conscience you must have,' I remarked, but he appeared not to understand that.

I kept him at a distance until nearly half-past eleven, and when he began to make love to me I broke away crying, 'Why do you come and do this to me once a year? It hurts, it hurts, it is so damnably casual . . .'

And he answered, ' Look Jean, I am married with a child! I can't help it! I know, I know just how you are feeling.'

And then I suggested that if he went home at once I would ask him for a weekend. He liked the idea of that. But he would not be tied to a promise. Why he had come this evening, he said, was because the family were away. He was to fetch them from Bognor the next day. If he arranged to come while they were at home he would have to 'sneak out, and you wouldn't want me to do that, would you? I have to come only when I am quite free to come . . .'

I do not understand his domestic situation but I imagine it must be something like this: His wife can have no more children (and he would like a large family, I found that out). She is cold. Either fears or does not want passion – his fault or hers, I do not know. They have to consider the child. He has, he says, some regard for the loyalties – he does not want to desert his wife or break up their home. But he is warm, passionate, and wants his passion returned. Close to me in bed, held tightly in my arms, he cried out with relief and deep joy 'Oh, to be wanted, to be needed – Jean, Jean, if ever I forget to thank you for this, forgive me.'

But the body says more than words. We betray ourselves utterly in our love-making. His reactions came quickly – too quickly – and although he declared again and again how happy he was, and burst into song and quoted Shakespeare (astonishing!), it was a whipped-up sort of happiness – he was stimulated, excited, but was not satisfied. I know how a man behaves when he is satisfied. He wants to sleep, turn over and forget one. M. was wide awake and still urgent – so was I.

He went about 2 o'clock, although we did not want to part. He made no promises, no arrangements for future meetings. Some of the things he said are flames of joy within me – yet they would all have been said to other women: 'The ties that draw us are long and strong . . . maybe longer and stronger than we know.' 'One has to go through many oysters before finding the pearl.'

What will be the end of all this? Will it be another year before he comes again? Can I stand that? 'You are all,' he said, 'that I thought you would be. And I have thought of you often, believe me . . .' Darling M., I do love you so. Imagination is now having a great time with lots of little Ms, and me as important, blooming, happy wife, hostess, mother. Idiot – you must not tell him that.

'I shall dream of this, Jean,' he said. 'Oh, you have no idea what it is like at home!' Come again soon my dear, please, please come again soon. Or are you, as Graham Howe suggested, the type who does not want to be loved, to be tied by the ties of love? The type described by Aldous in *Eyeless in Gaza* who refused, deliberately, to be loved, shutting it out? Who evaded confidences –'confidences were dangerous, confidences were untangling – like fly paper . . .' I am afraid you are, but probably for different reasons. Are you, as I have done, trying to avoid what can not be avoided? And will you find the answer, or will you go on as you are doing, developing into a successful, hot-tempered, paunchy little business man who in old age will maul and paw little blondes and be made a fool of by them?

I told Lydia that he had been round, that the situation was quite beyond my control. I dread telling Nockie. I saw her shaking with laughter: 'He is such a funny little man! One wants to pat him on the head and take him on one's knee . . .'

The things he said keep coming back. 'When we see each other accidentally, then you will say to yourself, "There is my man," and I shall say, "There is my woman".' (One of them, darling.) That is exactly what I do say to myself when I see him. A light is lit. Maybe the ties are longer and stronger than we know.

30.

No More Ghosts

Friday, 13 July 1945

I wrote and told Nockie what had happened, fearing very much her disapproval! She answered immediately. 'That M. has these five female friends seems to suggest to me that they have ⅕th of M. each and that he would be happier giving ⅘ths of himself to somebody. I think you are that somebody . . .'

I so much want to believe it. At this moment I do. But I may change. 'One has to go through many oysters before finding the pearl, and then one puts it in one's pocket until one wants to look at it again,' he said. But pockets can have holes, pockets may be picked, and pearls lose their lustre shut away in the dark – they must be worn and loved.

Tuesday, 17 July

In bed since yesterday with abscess in left ear. How I do love to be ill enough to stay at home with a clear conscience, but not ill enough to require nursing.

Thursday, 19 July

Entry in Barbellion's journal for 1904, September 8, 9, 10 and 11: 'Toothache, Toothache, Toothache and Toothache.' Entries in mine for July 16, 17, 18, 19 (1945): 'Earache, Earache, Earache and Earache.' And for how many more days? Doctor seems to think it will take some time to clear up. Not an abscess but a grossly swollen drum and infected glands. I feel very peevishly petulant and sorry for myself. As soon as I move about doing things the pain exerts itself – like a thousand needles pricking the drum. I lie and think of M., wishing he would walk in, make a fuss of me, sit and talk for a little while, tuck me into bed and leave me to sleep.

Friday, 20 July
I am a drowning, drowning woman. There is no relief, no satisfaction, no joy in anything. The pain in the ear is less, but the pain of the spirit intensifies. I start at shadows, imagine footsteps on the path, listen for the phone, listen to the cars outside. I shall tonight drink a tumblerful of Epsom Salts which will increase the tension tenfold.

It is this awful, intolerable, tormenting suspense, this silence – no, not just waiting for a period which I think will come – but the isolation, the loss of contact. Not a sign, sound or sight of him for a whole fortnight. It is no good saying, 'I will not put up with it, he must go.' I am committed, the way is chosen – there was no choice – I cannot dismiss him. I am caught in the tide and must be swept with it, a drowning, drowning woman.

Now Jean. You are all at a tension – taut, resistant. Relax. Open your hands. Open your heart. Let this pain seep through. Let go, drowning woman, slip into this sea of anxiety, this awful gulf. Let the darkness cover you.

Sunday, 22 July
I am better. The cloud is lifting.

Have just finished Andre Maurois autobiography.[148] He writes, 'A happy marriage is a long conversation that always seems too short.' And, 'Happiness, like wild anemones, is a flower that must not be picked.'

---

148 Maurois was a French author and diplomat, remembered among bibliophiles as the author of the first Penguin book (*Ariel*, a biography of Shelley).

Monday, 23 July

Not so good this morning. Definitely not so good.

Friday, 27 July

Three weeks and still no word. It's not, I am sure, that he doesn't think of me or even care quite a lot. He just wants to have his cake and eat it, without paying.

Confessed when he was with me that he liked doing things spontaneously. I do not want a 'spontaneous' lover. I want a man who will treat me with some confidences, who will share at least some of his life. I would honestly, at this moment, rather be married to Hugh, whom I do not and could never love as I could M. Hugh at least gives me his friendship fully and deeply. We are 'in touch' although he is in Italy and has a Greek wife. M. has gone from me, into the void. All his passion and his flattery is worthless. He isn't the type to write letters, as Hugh is, but there are other means. Chris Naude once phoned me from Geneva. Birmingham is only a trunk call.

I want no more ghosts.

Tuesday, 31 July

A delightful letter from Hugh this morning. 'You won't clear the Lucian ears by bedding with fools, no matter how passionate. It's easy to deal with "unwanted persistent young men". Just say "you bore me," or tell them that Hugh, the Terror of Turin, is on his way and would like nothing better than to complete the chaos in Lucie's kitchen by a trifling massacre of a man who, it would seem, can't even kill a kitten . . .'

And later: 'Have just re-read your letter. Am I jumping to conclusions about "the wrong lover in my bed"? Moogful, you were and are so good to me. When I come home . . .' (He has decided to leave the army and may be in London – with Maritza! – in October) ' . . . let me stay a few days with you and tire . . . you with talking. I'm told my operation scar is intriguing. Knowing your cookery I can see you now getting a slice of fatted calf for Hugh and putting it in that old saucepan and boiling it from now to October . . .'

Sunday, 12 August

Atomic bomb and imminent end of Japanese war have filled the news these last few days.[149] Office in still rather a turmoil. Firm is now a full member of Hawker Siddeley Group.[150]

Am trying to make myself concentrate on short stories. Always to have one on the go. I can find hundreds of excuses not to do it. But it is the only thing that keeps my thoughts off M. But it's a real effort – I'm trying to run away now by writing this.

What has all this to do with the atomic bomb? Just this: that one is so overwhelmed by the awful potentialities of this new discovery – what on earth, one feels, can the single, ordinary person do about it? Well, I think they can begin by setting their own house in order – learn to control and guide your own life so that in the aggregate we can control and guide such powerful weapons for the good and not the destruction of mankind. Eternal vigilance and discipline. Starting with yourself.

Tuesday, 14 August

It's not easy. You shut the thoughts you don't want to indulge away into a packing vase and sit on it. Busy yourself externally and forget for an hour or two the contents. This must be the masculine, the extrovert way of living. So busy with matters outside, one forgets what is inside. And then fatigue relaxes your guard. And out they swarm, like the evils from Pandora's box, worse than ever. But next day you pack them up again and go on. There seems to be no other way. You

---

149 Atomic bombs were dropped on Hiroshima and Nagasaki on 6 and 9 August, hastening the VJ (Victory over Japan) celebrations a few days later. The surrender was signed on 2 September, thus officially ending the Second World War.
150 The aerospace and engine conglomerate, responsible in future years for commercial and military aircraft, including the Harrier Jump Jet.

are conscious all the time of the emptiness and darkness and loneliness within. You go about hollow and unlit, tempted at unexpected moments to release the catch and lift the lid just a little – just for the artificial, imagined warmth those secrets can give.

One story has been sent to *Woman*. Now I am wrestling with one which, if it shapes as I want it to, might go to Penguin New Writers.

Saturday, 18 August

Story progresses well. 'Cri de Coeur' or 'Nuit Blanche'. Some such title. Am deeply absorbed. Think of it all the time, in buses, in queues, at the office – even writing at the office when alone. A transference of thought-energy – not suppression – into, I hope, more fruitful channels.

Attracted by my bedroom light, three hornets flew in at the window just now. Nothing terrifies me as do hornets. Three of them all at once circling above my head to the lamplight at my side, like stupid moths! I still feel weak, can hear the buzzing of a hundred more. My hell, I do believe, would be to be stung to death by hornets. Why this horror of them? I think because I was told when a little girl that one hornet's sting can kill a man. I must find out if that is true.

I skedaddled out of the room as quickly as I dared and fetched the fly swat and succeeded, trembling like a leaf, in killing them all, and have put their corpses on the dying kitchen fire. Am sure I can hear more buzzing – that sinister, terrifying hum, worse, much worse than the hum of enemy bombers.

The thing to do, idiot, is of course to shut the window and draw the curtains until I have finished writing this. Am much too wide awake now to settle. I can hear that buzzing still, all round me, and something beating its wings in a corner.

VJ days spent pleasantly. Wednesday afternoon at the cinema with Lydia. Thursday picnicking by the river at Hurley with Lizzie and Peter. But when alone in the evening felt my loneliness.

My dear Lydia. She does say some naïve things, I must admit. At lunch one day we were discussing cats with another girl who could not bear them, was really allergic. Lydia, talking of her Rusty, said she would rather share a room at night with a cat than a human being. And appealed to me, 'Wouldn't you?' I said I thought it depended who the person was.

Saturday, 25 August

In these journals a reader might well exclaim, 'which man is it about this time?' But I don't even try to be objective in these journals. They are a very biased, subjective view of a growing woman. What I am conscious of in this affaire, and may not have stressed sufficiently, is the difference in the quality of my feelings for this man. The feeling is always 'There is the male to my female.' I have never felt that before. Never as deeply, as surely.

Leslie and I have decided to sell 'Homefield' if we can. This gives me a riotously secure feeling. Possibly £1,000–1,500 coming to me.

Tuesday, 4 September

With Ethel at a guest house in Hove. The weather could hardly be worse. I try to forget M. and cannot. There's a man and his wife and two children staying at the guest house (oddly enough with the name of Pratt, and their little girl is Jean!). I liked the man at once as soon as introduced, a large, slow-moving very attractive male. Twinkle in his eye I couldn't resist for long if it pursued me with any intent. Perhaps because we own the same name we feel drawn. His wife is a nice but foolish woman, and later when the children are grown up if she's not careful she'll lose her husband. He likes, I am sure, a spot of fun in moderation, but she is all angles and nerves, striving to keep to rigid principles of behaviour. Will not go into pubs – afraid of starting 'a bad habit'. I can see she is tormented all the time by the fear of doing wrong, all tight inside herself with the effort to keep her husband 'good'.

Thursday, 6 September

Sitting on the Esplanade watching the familiar British holiday beach scene. Am rather conscious of people looking at me as I write this. The curiosity of strangers directed upon me does upset me – I like to watch but don't want to be watched. Am sure, if they think anything, they think seeing me with glasses, a prim expression and my shabby brief case, that I am a schoolmistress. 'Clever, you know.'

Tomorrow I am going to have my fortune told again by one of these many hags that make their living here from withered, wishful-thinking women and foolish girls.

Friday, 7 September

Exactly how much I wonder do these old witches pick up of one's thoughts and desires? How much was I unconsciously giving her? She was rather confused and confusing, saw several men, but I pinned her down to the one I wanted to hear about.

She saw him 'in commerce, a very good businessman, excellent prospects, will have a big position one day – something to do with engineering? I can see plans, drawings. Is he going to open up a new factory somewhere?' And so on. All quite possible. He will have something to do with patents. He is 'very fond of me and is thinking about me a lot, but doesn't at the moment quite see his way clear . . . But he will explain everything and make me an offer.' I may go abroad with him. I am certainly 'crossing water' (they always say that).

She said I have nothing to worry about. It will all come right. Well it's all very comforting and pleasant. At least she didn't warn me against him, she didn't see him as a bad man. He's not, anyway – I know he's not. (I do love you, Mac. I do really. You'd never regret making an effort to have me by you, with you. I am a nice person. Lots and lots of people have been reassuring me of this.)

Saturday, 8 September

Saw another hag this evening. She was much more precise. Told me more by what she didn't say. The whole affair seems so sordid. She saw me in his car. She saw me at work too, in a very large business. I am to stay in it. Promotion on the way. She saw me in the crystal walking in Slough (no one told her I came from Slough).

Monday, 10 September (War Diary)

I spent last week in Hove and feel much better, though could do with another three weeks at least. A fortnight's holiday in the year is absurd and no good to anyone. I would most earnestly urge for longer holidays for everyone. At the office great changes have been taking place. The firm is constricting in every direction and no one seems to know what is to happen next. We are told to 'carry on', which we all do in a very half-hearted way, but in every department are complaints of lack of work.

In Hove . . . there were no huts for dressing (I was told that on VJ night a pile of huts and chairs and other such oddments was burned by the populace gone mad). The front and gardens are wonderfully restored. All barbed wire removed and the long grass cut and flowers planted. The Hove Town Hall was reopened while I was there for dancing. It had been the Food Office during the war. Many troops still stationed there, but going gradually. The Aussies still occupy some of the big Brighton hotels. Went to two dances, crawled round many pubs and did not bathe once.

Thursday, 20 September

Apart from the Building pamphlet and our files which I am trying to set in order, I have no motive for staying at HDA. The situation gets worse and worse, and the atmosphere of discontent and uneasiness is appalling. Why should I stay on? I never see M. or am likely to (and it doesn't make all that much difference when I do). Rapid decay seems to have set in. I am not a metallurgist or engineer and not the least bit interested in these subjects. I will break away. Rest for a few months on capital, then try something else. Go abroad maybe.

Recently I have been glancing through back [journal] entries. How restless, restless you are all the time Jean. Will you never learn to cradle anxiety and be still? When will you learn how to wait – how to wait when no hope is offered you, when what you want is never granted?

Monday, 24 September
A postcard from Hugh written last week in Milan – he expects to be in England this week and will phone.

10.30 p.m. Phone call from Hugh. Just arrived in London. Almost his first thought – to phone me. Oh Lord, this is ludicrous! Why are men and situations so diverse and twisted? Damn and damn again. I have promised to meet him for lunch on Wednesday. He has no news of Maritza – she is supposed to be in England by now.

Tuesday, 25 September
Last Sunday week Dinah had four more Walterish tabbies. They were born in the usual confinement quarters behind the curtain under the water tank at the top of the stairs – and I found father Walter during Dinah's labour peeping in and making curious noises in his throat of great agitation. Tonight I decided to have a look at the family and to my astonishment discovered only two. Had Dinah decided that four were too much for her and eaten two of them or dragged them away somewhere to die?

Later I heard loud squeaks and found Dinah with a kitten in her mouth – she brought it, confusingly, into the sitting room, doing something with her family I couldn't fathom. I wondered if she had dropped the other two out of the bedroom window and went with a torch to have a look, but no. Dinah then jumped through the broken woodshed window with squealing kitten in her mouth. And at the bottom of a deep and I should have thought most uncomfortable woodbox were the lost portion of her family. What in the world has made her do this I can't think, unless the confinement quarters were too easy an access for the other cats, or she knew that Mrs Mop and her horrid little boy would be here in a day or two.

Thursday, 27 September

With my thoughts all on one lover I go to meet another. We are delighted to meet again. We have lunch, we sit in Hyde Park, we have tea, he buys me roses and I come home again. He may be here for the weekend. But my thoughts are still with the other man.

Hugh has a chance of a job in Australia. Supposing Maritza really does vanish (I hope she won't) and he asks me to go with him. He might. What should I do? Hugh is a pleasant and trying reality. I know him well. He is tangible, his friendship is tangible and hugely satisfying. M. has given me, promised me nothing, and from all appearances forgotten me. Surely the practical, sane move would be to go with Hugh. But I would not marry him, or only on the condition that we could each have our freedom the moment we wanted it. Haven't hundreds and hundreds of women decided this way in similar circumstances and probably made a much better job of the relationship because they did not expect too much and gave generously and fairly of what they had to give – unhampered by false ideals and sentimental tears for the moon?

Friday, 28 September

I hate him. I hate him. I suspend decision continually because of him. I have not asked Josephine to stay with me all this summer partly because I did not want her to be here should he suddenly make up his mind to come. I suspend decision on leaving HDA because of him. His behaviour points so obviously to the fact that he just doesn't care or think about me much. But Sentimental Heart won't let me accept that and forget him. Please God let this torment end soon. Let me know where I am, what I should do. I want him so much. But thank you that there is Lydia whom he treats just as badly . . . and all the other women who call him 'Swine!'.

I have sent M. a memo from the office – direct, signed personally, with regard to the pictures I know he is wanting. If he really wants to contact me again he has the chance. And if he doesn't he'll delegate the job to a subordinate and I shall crumple up.

Saturday, 29 September
Am in a rage waiting for elderberry jam to thicken. My own fault. I didn't dry the berries after washing them. Have now added apple.

Today one of those gold and blue days – everything burnished and heavenly. I spent all the afternoon in the garden divinely happy, and would still be happy but for the jam. Am reading, for the first time, some Proust, Part 1 of *The Captive*, English translation. Certainly one is held. But how small he is! Where did I read a reference to him recently as 'wallowing in his own dirty bathwater'? Not that he is smaller than most of us. Such grandiose language for such trivialities. But then life is made up very largely of such humdrum items for most people.

I have transplanted foxgloves, moved the Madonna lilies to a summer border, rooted dog violets away from dozens of young primrose plants. The elderberry jam is as solid today as the Rock of Gibraltar.

31.

The Problem of Palestine

Thursday, 18 October

The most marvellous birthday of my life. He came, he came. Out of the blue. My darling came. I'm not quite sane at this moment – haven't much control over my pen but because I feel I owe it to these pages, to sentimental heart, to all my urgent desires, dreams and hopes. He didn't know it was my birthday. Drove from Redditch to an empty house and phoned me at about 9.45 – took me for a drink to Beaconsfield, came back and is gone now, saying he would come again soon – and really I believe this time he means it. Means it deeply. I am sure of it at this moment.

Monday, 22 October

Hugh was here for the weekend. I am rather proud of myself, grateful again to Hugh. It would this time have been easy to slip – yes, literally almost, slip into the old intimacy. There he was in excellent health and spirit, charming, witty, attentive and willing – I am sure he was willing, but waiting for a lead from me. Sex means little more to him than satisfying an appetite. I don't think he'd have had any feelings of conscience towards Maritza, who is waiting somewhere in the Mediterranean in a transit camp, all transport delayed by the dock strikes. He would not be unfaithful while she was with him. But during this interval which may continue for weeks he'll take what is offered. And I did have something of a struggle not to make that offer. Chalk it up, please.

We had a delightful weekend – there is such ease between us now, so many jokes shared. But I know more definitely than ever that he is not my man and never could be. He has had dozens and dozens of women, really dozens; he has, he says, been very happy with many of them. And he does know in his superficial way how to make a woman happy. He uses his imagination skilfully, with Latin sensitivity and instinct – and he could have married any one of several of them at the time of the affaire if he had been free, and would have been sure of a certain kind of happiness. But whether he could have kept such women happy I don't know. Maritza sounds rather different – she has a strength he lacks and will keep him so long as she wants to keep him. She seems to be very much in love with him (although he suspects that she has had her affaires in the interval too). In some of the photos I have seen she looks to me older than he is, but she has a strong face, determination and courage in chin and mouth – is vivid, sparkling. Perhaps she is older, was caught by the glamour of a British officer's uniform, saw her chance (and maybe there weren't so many for a no-longer-young cafe singer) of a husband, and willed him with passion into it. I am sure she is the dominating personality. She is willing to go to Australia, is building her life around him, as most women do and want to do about some man.

And M., my dear, my darling? But I am so prejudiced there I cannot write clearly of him. I think he has many points in common with Hugh. Hugh says that he can be immensely attracted to and excited by a woman, but he goes to his work, becomes absorbed in it and forgets the woman entirely. I am quite sure that happens with M. That he came on my birthday is incredible. The memo about the pictures evidently had the effect I hoped it would. He told me that his wife is going to live with her people. And that when he comes to Slough he will stay at the Crown 'or at Egypt? May I?' (very shyly). It will be easier, now, he said, for him to come to me sooner and more often. But I wonder – I wonder if he means this. He certainly doesn't mean me to think that he intends anything of a permanent relationship. If he gets his house in Stratford, leaves HDA, and starts making jewellery (he talked about this more freely the other night) he may well start that new business in Birmingham, the centre of all such production, where he grew up and is known. Where would poor Jean be fitted then? In the same sort of pocket as the girlfriends in Sheffield? But maybe by then Jean will have achieved more wisdom, maybe she will know by then whether this obsession is just sick fancy or not.

I am tired now. Hugh was up at 6 this morning to be at his new job (his first day) in London by 8.30. I shall go to bed. Party on Saturday – phone call tonight from Phyllis and Gus. They can't come, because they are touring with *The Widow*. It is being an immense success – much to their astonished satisfaction. I am delighted. I was so good to hear Gus' voice again.

Thursday, 25 October
I had the day off today. My hair was 'Liberty' cut this morning and this afternoon I went to see Laurence Olivier's film of *Henry V*.[151] It is magnificent and I don't agree with any of the critics. Swarms of schoolchildren have been seeing this film every morning and if they are being 'taught' Shakespeare imaginatively and intelligently it should help them a lot. But I had to sit through the performance with soaking wet feet. I have hardly a pair of shoes now that don't let the water through.

At my suggestion Lydia and I wrote for 'Detailed (12s. 6d.?) Analysis' of our handwriting to the Institute of Graphology and Psychology. An appalling racket. One sends 25 words of anything, and signature, sex and age. I asked particularly for information concerning my creation and abilities. The reply I received is as follows:–

---

151 A boyish utility cut, in which the hair is heavily curled, pinned and set close to the head.

'This vivid writing is of a most intelligent and mentally active person. The writer is ambitious and wants to achieve the greatest possible amount of independence. Nevertheless she finds it rather difficult to free herself from all the maladjustments which have hindered a satisfactory development so far. In spite of accumulated knowledge and the good use of inborn abilities, she is not yet completely happy. There exists, deep within her, an experience, a disappointment, a deep grudge or something of the kind, which prevents her from ever getting complete happiness or satisfaction.

'The writer has fine abilities, such as judgement of character and excellent powers of observation, which combined will lead to the urge of expression in writing. Friendly, very helpful, the writer likes to assist others, helping them with her own manifold knowledge of life and its problems. It is this knowledge which qualifies the writer to be a real help, a person of true understanding, much initiative, and quite unselfish nature.

'Her abilities are intellectual and should engage with some literary work, such as play-writing, journalism, art critic etc, or become a teacher. Mere routine work is not for her, as she needs the human touch to be happy and also the chance to use her brain in her job. A clever person, she is also a sceptic with much practical knowledge and experience, possessing excellent qualifications for teaching humanity in some way or another.'

Now I could spend hours analysing this analysis. It is absolute nonsense to say I am a sceptic,* and I have no desire or intention to become a teacher unless I can do it through my writing. But it is interesting and encouraging to see that this ability and desire is apparent in my handwriting. What they have missed is my need for a happy, personal relationship. 'Complete' happiness is again nonsense – I don't believe that anyone is ever 'completely' happy – which implies con- tinuity, having everything one wants, achieving all one's desires. If that were possible . . . one would become static and dead. But I do lack a sense of completeness which is probably what they mean. I do need a man's affection and attention and companionship very deeply and if I have any grudge or suffer from some disappointment it is that I haven't yet been able to find and attract this man. This has always been at the core of my inferiority complex.

* NB Modern meaning of 'sceptic' implies cynical which I am sure I am not. But in the older sense of the word of being 'unconvinced of truth of particular fact or theory', 'inclined to suspense of judgement', perhaps I am slightly, particularly with regard to orthodox religion of the C of E and non-conformism and political faiths.

Saturday, 3 November
The variableness of moods.

I don't mind being alone all day when busy and with the knowledge of many friends in the background and interesting activities ahead of me – even the deadly routine at the office because that brings me into contact with people whom I have grown to know and like or at least find amusing to watch and be with. But it's in the evening and at night I feel my loneliness. Day over I want, yes, HIM (but I have no name, no particular person in mind – or only a sentimentalised image of M.) to be there to talk to, and laugh with and tease. And at night (let's be crude) sometimes but not always in bed with me.

Wednesday, 7 November
Always the unexpected bowling me over, setting the fire ablaze. Today Dr Lowe, who has replaced Mr Pike in the Library, and has just lost Miss F. the assistant who grew up under Pike, came and asked me if I would like to train to take her place . . . (he mentioned salaries of £850–£1,000!). With my training and experience and interests and intelligence I can't think why I have never considered this sort of work before. Librarians are usually rather dull, academic sort of people – but there's no reason why they should be. The type of work does

appeal to the timid intellectual who can find refuge in his sorting and indexing of knowledge for other people's benefit. But it could be – for me – a means of making many more contacts and might lead me into very interesting, enriching ways of life.

Thursday, 8 November

My first fine frenzy over the suggested Library job has quite died down. Was introduced to work by Mrs C. this afternoon – I can do it all right, given time and help, but whatever made me suppose that this was the work I've been looking for! After I had seen what would be required of me I had a moment of fearful revulsion. I'm not temperamentally suitable for a librarian – I can see that now. But I'll probably take on the job and do it conscientiously – maybe it's a way out of the present morass and it will be better than doing writing in publicity.

Tuesday, 13 November (War Diary)

Last week a doctor was reported in the press to have said that most of us were suffering from food shortage. One of the symptoms was an unusual feeling of fatigue, and particularly after doing extra work. Many people I meet seem to suffer from this fatigue. Lydia is one and has been to her doctor about it (she says 'One's heart feels almost too tired to beat'). Poked a toe through a sheet last night. So sick of Making Do.

Wednesday, 14 November

It seems that I may start work in the library next week. The idea of trying to work on a novel in any spare time waxes and wanes. If only I could do it! And so forget in these long intervals that continual source of torment over which I am alternately optimistic and in despair. Another popular song describes my state of mind – 'The Gipsy.' 'I want to believe the Gipsy . . . who said, my lover was always true, Although I knew in my heart, dear, somebody else was kissing you. But I'll go there again . . . because I want to believe the Gipsy . . .' Quite idiotic. I remember little things and 'suddenly the heart sings'! It does, indeed it does – The touch of his hand, the tilt of his hat, the life in him, the abundant if crude life in him that calls to the life in me.

But then again.

Friday, 16 November

10 p.m. In bed. The warmest, most delicious place on a sharp cold November moonlit night. The only other thing I would rather be doing is riding in his new car (an Austin 10, he had it two days before my birthday, and I was, he said, its first passenger). Either to or from some comfortable, attractive, firelit pub.

Sunday, 18 November

In a novel-forming mood all day. There is a character in *The Seagull* who keeps saying, 'when I was a young man there were two things I wanted to do – become a writer and get married. I've done neither.' And that is what I may be saying in my old age. When I think about my twin ambitions I get an icy feeling in the region of my heart, as though suddenly conscious of foreordained and inevitable doom, decided before I was born: 'She shall desire greatly both to marry and to be a writer, but shall do neither.' I must go on trying, I must never give up hope.

Tuesday, 20 November

There is some hitch in my move to the Library. Probably my salary, although Dr R.L. assured me twice there would be no change in that. I had a premonition about it last night, felt infuriated, disgusted and depressed and went to see Tom Walls in *Johnny Frenchman*.

I came home terribly hungry, wolfed some food and was then very sick. The second time I've been sick in a fortnight. I might be having a baby, I thought. I wish I were.

(War Diary)

At lunch today someone mentioned problem of Palestine. 'I don't think the Jews should be *forced* to leave a country – let them go to Palestine if they want to.' 'Jews get such a financial hold on a country.' 'That's true – all the same, a country is nearly always better off where Jews are powerful – they may make big money, but they circulate it.' 'They produce much talent too.' 'Pity they have such unpleasant characteristics.' 'Only due to long years of persecution – aggressive trait has developed.' 'Well, we all get aggressive don't we, when we feel looked down on?'[152]

Wednesday, 21 November

Extracts published today from Eva Braun's diary, 1935. Jean Pratt you should be ashamed. How familiar the tone of these entries: 'I am so infinitely happy . . .' Then, a few weeks later, 'Why do I have to suffer like this? I wish I had never seen him. I am desperate – I am going to buy more sleeping tablets; at least then I will be half dazed and will not think about him so much. Why doesn't the devil come and get me? . . . For 3 hours I stood outside the Carlton and had to watch while he bought flowers for Ondra and invited her for supper.'[153]

World is full of Hitlers and Eva Brauns. Eva Braun did marry her Hitler. But what a honeymoon. What a marriage! Bride and bridegroom disintegrated and destroyed within the hour – the inevitable penalty for their way of life, the just, slow stroke of time bringing the action's reaction. All who try to race time are in the end destroyed by time.

Friday, 30 November

Liz Cecil has been here for the evening. Sitting room is warm, has a happy, used feel in the air. Gramophone and record cases open, sewing

---

152 The Nuremberg trials began today.
153 The movie actress Anny Ondra, married to the boxer and Nazi supporter Max Schmeling.

oddments on the table, crumpled sofa cushions. An easy, friendly room.

Young people last night discussing on the radio 'Why should sex be a problem?' Lot of little prigs. 'Intercourse before marriage is wrong' – one or two very emphatic about this. Others not so sure, thought a trial period for engaged couples was excusable. But to talk or try to talk of sex isolated like this seems to me quite wrong. You might as well argue about constipation on its own. They came of course nowhere near an answer. Nor am I or can I give an answer. Concentrate, my dear reader, on your emotions not sex – sex is one means of expressing certain emotions or can be indulged in for the sensory pleasure it can give, but I can see no dividing line where you can stand and say, 'This side right, that side wrong.' Sex is a magical, magical power and should be understood and guided and then followed. It has its own deep significance and laws related to other parts of the personality. (But the importance or proportion of sex varies with different people. I am quite sure it is possible to lead a healthy, life-giving life without it. I have only to remember Aunt Janie.)

Saturday, 1 December
Always when on my own at the cottage I look forward and listen to *Saturday Night Theatre*. Always when it is over a great feeling of emptiness and isolation descends. All the life and the drama that has been filling the room and carrying me with it for an hour and a half suddenly recedes like a quick-turning tide leaving me stranded.

But now I remember a resolution I made earlier in the evening. I took the kitten – Junior, that quick, wicked splinter of life teasing his elders, pouncing on their lazily moving tails, winding my wool round table and chair legs, staring up at my cigarette smoke with button eyes just losing their baby blue – I took him to a new home in Slough and thought how wonderful and fearful was the night, the soft air and the lighted windows and the skeleton trees against the night sky. The fearfulness of the adventure ahead for the young thing in my arms, how small, how pitiful and helpless and yet how vastly surrounded and shielded from the terrors it could not face and understand alone.

I came home thinking that I did not enough appreciate the wonderfulness of this earth. Obvious beauty will move me quickly, easily to some slight passing expression of appreciation, but it is shallow – quickly come and gone. I am too much wrapped in peevish discontent for things I think I want and do not get – peevish, petulant, silly, selfish woman. It is a sin, a great sin not to look about you and think of life and history of the things around you. The things we use everyday, the cups we handle. Clay – through how many hands, fashioned by the thought of how many minds, contributing something to how many lives and taking in something from those lives it has touched.

It is a wonderful world, full, full of things to give delight. It must be part of hell to remember the beauty and the miracles one passed by daily with blind eyes – or rather, to remember that these were miracles to be seen daily which one was too ego-bound to notice.

Wednesday, 6 December

I receive now such a lot of nice attention, so many compliments from people and not only from dear, well-meaning friends like N. who say how pretty I am looking and what an owl M. is not to make more of this chance of a worthwhile friendship. But also people at the office – Dr R.H. for instance, 'Not thinking of getting married? Really, you surprise me' – oh, and meaning it, I know they mean it. And I know that I am a desirable, loveable, thoroughly marriageable person. That is a triumph, to have that confidence, and no longer the old fear of men and of other people – not in the same way. Shyness is still there, will always be there, but many people have dissolved that shyness, and that experience helps me to be less shy with new people.

I am to leave HDA in my own time, says Mr B., as the cancellation of my appointment to the Library (where everyone agrees I should have been well suited to the job) was the firm's fault. Well, I am going to plan a campaign and work at it. And then when I have one or two jobs in hand (as we hope) I shall be able to withdraw gradually from the ties of HDA.

(War Diary)

Have just been listening to BBC's *From the London Theatre* series – an excerpt from *Private Lives*. Saw Gertrude Lawrence and Noël Coward in the first production of this evergreen, then the film version. An incredibly fascinating play about really very stupid, tiresome people. Such delicious, delectable love scenes – that's what makes the play so appealing. All the women in the audience see themselves as Amandas, and see their men as Elyots. What, one wonders, are Elyot and Amanda like when they are not being brilliantly witty?

Thursday, 13 December

I've had a poem from Hugh – an Xmas poem which has been accepted by the *Sat Evening Post* and which is dedicated to me – in memory of last Xmas. A poem dedicated to me! Dear, delightful Hugh, what lovely things you think of; and how much his time with me must really have meant to him. 'My nice, unforgettable Moog' he writes. Oh, thank you God very much for Hugh and for N. sending him down to me. (Witch that she is and as much as I resented it.)

Friday, 14 December

Lydia dined out with him last night. He had come to tell her that the jewellery business was finished as far as he was concerned. He paid her for her designs, and that was that. Lydia was trying gallantly (my dear, my excellent friend – I hope I can do as much for you one day) to bring the conversation round to me but he would not be drawn. But her chance came eventually and (not being me) she had it out with him. He thinks I am taking him much too seriously – he had no idea I was such an – she couldn't remember whether it was actually 'hysterical', but it was around something like it, 'sentimental' perhaps or 'emotional' type.

He had finished, 'was washing his hands' of both of us, he said. He went on to emphasise that he had no intention of altering his domestic arrangements and he had given me no cause to think he was. She lectured him at length, said he had no sense of his responsibilities, that after all surely he realised I was very fond of him. She let him have it properly, I gather, told him he was vain and selfish and a lot more. But it was water off a duck's back. (Or maybe not. Maybe some of it he'll remember.) She says that he spoke well of me, that he is probably as fond of me as he is capable of being fond of anyone. She said it was a pleasant evening, he was good company, gave her a good dinner and plenty to drink.

I have got the solid evidence I wanted to help me out of the maze. If he wanted to he could still make me do almost anything for him. But I weep for him and his coming damnation. And I weep for myself that my own feelings are so unreliable, can be so easily tricked. I do not like believing the worst of people. But what a lot of proof I have been given of this man's falsity.

Sunday, 16 December

This is being much more painful than I thought it would be.

I must do nothing – I must just make myself realise that this is over, finished. I shall never see him again. None of my dreams can ever come true. It's the only way. Soon I shall be right away from HDA and all its associations with this unhappy business. For 18 months this stone has been in my path, I have been stubbing my toes against it. I must kick it in the ditch where it belongs.

I have many good friends to see me through the affair, the difficult days. Best help of all is when I see the funny side of it. Wonder what he'd do if I started sending postcards: 'Please send me more money for the baby.'

Shall I ever learn? Shall I ever, ever find someone who'll love me as I could love them, fully, freely, deeply?

Boxing Day

8.45 p.m. All knotted up inside, But have had a delightful Xmas. N. brought young Canadian scientist friend, Roger, a terrifying modern intellectual, like Aldous Huxley, but tall, courteous and interesting (I don't mean that A.H. is none of these). Brought with him all that forgotten Ivory Tower detachedness of the modern intellectual of the upper classes. A likeable, awe-inspiring person, but not loveable. He admitted to N. that he is terrified of emotional involvements – of being enveloped and 'possessed' by women. These men! They are all the same. But women must take some of the blame. They do, gener-ally speaking, want to catch, envelop and possess their man. Too much so. A natural desire which few women have yet tried to understand and discipline. It can become selfish and clogging – no wonder men are scared. Women forget the importance of their own integrity and independence. They shift the responsibility of their own lives onto the man – he has to make and direct their lives, often at the sacrifice of his own. The relationship becomes one-sided, and is not what it should be – a sharing of experience together, a mutual, integrated development of two separate entities – but a flopping on the woman's part, a selfish, greedy absorption of another person's life to feed her own. She becomes a vampire.

Friday, 28 December (War Diary)

I was not able to look for good and interesting presents this year and my friends and relatives had to be satisfied with Readers Union books, soap (from my store) and cards. For Ethel and Aunt Maggie I packed up a box of oddments such as Rinso, lard, tea, hand cream etc – it was just like a hamper for poor relations in pre-war days, but met with tremendous welcome. Myself, I received book and gift tokens, books, one pair of fully fashioned stockings, flower seeds for the garden and a homemade mince pie, shoulder covers for hanging clothes (made from blackout material and bound with bright tape), a much needed sponge bag, a lovely small glass bowl filled with homemade toffees, calendars, many cards.

Saturday, 29 December

Such a very pleasant surprise. Half-an-hour or so ago, as I was beginning the last of the washing up, Tommie Hughes phoned. Really I am delighted. He wants to hear all about HDA and what I'm doing and has given me his phone number and address. It was a genuinely friendly gesture on his part, I'm sure of it and I will NOT start looking for ulterior motives though no doubt they may be there. So yah! to Mac! Conceited little shrimp – thinks I'm wanting to marry him does he? So short of boy friends? And Roger now inviting me to see *Henry IV* (I) (Ralph Richardson as Falstaff) with him. I do feel good tonight. I also received an Xmas card from Peter Buckland quite out of the blue – he's with the RAF in Germany. Well, it's all exceedingly gratifying and I hope the twerp hears of it one day soon.

Monday, 31 December

Have just listened to BBC *Home Life* stories of C.B. Cochran, Alec James and John Gielgud. If the Cochran love story is true it is enough to twist the hungry soul of every woman like myself with envy. He fell in love with attractive blonde, pursued her against parental opposition and kidnapped her under the nose of uncle chaperoning her to a convent in Ireland. One doesn't seem to hear of men doing that sort of thing nowadays.

Last day of the old year . . . An undisciplined, lumber-filled mind is a great, exhausting strain. I never have any real rest. Lying in bed with all the morning before me free, walking the country, sitting in the pure golden light of the winter sun – wanting to relax and think of nothing – I can never, never do it. Am followed every waking moment by a zooming swarm of thoughts, a swarm for each subject, all hived away somewhere in my mind, and as soon as I am still and with nothing else to keep them back, out they come like hosts of flies on a summer's day.

Sunday, 13 January 1946

Life full and interesting, lacking only some one particular person to share it with.

I phoned T.H. this morning when I was in Hampstead, as I promised to do. His eagerness to see me again appears to be very genuine and is excessively flattering. It is largely I know that he wants to hear all the latest HDA news. I must beware, beware, beware.

32.

Of Course He Stayed

Thursday, 24 January 1946 (aged thirty-six)
M. in Slough again today. I sit now near a partition which divides
our offices from the main office corridor – and I heard his voice late
this evening. A few minutes afterwards in comes D.H. red in the face
and all secret dimples. I know that expression. I know what she was
feeling. He had said something extremely flattering, highly provocative. She is only 18, very pretty and just spoiling for experience. A
very succulent young virgin. I could have knifed him.

Sunday, 11 February
Only two more weeks at HDA now. Yorkie yesterday pronounced it
a 'sinking ship' and maliciously I hope it is, because then one feels
one is losing nothing by leaving it, just one of the rats.

It was real delight to be with Tommie again. He was so insistent on
my making a date as soon as I could that I suspected some ulterior
motive – to borrow money or something. But it seemed that he really
did want to see me again for myself alone! He evidently feels quite
emotionally 'safe' with me now. We had a terrific conversational evening.
I took him to see Joan and he talked communism solidly for over two
hours – besides hearing all I had to tell him of HDA and discussing at
length my future plans. 'It's a cure for sore eyes to see you again!' he
said and noticed at once my hair was shorter, liked it, said I was looking
well and two years younger – Dear Thomas! It seems that what we

wanted yesterday we get today when we have ceased to want it. When I know them well and am not 'in love' with them I get on with men extremely well. In fact I think there is much to be said for women like me marrying someone they are not in love with.

I may not have done much work at HDA that has shown solid, satisfactory results – but I leave it richer – in experience, friends, understanding, confidence. I feel a little scared about my future but also blandly optimistic.

Sunday, 17 February

I have a ring which was my mother's. I believe it is what was once called a mourning ring – it is of plain gold, the width of a narrow wedding ring and ¾ of the way round it a band of plaited hair (now black with age) is inset – the edges on either side of the space in the remaining quarter on which are the initials 'S.J.L.'. These were the initials of my mother and my grandmother – I have a hazy recollection that my mother once told me that grandfather had it made after grand-mother's death and wore it until his death. It fits my third finger and I sometimes wear it on my right hand. When the initial part is turned palm-wards it has the look of a wedding ring and pleases my silly vanity. But today I have decided to wear it permanently as a symbol of my bondage to my work – a bondage bequeathed me by my mother.

Tuesday, 19 February

Three more days now. I dread the 'farewells' and final clearing up. Feel full of the resentment and bitterness and impatience though of course no one would suspect it. But let it be recorded that this amiable-seeming, adaptable obliging creative is a volcano of wrath beneath. No one ever believes it – never never.

Friday, 22 February

Have written a detailed account of last day at office in Mass Observation diary, but of course much has been omitted. It's all over, finished. Don't cling to dead things. Don't listen to a ghost's alluring whispers. I'd have liked a last encounter with M., though it would not have been anything like what I'd have wanted it to be: 'Nothing but a common little cheat – I'm a human being, I'm not made of cast iron – I have feelings that can be hurt. You're a spoilt child – stealing the icing off the cake, that was all you wanted – you wouldn't even eat the cake . . .' But perhaps not.

Monday, 25 February
They'll just be finishing lunch in the canteen. The foremen in the corner still concentrating on their chess game. Groups still at their tables smoking, talking over the last drops of coffee. Outside in the cold works yard, people returning from lunch to shops and offices. No hammer to make the buildings shudder now – no flames in what was once the foundry. The estate steam train will give a whistle and puff its way slowly through our opened gates and along the track that runs through the yard and out the other side.

Remembered this morning, acutely, the interview with Miss White at school, in which she told me gently but firmly that she felt I had 'no backbone.' I was a silly little thing, easily influenced, much given to giggling. Now my physical backbone aches cruelly and I still doubt if I have much of the other kind, even now. 'Jelly where it should be diamond.' How does one achieve hardness without becoming brittle? Of course! Submit – let the flames consume you – accept the hammer blows. To the outsider they may appear trivial – not being able to defend an idea in conversation, for instance, or losing one's heart to a worthless man. A shrinking away from anything that might cause discomfort or pain.

8.30 p.m. Have just listened to a *Family Relationships* broadcast of great interest. It was called 'Asking for Trouble'. No names given in *Radio Times* of who the people are discussing these problems, but think the Marriage Guidance Council is behind the series. A very pleasant Scots voice seems to be the Master of Ceremonies and there are one or two pleasant women's voices. The Church is always well represented. They discussed tonight the reasons why people married and concluded that any but the right reason was 'asking for trouble.' They made a big effort to discuss the sex aspect as frankly as possible. Church was at first revoltingly sanctimonious and narrow about it but the MC and a woman came out boldly. Woman thought that the sex drive was so overpowering no couple should embark on marriage without cohabiting first – to marry only because of physical attraction is a great mistake and invariably led to trouble. The broadminded and intelligent view in this discussion did not condemn sex relationships outside marriage. Church was allowed the last word: said that while it held definite views and regarded such behaviour as sin, it did not consider it the only or even a priority sin.

An encouraging pointer of the way public thinking is now moving. Sex is actually allowed to be spoken of on the BBC! MC spoke of the Church's influence very emphatically – said he felt it had done a great deal of harm with regard sex problems.

I never have felt any guilt about my 'experiments' and I shall go on experimenting if I feel like it. But I hope and shall go on hoping that I shall marry – must try to soften this feeling of resentment that I haven't and may never. I want to be loved! I stamp my feet and whine that I deserve it, I'm a very marriageable person! I want to be loved, I want to be loved!

Friday, 1 March

I don't know how I can say what needs to be said. It was a lovely day yesterday. Went into Slough and Windsor and then to see *The Seventh Veil*. I fell for some very pretty shoes in Caleys – shouldn't have spent the coupons but they've gone now. After the pictures had to collect glasses which were being repaired and was not home until nearly 7 p.m. Was preparing a meal about 8 p.m. when the phone rang again.

Yes, it was my M. I shut the door on him and he climbs in through the window when I'm not looking. He said he had phoned earlier and been round in daylight to find out if I were in and left a footprint in the snow to prove it and then tried again. At first I had pretended I did not know who was speaking and kept it up well. He came round about 9.15.

Again I said none of the things that I've written here and thought that I wanted to say. He seems to put up a barrier instinctively. Of course he stayed. I could not love him more with my body. My body is all his, every inch of it, willingly, joyously. Katherine Mansfield, in one of her stories, speaks of the French phrase 'in need of a bed' – this is so strong when we are together I can not think clearly about anything else. And then, of course, he has to go when we are both tired and beyond talking. My darling, I do love you so . . . please let me love you with more than my body . . . don't be afraid of it . . . come and talk to me, come and relax here and learn to enjoy just being together. I daren't let myself think that it might ever happen.

I told him I hated the name 'Mac' and I am to call him 'Alan' now. Unfortunate that I know another one (Alan Dene). He said that when we met in the canteen or corridor at HDA his heart went 'thrrrump'. As he says, we 'click' every time. There is definitely something, but why, we don't know.

I believe that he has really, a very strong sense of duty to his wife and family, and because of that he does not want to take any other woman seriously – for fear of the upset it would cause at home. And what I want to try and make him understand is that he can, if he wants to, take me more seriously than he might other women who would demand more, without my ever trying to interfere with his domestic obligations. Or is that priggish of me? All I know is that my body adores him and is adored by his – oh it MUST mean something! I must accept him as he is and take what comes.

He said, 'Bless you! I won't fail you . . .'

Monday, 4 March
Weekend with Ethel, recuperating. Two things emerge. His casual

behaviour, apparent neglect and suspected infidelities during the long intervals between his visits to me are excellent discipline for my sentimentality. His physical love and respect for me are real enough when we are together but though this sends me waltzing in clouds of rapture am brought sharply to earth again quite soon by wondering where he is and what he's doing and why I don't hear from him.

Secondly, it is more essential than ever that I continue to make my own life, that I have independent, satisfying interests and work. I must go ahead with my writing and resist the temptation to daydream which is stronger than ever now.

Wednesday/Thursday, 6–7 March, 4 a.m.

Woke this morning with sore spot on my behind – logic and experience tell me it's probably a little sore of the kind I have had before but my whole being has been in a state of panic all day. Looked up all the literature I have on VD and can see N.'s wagging finger. Phoned T. late tonight to see if he could come here on Sunday and learned that he will be in Slough tomorrow driving for the Communists in local elections, and had intended to phone me. He has promised to come though may be late. I must talk to him frankly and get him to tell me all he can about VD, its prevention and cure. It is no use my trusting sentimentally in A., knowing what I do about him, although my heart wants to believe that he couldn't be so criminally stupid and selfish as to visit women (of any type) knowing he was infected. I should find it most terribly difficult to consult my doctor, as they urge you to do, and am so thankful that I know someone like T. in the medical world that I feel I can trust, talk to.

Friday, 8 March

Really I think T. is one of the nicest boyfriends I have. He was most sympathetic, kind and helpful and has allayed my fears – and is going to examine me again towards the end of next week. He stayed until it was time to catch the last bus, talking politics, and then discussing my possible work and has given me some really useful ideas. It's up to me what I do with them.

This silly business has shaken me badly. T.'s behaviour and help to me does more towards converting me to Communism than hours and hours of his talk.

Saturday, 9 March

Dying different sorts of deaths today. The thought of digging myself out and meeting new people leaves me half dead with terror. T. suggests I go around collecting information on the new Health Centre and Nursery Schools. A really excellent and sane suggestion, and he had given me a first contact. But I don't want to do it . . . I am a silly woman. Want comfort and security and sentimental love, a placid, domestic existence with no intellectual strain, no forcing myself into intelligent left-wing circles where my shortcomings will be so apparent. God, I can't do it, I can't! I don't feel well, I am tired, I have a sore throat – and am imagining more evils than ever. Feeble, feeble little coward. Run back to mother, whine for father's affection. Silly, sentimental, back-boneless child. That's how I feel tonight.

Trouble is I still feel so desperately alone. That's why I go on writing these journals – the strain is a little relieved, I have at least said something somewhere of what I feel.

Saturday, 16 March

Shall not forget T.'s courtesy and kindness. He has treated this silly scare of mine exactly as a doctor should – no personal questions, no sign of curiosity to know more of the story, although he must have been intrigued and amused. His student friend whom he called in as a 'second opinion' behaved in the same professional way.

Have arranged to meet his friend Bee Serota (who 'knows all about me and has always wanted to meet me!' – acutely unnerving) on Tuesday.

Wednesday, 20 March

Bee Serota very pleasant. Felt immediately at home with her – as though we had met before. She is an LSE B.Sc. (Econ.) works as a Labour member for Hampstead Borough Council, and is having a baby in 5 weeks time. Lives in delightful small old Hampstead house. Is going to get me an interview with a Mrs D. of the new St Leonard's Nursery School Committee.[154]

Wednesday, 27 March

Yesterday an interview with Bee's Mrs D. which was highly satisfactory.

Another current popular song, 'I dream of you more than you dream I do . . . you're mean to me more than you mean to be . . . I want you so . . .' And so on. How they do get to the point these popular songs.

Monday, 1 April

The most astonishing piece of information concerning the Pratt family has just come my way. Ethel phoned to say my cousin Martin had been asking for 'Uncle Percy's diaries', i.e. my father's 'diaries'. She did not know what he was talking about – nor did I, so I phoned Martin. He and his wife are living at Marlow now. He tells me that the Pratts are related to a Lord Camden who was Lord Chief Justice in the eighteenth century. But that one of the Camden Pratts was attached to the British Consulate in Paris during the French Revolution and had left some calf-bound diaries of that period which were at one time actually in my own father's possession, as Martin remembers seeing them once when he was a little boy, together with the original Book of Hours belonging to Marie Antoinette. These books were, says Martin, in our dining room bookcase. But I remember them not at all and am sure I should have noticed such interesting relics as I grew older, and particularly when we moved from Homefield. I think they must have passed

---

154 Later to become Baroness Serota, Deputy Speaker of the House of Lords. The baby born five weeks later is Nicholas Serota, later to become the ennobled director of the Tate Gallery.

out of our hands long ago – most tantalising. And most surprising to hear we have aristocratic ancestors. The idea flatters me enormously.

Thursday, 4 April

It is like midsummer. Too hot, too vivid to do anything this afternoon. Saw Hugh again on Tuesday. He told me one of his shocking stories of a little 22-year-old blouse who lives, I think, in the same block of flats as himself and his wife. She was a BBC engineer (so Hugh says) but found it more profitable to be the mistress of two wealthy business men, keeping the two apart of course. An empty headed little thing, said Hugh, but attractive. Fell for Hugh, who introduced her to an Australian friend who was staying with Hugh in the spare room of the flat. One night she went to bed with the Australian and early next morning (a Sunday) Hugh was roused by an irate 'real rat of a man' demanding to see the girl. Hugh went in to the bedroom where they were both asleep and woke the Australian. The Aussie came out clad only in pyjama trousers, socked the rat under the jaw, knocking him down the stairs, broke his arm, packed him into waiting car, knocked him unconscious to keep him quiet, and drove, still clad as he was in pyjama trousers only, somewhere along the Finchley Road, left him and car and walked back.

What people! What an age!

Wednesday, 8 May

The cleaning is done. The cottage is cleaner, tidier than it has been for years. All set for new scenes, for changes if need be – Oh, I am very pleased with myself this afternoon!

My plans now take this shape. To convert the front room upstairs into a double with camp and ARP beds, the back into a bedsit for myself and to take in couples for holidays throughout the summer. Feed them morning and night, pack them sandwiches and let them explore Bucks, Berks and the Thames Valley. It's a good centre. There is no reason why I shouldn't do this, and do it well.

If only A.M. would visit me more often I should be happier than

I have ever been in my life! If I could only make him come, say, once a month. Surely he could manage that.

Friday, 24 May
Josephine has been with me for a week. A little while ago she went with me and N. to a spiritualist service in Hampstead and the medium there gave a message from a Doctor who works through him, that was something like this: 'You suffer a lot don't you, from bad health? I think that some of these ills are unnecessary – you could throw them off if you wanted to.' I have thought on these lines for a long time and N. had come to much the same conclusion.

We don't know. Her way of life may be right for her. She is a very good and sweet-natured person. But I could not live with her (is there anyone I could live with?). Living with her is like living in a mausoleum. She likes going to bed early between 9–10 p.m. Is extremely sensitive to every sound and wakes at the least noise. Curtains are tightly drawn to keep out the morning light. Does not get up until about 9.30 a.m. Cannot do much walking on account of heart trouble. Finds a day out sightseeing too exhausting and prefers to stay in with short rambles in the woods between meals. One feels extremely sorry for her, but also extremely irritated. I kept myself at 'low' throughout the week and I hope remained amiable, but as I did nothing during the day I could not sleep at night. It seems to me all wrong that anyone at her age should be living like a spent-out woman of 70. Of course I do not think her illnesses are 'all imagination', nor was it ever suggested that she did not put up a fight. She seems to enjoy her illnesses – and they are real enough, she makes them real – she certainly enjoys talking about them. She has now abandoned her earthly 'Ghostly Lovers' – and she had as I did, several, and has now taken a spiritual one in the form of Leslie Howard.

My dear Josephine. I don't think she wants help. She goes about with a proud, disdainful expression – a 'bad smell under the nose' expression. Everything ought to be dainty, nice and oh, ever so refined and cultured and well bred for her. I am not surprised that the reactions of some people to her are violent, sadistic. Her attitude just makes the cruel element in one's nature want to jam stinking mud pies beneath that delicate, scornful nose.

Saturday, 15 June

Always the unexpected, the unthought-of, the incalculable X that happens. A picture postcard from A.M. this morning – dated May 28. He is in Canada and hopes to be in England again about middle of July. Oh God! Thank you. I am so happy, so happy, so happy! He says, 'I love this place, know you would too!! I hope to be back in England mid-July.' That's all. But it's all I need.

Sunday, 16 June

If I am ever to do anything outside these journals I MUST NOT re-read them. In time these journals may have value, maybe the only written work of value I have – but not yet.

10 p.m.: Trash, trash, trash. That's all I seem capable of producing outside these journals and I'm not sure they aren't trash too. For serious work, I must leave them alone. I must concentrate on articles. Now, tomorrow, or as soon as I have time I am going to begin again on that Bucks survey. Write up the places nearest – High Wycombe, Beaconsfield, Amersham. Camera has been repaired and I have a film. Go out on that bike and damn the weather and take photos. Go and talk to local habitants, vicars if necessary . . .

And let's try this: let us put the journals away with this present one. (They leave a record of my life as a slug leaves its trail – slime, slime.) Let us stop writing personal confessions until, say, the end of July. You still have various preparations to make in the cottage. You will potter in the garden. You will visit London and see more friends – Gus perhaps and so on. Reserve your writing energy for the aforesaid articles and Mass Observation Diary. Put this away, right away for six weeks. Just see if you can do it, if you have any guts. Adieu, adieu dear companion.

33.

Howl My Heart Out

Friday, 8 August 1946 (aged thirty-six)
Should be getting to bed but am in writing mood. What will my first official paying guests be like? Will my cooking and accommodation suit them? Will they go out all day as I want them to?

I have had some panic early morning dreams – trying to get breakfast, doing all the wrong things, cooking the bacon before I had heated water for their ablutions, the guests coming down before I was ready.

Monday, 12 August
It's a miracle – it's what a miracle must feel like, I mean. Thank you, God. The phone call that I have been eating out my heart for came this evening. Just to say, 'Hullo my darling, how are you, and will you come to a flick one evening – not tonight or this week as I have to go back to the Midlands – you're busy, too, are you, well, one evening next week? I'll phone you again then.'

Not once in all these two years has he done anything like this. God bless him, God bless him a lot. My guests have arrived – middle aged but seemingly very nice, homely, middle class. What a difference it makes to one's whole way of living, thoughts and feelings when one is happy, when something promises to unfold as one feels deeply it should. Is it really true, is he really beginning to take me a little more seriously, to think of me more, to want me more? I daren't yet believe it.

Tuesday, 1 October

Since I last wrote in here A. has been only once, and that was exactly four weeks ago this evening. I do not know why. He may have, impulsively, taken a much needed holiday and since been too busy on the firm's affairs and his own business to give me a thought. He may have been sent abroad again. He may have quarrelled with the HDA people finally and left them in a hurry.

Wednesday, 30 October

From tributes to H.G. Wells, just broadcast: 'His attitude was – "well, I've missed. May I have another shot?"' And 'He said to us – "Enjoy life and go out and fight for it."'

May I have another shot . . . fight for it. I need more of that way of thinking. We get the men we deserve. I am sure of that. All things come to those who know how to wait. They won't come to those who snivel and cringe while waiting – that isn't waiting, anyway, that is running away, avoiding the burden of waiting. Yet I seem to have spent most of this 2½ years 'waiting' for A. Should I go on? Is it worth it? Is he worth it? If he is a cad, then I am a fool. But I can't and won't believe he is as much of a cad as he seems. Am sending a letter to John Audrey of the *News Chronicle* 'Personal Problems' column, asking for his views on this type of man. I hope he prints a reply, gives it some publicity, because I am sure it is a fairly common problem type and causes many women much distress

Friday, 1 November

Still no period. It is now nearly 5 days late. I don't think it has ever been quite as late as this – it is usually a day or two early. A. has not been near me since early September and I have had two normal periods since then. All very baffling. I should be a lot more worried if he had been here this last month. I wish I had the courage to have an illegitimate child, but I haven't, and mixed up with that is a feeling of duty to the child – if I ever had one, then I would want it to have a legitimate father, a secure and happy home background.

I must go on with this journal. I know I must. This is the real diary. Here I feel free to write spontaneously, exactly as I feel and think – which is really what Mass Observation wants (and may in time get from me these diaries too). I must just go on writing them both. The one recording superficial activities, the other inner.

I must pay for my sins – although I don't think they are sins. But I must suffer the consequences of past action, right or wrong, and pay ungrudgingly. And why I don't feel as worried as I might is, of course, because I feel fairly certain at the moment that I could raise the money for a skilled abortion. This makes me wonder if there is anything I could do to help my less fortunate sisters (sort of conscience-gift). Certain people are trying to get the abortion laws altered. What could I do of a really practical nature? Why is society so hard towards the unmarried mother? I think it takes a lot of courage to be a mother, married or unmarried. Immorality? What is it? Society fears it, perse-cutes it. It's fear and lack of understanding of sex, I suppose, mainly. People are fundamentally shy of talking or thinking about it. I am. It arouses at once such complex, confusing emotions.

Saturday, 2 November
I changed my mind during the night. I would have the child. I saw it as a whole new set of interesting problems, concrete, manageable. All this morning I was planning what I would do as I did the house-work. How I would enlist Tom's services and advice, consult Graham Howe, break the news to Ethel, Leslie and my special friends. How I knew I could rely on them to stand by me and see me through. I should be so full of confidence and happiness myself they would be glad to help me. The more I thought of it, the more the idea of bearing A.'s child filled me with enormous happiness, even if he washed his hands of me altogether. I saw myself contacting him and saying to him at last all the things I have for so long really wanted to say,

pointing out that he would be free to take just as much or as little interest in me and his child as he wished. It seemed to give my whole life depth and meaning, to knit it all together, to give me something real to work and live for.

Sunday, 3 November

The body had its revenge in the afternoon. One of those terrible fainting, sickness and tummy pain turns that I have not had for years. Whatever the cause the result was an hour-and-a-half of indescribable agony. I knew what was coming and just had time to drink warm gin and water, fill a hot water bottle and collect basin and rag, then passed out with face buried in cushion on sofa – don't know how I breathed.

Coming to after a faint – one is first conscious of blackness, a deep, comfortable blackness where one was at rest, safe, still, knowing nothing. Then comes light in grey streaks and many confused images. Then consciousness of auto discomfort, difficulty in breathing and frightful pain and one remembers then, and knows what one has to go through in the next hour – sickness, diarrhoea and pain. All one's belly is cramped, distorted, wracked with pain. Warmth and a couch one must have – I have fortunately never had these attacks where it has been impossible to obtain these aids immediately. Rarely, if ever before, have I been quite alone as I was yesterday. One needs afterwards sympathetic, quiet attendance. One wants to be quite still and have hot tea or Bovril brought to me and more hot bottles and then be left to relax and sleep undisturbed for hours.

My fancy rides freely. Some angel of doom before my birth wrote with a cold finger, 'she shall be barren and never marry,' and a devil added, 'she shall not be unattractive to men and shall have womanly desires.' And this has been my life's burden, cross, conflict – in an age when many women are obsessed with the idea of 'leading their own lives' and 'pursuing a career', which has had its influence.

Thursday, 7 November

In my eagerness to find a romantic cause for last Saturday's sickness I overlooked other possible causes. A few days before the previous period, Kathleen Moneypenny suddenly announced that she wanted to come back to Wee and would I move into Gypsy East if we could persuade the C.s to move. This was a most frightful shock and kept me awake the whole of one night. I don't know when I have felt so upset about anything. I might have been living in sin with someone else's husband for seven years, it could not have been more painful. But she has compromised and thinks she could manage as well with Gypsy East herself. But the threat still hangs over me: Wee is not mine although I have grown into it as though it were.

As ever, my conscience has been nagging at me to do some writing. Out of that has emerged the idea of doing some research into the eighteenth century and writing up Peg Woffington.[155] I still want to do articles, though Peg W. might become a book. Further, it might be wise for me to specialise seriously, and I think of all things I might make Interior Decoration my subject. Study period furniture – start with that. And really make it your subject, Jean. Architecture and Building is rather too technical now that I have so lost touch with that world. There's Lydia with her new books on furniture and glass etc, and Luigi with her knowledge and contacts. There is still Vahan, the architect in touch with architects, and the RIBA library. So think on these lines. But don't spend all your time thinking.

Saturday, 16 November

A letter from Hugh today. He says: 'I often wish I could curl up beside your fire, stir the cat with a lazy foot . . .'

Hugh told me some time ago that Nockie had been to see them. Then N. wrote me:

---

155 Margaret 'Peg' Woffington was a leading eighteenth-century actress and socialite, and a paramour of David Garrick.

'Hugh informed me that he has told you of my meeting with Maritza. Rarely have I been so attached to another woman on sight and that he should have married such a woman shows that he has a good deal in him unsuspected by me at least. She is a real person, a bound book, with a deep spiritual side. I would have liked to help you to meet her in a casual way, but like me she has an extra sense and I am sure she would guess past activities and be miserable.'

I wrote back to emphasise that I never had wanted to meet her. I would much rather stay apart, meeting Hugh occasionally for lunch. But Madame N. continues, 'I am wondering if it would be possible to have Hugh and Maritza to tea on Sunday with your friend Tommy Hughes, if you would like it.'

There is something of a triumph for our dear N. in this. She refused to be Hugh's mistress and thrust him at me and then felt 'left out'. Now she can (and does) flaunt the fact that she is 'the only woman Hugh has never slept with' and can safely meet and be great friends with his wife.

Thursday, 28 November

It was getting almost more than I could bear, the silence, the not knowing why the neglect or what had happened, when help comes unexpectedly from my dear, faithful Lydia with news that he has changed his job and is now a Branch Manager for Langley Alloys.

Monday, 2 December

I shall write.

'I am afraid that this letter will make you angry. But before you burn it, please read it through – just once. It's written to appease my ridiculously offended pride and will probably flatter your own.

'I have been wondering what had happened to you. Now I learn that you have a new job and will not be in this district any more. I am glad for your sake that you are free of the other place and hope that the new appointment will be a big success.

'But why your long silence? What can I think? Only that you've decided I am not worth your time and effort to know. Perhaps you are right. I have to admit I am a coward. I fail to say things I should when I have the chance. But dear Alan – Mac – you do wriggle so. I was scared to say what I wanted to because of being misunderstood. Now it's too late. I am not a harpy waiting to destroy you. I would never have tried to interfere with your work or home life. But when you were with me I always felt you were thinking I would. It was a barrier I couldn't break down. I had hoped that you wanted us to be friends. I sometimes wonder if you know how to be real friends with a woman, though the fault may be in me. Perhaps, O man of promise and many promises! you are not the person I imagined you to be. I should be grateful if you would post back my 2 books, the Maugham and Meyer, when you have finished with them, please? I do not want to see you again. Don't think that I regret anything – except my reserve, which has carried more misunderstanding in my life than I care to remember.'

Sunday, 8 December

'Bad Girls Don't Have Babies' heads an article on the unwanted (illegitimate) child by Dr Eustace Chesser in today's *Pictorial*. Dr Chesser says: 'Half the sex troubles of our city population today – from outright deviation to unhealthy states of mind – are due to the widespread notion that sex is secret, sinful and forbidden . . . Deep in the hearts of millions of men and women of the last two generations is hatred and fear of sex, which renders them incapable to give any real advice or training to their children.'

Deep in my heart I want to know more, experience more, much more of it. I adore being made love to. I know no pleasure quite its equal – with the right person. But one must remember always it is not an end in itself but a means – a means to a better understanding, a cementing of the relationship. And my 'reserve' which I have so blamed, beaten and abused may perhaps have been and still be a very useful protection to me against making seriously foolish mistakes – mistakes with long, disastrous consequences. We sensitive introverts are now so ashamed of our shyness, as ashamed of our shyness as our grandparents were of sex.

11 p.m. My decision to work at a biography seems to be a right one (at last!?) and the choice of Peg Woffington a good one. All my friends approve and are interested – including N.! What is important is that the work absorbs me and I feel hugely confident about it. Am sure now biography is my 'line' and I should concentrate on it. Why haven't I discovered this sooner?

Xmas Eve

8 p.m. I have just had the best Xmas gift of all. A phone call from my darling in Warwick. My hand is trembling I can scarcely hold the pen – I have heard his voice . . . really it is true. He wanted me to know he was thinking of me at this time, he said. He wanted to try and apologise and hoped soon to come and explain. He said he knew what I must be thinking. Cards and letters were so easily written – he thought the verbal message might mean more. He had been through a bad time mentally and decided to cut right away – the only thing to do, but he wanted me to know he hadn't forgotten me. (Dearest, dearest I do love you so, forgive me please, all my bad thoughts of you . . . But this is what I did not say.) It is true, Jean, he phoned, just now, he really did phone from Warwick.

New Year's Eve

9 p.m. I have been trying to work but cannot. It is New Year's Eve and I have a great craving to be among people, to be having a party. I will pretend – I will summon them all to these pages though I don't know how they would mix in reality. Let us imagine that I have invited here tonight, and that they can all get home again by car after midnight, Joan and Vahan, Nockie and F., Luigi, Lydia and Curly, Lizzie and Peter, Liz Cecil, Leslie and Ivy, Hugh and Maritza.

No. I tire already, the contrasts are too many, too difficult. But I will think of them all – Gus and Phyllis, Josephine, Ethel and Aunt Maggie, Tom, cousin Joyce, the Devereuxs. And A. of course – all the time, but how would he mix with any of these people? I long for company, the right company. I wish I could have more of my own people popping in and out. (But of course if you will live in the country, isolated!) Wish them all a Happy New Year . . . Dear friends, a very Happy New Year!

Sunday, 5 January 1947

As I write the date I remembered it was my mother's birthday – in the year (I think) 1869 – (she was 27 when she married in 1896).

My thoughts have been on shyness. I can remember what torture it was to meet strangers, to have to go among strangers as at a new school. It was perhaps something I inherited from my mother and which perhaps could be traced back to her birth. It was not, in my adolescence, just men I was shy with. I was shy in any company, though women I always found easier to get on with. So I always aimed at the women and avoided the men – just as in schooldays I aimed at getting myself liked by the 'lower levels', the 'scum' – where I felt safe from opposition. I am still shy. It is still an effort and sometimes agony to meet new people or join mixed company, but I think I am a little better in my behaviour. I am not quite so often so confused and tongue-tied.

Monday, 20 January

I am looking through Esther Harding's chapter on the ghostly lover in her book *The Way of All Women* for something in connection with Josephine who was here yesterday. Josephine has for years hero-worshipped Leslie Howard from afar though she never met him when he was alive.[156] It has now reached such a state that he has really

---

156 Leslie Howard, the actor, died 1943. Best known for his roles in *Gone with the Wind* and *Pygmalion*.

become 'a lover who is not of this world, but belongs to the spirit or ghost world.' Since his death he has become more and more concrete to her and she now through mediums receives spirit messages of great comfort to herself direct from him. She is made so radiantly happy by these contacts and believes in them so fervently one dare not disturb her with one's own views.

Friday, 24 January

My family make me feel old, cold, frigid, spinsterish, 'booksy', neglected, lonely. This is a very secret confession and has in it only a hint of resentment and despair. But I must have it out and look at it. I love my brother and his wife and their daughter, very dearly. And they seem to love me. They are kindness itself in their manner, as friendly as possible. But there is a gap that I find difficult to bridge and it makes me self-conscious. Pooh and I have led such different lives that we are almost strangers. Small-talk – that is all we have in common. I long to make contact and cannot. Perhaps I try too much to go back in time and cannot or will not assimilate the fact that he has had a wife and daughter for 15 years. The life he lives abroad that I once so envied does not now appeal at all. And dear, little Babs – she is the colour of her parents and I fail to make contact with her as I do with them. They do not know or understand the sources of love that warm and move me. They only see me on the outside, a lonely, 'booksy' spinster – they have met scarcely any of my friends, know really less about my life than I do theirs and our time together is short. They expect to leave for their next post, Lisbon, sometime in February. I have spent a few other afternoons and evenings with them. We all went to the circus, Ivy and Babs came with me and Lydia and her niece and nephew to the local panto. In time, in time it would work. I feel strongly that if only I were married it would all be much easier. Though if they did not like the husband it might be much worse.

Monday, 4 February

Feel forlorn, miserable; perhaps it's the weather. Pooh sails for Lisbon on Wednesday. I hope to lunch with them all at Euston first, and then it's goodbye for another three years. Ivy and Babs follow as soon as passage can be found for them.

The feeling of isolation I get sometimes, of being alone – not lonely – is terribly hard to bear. I don't need company for company's sake, having many resources. But I am only half-alive – the other half is missing, the old cry, the old ache. How many other people feel the same? Is there always something missing, even in the happiest of unions, as Graham Howe suggests?

Love what you have in hand . . . It's not easy. When the wind blows from the east and there is slush underfoot and your only brother is always somewhere else, and the man you want never comes and you're alone, alone, always alone trying to fill your life with other things. The whine of complaint and resentment creeps in. Dreams are such a warming consolation on a cold night. I indulge in them far too much. My love must be spent on realities.

Friday, 14 February

In a London tube this morning I saw a red-faced, pop-eyed, sex-hungry business man with a dark eyed, voluptuous woman. His hand was fondling hers on her lap and they both looked very happy; they had pleasant speaking voices, the woman's deep throated, the man's a little high-pitched with joy. It seems as though he could not believe his good fortune, could not have enough of her, or nearing the moment of parting could not bear to let her go. I did not find it disgusting or embarrassing, but immensely disturbing. That wonderful physical glow of happiness – I know it. It's important. It shouldn't be abused. I hope they won't abuse it, I hope they'll go on being happy, I hope they won't be selfish and hurt others because of it. Don't sneer, or condemn or be cynical about sex happiness as over-whelming as that. Use it. It's here to help us. (But perhaps I was wrong? Perhaps she was his sister, daughter, good friend? No, I don't think so.)

My dear N. I do love her. We spent a very pleasant evening together yesterday. I read her my first two chapters of Peg Woffington. She was encouraging, genuinely. I think she really did like it and was not being kind. I feel good about it, too. I see it as a sort of mosaic. I must get all the separate pieces made first before I can put it together in a pleasing pattern and I may collect too many separate pieces, but that doesn't matter – they can be left out when the whole is done and I can start playing with the pattern. Wish I could work at it this evening but have to go to a Fabian meeting.

Thursday, 13 March
11 p.m. I think my Twinkle is dying. Why should this rend me to pieces so that I weep as much as I would for a loved human? More perhaps. He sleeps at the moment, and if he only lives through until I can get him to the cat clinic in Slough tomorrow morning – if it means only to have him destroyed. I shall be able to bear it better than if he dies this night. Why does it matter so much? Only a cat, one of many, yet as much a person in his way as any of my friends, and all his silly habits so well known to me. Every cat I have had has been a separate, individual friend with distinct, loveable personality, a miracle of independent life to watch and love. Every time they die or leave me, something in me goes too. It is replaced but never exactly the same, a similar plant in the garden but not the plant that was there with its individual twists, surprises and potentialities.

I have brought Twinkle up to my room with all the paraphernalia and am keeping the fire in. Nothing is too much trouble for anything one loves. He sleeps a sleep of exhaustion. After a battle we had to get a little milk and wine and oil down. He has eaten nothing for nearly a week and is now so thin, pinched looking, shrunk, his legs won't support him. He has sudden bursts of energy, tries to jump on the draining board as I do the washing up, climbs on the bath to watch the fascinating water fall and swirl as though to prove to himself he is not so ill, or as though he felt he must just once more indulge this favourite curiosity and jump to the window to look into the garden and watch the birds. He looks longingly at the back door when it opens but is too weak to make a dash for it.

Please God, please let him sleep like this all night. I have a throat on me I'm going to regret and think that I caught it from Twinkle but can't bother about it until I have found some ease for the cat. I'd have taken him today, but Mr Steward was busy with other matters and didn't encourage me. Expect he has a lot of hysterical fussing unnecessarily on the phone.

Friday, 14 March

My little Twinkle died in his basket on the way to the clinic this morning. I went into the bank afterwards and when the nice girl clerk made enquiries on seeing the basket I answered in hoarse voice as hard as flint, 'No cat . . . he has just died on the way to the vet . . . all very sad.' And I was wanting to howl my heart out.

I can't stop crying now I am home. There are so many cats, past and to come, why break your heart for one? My heart breaks every time. He suffered a great deal. The vet could have done nothing for him had I taken him sooner but put him to sleep. O my dear Twinkle. How you clung to life, wanted to live, wanted to play with my toes in the bath last night but couldn't. There was nothing, nothing we could do. Death is so cold, remorseless. There are no compensations, none. He was here, a fortnight ago, in his pride and beauty and now he is quite gone. An hour ago I saw his thin, tortured corpse with mouth wide in his last agony. It's so . . . understandable, horrible. Both my mother and father died in great pain and there was nothing we could do. My dear, dear Twinkle, little spark of life, where are you now? There must be something more for you, there must, not just the pool of life. The little bit of me that loved you so goes with you.

Later: The day wears on. I do things – shopping, notices of a local

Fabian meeting and so on. But the grief in my heart. Can I give it no adequate expression? All for a cat? Why are words so stiff and hard? I go over it and over it. I shall hear his feet on the stairs when he was well.

There is Dinah. Please God don't let anything happen to her. Don't let Dinah suffer like that, or don't let me ever let her suffer so.

Twinkle looked at me once or twice this week appealingly as though to say, 'look at the state I'm in, can't you do anything?' and then, 'well I suppose not. Just let me die, let me go into the garden and die alone quietly, it won't take long . . .' Are you at ease now my sweet in your Elysium? Is the grass cool and are there gentle hands to welcome you and give you real milk, you must be so thirsty, and lots and lots of delicious liver.

I couldn't feel more grief, more loneliness at the loss of a human friend, which goes to prove how much I need a human being to live with and love as I do my cats. They help to fill a gap and to satisfy some of the emotion that must be satisfied.

34.

Auragraph

Wednesday, 26 March 1947

Dear N. is now to be called Nicola instead of Nockie, a name F. has made for her and suits her well. She is I think my dearest enemy. She sat on my bed yesterday after she was up about 7 a.m. and lectured me with the greatest kindness and affection about A. I'm never at my best at that hour and her thoughts are always freshest and most forceful then. She had to tell me what she'd been thinking. Swept at me like the Charge of the Light Brigade and left me crawling after my dead and wounded. As many women do, as she did for nearly 10 years with her American T., she says I am clinging to a corner I won't spring clean. I am wasting myself on A., he is worthless. A man like that, who can behave as he does will NEVER etc. etc. She is *never* wrong about a man, the situation could never be a happy one . . .

I am dumb always before her onslaught. She means so well and speaks so much truth. But truth is never a plain tale and I cannot change my feelings to order. We are different people and behave differently. Her man must have the same intellectual stature – and in F. (whose friendship has lasted 5 years now) she has him. They are very happy indeed together, physically and mentally – as a lover and friend he is all she wants, the only 'snag' being their great difference in age. He is many years younger and looks it and this causes her much distress.

But my demands are not as exacting as hers. I know I must get my book on Peg Woffington done. N. is most encouraging and helpful over that and I am very grateful for it. I must do that because it seems the way I can use my talent and education. But to me it's a secondary matter, not the most important. I need to earn a living, to supplement my diminishing capital – and to have interesting work, of course it's important. To N. the idea of her work surviving in the British Museum and being read years after she is dead gives her great satisfaction. To me that doesn't matter at all though I dare not say so. It seems much, much more important to pour into the world and to create as much love as possible – that seems more likely to endure here and on the 'other side' as the spiritualists say, than anything else. Dear N. We all say 'dear N.' She'll never be anything but unique, attractive, interesting, giving forth original, bombshell views – living vividly, objectively, getting what she wants and always wanting something that eludes her.

Monday, 31 March
Sturt to Arnold Bennett in 1897:[157] 'Too much importance is attached to intellect. None of us have yet recovered from the surprise of discovering that we are animals who can think.'

Later that year Bennett goes to a Grieg Concert and notices among the audience two girls. One smiled all the time, 'the other had a fixed mournful face. She never stirred and seldom spoke; she did not join in the applause, which was frantic. Her thin lips were set, and her dark eyes were set . . . I fancied I could see her in her daily existence, secretive, self-contained and occasionally, opening the gates of her soul to some companion.'

When I read that I saw a picture, an exaggerated picture of myself, or as I think some people sometimes see me. It's too dreary and awful and I hope not true. But I think I know what she may have felt.

---

157 George Sturt achieved success for his depictions of rural life.

Thursday, 10 April

Mass Observation wrote recently that their aim was to collect private opinion 'with the brake off'. But I find I cannot do this as often as I might and would like to, because it involves other people living now and seems unfair and might be dangerous – though it might be of great value to future sociologists. For my own personal 'relief', as I use this journal, such matter is generally unimportant.

Sunday, 13 April

I went this morning to another meeting of the Quaker Friends at Jordans – no form of religion has appealed to me as this does.[158] It 'fits' Graham Howe's philosophy. I have been praying blindly for a long while for a 'sustaining' faith – and perhaps this is it. One has to experiment. A woman spoke this morning on our need to listen to the still small voice. It is of course important but there are many voices and we must listen to and train them all to sing in unison, like a choir – the clamorous, greedy voices of the senses and appetites, the thin, petulant, persistent voices of the mind, the dark disturbing voices of emotion and the rushing mighty voice of the spirit. All their discords can be resolved into harmony, all developed and disciplined to sing together. Well, it's easy to think about and write down. We have to live it.

Wednesday, 16 April

The British Museum Reading Room – somewhat terrifying at first but one gets over it.

Sunday, 20 April

Tomorrow I intend to buy a weekly season ticket and go up to BM each day, and the week after to work at home on results of research – probably carry on like that as long as I need.

---

158 Jordans, six miles from Jean's home, is still an active Quaker village.

Says Arnold Bennett in 1907, 'In reading Smollett's *Travels* it has occurred to me that I go about very blind, wrapped up in myself.' We all do. The effort of accurate observation is a very big one. I think I must try to read more of Bennett's work, and must certainly read again the last volumes of his journals which I don't possess and wish I did. It is the man more than his work that interests me. More and more do I think people more important and interesting than the work they do – their work is only a small part of the whole person.

'Water' dreams early this morning. Also, as I woke, was being courted by two men: one middle aged, good looking, wealthy and a little Jewish with greying moustache, and a younger man, thin, with sharp features and intense dark eyes who had something to do with a drapery department in a big store. The moment of declaration and honest proposal was at hand and I was filled with great joy – and woke! (when of course I had to complete this pleasant dream for myself in a daydream before I got up).

Monday, 28 April

I must record this. N. says the strain has gone from my face, that my skin is clearer, I look eight years younger, very well, pretty, happy. I really have cut down my cigarettes from over 30 a day to 15 (it's not easy to do this, and I should never have tried but for Mr Dalton!)[159] I don't want to give up smoking altogether because I enjoy it – I should like if I can to keep it to between 10–15 cigarettes a day, although at home it really is a struggle. I certainly do feel better than I have for a long while, and to have impressed N. with it is a real test – and all without a 'love affaire' too! Not that I don't still want him often and with great hunger and am swamped almost as frequently with wishful dreams and fantasies. When I think of him it's still basically: 'Please come again on any terms!' and it should be 'No. If you

---

159 Hugh Dalton, chancellor of the exchequer in Attlee's government, had recently increased tobacco duty.

really want to see me again don't come as a one-night thief: if you want me, woo me on a different level, or don't come at all.'

Friday, 2 May
Tomorrow, I hear, K. Moneypenny is paying her tenants a visit. I have to brace myself: to be courageous about this interview (two paying guests will be here too). Will she part with her cottage, or won't she, or will she still be indeterminate? I should like to know one way or the other. If it's the other then I shall re-orientate my life back to Homefield, incredible as that may seem, and plan to make it into a guest house for business and professional people for which I would advertise in the select weeklies.

Sunday, 4 May
No, she will not sell – she wants Wee. Well, it is her property. But she wants it as a pied-à-terre only. Fortunately she is a likeable person. We shall come to an arrangement. I am getting more used to the idea of possibly leaving Wee – I must not cling.

   All this evening: the sun through after a long day of rain, and everything is shining. The joy of living almost too much to be borne. Can one have a breakdown from the reverse-of-depression? What is the opposite of depression? Exaltation? Elevation?

Tuesday, 6 May
And underneath, all the time, snapping, snarling, screaming with frustration, stamping, hating, venomous, contemptuous as Judas, mocking, insatiable. All the time this conflict continues. I don't think that I am in any way abnormal sexually, but circumstances and current ideas and fears have moulded in me an abnormal longing for it – only because I don't have enough of it. It's like a deficiency of something important in one's diet, such as sugar. I pray and pray continually that this big need in my nature may be satisfied soon – It may not seem apparent on the surface, so that people might assume I am 'not

really very passionate'. I need a normal amount of passion! This doesn't mean I should turn into a Good-Time Girl and join the Vice Racket about which Hugh has been telling me – I don't mean that sort of unrelated, raw, material-only sex. A later age may marvel that anyone like myself should find this such a problem and that it should take so long to solve. But it is one of the big problems of this age.

Friday, 9 May

A few cocktails at the Dorchester (at expense of Ascot Heaters) and my mood rockets. Went with Vahan who suddenly suggested that if we could find suitable land we could both build: for myself a replica of Wee, and for him and his family the house in the country they want. It seems to me a miraculous and fantastic idea: would be a wonderful solution of housing difficulties for all concerned. He thinks we could get permits.

Thursday, 22 May

By chance today picked up the current *Woman* magazine and in it found an article by Dr R. Mace of the Marriage Guidance Council answering a letter from a reader asking Why do the Best Wives Get the Worst Husbands? His answer interesting and consoling. 'The average man has a greater field of choice – he accepts marriage in order to get the girl. The woman accepts the man in order to get married. The lower type of woman will resort to expedients to which the higher type would scorn to lower herself. Women of culture and refinement know that there is more in love than just glamour. They therefore refuse to conform to the pattern . . . which is "all lips and legs". Until men in general recover a true sense of values and see through the artifices of the girl who puts all her sex appeal in the shop window, the best type of woman, the "comrade wife", will have to go unwed or take any man who may be available. We probably all know fine women who would have made magnificent wives and mothers and yet have been passed by.'

And, he adds, (I note with immense approval) 'It must be said that often these "fine" women fail their husbands because they are too inhibited to be capable of full passionate response in their love-making.'

My observation on the type of woman that I make friends with was put by N. in another way last night. She said that of all her woman friends, or most of them, none had in their men their own equal. But I still think the fault may be in us. I at least seem to attract men or be attracted to those who reflect something of the 'weaker' side in my nature. I suppose I have been unlucky in my men friends, but none of them go to quite the same lengths or take quite as much trouble building the friendship as I and my women friends do. Largely they may fear emotional entanglement which doesn't enter into normal friendship between women, but apart from that they really won't put themselves out to the same extent, they can't be bothered, are too easily bored.

Met T. again on Tuesday. There is a case in point. I like him as much as ever and ironically enough can talk to him now with all the ease and freedom I once wanted badly. I'd like to continue this friendship very much, and shall do what I can to help it along. But I feel that he may not make the effort he might, not because of indifference but because of his natural indolence and perhaps some diffidence – a lingering fear or feeling of caution. He says himself that he is a confirmed bachelor, but one takes such statements with a pinch of salt. Yet I should feel some regret and loss and even some jealousy if he did marry.

Monday, 2 June
N. wants me to spend all Wednesday with her hunting for rooms in Hampstead. Of course I consent and willingly. When she is in distress my whole nature warms with goodness towards her and I am eager to do all I can. All I can to what? To quieten and restrain and soothe . . . the good doormat in action. And why not? Doormats are sound,

serviceable, necessary objects too often treated with contempt they do not deserve. They work hard, every house needs at least one, they are kicked, beaten, stamped on, shaken; they are dull to look at – no attractive colours or pattern, no softness to the touch, but are tough, humble, patient, enduring . . . In fact I think I lack some of its most admirable qualities and am not so much a doormat as I suppose, more's the pity.

Friday, 13 June

I am enjoying my thirties much more than my twenties and I hope to make this pleasure in living progressive decade by decade. May my forties be better and my fifties be better still. I should like to be able to say that when I am 70 if I live so long. Reported in paper today was a woman of 88 in trouble because of car she insisted on driving – and I have just heard of man of 73 about to remarry, with more vitality than his son. One shouldn't mind growing old. It gives one a chance to rectify mistakes, to benefit from one's experience – use it and practise it.

Friday, 20 June

In train to Paddington this morning opposite me were two elderly lovers. Thin, neat, grey-haired man – rather bachelor looking, and enormous middle-aged woman in skimpy coat and skirt, satin blouse, rose in button hole, awful tweed cap-shaped hat – she wore glasses, had broad, florid, kind face and rich North-country (or was it Irish?) voice. Was talking all the time about her family and past history. Might have been a matron or hospital sister – that type – and ecstatically happy. They held hands under newspaper. Am reminded of R.W.'s friend at HDA – a tarty, seductive, intriguing little bit, wiry, dark, exotic, rather French, who came out with things brazenly, impudently. Discussing news of an engagement she once remarked, 'fancy getting into bed with that'. Which after all is one of the first things one does think of at news of engagement or marriage.

Tuesday, 8 July

In town today, dined with Luigi and then paid flying visit with her to Gus and Phyllis. Coming home in train began an analysis of my friends. I say to myself vaguely that I know a great variety of people, but actually I doubt if they are so different. They all belong to some strata of the middle classes, upper, middle and lower. The upper grade have close and obvious connections with the aristocratic and ruling class. They are from well to do families with property or capital of some kind, familiar with comfortable, cultured living, with artistic or high class professional interests, liberal or conservative in outlook, their tastes refined, discriminating, and possessing a rather superior sort of tolerance for the rest of humanity. In this grade are, of course, Gus and Phyllis, Josephine, Lizzie Cecil, Luigi, Enid Martin. The next grade, in which I include myself, is rather more obviously plebeian. We are in touch with and know both higher and lower grades of the middle class and can adapt ourselves to either when occasion demands but do not feel we belong. I am always acutely conscious of the conflict within me between the happy, impulsive, uncouth, common little peasant Pratt and the educated, restrained, polite, timid little middle-class Lucey. Joan, Nockie, Lydia and Lizzie Mitchell – we all have a provincial, less sophisticated, less delicate background – we are coarser, tougher, not so confident of our social superiority. Hugh and Tom belong here too. But our interests are similar. We have strongly developed artistic or intellectual instincts. In politics we tend more towards the left, though this path becomes increasingly difficult and confusing. We distrust the Tory way but are shocked by present Labour antics and ashamed to own allegiance. Perhaps the people I know differ more in character and temperament than in social distinction or interests.

Saturday, 2 August

More paying guests today. Two nice women, about my age, plain, school-mistressy, sad-eyed. One, I think, an RC. A rosary fell from her night things when I took the cover from the bed. The hour before guests arrive is fearful. I wonder and wonder about them, imagining dreadful possibilities. The one I corresponded with most has an almost childishly script hand. Is active, pleasant-spoken – used, I should say, to command.

Sunday, 3 August

A day so beautiful, so perfect, that it hurts. Full of memories that go back and back. Full of foreboding. One should be with friends, a really jolly party, in some Cornish cove picnicking, in and out of the sea all day. Or with one or two special friends having a lazy tea in the garden. But I am here with an empty hour and an empty garden full only of sunshine and shadow and green leaves and the scent of phlox.

I have been given a talent for writing. This is a real fact that I must not try to bury and ignore. But the way seems long, hard and unfruitful. So many people can write, do write, have written. There are far too many printed words in the world today. But that is an old argument, refuge of the pessimist and coward.

Tuesday, 2 September

I keep feeling, more and more, that the small things we do, see, think and feel every day and forget are more important than we realise. We cannot capture them all: we should be drowned in words if we could. Yet in this moment I want to capture all mine. Hasn't Virginia Woolf written a book which covers in time only one day?

But I do not like to reveal too much to Mass Observation. This isn't delicacy, or consideration for my friends, but vanity. I am ashamed of my lack of strong male connection: no husband, no fiancé or lover to acknowledge and be proud of, and very few boyfriends. In revealing as little of this as possible I hope to conceal it and leave them guessing. As though they cared!

On Saturday we said goodbye to Hugh. He goes to India this week and then on to Australia. Shall we meet again? I don't 'feel' that we shan't. I have seen him little lately, yet I shall miss him. He has promised to write. I am very fond of Hugh. But I think there is little there for a woman to love. N. says his wife Maritza is no longer 'in love with him', that he does not sleep with her now. N. suspects him of having another affair. But he declares he has been faithful, and I believe that is true. Maritza is to join him in Australia, with his young son.

On Monday I went to see Gus and Phyllis. Gus read beginnings of 'Peg'. He went on reading it and wants to read more and gave me one or two most helpful points: not destructively as of old. That it is holding his attention is great encouragement. I make no prophesies, I have no 'feelings' about this book. I am getting it done. G. and P. cling to a colourful past and won't accept more than they must of the present to make life tolerable. But they are helping to keep alive and to continue traditions that make living gracious. They practise the art of fine living as far as it is now within their power, on the old lines, the ancient model. It is an art and must not be forgotten.

Supper last night with Ethel and Aunt Maggie. Home by 10.30, tired but happy. My path is set in pleasant places. I love my life. I am deeply envied by many people. (It is sometimes an immensely heavy burden, the envy of others.) Yet remember, remember all ye that pass by: I am lonely, lonely. No one comes home to me at evening. I sleep alone at night. This is becoming less of a whine than it was. But it is the price one has to pay for this lovely, enviable life that is mine.

At Hampstead I slept in a room facing the back of New End Hospital and on Sunday night was kept awake – it seems long hours – by a child's crying. Three nights in London are vivid now. One some time ago with Joan when the woman in Flat 3 had had an illegal abortion and was very ill (she eventually had to go into hospital, and recovered). The second when staying in flat with Liz Cecil near Paddington a few weeks ago. And then last night. The weight of misery in a city has borne down on me. It is terrible, suffocating. The sordidness of that woman's life in Flat 3 – a little dog that wailed, neglected outside a shut door near Paddington – and a child's bewilderment, pain, frustration. I can't properly recall the feeling now, but at the time it is what I think must be hell.

Monday, 8 September

This panic I get into about the future: sudden, vivid little pictures of a lovely, unloved, impoverished old age. Ill, neglected, without money, friends or any means of support. I want frantically to insure myself against such disaster and misery. It's a form of neurosis, a symptom of a neurotic attitude to life. Don't let it happen!

Sunday, 21 September

11.30 p.m. In bed and nearly asleep when I remembered something. Hugh has been fabricating the most monstrous tale concerning me. Made N. swear never to mention it but when she hinted at it last week she told me the whole without much persuasion.

From something I said in one of my letters to him. I wish I could remember exactly – it referred, obliquely, without names, to A.M. and my rage with him at that moment when he seemed to be behaving particularly badly; I felt very blue and let off steam to Hugh. I know Hugh answered promptly, most anxious about me, offering to come down at once and bump the offending male off for me. Very flattering. I laughed and forgot about it.

Hugh did come for a weekend that autumn – he slept on sitting room sofa. I did not encourage attentions though think he'd have obliged if I'd given the least sign – but I had become A.M.'s mistress that summer and was waiting ardently for the next visit. Well, out of all this Hugh composes this story: I am being followed and molested by an undesirable man in the neighbourhood who insists on visiting cottage late at night and is scaring me to death. I appeal to Hugh. There is 'fear in her voice'. He makes some excuse to wife M. and comes for the weekend. Of course because of M. he has no 'immoral relations' with me. I keep looking at the clock, expecting a footstep saying 'this is about the time he comes . . .' and so on. Then unknown to me Hugh goes to the garden gate about 10.30, sees a man walking up and down outside who says to him:

'What are you doing at that house?'

'I live here,' says Hugh.

'But Miss P. lives there—'

'I know. I live with Miss Pratt here. What do you want?' And the man vanishes and Hugh returns and assures me 'there'll be no more trouble'.

Well, really. Infamous story! I don't remember him going into the garden after dark. If he did I hope he didn't have that conversation with one of the neighbours, airing their dog last thing. I am sure he believes it thoroughly now – he is like that; and I wonder how many more he's made up like that; and of what other outrageous, sinister things N. suspects me of keeping from her. I am sure she thinks I went to G. Howe for the same trouble Monica H. did – her obsession with masturbation, which I have recently learned. I don't think the word was even once mentioned. I don't deny guilt where this is concerned but it has always seemed to me, long before I went to Dr Howe, the symbol of something much more important; that that in itself should not be worried over – and since reading Groddeck and other psychologists am all the more convinced and reassured.[160]

Wednesday, 1 October

All in a moment the bright day is darkened and my adored cat becomes a malevolent demon, a black stab of evil as I hold the frail, lonely husk of a small robin in my hands. Its body is still warm, but I think its back is broken. The inexorable law of life. Only humans feel pity and remorse and are aware of cruelty. If humans found some synthetic

---

160 The German physician Georg Groddeck, a pioneer of psychosomatic medicine, in which psychological, social and behavioral elements all play a part in diagnosis and healing. Acknowledged as an influence on Freud.

substitutes for food, animals would continue their slaughter of each other, parasites would suck the life from another organism, decay would attack and rot the living. And we who can feel pity can feel it falsely until we lose all sense of proportion in our feelings. Perhaps this is a means of escape from feeling real pity when we are powerless to restore what is destroyed, or mend what is broken. The still form of my mother's lifeless body, the closed eyes of my father's . . . That flesh will never again be quickened by them. Gone. These are the moments terrible to bear.

Sunday, 19 October
Last Tuesday I sat for my auragraph with Harold Sharp (am told he is a Communist) at the Marylebone Spiritualist Association. This is Lydia's birthday and Xmas gift to me. I sat in a deep armchair facing the light and Sharp, who began at once drawing and colouring a circle on cartridge paper. He is conscious when doing this, though his hand is being 'controlled'. He says that he cannot draw a line himself. He chats away amiably while I look through a book of auragraphs he has handed me. Amazing creations, all different, all colours, shapes pictures, patterns. He explained several. When mine was completed I sat in a chair by him at a desk and he went into a trance, when his Chinaman 'guide' came through and began to explain the diagram. It was a delicate concoction of pale mauve, primrose, green, red rocks, blue waves, and many delightful curly shapes, delicately drawn in the Chinese manner. Surprisingly like Lydia's. I took notes as he spoke and as far as I can remember he said something like this:

Upright rock-like structure in steps at base of circle in bright red: represents the slow magnetism, the heavy wavelength in my make-up by which I get things done step by step, determinedly. A tendency to plan my time, to make timetables and to get things done with steady patience. In youth some 'obstinacy' since overcome. A little blue sea lapped round my rock which showed adaptability, and the turning of this 'obstinate' force into a willing one which helped my progress considerably. The mauve all round outer edge of circle represents a 'rectification' ability – not 'creative'. Would make a good teacher, nurse, healer, psychologist or probation officer – the ability to put things and people right, to convert, to build up from given material: I could not design a hat or gown on my own from nothing, but could give an old one just the right touch and finish to make it into something new and attractive.

In the centre a green patch which showed a progressive outlook, that I had travelled a long way from the outlook and idea of my parents and early life. The yellow twisting its way throughout the pattern meant 'spirituality'. My religion was in my life and it did not matter if I never entered a church – not a 'shrine worshipper' was one term he used.

He saw a 'baby' influence in my life. I had thrown a protective wing over some child which had greatly helped my own growth. Did I understand that? (No!) It had helped me to 'expand' myself. Also, he could see no inferiority complex (I have to underline this!), usually represented by a brown patch near the base, this space now occupied by a pleasant little blue wave.

He thought he saw me at the start of a new period, opening new doors. I had to ask if he saw nothing about my writing and the biography I have been working on. He thought that would be my type of work exactly, my thirst for information seeking causes and ability to construct from given facts, the ability to resurrect a personality so that it lives again for others to see and recognise.

Wednesday, 22 October
I feel myself committed to the following confession. I have not thought of A.M. seriously now for months. The daydreams have altogether stopped: even daydreams of an imaginary lover do not possess me as they used to. But last night in bed before I slept I thought someone was saying to me, 'You're afraid of falling in love'. And I said, 'No – no – I am afraid of making the same ghastly mistakes all over again. I am so easily tricked. I couldn't bear any more of it.' And was once

more vividly aware of that look in A.M.'s eyes which I have always yearned to see in a man's for me.

The unmarried state is more than 'frustration at the biological level' of sex and motherhood. It is the deep need in a woman for emotional satisfaction that tortures the unmarried woman. Marriage does not guarantee it, but one expects to find it there as one can nowhere else. I am sure that is true. It is a warmth that fills one's whole being, makes every part of one leap into life. I wept again, bitterly, realising this – I do not weep often. But I do not want him back. I want him to go right away and stay away unless he can come to me honestly, with stable intentions and a love that is real.

Friday, 14 November
Ethel. Dear Ethel. She is growing so little, shrunk and old. I love her more and more, and see things so differently. But our relationship could never have been other than it was. She represents a kind of life and a class fast dying out.

Thursday, 27 November
Good resolutions coming up:

The way I lie down and let friends and lovers walk all over me and sit on my diaphragm must stop. There is no need for it.

Attend always to what I have in hand e.g. completion of 'Peg'. If it weren't for this I could be a lot more sociable to immediate neighbours and do a lot more in Slough. Fabian meetings, WEA etc.

Never to lose faith that I shall in time find the Right Man and not to be worried by highbrow cant about 'frustration'. All women, married or single, can feel a certain frustration if they are not being made love to, consistently, by the man who makes them happiest. That goes for men, vice-versa, in their sex-life.

Not to be bothered, either, by talk of escapism. I lead a more isolated life than I need at the moment but if I don't I shall not get

this book finished, which I am convinced is essential to my progress
– inner and outer (i.e. spiritual and material).

Sunday, 7 December

At Reading Room all day and meeting different people at night. The
book is progressing famously: by sheer hard work. Gus reading more
of it, is still very encouraging. I made an effort also to contact Tom
again and by a miracle his friend H.C. has just arrived from Dublin
to take up a good job in the BBC. H.C. is a poet, has been a sub-
editor on a Dublin highbrow journal and is a reader of manuscripts
– he volunteered to look at mine. He knows publishers and might be
able to suggest which one I could approach.

He is also a very charming young man, like Tom in many ways
but with more character. I could fall for him easily but mustn't.
Curiously, meeting him has completely subdued the fever (the last
phase of it) that clung to thoughts of A.M. But I do not want it to
become a new one – i.e. the old fever for a new object. Honestly, yes,
I would like to meet him again and often but not before he had read
the MS, for in his being an impartial reader lies his value to me at
the moment.

Monday, 29 December

I have done the forbidden, the unforgivable thing and read right
through this journal from April 10th. Once started I could not stop.
I must not, must not do this. Every time I do it I come to the same
conclusion. Do not look back. These journals are no longer for me
to read: only to write. And I think the time is here again when I must
exercise another check. So I will finish this year here and now and
resolve not to make another entry in it for at least a month.

35.

Guardian Aunt, Rather Exciting

Sunday, 15 February 1948 (aged thirty-eight)

Unfortunately, this is going to begin again with a really mean, bitchy outburst. Somewhere in Janet Whitney's biography of Elizabeth Fry[161] (excellent) she quotes Mrs Fry as saying of her journal that she uses it as an outlet for her overburdened mind, or to help induce a certain state of mind in herself. This is exactly what my journal is to me.

My poor dear N. who has had endless trouble with her sinus and for a very long time is now in hospital. A polyp, a complicated and bad one, was removed on Friday. Quite naturally the idea of it caused her anxiety – she has been away from the office for weeks, suffering, distressed in mind and on edge. She was afraid she would have hysterics when she got in the hospital, that there might be serious complications, that it would affect her brain and even that she might die under the anaesthetic from blockage of all breathing passages. Of course all her friends have rallied round wonderfully (though she took good care that all those she wanted should know of it). I said I was going to be mean.

It has been a tricky and very painful operation. They have pulled her poor face about and it is sadly swollen. She needs love more than ever and I never felt less like it towards her. What does one do with such base thoughts as these at a time when they may be most harmful?

---

161 The nineteenth-century Quaker prison reformer.

One cannot deny that they are there, if one is honest. Always I suspect that somewhere in these flaps of hers is a childish crying out for the dramatic, to be the centre of interest and attention. Yet however dastardly they seem, these thoughts, I don't think they should ever be too much exposed. They are destructive – to one's own self as well as others.

N. and I will go on irritating each other to the end of time I am sure. Well, I suppose – and posterity mark my words if they ever reach you – that it is just these kind of irritations and bad thoughts that we have to wrestle with greatest determination and patience. The small things, the smallest you can imagine, for it is they that compose one's shadow: the shadow within which one is perpetually at war.

Monday, 16 February

I have a most overwhelming desire – a real starvation hunger – to be made love to. And all the old dreams about A.M. suddenly return. Most disconcerting. If he came this evening he'd have a wholly undeserved and spontaneous success without any explanation and apology from himself. God, it is really a torment and a sickness – what a waste here of a good body, a willing woman with a spiritual consciousness and some intelligence! Does no one want her? No one want to marry poor Jean Pratt? Yet, apart from the perpetual ache for a lover who will be also a good and faithful companion, my life seems to be falling into some sort of pattern. The book progresses. I am typing it out myself, and have only the last chapters to write up properly.

Wednesday, 18 February

I sent a copy of my MS as far as it is typed to Tom for H.C., and last night heard from Tom on the phone. His enthusiasm and delight is simply staggering. I know how the Irish can rip the roof off with their blarney but really I think he is being sincere. It is all very very encouraging – I feel like another Fanny Burney![162] H.C. is going to read it properly in a week or two when certain important work of his own is finished. He is preparing a book of his poems for the Pilot Press. Oh dear, this all promises to be much too easy, I daren't start hoping!

Sunday, 7 March

From Tom and H.C. I have not heard another word. A plague on these Irish Communists! N. has suggested I make a bold gesture and contact our old tutor, now Prof Tillotson at Birkbeck, which if successful, would make me independent of T. and his friend. H.C. is tempting my imagination and I don't, I definitely do not, want to find myself in the same old frustrating entanglement. When we first met he seemed so anxious to see me again and sent me flattering messages through T. I might not have thought twice about him – I will not work myself into a fever over another 'ghost'! Though what I am really asking is that someone might work themselves into a fever about me for a change and do something about it.

Monday, 19 April

Pooh wants now for Babs to finish her schooling in England and to get her settled somewhere this autumn and for me to play role of guardian aunt. All rather exciting. I have been writing to Princess Helena College.

Monday, 3 May

It is cold, bitterly absurdly cold for May. Reading Ford Madox Ford's *A Man Could Stand Up* but not the war part which I can't bear, sitting in fire-warmed kitchen, drinking lemon tea. 'His hand was cool on

---

162 Burney (1752–1840) was a novelist and playwright, but is best remembered today for the journals she kept for more than seventy years. These were often written in the form of letters to one of her sisters, and although much of the content was expurgated by the author, the journals still provide a valuable female perspective on English society.

her **wrist**. She was calm but streaming with bliss . . . His touch had calmed her and covered her with bliss.' One knows this and longs for it again, but the heart is stabbed by the echo 'why should you receive this more than any other who longs for it as much as you, a dream cradled in every lonely woman's heart, nursed into wonderful, foolish fancies?' And I think with agony, 'supposing all the lonely women I now know find this happiness and I do not?' Cousin Joyce, Lydia, Luigi, N. I couldn't bear it, I couldn't bear it, and yet I should have to, should have to find fortitude, not consolation or compensation or substitute, but courage without bitterness and resentment.

On the train to Winchester I met Gus's long-ago boyfriend, Howard. This is the second time I have run into him within the last two years and he has recognised me and made the first advances with eager desire for further conversation. On Friday he stayed by my seat in the train for quite a while, invited me to have a drink when we could get one in the restaurant, then disappeared and did not return. In some ways I was relieved, for he was already asking questions about Gus and had revealed of himself that he was unmarried, in his father's business and living at home. I know Gus wants to hear no more of him, yet I don't think I should mind renewing the acquaintance for myself. He is of course much older, but seems still rather attractive, easily amusing and pleasant to be with. We once knew him so well – all of us: Gus and his despised harem . . .

Nice new neighbour Mrs Semple has been helping over the schools for Babs. No hope at P.H.C. – but through an agency a host of possibles which I have to answer and acquaint Pooh with. How shall I like being a guardian aunt? Will they invest me with full responsibility, will Babs like that, will she stay with me in the holidays willingly, and shall I like that?

Tuesday, 11 May
Said the *News Chronicle* last Saturday: 'We are living now in one of the world's great formative periods when the patterns are being fashioned

which will mould the future until the next great rebirth comes. This is both our misfortune and our opportunity: we shall only know tranquillity when we have made it for ourselves. What is needed is the confidence to forge ahead.'

It is in essence my own situation. I am living at this moment in a formative period, my misfortune and my opportunity . . . what is needed is confidence.

I am now well and truly committed to the Liberal cause, working as secretary of the Farnham Common group under our organiser, Mrs H. – drawn to it entirely by Mrs H.'s immensely attractive and likeable personality. I could not do it without the inspiration I get from her and I feel most inadequate. But I want to do it and do it well. She is clear-cut yet gentle in her approach, positive without being intolerant, quiet like deep water, sensitive, but courageous. I hope we shall be friends. I think she has suffered a great deal and is emerging like fine metal from a furnace – 'Quakerish' she says. It all fits. But a married woman with three children (and, I think a widow): has she time for me?

Sunday, 30 May
Babs is to go to 'Oakdene' at Beaconsfield and will arrive here sometime in September. Work at the Liberals and my liking for Mrs H. continue, but I am edging out of door-to-door canvassing. I can not do it, it tears me all to pieces emotionally. I feel raw, exposed and altogether too nervous – I hate forcing myself upon another personality which is what one has to do, and there's more reason for this than mere timidity. Virtue somehow goes out of one, exhaustingly, and I need all I have for 'Peg'.

Monday, 28 June
I wish I could capture everything, everything and imprison it here. But then it would die of its own weight, and I want this journal to live. I suppose I must always have wanted this, or I would not have

tended it, treasured it so carefully. I would like it to have a place among the famous diaries of the world, following in the tradition of Marie Bashkirtseff and Barbellion.[163] I may never read it right through myself now – it would suffocate me. But I would like to think of other people, years and years hence, reading it with interest, sympathy, perhaps some admiration? It is a secret whim, a secret vanity and if I thought about it too much and began to write deliberately for a future audience, visualising the audience as I wrote, then the whole thing would crumple to pieces.

N. says to me of some poor woman wanting marriage, 'She's not like us who want primarily to make a name for ourselves in writing.' Which fills me with quiet resentful rage (oh, I will not be chained and made to be exactly like N. in my aims and authorities and being!) so that I answer, 'Oh, I don't want to make a name for myself, I want to earn some money!'

It is wrong that I feel so enraged and impatient and hysterical inside about this, yet I do, so often. As though she were a vulture hanging over me, waiting to swoop and devour, to swallow all that is independent and individual in me and make it part of herself. I think now, honestly, I wish she'd find the right man and marry him. I'll relinquish willingly the silly desire – oh the silly, selfish, vain desire to be 'first' (to provoke her envy and astonishment, yes – and to hurt her back – for that is what her own unconscious cruelty provokes in others). Yes, I would see her married now most gladly, joyously, without a trace of jealousy or despair for myself – for it would set me free, free of that awful shadow! I'll even go so far as to say I'll try to manage without a husband myself. I'll be the doomed old maid if necessary for the sake of my freedom.

---

163 Bashkirtseff was a nineteenth-century Ukrainian painter, with work in the Musée d'Orsay. Her journal, begun at the age of thirteen, is highly regarded for its honesty, readability and psychological insights. For Barbellion see footnote accompanying 17 May 1940.

Saturday, 17 July

Peg is so nearly but not quite finished. The last stages, preparing the top copy for publisher with lists and illustration, revising, retyping. If the book is accepted right bang off I daren't begin to visualise the difference it will make to me. If it is turned down, I don't know how I shall whip up energy to support the humiliation and send it elsewhere.

The thought of that overdraft at the bank and the £100 I owe Pooh weighs heavily. If book is accepted I may have to wait nearly two years before I get any payment or see it in print – is it worth it, is it worth it? What can I do with no qualification and nearly 40, and Wee not mine. When I think of this gap, I am down in the depths, stricken with the idea of my uselessness and my loneliness, hedged in by women, always women (or will-o-wisp men like Tom), with world affairs threatening dire disaster, and uncertainty all round.

Rain without and rain within. It has been a wretched, cold, grey July.

Tuesday, 20 July

Little *Poil de Carotte*, I sit in my corner unregarded and in silence, and secretly, *Je Rage!*[164]

My nerves are worn to the raw edges and inside me muscles are tying themselves into tight knots with my anger, bitterness, fury. Hates of all kinds surge up and over me – hate for myself, hate for my friends. It's the sort of neurosis I am sure that can end in cancer, sterility, insanity or suicide unless treated properly. I am exceedingly tired and growing more and more so, yet must keep at my typewriter if I am to get the MS finished. I lie at the bottom of a pit, aching all over, my tummy hard with tensions. Oh, I can see far above a blue

---

164 *Poil de Carotte*, a semi-autobiographical novel by Jules Renard from 1894, in which a neglected red-haired child rages against the cruelty of adults.

sky and know that the world is a lovely place, there are beautiful things in it and fair people but I do not seem to belong there.

Friday, 23 July

It was a period. I might have known. And two hours gardening helped. I am a savage in these moods (oh who would think it, the gentle, kind and easy Jean!) and could tear the world and myself to pieces with chaos and fangs that seem to develop for the occasion. The MS is all but ready to go. I composed a letter to the publisher last night before I settled down and have since been dreaming – of some tall, well made, bronzed man at my side in dark crimson bathing trunks, who dived from me from a difficult perilous height and angle into a river and swam away magnificently. It was a joy to watch him.

Sunday, 15 August

'Peg' was finished and posted to Macmillan's on Sat July 24th – the day of Peggy Denny's (late Harding) wedding reception to which I went in my New Look clothes and then to Joan's for the weekend.[165] It came back with a kind letter yesterday morning. Naturally I felt disappointed, humiliated. But as Joan says, it would be fantastically lucky to have it accepted bang off the first time, and they excuse themselves by saying they have too many commitments to be able to add this to their very limited list of new books. Most publishers are now in this position, and it is about the worst possible time in recent history to try and get a new book accepted – even established authors have great difficulty. But the growing fact remains that there was a very small chance that they might have liked it enough to take the risk or they would not have offered to read it, and that for some reason or another they didn't. It has failed in some way and I wish they had given me their reasons.

---

165 Christian Dior's 'New Look' collection of 1947 proved hugely influential, evidently reaching Slough within sixteen months. The look was characterised by a tight bust and waist, and a fulsome skirt emphasising the hips. The fanciful and liberal use of material announced the end of austerity, in haute couture at least.

But the bitterness and chagrin of yesterday are fading away after a good night's rest and an easy morning, and I think I will try next the Porcupine Press which Lizzie Cecil has mentioned to me. After that perhaps the Pilot Press where Tom knows a reader. I won't give up.

I have been looking through two copies of *Tomorrow* (King, Littlewood and King Ltd) which Clinton G.F. left me last weekend. This is the organ of the Social Creditors and is nauseatingly anti-Semitic.[166] I think there is a lot to be said against the hold of financiers and bankers on world affairs – and I have heard and read a good deal on the subject in my Socialist days, but I cannot take seriously any creed that attacks another nation so violently as these people do the Jews.

8.45 p.m.: Read *Cranford*. Then began a letter to N., a stilted, unworthy letter, interrupted continually by little foreign boy called John Gussler who is a child of cook employed by John Clements (film and radio star) who lives in big house nearby. Little John is neighbourhood pest, has nothing to do in school holidays, speaks English poorly, wanders in and out of other people's gardens, is tormented by other children, eager to be friendly but is a nuisance. I feel sorry for him and let him roam in my garden – tonight he broke up firewood for me and cut the lawn and pulled up a few weeds. He did it all quite well and seemed pleased and happy. He responds to kindness and asks many questions but is difficult to get rid of. Other people turn him out sharply which I cannot do, but it is only because I don't know how. He seems an intelligent and likeable child if one could understand what he says.

Saturday, 21 August

Somerset Maugham's voluble Miss Reid in 'Winter Cruise' diagnosed by the ship's doctor: 'That inordinate loquacity, that passion for

---

166 The Social Credit party gained a little traction in the 1930s as the 'Green Shirts', a radical political organisation promoting the redirection of economic power from institutions to individuals. It was supported by British fascist Oswald Mosley. Clinton G.F., a long-time suitor, is elsewhere described by Jean as 'silly' and 'irritating'.

information, the innumerable questions she asks, her prosiness, the way she goes on and on . . . it is all a sign of her clamouring virginity. A lover would bring her peace . . . The deep satisfaction which her being demands would travel through those exacerbated centres of speed and we should have quiet.'

I still admire Maugham immensely (much to N.'s continued annoyance) but sometimes I think that much of what he has written will in time fall to pieces and shrivel to dust. There is something of a Miss Reid in every woman who is sexually unsatisfied, but the remedy is not in 'a' but in 'the' lover. I should like to know how true that 'Winter Cruise' story is. The attentions of the Radio Operator might have quietened her, as Maugham describes, but I should like to know if they did. If so I think he must have been a remarkably skilled young man.

N. and F. have come together again (and are coming here next weekend). I am, I admit, immensely relieved but a little uncertain, privately, whether it was the right course of action for her or not. The affair of last autumn with devastating Jew has come to nought – she has heard nothing from him or his family and was apparently just a passing episode in his life.

Meanwhile a Communist fitter in her firm, with whom she has been very friendly, has fallen in love with her. She phoned me when I was at Joan's on Wednesday evening and told me all about it and wants me to meet him. I am, she says, the only person she is confiding all this to, but I always take such statements with caution. I have a feeling she may be hatching one of her enraging match-making schemes and wants to push me off on to him. He is recently widowed and left with two children and is very unhappy. Was in love with N. before his wife (very ill with cancer) died. Oh, how can she imagine that he would be interested in me instead?

Tuesday, 24 August

Yesterday, just before lunch, came a tramp for hot water for his tea can. He had been before selling clothes pegs, the week of the heatwave just before Bank Holiday. Thin, with fresh looking face, broad, high cheekbones and pointed chin. Something elfish about him – sure his ears were pointed too. Bright blue eyes and walrus moustache, cloth cap, shabby clothes, but clean. In his eyes an engaging twinkle, the hint of an Irish accent in his voice, and a quiet, respectful manner. No bluster, no whining. Could I give him a drop of hot water? We began to talk of mushrooms and food while the kettle boiled. Then, could I spare a drop of milk in the tea can, and a drop in a bottle for him to take away. A cigarette? But no, that I could not spare. He picked up a butt end I had thrown away and showed me how to roll one in the fingers. Simple, really – what could be better than that? Would I like to buy his sweet coupons? And I gave him 2s. 6d. for them. Such is the effect of blue eyes and easy ways on soft-hearted women.

Thursday, 26 August
Leave house 10.30. In Slough get cigarettes, go to bank, buy cats' fish, go to Woolworth's where I get biscuits, Smith's for notepaper and other things, another shop for typewriter ribbon. Buy a mat for kitchen in the market, a salty, watery lunch (but filled in space) at Granada cafe; then home. Then settled down to Liberal work. Stead arrives with notices for next meeting. Stead seems a sound and conscientious man for his job (the party agent for this division). Is (I think) a bachelor and should be eligible but isn't. Something loose and wet about him. Large wet mouth, scruffy hair, slightly receding chin. Well, he's nice enough I daresay, but no, somehow . . . I couldn't.

Was going to study Liberalism but listened in to short programme on Holiday Camps. Shattering for people like me, such holidays, but evidently perfect for millions unlike me.

Sunday, 29 August
'Life is a never ending source of delight!' as N. said pouring rum. It has been an exceptionally successful and lovely weekend. N. herself

is a joy and inspiration when she's as well and happy as she has been these two days. She arrived tired and on edge again on Friday evening, but a little love-making with the right person works a miracle on what Maugham might call her 'exacerbated centre of speed,' and we do have peace, of a very entertaining and refreshing variety.

Little John Hansi Gussler was round again, and N. conceived an immediate and intense dislike for him. 'You amaze me,' says N. 'I thought you didn't like children . . . you have more patience than I'd have . . .' Whatever makes her think that I don't like children?

'All men are buggers!' has become a refrain with N. I begin to protest primly and she says 'well, all the interesting ones . . .' with which I cannot but agree wholeheartedly. I could at this moment swoon into a sickly daydream about the disturbing Harry C. whom I've met but once and dream about at night frequently (he is always cropping up in my dreams and sometimes very sordidly). But he is just the type for whom I could fall again, in the old way, heavily. I know. I knew when I met him. And I mustn't. I must get a hold on myself about it before we meet again, as I think we may. But I can see him, feel him here in the cottage, so intensely. A Communist, a temperamental Irish poet and almost, I suspect, 10 years younger than I am.

A thought has just emerged. Perhaps it has shot up from some long germinating seed. I don't think I shall keep the Mass Observation Diary anymore. I'll ponder on this further. But I would rather continue with this as I am doing it now – with MO as its possible destination in mind. Perhaps I'll write and tell them my intentions.

Monday, 30 August
At 2.30 start doing things with plums upon which busy since. Home-made plum chutney and bottled 4lbs in solution.

That mention of H.C . . . started the old imaginings, the foolish fantasies. And he was here with friends (a CP infiltration of Wee!) and I was with them, patient, adoring, listening, preparing food and tea and baths for the party, visualising all the sort of awkward situations that could arise, imagining his touch and tenderness and indifference. All so silly and exhausting. I woke this morning as tired as though I had spent half the night in hectic love making . . . and ashamed of myself. This hunger for rich, romantic personal adventures is I am sure very adolescent. But one does want them, one does.

Monday, 27 September

The strain of life. Babs arrives. We meet. We visit Granny. We do lots of shopping, we have fittings, we get packed off to school. Vahan comes for a few days' holiday, pushed off here by Joan.

I want to write all my irritation out of me. Poor Vahan! He is feeble where he should be strong, obstinate where he should be elastic. Cowardice, moral cowardice, is the curse – or one of them – of this age. I sympathise most deeply with Joan, can understand why she gets into such rages with him, dissolves into tears and long sulks. He is a nice person, intelligent, kind, sensitive. But he is a stranger in a strange land who has lost his way. There is much of the oriental in him and he could be deeply philosophical with a strong inner peace which would help him and his family, but he has lost whatever of it he inherited in trying to adapt himself to our nervy western culture.

Sunday . . . disastrous. It is another lovely day. We all go over to Beaconsfield, I see Babs into school, and feel utterly deflated – all torn to pieces. I knew so well what she was feeling and could have cried. Vahan then takes me to look at building sites in which he is interested. We eventually fall into a hotel for drinks and dinner. I see frothy glasses of lager or light ale and long for some, but Vahan has to order me brown ale. I could have poured it down his neck.

Then we had to walk another mile or so for our bus and just missed getting on it because of the queue. An hour to wait. Should we walk? (Another three miles.) I am dead beat, still weeping inwardly for little Babs and exasperated to the limit with Vahan. He makes such feeble, such ghastly feeble jokes. He is feeble . . . and tries so hard to please, to be kind and polite all the time. This was where I wanted the strong male to take charge of the situation and stop a car for a lift. It can be done. I have done it. I sit on the bus stop seat and sulk. V. waffles. I say: you go ahead and walk, I'll wait. 'Oh do go and stop a car!' I cry desperately at last. But he wants me to go with him – he always wants someone with him, he is really an extremely shy person and I should feel compassion, not contempt. Then I decide we must walk it – he of course protesting: but a car may pick us up. Which it does. Nice North Country folk on their way back from Oxford to Slough, their little car crowded with apples, picnic basket, petrol tin, but they make room for us. Vahan pinches my behind in the dark which makes me savage so that I ignore him during the journey and talk to the woman in front.

He was hating me when he left this morning, just as I was hating him. But why, why can't he take a look at himself, try to regain that inner sense of serenity and peace which he once had but has lost? We all need this, desperately. I gave him *Walk On!* to look at.[167] Talked about this Buddhist Society. He was very lordly, indifferent, condescending about it. Oh, nothing is wrong with Vahan! Perhaps he harboured a secret hope of an exciting affaire with me and feels outraged at his failure. Poor Vahan! That's all we say and go on saying. His daughter will make mincemeat of him.

I have also to remember that he is a foreigner and looks it. He is darker than an Italian, might almost be pale Indian, though not quite. It makes him different and conspicuous and oneself sometimes uncomfortably but I think unnecessarily self-conscious about it. When I have been with him I have never noticed any English man or woman treating him any different than they would one of their own race. Their behaviour is invariably impeccable which I should like to record to our credit, because race prejudice is such a deeply implanted bogey.

---

167 *Walk On!* by Christmas Humphreys, a British barrister who founded the London Buddhist Society. The book is an influential epigrammatic manual to the religion.

I am sorry if I ever let it influence me when I am with him but I sometimes wonder if it does. Even Joan, brought up in Beadles traditions of tolerance, has been troubled by it herself at times.

Thursday, 30 September

Joan has just phoned. V. does not seem to have complained at all but given her the impression that he thoroughly enjoyed himself! I can't believe it. He irritated me so much, and skilled though I may be at concealing these sort of feelings, he must have been conscious of some inner discomfort. Well, let it go. It only shows how much there is beneath the surface of any relationship that is never apparent or admitted.

I must confess in fairness that for the first day or two I enjoyed having him around, and he did help me enormously the day I had to go canvassing for the Liberals by talking over policy programme with me beforehand. It is just that kind of personal contact that I lack badly in my life – someone at home to discuss these sort of things with in a friendly and intelligent way. He was 'just right' on this occasion – he is a very sane supporter of the Labour government, not rabid at all, and thinks they have done and are doing really good work for the country. He is interested too in the Liberals and made helpful criticism, so that I was able to clarify my ideas and felt quite confident when I set out. Consequently it was not nearly such torture as I expected and I even found myself enjoying it.

I think I am going to be very fond of my niece. It is going to be hugely interesting having her under my wing like this. 'Very good for you,' says N. primly, which makes me laugh. Babs is immensely loveable.

'Babs is immensely loveable.'
Jean, Babs and Ivy at Wee Cottage.

36.

Destroy, Destroy, Destroy

Monday, 18 October 1948

Thirty-nine years ago today, in the very early hours, I think, my mother sweated and groaned and delivered me. If celebrations are necessary they should be in recognition of her travail and triumph and my father's relief and pride. I have been more or less ignoring my birthday for years now.

Today meet Peggy Denny to deliver Liberal literature for Thursday canvas. It pours with rain but we go. 'What good Liberals we are!' she remarks, handing me sopping pamphlets. We get cigarettes at a small store. We discuss Corbusier. She, as the former Mrs Val Harding, has entertained him, has seen his house and other work in Paris and does not think a great deal of either.[168] I think the only way of coping with the world's huge population will be to house them in the Corbusier manner as described in today's *News Chronicle*.

Peggy D. is an autumn tree, a brown and gold beech leaf. She chooses always those sorts of colourings for her clothes and furniture – and as she handles them they are very attractive, very right and justly expressive. She has a beech-bronze mackintosh, she wears browns, autumn

---

168 Valentine Harding, her former husband, was an architect best known for his work with Tecton, the partnership led by Berthold Lubetkin. He helped design Highpoint One flats in Highgate, parts of London Zoo, the Six Pillars building in Dulwich, and his own house in Burnham Beeches (which has been described by one architectural critic as 'adventurous'). He was killed during the retreat from Dunkirk in 1940.

yellows and old gold. So unlike me: severe white walls, plain furniture, no objets d'art. She does not like gardening, cannot arrange flowers, and yet we seem to have so much in common. What I like most about her is that she has a complete full life of her own and does not envy me mine, but is interested and sympathetic, is alive to what is going on outside her own domestic circle. I do like her, more and more.

This is the age of the middle-classes. I want to expand on this subject sometime. There was an age when kings predominated – the priests, the trading classes of the Renaissance, the aristocrats – and then gradually through these last two centuries, the business man, the professional and the artist. The working-classes may come into their own standards and way of life – a Butlin camp existence extended and refined and beyond our present comprehension – but today is still ours, we of the middle-class without vast wealth, power, or responsibility or bitter economic struggles.

Tuesday, 9 November

The days tick by quickly like minutes, busily, happily. I wonder when the reckoning will come and what I shall do if I can't sell 'Peg'. She has come back from the Porcupine Press (in financial difficulties) and gone to the Pilot Press under Tom's patronage. N. makes snarky infuriating remarks such as, 'I could have told you about the publishers but you have to find out for yourself.'

Tonight I am off to a Liberal meeting in Slough. I am enjoying this work though I am sure I shall never become a really good canvasser. I slide through my interviews as quickly as possible, hoping I shan't be asked awkward questions or expected to explain too much.

Wednesday, 17 November

Do the laundry, which has to be taken next door, where Lady S. detains me about an article by Aldous Huxley in *World Review*, and with remarks about my hair which raise all the old conflict. From my own family in early years onward I've been told I have 'such lovely hair – if only you'd take a little trouble with it!' It makes me feel I must be indeed a very lazy woman, and that the same comments could be applied to my complexion, figure, hands, and clothes. I am sorry, hair, if I neglect you, but you are temperamental, which no one understands, and we have only Mrs Hampton in the village to thank that people notice you at all. I can't manage you on my own but I daresay I should brush you a great deal more than I do – but there never seems to be time.

Huxley's article very good but very depressing. There is not and won't be enough food to feed world population adequately. What are we to do? My inner, secret answer to all these problems, but which seems too foolish to utter because I cannot defend it, is, 'God will provide.' This comes from my ingrained early training which I can not shake off. I still believe in a benevolent, fatherly individual who takes a deep personal interest not only in me and all my small concerns but in every other person in the world. Yet when it comes to prayer, to talking directly with God as so many C of E clergymen and others declare one can do, and that he listens and replies, I cannot believe. I believe there is immense help to oneself in thinking good thoughts, in formulating certain kinds of prayer and saying them over in the heart – even so little a phrase as 'God within me' – and that in this way, if persisted in, one contacts a valuable source of goodness without which one would drift into the path of self-destruction and disintegration. But when one prays for an immediate, concrete answer to something – say money, urgently needed, a fine day for a special occasion, or advice on what to do in a particular and troubling situation – then God doesn't [listen]. You have to work these things out for yourself.

Sunday, 21 November
As I drew out my dictionary, Virginia Woolf's *Walter Sickert: a Conversation* fell onto the floor.[169] Have just re-read it, wondering a

---

169 Sickert was often judged the most 'literary' and 'novelistic' of painters; his appeal to both Woolf and Jean is clear.

little why I had bought it thirteen years or more ago. There is a lot, I think, that I am forgetting about myself – of why I so much wanted to write, how easily I was moved by phrases, movements, a colour, or a scene. Encouraged by the Bartlett School teaching, I had developed something of a painter's sensitivity which I have let lie dormant too long.

I have often felt aware of things – atmosphere, other people's reactions – a sort of pattern of something that I can't put into words. 'Perhaps,' Graham Howe once said to me, 'the next time you come you'll tell me how you feel.' And not until today has anything of his meaning really filtered through to me. That I can feel – i.e. be conscious of feeling only, no words, no thought form in the mind at all – I know, and deeply at times. The trouble has been, partly, that I am always wanting to put all my experience into words, and when you stop to analyse and translate a feeling in the moment of feeling it, it begins to ebb away. Something is vitiated, lost. And why I have been doing this all my life is, perhaps, to escape pain. That is why in all major emotional upheavals I have rushed to my journal, as to aspirins. But I needn't start at this dramatic end of the scale. I feel, for instance, so intensely about my cats, I love them so dearly. I want to record their lives and their poses and absurd expressions and the light and shade on their silly, soft delicious little bodies, the tabby markings, the delicate eyebrows, the twitching paw.

The things one can 'feel' like this throughout the day are endless. The milk bottle by the kitchen door, the pail of 'pig' refuse, a cobweb on the stair, the movement of people in a crowded shopping street. Sordid, greedy, drab, but works of God also with life streaming from and around them. Let it all soak in, feel it, and then, like Sickert 'cloaked in the divine gift of silence, paint: lies, paltriness, splendour, depravity, endurance, beauty – it is all there . . .' without analysing, criticising, pulling it to pieces, pointing a moral, trying to rip away, or reform, or whitewash the lies, paltriness and depravity. It must all be accepted and endured, digested. The intellect tends to tear it all to pieces.

Monday, 29 November

Conversing with Lydia on the phone just now she told me some news that she herself only learned a few days ago. Some twelve months since A. Mc (Mac) was killed in a car crash. He had been suffering from blackouts, was driving himself and was thought to have passed out before the car crashed. Twelve months ago. I shed a few tears because for a long time now I have had only warm feelings for him, when I did think of him. I have never felt lastingly bitter, never. I could perhaps have loved him – I did as much as it was possible; now I don't know. If I ever deceived myself that I had not sometimes a shadow of a hope that he might walk again one day into my life, I can do so no longer. I shall not turn into a Josephine – I couldn't, I am much too of the earth, earthy. But when was it I went with Lydia and the others to that circle at the MSA? When someone with a smiling face and blue eyes and very fond of me was said to have been at my father's side? I had thought then that it might have been my S. African, Chris, of long long ago. Curious. It would be interesting to have another sitting and see if this man comes through again. I don't really want to try. I feel it might be so easy to get some sort of exciting message and then, there one would be – in the swamp. How simple, how satisfying it might be! To shut oneself off from the rest of this life and devote oneself to this 'ghost'.

The news makes little difference to my life, to what I am now doing and planning to do. Not one iota. It just puts the finale on any daydreams I may have been in danger of dreaming. Anyway there's not time for such indulgences. Phone went again just now, pulling me back to today again. Peggy D. re Liberal matter and a meeting tomorrow.

Sunday, 12 December

And not only day-to-day matters pull me to earth, but hard economic facts. I am becoming alarmingly impoverished and I must soon do something about it. Since Sept/Oct I have spent over £100. My overdraft is well over £250 and increasing steadily, my income (unearned) under £200 and no earnings coming in. Still have £3,000 war loan (1914–18 war) and half a house so that it may seem foolish to panic like this. But I want to reserve enough to buy a place of my own – say, at least £2,000. And meanwhile I must live, and costs are rising terrifyingly.

A job? Yes, but I want my job to be writing. All my training and experience and growing confidence point to it – and nowhere else. Not journalistic work in an office which calls for experience on a periodical of some sort, which I haven't had. But writing books, articles and doing work perhaps for the BBC. If K.M. still refuses to sell Wee (though I must somehow manage to stay here till Babs has finished her schooling) then it looks as though I must really abandon this 'cottage of my own' dream for a while. This is hard medicine to swallow but possibly what I deserve.

Perhaps I could go back to Homefield, even buy Pooh out, keep one room there for myself, and let the rest of the house furnished. I am in easy reach of London from there and could use it as an office and living quarters pro-tem very conveniently. A 'cottage in the country' must be kept for my old age, although I feel terrified now that if I ever let go of my hold here I'll never have another chance, that I'll just go on getting deeper into the financial slough and never get out again. I know I'm nearly 40 but I don't feel in the least middle aged or 'set'.

Thursday, 6 January 1949

An evening to myself. Wonderful. Babs and her friend A. are at a party. Ever since her arrival in the summer my niece has baffled me a little. She is a quiet little thing with adults, stolid, stoical and in between her pleasures sulky, bored, contemptuous – an overwhelming indifference, a shattering contempt for all one's efforts to get near her, to please her. While N. was here over Xmas she brightened considerably. N. has a marvellous capacity for drawing out children, but even with her I noticed the sulky mood.

Babs has much charm and sweetness in her nature which N. recognised and liked and it is this side of her I wish very much to see develop. But gradually I think I am discovering the other side of the coin – what lies at the root of her quietness and sulky moods. It is not the sensitivity, the timidity and uncertainties from which I suffered, although she possesses the normal little girl shyness. It is, I think, because she has managed to get her own way all the time with her parents and friends abroad. Used to much entertainment, to admiration and success, she wants it all the time. In her silences I perceive something cautious, canny, calculating. She is summing the other person up: saying to herself, how much can I get out of this sucker? This has become apparent since A. has been here. A. I do like immensely – a tall, gawky schoolgirl, with good manners and obviously not as spoilt as Babs. Babs is the dominant one in this relationship, and it is A. who does what Babs wants.

Babs is in danger of growing into a thoroughly selfish woman – she has quite a strong character already, and I am sure rejects everything an adult may try to say to her if she doesn't want to listen. I can see why her parents decided she must go to a strict school in England. Ivy wrote me something like this a little while ago, that in Portugal Babs has been thought the 'cats whiskers' at everything she did, meeting with too easy success and having no discipline at school. She hated Oakdene at first but seems to have settled down and be making friends there now. I think she always will make friends easily with girls and boys, but I am not sure whether I can like her for it. But Babs is my brother Pooh's daughter and for him I will love her and help her as much as I can.

Tom phoned on Xmas day. The Pilot Press is definitely interested in the MS and it has been handed from one VIP to another.

Saturday, 8 January
Darkness and country quiet outside. The still, brooding branches, like claws, like lace, and the light and warmth and quietness within the

room, ticking clock and occasional bubble from the boiler in the kitchen – these are the only sounds that reach me.

The wonderful relief at being on my own again! I must be at heart myself a very selfish woman, getting what I want, the sort of life that pleases me in my own way, just as ruthlessly, inexorably as Babs tends to do. And it may be that this cold, selfish side of me brings out the selfish side in her, so that I have only myself to blame if I sometimes find her difficult – she is a dear little thing, really, and real love will bring out the lovableness in her. Perhaps I have been over-anxious, wanting to please, wanting to establish myself as the trusted, admired and loved guardian aunt too quickly.

11 p.m.: I washed up, prepared mutton stew and put it on to cook, washed my smalls. Picked up the Mass Observation Xmas Bulletin devoted to Panel observers' descriptions of the traditional Xmas.[170] There was something vaguely familiar about the first quotation, and I discovered it was mine!, extracted from something I wrote for them last year and got lost in, carried back to Xmases of my childhood.

This is the first time I have found MO using anything of mine. I am designated 'Woman Architect, aged 36'. I have always felt a bit glum that from all the diary entries and Directives I have sent them they have never seemed to pick out anything for their reports. Now my vanity is appeased and my interest renewed. I shall start the diary again, which I think I have not touched since the spring. I also look on this as an excellent omen.

Friday, 14 January

When I woke yesterday morning I remembered having dreamt in the night of myself trying to learn the part of Lady Macbeth at very short notice.

Yesterday afternoon I went to hear Phyllis at the National Book

---

170 In addition to collecting random journal entries, Mass Observation frequently sent out 'directives' – structured questionnaires on specific subjects – to its co-operative panel. As with the journals, these were collated anonymously.

League – she was advertised in their programme of talks for this week as giving one on the 'Literary Detective'.[171] I had not let her know I was going and thought that it would be on the detective in literature, but it was nothing of the sort. It was on detecting and collecting good books, and mainly for school children, of whom quite a few present. She read delightfully from some of her own favourites – *Alice in Wonderland*, *Just So Stories*, – an extract from Emerson on friendship, Rupert Brooke, two of Shakespeare's Sonnets, and finished with Lady Macbeth's letter scene! Strange beyond belief.

Then I went up to the Information Bureau, as I had written for a lot of books on eighteenth-century women before Xmas and had no reply. Nice young females received me and as soon as I said what I wanted, one exclaimed 'But that is just what I am doing now! As soon as you came in I knew you were going to say eighteenth-century women!' We discussed further – they are finding, as I have, that there aren't many good books on this subject. 'Are you thinking of writing one?' said one of them. 'There's a need for it . . .' Just as when two years ago I was making enquiries at Slough Public Library for books on Peg W., the assistant Librarian said, 'Are you writing a book on her, how exciting!'

Wednesday, 19 January
She went back to school yesterday. Bless her heart, she does seem to like being here. Short, of course, of returning to her parents and Portugal where all the fun and sun are. She asked if she might come home every other weekend during the term. She says little about it herself but from other people and her parents it seems that she really has had 'a wonderful time' these holidays. Ivy writes, 'I don't think I can ever thank you enough for all you have done and are doing for the child. You have a share in her as an aunt, but there are aunts and

171 The NBL (formerly the National Book Council) was established to promote reading and the value of books. It became Booktrust in 1992.

aunts. Thank you again my dear.' Success of any kind always bewilders me. I get cynical about it – but that from Ivy is genuine, means something. Ivy is a reserved person and not given to gush. Definitely not.

Not being able to get on with my own work makes me bored, impatient, restless, but I hold it all in, I wait, I listen to what she has to say as amiably as I can, chiding myself sometimes for not having more to give her. But 39 and 15 is a big gap – bigger than I'd realised. All I want is her trust, her confidence in me and for her to make her own life while she is with me, and for me to be able to cope with any difficulties that arise, in the right way and with courage.

Sunday, 30 January

I started recently acquired Penguin edition of Elizabeth Myers's *A Well Full of Leaves*. Though thick fog yesterday morning and not feeling at all well, I went up to Joan's using up last day of the week's season tickets to Paddington, and was absorbed in this book all the long way to Golders Green. Forgot my ailments, entranced. At intervals while at Joan's I dipped in again and then on the crawling, dismal journey home.

The cottage is shabby, disgustingly dirty, cold. The cats had been shut in the kitchen all the time since I left yesterday, without much food as I expected to be home last night. They had upset my wood and odd paper boxes all over the kitchen floor, torn up spare magazine papers, helped themselves to a cake of shredded wheat and scattered the remnants, dirtied in the coal scuttle. In fact, the kitchen was indescribable chaos. Tomorrow I will set my chill little house in order and relight the fire. Tonight I will write of Elizabeth Myers' first novel.

I think this is a most remarkable, important book. Her characters are not real life portraits, the end most vulgarly dramatic, the whole effort a little over-indulgent and humourless. I have said all the worst things that occur to me about it, judged just as a novel. But it's so much more than a novel about ordinary people. The characters are not ordinary people, they are symbols. Beauty, Learning, Art and Religion – children of cowardice and stupidity. Beauty marries wealthy ignorance; Learning endures patiently his dull little life till Beauty and Ignorance give him his opportunity. Art, through the painful evolution of his character distorted by stupidity's cruelty, wins spectacular fame and worldly success. While Religion suffers and learns and sheds light on living, is wedded to Love and dies. It is all as simple, as medieval as that, but it holds the attention because of the way it is written, the lovely, luminous handling of words and the pointing to a way of life we have forgotten how to live.

This is what I was trying to say here on Nov. 21st. We do not drink enough of these simple idle things, these divine and matchless moments: 'The sunny window reflected on the door-knob, the look of candlelight on the scullery wall, coal-dust, the handle of the bread knife, the python in the hot glass cage in the Zoo, aspects of moonlight and water, the taste of marmalade, the furthest lamp at the end of the pier . . .' all these sort of things and a hundred, hundred more, in every hour waiting for our notice, to be absorbed and understood. Again and again I have had faint prickings, little gleams of suspicion of the truth of all this, but to discover this truth for oneself is more than I am capable of. I do not open my eyes and my heart wide enough.

Somewhere too – but I'm getting too tired and numb fingered to go on – she draws the distinction between selfishness and self concentration, and explains the difference between morbid introspection and trying to know oneself, deeply, fully. I believe in all this, as utterly as did Elizabeth Myers but not quite so fervently – or so dearly. It seems to me she was tearing it out of herself, anxious to get it all out, crystallised and in print before she died.[172]

---

172 Although now largely forgotten, Myers was a singular novelist and short story writer of the 1940s, with a passion for aphorisms and morality tales driven by her Catholicism. She died, after a decade of ill-health, in 1947, aged thirty-four.

Saturday, 12 February

About midnight. Outside is a full moon, a white still night. On the
kitchen hob a kettle sings, washing hangs on clothes horse round the
dying fire, Dinah sits on my manuscript files. I have finished at last
re-typing 'Peg'. It has been purgatory, standing between me and everything else I need to be doing. But it is done now and checked, and
tomorrow I shall pack the top copy to send it to Michael Sadleir
(*Fanny by Gaslight* and *Blessington-D'Orsay*) at Constable on Monday.
I pray and pray that something may happen about this effort of mine
soon. (Still no word from the PP, and nothing from Tom for three
weeks.) I seem to have gone on so long, waiting, waiting, hearing
echoes of hopeful tidings, hints of favourable news, but nothing
definite . . . always those shifting shadows, the deep and anxious
valley. I can't bear much more of it. When I dig down into myself I
strike a vein of deep, corroding cynicism. I don't believe in myself,
or the goodness or use of anything. But the silly thing is, if one can
only see it this way, cynicism has a value in itself and will only do
damage if dug up out of its proper place and put to wrong uses. I
must remember that. It is there to anchor one's optimism, to check
one's vanity and egotism, to help keep the personality balanced, and
to clear the air of sentimentality. A useful antidote to cheap emotionalism.

And my impatience, my disgustingly childish whimpers and moans
and storms – when I feel I could tear and crush and stamp and destroy,
destroy, destroy. When I want to do it in the grand manner, not as a
pygmy, but as a giant, causing earthquakes and whirlwinds and huge
tempests! (Oh no one, I know, would believe this of me, but never
mind!) There is at the core of these storms still that feeling of resentment and frustration, that deep sense of inferiority, of never being
very good at anything – mediocre, mediocre, watered down copies of
better things, an echo, a shadow, no substance, no strength. And the
40s ahead of me and still no sign of a husband! Just one of the 3
million surplus women, luckless, unwanted, unnoticed . . . Oh, I crawl,

I crawl! It's not fair O Lord, it is not fair, I do not deserve to be unwanted, unnoticed . . . and so on and on!

One does seem to reach a point where one can go on no longer self-sufficient, independent, alone in this way. Yet even as I write this I hesitate, not at all sure what I want. 'Someone who understands?' But haven't I been crying for this since my mother died and hasn't it always been better for me to work it out for myself? I think I do need the warm, personal exchange of the teacher – the living touch, which is what I have had only very briefly from Graham Howe in my life, and should have had much more in my earlier years. We all do, that heart-to-heart exchange, the living touch of wisdom. Not from books or lectures – that is only a substitute when you miss the real thing. Yes, it is this I am sure that I need, someone to draw me out and make me talk, make me angry, even confused, but make me talk, give me confidence to put into words all these dim thoughts that never receive expression, or at best are let loose to be lost in here.

Sunday, 13 February
Before I slept last night I opened Neville Cardus's *Autobiography* (and very interesting it is too) and fell upon these words: 'Humour is a necessary salt, and without a corrective of cynicism all seems foolishness and callow.'[173] I do not walk alone.

In my work I know I can do a job conscientiously, I can make a home, make people comfortable, give them good food and all the right sort of atmosphere – which is no mean feat, though sometimes I doubt my power of love towards them. But I want to earn money by writing – and I want it to be good, alive writing, useful and contributory, creative in a real sense, not dramatically clever, highbrow, or syrupy dope for the 'masses'.

When Cardus met Delius, Delius said to him, 'Don't read yourself

---

173 Neville Cardus, the influential cricket and music correspondent for the *Manchester Guardian*.

daft. Trust to your emotions.' And Cardus goes on, '. . . theory should . . . come after personal experience and much humble surrender.' And this I think has been one of the big problems, one of the big stumbling blocks for me and my kind. Cardus lashes out at us, the new generation, after the 1914–1918 war, 'unhappy and hot and bothered . . . dithering with self consciousness . . . Once on a time the young men from the universities looked to the Army, the Church, politics and the civil service and school mastering . . . (but by 1920) the discovery had been made of the possibility of careers for the educated classes in journalism and literature and music and theatre. Taste was better than ever no doubt (that was the trouble) . . . but it was all a product of education and middle-class breeding; there was no hint that these people, these dilettantes, ever felt deeply or were impelled riskily by imagination. We could anticipate their direction day to day, their preferences and prejudices; they would be as consistent as sterility.'

That is exactly the trouble with middle class education: theory is rammed into our heads and down our throats, stifling our hearts, from the time we start school and when we move on into the universities, it is a great banner that unfurls and wraps us round completely. With 'unearned' incomes to carpet our way for us we cannot help but become dilettantes to a greater or less degree – though I doubt whether many of the really successful writers today have had an 'easy' early life. But I don't think Cardus means such people anyway. He is hitting out at a type I just escape being because of my lack of confidence but can be classed with because I fit in nowhere else. I imagine there are quite a number of them working for the BBC at present.

Saturday, 19 February

I wish that something very pleasant would happen today – that Tom would come with friends to explain what has happened to the MS at the PP.

My hair is looking 'perfect' today: I wish it were always so. I could meet any of my old lovers without feeling age-conscious.

Sunday, 3 April

I have a difficult letter to write so perhaps it would be wise to sort myself out here first.

N. accuses me of not being strong-minded enough with Babs, of not keeping her 'in her place', and is making a bit of fuss about coming here this Easter weekend. It is all of course quite true. With her usual skilful accuracy N. hits the nail on the head. I am, I know, frightened, and this must be apparent to the child. I am not and never have been self-assertive enough – part of all my troubles, says N., and something she thinks that through being able to stay here at Wee, I have managed to escape grappling with and am now having to 'pay' for. How very formidable all this sounds. I cannot help wondering whether her criticism is not a little influenced by the raging envy she feels for my circumstances and opportunities. I see her now, grey faced, elbows on the table, biting her nails as she mentioned Wee and the 'leisure' I have here.

But it was a fair enough judgement and one I cannot ignore. It has cracked the ground between us and I can, by the way I write now in the letter that must go to her soon, widen the breach if I will. And in fact, I realised this morning, part of me does will, very much. The relationship has always been a little more than I felt capable of bearing.

After the weekend she was here in March, full of her new Theosophical adventures and 'expansion', I felt – as I told her – like a pack-mule trying to keep pace with a high spirited race horse (a very restless, rather vicious one too), and for nearly an hour after she had gone on Sunday I wept from sheer nervous exhaustion and no other reason. I just couldn't 'take it'. She had then said or done nothing to upset my vanity in any way, it was just the amount of her own life that she seemed to want me to carry that I felt to be too great. And not only is the thrust of her own life too strong for me, she overwhelms me with her desire to live mine for me. Her tyrannies still trouble me, her energies sap mine. But she realises nothing of this, I think.

I had a new sort of technique for my dealings [with Babs] before this came up. I think I try to come down too much to Babs's level. If I kept myself more occupied and withdrawn in my own affairs it would help to keep her in her place as the little girl she still is. And in this way I could be more firm with the ease and confidence that can only make firmness effective. I am too anxious to please, to understand and be sympathetic – and this only arouses contempt in the young. I must give her less of my own time than I did at Xmas. Oh, how I am dreading it all now, more than ever! How I wish I could talk it over with someone of wisdom.

The Pilot Press, who have had the Peg MS for nearly six months, has gone bankrupt. Tom and his friend have been very concerned and kind and have passed the MS onto the agents, Brown.[174] I have also heard from Michael Sadleir of Constables, who have sent the MS back, but with a really kind, encouraging criticism. This is the sort of battle I expected to have to fight.

---

174 The literary agency Curtis Brown is still a flourishing concern. When Jean's manuscript arrived, the company was celebrating fifty years of representing such writers as D.H. Lawrence, A.A. Milne and Daphne du Maurier.

37.

To Be Published

Wednesday, 13 April 1949

Have been re-organising my diary writings. Shall keep this book solely for those personal outpourings I cannot contain within myself – my inner griefs and tangles and disease. By which I do implore the reader not to judge me wholly but remember that I have an outer and busy life in which the inner may be detected by the discerning but which also brings me much happiness and content that I do not often trouble to capture in words.

My letter to N. last week produced two telephone calls and a promise to write. She has taken it all gallantly. She feared I had been taking her comments too personally. I must not forget to note, also, that plans are afoot in earnest for me to go to Portugal for the summer holidays with Babs. Our names are down on waiting list for passages on a boat due to leave about July 30th, and I am already getting clothes together.

Tuesday, 19 April

Another deadly, paralytic mood enfolds me. I feel I 'ought' to be doing many things but cannot get started on any of them. Babs is out, I have had nearly the whole day to myself and have done nothing except read Marco Pallis's *Peaks and Lamas*.[175]

---

175 A classic, from the late 1930s, about mountaineering and the application of

Wavell, on radio the other night, speaking on reading, said that books should never be a substitute for action, good conversation or independent thought.[176] He for one, he said, had taken refuge when young in reading when visitors came, and suffered now in trying to converse well; he could not grasp the idea expressed in the spoken word quickly enough or arrange his own thoughts in time to reply. This has happened to many of us, but Wavell has at least become a man of action with a sound reputation in his profession. I have read, and still do, so much too much, allowing myself no time to digest any of it before gulping at something else. I don't know what I want at this moment except release, or some sort of resolution, of the continuing state of anxiety. There is always something to ferment and perpetuate it – N., Babs, the book, my finances and economic future, the next book, my single state, my never ending faults and fears and failings – a perpetual grumbling and whining and shivering and moaning within!

It has been a rare and wonderful Easter, today cooler but still blue and gold and heart-breaking. One of the most difficult lessons for the westerner steeped in the Christian tradition who is studying Buddhism, must be the one of real self-denial, of relinquishing the popular conception of heaven in which 'I' is rewarded and preserved in perpetuity. We have a very strongly developed (and in fact deliberately encouraged) 'impulse to individual experience'. We do not like to lose sight of or hold on the thread that seems to be peculiarly 'us', or the idea that we shall continue with it, distinct and recognisable, after death.

Buddhism. The *Zen and the Art of Motorcycle Maintenance* of its day. Pallis travelled extensively in the Himalayas, and was the opposite of the 'conquering' breed of mountaineer, opting instead for a deep spiritual exploration of the local cultures and beliefs. It was this aspect, rather than the crampons, that clearly appealed to Jean.

176 The senior military commander Field Marshall Earl Wavell in his last broadcast. Wavell revealed that he would repeat lines of poetry as a calming device when under fire.

All these different religions and the varying diversions in each are very bewildering. Each seems to have a major snag on closer examination, or, shall we say, some difficult obstacle to be accepted. The need for a guiding religious principle in our lives today is paramount, and one that is within the reach of the average man and woman struggling sincerely with their personal difficulties. (That is, within the reach of their understanding and practice, to help them on to the higher path of their choice.) In the world now there seems to be such a need for some helpful religion, a re-flowering of the awareness of the spirit and its destiny. Even at this low level in our search for knowledge, I am sure it is true to distinguish, as Pallis points out, the difference between 'rational knowledge' and 'real knowledge'. The first comes from university courses and manuals of philosophy, the other is 'the fruit of a direct intuitive experience – not so much acquired by accretion . . . as . . . a thing already there from the moment that the obstacles to its realisation have ceased to be.'

Monday, 24 April

I must try and 'answer' Lundberg and Farnham's *Modern Woman* (Harper, New York, 1947). An able exposition of a pressing modern problem, presenting us with a formidable challenge we should not ignore.[177] According to these authors I am a complete and hopeless failure as a woman, my only possible – if at all – means of salvation or restoration to psychic health is through their sort of clinical treatment, here and now quite beyond my reach. Logically, therefore, this book could drive me to suicide, and although I may never hear of them I shall be surprised if it does not do so to others. It is quite

---

177 The full title was *Modern Woman: The Lost Sex*. In something of a cause célèbre, Ferdinand Lundberg and Marynia F. Farnham, a publicity executive and a psychiatrist, argued that women had lost their way. Feminism (classified as any striving beyond the kitchen or nursery) was regarded as a calamity, producing only 'a vain and foolish fancy, a she-monster'. The modern woman was cited as the cause of all modern ills, from war to the economy.

merciless to all who will or cannot accept their diagnosis and suggested cures.

But I am grateful to it for at least a few clarifications. Some useful information, historically. A good bibliography. A clearing up of any last doubt I may have had concerning masturbation. And further revelations of the reality of my relations with A.M. Or should I have said, release from some doubt and fear and feeling of guilt concerning my ability to experience an orgasm. This, they say, may be had – and should be – as much and more than in other ways, by vaginal stim-ulation. Which I knew nothing about and was not expecting, but experienced ~~intensely~~ (I wrote 'intensely' then felt I was trying to be dramatic) indeed and delightfully with A.M. (to some extent too with Hugh). And there were moments, too, when we were both 'suffused with tenderness.' This is not an exaggeration, I am sure, grown in retrospect, but true, and is vivid still. I cannot then be quite such a failure . . . or the potentialities for success are there yet.

The danger of this book – of perhaps anything like this, is that it enables one to sit back and pigeon-hole oneself and friends into damaging and arid compartments. One thing which makes it gravely suspect to me is that there is no mention whatever, anywhere, of Jung. The authors claim that they are not Freudian but discuss Freud's theories freely – and Havelock Ellis and others, but Jung might not exist. Is there really no alternative to the attainment of true balance and psychic ease except through full acceptance and development of one's maternal faculties?

I think this problem of neurosis is much more apparent and urgent among American women than here. I feel its views are limited – sound as far as they go, but dangerous, very, because they do not go farther. Women, obviously, cannot be saved by analysis alone.

Friday, 6 May
Babs back to school yesterday. I don't know at all how far I am being successful in my role as aunt or not. There were none of the sulks

these holidays that she had at Xmas, yet she still seems to give out in her silences a measure of scorn for me that I find chilling. In fact exasperating. She sometimes seems such a dull, self-centred, silly little girl. Oh, how boring teen-age interests and ideas can be! I do not seem able to 'touch' her at all. But she is not a demonstrative child and seems to have all the affection from her parents she needs. She has a great deal of sound common sense for her age and a turn for practical activities such as games, riding, dancing, dressmaking, cooking – although she says now and then she wishes she could write, and can write easily, and professes an interest in people.

Perhaps I see too many of my own faults in her: I was probably just as selfish at her own age (am I any less so now?), intolerant, unheeding, ungrateful. She makes me feel middle-aged and incompetent, and perhaps despises, instinctively, the childless, man-less adult female (though if I were married, with a troop of children, she might loathe her cousins and uncle).

Of course I want to be the child's shining heroine, adored and envied, but this sickening sort of vanity has no chance to develop at all – fortunately I suppose. The trouble seems to be, as always with my family (aunts, uncles, cousins as well as brother), I want very much to like her but find myself barred by an insufficiency of interests in common. I know so many more people who are not my relatives that I like much better than any of them.

Saturday, 7 May
[A loose-leaf enclosure headed 'Miscellaneous']
This weekend I intend shall be 'mine'. No more housework than necessary. No Liberal activities. No visitors – we hope. Just me alone with my diaries, book, meals, cats and conscience. It is such heaven to be alone, yet I have such feelings of guilt about it and know that I should not enjoy a state of solitude and relative idleness for more than a few days at a time. I am sure my mother longed for just this sort of life and was never able to have it. I don't know that it is worth

sacrificing husband and children for it, but I think it is a need that many women feel that should be fulfilled if possible. There's Lizzie M. She has two fine little boys, a nice home and a husband she loves and trusts – I don't know any family where emotional conditions are more favourable. Yet she is not happy. She has not a minute to herself the whole day, is worn out, drained, longing to be able to do other things, for some of my freedom, but can see no hope of it for years and years. Peter earns a steady salary but not enough to give her the domestic help to give her that much leisure. There must be thousands like her – intelligent, sensitive, interested in cultural things, young, wanting to enjoy the simple pleasures available (an evening out with her husband, a cycle ride into the country on a fine afternoon) but chained because of their own right and instinctive choice of man and family.

Joan's situation is similar although she is not really happy with Vahan and doesn't love little Hugo. But she is just as tied and tired and hungry for leisure.

Peggy D. too has her problems, although her children are all at school and she has a daily woman to help with the housework. She is very happy with her new husband except when it comes to politics. He remains blindly Conservative and refuses to listen to her at all. He naturally resents her going out in the evenings so that she feels she must restrict her political activities to the minimum when he is at home – and as they nearly all take place in the evening it is a bit difficult. I say, 'Yet if he wanted to go out in the evening on such affairs he'd go . . . it doesn't seem fair . . .' And she answers, 'Yes, but that is just all part of being a woman' Which does seem to be unalterably so.

I wait for my lunch to cook. All I want to do this afternoon is to read *Brideshead* here in the still sitting room undisturbed, praising heaven for these hours, adoring the lilac and forget-me-not in the green garden beyond. Quiet, quiet. How terrifying the thought that I may have to let this jewel go.

Thursday, 26 May

I pause in the middle of spring cleaning to record that I am feeling better than I have done for months. Am not sure whether it is due to i) course of cod-liver-oil and malt, ii) a really good haircut-and-set two weeks ago which makes all the difference to my appearance and morale, iii) realisation that my responsibilities as Guardian Aunt are nearly over for this (school) year, iv) news that landlady K.M. has really gone to Australia (will she stay there??), v) meeting N. again last week on most amiable terms, vi) Joan and Tessa coming here for Whitsun, vii) surprisingly good passport photos which reveal that at 39 I do not look soured or neglected, viii) finances being not too troublesome at the moment.

Wednesday, 8 June

But the black moods return, beating at me like vultures with all-devouring wings. Irritation upon irritation leading to despair. A grinding, hopeless impatience. I have gone on so long waiting for news of the MS. I can't bear it. I suppose I must up and make myself a nuisance again, write letters, push, push, push and stamp and scream to get a hearing, to get any notice taken. I have a longing for 'revenge' – to get back at life for always, as it seems, withholding what I most want – by tearing, wounding, destroying. See the good blood flow! Here and here and again here! I will stab you to death, to death I hate you so. All this milk-and-water mealiness about love and forbearance – pah! It doesn't work. I have tried hard enough, but what has it done for me . . . See how my dagger shines! There it goes . . . to the heart . . . And now there is stillness . . . at last, at last.

Sunday, 19 June

And in reply to that silly outburst, life gently bowled me over and boxed my ears. Have had the vilest cough I have suffered in years. Not one cigarette in a week, not even the herbal kind, and I lying awake at night thinking of pleurisy and pneumonia and my Will. Now I am with Ethel.

Some weeks ago I decided that what I have been trying to do for some time now is to de-N. myself. I must seem awfully dumb – no end of a sucker – not to have realised this before and that for years I have been living under an N. spell. She has, or had, such skill in convincing the feeble minded and gullible like me, that she was always uncontrollably right in her opinions, and for a long while her life and adventures seemed wonderfully glamorous and enviable. I have ceased to envy her for a long time now, in any way, but I am only just real-ising that her opinions also don't matter. I don't mean that they are necessarily wrong, or not worth noting (in fact they are often very right and worth consideration), but that my actions and the whole colour of my life [should not] be determined by them.

Friendship should not be conditional. One should not approach another with an axe to grind. But please please tell me what to do when the other seems to come at you always first with an axe ready to rip you to pieces? Does one lay oneself, undefended, open to the torture?

Thursday, 14 July
We are to fly to Portugal – a miracle. I had been dreading the four days at sea, at the mercy of the younger generation. But this week I learned there was no hope of passages for any Lisbon people this month or next, so Pooh has said we may fly. I am thrilled at the thought, beyond adequate expression. We shall be there in four hours, probably taking all our luggage with us. Josephine is coming to take charge after Bank Holiday weekend. There is no one else able to take on Wee as I had hoped and pay me something for it. But the cats' welfare is my greatest anxiety and with Josephine here I shall have no fears for them.

Having read this book through from April 23 entry, yes, N. has her witch-like, bitch-like phases. Let me state that courageously and adhere to it. But read Elizabeth Myers's story 'Second Sight'. People mustn't be profaned by total rejection. Grant people even what you hate in them, then on the wings of this tolerance will ride the things you can admire. You must forgive, and look for those crumbs of redemption that everyone, everyone lets fall. If you can meet a good man (said Confucius) try to emulate him; if you meet a bad man, look into your own heart.

Thursday, 21 July

I take with me Christmas Humphreys's *Walk On!*, T.S. Eliot's poems (Penguin) and some Osbert Sitwell short stories. There will be no more time for anything here – so au revoir my private heart.

Friday, 23 September

We arrived home at Wee again on Monday afternoon last, the threads all waiting to be gathered together and the pattern continued. Babs went back to school on Wednesday and Josephine left this morning. There is still a vast amount of sorting and clearing up to be done and the jungle in the garden to tackle. But I must pause for a moment, with a cup of tea after supper, to give my old love some attention.

I think the most important thing to note is the series of articles begun by Graham Howe in *Picture Post* Sept. 17th – a copy of which N. has sent me. 'Psychology,' he says, '. . . can show you to yourself, but it cannot give you what you want. It is an instrument of reflection, a mirror. It is not a mysterious cupboard from which hope, long disappointed, can at last be magically fulfilled . . . We should learn from our mistakes and not be ashamed of them . . . our mistakes . . . are our stepping stones to better travelling . . . Patterns repeat themselves like gramophone records that go on playing round and round: and we are blind until we are shown the point at which we dodged the real issue, the meaning of the situation by which we were confronted perhaps even in our infancy. Now we get our second chance to experience fully what we avoided then . . . the crucial fact is that the fate which has always so desperately dogged our footsteps is our own . . .'

Patterns repeat themselves . . . and my problems repeat, although I think I have been shown the point at which I dodged the real issue. I had a lovely holiday in Portugal, I tell everyone. And I did. But it is only half-truth. I somehow got myself thrust right back into the old slough: uncertain of myself, desperately shy, awkward and hanging back when I should have advanced. Again the little girl who couldn't make herself offer cigarettes to the Tommies until it was too late for them to accept.

My brother and sister in law were kindness itself. They couldn't have been nicer to me or made more effort, in their own way, to make me welcome and give me a good time. They gave a big cocktail party, made me a member of the club, would not let me pay for anything – not even cigarettes and letters – kept me in bed for breakfast, gave me huge meals and a tonic, sent up my afternoon tea, took me out and about, took me shopping, and spoilt me thoroughly. What more could I possibly ask for or expect?

Yet there was one thing which they did not, perhaps could not do and that needed only my own courage and determination to set right. I longed and longed to enter more fully into the social life of their circle. Going to the Club alone was agony, and one Sunday I ran away as I reached the door and heard voices within, and had to walk right down the beach by myself and back to gain courage to make the entrance I had to make. If I had played tennis, and been able to roller skate, or play bridge, if I had gone on my own at week-ends more often to watch the tennis and have tea . . . But underneath I know it was cowardice, lack of confidence in my own opinions and abilities. It was, I think, a very crucial and exacting test, and I failed.

And then came the voyage, by sea, home. But before I begin on that, what of the men in the community? Quite honestly, cross my heart, there were none who seemed even remotely eligible either for a passing affaire, or something more permanent. Most of them were youngish-to-middle aged, married men with young families, like my brother, pleasant, easy to know, easy to dance with, and a handful of junior bachelors ranging in age from early twenties to early thirties. All seemed quite likeable. In fact Colin Thomas, a lanky, slow but to me attractive 26 or so, I felt quite drawn to, but no opportunity gave me much chance for exploration. I never got really near any of them and felt that it did not greatly matter. I did not want any emotional complications, only to be one of the party, (fatal desire for a lone female when males are in a majority), and I was conscious of my age and had no wish to be thought cradle-snatching or after someone else's husband.

But one of the bachelors (31/32, I saw his passport) came home on the *Andes* with us. I knew him, as I knew the others, casually, and now I know him a great deal better and don't know how or why it has happened. He is a small man (Mac's height) but thin. In many ways a slighter edition of Hugh, the hands are the same and the set of the features, though D.B. has a much nicer nose. I am not in the least in love with him and cannot imagine myself in any permanent situation anywhere with him. But I like him, and physically the attraction is mutual and admitted, and admitted as such only. He confessed eventually that he was going to meet a girlfriend in England whom he intends to marry. But he is not sure. And now he seems less sure. It is all rather naughty by certain standards, but hugely gratifying. He phoned today from London and we have arranged to meet at the Cumberland Hotel on Tuesday. Perhaps I shall ask him for the day to Wee. 'I am a bad type,' he said. It seems to be, fatally, my type. But this time I don't care!

It has quite changed the colour – in retrospect – of my holiday, and I do say, with conviction, that I had a lovely time. But it was the voyage home that gave it that finish. Which only again shows what strange, unpredictable potency is contained in sex.

Sunday, 25 September

I have been stretched like a piece of elastic over a hard, bright interval and have snapped back into place with scarcely a pause. Everything here is exactly the same, the routine, the occupations, the people. It might have been a long dream, my holiday in Portugal, an extra day in bed. Only my clothes seem a little shabbier, a little more boring, the cottage dustier and more in need of new paint and clean covers than ever. Liberal activities are swamping all my spare moments again, I neglect the housework to clear the garden, cook and prepare the same kind of food in the same way, following the same round – wake, breakfast in bed reading papers, up, chores, shopping, see Peggy D., chores, lunch, garden, tea, garden, food to prepare, dusk at 7 p.m., more chores, meal, wireless, mending appointments, arranging visits, meetings . . . Tomorrow at 9 a.m., hairdresser, shopping, home preparing for rest of day, lunch [spent visiting] local paper with ad for insertion and to see an employment agency about a possible job, then on to stay with Joan at Golders Green.

Tuesday: what possibility can Tuesday's meeting bring but, we hope, a pleasant evening, shared memories and probable final parting? What more can come of it all than that?

Thursday, 29 September

And what did Tuesday's meeting bring? A very pleasant evening, yes. A promise that I would write to him now and then, and a promise from him to take back certain things for my family. He made, persistently throughout the evening, amorous advances that grew more and more intense and that I could not and did not want to resist, and he was saying all the time, 'Get married. Promise me you'll try to get married. A nice girl like you shouldn't still be free. You'll make someone a damned fine wife. And let me know when it happens, I'll be the first to send a wedding present.'

We met as arranged, we had tea, a drink, saw *The Third Man*, dined in Dean St and pub-crawled till 11 p.m. Then he insisted on coming all the way to Golders Green on the bus with me and to Joan's door. Joan insisted that I bring him in for a cup of tea (N. must be told of this gently) and then I saw him to the corner of Hoop Lane as we had missed our way coming and I was afraid he might lose his way back to the station. We sat on the cemetery wall saying good night. I almost became a fallen woman again among the gravestones. I could not get him to go. 'You're too darned attractive,' he said.

How my vanity has enjoyed all this! How desire wept for satisfaction! How pleased the hungry body, how appeased and touched the lonely heart. But now he is in Manchester, I have been for over 14 hours back at Wee, been to Oakdene, to a Lib. committee meeting and my mind is crowding out with other things the impression of Tuesday evening. Shall I see him again before he sails? I hope so, though we haven't a lot to talk about. I could not sleep for hours after he left me. I think he is unhappy. He said nothing about the girl he was supposed to be meeting here. I am much moved by his humility and his sympathy, but there is no fever in me. I think of him, fondly, gratefully, at intervals, and then forget the whole episode. I shall be hurt if he doesn't fulfil his promises, I shall be hurt if I hear nothing more and then later that he is to be married or something similar, but it would not be the inflamed and angry wound I suffered so often with Mac, and others.

Friday, 30 September
The cottage is at last beginning to feel normal again. I feel very well, full of energy, though period is late. No qualms of conscious about this (I am not his mistress, actually – yet), but it is curious that it should be so just now. I think it is because last month I was bathing in the icy Atlantic when it arrived and suffered some pain then. Or is it the new emotional upheaval or change of climate and rush of work?

I had told him quite a lot about myself on board, when his advances were even more intense. I hadn't married because, I thought, I hadn't wanted children. I had had lovers, four of them, and that the last one was killed in car smash. But I didn't say how shy I was, how I ran away from the men I really liked, got drawn to the pirate type, and could never rouse any interest in the men who were drawn to me, the nice, serious, dependable type.

Sunday, 2 October

O fabulous, wonderful weekend! The manuscript arrived back yesterday while Babs and I were having lunch. I cannot bear it, I thought . . . I won't look. But of course I had to. Curtis Brown have had an excellent offer from Hurst and Blackett, subject to certain revisions which I think I can manage easily, and on the whole want to do anyway.[178] There can be no doubt about accepting it and forging ahead with the necessary work. I still can't quite believe it – everyone thrilled. Little Babs squeaked and beamed all over with pleasure. Now she can tell her headmistress that her aunt's book is to be published (we hope, we hope – oh, how this excessive caution pursues me!). I phoned Gus and told him, he was delighted.

Cannot look for a job now (I need cash, but time for Peg's revision is much more urgent). What a joyous relief! I am still free to continue this life I love, see my friends, visit the BM and write.

Wednesday, 5 October

Lost: one period. It is now exactly a week late and has never been so late in my life that I can recall. What do I do? I don't know. The problem is teasing, casts a blight on all my activities. I can't be absolutely certain that there is no cause for alarm, that is the trouble. Could finger alone convey enough semen if the hand were covered with it? Considered in cold blood it's a disgustingly sordid affair and even farcical. The point is, should I take the immediate action necessary – I still have long instructions from Joan obtained from her sister on the procedure. I wish I could get in touch with Tom. I wish, but wishing won't help.

---

178 Established in the early nineteenth century, Hurst and Blackett was a highly regarded London-based house, specialising in biography and memoirs. Its reputation appeared not to be significantly tarnished by publishing Hitler's *Mein Kampf* in 1939.

And this morning another tiresome letter from N. No moment of triumph is allowed to go untrammelled when she is near. About the book she can say little except urge on me the seriousness of my future authorship. But of poor D.B., of whom I have given the lightest accounts possible, I receive a long lecture on my suburban tendencies and that marriage is not the only means of happiness for a woman. Just as though I had decided to marry him! Oh blast the woman! Her one instinctive and un-admitted satisfaction is I do believe to probe other people's weaknesses or be as upsetting as she knows how.

11 p.m. In bed. It has come, reluctant but definite and painlessly. With it lifts the cloud of uncertainty that marred my view of the immediate future.

Sunday, 9 October

Yesterday Tom sent an elderly lawyer friend of his to see me: shabby, unshaved, plump and exceedingly Irish with a passion for the eighteenth century, who has given me 31 introductions (he sat and wrote them all in the sitting room there and then) to VIPs in Dublin.

I have plunged into the eighteenth century and can see I may get involved with many other contemporary enthusiasts. But I am using (or trying to) this century as a means of living more fully in the twentieth century. That is what I want to remember: don't run away from your problems here and now however well you write and see the past.

Ethel, who is coming to stay tomorrow, is not well. She must be nursed, persuaded to rest. This is just the sort of thing I need to keep me firmly grounded in the present.

Friday, 21 October

This question of marriage. I cannot help now and then reflecting that there is much in what N. preaches (and Joan, but with less virulence) – that marriage is not necessarily the only fulfilment for a woman. I have always found ordinary day-to-day living with someone else fearfully irksome. I enjoy my solitude and independence and take it now so much for granted that when I get these spasms for 'love' and marriage I don't take into account what it would be like to have to adjust myself to someone else day after day, however deeply in love I might be. I am a self centred, selfish creature – it is so much easier, so much more comfortable and convenient to live alone.

And yet, and yet . . . No one has ever wanted (or said so at least) to live with me. That is what at forty makes me feel such a failure, that I have made such a poor show of my personal life. All my lovers slip away, as D.B. has done, without saying goodbye. Away they go, ghostly, unsatisfying, across the sea, to their death in a car, to study medicine, to Australia, to write plays, and that is the end.

Tuesday, 6 December

Seven weeks since I last wrote in here. I am extremely tired and feel [I am] looking older day by day, and it terrifies me. A stone in the heart. I see a woman in the mirror with untidy greying hair that I don't recognise. I don't inside feel older than I did in my twenties, I don't feel older than the young things between 20–30 that I see around me in bus and tube and crowded London street. I don't feel level with the plump middle-aged matron or the sophisticated woman of the world. I still feel as much hampered by inadequacy, inexperience, timidity as ever I did.

It is unbecoming, contemptible at 40. I have 'sold' a book. The contract is signed. But the terrible faux pas I made with the Agent over that has set me back years! I can't go into it now. Suffice it to say I was grossly clumsy, stupid beyond belief in my dealings and it has taken much grovelling and anguish to reinstate myself. I have not met him or the publisher yet. Work on revision proceeds apace, is enormously interesting but much additional labour. I am eaten up with impatience and all sorts of ridiculous doubts and fears.

I have had one letter from D.B. N. has joined the Freemasons. P.D. is selling her home here and moving with husband and family to Blackheath after holidays. When the election comes I am to be Sub

Agent for this area for the Liberals and everything else must cease. I am living again on an overdraft from the bank. It seems unlikely that I shall get any money for the book for 18 months or more.

My veins seem to be drying up. I feel chill, remote, detached, except when I am working full out on 'Peg', or when I am with Joan and her family, or P.D., or playing with my cats. I have, too, now an admirable domestic help who comes two mornings a week and so relieves me of the baser chores. And electric power on the ground floor which means a full fire in sitting room and kettle or iron in use in kitchen without danger of fusing the system. But joy, joy, the lovely, flowing warmth of rich contentment: where are you?

Sometime in Oct–Nov I met Priscilla Novy, the friend of Tom's who read the Peg MS for the Pilot Press, pushed it for me, and passed it on to Curtis Brown. A young, attractive, likeable person, unhappily married with two children, and crippled now from an attack of polio.

Friday, 23 December
[Newspaper clipping]

There are some people of superhuman energy and Mr Churchill is among them, who regard diarists as ineffective individuals who seek solace for their own ineptitude by recording, night by night, the vain ephemeral things that they have done. I do not share this prejudice. I find in any factual diary what Dr Johnson called 'The Parallel circumstances and kindred images to which we readily conform our minds.' Being fascinated by the mysterious passage of time and by coincidence of experience I can read almost any detailed diary with delight. All that I ask is that it should be true.

Harold Nicholson in last Sunday's *Observer*

Yesterday Babs and I met Pooh and Ivy and I handed over my responsibilities. Babs has been behaving quite differently this term. I mean her attitude to me. It is extraordinary and most pleasing. Ever since the sea voyage home when she saw me flirting with D.B. and also since the book was accepted. These two things seem to have caused the revolution I wanted and could not achieve in any other way. She does really seem quite to like me now.

Xmas Eve

'Xmas is forced on a reluctant and dignified nation by the shopkeepers and the press', says Shaw. Yet through the glut of food and tinsel, balloons, gifts and false snow something else struggles. It has me torn to pieces every year and in tears when I am alone. It comes over the radio and in the faces of children and the smiles of harassed postmen, in carols and the good wishes from distant friends.

I have sold a book, I have sold a book, and now drink sherry all alone and write Xmas letters. Am in a delightful, benevolent glow . . . but wish, wish I could be sharing it.

Wednesday, 28 December

Harold Nicholson in one of his *Observer* articles, refers to the 'illusion of hurry' or words to that effect: we are obsessed and harried on all sides by a sense of urgency, hustle, things waiting to be done that must be done. Maybe we manage our lives badly, try to cram them too full to avoid being left alone with ourselves. But there is another side to it. If I let things slide, as I am prone to do, idle over the morning paper in bed, spend a couple of hours on this diary, go for a walk through the Beeches, listen to a play on the radio . . . then the washing up mounts in the sink, I find myself without a clean pair of stockings to wear when I have to go out, or a shoulder strap loose, some Liberal duty is neglected or the cats have no fish. And how possibly can any average modern mother with very little domestic help ever find time for cultural recreation? It must be over ten days now since I did any work on the 'Peg' MS because of Babs and Xmas – I have just had to leave it, but no mother could neglect her child like that. When I think of this I feel that I am forever wasting time if not working at the book. Urgency batters at one on all sides, one cannot escape it.

Brother Pooh has just phoned. I do so wish I could make proper contact there. My brother, my only brother, and nothing but cloud and awkwardness between us.

Friday, 6 January 1950

I must stop using this journal as an escape, if I can. I need now, more than ever, practise in communication, i.e. direct, by means of conversation, with my opponent present and waiting for my answer. It is all very well after some failure in social intercourse to fly to these pages and say, 'But that wasn't what I meant . . . really, if only I had had the chance, what I meant to say was . . .' This may prove to oneself that one has it 'in the bag.' But it is not enough. I must learn to 'get it out.' (Why? One feels one is dying if one doesn't, that's why.)

I have re-read from May 7th 1949. I must not look back. One turns at once into a pillar of salt. I still have 'Peg' to finish, the Agent and publisher to meet. When the general election comes I must put all I have got into the fight for the Liberals. I will close this book now with this last resolution, that unless anything stupendous occurs, I will not touch it again until June. Keep to these resolutions, Jean.

Saturday, 7 January

10.30 p.m. I falter once more before I draw the final line. I am sure I am right in this discussion (to close the book). This journal has been a help, a consolation, a refuge and a pleasure, but something vital drains away through it. Latterly I have always left it feeling exhausted, 'virtue' of some sort has gone out of me, and is being wasted, because of the need to write here. The original purpose and use has ceased, or changed. When I was in a tangle, unhappy, and without guidance – it served. But now, no. I must move in another direction, divert all the energy usually spilled here into more creative channels. I must open doors and windows, and walk into the healthier spaces of more open life.

'My brother and sister in law were kindness itself.' A visit from Pooh and Ivy.

38.

X-Ray Man

Wednesday, 14 June 1950 (aged forty)

I have kept my resolution: silence here a full six months. I 'cheated' I think only twice by making entries in the MO Diary which will not be sent to them. But that diary I have kept only fitfully – my heart is not in it and I begin to feel a little annoyed with MO and disinclined to make the effort. It arises from a reference to the Liberals in their pamphlet summing up the Election. It indicated that they themselves have no great opinion of the Liberals – it was chilling, discouraging. Why should I 'open up' to a set of strangers who can, evidently, have no real sympathy for my particular attitude? Perhaps that is cowardly, but it dampens spontaneity to feel that what one is writing may be sneered at by the audience for which it is particularly written. It is better to have no particular reader in mind. A real diary will always find its readers.

A review of P.A. Spalding's *Self Harvest* in this month's *National Book League Journal*, by Georgina Mase, has pulled me back to this journal as much as anything, though I would have started again this month if I had not seen it.[179] 'A true diary,' she says, 'is one in which the diarist, with an irresistible urge to preserve experience, has recorded for the sake of recording . . . It really is a record of

---

179 Philip Anthony Spalding (1911–1989) was a literary critic whose diaries are in the Bodleian, Oxford. *Self Harvest* was subtitled 'A Study of Diaries and the Diarist'.

immediate experience and not a mere description or picture of the past "touched up" by memory. Maurice Chapelan . . . sums up the difference between diarists and writers of memoirs or autobiography by saying that the former seek to know themselves while the latter seek to make themselves known.'

By these standards I am a confirmed diarist and accept it joyously. Self-analysis may be 'carried to such lengths that self-consciousness obscures vision' – obscures vision, impedes action in living, can become such a shelter that one never progresses as a person. That is the danger for the diarist as an individual in the body politic. But I see no reason to restrain the urge if it is as insistent as it is in me. I am a diary writer, an addict, and shall continue if only spasmodically, although 'of all strange and unaccountable things this journalising is the strangest,' and although of all the great diarists mentioned by Georgina Mase I have read only Barbellion at all thoroughly, and have no settled notion as to whether mine will ever rank with these to be preserved.[180]

Let me collect the threads now since January. The bulk of the 'Peg' revision was finished and handed over to the publishers before the hard work for the election began. Then came a full fortnight for the Liberals.[181] I am still Sec to our reconstituted Assoc, but wish I weren't. I don't know enough and haven't the time to study the subject as I feel I should to be an adequate worker for this cause, though I still believe in it. We have a jumble sale ahead of us, on Sat week, and most of the organising for this falls on my shoulders, or rather finding people who will do the different jobs necessary.

Since the election I have been finishing 'Peg' and collecting the illustrations and have met the publishers. I took in almost the last batch yesterday and apart from about six more letters it is really done

---

180 See 17 May 1940.
181 Another disaster for the Liberals. The party won only nine seats, three fewer than in 1945. Labour, led by Clement Attlee, retained its majority, but its popularity was slipping fast. Churchill would return the following year.

until the galley proofs begin to arrive. H. & B. are a very old firm and published Fitzgerald Molloy's *Peg Woffington* in the nineteenth century – hence their interest. The first notice is in their spring catalogue. The manager, M.H., is a pleasant intellectual type (one could visualise him on the *N. Statesman* staff) with white hair, a young face, and blue eyes. I haven't met dragon Curtis Brown yet or even corresponded lately, but should like some of the advance money now if possible and will have to tackle him about it.[182]

Leslie and Ivy left in April for Barbados. I am once more Guardian Aunt. Babs has improved tremendously. She is to spend the summer holidays with her school friend at Bourne End, and I have been advertising for PGs again but have not been very successful to date. Only one definite booking so far – an elderly couple from Northumberland who come here on Friday for a fortnight. I dearly need (financially) to be booked up for August and September but have nothing so far.

I am afraid N. and I have reached another impasse. She is calling me a 'funny little thing' again – always a sign that she is baffled and irritated with me. Last March she was operated on for a fibroid.

Cats. Dinah has had her usual spring brood. The adored, persistent old monster tabby father was run over at last this weekend, so I am told. Dear darling pussies. Dinah with her family in the armchair, Squib asleep on the sofa at my feet. Full of fleas, all of them.

Wednesday, 21 June

Saw Vicary about the clock which still won't go. He had promised to come up yesterday evening. 'The day you come when you say you will, Mr Vicary', I told him, 'I shall have to be carried to hospital.' He vowed he would come tonight. Really when he makes these promises I do believe he means to keep them. Soon after 1 p.m. I have scrappy lunch and a pot of tea and top and tail gooseberries listening to *Woman's Hour*.

---

182 This is Spencer Curtis Brown, son of the agency's founder Albert.

[Later:] No Vicary, of course. Since 1940 he has had the works of my grandfather clock to clean. The case I put into store some time after the war. People tell me he has probably sold the clock part – he has been known to do such things. I keep asking for it. Except for the grandfather clock I have had everything back that I have taken to him and many small items of jewellery for other people. A little man and a born Bohemian. Works until 4 a.m. I am told, and is never available until after 11 a.m.

I sympathise. To each the life that suits him. I do feel vile for the first two hours in the morning. All minor irritations and deeper hates seem to come to the surface in concentrated attack. This morning I spilt cornflakes, upset mint sauce, and splashed tea over the table. I would like to have taken a jam jar or two into the garden and smashed them with a hammer.

Sunday, 25 June

The Jumble is over and we have made a clear £20 profit. I am shattered by a cat war in progress. Most of this evening I have been trying to catch a heartrendingly mange-ridden Tom, but he is of course much too spry. He really is in a terrible condition and his owners should be shot with him.

Monday, 10 July

We've been having a storming July, but yesterday was perfect: could not have been better for Babs's party. They entertained themselves with games of their own so aunt had only the cats to worry about and this was quite painless. But what should happen in the morning but Tom must phone and ask if he could come with a friend. Their entrance at 5 p.m., after the girls had had their tea, was the most effective that has happened to me in while. Me still busy in the kitchen, girls all on lawn outside, comes Tom 'Jeanie, Jeanie!' I run to sitting room, he to back door, this happens several times to delight our audience. He and friend Mac looking like a couple of strays, but the young are intrigued with anything male, and being Irish was a further asset. We went for a drink or two in Beaconsfield and got soaked in thunder storm at 10.30 – so much so that it did not take much to persuade them to spend the night at Wee.

The Irish are enraging and fascinating and never dull – I am steeped in it all again. Tom's latest affair – the femme fatale daughter of John Gilbert who sounds a bit of a nymphomaniac to me, flitting from one besotted Irishman to another – has been carrying on with Tom and Mac so that until a week ago they were ready to shoot each other on sight. But now she has left them both for another and they are weeping on each other's shoulders.

Tuesday, 18 July

Tom has been much in my thoughts, inevitably. He hinted, half seriously, that he was looking for a wife and that naturally set my undisciplined imagination flying. But if it came to the point actually, even if he got as far as asking one, I believe he would be off like an arrow from a bow if one did take him seriously and showed any real desire for marriage with him.

Friday, 21 July

I had ideas of going to see *Mr Ichabod and Mr Toad* this afternoon but did not feel equal to it. I must therefore be a little ill as I adore Walt Disney. But I do not much now like going to films on my own: it is so depressing coming out and home alone. I called on D. yesterday morning to see if she would go with me. Windows were open but there was no immediate response to my ring. Then she popped her head from an upstairs window and was I think in a dressing gown, and said she was busy packing. No other explanation as gardener was in drive, but it all seemed rather odd and curiosity-making.

Friday, 28 July

The doctor thinks I may have incipient jaundice. I have been given pills and medicines and ordered off all fats and to rest as much as possible. When I turn yellow I have to stay in bed.

The phone went. A Liberal call. The phone again. The same Liberal. I long for the luxury of a phone by my bed. It is something I have never had and I can't think of anything similar that would give me more pleasure – to lie here now, for instance and receive a call from Tom, or to gossip with Lydia. Dear God, what I wouldn't do for Wee if it could be mine within the next year or so! Let me indulge my daydream for once and spend, say, up to £1,000 on it. Completely redecorate, inside out. Have new flooring all over top storey. A new stair carpet. New settee and armchair covers. Line the new curtains. Have a larder built. Bookshelves. If funds would allow, I would have a sun porch built onto sitting room, a bay built out from the French windows about 3ft. I would do such a lot to the garden too, move the herb bed and have the lawn whole. Yes, and proper coal and coke bunkers built, along the back wall perhaps where the sun never reaches – except that that was where I once thought of having a bathroom. As someone said, it would be cheaper to build a new cottage.

Sunday, 6 August

As Peggy Denny said, their new home is a 'lovely little semi-detached . . . a come down'. But they are all adapting themselves gallantly and the rooms are furnished with simple good pieces of furniture to meet their needs. Life is not less full or interesting for Peggy because material means are reduced. They live very near a large sports club to which they all belong, her husband is secretary to the Royal Academy social club and there is so much work and many contacts in that. She is taking violin lessons. Life does not have to be constricted because you live in the suburbs; what you have made of your own goes with you. Peggy with her interesting, lively young family will never be dull or narrow. My complaint against the suburbs has always been their stifling narrowness of outlook, but if there were for instance several Denny families living in Wembley I would not at all mind having to go back to Homefield. But the country does pull. If one could only establish a colony. I only mean that I wish I could have all the people I like most living around me.

Saturday, 12 August
I knew it was rash to boast that I was 'never ill'.

Stomach pains. I had a temperature of over 102. Lady Spicer came round to borrow a lemon and insisted that I spend the night in her house, which I did very thankfully – after all it might have been appendicitis. Rest and warmth brought the temp down rapidly and by this morning was normal so I returned to my own bed and awaited Dr W. It is all a mystery. He says I am anaemic, probably underweight and is arranging for me to have chest X-rayed – but can't find the exact cause.

Well of course, part of me is loving all this. I am the centre of attention and neighbours being so kind. Mrs Semple sent me some lunch and got medicine for me. Lady Spicer comes to enquire and natters about the smoking. And I lie in bed or on the sitting room sofa delighted to think I have a real excuse to do nothing and perhaps put off all the things (like committee meetings) that I don't really want to do. In fact I feel a frightful hypocrite. The pains are never more than uncomfortable and I am always able to stop whatever I'm doing when they begin.

Monday, 14 August
To have my chest X-rayed. What am I in for? Months in a sanatorium? The thought drives me frantic. To look pale and interesting and be showered with sympathy and kindness is all lovely and diverting, but not at that price. Dear God, now I do go down into darkness, alone, but I will put my hand into thy hand.

Tuesday, 16 August
Really, I was in a panic last night. My main distress was for the cats. If I proved infected then they would all have to be put to sleep,

probably within the next few days. But the X-ray this morning revealed nothing.

I must say that what I have experienced of National Health Service so far is really not as bad as has been made out.[183] All the doctors or specialists (I had to have my eyes tested in the spring when it was discovered that there is a cataract in my right eye) that I have seen have all taken trouble and spent as much time on me as any previously paid privately. Sometimes there is long waiting at the clinics but I have been lucky, and learned to go a bit before the stated time so as to be at the head of whatever queue there may be.

This morning I was sent to the chest clinic at Upton Hospital in Slough. It was all rather shabby, obviously in need of new paint and room for stores, but all the people I had to deal with were pleasant and ready to be helpful. I did not have to wait long, was interviewed by a nurse whose face was very familiar and learnt that she came from Farnham Common – I have seen her about for years and am not at all sure I didn't know her in the Red Cross. She took particulars and weighed me. After another short wait in its X-ray dept I was shown into a cubicle and told to strip to the waist. A wizened, sad-faced little man in a dingy white coat (there were many dingy white coats about) was busy with a young woman already naked to the waist and unashamed. I waited with cardigan round my shoulders until he was ready and then stepped forth. The door was wide open, officials coming in and out but no one took the least notice of half-naked young women being pressed and patted by sad-faced little man. He pushed me up against a flat metal plate, so cold it made me jump, brought my chin up, my shoulders down, held my ribs in as I breathed in and out and then went away, telling me to breathe in and out again and to hold it, clicked something, and I was able to dress again. The next patient was a man. I think they kept him back until I came out

183 The NHS came into effect in July 1948, and faced a sceptical reception. The experience Jean describes sounds familiar even in 2015.

fully clothed but everything was so casual I couldn't be sure it wasn't just a coincidence. Poor little X-ray man – no wonder he looks sad, patting and photographing women's bare bodies all day long, he must be bored to death with the female torso.

Another short wait and the negative was given to me and I went to wait for the doctor. This was the longer wait but possibly not more than 20 minutes. I was shown into another shabby little compartment equipped for the doctor. He was young and nice, asked no end of questions, told me there was nothing whatever wrong with my lungs from that negative, and looked at old negatives taken in 1943 (a real cough scare then) which I had been told to bring. He seemed puzzled but took a lot of interest, had me stripped again and breathing for his stethoscope, and looking down my throat and thumping me here and there.

Of course the book had to come out in all this (my work). Was I a nervy person, was I worrying about the book? It seemed that must be the answer. My weight is now 8st 12lbs which really is a shock – it used to be on an average 9st 7lbs. I must then be getting thinner as everyone says though I have not noticed any big difference in the fit of clothes worn (and still wearing) over the last 10 years.

Friday, 18 August

Dr W. thinks anaemia is the seat of the trouble and I am to go on taking iron. And I prescribe for myself more fresh air, less browsing in libraries. Anaemia – yes. It seems to fit, to explain my months-long feeling of fatigue. Now I can be lazy, delicious thought, with a clear conscience.

Friday, 8 September

Of all my paying guests, Miss C. stands out as with the most character. She arrived a week ago in lavender and several inches of pink satin petticoat showing beneath her grey skirt. A plump, delicately rosy grey curled person with pale blue eyes and a difficult new top plate. 'Don't think I didn't like your nice food dear, I just can't eat . . .' But with a little manipulation of a nail file she made it tolerable and recovered her appetite. 'We did enjoy that, dear! We just ate and ate – as I was saying to my friend, till my corsets cracked!' On the first morning she wandered round to the kitchen in black satin flowered dressing gown looking for the lavatory. 'I've missed the door, dear.' She was frequently missing doors.

And never stopped talking for the first few days. Her conversation was sprinkled with people she knew or had met. Augustus John, Sonnie Hale . . . She was a delight. So vague, so silly, so obviously enjoying everything, and a personality in her own sphere, interested to the verge of inquisitiveness in all about her. She embraced me affectionately at parting.

Her friend Mrs G. was younger, more reserved but nice in her way too. The wife of the recent Liberal Candidate for South Shields, where, she told me, they had a much worse time than we did. No proper agent, no reliable organisation, an undercurrent of hostility between renegade National Libs and the old party. But her husband polled 9,000 votes and did not lose his deposit.

It is odd the knack English women have of making the worst of themselves. Mrs G. was really very pretty without her glasses and her hair loose prepared for a bath. But somehow we do our hair wrong, choose the worst sort of hats and the ugliest flower patterned materials. We look crumpled, neglected, as though we didn't really care about clothes, yet that is rarely true. There is so obviously no precision, no discipline in our thinking about how we should dress. I came upon a 1938 newspaper photo of the King and Queen of Bulgaria the other day. The Queen was Parisianly chic, nothing ostentatious, a plain coat and skirt and felt hat, but everything was diamond sharp in outline and suitability and finish. One hardly ever sees an Englishwoman looking like that.

I listened last Saturday to the play with them. Miss C. kept dropping to sleep with short starting puffs and would jerk herself awake every now and then with same comment: 'He's left her!'

Monday, 11 September

11 p.m.: In a rage. Have not done my ironing. Have not done any house cleaning and the place a slum. This evening after writing N. and shoving down lousy supper, spent washing up, washing up, washing up. That damned damned sink.

And now two enormous blobs of ink from this trashy pen on a beloved Maltese cloth. In my despair I have scrubbed them with pumice which will weaken the fabric. *Household Hints* says use 'oxalic acid' as though one ordered it regularly with the rations.

Wednesday, 13 September

Tonight, a resolution I must make. But word it with care. I must go on trying to become a biographical writer. I am not established yet. Peg came my way, and has been an astonishingly lucky choice. I worked hard at it, but in great ignorance – the more I learn about such work, the more amazed am I at my temerity and my good fortune.

Let me recall the start. After leaving HDA in 1946 and making one or two half-hearted attempts to place articles and more successful efforts to take holiday paying guests, my thoughts turned to the eighteenth century, still with the idea of articles in my mind, but also wondering if I should try a biography. I was remembering a remark made by a lecturer at the Truth Club (I think it was called), a club to which Constance Oliver took me, a literary affair founded to encourage beginners but run by elderly people. This lecturer was a young man, a biographer, and speaking on his subject, and the only thing I remember of his lecture (and his white evening dress shirt front) was his advice to beginners to start with a biography – it was good exercise, good practice, he said.

And then on the BBC in the autumn, I think, of 1946, I heard Handel's *Water Music* and the announcer's introduction. It seemed strange that I should be able to hear those same notes played 200 years ago – they were a stronger link with the past than anything I could think of. The printed word grew out of date, its meaning changed with time. Paintings and drawings also remained in and of their period – but music, the sound, still lived, like sap in a tree. And I wondered what living ears had listened to at its first performance in that year 1748.[184] And I began to go through, page by page, my (no, my brother's but I use it) Harmsworth's 1904 Encyclopaedia, picking out famous eighteenth-century characters who were alive in that year. Peg Woffington was on my list – Garrick's paramour and other love affairs. But it was not just because of that that I picked her out. It was, as I have told many people, because I stuck a pin in my list and fell on her name.

I took the names given of the authorities on her – Daly, Molloy and Reade – and ordered them from the public library. And then I started at the BM. This is what amazes me, the extraordinary good fortune of it all. It took me months to find my way about the Reading Room catalogues (and I am still learning), and only very gradually discovered how little in this century had been written of any length on Peg. I don't believe there can be another character with Peg's appeal in this period that suited my abilities as a raw recruit, blundering, fumbling, ignorant of sources and references – everything in fact necessary for a serious biographer to know. It is incredible to me now that I achieved what I did, and that I actually caught a publisher before making the revision I did last winter. And there again in knowing Tom, another astonishing stroke of good luck.

What I am trying to get at is this. I whine for a sign from Heaven to show me what I should do, but surely there's enough in all this to convince me if I will but open my eyes and heart to it? The way has been shown, fortune has been lavish. But I know what pulls me back and causes the doubt and confusion: the thought, hasn't there been rather too much good luck about this? It is more than possible that

184 Actually 1717. Handel composed the piece in response to a request from King George I for an eye-catching concert on the Thames. Peg Woffington was not yet born.

with Peg, in my urgency and enthusiasm and anxiety, that I have made some bad scholastic mistakes.

Sunday, 24 September

Two things to record.

i) I have resigned from committee of local Liberals. I came to this decision last Monday when there was much talk of another election in near future. The thought of going through all that again clinched the matter and I phoned the chairman. What surprised me was my firmness and clarity throughout. I did not feel clear in my own thoughts about it but found myself speaking with conviction and point, reasons all coming pat, no hesitation anywhere. He took it well, and there! I am free again. The relief is tremendous.

ii) Lydia and I went to see *The Cocktail Party* on Friday.[185] This is a really profound and most moving play, excellently produced and acted, though one could make niggardly criticisms. It had also – on Lydia too, I think – an extremely depressing effect. It left one feeling that here was truth, but without hope. Is the humdrum, then, all that is left?

But ordinary living isn't humdrum. That is the point. It is often difficult and sometimes tedious, but there is so much pleasure to be had from apparently trivial things.

Wednesday, 27 September

Today I was not up till after 10.30, went shopping in village, home again, finished clarifying the fat which I have in quantity and have now stored in a big stone jar bought for 1s., did the flowers, had lunch, washed up, complicated and messy with dishes and saucepans covered in grease, did the ironing, had tea and knitted; then bottled six jars of fruit salad according to *Daily Telegraph* recipe (peaches,

---

185 T.S. Eliot's psychological comedy was enjoying its first London run, and featured Rex Harrison.

pears, apples, grapes, blackberries in syrup with a teaspoon of sherry and using snap closures). Supper – deep-fried fish and chips and spinach; then more knitting and the wireless. There has been a surfeit of plays and stories today. A matinee at 3; 4.15 *Mrs Dale's Diary*; *Children's Hour*; at 6 p.m. a talk on modern literature on the Third; at 8 p.m. Jack Hulbert in *Madeleine* (delightful); 9.30 *Have a Go*; at 10 Hardy's *Withered Arm*; at 11 an instalment of George Orwell's *Animal Farm*. All the while I was busy with domesticities I have been entertained or stimulated mentally – I love it, I love it.

Doctor says I must take iron pills for another month.

Friday, 29 September
Yesterday Oakdene Commemoration Day. I escaped after tea, the speeches were as much as I could bear – they go on too long. The best was the headmistress, always such a gallant little grey haired figure on that platform, aflame with zeal, devoutly following her dedicated path. All that she has said, each year I have attended these functions, I have heard before, years ago. I wonder why no old girl is ever congratulated on the public platform for getting married and rearing a family. Degrees and public appointments are acclaimed but never the successful wife and mother.

39.

How She Smells

Thursday, 4 November 1950

Bernard Shaw died this morning. This was not what I came to my journal for, but it has some bearing on what I would record. I think my little cat Dinah is dying. Thoughts on death have been with me, on and off, a long while. It is so commonplace, so inevitable – all religions of the present day, or the ones I know of, say soothing, re-assuring things about it. But this only confuses me. In my heart I am frightened like a child threatened with loneliness in the dark. I have had to part with mother and father, Ethel has lost two brothers and a sister, she and Aunt M. will die, my brother will die, my turn will come. The light going out . . . that is what is so terrifying . . . into a darkness alone. It is having faith that matters but I seem to have so little. If I were faced with death without warning I might fly in a panic to the religion my mother taught me and hope it would carry me over.

Where will my little cat go when she goes at last? I cannot bear to think of her being anywhere unhappy. She has been the light of my life here at Wee from the very beginning, I have been thoughtless, ignorant, impatient with her, but her love for me has never lessened. Every time I returned home she would emerge from some secret waiting place, tail erect, ears eager, and then up on to my shoulder purring a welcome. She is too weak to combat the boisterous demands of her children, and I have shut her away in a box in my room. She hardly stirs from it and I know it might be kinder to take her to the clinic but I cannot bring myself to do it. Her little, delicate pointed face, with its tufted ears and amber eyes, her gaiety and patience with her babies, her tremendous pride when they were born, and her absolutely shameless flirtations in the amorous season in the garden. I cannot bear to think that my life with Dinah is nearly, maybe, at an end. This pain, this sense of losing things, of some sort of doom descending, has been haunting me.

Tuesday, 7 November
Dinah is still with me. She smells – dear, how she smells.

I have to reset my course. Publication of 'Peg' is to be delayed perhaps another year and with it my hopes of keeping the overdraft in check and all the possibilities of new contacts and interests that publication will bring. Lady S. cheered me somewhat this morning. The bestseller authoress, Doris Leslie has been in the neighbourhood and revealed that she also paints but chose writing because there was 'more money in it.'[186] I have no hopes or desires to be a bestseller, but I want to be able to support myself by biography. If only one could be sure. But there I go again with the desire for security instead of the hope adventurous. I don't want to be and couldn't be 'famous'. I couldn't speak on a platform or spontaneously in a broadcast programme. A real writer (like Shaw) has something to say which he can put into speech as well as on paper and I'll never be that sort of writer. I'm not sure that I don't distrust any other sort of writer as suspicious or deficient.

Wednesday, 8 November
I am starting seriously to plan for p.gs (P.G.s? – however one writes it, it tends to look like 'pigs') next year. I must get as many ads out

---

186 Prolific novelist and biographer, best known for *Paragon Street* and *Peridot Flight*.

as soon as possible from January, I am writing to friends in the north for suggestion for north-country papers, with eye on Festival of Britain visitors. If by having p.gs in quantity next spring and summer I can stop the drain on my capital and have something in hand for the next winter when money from 'Peg' may be coming in too – then I would forge ahead in earnest and without misgiving. I may of course fail in this plan, may make a horrid mess of it all, be unlucky with my guests, I may be ill again or get into trouble with landlady K.M., or the income tax authorities, and find myself in a worse state than before. Or we may be at war again or something disastrous may have happened that I can't possibly foresee.

And yet how can one know what the future holds? Inflation, war, revolution – and all my assets may turn to worthless paper.

Friday, 10 November

I have had a reply from Curtis Brown's office. They seem sympathetic about the delayed publication of 'Peg' and are trying to get the £100 advance money for me. But this will only be a small temporary (though not scorned) help. I suppose I can get no more after it until the book is out and selling and the £100 paid back – which may be another year or more.

Perhaps I shall be known as a good diarist when I am far beyond feeling any pleasure at such recognition. But as Frederick Laws has written, 'the best diarists are not always the most successful people'. Have been re-reading journals again – from the beginning of year till now. I can never stop once I begin to do this, and only the fact of earlier volumes being buried in my old school play-box prevents my looking at them. A good diarist? I don't know at all. There is a great thrum of passing planes overhead like a flight of bombers.

Sunday, 12 November

Yesterday afternoon as I cycled back from village through the Beeches I overtook Kay Hammond and John Clements with their two boxers.

I did not recognise their back view, but they looked interesting – she without a hat in a slim leaf-brown pony skin coat and slacks, he also hatless in camel-hair belted overcoat. Then she turned and I heard that unmistakable voice saying, 'You wouldn't lose anything by not having the second bathroom . . .' I longed to turn round and have a good stare at them both.

Je spoke of an Indian doctor at her hospital who practises hypnosis and took one patient right through an operation with it and also 'controlled' himself while having painful attention to his teeth.[187] He sat, said Je, quite relaxed with hands folded in front of him, and conscious all the time. The control of pain, he told her, was widely practised in India, with hypnosis for all operations, but can only be done by people who have studied and disciplined themselves to it from youth. It would be almost impossible for any adult in the West without such training.

Did I say I decked out the sitting room with new curtains early this summer? Gay cretonne bought from John Lewis. All with the thought of having a presentable sitting room for possible visitors when 'Peg' was published. Oh, irony, irony! I feel like the donkey after the evasive carrot.

Rain again. I am an idle, vain, pea-brained, vacillating, silly wench, and have eaten too much sweet cake. Hugh Laming is married again. N. sent me a letter he wrote her when he and his 3rd wife were on holiday recently touring England by car. I have heard nothing from him for months and do not expect to. I feel quite out of touch now, as I told N., without rancour, as though the wires had rusted and broken by mutual consent. I do not mind at all that he continues to write to N.

Sunday, 19 November
The Irish – who can ever do them justice, write of them adequately,

---

187 The mysteriously named Je was Joan's sister, a dentist visiting from London.

understand them? All words seem heavy in describing them. Their fey quality, their sensitive, imaginative, restless, nervous, defeatist natures . . . their endless talk, their recurrent laughter, their terrible despair, their idealism and their cynicism, their generosity and warmth, their heart-breaking casualness and unreliability, forever grasping at life and running away from it. Oh, I am thankful I'm not seriously involved with T.! I have learnt more about him in this weekend from P. and Mac than I could do in months or years of close association with him. I want to keep him in this perspective. I never want to fall under his spell again, never, he is not for me, not as I once thought I wanted him to be. He has a devastating way of flattering a woman's vanity and making one believe he means more than he does – but Lord let me never be deceived again.

Their way of living is fantastic, unbelievable, yet it is true. All the mad things they speak of really happen, and frequently. Their incredible parties where everyone gets stone-cold drunk. Mac called to the phone finds a body by it on the floor and sits on its face; drinks too much Pernod and finds himself alone on a mountain and nearly paralysed, and, making his way with difficulty back to civilisation, comes upon a parked station-wagon in which he finds a woman stretched stark naked without sign anywhere of clothes or coverings near her. He staggered back to the party where no one took any notice of his story, picked up a valuable handwoven rug and returned with it to the corpse. Later, when he could persuade someone to go with him to the spot, the wagon, naked woman and rug had vanished, and he never discovered who she was.

They are such a motley, brilliant, scintillating crew; brilliant and neurotic – knowing they go towards their own damnation, it seems ingrained, inherent this belief. 'The Celtic rot,' says Mac lightly. The tragedy and sadness in their eyes is sometimes almost unbearable. I hope T. can keep P. happy – as she obviously is now, in a trance, an ecstasy. But I do not envy her, I only hope she takes a little English sanity and stability with her to Dublin.

The Irish I think find us a little terrifying, our solidity and reserve which always increases when with them unless we have the knack of letting ourselves go with them. And perhaps they despise us too, for our dullness, our slow wittedness, our pompous attitude of patronage to them. Their faults are not unique to themselves – we suffer from them too, idleness, procrastination, impatience, and we could learn much from them in the way of living more adventurously, of taking life more easily. There is much to be said for their gaiety and inconsequence, their capacity for living in the present.

Wednesday, 22 November

I dreamt of slums: indescribable confusion. Trams in a narrow crowded thoroughfare all marked for destinations I knew not, and no link to anywhere familiar; policemen who could not help me; a butcher's shop; side streets; green-grocery stalls; decrepit houses, hovels, waste heaps.

Monday, 27 November

Woke this morning at 8, raw, foggy. Tea and cereal in bed reading *The God That Failed*.[188]

Decide to have some Nescafe and biscuits then go into village. Have to clean and tidy self. Been making my own 'Quickies' – little pads of cotton wool soaked in own-made astringent lotion and left in glass jar with screw lid. Highly successful and will be much cheaper. Make out shopping list, pump bike tyres. Go to grocers, no, fishmonger first, buy heads and beef sausages for cats; return a cream cheese to grocer. Believe that if local tradespeople find you honest, they will not cheat back, though I may be wrong. I rarely bother to check accounts; but did look at grocer's book today and found they'd been charging me for *Picture Post* which stopped months ago. Then to buy

---

188 A collection of essays written by Arthur Koestler, Stephen Spender and others, all discussing why they had become disenchanted with communism.

kettle-descaler from electricians and tell them clock had gained 10 mins since last week's power cut.

This is a very long bad cut, nearly an hour now. Ordered more coal and coke today after hearing report of Fuel Minister's gloomy speech. Economic outlook depressing too, according to today's *News Chronicle* leader. But this soaking of the rich – they keep saying that the rich can't be soaked much more. Yet I see evening sandals advertised at 12 guineas a pair, I see fur coats in the West End worth £1,000 and more; I hear of husband and wife each owning an expensive car; and in grocer's last week one woman calmly ordering 6 gins (at 32s. 6d. a bottle), whiskey, tonics, a crate of beer. Luxury goods can be had in quantity now, all kinds, at extravagant prices. Someone finds the money from somewhere to pay for them or they wouldn't be for sale. A lot of it may come, as mine does at present, from capital. We are still living on the energy and enterprise of our own Victorian ancestors.

Light again! And some play on the Light Programme: Maurice Denham in *The Ugly Duckling*. Someone being very hysterical and smashing mirrors.

Wealth is changing ownership – the old rich classes are impoverished, and the goods they were once able to buy go now to a different group. And it is all so relative. I am well off by some standards. I do not in fact think of myself as poor at all and try to be grateful for what I have. I have a modest fur coat (musquash, and I loathe musquash, I yearn to get something else); I keep a bottle of gin and sherry in stock for the odd occasion, I spend at least 14s. 7d. a week on cigarettes, I have a portable gramophone and records I never use (would sell it willingly if it didn't mean so much bother to try); an ancient hired radio but still serviceable (I would like a portable as well); an electric clock; sufficient clothes to pass muster (just) for smart dos – these are very rare so I get by; a stock of nylons, always adequate food. I think that I couldn't possibly manage with less and would like more – another coat, for instance, to wear on shopping expeditions into village when I always cycle; the one I own is now 10 years old and looks terrible.

Where does one draw the line between necessities and luxuries? I think it imperative to have my hair done every 2–3 weeks, to use good lipstick, face creams, powder and talcum, but do without bath salts which I adore. I manage without a car, but other people evidently find they must have one – each. And now it is 6 o'clock. And I had to fly outside to relieve nature.

Phoned Gus. Nice to hear his pleasant, cultured, witty voice – always full of a particular warmth for me. Prepared supper. Curry of mutton remains. It finished up as a revolting dish much too stodgy and fat and I have felt sick ever since. Did the ironing, tacked and pressed pleats of black skirt. Finished some mending, rinsed out the kettles, cleaned the bath.

It rains still lightly.

Sunday, 3 December

Have enjoyed having N. here again very much. There is no doubt at all that her contract with masonry is helping her greatly. Her joy and interest in living is as keen as ever it was. There is beginning to be – really and lastingly I think – a restraint in her. I know she longs for me to become interested in masonry too. Yet still my way can not be her way – not now, in this moment. I must plod on through the fog, alone. She is an inspiration and she shames me. I feel I have too often taken a mean view of her. I noticed her neck had thickened a little but she still had the slim delicate alluring grace of her youth – it was all very much there and I said so. Not until I saw her again this spring was the coarsening really apparent and quite shocking, plump now to obesity, no one could miss it. Hugh L. is in trouble again and wanting to meet N. His 3rd marriage evidently not a success and he is abandoning journalism. She is to meet him on Tuesday.

Say the mystics: when the master is needed the master will come.

I need this master now, now, more than I ever did. Help me into the way of finding him, or of finding what this need really is and how I may best fulfil it. I am so full of frets and worries, confusion and conditions. Help me to a greater willingness to learn, to real humility, so that I may see and hear and understand and live more strongly. The battle of living is never done. The less and less effort one makes, the more one tries to avoid it, the greater the difficulty becomes, the harder the way.

Monday, 4 December

A new toy, my first ball pen. Only 3s. 6d., but refills are 2s. 3d.,. I am enchanted with it and chose red ink because I need it for correcting MS and may use it for all proofs. At least perhaps it won't leak as my other pen does, though I hear they tend to do so as the filling runs out.[189]

Thursday, 14 December

This evening I tried on an old evening frock with next week's festive event in view. It is a model gown, bought for £1 off a naval Lt's wife in Malta. Hopelessly out of date, but still has something. I believe I'll get away with it. Have still all the etceteras – sequinned shoes and handbag, jewellery, a recently acquired white chiffon scarf tucked cunningly over shoulders conceals worn shoulder straps, a white flower in waistband. It still makes me look Upper Ten, but not only that – it makes me realise that there is nothing in my appearance when well dressed and groomed to cause lack of confidence.[190] It is a despicable habit this one, of always prancing before mirrors in one's mind.

---

189 It may have run out immediately: this brief entry is the only one to appear in red ink. She did, however, work her way through large parts of her journal, marking in red those passages that referred to cats.

190 Upper Ten Thousand: a phrase to denote the upper echelons of New York society, since shortened and applied to all privileged elites.

Wednesday, 17 January 1951

The dance was quite a success. (I did not wear the old model gown. When I tried it on for Babs it did not meet with the approval I'd hoped for. I think the low back shocked her a little, and anyway the hall was bitterly cold. The stalwart black velvet was worn instead and really did very well – everyone seems to like it.) I think Babs found her duties as hostess somewhat onerous but on the whole her guests seemed to enjoy themselves and the local caterer who provided refreshments for us came magnificently up to scratch.

The New Year weekend Babs spent at the Exiles Club at Richmond.[191] They had a fancy dress ball on the Saturday and B., her heart set on wearing a crinoline, persuaded me that Daddy would not mind cost of hiring a costume. We raced up to London and found what she wanted and she had the time of her life at the dance. Was more flattered and sought after than she has ever been.

One Sunday before Xmas, everywhere thick with snow and day leaden with more to fall and flakes in the air, Dinah went out during lunch and did not come back. She has not stayed out for any length of time all the winter and I was worried stiff, spent most of the afternoon, booted and spurred, out calling her till darkness. I disturbed neighbours, asked passers-by, searched in other gardens and then she appeared suddenly from nowhere, falteringly along the garden path towards me. Had she gone out to find somewhere to die, or collapsed with the cold and was unable to move? Shortly after this Lady S. cornered me in the village and lectured me at length on not having her put away. Called me selfish and cruel, I was thinking of myself and not the cat, she was so thin and so on and on.

I am being stubborn, I am unable to let go of this frail thread which has been part of the fabric of my life for nearly 12 years. And yet I would not hold on to it if I thought she really wanted me to let go. But her breathing gets more laboured and she is but a husk of her

---

191 The Cable & Wireless staff social club.

former self, so frail now she can scarcely stand against the wind. It seems on the surface that I should have no doubts, no excuse, and am being as selfish as the sentimentalist I abhor and would avoid being.

Saturday, 20 January

Dinah still with me, on my lap now after tea with me. One half of her – the top half – seems the same as ever, alert, eager, devoted, her delicate face and ruff, the tufted ears, clear as amber eyes, silken head, velvet nose. It is the sad, sagging, emaciated lower half that is so distressing. She follows me around, liking to be where I am and on my lap if possible, and always away from the other cats whom she detests, views them and their boisterous healthy activities with bitter loathing. I am the source of all the comfort, shelter, warmth, food and affection she has ever known. Perhaps now she feels that with me is the only possible solution to her difficulties. It is a big responsibility – and I wish I knew what I should do. Spilt a jar of currents just now all over crowded store room. Such treasure I could not bear to lose and set about salvaging them one by one.

Liz has a boy – in her last letter she said she was expecting a baby in January. I envy people now who have children. Not bitterly or passionately, but rather wistfully. They can be a tie and a burden, restricting one's development in other directions, but they also stabilise and determine one's life as other things we desire and go after don't. A career of any kind nowadays brings one into a hard, competitive sphere. But children lead one into a cooperative part of the community, where experiences are shared, there's no fight to 'sell' them or – unless you are a superlative egotist – make them better than anyone else's. The mother is chained to a regular dull daily routine but within it there seem to me endless opportunities for making new contacts and taking part in an absorbing sort of community life.

I don't know that I'd have the courage now, it grows so late for such an adventure (although my old friend Joan Silvester, now

married, my own age, had her first baby last summer quite successfully) and no use setting my heart on it if it's never to be. The point
that has been rumbling within for some time now, is that dimly I
begin to perceive something beyond one's own shadow.

Tuesday, 23 January

I phoned the cat clinic and asked if they could in this particular case
possibly send their ambulance. They only use their ambulance for
emergencies, but there is a possibility that they might fit in with
another journey tomorrow. I am to ring again. If they can do this I'll
never be able to thank them enough. I shall be spared that long
drawn-out agony of taking her there myself: it would be the best
possible solution all round and the idea of parting with her becomes
bearable. How she watches me now – can she possibly know? I must
write – or try to – a book about her.

Margaret Leigh's delightful *Spade Among the Rushes* answers
some of the criticisms always to be flung at a solitary woman and
gives her reasons for choosing to live as a crofter.[192] In lesser degree
I know them to be true for myself too. I no longer feel so doubtful
about it, or afraid of persevering in my efforts to combine writing
with the practical work of accommodating people for holidays. It
is curious how single women, if they are honest and of any integrity, usually express a regret that they have never married. But
remember always, O single ones, you have indeed a greater freedom
than wives and mothers and can use it to similarly creative ends.
And also that many wives and mothers, happy though they may
be with their husbands and children, yearn too for the independence and interests of their single days which they have sacrificed.
My friend Liz M. said last night on the phone that she had a greater
and greater urge to find herself a job as a commercial artist again

---

192 Leigh's lyrical books describe her experience of subsistence farming in isolated
Scottish communities, although she was briefly better known for riding a horse
from Cornwall to Scotland.

and employ someone to look after the little boys. The urge to experience life within the home and outside it will never be checked in women now.

Wednesday, 24 January

It is finished. Little light of my life is gone from me. When I can think of her without tears I will write more. Mine is such a pinprick of grief among the world's sorrows – I must bear it in silence and plod on. Squib sat on the table just before tea purring benignly and lifting his head eagerly for my hand. 'Do not weep,' he said, 'there is me, handsome, handsome me!'

Later: This is what happened. Last night in wave upon wave of torment I sat and wept over her, trying to eat some supper. She was on my lap, happily consuming most of my bacon. She elected to stay in the kitchen all night, seated on window sill, watching I think for a boyfriend. During breakfast she was stretched luxuriously in front of the electric stove and hitting out at Joey to keep him off her. I phoned the clinic as arranged at 10 a.m. and was told briskly that yes, Miss Hallam would call perhaps this afternoon but possibly this morning if I would be there? I would be there.

About 12.30 Miss Hallam arrived driving the ambulance. She has a very gentle, reassuring personality, a real love and understanding of cats – and their silly sensitive owners. Into the kitchen. Dinah was waiting to go out. Mrs Hallam opened her basket. 'Would you like to go away while I put her in? Some people . . .'

'Oh no, no . . .' But I turned my back. Dinah clung to me like a child, would not release her claws at Miss H.'s gentle touch. I kissed the top of her little black head quickly and turned to my handbag. I could not see the lid being closed. 'I'll be off now . . .' And away she went round the corner, down the path with the basket.

Tears. They do not bring the beloved back. They do not alter one jot of the years that are gone. Tears and tea and chores again. Now this, and more tears. Only those who have never known the strange, joyous, mystic communion that is possible with a loved animal will not understand.

Saturday, 28 January

Not a day has passed but some part of it is shadowed with grief. Even this morning when alone I was weeping again as I made the beds. That frightened, reproachful little face.

Tuesday, 6 February

I must try to do this summary. The whole point and purpose of these journals will, for me, otherwise be lost. Confession is good for the soul, a large forgettery also. I have tried to know myself, with self-concentration, not selfishness, but too often the problem patterns have repeated themselves. What are they?

> Timidity, cowardice, lack of confidence – fears of every kind
> Laziness and impatience
> A lust to destroy, particularly myself when apparently worthless
> Acute anxiety for the future

Fear has been one of the biggest governing forces of my life. If, like me, you are whipped perpetually by dissatisfaction, doubt and discontent, conscious that you are getting nowhere, stunted, left behind – then, as I understand it, there is only one thing to do. Dive in. Suffer doubt, humiliation, opposition, frustration, failure. Endure them. These are the problems that may not be escaped by being solved, but only by being lived through.

Fear in itself is not bad – it is not fear we must destroy, only our fear of fear.[193] Our object is to define fear and find the cause of it, as honestly as we can. Then having found the cause, to face it, and accept

---

193 Her main reference here is Graham Howe, but it is highly likely that Jean would have been aware of the lines from Roosevelt's Inaugural Address in 1933 ('The only thing we have to fear . . . is fear itself . . .')

it with open mind, open heart and open hand . . . and to hold it there without attempting to destroy it.

Laziness and fatigue have become in me so intertwined I don't know one from the other. But of fatigue – it is often a symptom of depression – and depression a symptom of unwillingness to be depressed.

Now, lastly, my anxiety about the future. For this there is absolutely no remedy, from the fearful possibilities no escape. It involves us all. All I can do personally now is to go on with my plans, living as I have done for some time almost from day to day, learning to love what I have in hand, learning to live in truth which is suspense, which is adventure: movement, growth, uncertainty, risk and danger.

Tuesday, 13 February

Took Ethel, for her birthday, to see Diana Churchill with Emlyn Williams in *Accolade* on Saturday, and stayed weekend at Wembley, visiting Joan for tea and supper on Sunday. *Accolade* a most intriguing play, cast and production excellent. But poor Ethel now so deaf she could not hear.[194]

Ploughing now through the Mass Observation diaries for cat material. Not as much there as I'd hoped. Oh, those war years! I am ashamed of these diaries – at least that is the feeling I have as I hurry through them. My attempts to be facetious, cynical, woman of the worldish make me wriggle. But there's a lot of useful data there. They were always written in a hurry, to record some passing detail, but my huge, burdensome vanity would push me into the picture wherever it was possible and I could find time for it – even when I thought I was concealing my own ego it seemed to pop out and take possession. It's been allowed to take possession here too,

194 Emlyn Williams's play explored double lives and double standards, an everyday story of high-ups and media folk. It was revived to great acclaim in London in 2014, with one reviewer calling it 'the most fascinating rediscovery in the British theatre for years'.

and there's a sort of passion behind the entries which keeps them moving and alight. MO wanted personal reactions to detail and that was what I was trying to give too. And my feeble attempts to explain and excuse why I clung to HDA and the cottage! However I can see how some of it might well be incorporated, by careful editing, with this – but fudge! You silly, conceited woman – stop being pompous and destructive.

From an interview with Sheila Hutchins (March 23 1950, *News Chronicle*): 'You have to allow time for writing and also for not writing. Lying awake in the dark is the time to be timid and humble . . . when you sit down to your typewriter you have to carry yourself across that fatal gap . . . on a great rush of courage.' This of course essential but it has to be, as she herself puts it, with a 'positive not a negative attitude' in oneself towards life in general. Writing is an attack.

Wednesday, 14 February

Available now in considerable quantity are varieties of Swiss roll. The chocolate kind are filled with thick mock cream – margarine I guess. Have just eaten two slices of this muck, some coconuts and cherry cakes and almond biscuits for my tea and feel heavy with indigestion.

The Mass Observation diary improves from 1946 on. It begins to peter out in 1948, falters badly all through 1949 and stops completely in May 1950. I might go on with it if they gave one more encouragement. One writes and writes, spilling oneself lavishly, recklessly and then what one has written disappears into a void. One knows it is received and read – or is alleged to be – but there is no response. It must be how an actor feels without an audience. One personal letter a year would be enough, something informal and direct, with criticism and guidance if necessary. This would be sufficient spur for me, but without it – no, I cannot be bothered. I don't imagine my diary is all that important, though I realise the value of apparent trivialities to future social historians. All detail, if accurate, is grist to their mill.

Wednesday, 14 March

I have now read Boswell's London journal 1762–63. Oh, I love it, I love it, whatever the critics say! Dear Boswell, how I sympathise, and how I wish that my journal might attain even half so much eminence. But I do not doubt that this is the wish, ambition and determination of at least a thousand others and we can't all prove so lastingly readable, or hope for so much luck granted to our MSS after death as Boswell's received after his. It is a miracle that the MS was not destroyed by his family long, long ago. I do not mean that it appeals to me just because of his detailed amours. It is the picture of the young man who 'sometimes approves of himself as composed, genteel, manly, firm, valiant, dignified, and feels sure he has the promise of unusual distinction but too often finds himself awkward, uneasy, timid, mean, bashful . . .' Aren't we all like this?

I now feel as bolstered and inspired as Boswell himself when Johnson praised him for keeping a journal. I would faint and fail if I 'knew' mine were to have such a high destiny, but as I feel pretty sure it hasn't I prattle on happily, hoping for a sympathetic reader or two in, say, 40–50 years' time.

Have been working hard at Dinah book, all last week at the BM and some days in the week before. Saw Luigi last week. Same as always, such a truly delightful companion – how she makes me talk. I don't think I know anyone I babble to quite so easily on fairly intellectual subjects as I do to her. Luigi has more to give back (without pushing it at you). Luigi and I are intellectually on a level – N. is above me, Joan below – though I don't mean any disparagement to Joan by it.

Babs home on Friday for the weekend. She is a prefect now and a very important person. Really she grows nicer and nicer. But I notice that she is always better during and immediately after the term, when still within immediate aura of school influence. It wears off as holidays advance. They are to have five weeks, heaven help me, this Easter, and I don't know how she will fill her time.

Thursday, 15 March

Looking through *Tatler*'s in hairdresser's I get seized with a longing for expensive clothes and to be moving in 'rich' society. I mean elegant society, but then I know I should quail at the outset and soon feel suffocated. I do not want luxury or fame, but I do like elegance and interesting – not neurotic – people. In fact, without being smug, I like my life well enough as it is. I only ask to be able to improve it where it needs improving and to maintain what standards of moderate goodliness I have already achieved. To go on growing, in short.

My own two apparently conflicting ambitions, to marry and to write. Since the A.M. episode, which for me concluded in 1946, there has not been the slightest possibility of marriage. I have met no one I have wanted to marry or could have married, and nothing has stood in my way of going ahead with the writing ambition. Until I could do this sincerely, without resentment and inner strife, I could not write, or could not achieve publishable writing.

The desire to marry, to marry rightly that is, is still there, but is set on one side. To marry because one ought to ensures no success in one's personal life as a woman.

Monday, 26 March

This is the cost of cooking for three people for four days. I will start with full menus.

Friday lunch: pork pie, boiled pots, tomato, beet, watercress, bread-and-butter, cheese, coffee. Friday supper: haddock in egg sauce with mashed pots, baked beans, sprouts, plum flummery, bread, coffee.

Saturday breakfast: bacon and fried potato, bread, butter, Vita-Wheat, marmalade, tea.

Sandwiches: grated cheese and chives, bread and marg, cake, oranges.

Saturday supper: pork hotpot (pots, onion, garlic, apple, herbs, seasoning and stock). D: peas and lentils mashed, cabbage, junket, coffee.

Sunday B: boiled eggs, as before.

Sandwiches: sardines and beet and watercress, as before but apple if not oranges.

Sunday supper: liver hotpot (in remains of last night's gravy with the bacon, more pots, tomatoes, last of the beans, peas) stewed bottled pears and apples in jelly, coffee.

Monday B: sausage and bacon as before.

Sandwiches: egg and tomato, oranges as before.

Monday supper: beefsteak stew in stock from last two days (including all veg water) plus onions, garlic, leftover peas and lentils, cauliflower, bread, coffee.

Tuesday breakfast: bacon and pots.

Sandwiches (if required): cream cheese and grated sprout.

Laundry: four sheets, two pillowcases. Two bath towels, two napkins, one tablecloth plus surcharge.

Total cost £1. 15s. 2d.

On top of this I have to allow something for kitchen stove fuel. I provided baths on Saturday and cottage has been aired and warmed this very chilly damp weekend, though stove would have been on anyway if I'd been alone. Also allow something for electricity – light at night in sitting room and bedroom and stove in sitting room all evening and for breakfast. Should allow something too for rent and rates but this very low – unless one throws in necessary decorations and repairs. I suppose too one should remember h.w. for washing-up, washing-up powder, and scouring stuff and h.w. for visitors washing.

I think £2 should cover most of it, including my own living expenses for the things mentioned. The profit would seem a good one. But I do all the work. It is a full-time job, from 8 a.m. to about 9 p.m. with an interval in the middle of the day varying perhaps from two to four hours. But add to this, or note, rather, that I dishonestly keep these 'earnings' from income tax declarations – if the venture were ever worked up into a proper business (as I often dream of doing) then I should have to declare them I suppose. Also, overall, I must remember that present advertising expenses, which are considerable unless I get many more bookings this summer, will swallow completely any profit whatsoever and leave me out-of-pocket.

On Wednesday I meet Babs and E. at the Ideal Home Exhibition.

Thursday, 12 April

B. a pet. Really so very nice now, pleasant, companionable, interesting. Is out tonight dancing with school friends. We saw *Kiss Me Kate* yesterday. On Saturday we go to see *Gay's the Word*.

But what sets me singing most is that yesterday morning I saw the jacket design for Peg. By Philip Gough, and delightful. It has quality. It sets the tone of the book. Distinguished, arresting. We are all pleased with it. To be done by lithograph – an investment for a long run I am told. I can't believe this is me: Janet Camden Lucey.[195] Dear God may I have the stability to stand the strain of success if it comes. October is to be the publishing month, and salesmen to start circulating the book in July. Please please let me not falter now.

---

195 Her pen-name Janet Camden Lucey derived from three sources. Her father's family name was originally Camden Pratt; her mother's maiden name and Jean's middle name was Lucey; and Janet was probably a play on Jean.

40.

The Latest Boogie-Woogie

Thursday, 19 April

Sometimes in my dreams at night I am back again at school and it is always nightmarish. I live again through that cold rush of hostility, of feeling I don't fit in, can't do things, will be jeered at or get reprimanded. All horrible, so that I wake with huge relief to my 40 full years.

Pepper's first family arrived in the early hours this morning. I found her purring ecstatically over three when I came down to the kitchen; she chose to have them in box placed under little table and curtained off. She swivelled right round to let me see them, and moved so that I could take away all the messy paper. Every time I peek in and speak to her she rolls over to show them to me. 'Aren't they the most beautiful babies?' she purrs. 'I am a clever cat, aren't I?'

Friday, 11 May

Guests who telegraphed last weekend that they would arrive last night have not turned up, nor have I had one word of explanation. They answered a *Liberal News* ad, address Bethnal Green. I hope they don't come at all now. As I worked about the house yesterday I wished that I did not have to give up my time to domesticities again, and when, with all things ready for them and the whole house clean and tidy, they hadn't appeared by 11 p.m. it seemed too good to be true. I can't think they'd turn up now expecting a pleasant welcome. I can only suppose that either something catastrophic has happened to them, or that they did write during the week but the letter went astray. When I have got into the writing swing again I detest the enforced change of rhythm to prepare for and entertain visitors. I worked at the Dinah book from this Friday until the following Sunday with only one day off in town on Tuesday, to the Foyles luncheon to hear Priestley.

Cats all behaving like savages with woodland wildlife. Garden littered with dead and dying corpses and remains. I rescued a baby thrush from Pepper the other day. Yesterday Squib was torturing a baby rabbit. I managed to get it from him and have had it in a box in my room ever since, but doubt it will live. It won't eat or drink. I don't know why I bother with these little creatures. I cannot kill them, and would see them live and free again if it were possible, although it might be only to die more miserably in a trap or live to eat my most tender and rare plants.

The warmth of the fire has revived my bunny. He fell out of the duster and has been making valiant efforts to get onto his feet, but keeps falling onto his side. The struggle costs much effort and he lies exhausted. It lies now wrapped in the duster on my lap, its head resting on the thumb of my left hand, and my fingers holding its forepaws. I have been feeding it with milk and water from a pen-filler. At least its fear seems to have gone – I hope it has. It is very still. I cannot feel it breathing. As I fed it with the filler it opened its mouth gasping – perhaps it could not swallow, the cats may have twisted something in its throat. I'm sure it is dead. I have loosened my hold, it does not stir.

Yes it is dead. It gasped its last in my hand. My kindness killed it, or saved it perhaps a few more lingering hours. If I had left it to the cats yesterday afternoon its agonies would have been over within the hour but it would have died in a pall of terror.

N. in trouble still. She has been having trouble with gums, had a poisoned elbow, and passed out under penicillin injections. Expects the end any day now, but retains, she says, her sense of humour. The

Powers of Evil have marked her down, she thinks, because she has refused to cooperate with them. Dear N. Forever and forever N.

Thursday, 17 May

The PGs never turned up and I have had no word. This evening the first batch of Peg proofs arrived. I read right through them (as far as they go) from 5.30 to 8.30 and then felt really exhausted and ill. The pains I had last year again across the diaphragm. I made myself eat boiled egg but then had to lie on bed for 20 minutes or more before circulation and appetite revived. I wonder if it's the smoking? I think that ever since I last mentioned it in here I have been smoking at least 20 day and sometimes back to the old 30 to 40.

Later. N. has been so urgent that I let her help me check the proofs and has sent me pages of advice: her job now involves a great deal of proof correcting so she is right on top of the technique. She makes me feel that what she wants really is to dig herself in somewhere so that it can be said that she was in one particular respect indispensable to Peg's production – she just must have her finger in the pie some-where, somehow. I can let forth about it in here and feel I am cheating. Other people have only the more ordinary outlet of 'pulling her to pieces' behind her back, which she discovers now and then and is fearfully hurt and shocked by, and makes me feel guiltier than ever of this very sly confessional.

Tuesday, 24 June

N. came for the weekend. She wrote later in a postcard, 'I didn't want any acknowledgement, my dear. I am rather overwhelmed to find myself in such distinguished company. But in a way it might even act as encouragement to me to do something myself at last, which I know would be your greatest reward for ever mentioning me.' Oh dear, oh dear!

Characteristically, she is going through the proofs with three times as much thoroughness as anyone else could. This I acknowledge is all to my advantage, and I'm grateful. But the price! She is, of course, 'saving' the book! Correcting grave faults, changing my writing style, revolutionising the punctuation. But I mustn't be pig-headed and stupid. It is not the superficial question of style that troubles me, but the old, old need for me to resist being over-whelmed by the N. personality – to resist it without spiteful feelings of resentment.

She says, 'The older I get, the less women seem to like me. The more I try to lead the good life the more antagonistic they become.' She seeks for the reason outside herself – concluding they are just jealous and resentful of her vitality, ability, culture and so forth, but there is this that she does not see: her very buoyancy is deflating. The accounts of her own exploits, achievements, activities make everyone else's seem stale, flat and unprofitable by comparison – she is a 'capper' par excellence – every anecdote will call forth one from her own life which puts the original in the shade. Also, her judgements and conclu-sions are not always right but she gives them with such conviction that only the very strongest could disagree without a tremor. She is almost – but I think this only in my lowest moments – like arsenic, needed in very small quantities for medical aids to health, but fatal in large doses.

Thursday, 28 June

Two more satisfied PG's go tomorrow. It is very gratifying to feel I can make a success of this job. They all say they want to come again (but never do!), praise my cooking, and promise to recommend me to friends. This is my first all-male contingent, and I must say I prefer looking after men than women. Not that I have had any difficult women. But the atmosphere is different, it's puzzling to know just why. With women, especially when they have a husband in tow, there is a feeling of competition, inquisitiveness and even suspicion, and always a sort of disconcerting, amazed, unspoken curiosity. Men bring much less clobber with them and seem somehow to demand less. Or perhaps it is that, all other instincts are being quiescent, they call forth the maternal.

Had been trying to persuade Tom to let me have his corrections, and finally he promised to bring them, plus latest girlfriend, on Sunday. Tom in ecstasy over *Lovely Peggy* cover. Everyone entranced by it.

Lovely, lovely life. Garden at a midsummer pause. Foxgloves are out, the dahlia is growing well but my rampageous cats will knock it about. Pepper's three kittens now at their most enchanting age, and I learn that the Cats Protection League can't place any more just yet, so what I'll do with them I don't know. Their names seem to have developed as Walrus (Walley), Tom-Tit and Starlet, two short-haired blacks and Starlet with a star of white beneath her chin.

Sunday, 1 July

Two of the proletariat this time: lads from a nursery at Walton-on-Thames, out-of-doors, uncomplicated young people with splendid bicycles of the new bright coloured light alloy. I saw a collection of these machines in the woods a little while ago, heaped against the trees by some club while the owners wandered, bright and dazzling, delightful as a rainbow. I can understand such a possession to be the desire of every adolescent.

Monday, 2 July

Truth is, I am slashed with nerves. A letter from Hugh about the cost of any proof corrections and a newspaper report of medical research finding people who died of cancer of the lung were all heavy smokers.

Tuesday, 3 July

My principal PG, the one who made the booking through the *Liberal News*, is a most interesting and likeable boy. Very, very tall, almost hits Wee's low ceilings. Tanned, pleasant, open face and intelligent brown eyes. He came back yesterday with newly purchased gramophone records and asked shyly and politely if he might try them out on my portable. I restrained my irritation, thinking 'Oh hell, now the latest boogie-woogie. But they are on holiday – don't be mean.' And what should follow but Tchaikovsky's entire Fifth Symphony – on four records! Abashed and moved, I listened with delight and suggested he looked through my records if he cared to. I have been guilty of sloppy thinking again. A boy who could choose this sort of holiday wouldn't like particularly the cheaper music – at least one supposes that if he did, if he had that type of mind, he'd want a resort populated with lush lassies and filled with noise. He sat listening to that music with passionate delight. And today persuaded his friend to buy a record of Yehudi Menuhin's. He is interested in embroidery too. His little friend hasn't anything like his character – talks as though he has no roof to his mouth and is just a little bit 'simple'. I suspect a very good-natured, and a willing, easy yes-man for the other, who with these interests must find companions of his own kind difficult to find.

Lunched with nice Enid R. today. She managed to stop smoking in Canada by chewing gum for three weeks, and says she can get enough sent over for me.

Monday, 9 July
Lunched at D.H. Evans cafeteria, did sundry small shoppings, then saw a coat for £3 in Jays and bought it. What exultation! What heaven! A Voguish, Brenner sports utility model in a fine navy check on cerise, wool, fully lined. Incredible. Then BL exhibition (modern books), and tea with Phyllis and Gus.

They in delightful turmoil. Gus seems to have found himself a really profitable business. With help of his Irishman protégée in basement, he is repairing antiques, upholstering, making curtains, decorating, renewing damaged structures, building. They want an assistant they have so much work. Really it is a joy to see them. In fact, I saw scarcely anything of Gus, he was busy finishing a sofa which was carted away at 6 p.m. Phyllis in background doing all the office work, phoning, scouring London for materials – hugely happy.

Tuesday, 17 July

N. said on Sunday morning as she pottered about the room and I lay still in bed knitting, 'My affection for you grows and grows with the years. Your book has made me love you more than ever.' This is generosity indeed. It came sincerely, spontaneously, from the heart. I don't know what I've done to deserve it. My journal will surely arise one day and pierce me to death. And that I shall deserve.

Her biggest quarrel with me is what she calls my 'reserve'. This is always being thrown at my head in moments of exasperation – I am always one of the most reserved people she has ever known. She picks up on the long forgotten Mac affair as an example, but that is all over, as dead as poor Mac. She senses acutely all the ocean of thoughts spilled into these pages and kept seductively from her.

There are no more PG bookings. B. comes home next week and is off to Scotland a week later. She goes to Eastbourne Domestic Science School in October. Peg illustrations have to be arranged. I want to get on with and finish the Dinah book. Sadleir has contact with the Golden Cockrell Press and I daren't let such a chance slip. Hurst and Blackett have option on my next book, so if I can I want to make that the cat book.

And at that moment the phone rang. Lydia. She has met a living Woffington, through her sister at Ealing. She is to bring him to tea on Sunday.

Tuesday, 24 July

More sugar has arrived from Barbados. Used some of my rhubarb to make more preserve.

Then Lydia and the living Woffington. He is elderly, pleasant, garrulous, and a Theosophist.[196] One is tempted to dismiss him as

---

196 The study of Theosophy is based on the pursuit of a unifying comprehension of the universe, combining a study of divinity, mysticism and human purpose. The quest is for a higher wisdom; the reward is enlightenment. It was to become a (temporarily) significant part of Jean's life.

insignificant and a bore. But Lord, how arrogant, how cruel that sounds! I must not let my impatience blind me to the miracle of having met, entertained and shaken by the hand a living Woffington. He cannot trace ancestry beyond a grandfather sailor who died at sea, but apart from his own family he knows of only one other Woffington – in Auckland, New Zealand. He is very probably a descendant of Peg's family. Has put me on the track of two more portraits which I must try to chase up tomorrow. But doesn't seem to have discovered more about her than I have (thank goodness!).

Wednesday, 1 August

Rereading *Gentlemen Prefer Blondes*. Lorelei seems to have missed something in this life. I mean, what halfwits all her men were. I wish I could meet gentlemen like Lorelei's gentlemen, but if I did they wouldn't even give me a bangle, so I get quite depressed.

Enid came and left a bag full of chewing gum on the sitting room table. She must have heard me typing and stolen away, thinking I was working. Now my ordeal begins. If I can do it – what an achievement! Very wisely she advises, 'Don't rush it, beware of wind, and try to keep your mind off smoking. Just don't think about it or talk about it, and do and say nothing to bring emphasis on the subject. Refuse quietly when offered one. You'll put on weight, your nerves, sight, breathing and health generally will improve. In fact, the benefits are so great that if you can only make the effort and stick at it, you'll wonder why you haven't tried before. Phone when you feel your grip slipping and in need of a pep talk. Shall follow your progress with interest.'

Of course I've since been smoking like a kipper. But here is the real kind of help needed. She never lectured or tried to persuade me to stop, but only when asked told me how she had given it up herself. She smoked since she was 14 and is now over 40. So it can be done. Whatever is that society for alcoholics called? They support each other when trying to break the drink habit. Something of the same could be organised for smokers.

Periods are behaving oddly: three in eight weeks and a flood on Monday when I woke. Can it be the 'change'? Am 43 in October. Suppose it is possible. But feel a little wistful. If it is, now there'll be no chance at all of my ever making good as a woman, wholly.

Sunday, 5 August

Work began again on the cat book. The first chapters seemed awful on re-reading and I'm glad I haven't yet shown them to anyone. Have been trying to tighten them up, set the pattern. It is a book about Dinah and cats, not me and Wee, though I and Wee have to be there in the background – but faintly, just shadows, the twist of chimney smoke, a lighted window. And talking of smoke, I simply cannot start this breaking campaign while at this sort of work. I tried, and I think if I were just doing the ordinary household round and social activities I could do it. After several hours of chewing it is a mistake to have even one – it only starts the craving again. I can see what Enid means when she says she found she had to give it up altogether. It is all or back where you were. And I still must have 'just one' when writing.

Yesterday came letter from Fry's, the people who look after my income tax, telling me what expenses I should submit in connection with work for *Lovely Peggy*. Have been busy at it all this bank holiday weekend. Quite enthralling. I find they come to over £300 in past three years. All this somehow makes me feel taller. I really am in the grown-up workaday world now. And it pushes me yet more surely towards the writing, and writing-only track.

Monday, 6 August

Managed to stop smoking from 11 a.m. until after tea.

Sunday, 9 September

Babs arrived home last Monday morning, bubbling over with her holiday. She brought back for me cigarettes, Sun Maid raisins, chocolates and a very pretty silk chiffon scarf. I was overwhelmed. I really had not thought of her bringing anything. She seemed genuinely pleased to be 'home' again and has settled down to temporarily quiet life with a wonderful philosophy. Her exam results arrived. She has passed in French and German, which means that she has her school certificate. This is a new version. All that is required for it is a pass at credit standard in one subject! It seems like money for old rope to me. Nevertheless it is an uplift to know she is through, and we celebrated by going to see the film *Tea for Two*, but came away with headaches.

Monday, 10 September

I have too many cats. Not for my own sake – I would willingly under-take more – but theirs. Each cat wants all of one's attention and would blossom wonderfully if they had it. They are great egoists. They like being adored more than anything and just hate you to adore any other cat.

I am entering the Black Babies for the cat show in October. Why I can't think. They won't stand the ghost of a chance against pedigree cats. I wanted to enter them as household pets, but there is no class in this section for kittens under nine months. It will be interesting and good experience for me, though I wonder if I should submit such innocents to an ordeal of this nature.

Thursday, 20 September

With enormous effort I finished the kitchen on Sunday and laid new carpet. Then began on Monday to tackle Peg's index. The vilest job. B. very good, took over housework and meals. Has been having driving lessons all this week and is to take a test tomorrow. She is absorbed and bothered with this and her own affairs. Don't think she has a clue as to how hard her poor aunt has been working! Adolescence seems such a long way from me now – I find it very difficult to remember how one felt and thought then, and the limitations of one's knowledge and experience and understanding. I of course am aching for sympathy – for someone to moan to.

And now this morning I wake to find election date settled for 25th October. It is really shattering. I phoned Halliday [editor at Hurst and Blackett]. It would be madness to publish in October now – in fact the scheduled day was the 25th! It has to be postponed again, until February. I feel like the donkey after the carrot.

Sunday, 23 September

The thought that really weighs me down is: no hope of any earned income now until next June. If I start thinking of the future it terrifies me. Suppose Peg flops. Suppose I can't place the cat book. Suppose I fail with Sadleir. Suppose in short I find I am a fraud and that the fact I have got as far as I have with Peg is just a lucky fluke.

But the point is, I do not believe that. Peg was an honest piece of work and I believe it has something. I believe it has a chance, if circumstances are kind and we are not, for instance, plunged into revolution with the Tories in power in February. I'm beginning to believe also that I can write. What I'm trying to confirm in myself is a determination to go on. I may know by this time next year the extent of Peg's success or otherwise. All I can decide now is to hammer down my fidgeting, fretful doubts. Give me grace that I may live in truth – which is suspense, which is adventure: movement, growth, uncertainty, risk and danger. I must not be afraid.

'Tomorrow I shall be an author!'
Lovely Peggy, published under a pseudonym in 1952.

41.

A Deadly Sting

Thursday, 4 October 1951 (aged forty-one)
This delicious hour must be shared. Free again to pursue my own interests with a clear conscience. Tea alone, once more relaxed on sitting room sofa, as I have not been, it seems, for months. Dear little B.! Really I am very fond of her but one can have too much of unadulterated adolescence. It is not good for adult or adolescent. The gap, which has to be bridged, is too wide. The adult has not stopped growing any more than the youngster – they may be a little further ahead, growing in a different way, and it is as important to allow for their growth as for the child's. Summer is over.

Wednesday, 10 October
I must get a grip on myself about this coming cat show. Was yesterday prostrate nearly all day with tummy pains and first day of period – I'm sure it was nerves. It had struck me all of a heap the evening before what misery it may be for the kittens: two whole days, confined and submitted to the public gaze. I felt I ought to cancel their entries and abandon my scheme. They won't stand a chance against pedigrees, though their coats are improving and I may with luck get them past the vet.

I feel better today and I must persevere. Have ordered a taxi to take us the whole way on Friday – cannot risk early morning congestion on Green Line. They are so sweet, submissive, affectionate, so totally unaware of what lies ahead for them. If I can only get good homes for them at the show, all the botheration and panic will have been worthwhile.

Tuesday, 16 October

The cat show I enjoyed, after all, hugely. And the kittens I do believe liked it too. They settled down well and loved the attention and praise they got at intervals. They won no award: not even a commendation. As for parting with them – I couldn't do it. Didn't even try, and put the whole thing out of my mind when we arrived. On Sunday, definite plans materialised. I will keep them both, have Starlet spayed, but keep Tom-Tit entire and try to obtain for him British Blue wife and launch into breeding true black shorthairs. Meanwhile, plans are afoot to convert one of the sheds into a cattery. With window mended, door made to shut and draught-proof, roof tightened up and tarred, and walls creosoted, the inside wholly reorganised, cleaned and furnished appropriately with clean comfortable sleeping boxes and a slow burning paraffin heater, I shall be able to leave them all there happily while I go away for 2 to 3 nights.

Sunday, 21 October

Election. Much to my relief there is no Liberal candidate for S. Bucks. Every Liberal I have spoken to is still of the same mind – many like me will not vote at all on Thursday. I don't think there is any doubt at all that the Tories will get in here. I hope in one way the Tories do get in, to see if they can clear up the mess they are always condemning. If they can't they are sure to blame Labour for it. I do wish politicians in all parties could admit more freely and openly that they are all fallible, and have made mistakes and will make more. To hear them talk before an election you think they were individually suddenly the only people who knew all the answers and had never done anything wrong.[197]

---

197 The Tories, under Winston Churchill, won with 321 seats, a majority of 26 over Labour. The Liberals returned only 6 MPs.

Friday, 2 November

I was determined to start again at the British Museum this week. Set off at noon, lunched in Slough, looked in at Selfridges to find they no longer have pets department. It was 4 p.m. before I reached the BM. There I found confusion – the Reading Room is being repaired and readers are poked away among the catalogues in the old music room. I found this most disturbing. After five years I was just beginning to know my way around and where to find essential ref books and now all at sea again and cramped into the bargain.

Friday, 9 November

I met Pat M. on train this a.m. – my doctor's daughter. She is a very clever little artist and now at the Slade. It is curious how with some people you sense a common bond from the start and are at ease and happy with them. But with my dear little B. there is always the undercurrent of suspicion and contempt. I'm sure she instinctively despises 'arty' folk – it is an inherited tendency and I doubt will never change now. All her friends are nice, but have the same ordinary tastes, although some of them may do more interesting things than B. ever will. Once she gets abroad again she will revert to type – she is conditioned to it now. The sad thing is that she thinks that because she has lived most of her life abroad she is unusual. But I have met no duller set of people than the English who live abroad, unless it be in the suburbs. Perhaps it's because when I've gone abroad I've only met suburbia again there.

Saturday, 5 January 1952

Peg is at last in book form. I went to see publishers yesterday and received my copy. But publication is being postponed again. Bound copies have only just come from the printers and Halliday is very anxious to push the book as much as he can before it appears officially. Although these delays are heartbreaking, I should feel flattered that he wants to go to so much trouble. He does seem genuinely keen to give it every chance. As I am a totally unknown writer with no academic qualifications (nothing at all to help publicity) it means extra hard work and perseverance from him. I am grateful, in a way even relieved for this further respite. Publication is going to be something of a nervous strain. Not as agonising for me as a platform appearance, but it will bring similar tension and palpitations.

Brother Pooh is sending me 5 pounds as an Xmas present, which I have already spent on a Parker fountain pen and a utility grey flannel Jaeger skirt. I resolved a little while ago to buy no more cheap clothes or jewellery, to wear out what I have at home, and try to concentrate on quality and grooming when the occasion calls for it. But God help me, grooming is a life's work, and quality is getting almost beyond my means nowadays. I get more sluttish at home, and when I go out seem to have no time to prepare myself. To get one's hair, hands, skin and clothes into decent condition after months of neglect needs at least a week's hard work on them beforehand.

Thank goodness tomorrow is Twelfth Night and I can take down decorations and cards. When Xmas is over they fidget me – so gaudy, so tawdry. We had a lovely display of cards this year between us. I wonder what I shall do next Xmas. B. will be in Barbados. N. may be abroad. I had another vision for Wee last week: to build a big studio room where the sheds are now, cover in the space between them and back door. There will be room for four visitors (two in each room) hanging space in one bedroom which would relieve congestion downstairs – oh, it would be marvellous. To have everything I needed for work around me, to hand, with room to spread typewriter and MS and books instead of having them scattered over floor, chairs, bed or sofa. Heaven, heaven.

Monday, 14 January

Peg book is being sent off to Allardyce Nicoll and will also go to professors Tillotson, Sutherland, Richardson. My dread now is to hear that Nicoll has turned it down because of grave errors or some sort of faultiness, and that other profs may turn it down too for reasons I haven't thought of. Some grave, grave mistake that they couldn't possibly excuse . . . [198]

Tuesday, 15 January

Mr Halliday of Hurst and Blackett writes this a.m. that he will let me know as soon as he hears anything favourable. But oh God, supposing it isn't? Where shall I put myself?

When I say that I am writing about cats I feel, after Peg, that I'm being frivolous, and am apologetic. I feel for cats intensely and want the book to be taken as seriously as possible.

Am sure N. is longing to lecture B. about sex, which N. always loves to talk about, suspecting that I am not frank or instructive enough with the young woman, and that B. may like a little wholesome information. But B. seems to me on the whole extraordinarily sensible about her relationships with young men and quite 'safe' to leave to find her own level. She is not at all silly about boys and likes to get to know them thoroughly. Though she hasn't many boyfriends in England, she has a few, and is quite content to wait until she gets to Barbados for more harmless fun. I am sure she will keep her head all right: I do not have to fuss about it and give 'little talks', thank goodness.

Sunday, 3 February

I heard yesterday from Halliday that the Book Society are not going to give Peg their blessing, though there seemed to be people in the office who hoped that the committee would. Nor has Prof Nicoll time to read or write the foreword. So Peg must go forth alone, unchampioned. I was disappointed and disheartened. Yet perhaps it is a good thing. Humility is a valuable possession. I must not, cannot, expect

---

198 Nicoll, a former professor at Yale, was an expert on the history of English and Irish drama.

too much. I do not deserve and could not support an avalanche-success. Though I hope, dear Lord, I hope I may have a little, enough to make me feel that the battle has been worthwhile, and encourage me to go on. I must be ready to go on whatever happens. Blinding failure itself must not send me backwards now.

Thursday, 7 February

The King is dead. We shall now be singing 'God Save the Queen'. I shall feel Victorian and expect to see soldiers in red coats. The idea of that shy, charming young mother Princess Elizabeth as Queen now is too massive to take in properly. One's heart aches for her. What a formidable, fearful task.

The news of the King's death was unbelievable. I had heard nothing when I left for London yesterday about 2.30 p.m. The sight of flags everywhere at half-mast startled me, closed cinemas were puzzling. I thought: it must be the king, but I did not credit it. Now it is finished. The burden was too great – he was due to go, one saw it in his face. In spite of all that modern medical science could do, his time here was over, and he slipped away so quietly, out of our reach.

I am more and more drawn to the theory of reincarnation. It explains so much, makes the pieces fit together. Have been to one meeting of local Theosophists with Lydia and may go to others – may even perhaps join. And now I think I have over-boiled the marmalade. What a curse. Last year I didn't boil the marm long enough. Does one ever learn?

A month today Peg makes her debut. Or so we hope again. Edith Evans has recommended it warmly, which will be used in the advertising.[199] This is really better, to me, than a Book Society notice. I rejoice and bless Dame Edith. But I have also nearly £40 for proof corrections to meet. That will mean £140 to be cleared

---

199 The actress Dame Edith Evans played several of the same roles as Peg Woffington, including Rosalind in *As You Like It*.

before I start getting anything. We can only trust in the Lord and wait.

Have just read Robert Reid's account of George VI in today's *News Chronicle*. It is very moving. He was, in a way which materialists will not be able to recognise, a great man. He was shy, unambitious, there was nothing spectacular or compelling about him. He had overcome a shocking stammer. But he did it – he got on to his feet, made public appearance after public appearance, quietly, competently. He spoke always directly to the ordinary man. He knew and voiced the simple and important values of life. He did an uncommonly difficult job remarkably well. Think of it, all you reserved, bashful, unassuming folk: how would you tackle it if suddenly forced into the limelight? George VI may not be so overlooked by the historian of the future as Reid imagines. The King set us an example of real courage: the courage of a man who was afraid but still goes on, and comes through well. We need more examples like this. We cannot all be Churchills, but we can be Georges.

Now redoing the marmalade with one apple. It would have set into toffee else.

Sunday, 17 February

I am on the edge of an ocean of self-pity tonight. If I walk a little further it will be up to my thighs, to my neck, I shall be comfortably drowned in it.

I want the larger security that comes from confidence in an established career: to be able to see my way fairly clearly for several years ahead, as one does presumably in a successful marriage. Here is our home, say the happy couple, here is our material, and now we can set about building our future together on a firm foundation. Oh I know. It does not always work out, one or other fails, the unforeseen bomb destroys the home. But I seem to have jogged on for so long alone, just seeing my way through the scrub, hacking the path as I go, laboriously and expensively with tools that have been provided for me. I cannot plan a broad road, though I may dream of it often.

I stood for four-and-a-half hours to see the King lying in state. It was well worth it. One felt part of a great tradition, an integral part of a great living, growing community with deep roots, an immense heritage. I'm proud to be British in this moment of our history. *The Observer* published a remarkably good leader last week on the symbolism of our monarchy – I think they are absolutely right in their views. In today's *Observer* a Debrett's editor discloses that Elizabeth II and Prince Philip between them are descended from every Royal house which has occupied the throne – Wessex, Godwin, Normandy, Blois, Anjou, Tudor, Stuart, Hanoverian. I can't find words for the feeling that this information rouses in me. But am uplifted, inspired, and turned away from the personal puddle in which I would have wallowed.

Tuesday, 19 February
Letters all yesterday evening – difficult ones, like writing to Edith Evans to thank her for supporting an unknown writer, which entailed a phone conversation with Gus to find out what plays I had seen her in.

9.30 p.m. Pharaoh [new name for Tom-Tit] has been sick twice again. With nothing inside him it was only froth and liquid. It seems I have spent the entire evening clearing up and slopping about with pail, rags and disinfectant, such is life with six cats.

Friday, 22 February
Starlet died just before noon today. This damnable, damnable enteritis – nothing we can do to help. I established them both in the spare room, where they just got weaker and weaker in spite of vet's penicillin. Veterinary science has no real answer yet for this virus. At 4.30 this morning I heard Star's little voice become husky and anguished. She purred when I came and quietened. I had to spend the rest of the night in that room with them – each time I returned to my own bed I heard Star crying. She was terribly weak when the vet came. He

thought there was little hope then, but gave another penicillin injection. Half an hour later, as I sat exhausted and sad, drinking much-needed coffee in the kitchen, she died, alone. I would have held her paw if only I had known. I was in and out of that room from 4.30 onwards – and it had to happen when I was not there. I felt bitterly that I had failed again, let yet one more poor cat down when she needed me.

Pharaoh just ticks on, but I never know when I may find him quiet and still too. He now lies just by my chair, he will not stay in his box. He is flat, with nose to ground, tense to the touch, but still breathing and will sometimes lift his head when stroked, and purr faintly. There is also the perpetual fear that one of the other four remaining cats will succumb too.

Priscilla will type the cat book for me and I hope to take the manuscript next week. I still have additions to make and now dear Starlet's little paragraph to alter. I hope I shall not have to change the tense for Pharaoh too. I want so much for him to live.

Monday, 25 February
But he did not. Here I may spill my grief. Release the knot that is tightening in my heart. He died, dreadfully, late on Saturday, sometime after 11 p.m. Poor little Pharaoh, growing colder, lying miserably, too weak to move, trembling violently after the least exertion. I would have spared him those last hours. I mourn for that little star of light who bounded purring to my shoulder, for the solid weight of Pharaoh to my breast, his silly sentimental nose at my chin. And for all my plans and dreams for a dynasty of magnificent Pharaohs that lie buried now under the blackberries.

Thursday, 28 February
Sickness continues amongst the cats, but not so severely. Pepper has been isolated and under observation but seems all right again. Squib is off his food and was twice sick this morning. People are so kind

– E.D., Lydia, N. who phoned with message from her sister, Ethel –
all expressing sympathy.

Sunday, 2 March

Pepper has recovered. Squib continues without any appetite but seems
otherwise all right. May our troubles be nearly at an end. And Peg
coming out on Thursday. Beethoven's Appassionata now being played
– lovely, lovely liquid blue notes.

Dear N. She sails for Takoradi in Ghana at end of March. Uplifted
at the thought of her new adventure, which I think she will at last
find really rewarding.

Wednesday, 5 March

I suppose that after tomorrow life will never be quite the same again.
I shall be in contact with new faces, new influences, and not all of
them pleasant. Morning mail is already exciting. Tomorrow I shall
be an author! Said my friend Teddy O'Sullivan, the village tobacconist
the other day, 'Feeling nervous?' Yes. Right across my diaphragm.

Lovely Peggy: A Life of Margaret Woffington *is a reliable and tradi-
tionally built biography of an intriguing subject. Jean displays both a
great admiration and knowledge of her heroine, pursuing her from a
modest upbringing in Dublin at the beginning of the eighteenth century
to her triumphs on the Covent Garden stage and her public role as the
object of desire for half of Georgian London. There are many passages
that mirror the author's own life, not least her strident independence.
But Jean's own claims for her book were unduly modest: 'I do not know
. . . that I have added much to what was already known about her,' she
wrote in the introduction. 'But at least, as far as I have been able, it is
all collected into one volume and in sequence . . . It has been the creation of a picture, a mosaic built from isolated fine pieces never before
related. If some of the glamour hitherto surrounding her role as courtesan
is thereby lost, I hope she appears more human and understandable.'*

In her acknowledgements she thanked those who had offered professional help, and also Priscilla, Tom, Gus and Nockie.

Wednesday, 12 March

Letters are a burden that grows heavier and heavier – it seems such a waste of writing energy, though I suppose that seems very rude. I like receiving letters, especially when they say in them nice things about Peg. I have heard from my old headmistress, Mrs Parker. She must be nearly 90, in her 80s at least. Was such an old gorgon in our day at Princess Helena College.

Friday, 21 March

In the *Times Lit Supp* today nearly three-quarters of a col on *Lovely Peggy*. It is a just, very well written, good review, but in its tail is a deadly sting. Scholarship, style, construction, logic. I was prepared for blows in any of these directions, but not for this one: The characters he/she says do not come to life. 'The book lacks living force.'

This is shattering. But I do not feel shattered – only disconcerted and confused. All day long I've been pushing the arrow aside saying, 'but it isn't true . . . Peg lived for me, she seems to have lived for N., for Tom, for G. . . . for Edith Evans . . .' The one thing I thought I had done, if I had failed in others, was to bring Peg to life, to recreate her in her surroundings.

I fear now that other critics may take their line from this one. I am then damned. All the little people who cannot think for themselves, the floating voters and the fungoids will follow and natter, 'Yes, very good, of course, but it doesn't live . . .' I wonder how much influence the *TLS* has? Halliday is anxious for the Sunday reviews.

I thought at first: I shall go to see Graham Howe about this. If the book really is lifeless then it has been a huge waste of time and energy. If all 'official' opinion agrees on this point I shall need help. Wait . . . wait.

Reading the review through again, I am bewildered further. 'The greater part of' the account of Peg 'is concerned with her private life.' But it isn't! There wasn't enough material about her private life. I thought it was almost too heavy with stage matters.

Sunday, 23 March

Am relieved to find a similar criticism made by Naomi Lewis today of the new Mrs Gaskell biography. Not so sharp, but still there, so that Miss Hopkins must be feeling as I do about her creativity.

I went to see Alec Clunes in *The Constant Couple*. It is astounding good fortune that he is putting on this play just now – his Wildair is a delight.[200] Show-cards of *Lovely Peggy* are being displayed in the theatre. I have written to Clunes expressing due appreciation. Such material here for a romantic situation! I cannot help dallying with it, though I know it is foolhardy. Author and actor meet. Flash, bang and a delirious ending.

I spent p.m. yesterday at the BM and when I got home a telegram waited. Ring Eastbourne at once. Babs has had her appendix out, and the poor head of the School of Domestic Education frantic because unable to contact me to know whether B. should go into a general ward under National Health or a private nursing home and dad to pay. They managed to phone Ethel and decided on the nursing home, to which I am sure Pooh will agree.

Friday, 28 March

N. will be now – where? The Channel, or the Bay of Biscay? She sailed yesterday afternoon, I cannot believe she is gone. Four of us saw her onto the train at Euston.

Must not let reviewers make me doubt my identity. More crits arrived this week, on the whole favourable, but again one said he found a lack of warmth in the book. (Quite kindly, and would like

---

200 Peg Woffington's portrayal of Sir Harry Wildair in George Farquhar's *The Constant Couple* was one of her most celebrated roles, and she is depicted in the part in a painting by Hogarth. Alec Clunes is the father of the actor Martin Clunes.

to read a book by me on Garrick!) But nearly all stress painstaking scholarliness. I find this unnerving – I wonder if I am really heading towards Reading Room Mole status.

Thursday, 10 April

I hunger and thirst for an encouraging comment from a reputable quarter. I don't mind how brief, so long as it contains no damning innuendoes. How I wish critics didn't have to be so cleverly critical. Even the local *Express* slights me by making no mention of the book whatsoever. I begin to suspect myself of persecution mania, for I find myself thinking up all sorts of dreary and futile reasons for the local cold-shouldering. I think of the queer little journalist woman I see often about in the village and Slough: shrunken and shabby with projecting teeth, and evil, weasel eyes that glitter from beneath the brim of the same ancient felt hat jammed tightly over bobbed hair – a stunted relic of the 20s. I do not know her at all, have never met her socially or officially, but am sure she knows who I am and all there is to know about me. A witch like this could well persuade her editor I was not worth bothering about if she had decided to dislike me. Though I have given her no cause intentionally, and it could only be that she has misinterpreted my abstracted moods for scornful indifference.

Not that the local paper could make or mar my reputation, but it would have been flattering to have been interviewed, as my publishers thought possible. It is just a month now since Peg appeared, and nothing shattering has happened. What I expected I do not know. To wake up and find myself famous?

Easter Sunday

Writing makes one of necessity very self-conscious. One has to be very sure about the worth of one's work and why one is doing it. The whole situation tends to encourage one's egocentricities. So long as one remains aware of failure and is not disheartened by it and can continue striving to achieve.

N. has here, I am sure, done the right thing for herself in going to teach the African young. She has shifted her focus of striving in the right direction. I do not mean that I should want to do anything like this, or to give up trying to write. I must just be more aware of its temptations and pitfalls, its tendency to encourage selfishness and the sin of pride. Peg has taken me 5–6 years to get done and published, and I shall be lucky if we sell 2,000. This would just clear my debts and leave me a profit of about £30.

Tuesday, 15 April

There is one thing that remains through the battle constant. I write. I cannot stop myself writing. If I get not a thing more published, not even a three-guinea article, I will not stop writing my journal. This seems to me potent. It may be a disease, a haemorrhage. I may get nothing more published (that is the most fearful doubt of all), yet I shall write. I have faith. There are I-don't-know-how-many notebooks like this one hidden away upstairs to prove it.

Wednesday, 16 April

This morning I woke all gloom and dumps again. The final straw was to see that my longed-for bath water was disappearing instead of mounting in the bath. The plug for some reason has gone on strike – it doesn't seem to have perished but simply would not stay in the hole. This brought on such a paroxysm of rage, I bit a piece out of the rubber.

Tomorrow I go into Slough, and then to lunch and afternoon with Liz. I shall look for a grey cardigan, and it is not going to be a nasty cheap thing that shrinks the first time it is washed.

Tuesday, 22 April

Recovery began on Friday with the tonic I expect I really needed: an excellent review of Peg by Susan Connely in *John O'London's Weekly* – a full page, not an unkind stab in it anywhere.

Thursday, May Day

I found the perfect grey cardigan and put my live cigarette end right through the back of it the same night. It has been mended professionally, but the place still shows a little. I could have strangled myself. Now I will have some tea, listen to *Mrs Dale* and then *Get On*.[201]

Later: I wonder why I listen to *Mrs Dale*. It's all such drivel. No – the matter isn't drivel really, it's the sort of stuff of which daily life is made for thousands. As someone else has said: it's ordinary things being said in an extraordinary way. Mrs Morgan, Susie and all the characters don't seem at all real to me.

Tuesday, 3 June

I feel profoundly sad, despairing, even apprehensive about Tom. I have lost real contact there. Always with the Communists one is aware that one isn't on their side of their fence. Theirs seems such an upside-down, distorted, turmoil of a world. With Tom it becomes a nightmare, without love, hope or charity for any thing or person that cannot be dyed vermillion. He irritates even his own best friends. I wish him luck and success – but Tom, dear Tom, do not destroy the world instead of building it. What is terrifying about Communism in Britain is that it seems to attract so many of Tom's type: violent, abusive, unstable, obstinate and unscrupulous. The embittered have-nots, the army of the maladjusted.

Wednesday, 2 July

My story about biting the bath plug has met with huge success. E.D. suggests that I keep the plug hung in a convenient place and bite chunks out of it whenever overcome with rage. But not to let myself be seen doing so, or I should be locked up.

---

201 *Mrs Dale's Diary* ran from 1948 to 1969, a radio soap opera that preceded *The Archers* by two years. It was a cosy, middle-class drama, much prone to parody.

Thursday, 10 July
Wee Cottage, Egypt,
Farnham Common,
Slough,
Bucks

My dearest Nockie-Leo,

I thought you might like a long letter by ordinary mail for your birthday. I managed to get a *Silas Marner* and sent it from Slough about a week ago. It was the hottest day of the year (92 in London!). It was only 5s., so I still have 7s. 6d. in hand owing to you and am keeping an eye open for short stories. I was in Charing Cross Rd the other day, in Watkins for a special cat book which they had obtained with difficulty and were keeping for me. The price – second-hand – was 27s. 6d.! Which so took the wind from my sales and money from my purse I could only crawl home without daring to look in other bookshops. But I hope to be in the vicinity again before long.

The cat book was sent off about 10 days ago. I don't suppose I shall receive a verdict for some weeks. Rather a bad time just now, readers and executives will be on holiday. Saw H. and B. publisher Halliday last week. Peg sales are not exactly staggering, but he is very pleased with reception and says that it was well worth publishing. Thinks biography is my 'line' and urges me to persevere. Some comfort to one's pride if not one's pocket. Then there is the novel to which I am now committed and can hardly withdraw.[202] Have been trying to read some contemporary historical novels, to find out how others set about it, and find most of them so far such drivel I can't even finish the first chapter.

Your letter of the 6th arrived today at teatime, so I was able to enjoy it while having a cuppa. The kittens sound great fun; you will find them good companions. It is delightful to know how much you

---

202 The novel, an adventure set in the eighteenth century, is called *Heiress Caroline*.

like the Africans. Felt that you would, and I am sure they will love you. Europeans always seem to get 'crusted' when they settle abroad. It is probably, as you say, when they find themselves in unaccustomed positions of power. Did you ever see *Banana Ridge*? It was a silly farce with Robertson Hare in leading role. I forget the plot, but have always remembered the wonderful caricature of the stupid little Englishman abroad, lording it over the natives (Hare played it beautifully) and then at home finding himself just nobody! It is sad that so often this type gets drawn abroad. I've seen it among the English where my brother has been stationed.

14 July: I had a letter from Luigi today – the first squeak out of her since March. She is in Melbourne now, and has found herself a good job as a draughtsman in a government department, working with a Lithuanian, an Austrian, a Pole, a Swiss, and another from S. Rhodesia! At present she is engaged on army kitchens and canteens – a change from luxury Mayfair hotels and chapels. She finds the native Aussie much less bumptious and more likeable than those who come over here.

Tuesday, 22 July

It is an afternoon in which to be idle. It is a good thing to know when to be idle and how to be idle. I don't think I do, or have ever done – this has only just dawned on me. I read Graham Howe's books over and over, and am forever making discoveries, finding what I have missed or failed to understand before.

'The characteristic of the spoiled child and of the nervous state is,' (Graham Howe writes) ' . . . that there must be neither time nor space unfilled. We must learn to suffer emptiness . . . To come to terms with nothingness.'

This is at the core of many of my fretful moods. I am often conscious of emptiness, a hollow, a cavern which I have seen as a fault, a lack in me (the empty womb) – particularly when some heavy piece of work or special activity is concluded. An unhappy space within is suddenly apparent as the bustle and pressure of work and obligation subsides. And so the space has to be filled. Be busy now: clean the house, weed the garden, sew, listen to the radio, go to the pictures, have a cigarette – or write in here. Or sleep. Yes, even sometimes one can fill the space for a little while with sleep until one's dreams grow too troubling.

Far too much of this journal – I now can see – is an attempt to fill a vacuum which should have been faced and suffered, not avoided. There are certain intervals in time which are meant to be silent pauses. If I could describe this in musical terms I could make it clearer: music does not fill the listener's ear with notes continually; the pauses, the intervals, are all part of the whole composition which could have no value without them. We have to learn how to wait (idle) in peace, alone, suspended like stars in the sky.

'Cigarettes and pipes,' continues Graham Howe, 'fill up our empty spaces. We seem to need a lot of these soothing stimulants to satisfy our restless and unfocused energies, but it cannot be good for health in body or mind to rely on these external "dummies". They are nervous props, false substitutes for real limbs. The cure, I think, is not to stop our smokes and drinks . . . But to develop instead our own real limbs, strengthening our positive interests and attitudes by making them do some work themselves, until we no longer need narcotic comfort.'

But do not suppose, dear gentle reader, that because you have managed to give up smoking, or do not like it, that you are therefore one of the elite with all limbs grown and working. I can think of half a dozen people, straight away, who do not smoke but they do not seem to me any better psychologically. This is not to excuse myself, but only to warn myself and others that to be without or to rid oneself of one particular nervous prop does not mean we have no need of others.

This then I must do: learn to come to terms with the hollow within, the vacancy, the gulf where no bridge is. And I must not do it by rushing to these pages. Wait. Endure the silence, the suspense, the uncertainty. The music has not ceased.

The road to self-knowledge is long and full of blind alleys.

Thursday, 14 August

Today Eden married Clarissa Churchill. A surgeon was lowered 1,235 feet into a cavern in the Pyrenees to attend an explorer lying unconscious with a damaged spine. And little Babs Pratt sailed in the *Golfito* for Barbados.

I am free. My four years of stewardship are over. I wondered on the way home from seeing her into the train at Waterloo whether the experience has washed through or over me. Tonight as I went through the things she has left behind – discarded clothes and trinkets – I knew. It was an experience we both hated and wanted done with. I realise how much she hated it when I found odds and ends I had given her which are now as it were thrown back at me. None of them of value – most in fact are rubbish and only fit for the wpb, but there were two which have a certain quality she failed to recognise, and I felt that if she had had the smallest real feelings of affection for me she would have kept them. Both are so small they could have gone together in her handbag.

I saw behind that sullen barrier and felt the wave of her hatred and impatience for England and everything that I love and value in it. I tried to make her happy. God I did try to make Wee the best possible substitute for the home she lacked here. On the surface I succeeded – she reached a measure of content. I could never of course give her what only a parent can, but I failed to give her what even an aunt can.

My heart wasn't in it. My heart was numb with impatience and pride and fear – there was no spark, no living link between us. Our differences seemed and still seem so insurmountable. I feel that my brother and his family are lost to me.

B. gave me some irises for the garden as a parting gift – quite unexpectedly – which was sweet and touching. But the giving of gifts is a formula with her – she's too easily generous in this way. It is the word, the feeling of gratitude one hungers for. If only she could have said 'thank you for looking after me'. Youth is always the same. Too young to know, to understand. I hear it echoed on all sides from hurt, exasperated parents.

Not a sigh of regret from B. at leaving Wee, not a turn of the head or one word to the cats. Then the wait at the station where (four years ago) I had met the rude ragamuffin little schoolgirl. The polite farewell kiss. And we both I do believe heaved huge sighs of relief. Only tonight among the abandoned trinkets did I weep, realising my failure. Dear God forgive me, forgive me.

Later: I do not blame B. I did not expect her to share my intellectual interests or to see life from my angle. I tried to reach her level and not be scathing or critical of things she is not yet able to understand or view as one does from mid-maturity. I tried to be patient, to listen, to share what I could of her activities and interests. I must not forget the action of time on seeds sown in these past years. What I have done and what I've neglected to do: all will bear fruit of some sort in due season, the good and the ill.

I have learned something. I've seen my own adolescence again from a middle-aged viewpoint. How cruel we were. I have been despised as I once despised. B. despised me because I was not a Tory, I lived alone, was manless, and I did not spend my days in a whirl of social engagements. I was never, as far as I can judge, a positive influence for good in moulding her ideas, nor so acceptable as an aunt that she showed any pride in the relationship to friends and acquaintances. There was never any 'auntie you must meet so-and-so'. I wonder sometimes what sort of impression she must have given of me to people I didn't meet.

I never forced any of my ideas on her: I was probably much too hesitant and cautious about this. Once she exclaimed 'how stupid!' when something was said about the segregation of the coloured people in

South Africa. I might have started a discussion then of the colour problem which she'll meet sharply in Barbados (see Patrick Leigh Fermor's opinion of Barbados in *The Traveller's Tree*).[203] But would anything I, the despised aunt, have said made any difference? She is too lazy, too eager for a good time, too practical and matter-of-fact to let such things as principles, ideals or politics disturb her. This is not to say she has no feeling or imagination. I can see her making a fair success of her life, if she keeps within her limitations and never feels an urge to move from the familiar sphere to a larger but less kindly one.

My point is that unless one is sure of youth's affection and respect, anything controversial will be taken with a sneer, and to press one's opinions may only increase the opposition to them, doing more harm than good. So that the first aim in a relationship of this kind is to win and establish a bond of trust and affection which isn't done by being dogmatic and pompous.

Well that is off my chest now. I have finished this in bed on Saturday morning and must get up and on with the cleaning up and tidying. She is a dear little soul, with lots and lots of sterling qualities. One must be amused not angry when, after she has with a flourish 'spring cleaned' her room and beaten the mats (a minute or two of banging at them in the garden) one finds inches of fluff in a forgotten corner, the empty bookshelves undusted, the wash basin still dirty. (One is only angry at the thought that she may have thought Auntie wouldn't notice.) She likes, thoroughly enjoys, she says, house work. Good luck to her, the poppet. May she still enjoy it after years of doing it daily.

Monday, 1 September
Cat week over. The Pewter Puss triumphant with a 2nd and three reserves.

---

203 This was the great travel writer's first book, a flowery and highly opinionated guide to the Caribbean. Modern readers may baulk at his descriptions of natives and native customs, including cannibalism.

A letter of thanks from Babs. Prompted by her own conscience or Mama I know not, but it was welcome.

Tuesday, 2 September

I am trying to live, to pay for everything, on a limit of £5 a week.

Monday, 8 September

I don't know how anyone manages to live on £5 or less a week these days. Insurance, cleaners, milk, bread, laundry – all these bills last week were heavy, so that I had to spend £4 of my allotted £5 on them alone. Now I am faced with the August grocery and butcher's accounts, which will need nearly £6 to settle. The quarterly electric light and heat bill came this morning – not formidable, but still another £1 4s. 6d. to find somehow.

It's a headache, and I have decided I must sell my fur coat. I never much liked it and didn't wear it all that often. Nice to have for an occasion, but the occasion is seldom, if ever, one when the good winter coat would not do just as well. I do not think there is anything else I can sell now, except my mother's engagement ring stored in the bank, and old-fashioned diamonds aren't of much value today. Anyway I do not think it can have been an expensive ring as Pop was then young and poor.[204]

Monday, 15 September

Autumn has come too soon. One thinks of the thin frocks and blouses hanging in cupboards, behind doors, left over chair-backs, in the hope that tomorrow we may don them yet once more before we settle into coats and skirts and twinsets. (The well-dressed English woman's winter day uniform is the tweedy skirt and soft wool twinset – it has been an essential part of the wardrobe for years now.)

---

204 Note added later: 'I retrieved it from the bank and find it better than I thought. I shall not sell it yet, but wear it sometimes.'

Thinking about an essay for this year's *Observer* competition, announced yesterday. I must **try**. Oh how lovely to win £100 (or even £10!) and a little success.

Saturday, 27 September
More reviews of Peg have come. All very encouraging.

I am only just living within the £5 a week limit. The only things on which I could cut down with effort are smoking and cats. On smoking, if I could give it up entirely, I should have an extra 20 or 30 shillings a week, and if I reduced my cat family to one or none I'd save at least another 15s. to 20s. on the food for them. I urgently need new bedroom slippers, must collect secateurs being repaired, want to have a frock dyed, some shoes mended and hair done, ought to visit Ethel one day, and so on. I must see about selling the fur coat. After that? Deluge?

42.

Self-knowledge

Friday, 3 October 1952

'When a woman is able to sit down to make the most of the evening – most of the evening's gone.' (Harrabin, *News Chronicle*)

It is despairing the way housework and other obligations rise like a barrier before one. Life is full of little things – they clutter one's day, and one forgets them and then wonders why one has 'no time'. The light in the sitting room that went wrong. A new hook I put up in this room. The fur woman, Mrs Read, whom I phoned about the coat, which had to be carefully packed and registered to her – I wait now for the verdict. I doubt if I'll ever have another fur coat. For one reason I may not be able to afford it; for another, am at last receiving literature from the UFAW,[205] learning something about the abomination of trapping.

This place is old and damp and badly in want of a good paint. Walls peel and flake and create dust, and the old stone floor in the kitchen is cracked and its rough surface catches ash and grit from the fire. Every room and stairwell needs redecorating thoroughly. I would have good hard washable paint on all walls. New flooring for the bedrooms – close compact flooring which will polish easily. All this and more is really urgently necessary, would run into several hundred pounds, and would in the end reduce my labour considerably.

205 Universities Federation for Animal Welfare, established in 1926.

The maddening, irritating thing is that I might have had much of all this done if I'd known I was going to be here so long. Ever since I came I have looked on Wee as a temporary lodging, not knowing what new change the next year might bring in my life – yet all the while feeling myself growing roots here deeper and deeper.

Thursday, 16 October
The Dinah book came back from Hurst & Blackett via Curtis Brown yesterday. It is 'not in their usual line of books,' but they will always be interested in my 'straight' work. This is galling, though not perhaps surprising.

I've sent it personally to Michael Joseph with a letter. If Joseph shows no interest then I must face defeat – I shall be bitterly disappointed and despairing. But I hope, positively, determinedly, that he, a great cat lover, will see what I am trying to do and give me some encouragement.[206] I believe the Hurst & Blackett readers did not get beyond the first two chapters. Oh, the humiliation!

Cannot find a buyer for the fur coat. Don't seem able to sell anything! One feels bruised and ashamed, as though one had exposed one's naked body to the wrong man.

Sunday, 19 October
Study of theosophy draws me so much that I cannot keep away from it. One has to make a feature of surrender and accept what the teachers say are fundamental principles as true. In all religions one has to start with an intuitive belief in God or goodness, and it cannot be 'proved' technically by the intellect. If the tenets work for you, help you to become a better person and to 'see' what was

---

206 Joseph, the renowned publisher of H.E. Bates, Monica Dickens, Joyce Carey and Vita Sackville-West, personally wrote or edited at least seven books about cats, including *Best Cat Stories*, published by Faber in the year of Jean's submission.

before obscure, then they have value and may be used without misgiving.

I must pull myself away from this, down to mundane matters. Yesterday my 43rd birthday was spent very pleasantly with E. and Aunt M. at Wembley. Today rain all day (I love rainy days – they enclose, isolate me, leaving me free to indulge my idleness and contemplation). My overdraft has reached £100 again and I must visit the bank. That, work and chores are the main activities I see before me this week. Oh the chores, chores. In emancipating themselves, women also emancipated the char, as men keep telling us; we have freed ourselves only into the bondage of the sink.

Monday, 20 October

Had tea and received my neighbour Lady S., who is involved in altercation with new neighbour, Joan Hammond, about trees which overhang Lady S.'s garden and which Lady S. wants to cut down. She thinks J.H. is a lesbian, but this does not worry her. Conversation concerning other people's morals led to discussion of our surrounding 'soaks', which does disgust us.

Nearly everyone around here seems to drink heavily, and we wonder how they can afford it. Really the people in the Avenue are a frightful crowd! (I'm not being 'superior'.) The G.F.s, Jasper G., the L.D.s, Mrs H. (a 'kept' woman unashamedly), Mrs F., another soak, old M., another heavy drinker. It is sad, for they are all attractive-looking decent people, most of them young, with children and lovely homes. Such a waste of vitality, and all, as the Theosophists would say, making bad Karma for themselves. I can't say that I've kept apart because of anything specially virtuous in me. Only my shyness and inability to be what they would think a good 'mixer' have kept me from this puddle.

Tuesday, 21 October

I am now within a few pages of that part in *Light on the Path* reached by the group, and shall be able to relax this small intense effort to catch up, and follow on with them.[207] I think theosophy may help me greatly. If it is 'wrong' – i.e. if the originators of this modern movement have in some way erred and are leading us a little awry, which may be so – I am in no position to judge at present. If it helps me to become a better and bigger person – or, as they would say, if it helps me towards merging 'personality' with 'individuality' – then it is the right and good thing for me now and I must pursue it sincerely.

Now I desire power. Not worldly power, but the power a disciple must surely have before he can even begin his training: the power of inner stability, to be able to go one's own way steadily without being intimidated, swayed or pushed by others. To be able to hold steadily to one's independent thought, and without being intolerant; to be able to withstand attack without cringing; to be able to speak out plainly and calmly when the need arises: in a group without being paralysed without self-consciousness, and to another person without being confused by fear.

I desire also some return for the labour I love most. Without my writing I should be very depressed and unhappy, and without some material reward within the next four years I do not know how I shall be able to satisfy the needs of my physical body.

Sunday, 9 November

The Dinah book came back from Joseph, but with an extremely kind letter. He liked it but cannot take it, as it is their policy not to publish too many books on one subject, and their cat quota is well filled.

Sunday, 22 November

Phone Miss Barry. She (furrier and dressmaker in Windsor) suggested I bring the musquash for her to see. I have advertised the musquash

---

207 *Light on the Path* by Mabel Collins, a seminal introductory theosophical text, first published in 1888.

in *The Lady*, had several enquiries, but unfortunately all lost while coat was kept on approval for a week by one lady and returned because it was too small for her.

Later: Miss B. could not take the coat (like all my things, too shabby for a good sale).

Yesterday I invested in a pair of Dolcis woolly lined bootees for £3. I can't afford it, but I know I have done the right thing. They are navy suede without zip or laces, reach only to the ankles, with opening down instep for easy access. They are for fine weather only and I must not garden in them. Have been wearing them ever since my return yesterday p.m. (except in bed) and know I shall live in them. I had also to buy some Marks & Spencer winter lock-knit woolly pants, hideous but warm and cheap.

Sunday, 23 November

I have just typed out new instructions for the disposal of my journals in event of some disastrous accident or sudden death to myself. I have been wanting to get this done, though if God wills and I am spared I would like to prepare them for publication myself in say 20 years' time. It seems as though I am enormously conceited about them. There must be hundreds of other writers and diarists with similar plans.

Yet I feel that they should have their chance. Once written, they lose (as Peg has) their link with me and take on an identity of their own. It is for this, their opportunity, that I prepare now, in case I am not able to do all that I should like to do for them. Not knowing who my executors may be yet (one might even be Babs) I must leave some guidance to those who have to clear up when I am gone.[208] I have no intention whatever of dying yet if I can help it, but forethought of emergency is part of my nature, just as I keep rather too many tinned foods and preserves.

---

208 The instructions were not included within the journals, and have since been lost. Babs was indeed her principal executor (see Introduction).

I have grown a little suspicious of Mass Observation. Tom Harrisson has settled in foreign parts, and from what I hear, it sounds as though organisation is now rather Communist dominated. I do not wish to offend my own Communist friends, but I do not feel I can trust the English Communists, as they are at present, to take on the guardianship of my journals.

Thursday, 27 November
The Princess Helena College Old Girls newssheet arrived yesterday. Miss Parker is reported as having read and 'so enjoyed' Jean Pratt's book *Lovely Peggy*. This really is very high praise.

Saturday, 29 November
Oh I do wish I had a portable wireless – then I could get into bed and listen to the play.

Sunday, 30 November
An interesting article on creativeness in a recent *TLS*. I think mentions one of the old philosophers who lay in bed until 11 or later, finding that his ideas during that time flowed most freely. One is much too afraid of being lazy, or of being accused of laziness.

8.45 p.m. My jobs for the day done, I had a sudden whim while reading Boswell's *London Journal* to collect all the journals I have in my 'library' and see what others did on a last Sunday in November. In 1662 Pepys woke on the morning of the 27th to find 'the tops of the houses covered with snow, which is a rare sight, which I have not seen these three years'. The next day . . . he went off to attend the funeral of Sir Richard Stayner at the Ironmongers' Hall.

On Sunday, November 28th, one hundred years later, Boswell breakfasted with Margaret Douglas, heard a sermon on the advantages of early piety at St James's while he planned his next amorous adventure, walked in the park, dined off veal and pudding and went to Sheridan's in the evening.

Kilvert does not seem to have recorded many last Sundays in November, but his entry for Monday, November 28th 1870 begins: 'A plaintive mew outside the door. I open the door and tabby Toby comes trotting in with his funny little nod of affection.' On Sunday, November 28th 1897, Arnold Bennett's friend Webster told him a true ghost story. In 1914 Barbellion heard a Sir Henry Wood concert at the Albert Hall. Katherine Mansfield seems only to date the first months of the year in her journals, as though she began each year with a good resolution to keep a diary and petered out by March. The only other diary I can find is Mr Pooter's, which cannot be extracted from its context.

And I have to finish my Sunday cleaning up a mess made by Spot, who has diarrhoea and worms.[209]

Saturday, 6 December

Most strangely I am a stranger in my own house. I left an hour ago to go to town, but the worst fog of the year has clamped down on us (AA reports the worst fog in London they had known). No buses are running, and one or two people have walked from Slough to Farnham Common. I walked into the village to buy cigarettes and collect my paper and came home again through the mystery-heavy frost-white woods. The fog shows no sign of clearing. The cold penetrates everywhere.

Sunday, 7 December

I went to town yesterday. I felt tremendously bold and adventurous not knowing what lay ahead. The fog in London was dense and yellow, penetrating every corner. At Paddington the air was so thick it was really like pea soup. What surprised and excited me was the great movement of the populace. Everywhere was thronged with people,

---

209 At this stage, Spot (sometimes referred to as The Damned Spot) lived with Jean and Pinnie, Pewter Puss, The Senator, Joey, Nicky, Pepper and Squib.

keyed up, friendly, determined not to be beaten by the elements – it was worth the journey to have experienced that.

The British Museum portico was shrouded, one could not see the pediment properly. One felt one was entering an ancient temple in another age to take part in mysterious rites. Fog hung all over the Reading Room. I worked for little more than an hour and started home again.

In Slough it was like a blanket. I found a long queue at the 441 stop. We waited and we waited. There were no 441s. A conductress in a passing bus for the station shouted that there were no more buses. If only, I thought, I had begun to walk home at once, I would by then have been half way home. I fortified myself with tea and baked beans on toast at the cinema café, turned up my coat collar and secured it with scarf tied round beret and under my chin, and set forth. Worse things could happen.

Until well past The George stop at Farnham Royal the main road was well-lit and the way was easy. But then the road lamps cease, hedges are high, and lights from houses few and far between. I had a torch, but the battery was nearly finished and I feared it would not last. As I stumbled upon a grass verge I heard footsteps and voices behind me and saw a beam from a stronger torch. Warily I fell in with the travellers – two girls and a man. The man was going to Farnham Common, the girls had to get to Beaconsfield. They dropped off at the Jolly Butcher, looking for adventure perhaps ('Will some kind gentleman see me home?'). I plodded on with the man who had the strong torch.

My companion was an assistant at one of the tailors in the village. He had gone to meet his daughter from the Slough telephone exchange, but missed her. One can walk 10–15 miles in fine daylight without resentment or fear – it is the thought of 5 miles through a fog at night which is the main obstacle, and of losing one's way, becoming ill, meeting with robbery, rape or assault.

As we climbed, the fog thinned rapidly and in Farnham

Common stars were visible. The village lights welcomed us and people were about. One man was anxious for his wife who had left at 1.30 to go to Hounslow. There must have been many held-up, lost, frightened . . .

I was indoors by 8.30, and within the hour had fed and settled the cats and was seated on sitting room sofa consuming an enormous salad and fruit meal and listening to Noël Coward's *Hay Fever*, feeling thoroughly happy and triumphant. I have not felt so happy for months.[210]

Tuesday, 9 December

Modern Theosophy: the meetings I have attended excite, confuse and exhaust me. It is an intellectual excitement, new ideas helping to crystallise already present knowledge. What I want is to learn to be calm, to attain that stability which stands in storm (strength without rigidity; confidence without conceit; humility without servility).

How does one learn to become calm? I am now looking at the Theos Soc's 'Study Course in Meditation' published this year. Earnest meditation, or Christian prayer, is the answer. It is as simple, and as difficult, as that.

There is in me a hard crust I cannot break down. It is (I think) the result of mental habits which developed early, which I used as a refuge (as so many of us do) from experiencing pain. But my mental

---

210 The fog – or Great Smog as it became known – hung over London and its suburbs from 5th to 9th December, and is generally acknowledged as the worst of the century. It was caused by a combination of industrial pollution, a cold snap leading to the mass lighting of domestic coal fires, and a perverse high-pressure weather front that prevented the smog from rising. The smog, often highly toxic, crept into cinemas and theatres and almost all public buildings. Only the Underground was spared. An estimated 4,000 people died as a result, most of them elderly with bronchial disease, some from collisions. The calamity led directly to the Clean Air Act of 1956, which restricted coal burning in urban areas, relocated power stations and encouraged alternative sources for domestic heating. It was one of the first significant acts of environmental urban planning.

powers are not, perhaps fortunately, strong enough to have made me into a successful intellectual at the expense of my emotions.

The Theosophists have a much larger and deeper explanation for all this. I am, they will say, still chained to my personal nature, entangled with environmental difficulties, and no amount of mental gymnastics will be likely to alter this attitude. Now, say the Theosophists, meditation 'will bring about noticeable changes in the whole personality'. It brings 'serenity of mind' and 'stabilises the whole psyche in its reactions to living'. The true goal of meditation is 'to prepare the personal nature . . . to change the habitual, automatic reactions of the personal nature so that this becomes tranquil and more open to influence of the spirit . . . so that in time the personal enters into conscious relationship with the Universal.'

I desire tranquillity in the true and deepest meaning of the word.

Friday, 12 December

The Dinah book back again, not wanted.

What a perpetual, remorseless battle living is. I think my heart is numb. It's crept away into shelter from this fresh setback. It is so tender with swollen conceit of itself that the world's indifference to its good intentions is just too much, cannot stand it. Oh well. On, on.

Tuesday, 16 December

I have invested in an 'Apal'. This is an imitation cigarette filled with certain harmless chemicals which when drawn upon give off a cool, faintly pepperminty flavoured vapour. You keep the 'dummy' in your mouth and pull hard for as long as you have a craving to smoke. I only started this after tea when all my cigarettes were finished. If you can keep it instead of a cigarette for two or three days, the craving for nicotine will subside (say the Apal makers) and gradually disappear altogether, but you will not be left with a craving for the Apal instead. It helps you through the transition period.

If I cannot break the habit with this, I never shall. It is, I feel sure, my last chance. The Apal makers publish dozens of testimonials of its success with every variety of hardened pipe and cigarette smoker, some at 60 who had smoked 40–50 in a day. I cannot be so different from all these people. But oh, if I do it, what joy and jubilation! What triumph! What a crying of the news in the market square!

Boxing Day

I persevered with the Apal from Tuesday evening until Saturday midday, but found not the slightest alteration in my desire for an ordinary cigarette. If anything, the craving increased. All very disappointing and shaming – since Saturday I have been smoking as much as ever. It seems to be much more than a superficial physical craving. As for sweets, for instance.

Against my intentions I have been drawn into the Xmas whirlpool of good will and overeating. The Mitchells persuaded me to spend the day with them yesterday. I had breakfast in the sitting room by a fire kept in all night, and opened some parcels kept for the occasion. Room is gay with many cards and some decorative greenery, tinsel and baubles. I am a very lucky, spoilt person.

Sunday, 28 December

The kind of success I want will come when I have earned it, but whether it will ever do so in this life sometimes seems remote. Reading the winning essays on 'Eyes' in today's *Observer* I can see where mine fails and how much more worthy of reward are the three first winners. Yet it is bitter and disconcerting that I couldn't achieve even a £10 reward. I felt that really my little effort stood a chance. It was competing against 4,855 other efforts.

Monday, 29 December

One ray from a brighter day comes to cheer me. Hurst and Blackett are at last advertising *Lovely Peggy* in *The Observer*.

Friday, 9 January 1953

What have I done since Christmas? I have attended a lovely cocktail party given by Gwen Silvester (now Mrs Derrick Franklyn), and received there much praise and encouragement re Peg. Have found homes for two kittens and am advertising in *The Cat* for the third. Have had drain dug up and repaired. Went shopping in Windsor. Prepared for a tea party for Lydia and her nephew and friend Rita, but nephew had bilious attack so they could not come. Went to town shopping, trying to sell fur coat once more and was told it was hardly worth £10.

I still feel hard hit from recent disappointments, and an article in *Daily Telegraph* by H.E. Bates about the difficulty of the 'young' (i.e. not yet established) writer today. One's work now must be absolutely first class before anyone will look at it, and not only that but saleable. It must sell, sell, sell, and therefore Women's Mag drivel is better from a worldly standard than half-baked highbrow efforts. I am indeed, when I look into it, in a fearful rage: an inner sea seething and tumultuous with cross-currents of despair and self-contempt. What is the good of my going on trying? Go back to your suburbs – back to the village street, the carpenter's bench, you poor and puny, despicable stupid woman.

Tuesday, 20 January

It requires training and discipline, said someone on a radio programme recently, to make good use of leisure. It certainly does. And I fear I am not proving worthy.

Is it vanity that makes me want to go on writing? I think I shall always want to write – what I am up against are defects of character. Now it is inertia I am having to fight. At other times it is timidity, or impatience.

Let us now look on the credit side of this depressing picture. The cottage is moderately clean and tidy in all the rooms. The cats are in good health, well and regularly fed. I have managed to date to keep cigarette consumption to 20 or less a day. I can still dress myself adequately for modest social occasions.

Sunday, 1 February

My *Observer* essay returned with printed slip to say it was one of the 214 chosen from the total of 4,855 entries for consideration. This was the 'sign' I so sorely needed. My labour and judgement were not in vain.

Saturday, 14 February

This morning woke to find a world white with snow. I was the only passenger on the 8.24 bus at Hedgerly Corner. A world in white. Even the Trading Estate and the first drear reaches of Slough were transformed.

Sweets went off the ration last week. I've died laughing since at the number of men I've seen nibbling chocolate and sucking toffees. Bless them – did they before all hand over their rations to the kiddies, or were they ashamed to exhibit their sweet tooth, or are they now revealed as plain greedy?

A Theosophist public meeting on Tuesday. This was I think the only Theos gathering I've attended this year. I find I am a little put off Theosophy by Theosophists.

Yesterday morning in the tube I was attracted by a couple obviously at the start of an illicit love affair. Do not ask me how I knew. Something in the man's pink, excited, nervous, pop-eyed face and the way his body leaned towards the woman's; something in the way she looked at him – assurance, triumph, a sort of proprietary attitude that hadn't deep roots. To my utter amazement I saw them again in the evening in the carriage I was in. In identical seats too – the woman looking rather more puffy and lewd, her leer at him quite revolting. But for the fact that she wasn't busy with the crossword she was doing in the morning I'd have believed it was a sort of mirage. They did not on either occasion once touch each other, no linking of hands or meeting of elbows or shoulders, but each body yearned towards the other. Neither was striking in appearance, both near 40 perhaps, nor were they ugly or ill-dressed (and she was not a professional tart). I wonder if I ever struck anyone like this during one of my own silly amorous adventures.

This evening I found awaiting me a letter from my new accountant to say I have about £20 income tax rebate to come; and liver from the butcher; and coal. All unexpected good things.

Sunday, 15 February

'During one of my silly amorous adventures'. How very superior that sounds. I did not mean it so, as though beyond such folly. Indeed I am not, but chance is a fine thing, and all my energies are directed to my writing now.

Lydia has left her job and plunged recklessly into doing what she wants to do. She had suddenly decided she could not bear an office job a moment longer and gave in her notice, and now she is settling in (with a knitting machine) to keep herself by the hand-craft work she loves and is so good at, though she does this accompanied by many fears and doubts of the kind I know well. People tell her that she'll never make a living on her own, and I'm sure it will be uphill work at first, but I am sure also that she is right to try. Making loose covers, clothes, decorating a room, cooking, sweet-making and so on. I admire her for taking the plunge.

Monday, 16 February

'I never noticed this before,' he said, touching the high book rests where I was poring over an encyclopaedia. And so a casual conversation began, until someone turned round and frowned at us. Conversation is not encouraged in the Reading Room.

He was elderly, muffled up in scarf and greatcoat, might have been 60, with fairish hair, pale blue eyes and light lashes. I found myself saying that I had written a biography of Peg, loved the research, had been to London University. 'You must come and have some tea with me, I won't disturb you now.'

And panic seized me. He smiled and patted my hands. I won't be pawed, I thought later. Yet there was something warming about him. He'd have had my life history out of me before I knew where I was, and at 4.15 I ran away.

Here is the beginning again of the same old story. I was deeply immersed in my subject, and shocked out of it by this friendly approach. But I think a woman's loneliness sometimes outlines her like an aura, and just as some people can see the psychic variety, so others can sense this. There she is, over 30, still rather attractive, ringless left hand, and beneath that surface absorption her hungriness apparent, solitary in that single bedsitter – easy game. A little flattery ('You look very clever.' Oh God, who wants to look clever? 'I am sure you are someone famous . . . were you at Oxford or Cambridge?'), a few leading questions and her story is out without knowing the first item in the hunter's. Beware, lonely women, of this bloodsucker, and don't be easy game, or you'll be over the tripwire and then God help you.

This isn't being cowardly or even prudent, just wise. This kind of trickster can see that your vanity is at low ebb, has long desired fuel, and if you're not aware that it's your vanity he's playing up to, you are in for much heartbreak and humiliation. Be wise, run away, with-hold yourself. If the man is really interested in you and not feeding his own vanity (which is what the trickster is always doing on these occasions, so never imagine that you yourself have much to do with the situation) – if, I repeat, he is interested in you and not in himself, he'll come back, he'll pursue you in the orthodox and civilised manner. Remember, shift the focus from yourself to the stranger . . . and don't give yourself away in handfuls in the first five minutes.

My imagination got busy at once after he'd gone. Supposing he was Osbert Sitwell, I thought.

Saturday, 21 February

I saw no more of the old boy who made advances last Monday. I may have maligned him, deeply hurt and offended someone with quite honest, honourable and kindly intentions. Or he may of course have forgotten all about me and his invitation. I had my apologies ready next day (shopping in Oxford Street and a train to catch – all true), but he did not appear. It was the way in which he patted and pressed my hands when he left me that got my hackles standing. I don't think I was wrong.

How sick I am of train and tube and bus filled with the world's workers! Oh dear Lord, make me more charitable and generous and loving. They do bore me so these people. There they are, day in and day out on platforms, in carriages, in the streets, tramping, standing, sitting in crowds and crowds, moving all the time like one river there is no stopping – I cannot bear it! When much in London, my dreams are always choked with these images.

Perhaps it is because they emphasise my own loneliness. There are among them hundreds much lonelier and more unhappy than I am.

Monday, 23 February

I have got Elizabeth Taylor's *Wreath of Roses* at Foyles. I remember vaguely the glowing reviews when it first came out, and Liz M. reading it, unable to put it down. And N.'s friend Ara telling me she had met Elizabeth Taylor: 'A little, quiet thing. She said she had written a book, and I said, "How nice, what?" in a patronising way.' A year or so later I met Ara again with N., and she said I reminded her a little of Elizabeth Taylor, not in looks but in her quiet manner. It fills me with rage, a rage of which I am ashamed when I analyse it, that people like Ara (whom one thinks of as intelligent, cultured, sophisticated and therefore perceptive) should express astonishment when they find that quiet little things have depth.

'She sat there without saying much but must have been taking it all in . . .' How else can you observe and absorb? When you are active in a crowd you cannot see the crowd; when you are in a state of flow you do not ebb.

But reading the book now, I cannot put it down either, finding so much of me and for me in it.

Friday, 6 March

Last week a note from the bank reminded me that my overdraft had again reached £100. Terror of the future again descended, eating me up. But there is only one thing I can do, and that is to sell more stock. Yesterday I decided quite definitely I would realise £500 out of the remaining £3,000 war stock. This should keep me going for a year at least, perhaps longer if I keep to my rigid economies (without starving or looking shabby). This money is for living, for the things that are of practical importance now, and not for any frivolity or extravagance. I am especially blessed to have this capital, and must employ it gladly, creatively, with hope adventurous. If it is God's will that I am to suffer a lonely and impoverished old age, I will submit, with gladness if I can.

Sunday, 8 March

I may invest in a very small electric cooker – they're to be had for about £7. And sell the oil stove with oven and stand. I have dug out the last of the family plate which has been in the bank, and am going to try to sell that with the china and glass packed away that I never use. I cling too much to my possessions.

Mid-August

I desire to change, to improve, I see the necessity for it, in myself and in others. In my own experience I have seen that nothing – none of the more ordinary religions, nor philosophies, politics, psychological analyses, nor the odd groups who try other means – nothing seems to have made a great deal of difference. A little, perhaps, here and there, but fundamentally the jealousies and greed and self-centredness within, the external rages, remain. What is it one wants, in essence? What is this thing, this quality one is always seeking, feeling sure it can be found if one's self were a little more able? One wants not only to feel sure of one's power of endurance in big things, but also of one's ability to cope with the minor irritations of ordinary life.[211]

Tuesday, 18 August

I must accept this: that there is a condition, somewhere, somehow, that is mind-less, time-less. I only know that the mind is always busy: too busy, sometimes a burden, so that the head aches and the soul is limp. I know this; I wish very much I could make it stop, just for a minute or two, so that I could rest. I can at least drift into sleep, but there is no rest even there from the mind. One is conscious on waking that it has been churning and chattering to itself. On waking . . . it is like opening a door on early morning and letting in a swarm of insects.

I know also that now, in this century, we seem to have got ourselves

---

211 Between mid-August and late-October 1953, Jean abandoned her usual pattern of writing to consider the teachings of the Indian mystic Jiddu Krishnamurti. Jean had been to see Krishnamurti (or K. as she often referred to him) deliver a lecture in London, and was impressed with his spiritual insights and detached, calming aura. (His teachings were later regarded as significant influences on both Nehru after independence and Indira Gandhi in the 1970s. Krishnamurti died in 1986 at the age of ninety. Aldous Huxley had been similarly captivated, writing that seeing him had been 'like listening to a discourse of the Buddha'.) His teachings were not entirely new to her: Krishnamurti was in his late fifties, and was a leading Theosophist. He had written several books on the importance of the individual psychological change that was required to bring about greater transformations in society. In her journal, her 33rd, Jean attempted to suspend the record of regular passing thoughts, and strove instead for a deeper understanding of her nature and her actions.

She was aided in her quest by a new literary approach: she wrote out in red ink some of the more salient passages delivered from talks Krishnamurti had given the previous year in his base at Ojai, California, and she would then consider how his observations reflected or may enhance her own life (in her regular blue-black ink). One may detect an early manifestation of mindfulness. These entries were dated, but were effectively written as one sustained meditation.

into a state of no-time in another sense. We have no time to do things we want to and should do. There's so much else to be done, there's no time to be leisurely, to stand and stare. I hear this complaint on all sides, everywhere. Time flies, races, we are raced off our feet by it, and I have no time to meet you, read this, look at that, listen, feel . . . no time, no time . . . Is it the mind that is rushing us off our feet like this?

It is therefore arresting to hear someone say that there is a source (of strength, wisdom) which is not of the mind, which is not of time.

Sunday, 23 August

K.: When so-called religions fail . . . political parties become all important, they offer a vision, a conviction, a hope, and we jump at these things because in ourselves we have lost the source, the spring of that which is un-nameable.

I know that this last quotation is true of myself. I have worshipped authority, and do, and have even looked to political parties – Socialism, Fabians, Liberals – not with ardent conviction that all could be solved through politics, but with the belief that their influence is powerful, and the more people voted for the underdogs and have-nots and tried to restrict 'the grinding of the faces of the poor' (mock the phrase if you will), the better.[212]

Is not K. implying that the majority of people everywhere are up against the same sense of failure and frustration?

Friday, 28 August

N. threw in a sentence in her last letter: when she comes on leave she might not go back, it has been such a hard year. This put me into a mood of terror and exasperation for days. I hate her, hate her, will not have her here. We don't want her in England! She is such a menace to everyone when out of work, and is bad enough when she has a

---

212 The phrase dates as far back as the 1830s, and was popular in the arguments promoting a more progressive Poor Law.

job. She is always provoking the worst in people. I fear her interference and her cruelty, the weight of her. My idea of hell is a heaven full of N.s and Josephines trying to help me.

What can I do with this mood? Does K. say anything about that? I've somehow got the idea that when he talks of fear that it is . . . within the mind-field, and that really there is nothing to fear. But there is. There are destructive forces within oneself and without. How does one find the courage and strength to meet them so that one is not swamped, defeated by them?

Sunday, 13 September

One must be everlastingly aware, says K. This is possible, but it leads one into dangerous paths – one becomes self-conscious, self-centred, morbidly introspective. And then one begins to feel, very slightly, how wearisome is the burden of the ego. Can't one get rid of it altogether? Discard it completely and so escape its tyranny?

9.45 p.m. A peaceful, busy day, alone with cats, listening to wireless. And so a guinea goes to the Wireless Bedridden Society for which Gilbert Harding spoke. I have great admiration and liking for G.H.[213] This isn't recorded here to illustrate my generosity. The gift goes on impulse – there are many other causes to which I should contribute. I do not feel for this one more than I do for cancer relief, displaced persons, distressed children, oppressed nations, animal welfare. One cannot give to them all: one has to give now and then when prodded to it or by 'sticking a pin' method.

One thinks of the things one buys for oneself which one could do without – those extra shoes, blouse, frock, cigarettes and so on, and the money spent on them . . . There will always be rich and poor, said K. to children in India last December, so long as some people must have more and more. More power, position, success. Success in

---

213 A guinea was £1 and 1 shilling. Gilbert Harding was an irascible journalist and presenter, a favourite on the panel show *What's My Line?*

fact is bought always at the price of other people's failure. Giving to charities is a very easy way of seeming generous.

Sunday, 20 September

My problem is to experiment, to find out through self-knowledge. To watch patiently every movement of the ego, to observe without judgement. To do this, to understand self, what other way is there but through the science of psychology?

But so many people are frightened of this way – they think it leads only to confusion and greater disease. We are afraid of knowing ourselves and have remarkable skill in shutting doors and blocking awareness that would reveal us fully. We all in greater or lesser degree suffer from some form of neurosis – irritability, tempers, cowardice, vanity, arrogance – all these things indicate a lack of balance and maladjustment in some way.

Sunday, 4 October

Fundamental change comes when the mind is quiet, still. There is no freedom from struggle, pain, inertia, until the mind is stripped and empty: purged of all images and things acquired and stored in the memory.

We cannot put an end to thinking, but we can understand the movement of thought; we can be everlastingly aware. We must watch, patiently, continually, without judgement. Observe the fact without condemnation. When I begin to understand the ways of my own mind, its chatter will cease. Let us understand our own conflicts without going with or against them. Let them come up from the depths of our being.

Watch and listen for what is true.

These aphorisms should be learnt by heart, so that one can say them during the day to oneself and ponder their meaning. I carry them written in my handbag, but do not study them as often as I might.

The most difficult of them to apply is 'observe without judgement'. When I am with people I admire, respect, and know to be cleverer or better in some way than myself, I despise myself for not being their equal. I am awkward, gauche in my manner. If they are people of my own stature I quickly spot faults and failings, probably similar to my own, and despise them. Even with individual and valued friends whom I love sincerely, this contempt creeps in. When I realise that I am behaving or thinking in a despicable way, I am torn with fury at myself, for being so mean, so petty, unbalanced and without compassion.

Why do I despise others? The mob. Their tawdry, vulgar, ugly clothes and voices, their common, common silly chatter. Partly perhaps because I am afraid of being enveloped, drawn down to it and drowned. I am trying to get above the mediocre, the slovenly, slipshod habits of the average person. I know these failings are in me and I hate them, despise them intensely.

Tuesday, 13 October

Today heard that Peggy D.'s youngest son died yesterday morning. This is one of those completely inexplicable tragedies. I can feel her grief acutely. He was the apple of her eye, full of promise, unusually intelligent and never seemed delicate like the other children. It was no one's fault – no road accident, or carelessness of the boys or anything like that. A tumour that couldn't be reached, and an asthma attack.

Peggy's life has been full of blows. Her first marriage was very happy, but he was killed at the beginning of the war, leaving her with three young children to bring up. Her second marriage was not a success. She had to sell the lovely house here in Egypt and lives now in a near-slum in London SE. One of her brothers is always causing anxiety, and so on. And now this. It doesn't seem fair that one person should have to bear so much, when it doesn't seem deserved.

Tuesday, 20 October

40 – what was I on Sunday – 3/4/5? Does it matter? I am over 40 and have so little to show for all these years. They have been spent

in struggle to understand myself and to improve; to change and
become what I think I want to be.

*Neither her cat book nor her novel (Heiress Caroline) found a publisher.
Even her journals became less central to her life: having filled 34 exercise books between 1925 and 1952, in addition to hundreds of personal
loose pages before this, Jean would write only 11 further (and far thinner)
books before her death. Whereas once she would take one book to
describe three months, increasingly, a single volume would cover two
or three years. Several months would often pass without an entry or
explanation of absence.*

PART FOUR:
The Village's Book Supplier

43.

The Colour of Nurses

Wednesday, 3 February 1954 (aged forty-four)
Our world is frost-bound. Hard, hard, everything tight and solid with frost. I keep fires going in sitting room and kitchen, all doors closed. I fear there will be terrible mortality in the garden.

Yesterday the Southern Counties Silver Jubilee Cat Show in Westminster. I entered Pye and Bum (Bumphrey). Pye was only entry in her class. She was awarded a 1st.

Bum, competing with fully pedigreed red and silver tabbies, won a 2nd in a kitten class. This is very cheering. I tried to sell him yesterday – but custom was bad. I failed to find anyone for Pye too, so here we are, all home again, seven cats in fine form.

Wednesday, 10 February
Now Pinnie is missing. Oh these cats, unending anxiety and heart-break. She must have been coming on heat last week. Nick the local stud seemed very interested. I shut the pair up together in shed for two days and nights. But she would have nothing to do with him – just batted him on the nose and went to sleep. On Monday afternoon I idiotically let her out. She went off, yelling madly, and was seen by a neighbour that afternoon heading towards the Common.

I've been writing a review of Virginia Woolf's published diary for the Society of Women Writers Festival comp. Could have written pages, but had to compress into 750 words. Somewhere she remarks something to the effect that a diary is often the resource of the potential writer unable to make the sustained effort for other work. But is useful for writers as a means of loosening the ligaments. The result is enthralling.

Later: I have supper, do ironing, and wash-up listening to *The Unguarded Hour*, and now silence.[214] Pinnie is missing. Does it matter? One little cat in seven? Can I endure it again, this not knowing, maybe never knowing, the long search, the asking? My little grey cat galloping after me through the woods, here I come, here I come.

Thursday, 11 February
She crawled in this morning – no, trotted, when I opened door to postman. Very hungry and peevish. Is sulky, arrogant, and only now and then condescends to be gracious and playful.

Aunt Maggie is to have an old friend's bungalow rent-free for the rest of her life, and when she is settled, Ethel is to join her. This is a miracle. One could not imagine what these two old ladies were to do, and now here is a home for them, secure, till the end.

Saturday, 13 February
Yesterday's evening and this morning's papers have been full of the research being done on the 'relationship between smoking and cancer of the lung'. It is established now that there is a connection, though other factors may contribute (e.g. air pollution in urban areas) and some people who were not smokers at all have died from it. When I mentioned that to friend tobacconist he brought out the names of seven locals who had died recently of the disease – and all of them excessive smokers. But I still get my supply for 30–40 a day. 'Well goodbye,' he said, 'in case I don't see you again.'

Not that I mind dying – I have to face it one day. But I don't want to die just yet. I'd like to feel I'd done here what I have to do. I'm still

---

214 A courtroom thriller featuring a spritely Arnold Ridley, Private Godfrey in *Dad's Army*.

very much of a 'failure', and shall go on feeling so until I can earn my living by writing. If I have any luck with the V.W. review it might lead to something. I have been thinking of *Woman's Hour* possibilities too. Might try a talk on breeding cats for a hobby (NOT Siamese), and could chat endlessly about Wee and garden.

Friday, 5 March

British Museum again this week – Monday, Wednesday and yesterday. On Tuesday to the annual meeting of the Red, Cream, Tortie, Blue-Cream and Brown Tabby Society. At 7 a.m. Pinnie had another alarming 'attack' in my bedroom, nearly fell into the electric fire. I stayed at home and summoned vet. He thinks she is epileptic. This really is a blow to my breeding hopes.

Sunday, 2 May

Finished typing the novel yesterday and felt all-in. I wheedled drugs and tonic from doctor to carry me over Easter. He gave me mild sleeping tablets which do seem to work, wonderfully. They stop the brain-buzz, and get me off quickly and soundly. When one has to wake early, as I did when paying guests were here, one feels a bit drunk at first; one bumps into things.

Monday, 10 May

Last night Lady S.'s little brute of a dog began to bark furiously in her kitchen at about midnight – it seemed just under my window. I was falling off deliciously, but the noise made me think of night prowlers, sex maniacs and homicidal lunatics. Torment. Couldn't relax. The old panics returned. Krishnamurti useless in these night hours of desolation.

Friday, 4 June

Ethel came and was with me three weeks. She took over all the chores and catering while I finished *Heiress Caroline* – it was posted to

Harper's on May 22nd. I went flat after that for several days, felt like a tube of squeezed-out toothpaste. E. kept me in bed one whole day, spoilt me thoroughly.

This morning I was at hairdresser's by 9 a.m. Have taken to a horse's tail – oddly, it suits my temperamental hair and is the one style that seems to keep moderately tidy in nearly all circs. I thought I would never wear this absurdity: too young for me, altogether too eccentric and silly. But it isn't. It meets with general approval, at least with my own.

I have my longed-for portable radio – a Champion (£9 5s), and have finished with Radio Rentals. I can listen in bed, or in any room at any time. Runs off the mains; plugs into each room.

Phone rings. I am to join the M.s on a picnic excursion to Whipsnade tomorrow.

Whit Monday, 7 June

We all set off in grand style in thin frocks with picnic baskets. Then came the storm – torrential rain, thunder and lightning. We sheltered beneath trees while Peter dashed out to get the car for us. We were eleven in all: seven adults and four children, in two cars.

I enjoyed it all, on the surface. Why have I this urge to be alone, this feeling of relief and pleasure when I am? Not that it lasts, but the need mounts until I must have the breathing space: an interval in which I can stretch, relax and be myself. But am I never 'myself' except when alone? What do I mean by that? I think I mean freedom to think and feel without restraint. Always, the presence of another person or other people sets up resistance, barriers, obstacles. One is aware not only of one's own limitations and shortcomings, but of the prejudices and barriers and limitations in other people. One is stifled, wounded, or made impatient by them. I long for the opportunity to withdraw into silence.

Saturday, 12 June

I was thinking of brilliant people who achieve big things. People who do brilliantly at school from an early age and become leading politicians or lawyers (I listened to Cambridge Union debate on Third Programme last night), or psychologists, or doctors, or poets, or artists, or business men . . . They have it in them from the cradle; their potentiality is apparent, is nursed in encouraging circumstances, and flowers naturally. They are born to be great, and become great in their particular line, and rarely, rarely if ever can they understand the mentality of mediocrity, the also-rans.

Our littleness, our second-rateness in this age is a very big problem. There is so much of it. It's no use being envious of the giants above us and trying to imitate them. We have got to understand ourselves, each individual separately, our limitations and apparently endless capacity for failure.

Yesterday I was absolutely sucked under by Witch B.'s oppressive, malevolent mood.[215] She is an abominable old woman, though an excellent worker and thoroughly trustworthy with one's possessions. With one breath she tells me that if she had the chance again she'd stay single, and in the next can't understand why I live here alone. Again, she thinks I'm 'crrool' to rear kittens and then let them go to new strange homes, then wants me to get rid of all the cats except one. These two themes repeat and repeat like a gramophone record, whatever I may do or say to try to enlighten her. When I say I like living here on my own, and that I adore all my cats with passion, she obviously doesn't believe me. She only wants to see me behaving as she thinks I ought to behave. I don't know how one is supposed to deal with this type of ox-like stupidity. I am torn inside with rage at it. To tolerate intolerance is perhaps the hardest kind of tolerance to practise. The trouble is, I'm still too anxious for universal approval of all I am and do.

Tuesday, 22 June
Was in a jangle today, all because of a hat I wore to town yesterday and which I soon realised – but too late to do anything about it – was

---

215 Jean's cleaner.

hideous on me. But I endured it, and as soon as I was home again I ripped it to pieces and spent the afternoon remaking: the result I think is going to be a success.

Does it matter what one looks like? Should one mind so much? Isn't it vanity? Desire to attract attention, to be thought well-of and so forth? Not entirely, I've decided. I don't see why anyone should look plainer or more ugly than they need. I think one should try to be as pleasant as possible to look at: well groomed, neat but not gaudy, to wear colours and clothes that become one without being conspicuous – to be easy on the eye, as the saying goes, without necessarily attracting the wrong sort of eye.

I am determined to master the hair and hat problem. Luckily my figure is easier to manage. It causes me no anguish or anxiety, and for that at least let me be truly thankful.

Wednesday, 23 June

Heiress Caroline returns from Harper's. The whole mood of living darkens as the weather brightens.

Oh the dreariness, the utter abysmal hell of rejection, of being shut out, not wanted, a failure. All the success and happiness of one's life depending on capital inherited – unearned, perhaps undeserved. But I've got to live with it. Must try to understand the sensitive, spoilt, imaginative little girl – so easily hurt, so easily made to feel deprived. Oh, the scent of roses: heavenly, heavenly indifferent summer's day.

Long ago, while my mother was alive and I was still very young, Ethel was Miss Watson who came sometimes to tea. She was told one day by my mother, 'Jean's writing a story.' 'Put me in it, won't you?' asked Miss Watson, and little Jean answered, 'Oh yes, I will!'

11.15 p.m.: And how could I have forgotten! Hurst & Blackett are selling off the 1,000 remaining copies of Peg.

Midsummer Day

Pet Shop woman in village tells me there's a big demand for cat kennels. If only I could take the plunge at once! If only I knew what it is I should do. In this mood I'd welcome another war. Then the decision would be taken for me.

Sunday, 27 June

Yesterday a letter arrived from Halliday at H. & B. saying how sorry he was that they have to remainder Peg, but urging me not to be discouraged. In the circumstances, he and the MD were prepared to write off my debt for proof correction (standing at £25). My joy and gratitude for this thoughtful gesture are inexpressible. £25 won't mean much to H. & B., but was bothering me quite a bit. I have written H. mentioning 'Caroline', though not of course that she's been rejected by Harper's. Still thinking about cat kennels.

Tuesday, 13 July

Too excited tonight to fall asleep easily. I've seen super excellent cat kennels this p.m. Mrs Turney's at Holyport, just outside Maidenhead. They are an inspiration. She can take up to 40 cats at a time, and must have accommodation for nearly as many dogs. The boarded cats live all the time in single roomy pens in spotless, warm, dry sunny sheds. All looked perfectly happy and in good health. She says they do not need exercise. The precautions she takes against disease and infection are admirable. She charges only 15 shillings per week per cat. I begin to feel my way a little.

Sunday, 14 August

I've had paying guests – all nice, very nice. But I realised that I didn't want to depend on this means of a livelihood. I get sick to death of having strangers about the place. When they are here, however pleasant, appreciative, interesting, I just long and long for them to pay up and leave. The work is endless drudgery in the main.

As for the cat kennels. I would at least have a shot at it if Wee were mine. I could start here in a very modest way and build up a reputation. But with the very minimum of alterations to garden sheds necessary, would cost between £40–£50. I don't feel like spending that on someone else's property.

Tuesday, 17 August
Babs·is engaged. An ecstatic letter to me, omitting to mention the young man's name. We wonder, granny and I, if it'll come to anything. As Gran put it, Babs is very 'susceptible' – i.e. she has had many boyfriends. And the West Indies, as someone else remarked, has a troubling climate.

Friday, 3 September
Babs's fiancée is Roy Everett and works in Barclays Bank in Port of Spain, Trinidad.

Phyllis is now in the new Rattigan play which opened in Liverpool last week.[216] I met her old friend Estelle. She writes too, but gets nothing but rejections. I admire her perseverance immensely, take new heart from it. She has just had a children's play for TV accepted – there seems a great opening here. But I should see more TV before I try, and how may I do that?

Monday, 20 September
Perhaps it's the sweep of autumn in the wind and sky; perhaps it was E.D.'s frenzy this weekend, her wracked absorption in a Pyramid Party – an absurd, adventurous gamble for making easy money which has got hold of London, into which I might well have been drawn had my circumstances been a little different.

Wednesday, 22 September
Our miserable summer seems over. I have not once worn my nice

---

216 This was the first production of *Separate Tables*. Phyllis played the demonic Sybil Railton-Bell, and reprised the role when the play transferred to the West End (where Jean saw it) and Broadway. In a later production, the part was played by Julie Christie.

nylon summer vests, but went into a semi-weight, which I am still wearing, with a skirt and cardigan set. The few some summer frocks I've worn hardly need washing before they are packed away.

Monday, 22 November

Caroline came back from Curtis Brown early in October. Hurst and Blackett have turned it down, and C.B. doesn't think he can place it elsewhere. But after Harper's rejection the edge was off the blow – it doesn't seem to matter very much. Gus is reading it for me now.

Am in touch, through an ad in *Our Cats*, with a woman in Dorset who was looking for a working partner with a car for various country enterprises, including the serious breeding of Siamese and small dogs. I like her letters extremely – but this idea of me removing myself and cats to Dorset and driving a car again seems so remote and impossible. I have got as far as arranging to meet the advertiser at the National Cat Club show on December 8. The choice will be: cats and country life among strangers, a really new start, or London, a job and all my old friends there, and maybe not more than two of the neutered cats as pets.

Tuesday, 7 December

I'm in a panic. Tomorrow I meet the woman from Dorset. Her letters have been friendly, encouraging, exciting, but I'm so convinced from them that she is another 'difficult' character. Perhaps it will all fall through – I'm now at the stage where I hope it will. She may not think me suitable, I may not like her, I may find her too overpowering. And after all I don't know a thing about her past. She may have a criminal or a mental record. She has confessed to trouble in her own family: a mother of 82 who seems, shall we say, petulant.

Monday, 3 January 1955

Krishnamurti, the more one reads him, becomes more and more difficult to understand. I want to understand, to change myself. But if that motive wasn't there – the divine discontent – I should not move a finger in K.'s direction. I wonder if there is not something immensely profound in the saying of an American who was so horrified when he read of the effects of smoking that he gave up reading.

I must go back a month, to December 2nd, when I went with Lydia to see Harold Sharp. There was still red rock at the bottom of my auragraph.[217] It had expanded, was thicker and heavier. This indicated drive and steadfastness, and being at bottom of the circle was good, giving ballast – at top it would have meant unbalance. A wash of green behind it, suggesting sea, meant adaptability. Violet colour was again predominant – this, said the guide, was the colour of rectifying or healing vitality and was very strong in me (the colour of nurses, psychologists, teachers). The circle on the left hand was edged thickly in blue. This indicates personality, but being on this side doesn't mean egotism.

He saw me writing small, short items. Short, short he kept saying – not a long book, but articles or stories. For the first time with a 'seer' of any kind (except, I think, in one graphology reading) did my writing tendency come to the surface. For this I am thankful: I cling to it, in the hope that it confirms that my passion for writing is not an illusion and that I shall be able to make a living by it. It has occurred to me since that the short items he saw me writing might be these journal entries.

I take the wider interpretation, and on the strength of that intend to turn again to freelance work. There is more scope now – a bigger market. Correspondence schools abound, and though they may be catchpenny trick-wires, there must be some foundation for them. If some of their students didn't succeed they wouldn't keep going as they do. Anyway I've fallen again (sucker that I am), and have enrolled with the British American School of Successful Writing. The whole affair makes my academic layers writhe in agony, but this school

_____

217 See 19 October 1947.

guarantees legally (in large black type) to refund one's fees if one hasn't covered them by one's earnings at the end of the course.

I must record the touching concern of my accountant L.J.N. for my affairs. He knows, better than anyone, how alarmingly my capital is dwindling, and he took it upon himself to send me an ad he saw in *The Times* for a research assistant. He also invited me to lunch with him in the City last Friday. I am sure this interest arises from sheer kindness of heart, perhaps a little curiosity also, and nothing more.

He is an odd little man. One doesn't sort of 'see' him at all. He has no obvious personality, is grey, lives in a miasma of sums, and needs perhaps this personal contact with some of his clients to brighten his existence. I think he wished only to warn me of the dangers of 'living on capital', and may not have realised how acutely I was aware of them. 'We are,' he said as he parted, 'the money doctors. We like to keep our patients in health.'

And then my dear Peggy D. I stayed the night with her after meeting the Dorset woman. Peggy asked me if I wanted to 'expand' or 'close in on myself'. I wish I'd had the courage to penetrate this further. Did she mean that I don't give enough? To every one of my friends I give what I can, but with each individual, and there is no exception here, I withhold some part of myself. With Peggy it is much in my life that happened before I met her – all my sordid ineffectual love affairs. With Joan it is the Krishnamurti side, because I do not know how to put this across to her. N. may winkle some of it from me, but from her I have to withhold a great deal now, in self-defence, for the preservation of my integrity. To Lydia all my pre-war life is more or less a blank, the Gus and Malta periods, the Graham Howe influence. And with Gus, all that he doesn't know about me doesn't seem to matter. It doesn't make the least difference to the warmth I feel when with him. He couldn't care less about the love affairs and spiritual explorations – it is what I am at the moment, when we meet, that matters. So I could go on, through the whole list. And why should

I think it in any way unusual that a woman of 45 cannot disclose the whole of herself to every friend?

The Dorset woman, J.D., was certainly a 'tough' type: a very hard-headed business woman, frankly out to make as much money as she could by fair means or foul. She would have to be the boss in any partnership. It wouldn't be easy working with her and I should have many moments of cowardice and submission for the sake of peace. But it wasn't just this that deterred me. I woke in the night asking myself urgently why in the world I couldn't make more effort with the articles, children's stories, TV programmes and so on. To break away and settle in Dorset seemed monstrous, foolhardy. I wrote to J.D. saying that I feared I had not the funds to cover all that would be required of me. But she wrote again, very sympathetically, and has left the matter open. If in a few months' time I feel differently about it. Which was generous (and flattering).

Tuesday, 18 January
On Sunday I found Pinnie on heat and arranged for her to be mated to Mrs Hughes's stud in Cheam. Tonight Mrs H. phoned to say the affair has been happily concluded.

Tuesday, 25 January
I bought this horoscope in Woolworth this afternoon for 6d. and thought it would be amusing to start the new book with it in this first month of the new year.[218]

Much more important is Elizabeth Myers' book of *Letters*, borrowed from the public library. I am already twisted with admiration and envy. There she was in London, three years my junior,

---

218 The horoscope was pasted onto the first page of her 35th journal. One line was marked with ink: 'Your income is likely to increase before the autumn'. The front of the journal also contained a small piece of paper with some crossword markings, the name 'Dr Whoe', and a quote from Socrates: 'Beware the barrenness of a busy life'.

succeeding while I flumped and floundered and failed in jellyfish fashion at UCL.

But I'm not writing this just for the luxury of a moan. It is in the hope that one day it may catch someone's eye, someone who understands what happened and can prevent it happening to another youngster. I do feel that somehow in some way my life has been crippled psychologically – just as much as a child's leg may be crushed and made useless by a careless car driver. I'm not trying to make excuses: I must do the best I can with my deformity, but if it's possible to reach future generations by these pages, I hope they will understand more clearly than we have what psychological damage can be done in those early formative years. Damage beyond repair, if it's not treated in time, through ignorance, neglect and carelessness. I do believe I had a chance to become a fairly successful writer long before I was 40, perhaps also to have made a happy marriage and had children, if someone (or people) had not left me by the roadside.

I do not know when this 'accident' happened – perhaps before my mother's death, though I think it was probably then, that sad October in the year 1923. My really miserable years began when I was 13, no, 14, and lasted until I went to UCL in 1930 (7 years). Oh, I've enjoyed my life all right since then, on the whole very much. I've had lots of fun, made marvellous good friends, had much interesting experience, learnt a great deal – but it seems now that it all came too late to help my growth. I don't like to blame my father, stepmother and school teachers for this – it was not their fault so much as perhaps their ignorance. It is this 'spiritual lack' in our day and age. To refer to a recent correspondence in *The Observer*, we must learn the 'knowledge of the heart'.

Wednesday, 26 January
At home what chance was there? After my mother died, nothing was read or discussed but the *Daily Mail* and novels by Ethel M. Dell and

the Tarzan books.[219] I was left to choose my own reading, but one needs someone to talk over one's discoveries with. Musical standards did not aspire beyond the Grand Hotel Palm Court Orchestra. My brother sneered at Shaw though I doubt very much whether he had so much as seen one of Shaw's plays. I'm not saying these standards were wrong or to be despised, but there are others.

The trouble with me was, I think, that someone long ago made a sensitive, imaginative child feel insignificant and unwanted. Something touched the inferiority complex into life, and it grew and grew unchecked, unspotted, unhelped by any of the guides or teachers in my life who might have done something to right the balance. And so here I am at 45, without any definite occupation, unmarried, rudderless, feeling homeless, not 'safely nested down' as I should be. Not that I want material security – I want something much bigger and more difficult to achieve.

I am trying to give myself as an example and warning to all the parents and teachers of future generations. Do not jump to conclusions about them, however dearly you suppose you love them, however much they may exasperate or disappoint you. Learn to listen and know with the heart as well as the head. It doesn't matter in the least whether your children are brilliant or famous or make a great worldly success of their lives: but it matters very much that they find the way of living creatively, out of their own true selves, however small or poorly paid their actual everyday job may seem. It is sad to think that those who need this advice most will heed it least. Ambition and power lust have such a hold on the human race.

Thursday, 27 January

I have this moment just come to and made a resolution. It is to write, for myself, an 'Uncritical Study of Elizabeth Myers' in special note-

---

219 Dell's popular romantic novels included *The Knave of Diamonds* and *The Way of an Eagle*.

books, with full quotations. There is nothing I should like better than to be the means of bringing Elizabeth Myers's work to the notice of more people. The mind flies ahead too, with all the kudos and profit such an achievement might bring one in person, but this must be chastened. It must be written secretly, like these journals. Oh, I think this is a lovely idea!

Saturday, 29 January

I am living at the rate of £10 a week. This includes my one extravagance (cats) and my one vice (smoking), but together they don't come to more than £3 a week. The rest of the money goes on food and the very small necessities of my tiny household. I never go to the pub, or buy any alcohol, eat very little cake or sweet things. My meals are of the simplest – little meat, no fish or very rarely. I must earn more.

Sunday, 30 January

I don't think I shall 'study' Eliz Myers. Am re-reading *Well Full of Leaves* and suffering a sharply critical reaction to my first splurge of enthusiasm. Is she a little too intense, too sure? Was she just a little too wrapped around by dazzled, adoring old philosophers and poets? Why did she so ruthlessly and scornfully reject all the psychologists?[220]

Tuesday, 1 February

What new hare-brained scheme is this? Yesterday Miss B. of the Pet Shop informed me that she was leaving her present premises for a larger store in the village: did I know of anyone who would be interested in taking over her present shop? I immediately saw myself in it – with books. Books, books and perhaps a sideline in high-grade pottery.

Sluggard, slut, craven and snob in me all shriek, 'Oh, you can't!

---

220 In June 1957, Jean added a footnote: 'A book on Eliz Myers by Eleanor Farjeon is coming out this summer.'

You couldn't!' They always do at the first hint of hard work, orderliness, risk and menial labour. At the same time, above or beneath their clamour, another voice counsels prudence. What exactly is involved? How much do you stand to gain or lose by such a venture?

I had a very brief consultation with the nice, efficient Mr M. across the way in hardware (doing very well too, and his wife next door managing a drapery section). When they had a café in the village they had also a small lending library. There is none now and it is quite a lot wanted. Foyles will provide stock and advice. Miss B.'s shop would be ideal, he said, with a lady to run it needing a little pin money (I said I wanted rather more than just pin money). You could sell a few books too, he said – take orders for Foyles. You wouldn't need much money: outlay very small, overheads negligible.

Rent and rates are certainly microscopic (8 shillings a week and £7–£8 a year).

There'd be lighting, heat and insurance. But would it be worth my while, economically? As an adventure yes, every time – it's just the sort of part-time job I'd adore. Getting pottery would be exciting too. There's Lydia's friend M.T.J., I could start with a few things from her. I'd go to the Odney Potteries at Cookham.[221] And then perhaps a second-hand book tray outside.

Can I face it? All those rich, starchy, atrophying Farnham Common women I see around? They all would be potential customers. And what reaction would there be from the other shopkeepers – any hostility? Rivalry, cut-throat competition? Am I tough enough? Not tough at all, and will probably collapse at first sign of opposition.

Still, if I could work up a business like this while I hammered away at the writing in my spare time, it might be just the thing. Though when one calculates that 1,000 borrowers a month @ 6d. a book bring in only £25 – and Foyles probably want a large swipe of

---

221 Before Jean became interested, the most notable purchaser for Odney pots was John Lewis of Oxford Street.

that – one isn't fired with enthusiasm on the money side. I can't see 1,000 borrowers a week in FC somehow.

And another thing: I should be putting myself right in the lime-light, which I should loathe. 'A bookshop in the village, my dear, run by a dolt of a woman – she'll never make a success of it . . .' Or, 'That nice Miss Pratt – I'm sure she means well! I wonder if she'd subscribe to our so-and-so, or join this and that . . .' Says my horoscope, 'It is important that you fix something worthwhile for the whole of the year. You can now afford to plan in advance, without much fear of disappointment.' At what straws do we clutch in our groping uncer-tainty. In this moment now – scared, tempted, impatient, uncertain, void, hopeful, confident, and slaughtered by doubt.

Later: I follow with interest Princess Margaret's Caribbean tour beginning today in Trinidad. The Poohs will all be at the Government House reception tomorrow. A letter from Ivy today says, 'It is no thrill and pathetic these days to see what goes to Government House. Blacks, Indians, Chinks and what you will.' That this is my family's attitude makes me sad. I do not know how I may combat it.

A pleasing off-the-record story of the Queen given me by Lady S. a little while ago. Lady S.'s lawyer has clients among the Sandringham estate personnel, and was told on one occasion that when the Royal Family were at home *en famille* and were playing 'Treasure Hunt' or some such, the Queen rushed into the kitchen, her hair dishevelled and shrieking her head off with laughter.

Wednesday, 2 February

My hope and confidence mount, and the imagination flies off into realms of ecstasy. I long now to get cracking. Life is heavenly at this moment, and I mean that; heaven here, within me. I feel I can not only do this job, but make a moderate success of it.

44.

Hags and Bitches

Friday, 4 February 1955 (aged forty-five)

I know exactly how I want it, and have it worked out almost to the last detail. 'The Little Bookshop and Lending Library'. Paintwork in black, picked out with lemon, walls within pale lemon, steel shelves for the books, a narrow long table down one wall, hung one side with a curtain (a tasteful modern design in lemon and black). I can lacquer an old chair black, cover a cushion in the curtain material, and have one little stool for the odd customer who wants to sit or for me to reach higher shelves. Little display stands in the window. Oh dear, I still can't believe it will happen! If it does, I am the luckiest of women.

The shape of it, on plan, is something like this:

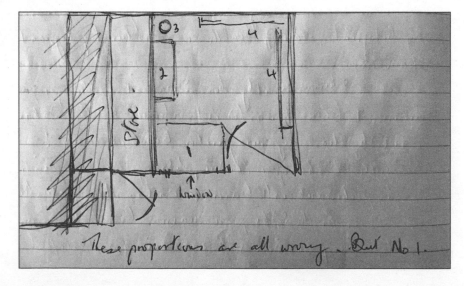

These proportions are all wrong. But No. 1 is a shelf for display just inside the door, beneath the window. Nos. 2, 3 and 4 are the 'fittings' I should have to provide, i.e. table and chair, shelves. I'd sit right in the corner (at 3), out of the way, with my cards and rubber stamp and records.

'Drink to Me Only . . .' on the radio has just reminded me. Ethel told me at Xmas that my father once tried to get into the D'Oyly Carte company but failed because his voice was not powerful enough. How curious to think what might have happened if he had been accepted.[222]

Sunday, 6 February

A good profile of Stephen Spender in today's *Observer*. He is exactly my age, has much the same background, had exactly the same kind of education and opportunities, has the same temperament, the same turn for self-examination and had the same urge to write. He succeeds, I don't. Why? I think because he has a tougher psychological constitution. He is not only poet and writer, but is able to lecture, to be a conference delegate and an editor. He is, in short, able to talk.

Well never mind. Am trying to possess my soul until I see Foyles rep.

I am now going to wash my 'smalls'.

Monday, 7 February

Mrs B.'s landlord is pleased as Punch to have a new tenant waiting to take her place, and will redecorate for me – but, as I feared, to his own atrocious colour scheme: paintwork the colour of chocolate blancmange, walls custard cream.

I've been studying the *Encyclopaedia Britannica* on subject of bookselling.

---

222 D'Oyly Carte specialised in Gilbert and Sullivan operettas.

Monday, Valentine's Day

I have been full of hatred all day. Hatred for east wind, leaden sky, Monday morning and all the things that choke one's path.

Was in town on Friday and penetrated the rambling, monster premises of Foyles, to their lending library department. My letter had not reached them, 'lost among W.G.'s mail' said the head – charming, apologetic and helpful until he heard I was thinking of selling new books also.[223] This turned him frosty and discouraging, so that I felt like a schoolgirl making some hideous gaffe, and all around that end of Oxford Street I could hear the roar of the jungle powers that rule and fight for dominance, laying snares for the unwary, living on man's credulity and ignorance, and crushing with a flick of contemptuous paw any solitary person that stands in their way and dares to challenge them. Small, alone and scared, I crept away.

My 2nd correspondence course assignment exercises on short stories, these seem to be complete balderdash. I enjoyed the first exercises (on article writing) but have not heard from the school a word about them and I wonder now if they too have gone astray. The no-time-limit bait cuts both ways, obviously.

Sunday, 20 February

I have the books I need now on the subject of bookselling and questionnaire for completion from the Publishers' Association (formal application for trade recognition to be sent with £2 2s.).

I heard from friend clockmaker Vicary (on whom I called quite by chance the other day because snow prevented me from bicycling and I was walking past his shop) that the cleaners next door but one to him have been having the same idea about a lending library. The proprietor has been negotiating with Foyles and has a stock of their library books already in his shop. They were intended originally for

223 W.G.: Probably a reference to the shop's founding brothers and the firm's original name: W & G Foyle Ltd.

the little store which Miss B. is now taking over – he had taken it for his daughter who was going to do knitting orders there and run a Foyles library on the sideline. He still has the books, and Vicary is trying to find out for me what he intends to do with them. I am touched by V's consideration. He is a genuine Liberal and believes, says he, that we must all help each other and not try to cut each other's throats.

Saturday, 26 February
Bliss, bliss, bliss. Ever since I left it this morning I have thought of bed with longing. Now here I am at last, with two h.w. bottles, bathed and smelling of Vapex. Cats come and go, mystified. It's nice sometimes to be just ill enough to enjoy this indulgence, able to get oneself organised for it, the coals in, kitchen fire stoked.

The more the news of my proposed bookshop venture spreads, the more encouragement I receive. Village folk are movingly interested and helpful; tobacconist is putting a notice in his window for me. The poor cleaner man is no rival. His books have been collected again by the Foyles agent, with whom I have now spoken by phone. She sounds exceedingly nice.

Friday, 1 April
What a long interval. Life has been too full, exciting, exacting for words here.

The Little Bookshop was launched on Friday, March 18th. During the 10 days that preceded I hardly had time to eat or sleep. Only the library and pottery are started. I started the National Book Agreement only last week and am now a recognised bookseller. It is quite a thrill. But I have to get more shelves and the shop reorganised for new stock. I started with two steel stands, but they take up too much space and are the wrong colour.[224] Everyone has

---

224 In fact, much of it seemed to be the wrong colour from the scheme she envi-

been so kind, things have fallen my way so miraculously I dare not boast about it yet.

It Couldn't Be True was sent to Fred Muller last Monday.[225] We have had wonderfully encouraging reactions from the few people who have so far read it in script – including Mrs K.R. Williams (the Siamese judge and breeder).

Saturday, 2 April

Hags and bitches . . . hags and bitches! I find myself pitched into a Reading Deposits battle. Mr M. (now Hardware) found that he had to change from the simple '2s. 6d. deposit and take as many books as you like' to '2s. 6d. deposit for each book borrowed'. He was losing too many books, and warned me to insist on the 2s. 6d. per book scheme also. Most people accept this, but every now and then there is trouble. I lost my innocence a fortnight ago at 10 a.m., when a bitter-eyed old woman stormed out of the shop muttering, 'Absurd! Absurd!' Now I am getting people who declare, 'Oh, but Mr M. didn't!' Hags and bitches . . .

I have to learn to be firm, kind, polite I suppose (to know fear without being afraid). I am having now to accept what I have in the past rejected – the discomfort occasioned by differences in opinion.

Saturday, 9 April

ICBT has come back from Muller's with the usual formal apologies and scrape, and not a word of explanation. Oh, I am sick and numb to the core of manuscripts being thrown back at me. Four books now written since the end of the war, only one of these accepted, and that

----

sioned in early February. In a later entry, Jean notes that the landlord has painted it in dark brown, pale cream and turquoise. 'I sit facing wall, not door.'

225 *ICBT* is Jean's second attempt at a cat book, a more expansive guide than the first, with illustrations by her friend E.D. and some semi-professional photographs. Frederick Muller Ltd was a British publisher most fondly remembered for producing the first *Doctor Who* books.

has not kept me in cigarettes for more than six months. People are still reading Peg, and telling me how much they enjoy it. If only it had led to something better, had been a beginning rather than a dead end.

If one could only understand the policies and mentality of publishers! I am sure there is a big cat-reading public who would admire *ICBT* and buy it eagerly. I've just no idea at the moment where it should go next. There is one advantage of being in the Trade: I am getting publishers' lists and the trade papers, and finding out the kind of books each firm goes in for. Their ads and prelim publicity are more revealing than statements in *Writers & Artists Year Book*.

Tuesday, 3 May

I've had no time to do anything more about *ICBT* – except to send it to Hart Davies, who returned it immediately saying it was a 'charming book' but just not their kind. Well that was something.

I seem to get nowhere with the shop. Unable to find a wholesaler (the one I'm in contact with now seems laggard), unable to make up list for the initial stock. My first lot of Penguins displayed on Saturday, but not one sold.

I am really tired though wonderfully well – now living on a Hauser diet. I can't speak highly enough of this system, the most sensible and logical I've come upon.[226]

Friday, 3 June

My panic is the old one regarding money. I must make the Little B. pay. I need to bank between £30–£40 a week. It seems a target I'll never reach: last week my total takings were about £2 12s. The library

---

226 Formulated by the German-born Americanised nutritionist Gayelord Hauser in the 1930s, it promoted what we may now regard as a cornerstone of good nutrition: low sugar and white flour intake, plenty of vitamins. Jean may have been reading his most recent publication, the 1955 slimming manual *Gayelord Hauser's New Guide to Intelligent Reducing*.

is just about paying the rent of books loaned – i.e. the supplier's charges.

I shall have to open every day – instead of just Wednesday a.m. and all day Thursday, Friday and Saturday as I have been doing. I'm going to start a 'Bookseller's Diary' and shall make entries daily while at the shop. The idea pleases me mightily – I see it already selling in thousands (what a hope!). Delightful new neighbour Mrs D. (Lady S.'s new housekeeper since January) said, 'But you don't panic about money, Miss P.? I shouldn't have thought you were the type.'

Sunday, 31 July

The 'Bookseller's Diary' did not get very far. I couldn't write it in the shop, and the accounts are the key to the story and are such a bore when recorded. Yet have patience, dear reader. On June 3rd last, total weekly takings were £2 2s. (and that incidentally, was the total for the first month). For the last three weeks the total has averaged £10. Does that not tell an exciting tale? Since Whitsun I have spent just over £100 on new books stock, and I have sold more than half. This is quite apart from the lending library, which is now paying for itself royally. I am more full of confidence than I have ever been about anything. I feel now that if I could find another shop locally just a little bigger and with more conveniences it would be worth the expense of moving and the bigger rent. I daren't think about it too much (though of course am doing so to exhaustion pitch).

Monday, 1 August

I very rarely take purgatives, having had the good fortune to escape the influence of advertising which makes so many people whip their poor bowels into action until they are nearly paralysed. But last night I decided to try two of Heath & Heathers Constipation Pills. Never again. They nearly killed me.

Tuesday, 2 August
Sold a Penguin, and loaned out a book to one regular. *ICBT* has been returned by Michael Joseph and The Harvill Press.

Saturday, 27 August
Several people have said within the last few months that I look so much better, and that the life I am now leading – meeting people – must be so much nicer for me, meaning that it is unhealthy or anyway not quite right to live so much in the narrow circumstances that I did. This makes me boil inwardly, and also leaves me sad. What the commentators fail to see is their own terror of loneliness. That anyone can live alone and like it makes them feel uncomfortable. 'So good for you again to be out meeting people instead of staying at home all the time.'

Saturday, 15 October
Babs's wedding day in Trinidad. The knot must be tied now, 10 p.m. here, 6 p.m. there. Bless the little oddity, Mrs Roy Everett, she was made for marriage and motherhood. And do not prate, dear reader, that so are all women. In my generation there were 3 million too many.

Tomorrow E.D. comes for the day, about the Christmas cards we're trying to produce for sale this season. She's about the only person I've seen this summer of my London friends. I do miss them. I miss my leisured days very much. That sort of freedom is precious beyond measure. My only hope is to work hard at my business until I can engage a regular part-time assistant. I will not let myself be submerged, if I can help it, in this repellent race for enough lolly to keep oneself alive.

Monday, 5 December
Can think only in terms of filthy lucre. Can I take £100 between now and Christmas? Saturday was the best day I've had yet – nearly £9,

as much as I've taken in a week formerly. If this could but be the turning point, and that I might average £5 a day until next year begins! Trade has been very slack for many of us this last month since the budget. Cost of living is so terrifying that people cut down on everything but food.

By strange, devious routes, *ICBT* is now in the hands of John Murray.

N. is on leave again and has been with me for a week. Gay, exuberant, warm, generous and as egotistical as ever. Giving abundantly with one hand and taking with the other.

I am in the process of forming a new friendship. Another woman, as unusual, stimulating and alarming as N. B.P. is a large and not unhandsome woman, with very dark, vividly alive eyes. Musically and spiritually she is very highly developed, is married to a local lawyer and has one small son at school. She comes and talks to me often and I enjoy her conversation enormously. I don't really know what she thinks of me. Every now and then I receive a salutary shock, e.g. her surprise that I actually selected the better-class books in the library (she had thought that I just took, lamely, what was handed to me). She asked to read 'Peg' and I have lent her a copy. When she came in this morning I was hoping to hear some favourable comments, but she was full of the new Jennings book she bought off me on Friday. How good all this is for my ego.

God, oh God – and I am, what, 47 now? And still looking for security, reassurance, the spiritual or psychological anchor of the mind and longing heart which just doesn't exist. If one could only realise that. Prayers and meditation and study are unavailing.

Monday, 27 February 1956

Something does lift or drain away after a session here. An easing of tensions, a releasing of inner tides. I want often and often to turn to it, but there is no time, I am too tired, too distracted or burdened with other things.

Tonight I make time for it. Events are taking such an unexpected aspect I must. I fret and fume and pray for capital – a football pool win, a prize, an undreamt-of legacy or surprising rich lover, anything of this nature to help me finance my little business. And out of the blue descends Lady B. A month ago I didn't know of her existence, but this was my fault, my ignorance of the powers that rule the Trading Estate.

She is wealthy, influential, forceful, of heavy build with a slow, powerful kind of vitality. Her husband is in his 80s and potters about the village with push-stick shopping basket. He came in about three weeks ago to ask if I could get rid of some old books for him – he asked me to have tea with him and see them. He makes delicious wholemeal bread and promised me a loaf. And of course during polite conversation I said I much wanted a larger shop: I'd heard some time ago that tobacconist's Allan's was on the market, but was quite beyond my means. And Lady B. said, 'Find out more about it – I might go in with you.'

The possibilities here are endless, complications fearful. Lady B. is set on making the basis of the business newspapers and magazines – bookselling alone isn't enough. A good newsagent's, plus books, library and cigarettes might well flourish. I, however, am not going to be up at the crack of dawn to organise a dozen or so maddening little boys.

Sunday, 6 May

And now it has all frothed into nothing. Allan's went long ago. Lady B., having gone into figures, decided that the project was too expensive, the returns would be too uncertain. I have struggled on, just paying my way but no more, not a penny profit yet for me and my resources dwindle, dwindle. A local trader suggests that I approach some other, established, bookshop in the locality and ask them if they would be interested in opening a branch here. Make your own position safe, don't risk more capital, let someone else be your boss. As the book trade is at present I doubt very much whether any other bookseller – short of a firm such as W.H. Smith – could possibly undertake expansion. It is all so humiliating.

Aunt Jessie Holford died in January and has left me £200. I have had to break into my last £1,000 of war stock, and have £700 left on paper, worth actually at present less than £500. This is what the credit squeeze, inflation, universal greed and fear does for one. Thank you, Aunt Jessie, whom I never went to see, for remembering me. It is a greater gift than you know.

Thursday, 14 June
Old Mrs W., as always in straight-cut dark brown coat and Henry Heath hat, came in the other day saying, 'This is the first time you have disappointed me. Filth!' And she flung Sylvia Townsend Warner's new collection of stories *Winter in the Air* on my desk. 'Filth!' I must have looked startled, for she added, 'I hope the author is not a friend of yours?'[227]

I should have known better than to suggest this book for her. I am enjoying it immensely, but not because I find it filthy. I discovered S.T.W. a little while ago, and my judgement seems for once sound. I am glad of this, that I can recognise a writer of quality.

One must not dwell on the things people say that cause irritation. You are tired out, then anything anyone may say can inflame you and inflame old wounds. At that point, when you begin to find yourself on edge, bristling with resentment, let go. At what seems the 'nervous breakdown' stage, unable or unwilling to let go because you are sure your world will drop to pieces if you do – that is exactly the moment when you *can* let go. And when you do, the pleasant aspect of living returns. You discover or rediscover the pleasure of living in the immediate present. Which is always right. The eternal moment Now.

---

227 She wasn't a friend, but was born and grew up a few miles from Jean. She was popular in her day, and was later championed as a significant feminist writer.

Wednesday, 27 June

I've decided all of a sudden that lino is the answer to the floor problem.

Tuesday, 3 July

Nurseryman S., deploring the lack of good writers today, stirred my sense of responsibility as the village's book supplier.[228] For him and one or two like him it is in my power to provide the new and better authors I read of. The sad truth is, so few people are interested. One tends to get lazy about it – as sapped and woolly as one's customers. They don't like what they call 'horrors' (I don't mean murder whodunnits). Nothing different or difficult or painful, nothing to disturb their illusions. Colin Wilson has pointed out that 'the instinct of self-preservation fights against the pain of the internal widening, and all the impulses of spiritual laziness build into waves of sleep with every new effort.' Must try to get hold of his book *The Outsider*.[229] Also Angus Wilson's *Anglo-Saxon Attitudes*.

Friday, 13 July

A gypsy with basket of lace nipped into the shop this morning and wheedled 25 shillings out of me. I could burst into anger at myself. She sold me 5 shillings' worth of lace that I do not want, then read my fortune in the crystal for £1. She told me nothing that I hoped to hear. They never do – why do I always let myself be exploited, made a fool of? Now I must pay, not only in cash, but in deep mental humiliation.

She was emphatic that I should be selling the business, and be married by the New Year and go abroad. I was to marry and settle down and be happy in a little house with no stairs.

If I am to meet a man who wants to marry me, well let that be so, I'll deal with this situation to the best of my ability when it arises.

---

228 The name is uncertain; possibly a customer in the shop.

229 An existentialist study in artistic and social alienation, it was flavour of the year for a generation still finding its way towards a modern future.

But as the reader must surely realise by now, there is not the merest whisper or smell of such a person on my horizon. Why do they never see the really important influences in my life – Wee, the cats, my desire and efforts to write, my love of literature, my search for something 'higher'? My urge to be married, to be 'Mrs', has died, truly that is so – it does not seem to matter in the least now, with a business to build. I love what I have, the life I am living. I no longer waste my energy on ghostly lovers or wishing I were someone different. If that sounds smug, it is not. There are enough difficulties, anxieties and hurts in my present to keep me from becoming smug – I only mean that I am learning to accept what I am.

Sunday, 15 July

Lydia phoned at 8 p.m. yesterday and swept me off to see *Seven Brides for Seven Brothers*, the first film I have seen for ages, a diverting, stimulating musical trifle of backwoodsmen in America, with some marvellously disciplined and agile dancing in it. I think she had had a row with husband Don and wanted to get away from him for the evening.

Sunday, 29 July

Sitting room is pale *eau de nil* green with white paint on ceiling, perfect background for dark oak, coloured books, old coloured cushions. The bath in kitchen has been boarded in at last. Kitchen walls are still cream, window and sill pale green, curtains dyed rust, the storeroom is white with a green door, green handles on doors, green medicine cupboard, green telephone shelves, broken walls mended with cement.

Tuesday, 18 December

Pooh and Ivy have been on leave since September. Babs and Roy arrived in October and sailed for Jamaica today. I am to become a great aunt in April/May. Pooh has finished his service with Cable &

Wireless and intends to settle in Jamaica. We spend Xmas day together with Ethel and Aunt Maggie – he has been saving the petrol for it.[230]

Babs is very distant. I cannot reach her at all. She and Roy stayed with me a fortnight. Him I like exceedingly, a lanky normal healthy young man with nice sense of humour and devoted to Babs. Perhaps there is too much of the Pratt/Lucey reserve in her for me ever to know her better – I feel all the time repulsed, just as I must have repulsed many people when I was that age. I suffered for it, but she can escape into doting affection of her husband, sanctuary of her own home and coming child.

Joey is lost. My dearly beloved philosopher Joe. I have not seen him for nearly a fortnight. What happened, my little love? Did car lights one dark evening dazzle you? Did a fox surprise you? Or did you find more loving, patient friends and wander away with them?

I mentioned two books on 3 July, *The Outsider* and *Anglo-Saxon Attitudes*. Angus Wilson's highly praised work was disappointing. I got through it, but was limping towards the end. I saw for a moment clearly, exactly, the homosexual as described to me by Graham Howe. Only a homo could have written it – brilliant, perceptive, but disintegrated, all his characters were separate, striving for separateness and isolation, afraid of real relationships. And what a phobia he has for the colour mauve.[231]

Thursday, 27 December
Christmas all over now. Sadness and silence fall.

Pooh and Ivy spent Xmas Day very pleasantly *en famille* with Ethel and Aunt Maggie – huge meals, fires, welcome. Yesterday afternoon

---

230 This is Jean's oblique reference to the Suez Crisis. The petrol blockade in the Middle East had led to the introduction of petrol rationing on 17 December, restricting private cars to travel only about 200 miles a month. The rationing lasted until May 1957.

231 Angus Wilson was indeed gay, and made no secret of this when he worked at Bletchley Park as a code-breaker during the war.

was spent with Pooh and Ivy at Richmond playing Scrabble, then by train to stay with Joan at Golders Green, and today on my way home have called in to see Gus. Phyllis is with *Separate Tables* in New York – both hate the separation. He is haggard with various stresses and strains in her absence, but charming, charming as always.

Why am I not happy, content, at peace, as I should be? I didn't want hectic gaiety and noisy parties, I didn't want romance, glamour, excitement. I wanted no more than I actually had. We are losing touch in some way, through circumstances that have got out of our control. We have to break away and learn to understand loneliness – the loneliness that each individual must know and not try to avoid . . . we've left youth and its exuberance behind. We are sober, respectable, middle-aged – but not from morality or pride, simply from the pressure and edge of the times. All of us, one way or another, struggling against financial worries, fatigue, anxiety about families or elderly relatives. There is no security for us, not even the false security of fixed adequate incomes and capital.

It was laughter I sought, a catharsis of laughter as we had in the Gus 'harem' days, wonderful sensation of lightness and ease out of nonsense. No, it doesn't happen anymore. It is depressing, longing for the drink that satisfied one in youth.

Monday, 7 January 1957
A little concentrated grief, then it will be over. I've said goodbye to Pooh. Dear Pooh, whom I love dearly, God bless, keep and prosper you. We went this morning to the agents at Wembley to discuss Homefield; shall probably sell it when the time is opportune. And we stood for a few minutes outside the old house like ghosts. I dream of it often, but it is never quite in my dreams as it is actually. The district has changed so much. The buttercups and cow parsley, owls in the oaks, that small unmade gravelly road where tramps lurked, the still summer evenings, Pooh cycling before breakfast in the holidays, the Burlington sweetshop where I spent my Saturday pennies, all echoing,

miraged faintly in the dim winter morning – goodbye goodbye! It is over, over long ago. We cannot go back.

Yet I cannot let go quite so abruptly. Our father built that house more than 50 years ago, full of bright hopes, establishing a home for him and his family, expecting the place to take root and grow, be a centre for grandchildren and great grandchildren. I feel that something is lost, that somehow we have bungled things. I don't mean just our small family, but ours multiplied, the whole generation that has rushed into being and made Wembley into such an outrageously sordid suburb. All the Wembleys that have tramped down the buttercups . . .

45.

Terminex

Tuesday, 20 August 1957 (aged forty-seven)
This is an instrument, not an indulgence or means of escape, not a discipline nor an end, nor an attempt to embalm the passing moment. It shall be a clearing house, a sifting ground.

Really, what bliss to sit here again writing this. It makes me feel better at once. About this time every month I get fearfully depressed. It is the time when I have to make up my accounts and pay as many bills as I can. I must face it: more money goes out than comes in. One feels hemmed in by rapacious beasts, always roaring, demanding their pounds and pounds of flesh. They all seem so much more powerful and better fed than I am. They couldn't care less that they are draining my resources. I get panicky. I think I can't go on, I must give up this silly losing battle, find a more safe, well-paid job before disaster quite overwhelms me. Why do I bother? What am I living for? All the old torments return.

I meant to do the ironing. I must go and mince the cats' supper.

Sunday, 25 August
I had £5,000 when I was 21, and now I have only £500 of it left. It has helped me do quite a lot of pleasant things, but I don't desperately want it all back again. I think it's such a false idea to suppose that if you had that amount or other fat sum that everything in the garden will be lovely.

My neighbour Lady Spicer died about five weeks ago, quite unexpectedly, one quiet Tuesday afternoon. She had been longing to die, for months and months, it must have been a great relief for her. She was a miserable old devil in many ways, cantankerous and selfish, but she was elegant, had lovely things and a nice sense of humour. I had grown very fond of her, though dreading always any reference to politics and current affairs. We were always, according to her, on the brink of war, and it was always Russia's fault. She would lie in that delicious bedroom against snow-white pillows, in delicate pale pink bedwear, plucking at the silk eiderdown and murmur, 'Isn't the world in a mess! What a mess we're in . . .'

I found her pearls one day this summer. They were lying in the grass on the triangle in front of our houses, where I cut across on my bicycle daily. I didn't know they were hers when I picked them up, but it dawned on me slowly that they were unusually handsome – in fact they were alive, they glowed. They became more and more beautiful as I looked and handled them.

She was so grateful to have them restored that she gave me a cheque for £5. It was during one of the periods when she felt well enough to get up and walk outside a little in the afternoon. She always wore her pearls, but her hands shook so much she had not been able to fasten the safety catch.

It was a thrill to have held a small fortune in my hands. They are being sold, I'm told: her heirs don't want them. Her heirs don't want her charming house either. We all wonder apprehensively who our new neighbours will be. I do miss her. I have known no other neighbour that side all the time I've been here – 18 years.[232]

232 The journal contains a cutting from the *Windsor, Slough and Eton Express* dated Friday, 18 October 1957. Above a small photo of Jean, the headline ran: 'She's Woman Parish Council Clerk No 4'. The article began: 'In a few weeks time a slight, dark-haired woman will have her first opportunity of coping with what until recently has been an all-male task. She is Miss Jean Pratt, of Wee Cottage, Egypt, who was recently appointed clerk to Farnham Common Parish Council. Already well known in the area as proprietor of a small but intriguing bookshop in the Broadway,

New Year's Day, 1958

Two resolutions:

8. To remove sign saying 'Agent For Foyles Library' outside the Little B. This has been achieved, and fills me with relief. I am sick unto death of being thought part of that hugely untidy concern. 'Foyles would get it for you, wouldn't they – you're an Agent. They have everything, surely.' Such is the power of advertising.

9. To keep this again as diary. But the resolve weakens already – frustrated by overwhelming urge to make up for lost sleep, having seen the New Year in until 2 a.m. at Lydia's.

Saturday, 18 January

Today has been a typically busy one, so I'll inflict it on you in detail. I do not drag myself from bed until after 8. BBC News is already half over as I plug in my electric kettle. By nine I have fed and smoked and dressed, but have left the bedroom and breakfast things. Off I go in my shabby winter coat and head scarf on my bicycle through the dull, cold January morning. Must stop at baker's to collect bread, at PO to post parcel and buy stamps, at Lund's to order greengroceries for today's delivery, at Foley's to buy cheese and other oddments. Then to tobacconist's for the daily drug and to collect my mail. And so at last to open up the Little B.

It is after 9.30. I have to put out the mat, the '1s. 6d.' tray, turn on the electric stove. A letter from Grig – what joy! And another cat book order with blessed postal orders for £1 16s. Things do not get really hectic until after 11 a.m. I have my milk and biscuits in comparative peace, reading *The Bookseller*. Then everyone comes all at once,

---

Farnham Common, Miss Pratt is thrilled with her new job: "I never dreamed of doing such a task. I knew they needed a new clerk, and when Mr Sachs, who is on the council and comes into the bookshop regularly, asked me if I would like to take over – I agreed." The article explained that the shop was going well, and that Jean also volunteered to campaign for the Liberal Party, was a member of the village dramatic society, and, when time allowed, bred short-haired British blues.

and I hardly pause until 12.30. Many weekend library customers, children for small items, a man buys one of the Don Camillos.[233]

Home. Open up the kitchen fire, put on the soup, dash upstairs and make the bed, empty the slop pail, clear up the breakfast tray, make the afternoon's thermos of tea, sit down to soup and egg and cheese, bread, honey and a banana. Comb hair, smear on more lipstick, must buy some more stamps, get more cigarettes and a Crunchie for my tea.

Must finish off the week's *Clique*.[234] Harrods' van with the week's library exchange arrives about 2.30 – I get these books checked in and sorted. A new man joins the library. Library, constant planning and organisation and niggling detail, constant watching of book reviews, tracing books people ask for and keeping customers satisfied, keeping records up to date, mail, letters to be answered, publishers tackled, orders sent.[235]

Just before 5 I go across to the Ladies at The Feathers. Yesterday's headache still threatens at the back of my eyes. At 5.30 I go out again to buy in the weekend's cigarettes and some greens from Mrs Ford. We gossip mainly about the coal situation. I am quite out of coke and burning the dregs of slack in the kitchen fire. The coal merchant can promise nothing. I feel tempted to burgle my late neighbour's store.

I buy a 3d. ice cream and eat this while I balance the day's takings, which I make 1s. short. Bring in the book tray, padlock the cases, stove off, lock up. Back lamp won't go on, must cycle home without. A light darkness tonight, not unpleasant. Home again – little shadows in the dark garden emerge. A warm, enticing meal all ready for me? No, of course not.

---

233 The fictional WW2-era priest created by Giovannino Guareschi.

234 The weekly trade magazine offering bookseller directories, library information and lists of rare and out-of-print publications.

235 The loan terms at Jean's library were elaborate, a scheme involving 'A' category and 'B' category books and a subscription service offering two 'A' books or three 'B' books for £3 7s. 6d. a year, or two 'B' books at a time for £2 2s. Other options were available. ('Romances * Thrillers * Westerns*', her leaflets proclaimed. 'Change as often – keep as long – as you like! No fines.')

Here is a surprise for you. This autumn I was appointed Clerk to the Parish Council. Am very glad of the extra money. (The job has to be learned slowly, item by item – all the Councillors and late clerk are being very helpful and tolerant.)

So it goes, dear reader, day after day much like this one, until I can stand it no more and go to bed early with hot milk and a couple of Veganin tablets. Most people haven't a clue of the work I have to get through. 'You wouldn't think it, would you, with a little business like that . . .'

But it is beginning to pay, just a little.

Tuesday, 21 January

I feel tonight as must people of the frozen North when they see the first signs of the winter's ice breaking. The Scheme may fruit. We have waited so long, bound in for nearly three years by ice I couldn't thaw.

Why does anyone worry about 'love', about being loved and finding the Right Person, and about missed opportunities and 'I've never had a chance?' and 'It isn't fair!'? There is no need to let these moods colour your life. Love can illumine every moment of it, whether you are 'loved' or not. But let us not nail that poor butterfly. Make your own discoveries and keep them secret.

Today, snow fell early in the morning. Could not get up, having grown roots into the bed. Mail-order cheques amounting to over £10 awaited me. This is what maketh the heart rejoice. All down to my cat passion: nearly all my biggest and most rewarding orders are for cat books.

Lunch today supplied by my neighbour Mrs S. – lovely hot meat, two veg, treacle pud and coffee. We have had this arrangement since the summer, twice a week for 3s. 6d. a time. I cannot praise this service enough.

Sunday, 26 January

Birch trees being felled by Wee and the woodsmen burning the thin branches in huge fires. They were nice men, and gave me some long lengths too. By Friday night I knew I must have a day in bed or crack up completely. I was beginning to get the old duodenal pain again, as well as headaches and general feeling of tension, irritation and panic.

Nothing could have suited me better – smug and relaxed in my little nun's blue and white bedroom, with four cats stretched on the eiderdown, the 5th around somewhere.

It has been a day like the one I once spent in the Sick Room at school – restorative. I think I had a poisoned heel but was not otherwise ill. I was then absorbed discovering Rupert Brooke. I believe I wrote some Journal which I still have. I can reach back over all those years and touch that day again.

Friday, 28 March

How many times do shopkeepers discuss the weather? And how many get bored to death with the subject? And what else should we speak of with our customers if weather were monotonously consistent?

Must confess this out of my system: have been giving my eczema-plagued Pepper a course of Benadryl. The capsules have slipped down quite easily, but the other night I was tired and late and consequently clumsy. She resisted and lashed out at me with her claws. I lost my temper and slapped her nose hard. With a whimper she sprang from me, and when she lifted her head there were huge tears in her eyes, slipping down her nose. I have never seen an animal cry, and she was really crying. Her expression was anguished. I could have killed myself on the spot.

Tuesday, 22 April

Yesterday I took barely 10s. I have just over £8 in my current account, and bills amounting to £30–£40 waiting to be paid. I am owed perhaps £10 – not much more.

Overtired, I wake in the small hours feeling choked, as though

I'll never be free of this situation, held in that small space as if by a vice. The only capital I can raise is tied up in Homefield. We have served notice to quit on the tenant, but solicitor has received heart-rending appeal from the tenant's daughter. Tenant is now 81 and has chronic invalid son living with her – they cannot find other accommodation and so on and so on. It would seem to be a case that a court would view with favour, and we judged harsh landlords. I would not like to think of Ethel and Aunt Maggie in such a situation. We are not wealthy or selfish people, we don't want to turn old and ailing people into the street. Let us see what may be done with cooperation and goodwill.

Sunday, 7 June

The struggle for money becomes so ghastly it excludes all else. I need another £100 in my current account to meet all the bills due for payment this month, and there is no hope of the business producing that much in that time. In other words, I am theoretically bankrupt, and shall have to plunder my last little bit on deposit. I've kept it intact, earning interest, for nearly 16 months.

I long to write again. A book about the Little B., of course. There is agitation in the book trade now to publicise bookshops nationally – a 'Buy More Books' campaign (I am not the only bookseller in difficulties). A light, amusing little volume, if well written, would be timely.

Tuesday, 15 July

The sourness of this summer eats into me like acid. Should I throw in my hand, give up the whole venture? Who would buy my miserable little business as it is? The cats hold me to Wee. If it weren't for them I might feel capable of abandoning everything.

And suddenly came a near-neighbour, Little Miss H., with a basket of wonderful raspberries from her garden for me. I am more touched than I can say.

When I went into PO this morning, absorbed in the addition of stamps, nice Mr M. exclaimed, 'You have been looking worried lately'. That my anxieties should be so obvious really shook me. I wanted to rush away somewhere and cry a lot, but there was no escape.

It is not only that I am not paying my way, nor the present difficulties of trying to work in two places and the smallness of the shop giving me claustrophobia. It is the apparent indifference of the public in general to books. They seem to be the last thing that most people ever think of buying.

Wednesday, 16 July

It is quite possible that within the next five years they will have widened the village street, which it badly needs. More and better shops will be built and local trade will improve, though our rural character will be somewhat lost. This doesn't worry me greatly. It is a hideous village, there is nothing attractive about it at all, no buildings worthy of preservation except the Stag & Hounds, which won't be pulled down anyway.[236] In fact, good modern building should improve it vastly if planners keep in mind that we could still remain a village and don't let Big Business get its claws into us. Or speculative builders for that matter, who are already ruining the area with suburban housing estates, badly designed and built. There seems to be no control over this sort of development whatever.

Wednesday, 23 July

Am about to try once more to stop smoking with aid of a new product called Terminex. God help me. If by this time I'm not near suicide I'll go down on my knees and thank Him for Terminex.

I like their sales talk approach. It is all reasonable, possible and promises no miracles. It seems to be what I've been whining after for years, and therefore I must try it. After all, it is insane to burn away

---

236 It still exists. Pub quiz every other Tuesday.

over £2 a week when one really hasn't got it. I smoke at least 40 a day now at 3s. 3d. per 20. It could mean for me a short holiday or new clothes, Mrs Mop's wages, Lund's bill, the milk and laundry. I have gone without new clothes; I like a little alcohol occasionally, sweets, cream, an occasional theatre in London, but can do without them without my becoming a raving lunatic. Cigarettes however, no never. Must, must, must be able to smoke when and as often as I desire. It is this desire that I have wanted help in breaking down. I feel about to face the dentist's chair or prison.

Penguin traveller came round to Wee this a.m., sent from the shop by Mrs H. He caught me in the lavatory. As this is next to the back door I can never pretend I'm not there, and am so used to the situation I can usually carry it off with some aplomb. A tactful kitten was attracting his earnest attention when I appeared.

He encouraged me somewhat by pointing out there is no good bookshop in Gerrard's Cross, Beaconsfield or Slough (except for Carter & Wheeler at the far end of town). The Smiths in these towns are not adequate, run by 'nice little men, but harassed by head office'. He could see from the sitting room that I had a genuine interest in books, and Penguins, and had me revealing my literary past and the sad tale of *Lovely Peggy*.

Friday, 25 July

I do believe it is going to work. Only 10 cigarettes yesterday, and not 8 today. Frightfully hungry and frightfully tired.

Sunday, 27 July

I do indeed thank God for Terminex. The craving is certainly checked. There is no longer that tormenting and positively irresistible urge to smoke continually. But I feel a little lost, as though I have nothing to do. The physical gesture of taking, lighting, holding had something soothing in it. Chewing gum and sweets help a little, but one soon tires of them. I long for meal times, I long for sleep.

Tuesday, 12 August

I am still smoking up to 10 cigs a day. I do not seem to be able to keep it much below this. But to have reduced to that amount for three weeks is quite incredible for me. The treatment itself is nearly over and I may try another bottle. I think the chemical compulsion has been checked, but not the psychological compulsion.

Parish Clerk salary and Homefield rent have both come to alleviate the financial crisis for a few weeks. The fog checking the Homefield sale shows signs of lifting also. We do not need to make a court case of it. I now learn that we can renew the agreement on a monthly basis and at a higher rent.

Wednesday, 15 October

N. has been on leave again. I went to London for a day, saw Charles Laughton in *The Party*. She has had a book accepted by Collins, bless her (God help us all). But really I am delighted for her sake. She has written it during her heavy school work in Ghana, about a little black boy in West Africa and his struggle to get educated. Collins think highly of it – had it read by Naomi Mitchison who wrote N. a personal letter praising it.[237] Publication is next autumn, in time for the Queen's visit, and it is to be sold in America. It seems an almost certain winner.

And now of course whatever I may say here will be interpreted as raging envy and gall and wormwood. I do not find her different: she seems to me still the same restless, volcanic, unstable, ego-bound unreasonable person she always has been. She doesn't seem to soften, to mature in spite of all her achievements. I cannot share things with her. I am still too scared to relax with her. I am left after our meetings feeling like a tossed, bruised kitten.

Then there is B.P.[238] She is another stimulating, forthright, forceful character to whom I am attracted and wish to talk to about all manner

237 Mitchison was a successful novelist and active socialist. Like Jean, she kept a wartime diary for Mass Observation.
238 See 5 December 1955.

of things, but, just on the edge, fail. She is the one who talks, to me
– endlessly, brilliantly, searchingly – and listens only when she wants
to, never when I want to be listened to.

I long, long to find someone with their sort of intelligence, interests and outlook with whom I can really and deeply share my own,
but I never do. I try to explain it away as fear: I cannot face their
anger and scorn if I try to express an opinion or an idea that contradicts their own. But is it perhaps more an anxiety to please, to be
pleasing, applauded, approved of? I want their approval, their favour,
their love.

Sunday, 9 November
I think it was the next day that B.P. discovered me breathlessly scurrying
between shop and Wee to get parcels packed for the afternoon carrier,
and money in the bank by 2 p.m., sacrificing my lunch. 'But you mustn't
do that!' she exclaimed, and raced off to provide a meal, returning to
shop with eggs baked in tomatoes and sauce in special ramekins, rice
pudding, bread, tea, apple – the lot! I was very grateful for it.

I'm getting numb, go through the working day in a trance, feeling
nothing, not caring. If someone said to me tomorrow, 'Miss P., here
is a thousand pounds and the shop premises you want' I should feel
nothing. I cannot do more that I am doing in the present circumstances, and they are slowly, slowly destroying me.

Friday, 21 November
I 'pulled myself together', put Mrs J. on duty at the shop and stayed
at home to bring some order to my work room here. A miracle
(apparently) was achieved. Mrs Mop can get in to clean floor. I can
dust. I have things so arranged that I know, on the whole, where to
find them.

Business improves slowly as Christmas approaches. I do not care
now if this precious festival is over-commercialised. It is the only time
in the year when I can feel sure of making a little money.

Saturday, 31 January 1959

Scrape, scrape, gasp and hope, all the time. Lucky in many things, if not as money-maker. My Mrs Heron has left me for a post as secretary to the new primary school, but her friend Mrs Faulkner has taken her place. I am very lucky indeed – she too is a married (i.e. supported) woman, interested in books, reliable, kind. In fact, I was staggered to discover that when the news went round that Mrs H. was leaving, no less than three people were after the job at the Little B. And I can't pay as much as I pay my cleaner. (Mrs F. on phone last night: 'You have "Cash on Delivery" down for him.' 'That's the *Concise Oxford Dictionary*,' I explained.)

Wireless playing 'Stormy Weather' – tune of the summer I went to Jamaica (or was it 'Smoke Gets In Your Eyes'?) I was so young, so ignorant of my instincts, which were those of a trollop. I still believe too much fuss is made about sex. I wish I could have let those instincts rip, freely and lightly, instead of forcing them into remote, romantic, dangerous daydreams. They distorted and frustrated my development, I am sure of it. Yet if I had been able to let those instincts have freedom, I should have become in this day and age what is termed a bad woman. Well really – that was the last sort of confession I expected. Just shows the potency of cheap music.

Lady Spicer's house was bought by a friend of hers, Mrs Rundle. Mrs R. has a perfectly charming daughter with a 19-year-old son – Vera and Edward.

Am smoking again, much too much. There is no cure, no hope of salvation here.

Saturday, 28 February

Today ends an absolutely bumper Book Sale fortnight. I've already taken at least £30 more than I did at either of the last two national sales. It is odd: book buying is such an individual urge and so very thinly spread over the population. It seems to come in waves, independently of the economic condition of the country. Bad weather is

particularly disastrous for me, with my two showcases outside. This
year people have been able to potter and browse in the sunshine at
leisure, and buy, bless them. I think that locally I am at last being
taken seriously. The real booklovers have nosed me out – alas that
they are always among the poorest in the community.

Sunday, 5 April

Have just finished Peter Wildeblood's *West End People*. I think it's
gorgeous and must push it in the library – his homo associations
make people a little wary.[239]

It must be all of six weeks since my last entry. The Dram Soc has
put on *Love in a Mist* with some success at last, and again I looked
after props. And then there's been annual Parish and Council meetings, and a visit to the Ideal Home to see W.H. Smith's stand, and the
new little boiler I've decided to have in the kitchen, and stocktaking.
And on Tuesday there's a Village Hall development meeting. That
seems to me a fairly full and varied programme, which I mention to
reassure myself I am not the work-grubbing, money-bound recluse
B.P. sometimes makes me feel.

'Marvellous what people think is Life and what isn't, ain't it?' says
the recumbent clip-joint hostess to Cherry in *West End People*. ' When
I came out of school, I thought Life was stopping out late after
midnight and going to nightclubs and having handsome foreigners
licking the back of my hand. Well, I've seen plenty since then, and
now I know what Life really is. It's mending someone's socks and
having kids and staying in with the telly in the evening. Sounds
terrible, it probably is terrible, but I just lap it up.'

---

239 Wildeblood was a writer and television producer, but it was his frankness as
a campaigning homosexual (when such a thing was still illegal) that made him
famous. In a distant echo of the trial of Oscar Wilde, in the mid-1950s Wildeblood
was prosecuted with two others for inciting indecent acts with men, and the case
was instrumental in the recommendations of the Wolfenden Report of 1957 that
homosexuality between consenting adults be decriminalised. *West End People* was
a satirical novel of gangland Soho.

Wednesday, 8 April

Went to a new hairdresser's in Slough today. It was quite terrifying. A nice, long open salon, no cubicles. Before mirrors along one wall sat all the women whose hair had just been shampooed somewhere at back of shop, being put into curlers. Along the opposite wall sat others under dryers, placidly reading magazines. There were little tables with mirrors and chairs in the middle of the room too, and scores of little teenage girl assistants in pastel overalls attending two male operators. It was like a launderette.

I wanted to bolt as soon as I entered, but there was no escape. The till near the door was partially screened off by plants and rubbery creepers on a bamboo frame. The principal of this modern establishment is small, dark, autocratic, could be Greek, Italian, Armenian. Cut my hair himself, as the assistant I had booked the appointment with is away ill. I needed only pruning – my hair has not seen the dresser's professional scissors for over a year – and certainly the little fellow trimmed it very well, though he took his time over it, darting away at intervals to attend to this and that and welcome another foreigner (large and fat, who disappeared up some stairs). One was reminded of a film, set in Soho. And as I sat waiting, watching all the other women in stages of disarray, they seemed indistinguishable one from the other. We are being moulded to one pattern, made to look as the hairstylist and fashion designer dictates. We haven't a chance to be individual.

Saturday, 25 April

Builders arrive to install new Ideal boiler.

Tuesday, 28 April

Woke at 6 a.m. and went out to outside lav. Then breakfast, and at 8.15 BATH. Have never been able to do this in all the 20 years I've been here.

Trying to read Sillitoe's *Saturday Night and Sunday Morning*, but don't think I'm wildly interested in the vigorous working-class life of Nottingham.

Thursday, 30 April
Gregory missing since last night. No sign of him.

When, oh Lord, shall I ever show a nice balance to my credit? Never, I feel. Semi-bankruptcy is the state and lot of all honest booksellers, let us accept that.

Friday, 1 April
Just before 9, phone rang. It was Gus – Gus of all people. To say that Luigi was dead. I have been stunned all day. Sat for 15 minutes thinking, remembering dear Luigi and the fun we all had, and that she was planning a trip home next summer. Gus phones again. Luigi had died very suddenly of a haemmargh, no, I cannot spell it. Still no sign of Gregory. Am so worried but can do nothing.

Sunday, 3 May
Determined to make enquiries, I embarked with gumboots and mac, ending finally at Mrs Ken's by the bus stop. She said at once, 'Oh, Miss Pratt! That must be the one my husband buried yesterday . . . we found him by the hedge.' He had evidently been courting next door to her bungalow, but of course was not accustomed to that vile main road. And I trudged home again, weeping, weeping in the rain.

Friday, 21 August
'Isn't it a lovely little shop?' said the woman to the children with her. And Lady B. earlier in the week: 'But its smallness is such an attraction – don't you feel people come because of it?' These sorts of compliments I get quite often. They help to make bearable the insults and frustration. Perhaps I should fail to create the charm that attracts the discerning in a larger shop.

Sunday, 23 August

'It is a struggle, isn't it?' said accountant K., for once sympathetically, as he surveyed last year's figures with me. 'You need a bigger shop,' and suggested little sidelines such as tobacco, sweets and stationery. Oh God help me! I will not descend to that level.

Collins sent me, at her request, an advance copy of N.'s book, *Ashanti Boy* by Akosua Abbs.[240] It is excellent, a limpid story of a black boy's efforts to get himself educated. There are no love affairs, but the tale holds one's attention.

Thursday, 31 December

We stand at the door of a new decade. It promises to be a decade of moment for me.

In August Miss Drumm, an elderly, faithful library customer, had been wanting me to see if some old books of hers were of any use to me. I have quite often had this sort of invitation, but not combined with a lunch. At the end of this pleasant meal she announced that she would like to back my business. She lost her friend and partner at the beginning of the year and was seeking new interests. I left in a haze, not quite being able to believe this offer.

At the end of the month, Florence Cottages suddenly came on the market again.[241] There followed weeks of agitated thought. Miss Drumm is lending me practically the whole of the purchase money, plans have been drawn up and submitted to the Rural Council's Planning Committee, and builder has already started work on the ground floor. Is not there, then, a wonderful new year ahead of me? Added to these plans is the now definite prospect of our selling Homefield to a developer for £6,000. It reads like a fairy tale.

I'm fighting to preserve something worthwhile. I can't at the

---

240 The origin of N.'s pseudonym is unclear. Her subtitle is 'A Book for Young People of All Ages'. Judging by the number of editions, the book sold well.
241 Jean had been eyeing this site for a few years with a view to expansion. It was a larger shop on the Broadway, the main thoroughfare in Farnham Common.

moment think of another word, but 'culture' was the one Peggy Denny used. She arrived one bright morning unexpectedly and took me out to lunch. It was one of those days when I was feeling uncertain – was I doing the right thing? 'Go on,' she said. 'We must have culture – there is so much of everything else.' Culture, yes, the things of value, or the means by which we can assess values. Not money and security which is all this age clamours for. Quality. Taste. This word was used by another new friend: 'There is no taste in the village,' he said. 'You could supply it.'

Tuesday, 2 February 1960

The cottages are now definitely mine, plans passed, mortgage all arranged, the village agog with curiosity, and people besieging me for the flat that is to be made of the top two floors. But ready money is lacking and seems more unobtainable than ever. Wembley Council has been moved to refuse the Developer's plans for Homefield – people in Crawford Ave started an agitation, disliking the idea of flats at No. 4, and have brought pressure to bear. Agent Ward is fighting mad about it. It means months and months of further delay. But for the hag – who, I understand, was responsible for the Council's refusal – it would all be settled by now, and Pooh and I together richer than we have been for years. I really do hate that old woman at this moment and feel very sorry for myself. I have about £50 left on deposit. All of it will be needed this month to pay outstanding debts and publishers. I have therefore, you horrible Wembley bitch, as though you cared, nothing whatever of my own for all the things I'll be needing for the new business. Meddlesome, pompous, bigoted old sow.

The enraging thing about the whole affair is the Wembley Council's inconsistency. They have allowed similar development, flats to be erected next to Churchill's old house, and other developments opposite Homefield. There was, I must confess, a pang at first at the thought of Pop's home (planned and built with such pride and hope) being destroyed. But my solicitor hit me sweetly on the head about this. If we for sentimental reasons tried to prevent it, there was nothing to stop the next owner letting it go for development, so why should we not reap the benefit?

Sunday, 7 February

Babs, Roy and Sue have been home on leave since the beginning of January. They now have a flat in Putney and today we have all been celebrating Granny Ethel's 80th birthday. Sue is a perfect sweetie. A little shy at first, but it does not last. Once she knows you and feels secure, she is enchanting. They are in fact really rather a nice little family – Babs has chosen well and I am quite proud of her. Adolescence is an abominable age. I am becoming very fond of my niece, it is a heart-warming relief.

Babs with sprout at lunch to Sue: 'Do you want a dolly cabbage?'
'S, please.'

Babs to me: 'I used to call them dolly cabbages!' And so did I. And so does a family tradition continue – from Victorian to New Elizabethan, for I think it came from my mother's childhood days.

Thursday, 11 February

Someone said on *Any Questions* this week that he could relax every limb on getting into bed, block out his mind, and be asleep in five minutes.[242] I long to be able to do this.

Phyllis is playing at Windsor next week for a fortnight. One of the Langton boys was in this evening and seemed quite impressed that I knew Phyllis. It is very vanity-enlarging: 'You know Phyllis Neilson-Terry?' (with awe).

'Yes,' (nonchalantly). 'But I know her husband better.' How could I ever explain to anyone how much? Dear old Gus. He was speaking recently on *Woman's Hour* with two woman decorators in a little 'My

---

242 *Any Questions* began on BBC Radio in 1948.

Worst Mistake' item. His, apparently, was to line, at great expense, a bathroom – floor, ceiling, walls, the lot – with mirrors. When the light was turned on the effect was paralyzing – you couldn't find the door. This Luigi would have enjoyed hugely.

The first step of the move on Monday was not as enthralling as I'd been hoping.

Sunday, 28 February

I scrape the till each day and come home sick at heart, wondering if it will be the same in two or three years' time. And what shall I do then – slide gracefully into bankruptcy?

Saw Phyllis in the play last week. I adored it.

Thursday, 1 March

A sad interview today with a little man and his wife from Willesden. They had traced me down about Homefield – they want the house very much because of the garden. They have a son who loves gardening, the greenhouse, all the things we once cherished. He quite understood that we should accept the highest offer, but I did not tell him that I had this morning a further offer via Ward from the developer, who is willing to take a chance on the permit he wants.

I think he is genuine, this little man from Willesden, with a pale, rat-like face and a somewhat sluttish but pleasant-looking wife. There was something I liked about them, but they were not the type either my father or mother would have rejoiced to see in possession of the old home. It is all sad, sad, but Wembley is degraded . . . like Slough, a perfectly revolting suburb.

Wednesday, 23 March

I have sickening doubts about the future. On Monday morning at the shop I took the large amount of 6d. I left Mrs J. to carry on after lunch. She managed better and took nearly £3, selling one of the Eden memoirs which I feared were going to die on us.[243] This is one of the heart-breaking hazards of bookselling which may well kill one stone dead. I was sure Eden would sell, like *The Turn of the Tide* and George VI and Queen Mary (I sold 6 copies of QM), but the two copies of Eden were still with us months after publication. I hesitated and flopped over *Born Free*. I had read all the advance publicity and was fascinated, knowing I'd adore the book myself.[244] But I failed to order – could have sold 2 copies by now if I'd had them. Have ordered too late; first edition is out of print. I still have, weighing the stock down heavily, 2 copies of the last vol of Churchill's *History of the English Speaking Peoples*. We've had them I think nearly two years, and Cassell's have said they won't take any back.

Sunday, 27 March

I am being given the chance to purchase Wee. It is quite fantastically incredible. The Moneypenny has decided to sell her property and each of her tenants is being given the opportunity to buy if they wish. I shall do so somehow. With a really excellent solicitor in R.P. behind me I am sure it will be managed.

I gave up all hope of owning Wee years ago, and have never felt as desperate over my home life as I have done over the business. I am still a protected tenant and knew that unless the law was changed I couldn't be turned out. The feeling of freedom so floods through me now.

Thursday, 7 April

Back rooms still in chaos, but shop looking really lovely, though not

---

243 Anthony Eden, Conservative prime minister 1955–57, undone by the Suez Crisis.
244 *The Turn of the Tide* was an annotated collection of diaries kept by 1st Viscount Alanbrooke (edited by Arthur Bryant) during the war; it was highly critical of Churchill. *Born Free* was Joy Adamson's moving account of protecting lion cubs in Africa.

enough shelving yet. We have had a very good first day, everyone very kind and extremely flattering. But how much will they buy?

Friday, 8 April

B.P., as we stood drinking coffee in the still untidy 'cloaks' of the new shop this morning: 'You were introvert and are now becoming extrovert!' Everyone, everyone comes into the new shop beaming, ecstatic with delight and wonder.

I hope B.P. is not quite right. I hope I never lose or live to regret or neglect the introvert in me. Are there not both in everyone? Isn't it only when the introvert is over-emphasised, when the shadow in one overshadows the personality, that there is misery and frustration? 'If a man learns to deal with his own shadow, he has done something real for the world.'[245] And if that is what at last I am doing . . . oh, I hope it is true, just a little bit. It will mean that everything in the past was right. All the pain, the anguish of stumbling about in the dark alone. Now we emerge into the light.

Wednesday, 4 May

That damnable little Penguin rep – promising over a fortnight ago two display stands which have not yet arrived.

This evening to a Dress Show at the village hall in aid of World Refugee Year. Packed with local women, show put on by a firm from High Wycombe. I saw nothing I felt I couldn't live without, but it has made me terribly dissatisfied with my own wardrobe. I did buy a new suit for my cocktail party, the 'shop warmer' I threw on the premises on Easter Monday. Smashing, as they say.

Friday, 22 July

The Homefield money has still not materialised. I begin to think of it as a myth, but my bank won't. I don't dare calculate my overdraft,

---

245 Paraphrasing Carl Jung.

keep putting off payments in the same old way, exactly as I have been doing for five years, gritting my teeth, telling no one.

Babs is to have another infant in January. It is pleasing to think of one's family going on like that. The cats also multiply. Three quite adorable ginger kits disrupt the routine.

Sunday, 14 August

Shop phone was installed on Friday. Now disconnected at Wee. I may be able to have an extension in about two years' time, but until then must do without. In a way it's a relief to know one can't be 'got at' by anyone while one is at home.

Monday, 15 August

And it was N. who, quite without intent, called first on the office line.

Oh dear, oh dear, please help me now God to be patient, generous, kind, without giving in to her, making myself into the same old doormat. She sounded quite unchanged, peeved and aggrieved because now my friends (meaning herself in particular) would not be able to get me – i.e., only all day everyday between 9 and 7, except Wednesday afternoons and Sundays. What a woman! Everyone else has accepted the conditions quite calmly and reasonably. She wants to come for the day on Wednesday and may stay the night. Of course I want to see her and for her to see the shop (my vanity, which will no doubt soon bite the dust). But I am shaken with dread. I shall be pounced on, poked and prodded and badgered with unanswerable questions, without pause for the answers, until I am in the limp state she enjoys of her victims. But about Wee I must be very non-committal. I have not breathed a word to her about the possible purchase. She will want to 'help'.

Thursday, 18 August

Dear N. She was more tired and 'down' than I think I have ever known her. The mechanism I dreaded was still there and operating, but the generating force was so low I scarcely felt the effect. I hope she will take things more easily when she returns to Ghana. It is sucking her blood, though she loves the place. I do love her dearly, and hope that she will never, never have the chance to read this journal.

Monday, 19 September
[The entry is preceded by a small, pasted newspaper cutting from the Death Notices.]

PRATT – On Sept 12, 1960, Ethel Mary (nee Watson) aged 80 years, beloved sister of Maggie. Cremation Breakspear Crematorium, Ruislip, Thursday, Sept 15, at 12.30 p.m. Flowers to James Peddle, 65 High Street, Rickmansworth.

A desolate day, grey, cool, unlovely. I'm not yet over the shock of Ethel's death. I feel I never shall be. For 35 years she was an intimately integral part of the pattern. And though we knew it was coming, it was just desolation when I heard finally.

She had been for a month in Chesham Cottage Hospital, very ill. Aunt Maggie went to see her every day, I went every Sunday. Fluid against the left lung was causing pressure on the heart. Her breathing was so painful she could not talk, and then she became gradually weaker and weaker until she lapsed into unconsciousness. I am sure she was longing to be through. The hospital complained a little that she would not cooperate. She felt herself becoming a nuisance, saw only a failing old age ahead. I would not have wanted her to live for this.

But I miss her. There was a bond between us, grown unnoticed since my father's death, a sense of companionship, a sharing of many mutual interests, a delightful kind of communion. This is the loss, the cause of the pricking eyeball, the lump in the throat. Her flower-laden coffin slipped so smoothly away.

At this moment Babs and Roy and Sue are airborne on their way to Lagos. I took the afternoon off to see them go at London Airport, but their bus was late, so it was Hullo, Goodbye and I was alone again in the gray day, watching distant impersonal aircraft, not knowing which was theirs. Roy escorted me to Ethel's funeral while Babs stayed at Wee with Sue. I have delicious mental pictures of Sue romping through the golden Beeches with her father, shrieking with laughter, tugging at Roy's hand, hiding behind trees to 'boo' out at Mummy and Auntie as they passed.

And in the morning, climbing to my room where I was making the bed:

'Can I have another biscuit?'

'You must ask Mummy.'

Face falls. 'Oh, then I can't.' Pause. 'Perhaps I'll just go and ask if I can or can't.'

'All right. You go do that.'

She does, and returns, shaking her head mournfully. 'I can't.'

Desolating news, too, about Wee. The building society to which I applied for a mortgage sent surveyors, and has turned down my application flat. Apparently the cottage is in such a bad condition that it couldn't be improved or altered without collapse of the whole fabric.

Tuesday, 25 October

'Everything gets killed by words sooner or later.'

From 'A Rose by Any Other Name' by Anthony Carson, 1960

Wednesday, 7 June 1961

October, November, December, January, February, March, April, May and now into June and not an entry made. That could mean such disaster it was beyond recording, or such absorption in living there was no overwhelming urge to find a refuge. I have no particular reason to be starting again tonight. At least I may as well note, since the economics of living have so dominated my life in recent years, that I am not bankrupt yet. I still have anxious moments and scraping of the till on occasions, but the rent from No. 1 Florence Cottages is an enormous help. The mortgage interest arranged with Miss Drumm is unusually modest for nowadays – only 3-and-a-half per cent. I have so much to thank her for.

Jung is dead. The BBC speaker tonight was not, I thought, very inspiring about him, but did sum up his significance by saying that his teaching had aimed at presenting a concept of man complete: his good and bad aspects, his inner as well as his outer life, instead of the ideal man with which we had previously been plagued and confounded.

Babs had a son at the end of January. Colin (wonder why they called him that). Now they are all in Ghana and maybe meeting N.

Have been going to art classes once a week since last autumn at the Slough College of Further Education, with Kay Faulkner and Sheila Hiron. We are none of us very good but enjoy it hugely. I ran an art competition for local children recently. It was a big success, though I went through agonies of panic beforehand. Am suddenly up to my neck in something that apparently calls for Initiative, Imagination and Drive.

Wednesday, 19 July

Our art teacher at Slough, Ralph L., whom I have commissioned to do a watercolour of Wee (he has a picture in this year's Royal Academy summer show and was mentioned by a *Sunday Times* critic), dropped into the Little B. yesterday afternoon unexpectedly. He came into the shop with a woman and two small girls. 'Is this your family?' I exclaimed. He answered, 'Good heavens no! I wish they were.' I stood looking at him with my head on one side, thinking what a darling father he'd make, and suddenly realised from the way he was looking back at me that he might be thinking I'd make quite a good mother. I managed to pull myself out of this clinch and we discussed future possible arrangements for his coming to do this picture.

It is all at least 20 years too late for me, but he does attract me and I'm pretty sure he likes me too. The local paper says he is 28, but he has told me he was stationed at Beaconsfield during the war, which must make him quite 35. I'm nearly old enough to be his mother, and all I can hope for is a satisfying friendship with a sensitive intelligent young artist of promise, and that I don't get too maudlin about it. Oh, let it rest.

Thursday, 20 July

For the first time ever, accountant K. met me with a beaming smile of approval. The business has much improved, I've done very well this year, it's a good little business now, and so on. Perhaps this was to soften the blow that accountant's charges will be higher. Nonetheless it was a pleasant surprise to leave his office without feeling that the best thing I could do was to drown myself.

Ralph L. never speaks of his wife. I don't mean by this that I'm thinking or hoping he's unhappily married. It's been quite a battle for me to get the affair onto a realistic level – to steer clear or to ride the familiar and terrible waves of emotionalism that threatened to swamp me, to swamp both of us rather, and destroy something that may be of value if allowed to develop freely in its own way.

Wednesday, 2 August

Discussing cheaper brands of cigarettes last week in tobacconists, I said I'd resort to Woodbines. 'And where will you go from there at the next increase in price?' asked a traveller.

On Saturday, obliging villager S.P., who was providing the transport to Cat Show for me, called me Miss Bray. 'Miss P., please,' I corrected him, adding, 'Ever since I took over her shop (the original Little B.) there's been this confusion.'

'It's only that,' he said kindly, 'you both wear glasses, have something of the same look, and are about the same age.'

This absolutely stunned me for about 10 minutes. Miss B. started receiving her old age pension last year. My answer should have been sharp and instantaneous: 'Good grief! She is 15 years older than I am!' Not quite accurate, but near enough to check grossly inaccurate village speculation about me. Oh, I can't possibly look that old! To be thought to be anything like Miss B. is so deeply humiliating.

Monday, 21 August

What saddens me is that the 'sparkle and life' Ralph L. said he found in my last two paintings (before the whole class, at the end-of-term review of our work last month), and which I know to be there in me, is so often swamped, obliterated, in the wrong atmosphere. With my family I seem always to become dull, fearful: it is so rude to them.

Wednesday, 11 October

'I just love painting.' Yes I do. And it seems to be bringing about astonishing results, though I doubt it is wise to record this. I did three or four more pictures on my own during the holidays – two of cats, a still life, a little flower piece – and the few people who have seen them so far seem genuinely impressed. I am encouraged to go on, to work at it, not simply dabble to satisfy my vanity. It is the stillness that counts, the silence, the absence of nagging at oneself.

I am not trying to compete, I really have no ambitions about it. Am discovering through trial and error, not minding the errors, but here is a point: what I find I can do I seem able to do quite well. It is encouragement received from others that fills me with warmth and makes it seem worthwhile. (A small group of local amateurs meet every Monday evening at Farnham Royal Village Hall and just paint without instruction. They are a nice little group – there's a feeling of expansion when working with others.) Ralph L. hasn't seen my 'homework' yet, though I long for him to do so. I need his judgement. Oh my God he is growing a beard, and seems younger to me than ever.

I am glad I have 'given up' writing.

The deepest humiliation I suffer is in trying to answer the question (which I am always being asked or see in people's eyes) 'Why haven't you married?' The only true answer, in my heart, is 'Because no one has ever asked me.' I shall never be able to bring myself to say this. I don't think it is entirely my fault.

Thursday, 9 November

I seem to have come to a dead end with Ralph L. Every Thursday it is the same. I come home disturbed, disappointed, and there start all the fascinating conversations I want to have with him and never do. His wife turns up at the end of the evening. I was introduced a few weeks ago, not I think deliberately, but because I happened to be almost on top of her. My spies report that 'she doesn't understand him' but I thought her rather nice, a good balance to his vagueness, solid where he is ephemeral.

Sheila Hiron returns to work at the Little B. next week, another miracle. I have a great affection for Mrs J., but as one of my staff she was beginning to drive me up the wall. After six years or so of faithful attendance you'd think she'd remember something of the work, but the mistakes she continued to make were quite incredible. Now I shall have two excellent helpers: Sheila onto the secondhand books, K.F. does practically all the library work. We have been improving slowly and steadily. I think we can do better yet.

Thursday, 8 February 1962

I am drawn to this journal only because I have a feeling I want to tidy it up. Its purpose is over, finished. The pattern of my life seems set. Day-to-day work at the bookshop, which I love, and am still managing to keep my head above the financial waters. Parish Council work six times a year. Wee and the cats as my home background, painting and gardening and the social round to fill whatever leisure time I may have. Family connections seem to be expanding too. I hear from Babs that Roy wants to buy a house in Bucks. I might then seriously, with Pooh's help (moral not financial), get a car. And so it goes on, unfolding and unfolding, sheer delight.[246]

Friday, 21 September

'There was light in the sky when I woke up. Sylvia was asleep, her arm under my neck. The light grew, and I lay for a long time . . . then Sylvia's free arm came up over the bedclothes . . .'

From *I Met A Lady*, Howard Spring. Oh my gawd! The moment I wake I always want to pee, but they never seem to in books.

---

246 She bought a 1947 Ford Prefect for £40. Immediately afterwards, it was in a garage in Beaconsfield being fitted with a new engine. She called it Freddie. 'I think it will prove a good partnership,' she noted two months after it arrived, 'but it will take time. I'm fairly sure I could get to Slough and back now.'

'What a woman!' Jean and Nockie in full bloom, 1960s.

46.

Gloss and Plastic and What Have You

Wednesday, 9 January 1963 (aged fifty-three)[247]
The worst winter for 82 years. For 10 days I couldn't move Freddie. Spent most of the morning digging him clear and making a track, and finally got him to Slough. Miss D. skidded into a tree. A cruel and beautiful world of wonders, terror, pain and delight.

Friday, 2 February
This winter will pass and we shall forget the details. We shall say, 'It was so cold and went on for so long . . . there were electricity power cuts . . . transport difficulties . . . fuel shortages and delays . . . the usual burst pipes, illnesses, deaths . . .'

We've been without water at the shop for nearly a month. All the trees were etched heavily in feathery white, a clear frost of exceptional density. I haven't been to the painting group on Monday evenings. The weather has taken the heart out of one's enthusiasms.

Sunday, 10 February
It is bliss now to be relaxing after tea in sitting room, buried by cats and cushions. How thankful I am for the plastic cover bought as part of Pooh's Xmas present for Freddie, tiresome as it is to get on and off

---

247 From January 1963 to May 1986 Jean wrote only six slim journals. She didn't admonish herself for the long intervals between entries; she now regarded her diary as something to slip into only when the occasion arose, a rarer comfort.

and keep tied down. With engine covered by old dust sheet and an oil lamp inside the bonnet, the little car is well protected and is not at all reluctant to start when unwrapped.

I must remember that many other people are much worse off and have suffered terribly this winter. In remote country places, old couples have been found snowbound without fuel or food. People have been caught in drifts in their cars and died. Farmers have been having the most appalling difficulties and what animals have been through one daren't contemplate.

Tuesday, 12 February

Relax, relax, forget the undone things, the semi-frozen slush, the shrouded woods, the tiresome old women: 'Not my sort of book at all, dear. Complete waste of time, couldn't you allow me something on it?' Sixpence she had paid to borrow it over the weekend. And, 'I heard a book reviewed, can't remember the title, it was about children or something, I think the author was Mary Smith or it may have been Brown, quite an old book they said but I should like to read it, No, I don't want to buy it . . .'

Mrs A. is small, with plump little appealing face, comes dressed in sealskin coat, 'I shan't survive this winter, I just shan't survive, bury me quietly.' We discovered that we both like salads and can eat them all year round.

I had hopes, ten days ago, that I had found someone to replace Mrs D. the cleaner. She came and looked, as it seemed to me, in stunned silence about the place, slapped around for an hour and fled. I heard indirectly that she has an allergy for cats, but I am left with the feeling that she was so shocked by the shabbiness and poor equipment at Wee that she could not face it, and this has filled me with rage, despair and contempt. Wee can be made to gleam and sparkle and glow. It is not a slum. Young women nowadays just don't know what real housework means. They have highly efficient vacuum cleaners and electric polishers. Their beastly little kitchens are all so well fitted and finished in gloss and plastic and what have you, they don't have to contend with old fireplaces and old oil stoves, old stone floors that wear out one's lino, ill-fitting doors and outside lavatories. They have kitchen cupboards, larder, refrig and washing machines. Well I don't care. Snobs.

Wednesday, 7 June

Aunt Maggie died about three weeks ago. My last link with the Homefield days. I'll never go over to that bungalow at Little Chalfont again. Every room, every bit of furniture was so familiar, so much part of my background, and now it is finished, like a shutter suddenly clamped down. I have no part even in its dissolution: I knew her intimately, but none of her relatives sufficiently to be drawn into the winding up of her affairs. I doubt I shall ever know what is being done with her things. There are books which I have given to her and Ethel which I should have liked. Not very important really, it is only that once more I am shocked by the silence which follows death.

An American yesterday bought over £9-worth of art books and has ordered 5 or 6 more @ 35 shillings and 2 @ 42 shillings. I do love Americans.

Sunday, 25 August

Lydia has now bought herself one of the small new Wolseys. Smashing. On an overdraft, against the deeds for her house in Upton Park. And why not, indeed, if it makes her as happy as it seems to. Freddie's trouble now is body rust. I wish Peter or someone had warned me of this last autumn. I am treating the worst patches with Jenolite and car paint.[248]

Mr E.B., for whom I collect Bucks material for the history he has been compiling this last 10 years or more, breezes in. 'What a nice

---

248 'Ruined by Rust? Then you haven't used Jenolite!' ran the advert in the *Practical Householder* from 1956.

little shop! I always say,' (as he always does) 'that a place without a bookshop is a place without a soul. You give the place a soul.'

Monday, 2 March 1963

The cats are my great love, and through them must therefore come the great griefs. Suzie was born last September, a delectable blue-cream with white splodges. One night early in November I had drawn a bath of unprecedented heat, as near boiling as it has ever been. I was in a dazed and with-fatigue phase, but that is no excuse. There is no excuse for me – that is the terrible, unbearable point of the tragedy. I had pushed chairs from the bath edge, but Suzie and her brother were an active two-months. I should have known the danger of leaving them with the bath flap up. I went outside for less than two minutes, heard cries but thought it was adults squabbling, which they often do, and returned to find Suzie swimming desperately. I can't bear it, please God forgive my completely unforgivable carelessness. No, I cannot be forgiven – what I want is that ten minutes back again. She must have been struggling in that scalding water for a full 60 seconds.

She screamed for an hour and a half afterwards. I dried her, warmed her, poured on olive oil. It was a miracle that she survived the shock as she did, and was one reason why in all these laborious, patient and determined months since I hoped to pull her through. Twice at the clinic they urged me to have her put to sleep but I could not give in. The burns were frightful, paws, legs and the whole of her undercarriage. I realised the tail would have to be amputated. The vet came to the conclusion last week – so pleased he seemed, and so confident of success – that he could operate and do some plastic surgery on the back muscles. He operated this morning, but my darling succumbed to 'operation shock'. It is over, over.

I was so sure she would come back and charm us and enjoy her little life at Wee. Was it really necessary to have operated now? Could we have waited? What I feel, fear, is that it was a betrayal. I was keeping that kitten alive with my love – away from this contact she was bewildered, frightened. The clinic surroundings are, well, clinical. If the operation could have been done on my lap . . . Stupid, you say, well yes, but think of the trust she had in me. How can I explain? We live in too cruel, too insensitive an age. Science, science, but no understanding of love.

Wednesday, 4 March

I went to the art class this morning, lunched in Slough, shopped at Sainsbury's, called at Cats Protection League. I have asked them to find another kitten for me (mad, all cat-addicts are mad), a blue-cream if possible. This is not just a selfish replacement urge, but I hope will save another life.

Easter Sunday, 29 March

The little grey ghost still lingers, can still reduce me to anguish and tears, but life pushes one on remorselessly, and the pain lessens. Or, the intervals between the memories which bring the pain lengthen. To stifle it, I have been playing patience at the time I usually spent attending to Suzie. It's an occupation I despise and feel no better for, just another sort of drug.

Saturday, 27 June

Shop garden is yielding strawberries, gooseberries, raspberries, spinach, roses, pinks. I could not give all this up. Developers are after the whole block, have already swallowed old grocer Spong, and are tempting my neighbours. No amount of money seems to me worth being dispossessed of my freehold, uprooted, broken.

It may not be easy to maintain refusal. I have to face, sooner or later, the county's road-widening scheme. This, some people think, may give the developers a lever with the Planning Authority for compulsory purchase of obstinate land blocks. I couldn't have better legal advice and backing, but I still feel small, vulnerable and frightened, a pebble in the way of a tidal wave.

Thursday, 2 July

There's a nice woman comes sometimes into the shop. I don't know her name. She buys with discrimination, usually Penguins, and told me she was at Oxford. I remembered her tonight as I began on H.E. Bates's new collection of short stories *The Fabulous Mrs V.* After she had wandered around for a little, she asked me, 'Do you write?'

I said, with some hesitation, no. And she left it at that. No, I do not write. I am not even painting very much these days. There never seems to be enough time.

Ralph L. leaves us this term. It was bound to happen. There again I have failed utterly, but probably because I wanted the impossible. We have never got beyond the most frivolous of exchanges. A gulf too wide, too deep, unbridgeable. Yet I feel I should have been able to bridge it.

My Mrs D. has come back. After 18 months of battling with housework on my own I ran into her one morning in Slough. She volunteered to give me a morning a week, as before. This is such sheer bliss I can hardly believe it is true. Also, I have had the phone put on again at Wee – a party line with neighbours.

Wednesday, 12 August

Mrs D. survived three weeks.

Last week I closed the shop and spent the week at leisure – seeing Lydia, a night at [hairdresser] Surge's entrancing top-floor flat overlooking Clapham Common, Mitchell family to tea, gardening. Incidentally, saw the Beatles' *Hard Day's Night.* They are amazing.

The threat to Florence Cottages has not been lifted, but R.P. has been whipping me into a state of confidence.[249] Most of the men with

---

249 Her solicitor R.P., the husband of her equally mysterious friend B.P., is praised by Jean elsewhere: 'He was chosen to sit on the Government's Committee now going into the landlord racketeer problem (Peter Rachman), and has to negotiate very big deals indeed for his own firm. He should have no time for me at all, but the just spirit still exists and has its powers also. R. himself has great integrity and despises the get-rich-quick contingent and I think he enjoys fighting them.'

whom I've discussed the problem urge me to consider the advantages of accepting a good offer: 'You could be made comfortable for life.' But I do not want that sort of comfort. R.P. says, 'You have a valuable little property, a good little business, you'll never get another freehold in Farnham Common like it. A Compulsory Purchase Order will require the Minister's consent. If he grants it we shall then appeal and this will mean a Public Inquiry. The council will look very foolish, and they won't want to risk that. You are perfectly safe – it's a cinch.'

It is a battle for the 'small man'. He is being bullied and crushed out of existence by the greed of the powerful. Their influence is so insidious that practically every man in business has his outlook distorted by it. Nothing but money seems to matter.

Thursday, 4 February, 1965

Village development plans are halted. First, probably, because Labour was returned in October, and since then on account of the county's new road proposals. They threaten a huge widening all along the route from Slough to Beaconsfield, with dual carriageway to link a new M road at our North with the M4.[250] But there has already been so much public protest from local residents – it would destroy the village utterly – that the county authority is reported as seeking a diversion. We are not out of this wood yet.

Saturday, 6 February

This time last week we were all rather under the pall of Churchill's funeral. I saw some of it on TV and was immensely impressed. But the general depression was heavy, I could not escape it all day, or the next when I crawled into village to collect Sunday newspapers. Several personalities have passed recently – T.S. Eliot and Dame Edith Sitwell – but none has made the impact on the nation that Churchill did.

When tired I do get so fractious, grinding my teeth, wanting to

---

250 This was the M40, which began construction two years later in 1967.

destroy – impatient and full of bile. It's the pressure of the age, all such huge ghastly haste, so much to do and never enough time.

August 1965

Wee boasts a larder and I have another car. These are the season's big events. The larder, planned for years, materialised in March and was followed by an orgy of redecorating and clearing. Car is a 1954 Anglia and an astounding bargain, available at my garage just as Freddie cracked up in May. I'll never know such joy as when we were trying out the Anglia and discovered how easy it was to drive. Freddie's bodywork gave way, literally falling apart. The wiring too was in a dreadful state; I had been able to use the fog lamp only.

Sunday, 6 March 1966

This is being a year of trouble and tragedy. I had recovered from flu setback when disaster struck the shop with a thump. Just over a month ago, in the early hours of a Thursday morning, the Aladdin heater started to smoke. It must have smoked at least half the night. The shop was thick with heavy black soot everywhere, right through to kitchen at the back. It was terrible, an absolute and most ghastly nightmare. Kay opened that morning and nearly fainted on the spot. It was hard to believe so innocent a thing as an oil stove could cause so much damage.

I phoned the insurance company immediately, but I think they thought I was being hysterical. It took over three weeks of intense hard work to clean through the premises. It was a snow storm in soot, a fungus on all exposed surfaces, a drift of black scum into every cupboard and drawer. Every single item of stock has had to be gone over – books, greeting cards, wrapping paper, drawing paper, every book has had to have its jacket removed, pages flipped through. At least two-thirds of the stock has had to be discarded. My claim is for £300.

People were wonderful, so many volunteers came forward. It has been trouble for me, a great shaking, but not tragedy, such as has troubled others this year. In January my acting landlord died of a coronary – we were in the middle of negotiations about electricity. Hairdresser friend Surge is threatened with blindness and is fighting gallantly and gaily. And last week the young husband of enterprising young woman in the village committed suicide. Last summer she took on little shop where I started and was making quite a success of good-class ceramics.

Wednesday, 27 April

My dear fairy godmother Drumm died at the end of March and was cremated on 1st April. By her will she has cancelled the mortgage on Florence Cottages and left me her books.

The assessors say that as there was no fire there is no claim. Shall soon be suffering rather more than usual financial embarrassment. Cannot hold out on creditor publishers much longer.

Monday, 19 September

A week ago last Saturday a young man came late in the afternoon and asked if I could give his young brother a job. 'He's a bit slow but he loves books. Just left school and we don't know what to do with him. I don't mean he's stupid, but he can't cope with exams . . .'

I asked a few questions, hesitated, said I would think about it.

On the Monday, mum arrived with the boy. They live in Beaconsfield, father is a doctor, Mrs is also I think a doctor, eldest son has just left Cambridge where he did splendidly, the youngest has just won a top scholarship to Shrewsbury. All this brain and brilliance has had adverse effect on the middle one. He has a Billy Bunterish face, and with his mother appeared almost idiotic. The whole proposition terrified me. I said I would phone her.

I couldn't stop thinking about it, something nagged me all day: 'you've got to help, you've got to. You're the one who can.' I phoned in the evening and said I would take him strictly on trial. Mrs L.

nearly burst into tears. He started last Friday. He is a very sweet-natured and good sort of person, but must do things in his own time. All my heart goes out to someone like this. I know their terrors.

I have put him on to filing the catalogues and leaflets, he seems to be very happy doing it. He came with Irene Babbidge's *Beginning in Bookselling* from the library, and said he was taking *The Bookseller* weekly. What a marvellous and fearful thing to think that I may be able to influence his whole future.

Sunday, 11 December

Poor, retarded, abnormal little Ian. We were getting on so well. He came regularly two afternoons a week, was so keen and was beginning to be of real use. Last Wednesday he had a fit and died. He was learning typing and office routine at a school in High Wycombe and it was at that morning class when he was taken. I was told nothing of his tendency to fit until this week, which was perhaps as well. He had been subject to them for the past five years, but had not had one for over a year, and they were hoping the treatment he was having was being effective. A week ago he came to help at the big Olympia Cat Show and I was thrilled to the core with it all – felt he was really a bookseller.

Thursday, 29 December

This morning I bought two new (sale) Jaeger jumpers, a skirt, a saucepan, at John Barnes in the Finchley Road. Lovely, important trivialities. And all the crimes committed, the ghastly bombing of Vietnam, prisoners escaping from our gaols like insects through fishnet, the car maniacs let loose on our roads (the aggressive, thwarted male?), the terrible greed devouring our body politic – all these bad things to depress and bewilder and terrify.

The latest improvement to Wee kitchen, installed three weeks ago, is a formica top to the bath.

Friday, 13 January 1967

In bed, listening to Barbirolli conducting the BBC Symphony Orchestra in Moscow. This is a wonder, a magic of our age. Music transcending political discords. I wonder how many people are listening to it in preference to watching TV? I have no choice, as I have no TV nor want one (except to have seen, for example, the recent *Alice in Wonderland*). And I would not probably be listening now if a gastric bug hadn't mysteriously attacked my guts. Everything sliding crudely straight through me. Oh, the tedious washing and changing of bed linen.

Monday, 3 April

At the shop we have at last finished with the Lending Library. For two years or more I doubt if I had five shillings a week from it. This created the wildest crop of rumours. I am closing down altogether, I have sold out, I am taking on one of the proposed new Council shops. 'And where are you going?' I have been asked. 'Are you moving out of the district?' For years now the Library has taken up no more than one-eighth of one wall. The rest of the shop is stiff with new books and greeting cards – what do these deluded library folk think they are there for? Decoration?

Friday, 2 August 1968

Sixteen months since I wrote in here! The road problem, which has frozen village development for the past 4–5 years, is erupting like some ghastly sickness. An answer has to be found for the increasing traffic that roars and rumbles along the Beaconsfield Road through the two Farnhams (Common and Royal) to Slough daily, and the Authorities have been sitting together weightily in committee and scratching about in drawing offices. Recently I have attended several of these hush-hush meetings and heard their proposals. One monster project threatens to cut through Burnham Beeches from the top of Egypt Lane, passing behind these cottages.

The whole idea is diabolical. The county planning dept thinks that this will be the best solution ('easiest' and 'cheapest') and to my dismay the parish council supports them. There are two other proposed routes. Today, Dr H., a dynamic character in Farnham Royal whose property is, I understand, a direct obstacle in the BB route, phoned to ask when the public were to be let in on these secrets. 'We behave like sheep. Why do we have to wait and do what we are told by the County? We shall find the whole thing is a fait accompli and it will be too late.' He may well be right. I hope he will go on agitating.

Sunday, 5 January 1969

The road problem continues to bedevil us. A nightmare of uncertainty and rumours, and no indication from Authority of what the decision may be. Agitation goes on, letters have been written. Meanwhile, I am giving up the work as Parish Council clerk. I am not really a local government type, and while I battled with the work conscientiously, I found it an increasing burden. I had no complaints from the council about my work, but I know I am doing the right thing.

Changes must come in my business too. My tenants want to vacate, and this means that I can take over the front room of their shop to incorporate with mine. Now is my chance. Now or never, I shall not be able to resist the pressure of developers indefinitely, but might evade the issue for another 4–5 years. The possibility that Egypt may be bulldozed for this bloody bypass will not be defeated easily.

Babs and Roy have settled in Surrey – he has a job in London. It is lovely to have them nearer and see something of them occasionally. I spent Christmas Day with them, a big Everett family party, and they have all been over to tea with me today. The children are so sweet. Also, I have very nice new neighbours – an army colonel, now at the Foreign Office, with wife and three school-age children.

Bookselling gets no easier and is less profitable than ever.

Thursday, 3 April

This living instant is joyous and good, compounded of warmth and cooking food and work achieved and a holiday in view tomorrow. There is the memory of yesterday to savour, as sweet and thrilling as the sherry I now sip while fish and chips fry for supper. Babs and the two children and me, touring Mme Tussauds and then the Zoo – in spite of the bitter wind, enjoying every minute of it. Auntie losing all her earlier fatigue and mental stress in the joy and tonic of being with those little, responsive, happy beings. What a wonderful gift they are. 'Auntie, come and look! Look!' Pulled by little eager hands, little eager upturned questing faces and mummy smiling at our side. Pearls of great price. And now the boiler alight again after weeks of surly behaviour.

Wednesday, 9 April

Last night I kept waking with a pain over my heart, or where I think my heart is. There has been pain around my diaphragm all day, making breathing uncomfortable. I have not had one cigarette since last night. Have made an appointment to see the doctor on Friday. I do not want to cause embarrassment and inconvenience by dropping dead without warning.

Saturday, 31 May

This time last night I was battling with flood water in the sitting room. The most incredible freak hail storm. I suddenly saw a pool seeping from under the bookcase – thought at first that one of the cats, scared by the thunder and noise of hail, had 'forgot itself'.

On Wednesday I had tea with Alison Uttley at Beaconsfield. She is to pay a personal visit to the Little B. next Thursday. Great event.

Doctor found my blood pressure normal and nothing whatsoever abnormal with my heart. She sent me for X-ray and blood test. Nothing sinister was to be seen on X-ray, and blood test was 101 per cent. Doctor was very impressed.

Alison Uttley is a spry, interesting woman, still active, and though she 'has no time for cats' is witch-like and approachable. I hope I can make her visit to Little B. a success. She must not be made tired by importuning children or too-eager autograph hunters.[251]

On Monday I attend my first meeting as Parish Councillor. Well what do you know, aren't I the one.

Monday, 15 September
Important, important local events. I have seen democracy in action, have been part of it, even some influence. This evening at Farnham Royal, The Farnham Villages Association was formed to prevent if it is possible Authority riding over us roughshod with their Bloody Bypass proposals. We are united on the central point that no one wants the road anywhere – East, West or Centre. The essence is that such terrible uprooting and destruction must be proved absolutely necessary, and part of a well-thought-out overall road plan for a very wide area, not shoddy piecemeal planning to alleviate a current congestion. 'The people' have a voice and must be listened to.

The Parish Council has had nothing to do with this evening's work and I am ashamed of them. I have never been at such a huge local public meeting, people standing two-deep round the walls. The last thing I remember is DS strung about with tin collecting boxes, like modern jewellery, at the hall entrance as the public streamed out, stuffing in notes and coins.

Sunday, 21 September
One sinks from last week's elation. There is so much division and

---

251 Uttley was the author of *A Traveller in Time* and such popular children's stories as *The Squirrel, The Hare and the Little Grey Rabbit, Little Grey Rabbit's Washing Day, Sam Pig and His Fiddle,* and other adventures enjoyed by the Little Grey Rabbit and Sam Pig. But it wasn't all softness and cuteness. Uttley also kept personal diaries, in which she expressed a marked distaste for some of her illustrators. Jean notes later that the visit was a great success, and the two became friends.

selfishness underlying our moment of unity. All we are really united on is that The Road shall not interfere with or destroy any of our own personal lives and property. Many of the village people bawl, 'Let it go through the Beeches!' Those who are ruled by it will slaughter the soul for expediency. I do pray with all my heart that just now and then . . . some things of the spirit must grow and be encouraged to grow.

Saturday, 4 October

The County meeting last night. A shocking affair. Chairman of the Planning Committee, the County Surveyor, the County Clerk, a Planning Officer and the County Architect. They were there, we know, to listen, to receive public views, and not to make any decisions. But at least they might have answered some of the decisions hammered at them from every part of the hall. They evaded, shuffled, mumbled. Obviously their tiny minds are determined and dried on the Eastern fringe route of the Beeches. 'We are here to note your views, we shall make notes of what you all say.' Yes, and then what? Everyone today was speaking of it as a perfectly disgraceful exhibition.

Tuesday, 6 January 1970

Car starts perfectly. Have I recorded the advent of Jolly Morris? Poor old Anglia failed its MOT in July, more money found, and eventually invested in 1964 Morris 1000 Traveller. At end of November during frightful cold spell, when roads were like glass, a Humber slid into me, crumpling the whole near side.

Saturday, 10 January

Angela with me this afternoon. She is 18, and has given spasmodic help on Saturdays for the past four-and-a-half years. Very tall and mini-skirted, casual, but loyal. A type I enjoy, and we are very pleasantly rude to each other. I think she is attractive, but her height makes her self-conscious. At the moment she has a crush on N.G., a young local artist who does picture framing as a sideline, and for whom the Little B. has been an agent since the summer. He is quite the opposite of the modern beatnik longhaired type, a clean-shaven, fair, handsome normal young man of '30s era. Angela drools over him and I suspect her present faithfulness to the Little B. is because there is a chance he may come in on Saturday.

Sunday, 18 January

I must write to Kay M. and see if I can move her into action about selling Wee. (Solicitor says, in view of road situation, it would be to my advantage to own the freehold.) The Farnham Villages Association seems to be going from strength to strength. As far as we know there is to be a Public Enquiry about the road in the summer, when the Association plans to employ a QC to put their case.

Monday, 27 April

I should like to get sodden, sherry-warm, but there is little sherry left and I cannot afford more. Yesterday I drove without trouble to spend the day with my young family. Sue (it was her 13th birthday) was at school, and after a gorgeous Sunday lunch we went to Bramley and took her out to a luscious fresh watercress tea.

I was contemplating writing to K.M. but I received a letter from her before I got round to it, to say she had at last decided to let me buy Wee if I wished. As far as I know, our solicitors should now be negotiating.

Letter from beloved brother Pooh, the first for months. He has had an eye cataract removed and is progressing splendidly.

Wednesday, 29 April

Group 13 discussing proposed exhibition at lunch today.[252] I still tag along as honorary treasurer, and have long wanted them to display

---

252 The new name of her local art gathering.

some of the work they have achieved over the last 7 years or so, which no one but ourselves know of. Enid R. might be able to persuade John Snagge to come and open.[253]

Liz has produced the most marvellous abstract painting – it is full of feeling and has lost all the hard lines and shapes which are imposed on her other work.

Friday, 1 May

Mrs V.N. came in this morning. She thinks that Liz's abstract betrays great psychological disturbance, that she may be on the edge of a nervous breakdown. I wonder if she could be right. My poor Liz! She had flung what must have been a whole tube of pure cadmium red in a great billowing bar across the picture, diagonally branching at one end in a cruciform. 'That red is a very bad sign,' said Mrs N. 'All that dripping paint.'

It was a great explosion against a turmoil of darker colours, a wound exposed, a great release. I still think it is a gorgeous picture.

Thursday, 5 May

Angela in again this afternoon, pale as death. The firm she was working for were money-lenders, and every one of them has been arrested by the police this week for various shady deals. The police picked her up last night and questioned her at the station until 3 a.m., but she was able to convince them she knew nothing of what was going on. She has eaten nothing for days, and fainted twice yesterday.

Thursday, 23 July 1970

General Election has come and gone, shocking us all rigid when Tories were returned. I supported the Liberals as usual, and for the same reasons, trusting neither of the large parties and sick to death

---

253 Snagge was an old-school BBC newsreader (although when he began in the 1920s he was new-school).

of Wilson and his braggart mob. Now we have a dock strike threatening the country with disaster.[254]

For good or ill I must record what now follows. At the end of May, I went to National Health oculist to have routine check-up. For some time I have been troubled by fuzzy vision, particularly noticeable when driving. Cannot read the smaller road signs and directions, letters are all a blur, disconcerting when trying to find one's way in new territory. Oculist maintains it is due to cataract which I have had in right eye for years, making it virtually useless. All the work has been done by the left. Specialist at Windsor thinks I should have the right eye dealt with. It will mean two months completely off work. I told the specialist that my business would fall apart if I couldn't be there, but this won me little sympathy.

And then a week ago last Sunday, Lydia appeared. We went into the sitting room for a good gossip and glass of wine, and when I told her I might have to have a cataract operation she said, 'You must go to George Chapman.'

If you don't know to whom I refer, dear reader ... George Chapman is a medium for the spirit doctor M. Lang. I am to see him (Lang) on Sept 29th. In the meantime I correspond with the medium and am being given Distant Healing.

Sunday, 2 August

Tired but triumphant after long hot day at Cat Show selling cat books. Friday afternoon was torture driving to Westminster, tensed up, hot, doing all the wrong things, taking wrong turnings, being cursed at by pigs of men in huge cars (though I insult pigs by the comparison). A sweet young policeman flagging me to a standstill because I had entered a strip sacred to buses only in Vauxhall Bridge Road: I had

---

254 In June, Edward Heath defeated the government of Harold Wilson by 330 seats to 288. The Liberals, led by Jeremy Thorpe, had suffered a disaster, winning only 6 seats (at the previous election they had won 12). When it was over, the Liberals again rallied for proportional representation.

seen no notices whatsoever. 'Just drive more carefully in the future' – as though I had bumped into the back of the bus I was in all innocence only following.

Thursday, 29 October

I have met and received a psychic operation on my eyes from Dr Lang. Four weeks he said it would take for the cataracts to dry and wither away. But I do not know, cannot be definite yet.

K.M. has accepted my offer for Wee, and bank manager has promised to grant a loan to cover the amount. A step or two nearer, and of course still in legal hands.

Tuesday, 29 December

I am a little drunk with sherry. I have had two stupid little bumps with the car within the last week. No lives endangered, no person even scratched, only wings dented, a backlight smashed. I know of nothing which arouses male aggression and fury so much as a car incident.

Wee. Contracts have been exchanged. I have sent deposit. Purchase completion date is Jan 17th.

Eyes. Are better. Certainly no worse. I am in fact sure I am seeing more with my right eye than I ever did.

Two bright stars illuminate this mid-winter darkness. Last week I sold Krishnamurti's *The Only Revolution* to a young man who had seen him on television. My young customer's face lit up. 'I must lash out on this!' It is the sort of thing that makes bookselling so rewarding. And tonight in greengrocer's, a girl said, 'Congratulations on your choice of books!'

There is one muzzy resolution coming up for the New Year. As it seems that I am in truth to become the owner of Wee, may I not become withdrawn and selfish because of it – retire here from the world and this terrifying age of 'speed and greed' – but give out, give out, share all that I have and can to the tormented and eager young.

I mean that when forced to retire, as I may be, may I be able and guided to do something useful with what remains of my life. Not just shrivel and grow old.

'I must go and mince the cats' supper.'
Jean and her protectors at Wee Cottage, probably 1960s.

47.

Slough of Despond

Sunday, 14 February, 1971 (aged sixty-one)

Dockers, dustmen, electricians and now postmen for the last month have been bedevilling the country. Consequently nearly 40 publisher's accounts are in limbo. Wee negotiations are held up too. Mail order business is at a complete standstill, daily takings down perilously. (I heard yesterday that Blackwell's of Oxford have been losing £200,000 a week.) General sympathy seems to be with the postmen.

It has been a wonderful rest. Nothing in the post, nothing to bring the usual daily train of fret and frenzy. If only I could go on living at this more leisurely pace – but one cannot afford it.

As I was parking the car this morning, a whacking big saloon car (I never know the make) drew up beside me, and a slick young man with longish hair, smoking at the wheel, leaned out and asked if I could tell him the value of any of the properties around here, pointing to my neighbour's house. 'Thinking of buying,' he said in a lordly way. He looked about 18. The girl at his side, not much older, pale, fair, detached and a little apologetically amused. What an extraordinary request. I would never divulge values of adjacent properties to callow strangers, even if I knew the value. What on earth were they up to, that with-it and brash young couple?

D-Day, Monday, 15 February[255]

First customer wanted paperbacks. They came to (14s.) 70p. That was easy. During another transaction, when I was valiantly adding up decimal value of several greetings cards, customer added wrapping paper at last moment, and I just stopped myself adding another 8p instead of 3-and-a-half p to the total. At tobacconists-sweets-newsagents The Bon Bon, Mrs Bon Bon was doggedly taking and giving new money at her till on one side of the shop, while on the other veteran Mrs H. (who at 70 years or so still has a newspaper round in the mornings) said, 'I'm not doing that money!' and firmly gave me 2s. 10d. change for 50p.

Peter M. popped in just before closing time. He reported chaos at one large factory he visited today, where authority had changed all the tea machines over the weekend to take new coinage, but employees this morning had none, and queues formed outside accounts dept for change.

Monday, 8 March

The post strike is over. The Government has won. 'We are not defeated!' cry the postmen. January mail is delivered. Bills will pour in, money will pour out. No more rest, no more ease. Day that I loved, the night is here.

Tuesday, 9 March

Local Dr Barnardo's group is giving a lunch tomorrow. Tickets @ £1 a time via the Little Bookshop (because of postal strike). A fashion show is thrown in and the whole affair is being held at a private house.

---

255 Decimal Day: the UK and Ireland changed from pounds, shillings and pence (£, s. & d.) to decimal currency, moving from 240 pence in the pound to 100. Despite months of advance warning and educational programmes, the public and banks appeared surprised by the finality of it all and confused by practicalities. There were no longer 12 pence in the shilling and 20 shillings in the pound. Tourists and the international exchanges found life easier; everyone else seemed to feel that the 'rounding up' that occurred inevitably worked against them.

The committee organises and cooks lunch for what apparently will be well over 130 people. About 50lbs of deep frozen fresh salmon is being dealt with today in someone's oven. Salad is bought I think from a 'Cash & Carry'. I record this because Left Wing intellectuals tend to sneer at this sort of activity. I wonder why, and if they have tried to do anything similar themselves to help the community.

Friday, 28 May

Wee. The conveyance came through only last week. Today final arrangements for loan were made with the bank, and I handed cheque for purchase money to solicitors. I felt like a millionaire and have been promised a further few hundred to help with the badly needed improvements I have in mind. Thank you God, here is one prayer answered.

Sunday, 4 July

Last evening, Peggy Denny took me to the new Chinese Restaurant in the village and we sat drinking coffee upon coffee after the lush meal. P. is a dear, large, ugly woman, and such a snob – I can't understand why I like her as I do. I am ashamed later. She has a very good job with British Aluminium and lives alone comfortably in the house left her by her parents. She is large and clever and comfortably off and respectable and has not a wisp of imagination, but a huge sense of humour breaks through the dust and makes her more than tolerable.

Monday, 6 September

Wholesalers seemed to have abandoned me, but they both arrived today with usual sort of excuses, van breakdowns, new schedules etc. I forgive them as I now have new stock (needed at least three weeks ago) and have spent greater part of the day sorting and rearranging and putting on a new window display. It is a good feeling – something to offer people, Come Buy, Come Buy.

'A place without a bookshop is a place without a soul.'
Jean drums up business in *Our Cats* magazine.

Tuesday, 28 December

I now have the great comfort of an enclosed loo and a little greenhouse against the kitchen. No more paddling out on cold wet nights
and mornings. And new French windows in the sitting room.

Thursday, 3 February 1972

Ghastly things are happening in Ireland. I begin to feel drawn towards
a growing feeling in this country that we withdraw our troops and
leave the Irish to fight it out amongst themselves. IRA snipers appear
to be everywhere, and any youth who can make and throw a bomb
can do so at any time through his own initiative. Violence bubbles
up in me when I hear these things. I know in my heart that we must
get rid of this feeling of violence in oneself, one must not feel exasperated and impatient.

Must feed the cats. Have not recorded yet that three more have
gone. Modest Wendy lost weight, went off her food and died within
it seemed a few days – kidney disease again. Monty, my beautiful
marmalade, went the same way a few months later. And just before
Xmas my beloved Roger, so loving, talkative and altogether dear,

disappeared on Sunday evening. It was the Olympic Cat Show weekend (such a big success too!). Weather was mild, and I found all the cats safe and well on my return, Roger indignant at his captivity and eager for garden air. And evil young tom was on the prowl. We were plagued by him for months last year. He was in fact a cat with no fear of the human race whatsoever, and would always try to seduce me. His intention was clear – he wanted to come in and dominate the cottage. More than once I rescued Roger from a cowering position in the bushes. But this Sunday evening he did not come back. He was not there in the morning, nor all day Tuesday. Just after Xmas I met neighbour Mrs B. Had I lost a cat? A friend of hers had seen 'that beastly tom eating a black and white cat' near our cottages.

If only I hadn't turned him out.

Wednesday, 15 February

Last Wednesday I had another interview (the third) with spirit healer Dr Lang at Aylesbury. My eyes do not seem to have improved, though they are no worse. Some doubts, indecision and a little despair were making an attack, but Dr Lang reassured me. He found definite progression in the spirit body not yet apparent in the physical, and thinks it will not be long before it becomes evident. You may sneer if you must, but I believe him and came away trailing clouds of glory. Meanwhile, my big brother has had a second cataract removed in Jamaica by surgery.

The Miners' Strike. Biggest and most paralyzing event we have ever had. It is not just the temporary inconvenience of power cuts. We have candles, torches and alternative means of heating and cooking facilities. We cope. We try to plan our meals and domestic routines ahead, we buy in extra tins of this and that, we fill the odd thermos.

It is the thought of what the long term effects may be that frighten us. If you tend to be over-imaginative, the prospect is terrifying. I was lucky earlier this week when I phoned the local fuel office. I think I have enough stock at the shop to last us well into late spring if weather continues mild, but was doubtful if I could last out till end of March at Wee.

Ellen D.'s daughter came into the shop the other day. We were discussing the situation, when she said how much she enjoyed sawing up pieces of wood. Eagerly I said she could come and saw up some of mine. Bless her, she came round this afternoon in deluging rain and has tackled at least a quarter of it. She glowed as she worked, clothes soaked and hair dripping, and rushed off full of energy at 3.30 to go to collect her two children from school.

Sunday, 25 June

I wake to 8 a.m. news. Two more deaths and more violence in Northern Ireland . . . floods on east coast of USA subsiding . . . the floating £ . . . and the coldest recorded June due to quantity of icebergs adrift in the North Atlantic. The troubles in Ireland become like the war in Vietnam, part of the news pattern which one ignores.

One morning I heard H.A. Williams being interviewed on his new book *True Resurrection*, it impelled me to order the book for myself.[256] Live to create, he says, do not live to conform. I am timid, weak, and conform too often when immediate pressures are strong, but always regret it. I do not know at all how much of the joy I often feel overflows to influence others; I think very little.

Have I recorded what the children did for me last autumn? How they spent one Sunday laying crazy paving all round back entrance so that I have a clean, dry walk to fuel and dustbin? Made a new herb bed, smashed up the old well, so that I now have another flower bed where oriental poppies are in glorious flower, some irises, new rose bushes.

Sunday, 20 August

Roses have blackspot and mildew.

My car was badly smashed up 10 days ago. Another, travelling in opposite direction, went into a skid which driver couldn't control,

---

256 Harry Williams, an Anglican monk, wrote several bestsellers exploring alternative religious paths.

and crashed into offside of mine. I had three passengers, but mercifully no one was hurt. My car towed to local garage, where it awaits
insurance wrangle, and police eventually brought us all home. Friends
and neighbours are very kind with lifts.

Wednesday, 18 October
A super birthday, quite unplanned. I don't like being reminded of the
passing years. But nice cards and letters arrived this morning, and,
just as I was leaving, the Coalite.

News of 'The Road' broke officially today. This great shadow which
has hung over us for the past five or more years has moved away. The
Minister has refused all seven (I did not know there were so many)
applications for a bypass route. The need, he concludes, has not been
proved, and we must now wait to find out what the effect of the new
roads already under construction to east and west of us will have on
the one through the villages. This is in effect what The Farnham
Villages Assoc has been hammering out all along.

The poor little Morris was pronounced a write-off. And then
miracle of miracles – Babs's neighbour (a Lloyds underwriter) is
retiring and buying a new car in November, and is willing to part
with his present one at trade-in price (£150!). A 1964 Singer Vogue
meticulously maintained.

I was describing the birthday, wasn't I? Sandwich lunch with the
art group. Liz had organised a small 'reception' and a hastily designed
greetings card signed by all of them. Really heart-warming. The side-
board in the sitting room is gay with cards, I am amused and charmed
by them all, particularly one from my rude young family: 'You are at
a difficult time of life (picture of distraught little man at desk). Too
tired to work, too poor to quit.'

Sunday, 12 November
The Singer was brought over this afternoon. Roy (with Babs as back-
seat driver) took me for trial run in the Beeches. I think I managed

fairly well, but am loaded once more with dreads and fears. All switches differently placed again, a different set of gears to master, handbrake on the right instead of the left, pedals larger and more widely spaced.

Friday, 2 February 1973

Mrs H. at The Bon Bon is telling the village that I have had a breast removed. Why these fantastic sort of rumours still shock me I don't know. I should be hardened by now. I have heard so many distortions of truth not only about myself but about dozens of others in our community. How do they start, who first actually said, 'Miss P. has had a breast removed'?

I went down with flu on Xmas eve and spent the whole holiday in bed. Was beginning to recover, idling in front of sitting room fire, when I felt acute pain and was very sick. I managed to crawl into bed with h.w. bottle, and then discovered a small hard lump in my groin. I staggered down to the phone and spoke to the on-call doctor, who was round within a few minutes, diagnosed a strangulated hernia and ordered an immediate operation.

I think I have never lived through such a nightmare as the next few hours. It was 10 o'clock at night, the day's washing up not done, five little cats waiting to be fed. 'I can't go to hospital!' I cried. 'Oh yes you can,' answered Dr S. 'There must be someone you can phone.' Neighbour Nan F. came at once and took complete charge and got me ready for the ambulance, and next day telephoned key people like Kay and Babs.

I was bundled up and carried through freezing fog to the Canadian Red Cross Hospital at Taplow, too tense and dazed for tears. They operated at 2.15 a.m. The hospital, the subdued bustle, the questions. A West Indian nurse asking who was my next of kin and me replying 'they are in Jamaica' and seeing her eyes grow enormous. The pale green light in the anaesthetist's room, two Indians I think hovering about and telling me to breathe deeply. Then deep oblivion and coming to in the ward bed feeling as though I had had a wonderful night's rest.

Kay turned up in visitors' time that afternoon. I could hear her at foot of my bed asking for me. I must have been quite unrecognisable, and I didn't even have my plate in. Dear, loyal, wonderful Kay. She and Anne would look after the shop, they would bring me the mail, they would visit me often.

I have received so much attention and loving kindness. In fact, I think this last five weeks have been one of the most exciting and rewarding periods of my life. Two weeks in hospital, then two weeks with Babs and Roy, able to provide just what a convalescent aunt needed, a quiet, warm home where I had nothing to do but be pampered.

One is, astonishingly, as weak as water. Recovery was also complicated by my fiendish cough. I coughed so much in hospital I kept the whole ward awake, and would stagger to the toilet in the morning hacking away like an old bronchitic and could scarcely get my breath. More than once a nurse found me gasping as I clung to a wash basin. The cough continued at Babs's – kept them awake at night too.

A week ago today Babs brought me back to Wee. Her doctor advised two weeks off work. It has been heaven, heaven, heaven. All the cats rejoicing. Have not smoked since Xmas eve and so far have no desire to.

Saturday, 10 February

And then one morning one wakes at daybreak, the whole soul rejoicing because one feels better. Really better – the days of shortness of breath and lack of appetite are ending. There is a faint itch after breakfast or coffee or any good meal, or a sudden little wave of excitement for something, some extra small satisfaction, and one thinks of a cigarette. But then one thinks, 'but it is not going to promise any pleasure – I do not want one.' And one finds something to nibble or suck, a nut or a lozenge, and one forgets the irritating thought.

Have only popped into shop occasionally to see how things are going, answer queries, pick up mail. I have a nasty suspicion that I am not supposed to do even this while drawing sick pay, but am not going to declare it.

Friday, 30 March
Dear Lord. I sit on the little stool by kitchen fire (heavy with good supper and too much Dubonnet) and turn off *Any Questions*. For two months I was the centre of sympathetic attention and basked in it. I had leisure, had a taste of what retirement in the modern sense could be like, and life had a different, richer sort of quality. One could move from day to day without harassment.

My business that I once loved has become a teasing, tiresome and unprofitable burden. I can see no future for it and am losing heart. Yet I wish to complete two more years so that I can say '20 years'.

Monday, 9 April
The new *Cats and Catdom Annual* arrived. A.A. has given me a tremendous 'paw-pat', and this has done much for my morale. 'A great character in the Cat Fancy . . . 17 years specialising etc'. And yet still I walk on the edge of melancholy, a slough of despond lapping at my ankles.

Photo of a January bridegroom in an old newspaper on kitchen table catches my eye. He wears a grey topper on top of shoulder-length hair, and looks fantastic.

Monday, 22 April
I picked out, carelessly, from the bookcase, Shane Leslie's *The End of a Chapter* (inscribed 'To Lucie the Moog from Hugh, 1945').[257] Except that I recognise Hugh Laming's handwriting, and remember that this is what he called me, I recall nothing about the presentation.

I am still not smoking. I realise that whatever one thought one

---

257 Leslie was a career diplomat and the first cousin of Winston Churchill. His memoir of 1916 considered not only his family life, but also the future for English and Irish society at an uncertain time.

got out of it is an illusion, like all drugs. What is it one wants so desperately and never finds? Cigarettes, drugs, alcohol, sex, food, reading, music, sleep – none of these bring any lasting satisfaction, real fulfilment. One knows only that one is forever dissatisfied and hollow and agonisingly alone. All round one is a vast wilderness, or there may be if one moves from the familiar daily circle of known living. Why have we lived? Have we lived? The flower at least may have given some pleasure, joy, perfume to the world. Or it may have lived to blush unseen.

Thursday, 17 May
It seems to go on and on, this tiredness and despair. For a few days at a time, maybe, all seems fine again, I work reasonably well and even feel happy at it, especially if I can do some useful gardening as well. Then wham! down we go, no energy, no inclination or wish to be doing anything but what I am doing. Cannot make decisions or plans. People say 'you need a little holiday,' which I suppose I do, but this calls for more effort and organising than I can summon. The thought of journeys I may have to make by car fill me with cold, paralyzing horror.

I look so well now, that is the trouble, have put on some weight and my face has filled out, making it less haggard. More colour too, it's all rather misleading and tiresome. I fear now that I am a fraud and evading all sorts of important challenges, and am in danger of growing 'soggy'. Declining into a vapid and fretful old age. Horrible!

Sunday, 24 June
Today I spent with Babs and family at Pyrford. I did not want to do this journey – the first time I have driven further than Slough or Beaconsfield since my illness.[258] From the time I woke at 7 to the time I started at about 11 I went through the tortures of the damned. I

---

258 Pyrford in Surrey, Babs's new home, was a thirty-mile trip.

wanted to die, to be seriously ill, so that I could phone and postpone the visit. Feeling sick with knots in the stomach and gripped at the throat – just what actors go through before a performance. I got there adequately without trouble. I need to take a few driving lessons from a professional, just to tighten and polish and sort out my confusions.

Roy has given me some very helpful suggestions for possible plans ahead. Developers are beginning to nibble again for the Florence Cottages property. I have to look ahead now, to old age, decline and senility and accept that I need capital.

Sunday, 8 July

I have been offered £30,000 for the shop property.

I cannot take this in and all its implications. How much will be left once the Inland Revenue have sucked their fill? Will there be enough to keep me in comfort for the rest of my life (20–30 years at most and perhaps much less)?

I do not want to give up the business. I have been thinking in terms of finding space cheaply somewhere where I could carry on with second-hand books by mail order, still specialising in cat books. But there will be an end to the Bookshop as such in Farnham Common, and this I find bitter. I have established one now, and if circumstances were different I could have retired, selling to the right people to carry it on. This would have given me the feeling of having contributed something solid and real and growing to the community.

Sunday, 12 August

My solicitor R.P. is ill, so I have progressed no further. I am ill too, sick to the heart's marrow, but I do not know why. The invasive melancholy which has haunted me throughout convalescence increases and increases. I do not know how to combat it.

I wake early and doze fitfully until it is time to get up. And as soon as I reach this wakeful state, beyond the blessed peace and oblivion of night, I am conscious of weight across the diaphragm like lead. It lessens but doesn't lift all day, and I long only for bedtime. The garden is being neglected. I force myself through the work at the shop that must be done, but my enthusiasm and interest is dead. Minor worries become monstrous – recently, persecution from Beeches authorities about the parking of my car on their sacrosanct land upset me hugely. Mercifully, a very kind neighbour has given me use of a piece of waste land outside his property only a few yards away. A great relief, but the desolation and despair continue. So much so that I have to confess to it openly. I have been again to the doctor who has prescribed further tonic (Beconite) and a holiday.

The holiday is booked at end of September, to Newquay, with my ponderously kind P.D. It must be endured, this malaise, and lived through. A cancer of the soul – is it?

Sunday, 19 August
[Glued clipping from *Radio Times*:]

Radio 4, 7.30 p.m. *New Lifelines in Medicine.*
Seven programmes about the developments which in the last decade have transformed the science of medicine.
7. *Depression*
Being 'down in the dumps' or having 'the blues' is a common enough experience for most of us. It is not pleasant, but it passes. We cannot easily imagine having the blues permanently, and so severely that life seems either pointless or worse – daily torture. This is depressive illness at its most severe, and it demands medical treatment.

I listened to this programme and recognised all the symptoms. Sensations of isolation, anxiety and guilt. A great fatigue, escape into sleep whenever possible, night and day. Is too much hope and emphasis being placed on the drugs now found effective towards a cure? Do we want to cure or heal?

Sunday, 2 September

Yes, I am a lot better, and on Friday a letter from brother Pooh with tremendous news. He and Ivy have decided to sell up and come home. The children and Roy have spent summer holidays in Jamaica, and full discussion was therefore possible. This is glorious, glorious news for me. I had thought of them as dug in and settled forever, and that unless I could make a huge effort and find the funds to visit them, might never see them again.

Yet I wake this morning still with a black cloud in the head – despair, despair. Why? Where does it come from?

Monday, 10 September

I made up my mind to find the location of a new wholesaler in Slough. I knew it would be difficult among tiresome back streets, 'No Entries', 'No Right Turns' and so on, obscure, difficult access with difficult parking. All of which proved true, so that I nearly gave up and drove back to FC more than once. Resolving to pluck up the heart, I pressed on.

This is the wholesaler I need and will be our salvation. I hope. Van service of W.H. Smith and Bookwise are now virtually non-existent. I was in despair about our daily bread-and-butter stock, and now I have seen what can be had on our doorstep I can finish with W.H.S. Their service has been becoming more and more atrocious for 12 months or more. I can see my way ahead now, without stumbling.

'Eighteen years old, long blonde hair, Indian headband . . . suede jacket, fringed skirt, green eyes . . . Her companion, a morose bearded creature . . . sported an Afro hairdo . . . festooned with love beads . . . his heliotrope bell-bottoms kept up by broad leather belt, the buckle of which was fashioned in shape of a penis.'

This image of our new generation is quoted from last pages of David Niven's *The Moon's A Balloon*, just to remind me how really repulsive it has become to older people, but isn't universal. The young that I know aren't like this, but the shadow, the influences, are there, and make one shudder. Shudder.

Wednesday, 31 October
Pooh and Ivy are flying home tonight. I have had my holiday in Newquay with that appalling woman P.D. Kay and her husband have moved to their new home near Chepstow. I have a promising replacement in the shop in D.W.

The developers have withdrawn their offer. After much discussion and digging around, I discovered that their scheme was too urban for our County Planning approval – huge office blocks were intended. I might have known it couldn't come true, that offer.

N. came on Sunday. It is years since she visited Wee. She has bought herself a little terrace house in Yorks but is not very happy about it.

Saturday, 3 November
It takes alcohol to release me.

Tomorrow I am due to meet again, after 16 years, my big brother Pooh. They arrived at Heathrow on Thursday, early, and at 9 a.m. phoned me from Babs's home in Surrey. I could only remember with icy anguish that tomorrow morning I had another hour's cross-country drive, possibly through fog, before any pleasure could be realised. That would be damped, torturing me, by the thought of the drive home again.

Now, after 2–3 glasses of Dubonnet in warm, loving kitchen, waiting for supper potatoes to bake, I am happy, filled with longing and wonder. How shall I find him? Babs says that his nerves are 'all shot to pieces'. All the Pratts, i.e. my father's brothers and their children, tend to this high-strung response to living, almost a stutter, an inability to be coherent, to express themselves calmly. I am like it, too.

Tuesday, 13 November
Life has withered him. He is a husk. But I love him, I love him, and he loves me and that is very warming. Ivy is splendid, and surprised

me with her welcome. Both are delighted to be home again, are thrilled by all the privileges granted by National Health to OAPs, and by how much cheaper are commodities here than Ja.

Last Friday/Saturday, dear old lady Priss went on her way, another dear little cat gone. For months she had been failing, so frail, but her eyes still big and lustrous, her appetite healthy and her affection immense. Until Friday evening, when she refused all food and wanted only to be left in her basket by the fire. On Saturday I found her curled there, very cold and still. That is how I wish them all to go, in their own time. But my heart again was torn apart – goodbye, dear, dear little Priss.

Now we are four. MaryAnne, Buster, George and Tweezle.

48.

Now We Know

Sunday, 25 November 1973 (aged sixty-four)
I have been slipping down a riverbank, saved from immersion by my hold on an old strong tree trunk. This feeling has continued day after day all the summer. Last summer I caught another chill which went to the chest, and I had a fair excuse to visit doctor again. He examined the chest and pronounced it clear. No undue shortage of breath, no anaemia, nothing at all in my body to blame for this dreadful darkness of the spirit. I tried to explain it a little: Dr S. was as sympathetic as I suppose a GP can be. He told me to take heed of my age and suggested that I make an effort to wind down business responsibilities.

But I do not think I can do this yet. I do not want to be enveloped in Old Age. I am 64 but don't feel it – I want still to do the things and at the pace I did at the age of 54 or 44.

Monday, 3 December
I am overfull of Dubonnet again. Following confession to Doc S. and his course of antibiotics, I was feeling wholly able to cope with this last weekend, when I went to London for the NCC show at Olympia. It was a terrific day, we took over £500, nearly half of this due to sale of two spectacular cat encyclopaedias. I can do it. I can. This is the boost I needed, leaving me with nearly £100 in the bank, towards meeting at least two-thirds due to publishers. And today I heard from

Babs that they can put me up for the night at Xmas, and this will make the day for me, not having to get into a frenzy about driving home. Yes, I am better, better! (And very drunk.)

Sunday, 16 December

The 'betterness' really continues, thank God. How can one explain this? I did not imagine that black pall. It did envelope me all those months and I could not escape it.

Was it partly premonition of our present troubles? They become a challenge, like a war. Fuel shortages, threats of blackouts, railway chaos, paper shortage and the 'three-day' week for industry and commerce. No developer is going to come to my rescue at this moment of doom and gloom.

Still not smoking. Not one cigarette since last December. There is no virtue in it, no struggle, no anguish. I simply do not want to smoke.

Wednesday, 2 January 1974

Mr H. heard on TV that small shops may use three hours of electricity per day at any time. I think we may get by with shop lights only in the afternoon.

Tuesday, 12 February

Said Anne C. today: 'I am not in the least interested in this coming General Election. Each party will promise wonderful solutions to our crises which none will be able to carry out. I am not going to listen to them on TV or read the newspapers, I simply do not believe a word they say.' This is exactly how I feel, and am quite sure we are not the only two in GB who do.

Tuesday, 12 March

Election now over, and Labour back, stepping very cautiously. Emergency measures removed, and full light and heat (electric) restored to industry and business, and the five-day week. Though some firms have found that their men work so much better and produce more in three days that they have started them back on a four-day week only.

I have a dream, I know now what I want to do. I want if it is possible to forget the possibility of being swallowed by developers, or beaten down because of a road improvement. I want to divide the shop into two units and sell the goodwill of the new book business to Carter & Wheeler in Slough, and rent them the original front shop so that they could carry on a branch of their very excellent Slough business. I to withdraw completely from this side of the business, taking only the secondhand portion and my cat book speciality, keeping the backroom office. They would of course pay me an agreed rent.

I could carry on mainly by mail order and open one day a week (Saturday). I could do work of interest in my own time, relieved of all the present pressures. FC can be sure of its bookshop for at least another decade.

Sunday, 12 May

I had a dream, but it died. I approached L.W. of Carter & Wheeler but he was not impressed. He has now a super-modern business in Slough, his whole overlook on bookselling is urban, up-to-date and quite different from my slapdash rural cosy and intimate attitude. No, he was not impressed. Forget it, Jean.

The new business rates are paralyzing. As foggy a future as I have ever faced.

Tuesday, 16 July

Throughout May and June I struggled on at shop, trying to get the year's accounts prepared for an audit. Preparing for invasion of primary school children bent on securing prizes. We have had nearly 60 so far. I had forgotten how sophisticated the 10, 11, 12 year-old can be.

Saturday, 10 August

It is midnight. Somewhere nearby the young are holding high revel with a discotheque. It is the most ghastly noise. I have not been sleeping well, not for months. Radio can soothe me sometimes. I discovered not only the BBC World Service, but LBC (London Broadcasting Company) which often keeps me wide awake. Astonishing phenomenon of the times these phone call-ins.

Sunday, 11 August

Another bad night, maybe because of the discotheque. I wake as depressed as ever. Money and what best to do with the business dominate, but also at the core is an increasing sense of my loneliness.

And also the problem of my eyes. The left eye is slightly worse: very small print now almost impossible to read without a magnifying glass. Am haunted by the thoughts of an operation. Have started again to link up if possible with Dr Lang.

Sunday, 29 September

Dr D. came again on Friday, and is to call for third time tomorrow. When a NH patient has to have three visits at home from their doctor, you can be pretty sure they are ill. The fact that I had been sleeping badly slipped out, and he at once asked if I had been feeling depressed. It is true – the medical profession does recognise depression as a sickness now. This is itself a relief. My problems (some of them) began to tumble out. He seemed to understand and prescribed an 'anti-depressant' (Surmontil).[259] I wake with a headache and feel heavy all morning.

I have done it – once more back into one little shop. Anne and Sarah met me at 2.30. Anne began to get anxious that I was overdoing it but it was a tonic: the fact of achieving this long-planned move

---

259 Surmontil is still prescribed for serious depression and insomnia, and is known generically as Trimipramine.

'back' and finding that the stock all fitted in reasonably well. 'But why are you doing this?' I shall be asked. For reasons of economy. To cut the rates and reduce overheads. You have only to listen-in to know how rising costs are hitting the small man; the retailers' problems were mentioned only this morning on a BBC programme. Also, every time I am forced into an illness I have to call a doctor and am told I am doing too much.

Old Hys who travelled for Batsford turned up again last week.[260] He is a fearsome old gossip, and what intrigued me to learn was that so many of the surviving smaller bookshops survive as they do because there is money behind them, a rich stockbroker husband/ father/boyfriend, or just money of the owner's own to burn. I have kept going for almost 20 years without subsidies, except for the capital obtained from Homefield and Miss Drumm's help in securing the freehold. It is very doubtful I could have managed without these aids.

Which brings me to the most wonderful, most unlooked for, most undeserved gift I have yet received. In August I took time off to visit Joan and Vahan in their new home at Radlett. I babbled to Joan about my woes, when she suddenly asked how much money I needed. It seems with the inheritance from her parents, and Vahan's fees recently scooped in after some delay, they now have too much capital and are in the 'Super Tax' bracket, and therefore want to get rid of, tempo-rarily, as much as they can to relieve the tax situation. I am to have £2,500 interest free for two years.[261]

I cannot quite take this in. It is so rare in this frightful age of grasp and me-first. This is of course another great boost to my flag-ging spirit. I can clear the bank loan on Wee, and the overdraft, and have a few hundred in hand for repairs and improvements.

---

260 Batsford specialised in games and gardening books.
261 In the 1970s, Super Tax stood at up to 83 per cent of earnings, and was responsible for the 'brain drain', higher earners leaving the country for lower tax bands abroad.

Monday, 2 December
How pleasant it is to have money.

Sunday, 8 December
Tomorrow my new shop tenants, the florists, open. Yesterday was opening day for an antiques shop, very splendid and lush and Cotswoldsy. So now at our end of the village we have antiques, a picture gallery, flowers and books. Highly cultural.

I eat nut roast (rather over-cooked) with baked pot, sprouts, carrot and turnip, and apricot tartlet with tinned apricots and sour milk. I have not suffered at all from sugar shortage or bakers' strike. Because of Joan's loan I am lashing out and having the kitchen rejuvenated. My ambition was a 'pine' kitchen, but this far too expensive. But that is the motif: two new cabinets – formica, pine-faced, and the two kitchen rooms repainted to a 'pine' scheme. (Airing cupboards built round hot water tank and pipes last year faced with 'knotty pine' special boarding.)

Saturday, 28 December
This Christmas I have been guest at three separate groaning boards, each beautifully and lovingly decorated. What a feast it has become for us in this section of society: the enormous turkey, stuffing, roast pots, sprouts and other vegetables favoured by the hostess, sauces, gravy, wine to drink, plum pudding, mince pies, cream, lard sauce (i.e. not butter), nuts, sweets, crackers until one feels like dying quietly.

Next week we begin the new shop regime. This will in theory give me Monday and Wednesday at home. It is what I have been aiming at, the planned retirement operation.

Wednesday, 12 February
Margaret Thatcher has been elected leader of the Conservative Party. I am fascinated.

Trying to read Margaret Drabble without success. I find her too heavily influenced by Henry James, yet feel I am shirking something.

In *The Needle's Eye*, for instance, Rose suddenly says splendidly, ' . . . the things I do now, they're part of me, they're monotonous yes I know, but they're not boring, I like them, I do them all – I do them all with love. Getting up, drawing the curtains, shopping, going to bed.'

This is how we can all live, if we will. What a formidable array of talented women writers the post-war years have thrown up.

Monday, 14 April

Two months have frittered by. Have just turned off radio Monday play *Now She Laughs, Now She Cries* by Jill Hyem. I just cannot stomach this sort of thing. I am sorry for them – the lesbians and homos, but don't ask me to sympathise or join in.[262] And don't say to me that this attitude only proves that I have similar latent tendencies. If anything I am a frustrated nymphomaniac but perversion for me could go no further. I loathe the very idea of the other, but do not at all loathe the idea of being a successful courtesan. Am still tormented sometimes by erotic fantasies on these lines. Men. Lovely men . . .

I did not have this in mind to record – it was that stupid play that provoked it (now am being unfair – I think it is probably a good play. I should have heard it to see whether in the end she is left crying . . .)

Tuesday, 6 May

I am only finding the words, put by someone else, that express or explain part of the great feeling of desolation and despair that is enveloping me. The hounds of hell perpetually at my heels. I don't know what to do, where to go, what is worth doing. Truly this despair has pursued me, and no drugs, no props, no escape in any form rid me of it or change the mood. I wake each morning full of dread when I should be shouting with joy.

---

262 The play, in which a woman leaves her husband for another woman, was regarded as a watershed in gay drama. The BBC pronounced itself proud to broadcast a play about such a controversial topic, but then refused to air the repeat in the afternoon lest it cause offence.

There is too much ghastliness on the news to be borne, it goes on and on, IRA atrocities, Vietnam disaster upon disaster, famine and starvation in the Third World, perpetual cruelties to animals, perpetual greed and aggression all round one, brainless and juvenile violence. How can one not be aware and influenced, and threatened by destruction with all this bombarding one daily? And all the time one's own little life continues, fretted with the same old anxieties about money and one's eye defects, making long journeys alone by car; and then insurance of one's rotting property problems, and the nagging of the well-meaning male, intent on boosting his own ego, exploiting the fears of small people. I took the Surmontil for only about five nights. But dreams are ugly – confused and bewildering.

Later: What I have to do is to 'stand fast in my surroundings'. In old-fashioned and out-of-date terminology I must 'pull myself together' and 'not give in to these moods'. Can't you hear all the nannies down the ages chanting this? Now. Concentrate on the nice things that happen each day, and at risk of being an excruciating bore, record them here. After all, why do you always suppose that someone, in fact many people, are in the years ahead going to read these pages, or have the least interest in doing so? Maybe they'll just rot away, unread.

Wednesday, 7 May
A strong NE wind was whirling last year's dead leaves like a dust storm through the woods. Someone I knew but could not name as I walked down road smiled and said 'Windy, isn't it?' This was the first warm lift for me in an otherwise bitter and frustrating morning.

Another little warming incident: one of the village bods preparing for an afternoon function at the Hall grinned at me cheerfully: 'Hallo Miss Pratt! How's your pretty garden? I passed it the other day . . .' So people do notice.

Sunday, 22 June
Years ago, Gus said to me: 'You will never be happy – you want too

much.' I see this now as meaning that I want more than I am capable of achieving. You are a poor, mean little thing really. You want to be so wise and strong and admirable, but you are not. You want to be astute, clever, to be able to answer back smartly, to make clever quips, to contribute solidly to conversation. To be a much-loved, warming person – and you are not. You don't have people turning to you for advice and comfort, you are empty, alone, unwanted. You can appear to be busy and popular. You can crowd your life with social activities and contacts, but your inner life is vacant, a cold cavern where no one comes for shelter.

Monday, 30 June
I am still a member of Parish Council and am on three committees. I record all this so that it may be understood (why?) that I am no recluse, and have not yet withdrawn entirely, as so often in the black moods I long to do.

Thursday, 3 July
Yesterday a good day. I spent p.m. at local wholesalers gathering more stock for the school prizes and felt I achieved a good selection.

Tonight tired and deflated. Parents will tell me what a lot of such beautiful books they have at home, though I cannot remember ever seeing them in my shop before . . . the child with the delicate cough wanting impossible history books, and other children wandering about with pale, bored faces – oh, they've read that, that's in the library. I loathe the whole boiling lot. ('Oh no, I saw *Black Beauty* on TV . . .')

Monday, 8 September
I feel so much better, dare hardly mention it. Evidently the holiday was what was needed, just to get away from the daily nagging of petty affairs into a refreshing atmosphere with old friends.[263]

---

263 In the space of a few weeks she visited, after much agonising over the driving, her brother in Byfleet, Lydia in the Cotswolds, Babs and Roy in their new home in Dorset, and Joan and Vahan in Radlett. Still no sign of N.

Monday, 2 March 1976

And what do I do all day, each day? For a year now, shop opens 10–5 on Tuesday, Thursday, Friday and Saturday. On Saturday morning I now have 14 year-old Jane Kerr, a delightful and conscientious Scots lassie who manages very well indeed. On Monday I try to do all the chores at the cottage. On Wednesday during 'the term' I take a sandwich lunch to eat with artist friends who spend the day together at the village hall. On Sunday I am monstrously idle, except when I can get myself into the garden. Weekday evenings, unless there is a meeting to attend, are spent at home by myself. I like to get in, relax, have a drink, start preparing a substantial meal, a little washing or mending perhaps, usually much too tired to do anything but the washing up and feed cats. That is the slow pattern of my days, but each day is pretty crowded.

Have acquired another car. A Morris Mini Traveller, G registration, advertised in local PO. It is a joy, so much easier to handle than that elephant Singer which I must sell but think it is going to be a problem.

Wednesday, 26 May

Ivy went down with a stroke at the beginning of March, and brother Pooh was in for a tough time. Babs helped for the first days until her mother could be got into hospital. I went over two weekends to help. Ivy is much better and is coming home this weekend 'on trial'.

Sunday, 1 August

The heatwave of heatwaves. Never do we remember it so hot – all the news media has been full of it. At times almost unbearable.[264]

Dear little MaryAnne . . .

---

264 The summer of 1976 was a 'hottest since records began' event, and will not be forgotten by those who lived through it. Droughts, forest fires, hosepipe bans, water-rationing, washing up bowls emptied on parched gardens, campaigns to 'bathe with a friend', joy at Wall's Ice Cream.

Sunday, 8 August

P.D. is wanting me to go again to Newquay with her in October. Poor, dear P.D. I am sometimes so filled with revulsion. When away with her before I found her overwhelmingly gross, greedy and sentimental. But she has a large heart, and is also a heavily brilliant Oxford graduate. This one is never allowed to forget. I feel so mean, and treat her cruelly. I doubt whether she has ever had the remotest sort of love affair in her life. She is in her 50s, and all one ever hears of her past is Oxford and 'Mummy and Daddy', to whom she was very devoted.

A long, long letter from N. last week. She is now in Norwich and seems happy enough. Though still hinting that she may return for her last days to Ghana.

Collected Suzie Min (the Mini Traveller) last Wednesday. Her radiator collapsed on the M4 on way to the Cat Show.

Tuesday, 31 August

My week with family in Holt Forest, Dorset nearly over. Still scorchingly hot. I arrived soaked through. Roy's big Triumph was much cooler than the Mini. Visited Thomas Hardy's cottage, collected Colin from a day's fishing on the Stour, greeted Sue from her first holiday job in Paris – very tired but still shining with Parisian sparkle, full of confidence and conversation, her parents bubbling with pride. I am lodged in what I call the Royal Suite, a large twin-bedded room with its own shower basin and loo adjoining, all very splendid. Spacious cupboards.

Jottings from scraps of paper:

In April I read *Miss Seeton Sings* (Heron Carvic – my old friend Gus).[265]

---

265 In addition to his career as an actor, Gus invented the literary character Miss Emily Seeton, an art teacher whose sketches help a team of detectives solve crimes. Classified as 'cosy mystery thrillers', the series ran to five novels with Heron Carvic as pseudonymous author, with other authors reviving Miss Seeton after Gus's death

Barbara Cartland on *Woman's Hour*: 'People are frightened – so frightened of the future and present they drug themselves stupid to escape it.'

'There is a brief time for sex, and a long time when sex is out of place. But when it is out of place as an activity there still should be the large and quiet space in the consciousness where it lives quiescent. Old people can have a lovely quiescent sort of sex . . . leaving the young quite free for their sort.' (D.H. Lawrence to Lady Ottoline, 28.12.28.)

Authors I can stomach: Mary Hocking, Elisabeth Taylor, Lettice Cooper, Frank Swinnerton. Not, oh please not Edna O'Brien and her ilk! What a waste of talent – like all such modern younger writers, each trying to be cleverer and more perceptive and dirtier than the last. All with such immense talent, skill and feeling wasted, wasted.

Sunday, 3 October
I feel extremely well – depression niggles away in the depths, but doesn't overwhelm.

Thursday, 11 January 1979[266]
And now laid low with bronchitis. Woke Wednesday after a bad night with chest afire and coughing a lot and painfully. Thick phlegm

---

in 1980. Under his real name Geoffrey Harris, Gus is better known to sci-fi and fantasy connoisseurs as the voice of Morpho in early episodes of *Doctor Who* (with William Hartnell as The Doctor), and as Gandalf in the BBC 1968 radio version of *The Hobbit*.

266 No journals survive from 1977 and 1978, but there is no suggestion from subsequent entries that Jean didn't maintain them. Her brother Pooh died from heart failure during this time, and she planned her retirement from the shop – both of which she would have written about decisively. Her remaining years are catalogued in just two journals, and it is indeed mostly a catalogue: weather reports, gardening updates, cat shows negotiated, meals destroyed when she dozed with the oven on, doctors' visits. Several times she questions why she is making her more cursory entries at all (it is no longer habit, but increasingly a resilience; her endurance is now one of her strongest assets).

threatening to choke me. Thank goodness phone is working. Summoned doctor, a new one, nice young woman, who confirmed congestion: 'Your chest is full of gunge.'

Saturday, 20 January
The first drug did no good. Another drug prescribed which has worked and I now feel better. Longing for the old days when Home Nursing was a skill and an art practised assiduously. I must not grouse. My new neighbour, whom I have treated shamefully, brought me two huge bunches of daffodils.

Monday, 29 January
Yesterday Enid tempted me to view with her a TV programme on a local Surrey dog show.[267] I was home again by 5.30 to prepare a delicious piece of stuffed rolled breast of lamb. I larded and put it into a Roastabag with cut-up onion, leek, parsnip, potato and mushrooms. It promised to be absolutely delectable. I then went off to write to N., neglecting to turn down my vicious little oven. When I came to it again, veg were burnt black and meat encased in shrivelled skin. Not a happy ending to the day.

Friday, 7 September
Coming home at night, 6–7 p.m., is the bliss of the day. I return to warm welcome, I can potter in greenhouse and garden, a comforting drink (or two) of sherry or vermouth, and then to prepare supper listening to *The Archers*. Tweezle had one eye alarmingly bloodshot and filmed over. Was able to rush her to vet and have been given pills and drops. Of course she resists tooth and claw.

---

267 A very old friend from architecture school, who now helps Jean run the shop. Elsewhere, Jean describes their relationship as consistently 'stormy', stemming, perhaps, from the days when Jean threw a watering can at her from a Hampstead rooftop when they were starting out.

Wednesday, 12 September

I never mentioned the Olympia Cat Show. It was a spectacular success. After traumatic difficulties (my regular driver collapsed a few weeks before the event with a severe heart attack) we got there and Rolf Harris came to sign his super *Picture Book of Cats* and I have never had a more successful signing party. He had only to appear by our stall and the public flocked round us. It was Enid's idea, from her watching TV, but of course she thought I could not possibly draw such a personality into our humble orbit. However I am quite used to approaching publishers on such issues, and his were remarkably keen and co-operative and one of the executives came in person to feed us with sufficient stock in the afternoon, which we did need.

Sunday, 27 April 1980

Business has been very good. In fact I have nearly £1,000 in credit, so that I have promised to pay back £500 to Joan of the loan.

Did not stand again for Parish Council. I have joined the Women's Institute – new experience and pleasant.

In the new *Cats and Catdom Annual* Alison Ashford refers to me as the 'Fairy Godmother' of the Cat Fancy, for obtaining and stocking cat books. She has always been very generous to me.

In the middle of Friday morning Ralph L. suddenly appeared. I was so amazed and delighted to see him I rushed into his arms and kissed him. But he did not stay and would not make a definite promise to come again or visit the group on Wednesday.

A decision at last reached and discussed with colleague Peter B. It is time I 'retired' if it can be contrived. He is willing to take on the front shop for his second-hand business in September, and I will withdraw into back office, keeping on with mail order and cat book business.

Wednesday, 11 February 1981 (aged seventy-one)

The periods of intense tiredness, of pushing myself into doing things, of getting breathless, of rages in getting the housework done, and feeling exhausted when completed – these conditions continued and increased, so that I went at last to the doctor. He diagnosed a tired heart and advised a general slow-down and rest.

This I was trying to do when I caught a chest infection. I have had wonderful help from neighbours and friends. The boiler tended, meals brought in, flowers, sweets, fruit, magazines – oh, spoiled old woman I am!

This is, I think, a warning. I have no desire or intention of dying yet. I still have a great deal to clear up, and it wouldn't be fair to leave all that to my family. I must remake my will.

Saturday, 21 February

This morning I woke to brilliant white frost, and knew I would do more today than I have done for nearly three weeks. It is well to remember how ill I felt, a rubber band around my diaphragm allowing me breath only in gasps. 'Are you all right?' I was asked. It was torture to get up in the morning.

How lucky I am with friends and neighbours. I hope I shall in some way be able to repay their kindness, their concern for me.

Anne Coote has returned as a part-time employee, and brings the mail from the shop. She has packed and posted parcels, took me to see specialist at Wexham Hospital and then last Monday to Hammersmith where my thyroid region was 'scanned'. Such a nice girl operated this fearful-looking machine. So far the doctors have decided I have thyrotoxicosis. Glands are doing something they shouldn't, and putting pressure on the heart. We await the report of the recent scan.

Tuesday, 24 February

On the eve of the announcement of Prince Charles's engagement to Lady Diana, I hear on radio from astrologist Sheila Geddes that most doctors agree that 80 per cent of illnesses are psychosomatic. I can go along with that. I am certain that this one of mine has made me stop when I couldn't make myself. Now the thyroid has taken over. I am in bed and have time to pause and replan.

Sunday, 11 October 1981

It is nearly a year since Taffy S. gave the retirement party for me as reported in news cutting I have just pasted into beginning of this book.

[The cutting, from the *Slough Observer*, was headlined 'Now Jean has more time for her feline hobby'.]

After 25 years of running Farnham Common's well-known Little Bookshop, Miss Jean Pratt has gone into semi-retirement to concentrate on her lifelong interest – books about cats.

Every year she sends a thousand parcels of books about our feline friends to animal lovers the world over. To mark her semi-retirement, a good friend, Mrs Spence Sanders, threw a lunch party on Sunday[268] where Miss Pratt was given a pretty posy with pink ribbons . . .

Born in Wembley, Miss Pratt did a journalism course at London University and some freelance work for architectural magazines. 'I always wanted to be a writer and I'm a great reader,' she said. Her wide knowledge of cats and the many books about them came during two years of research at the British Museum, working on a novel about a cat and her kittens which she never got round to writing. In 1955 she took over the Pets Corner shop in the Broadway for six shillings a week rent, selling and lending books. In that time she wrote a biography of Peg Wolfington [*sic*], the famous 18th Century Irish actress.

Moving to the present site five years later, she ordered books

---

268 Jean writes on the newspaper cutting: 'No! A mid-day gathering for sherry and nibbles'.

for the old Farnham Common primary school and had many book-signing sessions, most recently with local TV presenter Johnny Ball, who does the BBC's 'Think of a Number' show. Customers from as far afield as South Africa and Japan have dropped into the shop and she said: 'It's fascinating, you never know who'll turn up next.'

It was such an event for me and I was so moved by all the interest and attention. I kept a list of the guests: Catherine Altham and her mother (she presented the sherry). Taffy's son dictated that she have a caterer to provide the food (it was all super!). David and Sheila Milward (David made a touching little speech – I was nearly in tears!). David Gladwell (why I don't know, except that he likes to be in on all Taffy's parties). Muriel and Peter James (M. always a good customer, and Peter on the Council all the time I was there). Mr and Mrs Ripley. Mary Bassett, Peggy D., Lilian Gawthorpe (WI, is a very good customer). Nellie Bishop, my architect's widow. Irene Chinnery, Lesley Furness, Tom Steel the current parson, and me and Taffy. It was altogether a famous occasion.

Thursday, 31 December

Have tonight been listening to a repeat of BBC broadcast of part of the Royal Wedding, which enchanted us all last July. I watched it with E. on her colour TV.

I am better thank God, but still have to go to Wexham Hospital for thyroid check-ups.

I have managed to replace the old Mini Traveller for an ordinary Mini. Was really falling apart with rust.

Friday, 1 January 1982

Have just been listening to BBC Radio 'diary' item. It makes me wonder how many thousands and thousands of other people have this urge, therapeutic as it may be. And makes me wonder how I have the nerve to continue in competition with people like Antonia Fraser, Hugh Casson,

Mary Whitehouse, Peter Barkworth . . . Was it Hugh Casson who said it was the detail that interested him? Quoting Proust's 'tell me the colour of the blotting paper'. I think these are important things too, not 'the future of Northern Ireland' or who will win the next election – even the local politics of Farnham Common. I hear now a tap dripping, a clock ticking. Always there has been a clock ticking in the background of my life.

Went to a lovely mid-day party today of near neighbours. I've lived in Egypt now for over 40 years and find I know so many people. It is very warming. And flattering to have one's host kiss one on arrival and twice on leaving. Expect he just thinks, 'Poor elderly spinster . . . I'll cheer her up.'

Thursday, 13 May

My writing gets worse and worse. Partly, I believe, due to the thyroid trouble. At Wexham Hospital in Feb, the doctor there (a new one) decided that after a year's treatment the gland in my throat should have subsided. I'd been feeling so well – what did it matter? But I was sent again to specialist at Hammersmith and more scans. Radioactive iodine was prescribed, one small initial dose, the next day a massive one. Was warned that I would be highly radioactive for three weeks and must avoid pregnant women, babies and small children. I wondered about the cats, but had a word with the vet who said, well don't pet, don't let them get around your neck.

In a few weeks I was right back to palpitations, shortness of breath and no energy. And this blurred vision and seeing double which also afflicts me. Will need more iodine they say.[269]

---

269 Jean wrote only a few disjointed entries between October 1982 and May 1985. Her handwriting became larger and scratchier, though her mood remained steady, even content. Medical drama was limited to her eyes; she needed an urgent cataract removal, and was delighted to find that her NHS specialist at the Prince Charles Unit at Windsor was Dr Richard Packard, the same man who operated on Mrs Thatcher's detached retina. There is no mention of a serious operation she refers back to in her final entries. She managed to attend the Olympia cat show each December and spend two Christmases with Babs and Roy in Taunton. Developers

Monday, 20 May 1985

Have been trying to salvage what I can from the doomed land behind Flo Cottages. Two double white lilacs, white raspberries, one goose-berry and rosemary have been transplanted to miraculously reclaimed land at back of Wee garden. Two good apple trees are doomed, but I have saved young Coxes and maybe a conference pear, though it's not looking very happy yet.

This sort of thing is what delights me and makes me feel fulfilled – I am 'creating'. A slow developer, but now at last coming into full flower. And to discover, you silly young idiots, that sex does not matter!! Shut up, you argumentative, neurotic lot. It doesn't. One can live a full and joyful life without it and still stay reasonably unshriv-elled and unembittered. Believe me!

I plan to withdraw from shop altogether, to have good storage accommodation for book stock, built on old shed site here, and carry on mail-order cat book business from here.

Monday, 5 May 1986

Nearly another whole year gone and I am still as happy – even more so! The other day, meeting Enid R.'s sister Rae in village, she asked tenderly after my health (there has been touching concern for an ailment which has plagued me and mystified medicos since Feb). She said, 'I was saying to Enid, I think that all people over 70 should be put to sleep!' She, Enid and I are now all well into the 70s (don't ask me exactly, I don't want to know).[270] I exclaimed in horror, 'Oh NO! I don't want to be put down yet!'

Really, I am enjoying life so much. What a little extra capital can

---

continued to sniff again around her shop, and were particularly interested in the garden area, which they hoped to convert into a car park. The second-hand book-shop established when Jean retired to the back office failed to pay its way, and was replaced by a jeweller; there is passing mourning too for the disappearance of her local haberdashery and ironmongery shops. Amid much upheaval at Wee, Jean had a new bathroom installed with a knotty pine finish. Three cats left.

270 Jean is 76.

do to one's ego, so long as one doesn't lose all control of reasonable-ness. I have been awake since 3 a.m. looking through mail-order catalogues and by chance came upon 'shower coats' in thin nylon which I sought in the stores all last summer. Only £13 each, so woke up properly and have written an order for one each of two different colours and an attractive casual summer dress which seems worth having (three items for £40). This is what I can do now, be self-indulgent though not extravagant. Have just acquired a 14' screen TV set. The novelty here is not in TV as such – have seen so much of it when with Babs or at Elsa's and other places – but in having a set of my own which I can control.

I have help in the house and garden now, which makes living easier. It is not just a question of being able to afford today's high wages, it is knowing the right 'types'. Dressmaker's husband is a pensioner, but by trade a jobbing gardener and glad of extra money. He is a stalwart, excellent at rough digging and slashing back shrubs. Cuts back too much sometimes, and would clear garden of all my sedum ground cover if he could.

Domestically an attractive Finn comes one morning a week. Is a meticulous cleaner, and disapproves of all my little ornaments and general untidiness. In spite of years with an English family is difficult to understand. I like her.

All shrubs and trees transferred last year are doing extremely well. My cat book mail-order business is now established in rebuilt garden shed behind kitchen. There is still a lot of sorting and filing to do there.

Delay has been due to my recent affliction. It began with a monstrous tummy upheaval early February. Have never been so shat-teringly sick for so long. Think it was due to an extra extra hot curry of my own composing. I got over it in a few days, then tum pains, sickness and diarrhoea began. Pains, acute, continued, until my GP sent me to see surgeon. Was then sent for a massive barium follow-through X-ray, and had blood tests. Was so surprised and delighted when he said he was turning me back to my GP and would prescribe certain medication.

Acute, acute tum pains continued all this while. The tummy rumbles are fantastic – like Niagara Falls plus a crashing thunderstorm.

Lunch, cup of Oxo, half avocado (not quite ripe enough) stuffed with delicious cream cheese I made from sour milk and a little soured cream, chives, garlic crystals and other seasoning. This mixture, on Hovis crackers which Babs brought yesterday, went down very well.

Wednesday, 7 May

This morning a great improvement but only following a ghastly 24 hours of tum pains, acute, sickness and diarrhoea. What caused it all I'm not sure, except for an over-rich aspic jelly stuffed with creamed chicken, cooked veg, hard-boiled egg, soup and wine vinegar. Certainly it all came back at 6.30 a.m.

Yesterday no food at all until very light supper. Only soda water, half cup of milk and soda for lunch, and later Lucozade. This latter really does seem to restore energy.

Saturday, 10 May

Pains again, acute. Why?

Telephone surgery. My own Doc (Salmon) was not there, so had a word with Dr Scott. He came to see me at noon. Very charming and sympathetic. (He has two cats of his own and was flatteringly impressed with Jubie, who would sit on his notes.) He poked tum again (how many times has that poor item been pummelled?), listened to my tale of woe. It really does seem to have been getting worse since new pills started.

Letter from surgeon C. had arrived. He read out relevant bits. Must expect good days and bad days. There is a tendency to a blockage, and because of something connected with the '84 op, the liver is affected. I want a name for this affliction, as I have a number of neglected cat book customers to whom I must write my apologies and excuses.

Sipping Lucozade. It is marvellous! Read (*Strong Medicine* by Arthur Hailey in a large-print edition – good story but volume is very heavy), dozed, did one or two easy crosswords. Hot honey and milk, a saucer of rhubarb, a slice of bread and Marmite with a leaf or two of chicory and repeat the medicines. The whole ground floor of No. 2 Flo Cottages is let to a Railway Model dealer who seems to be doing well.

12.30. Dr Scott has just been. Now we know and I would much rather. He said, 'I am not good at telling lies.' Nice doc. 'You've had a rough time,' he says.

There is a little cancer of the liver – spread from the guts, though guts are not re-infected. (Did I note that they had removed cancerous growth and I was assured that they 'caught it in time' and that it would not recur there?) Doc wasn't positive, but there is hope that the liver trouble can be 'suppressed' by Prednisolone.[271] I want to cure it, to prove it can be cured. Herbalife? Must get back to dear alcoholic Rosalind.[272]

Meanwhile I go on with the Preds and the other medication to control the sickness and diarrhoea, but must not get too constipated. I'll fight this, with God's help.

Did not want any lunch. Dressed and went straight off to garden centre. Bought strips of seedling lobelia, purple alyssum, seed packets and white clematis. Had forgotten pain killers, and pain became so excruciating had to come straight back home, take the pills and lie down for half hour.

Back to village and to see E. She can be sympathetic and supportive on this sort of occasion – no wise cracks, no sneers, no snide remarks. Some helpful suggestions from what she remembers

271 A commonly used anti-inflammatory steroid.
272 Herbalife was founded in 1980 with a mission to improve its customers' diet and health regime through protein shakes and other products. Jean's new friend Rosalind was apparently one of Herbalife's local reps: as with Avon, the company relied on a network of personal distributors to boost sales.

of hairdresser S.'s combat with cancer. S. went into it all in depth, refused surgery and believed in special diet. No red meat, perhaps no meat at all. Alcohol a favourite weapon. (An old friend who lived till she was 90 fought it with whisky, saying 'I've pickled it!') So when I got home I started again on the gin and tonic. Thank God for alcohol.

Spoke to neighbours B.s. They really distressed. I shall get a lot of sympathy, and must beware getting conceited and trading on it.

Also heard from another source that quantities of vitamin C are good for this.

Wednesday, 14 May

A very satisfactory morning. But first, have embarked on what I hope will be 'the cure'. Knowing my need in particular now for herbs, vitamins etc have twice this week visited Health Food Shop (on Sunday dug out Gayelord Hauser's *Live Longer; Look Younger* – this inspired me to further research).[273] And found Brenda Kidman's *A Gentle Way With Cancer*. Based largely on the findings of the Bristol Cancer Help Centre, you may, dear Reader, study it for yourself, unless of course you have the sense to know it and what it's all about.[274]

To start with: A rigorous veg diet. No meats, fish, poultry, dairy products: eggs, cheese, butter, margarine cream; salt, sugar, tinned or processed foods. How dreary that sounds. But there are delicious substitutes if you work at it. As much fresh green salads,

---

273 See footnote on p. 605.
274 Launched in 1979, BCHC proposed an alternative, holistic approach to traditional cancer treatments, focusing on a strict (largely raw) vegetable diet, meditation and other non-invasive therapies. It was tainted with controversy in 1990, when a report in the *Lancet* suggested that women attending the centre with breast cancer fared worse than those who received conventional treatment only. It is now known as Penny Brohn Cancer Care, after its co-founder, and these days offers a less stringent diet and more of a complementary therapeutic package to run alongside traditional treatments.

raw vegs, pulses, grains, nuts, fruit, brown rice and so on. I am
having an adventurous and exciting time planning menus. I have
been conditioned to all this anyway – wholemeal bread and unre-
fined sugars – for years. I'll beat this vile disease! Doc approves
wholly of my attitude. 'Don't give in: think positive.' Salads and
fruit I have always enjoyed, and see now what opportunities my
loved little garden will provide. Also, I have no lusty, greedy
husband, children or grandchildren screaming for meat, sweets
and junk food.

It is all immensely heart-warming. Drinks are available of assorted
herb teas; unsweetened fruit juices are readily available in the village.
Am also allowed two glasses of white wine or spirits daily. Anne Coote
telephoned this a.m. I told her, of course, the full sad story, and
confessed to longing for champagne. Believe it or not she rushed in
later with a half bottle of Moet & Chandon.

Thank you, thank you God. Grant me confidence without conceit,
humility without servility.

Saturday, 17 May
A glorious early summer day yesterday – basked in sun all p.m. At
3.30 p.m. E.J. and Josephine called. This was a great delight as have
been wanting E. to come for weeks to see garden and new arrangements. Jos also I much wanted to see, hoping that I may be able
to persuade her to come and help me with filing, now piling up
horrendously.

Awake this a.m. at 3. Did easy crosswords. Brought breakfast
back to bed (grapefruit puree and molasses with hot water, half
grapefruit and honey) and renewed h.w. bottle. Bliss. Relax and doze
and plan.

This p.m. P.D. has promised to come and help with liquidiser and
blender. Now I need them.

Tomorrow I want to do the garden path border, where dying bulbs
need feeding, and growing everlasting pea must be staked with

bamboo sticks. Can't leave this to gardener – he'll be wanting to chop leaves off bulbs. This p.m. shall try a veg roast.[275]

Thursday, 22 May (final entry, Journal 45)
I did so enjoy yesterday. After two more grim days in bed with acute pains etc and starvation diet, Babs came. It was pouring, so no gardener, but was feeling better and she took me into Slough.

Had not been since Jan., and I badly needed small repair to new portable typewriter, stationery from W.H.S. and to explore Boots Food Centre products. We achieved it all, she carried all the heavy loads, and we were home by 2 p.m. I felt really hungry and not at all over-tired. She had brought her own sandwiches and would have nothing from me. And champagne! This does me a lot of good. Sun came out. She helped with more chores and went back at 3.30. Bless her!

I had to get a letter and sketch map and list to dealer D.D. who is visiting the cat book stock on Sat, and wanted to catch 4.30 post at nearby mailbox. In pops neighbour M.K. for a chat, then the two R.s to enquire. All delightful, but I was in a fidget. However, they had gone by 4.15 and I just managed to get letter scribbled and posted in time.

Then rest, rest and lazy sun-filled evening. I have had a lot of visitors.

---

275 Added later: 'No – it didn't get done.'

'I am in heaven. I am in love.' Jean and friends walk away from Wee Cottage.

Epilogue

Jean died ten weeks later in a local nursing home. She was cremated on 21 August 1986 at Slough Crematorium, and her ashes scattered beneath a flowering rose bush planted for her brother Leslie. When I visited in January 2015, a grey Sunday, the ashes were geology. I placed a stone in the garden, a Jewish tradition that usually helps mark a gravesite, but also suggests that the deceased has not been forgotten.

There are different types of ashes, of course. Jean's journals and papers serve as their own remarkable memorial. They do not 'rot away, unread' as she feared, but instead provide an extraordinary social document. I think Jean Pratt has come closer than most in the twentieth century to record the emotional disarray of a single mind, and the affecting life of a single woman. The achievement is an art beyond value.

I have found three brief obituaries. *Bookdealer* magazine, a weekly to which she subscribed, ran a piece on its front page. 'Despite being a very private person, her interests were many and varied,' the article stated, before listing some of them – her local parish duties, her art group, her garden and her cats. There was a description of her architecture and journalism training, and her time at High Duty Alloys during the war. 'Friends and fellow dealers remember Jean Pratt for her consideration, straightforwardness and great kindness. She will be sadly missed.'

The other two were from local papers. One, entitled 'Death of Bookshop Owner', noted that 'She ran a worldwide book order service from the shop in the Broadway, and soon became the largest supplier of specialist cat books in the country.' The second, headlined 'Tributes to a Cat Lover', observed 'Her enthusiasm was not restricted to the printed page, and at one time she kept 13 cats in her cottage. Lady Anne Coote, who worked for Miss Pratt for many years, recalled how many American and Canadian cat lovers would make a special detour to The Little Bookshop when they visited England. She said, "She was a very private person."'

In editing her writing, I have tried above all to be true to the variety of her concerns and the depth of her struggles. To avoid an endless river of ellipses I have not usually indicated where I have made excisions. My main changes have been grammatical. You may have noticed a fondness in Jean's writing for the dash – her thoughts seemed to dart around so swiftly at times that orderly presentation just went out of the window – and some of these I have turned either into commas, colons or full stops to smooth the read. And I have also removed a great many exclamation marks (as she tended to use them a great deal!!).

I had a decision to make about the felines. I'd never dare admit it in Jean's presence, but after a while one cat's antics was very much like another cat's antics (at least in the journal). At one stage one would have required a detective to keep track of them all, in the cottage as on the page, so I have lost a great deal of their fur-balling and temerity and impressive range of calamities. To her credit, Jean appreciated the hoary cliché of the spinster with only feline company, and in her last years I think she played up to it. I can only hope that I have given full weight to the love she had for her companions, and the howling loss that accompanied each passing.

Babs Everett, whom Jean recalled being born, is now in her eighties. She cannot remember as much about her aunt as her aunt has recorded about her, but her final days are vivid. 'Just towards the end of Jean's life she came and stayed with us for a week to ten days as she was not able to look after herself. She then returned to Wee to be collected by ambulance to be taken to a nursing home where she spent the last days of her life. She was in a lot of pain as the cancer had spread throughout her body.'

Babs was pleased that her journals were finally being published. 'I was never privy to her private life. She was a kind and gentle Aunt who had to put up with me for the Christmas and Easter school holidays.' She remembers having a bath in the kitchen 'with the cats sitting round the rim scooping up water with their paws. Thankfully no one ever fell in. A hinged wooden board came down over the bath to become the kitchen table.'

'A little story you might like was when Leslie went to visit his sister in boarding school taking a box of chocolates for her. They sat in the school grounds talking and Jean ate the whole box never offering him any. He then told her she was a pig and would call her Piglet after A.A. Milne's stories. She replied, "Right, I shall call you Pooh with very little brain." The names stuck and I and my children always called her Aunty Piglet. I think she rather liked being called that.'

All gone now, of course: Spong the grocer, Lund the hardware shack, Mrs H. at The Bon Bon. The Methodist chapel, The Little Bookshop's onetime neighbour in the Broadway, is still there but dilapidated. Her first, tiny, shop has been subsumed by Tesco Metro, while the second was most recently Sherriff Mountford estate agents, but is, at the time of writing, empty and to let. Opposite is Costa Coffee, where I meet Judy Tipping, Farnham Common's local historian. Judy was born in the village in 1940, the year after Jean moved in. Peter, the garage owner from whom Jean bought several cars, was her uncle. She remembers Jean as a rather prim, school-mistressy sort, a bun on the nape of her neck, 'but not standoffish at all, would talk to everyone. She liked to joke. I wouldn't say she was a typical spinster.' She remembers there were usually cats in the shop, something Jean never recorded. Tipping also remembered that Jean was quite terrible at parking her cars.

I had first met Tipping about ten years before, when I had come to talk to the Farnhams Society about Jean's appearance in the Mass Observation archive. After the meeting I was approached by a man who said he was a regular visitor to The Little Bookshop. He was also dyslexic, he said, and would be forever grateful to Jean for helping him learn to read.

Wee Cottage still exists, deep in the woods. Its present owners, a professional couple and their daughter, point out the extension built since Jean departed, and wondered at how cramped it must have been when she had guests. Inevitably, they have questions: what did Jean write about the cottage? What did she do there for almost fifty years?

In 1934, when she was living in Wembley at the age of twenty-five, Jean wrote in her journal that the diarist had a purpose both special and peculiar. The skill lay not just in sifting the significant events, but in combining facts with the feelings and ideas they aroused. A diarist must have 'intuitive knowledge of the values of these fragments which pile up', in order to 'capture and crystallise moments on the wing'. And there was one more requirement, a promise to the reader: 'This,' future generations should be able to say as they turn the glittering pages, 'was the present then. This was true.'

Acknowledgements

The task of editing Jean's writing has been a pleasure. I was frequently grateful for the shared enthusiasm and creative suggestions shown by my agent Rosemary Scoular, my editor Jenny Lord and my wife Justine Kanter. The support for the project shown by the great team at Canongate, led by Jamie Byng and Jenny Todd, has also been unstinting. I would like to thank Seán Costello for his sensitive copy editing, Jake Lingwood for getting the ball rolling more than a decade ago, Martin Bright for making the initial link with Jean's family, Ella Frears for her careful transcription of several journals, Judy Tipping, John Conen and Paul Townsend for their knowledge and friendship in Farnham Common, and Cats Protection for its current guardianship of Jean's writing. Finally, thank you to Babs Everett for supplying the photographs, and for placing her faith in me with something so valuable.